Drupal® 7 Bible

Ric Shreves

Brice Dunwoodie

Wiley Publishing, Inc.

Drupal® 7 Bible

Published by
Wiley Publishing, Inc.
10475 Crosspoint Boulevard
Indianapolis, IN 46256
www.wiley.com

Published by Wiley Publishing, Inc., Indianapolis, Indiana

Published simultaneously in Canada

ISBN: 978-0-470-53030-6

Manufactured in the United States of America

10 9 8 7 6 5 4 3 2 1

For general information on our other products and services or to obtain technical support, please contact our Customer Care Department within the U.S. at (877) 762-2974, outside the U.S. at (317) 572-3993 or fax (317) 572-4002.

Library of Congress Control Number: 2011926342

About the Authors

Ric Shreves is a partner at water&stone (`www.waterandstone.com`), a digital agency focused on open-source technologies and new media. He's been building Web sites professionally since 1999 and writing about technology for almost as long. He's published several books on open-source content management systems, including titles on Mambo, Joomla!, and Drupal. This is his fourth title with Wiley, having previously released *Mambo Visual Blueprint, Ubuntu Visual Blueprint,* and *Joomla! Bible.*

Ric is an American who has lived in Asia since 1995. He currently resides in Bali, Indonesia, with his wife Nalisa. You can learn more about Ric and his most recent work by visiting his Web site at `http://RicShreves.net`.

Brice Dunwoodie is the founder of Simpler Media Group, Inc., and the publisher of CMSWire (`www.cmswire.com`), a niche online magazine focused on information management, enterprise collaboration, and Web publishing. He is also the co-founder of Cylogy, Inc. (`www.cylogy.com`), an information technology consulting firm based in San Francisco, California, since 2001.

Brice started his career at Oracle Corporation in the mid-1990's and worked with San Francisco-based start-ups and Macromedia during the Internet boom before taking a more entrepreneurial path. For the past 15 years, he has consulted with a broad range of international clients, including Singapore Telecom, IBM, France Telecom, Gawker Media, Union Bank of Switzerland, the United Nations, SX2 Media Labs, and the U.S. Federal Reserve. He currently splits his time among San Francisco, Budapest, and Paris.

Few outside of the open-source world realize how many people it takes to create and support a project like Drupal. Without the (largely anonymous!) efforts of these people, Drupal would never have achieved the success it enjoys today. We'd like to dedicate this book to the many volunteers who have put in innumerable hours building the Drupal system and creating the community that is the heart of the project.

Credits

Senior Acquisitions Editor
Stephanie McComb

Project Editor
Martin V. Minner

Technical Editor
Joshua Brauer

Copy Editor
Gwenette Gaddis

Editorial Director
Robyn Siesky

Editorial Manager
Rosemarie Graham

Business Manager
Amy Knies

Senior Marketing Manager
Sandy Smith

Vice President and Executive Group Publisher
Richard Swadley

Vice President and Executive Publisher
Barry Pruett

Project Coordinator
Kristie Rees

Graphics and Production Specialists
Melanee Habig
Andrea Hornberger

Quality Control Technician
Rebecca Denoncour

Proofreading and Indexing
Christine Sabooni
Potomac Indexing, LLC

Introduction

Welcome to *Drupal 7 Bible*. Like all books in the *Bible* series, you can expect to find both hands-on tutorials and real-world practical applications, as well as reference and background information that provide a context for what you are learning. This book is a fairly comprehensive resource on the Drupal open-source content management system. By the time you have completed *Drupal 7 Bible*, you will be well prepared to build and maintain a Drupal-based Web site.

Drupal is in the forefront of one of the most dynamic trends in open-source software: the rise of the open-source content management system (CMS). Historically, a Web content management system was a very expensive investment. Open source has changed all that. A number of options now allow site developers and site owners to tap into the power of building CMS-powered Web sites.

Of all the options that exist in the market today, perhaps none is more powerful and flexible than Drupal. Although the system can be used for simple sites, it is also suitable for highly customized and complex Web sites; indeed, with its open API and support for a variety of databases, it has many of the attributes of a Web applications framework.

If you are a designer looking to build functional Web sites for your clients, Drupal is an excellent tool. If you are a developer looking for a system upon which to develop custom functionality, Drupal can meet your needs. And if you are simply a Web site owner who wants to take control of your Web site, then you need look no further than Drupal.

Who Should Read This Book

In keeping with the comprehensive theme of the *Bible* series, this book seeks to provide a wide range of information suitable to a variety of potential readers. We strived to present information that is relevant to the largest possible group of users, but certain sections of this book are logically more relevant to certain categories of users.

For those looking to take their first steps with an open-source content management system, the book progresses logically from the first section of introductory materials through the final sections on customization and site maintenance.

For those who are already familiar with Drupal, the opening sections will probably add little to your understanding of the system, but the sections that follow will help you unlock the full potential of the system. Drupal is a fairly complex system, and the middle sections of this book explore in depth how to get the most out of it.

For designers and developers, the middle and final sections will be your focus, as they take you through creating and configuring a Drupal site and cover the basics of customizing the appearance and functionality of the system.

Finally, for site owners and administrators, this book should serve as a reference work, providing you with an easy-to-use guide to the ongoing ownership of a Drupal site.

How This Book Is Organized

The book is organized in a way that enables you to start at the very beginning with Drupal and proceed to the point where you can build, customize, and maintain a Web site based on Drupal.

Part I covers the basics of getting started with Drupal. It assumes you know nothing about the system. In Part I you learn the following:

- The nature of open source and content management systems (Chapter 1)
- How to obtain and install Drupal (Chapter 2)
- What's in the default system (Chapter 3)
- How to configure a new installation (Chapter 4)

In Part II, you learn how to use Drupal to build your Web site. These topics are covered:

- The themes included with the system (Chapter 5)
- The modules, which provide the functionality in the system (Chapter 6)
- The blocks, which provide part of the output in Drupal (Chapter 7)
- How to create menus and menu items (Chapter 8)
- How to create custom actions and triggers for your site (Chapter 9)

Part III focuses on the heart of any CMS—that is, working with content. These topics are covered:

- Understanding the key concepts in Drupal's approach to content management (Chapter 10)
- Managing Drupal's taxonomy system (Chapter 11)
- Formatting content and media (Chapter 12)
- Managing the front page of your Web site (Chapter 13)
- How to employ advanced content management techniques (Chapter 14)
- Working with Drupal's comments system (Chapter 15)
- How to work with blog content in Drupal (Chapter 16)
- How to work with Drupal's book content type (Chapter 17)

Part IV deals with the additional Drupal modules that provide other types of content. You will learn about these topics:

- How to use Drupal's RSS aggregator to bring feeds into your site (Chapter 18)
- How to create and manage the basic forms in Drupal (Chapter 19)
- How to enable and configure Drupal's forum functionality (Chapter 20)
- How to create and manage polls and surveys (Chapter 21)
- Working with multi-lingual content (Chapter 22)

Part V covers Drupal's user management system. Topics include the following:

- Understanding how the user management system works in Drupal (Chapter 23)
- How to control user access to content and functionality (Chapter 24)
- Setting up user registration functionality (Chapter 25)

Part VI focuses on customizing and extending the system. These topics are included:

- How to customize Drupal's themes to create a unique appearance for your site (Chapter 26)
- How to control the display of content on the site (Chapter 27)
- How to customize the modules that provide the functionality in Drupal (Chapter 28)
- How to find and install extensions for your Drupal site (Chapter 29)
- Implementing ecommerce and catalog management with the Ubercart extension for Drupal (Chapter 30)

Part VII looks at using Drupal in the enterprise. Topics include the following:

- Securing your Drupal site. (Chapter 31)
- How to manage and improve site performance. (Chapter 32)
- Making your site search engine friendly. (Chapter 33)
- Improving handicapped accessibility on your site. (Chapter 34)
- Handling change management and managing site updates and patches. (Chapter 35)

Icons

Whenever the authors want to bring something important to your attention, the information appears in a Tip, Note, Caution, or Cross-Reference.

Tip

Tips generally are used to provide information that can make your work easier—special shortcuts or methods for doing something easier than the norm. ■

Note

Notes provide additional, ancillary information that is helpful, but somewhat outside of the current presentation of information. ■

Caution

This information is important and is set off in a separate paragraph with a special icon. Cautions provide information about things to watch out for, whether simply inconvenient or potentially hazardous to your data or systems. ■

Cross-Reference

This icon directs you to related information in another chapter of the book. ■

Minimum Requirements

To get the most out of this book, you need access to an installation of the Drupal CMS. Typically, this requires a server running a combination of the Apache Web server, the MySQL database, and PHP. Site management is accomplished through a browser with a connection to the server. Full technical requirements and recommendations for optimal versions are discussed in Chapter 2.

In Part IV of the book, where the topics turn to customization, you also want to have access to your favorite editor for working with the site's code. In Part IV and in several other points in the book, having access to an FTP client will be useful.

This book focuses on version 7 of the Drupal CMS. Although there are some similarities, this release varies significantly from older Drupal releases.

Where to Go from Here

It is our hope that you take away from this book an increased awareness of the capabilities of the Drupal system and a higher comfort level when working with sites based on Drupal.

If you spend a bit of time around open-source software, you quickly discover that the rate of change in systems can be impressive (sometimes even a bit daunting). Drupal is community-driven open source. The community behind it is large, dynamic, and ever-changing. New features are developed at a rapid pace, and new extensions, tips, tricks, and tools arise even more quickly.

If you want to get the most out of Drupal, I strongly suggest you make an effort to keep up with the project. In Chapter 1, we list the official Drupal project sites. You should bookmark those sites and visit them regularly. The Drupal Forum is a great place to visit and learn what is new and of interest. Several of the official sites also provide RSS feeds and other easy ways to stay abreast of developments with the project. The final appendix also includes tips for where you can find out more.

Please feel free to visit the official Wiley & Sons Web site (`http://www.wiley.com`) if you want to provide feedback on this book.

Acknowledgments

I want to thank my wife Nalisa for her love and support. She kept things running smoothly both at water&stone and at home while I spent many long hours working on this manuscript.

— Ric

I dedicate this book to El T, the one who had the courage to cross the road and, like me, the luck of stumbling upon a fabulous Francaise.

— Brice

Contents at a Glance

Contents

Part I

Getting Started

IN THIS PART

CHAPTER 1

Introducing the Drupal Content Management System

IN THIS CHAPTER

Discovering open-source content management

Discovering Drupal

The Drupal community

Drupal is a Web-oriented content management system (CMS) that grew out of a personal project started in 2000 at the University of Antwerp, Belgium, by a student named Dries Buytaert. The project founders designed the original software to allow a group of people to share their thoughts and files via electronic means. The first public Web site built with Drupal was Drop.org.

In 2001, the software behind the project was first released with the name Drupal. The word Drupal is pronounced "droo-puhl" and derives from the English pronunciation of the Dutch word druppel, which means drop.

Today thousands upon thousands of Web sites are built using Drupal; it is one of the most popular Web content management systems in the world. And it's this success story that probably led you to consider Drupal for your project.

This chapter introduces important Drupal concepts, provides you the vocabulary you need for moving forward, and explains how the Drupal community functions.

Discovering Open-Source Content Management

Engaging in open-source software projects is always an adventure. No two projects are alike, though many share characteristics. Importantly, you should remember that when it comes to open-source communities, you typically get out of them what you put in. And if you are to contribute, you must first understand the basic concepts.

What is content?

There are two general categories of content: structured and unstructured. A blog post is an example of structured content. It is structured because it is made up of sub-elements. For example, a blog post might have a title field, a body field, a field for the date created, and a field for the author's name. A typical blog post may have other fields, but the point is that a structured content type is composed of other smaller units of content. These sub-elements are of a specific data type (for example, text, date, or image) and are typically understood by the system in which the content lives.

Unstructured content is different; it's a single piece of data that the system holds and presents but typically does not understand. A Microsoft Word document is an example of unstructured content when it is stored in a content management system.

Note

You often see structured and unstructured content types mixed together. For example, an article content type may be composed of several sub-elements, including one or more image fields. In this case, a structured content type also contains unstructured field types. ■

You can put a Word document into a CMS, but only the Microsoft Word application understands what that data is and how to manipulate it. Unstructured content like this is self-contained; it is not made up of sub-elements.

Drupal content types are structured. They are comprised of sub-elements called *fields*. Fields have a data type and can hold various types of content. We discuss fields in more detail later in this chapter.

Cross-Reference

See Chapter 10 for a full discussion of Drupal content types and the new Fields functionality that is part of the Drupal 7 core. ■

What is a CMS?

The acronym CMS means *content management system*. This is quite a broad term, and in practice it refers to a range of different software types. In this book, CMS means *Web* content management system. A Web CMS is a software system you use to create, manage, and present content via public or private Web sites. Figure 1.1 shows a typical online publishing site powered by a Web CMS.

In other contexts, the CMS acronym can refer to a document management system, a Web publishing system, a file-sharing system, or even a micro-blogging system. The lines between these types of systems are often blurred, because many of them share the common goal of facilitating the orderly management and publishing of electronic information.

FIGURE 1.1

The CMSWire.com Web site is an example of a typical online publishing site that is powered by a Web CMS.

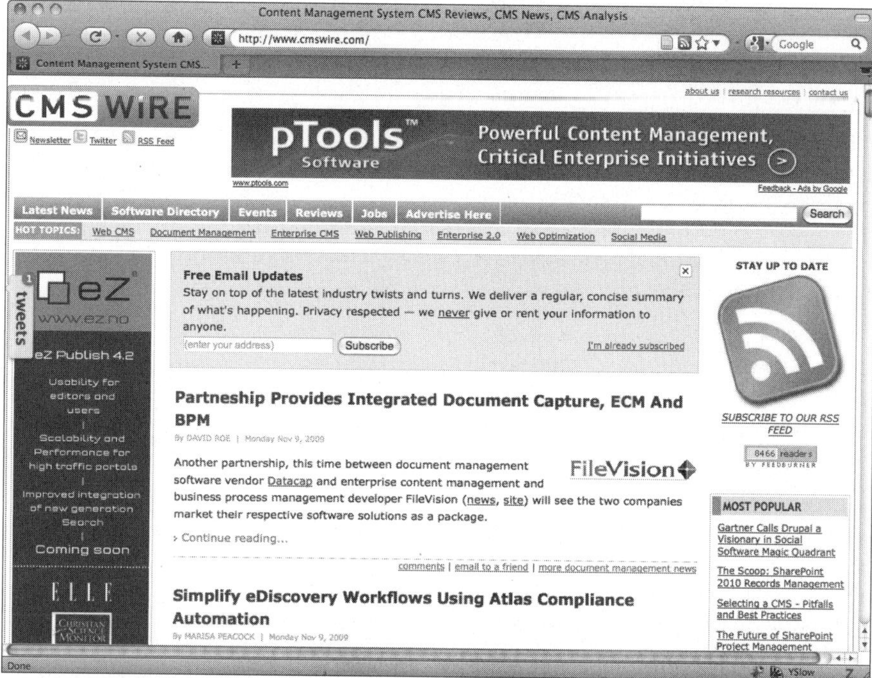

Why should you use a CMS?

Using a content management system should make your life simpler. Exceptions to this rule exist—for example, if you create a very simple Web site with just a few pages. But in general, a CMS provides a rational framework and some tools that make creating and managing a Web site easier.

Empowering content authors

One of the early justifications for implementing a CMS was to empower content authors who either desired to or needed to manage Web site content but did not have the necessary technical skills to edit the raw content or did not have the security rights to access the publishing systems.

Historically, content authors might have done their editing in a desktop word-processing program and then given it to a technical team for publishing on the Web site. The process involved at least two people and was typically time-consuming and often frustrating for everyone involved. If changes were needed after publishing, the process would be repeated.

Content management systems like Drupal bypass this cumbersome process by providing simple Web-based tools that authors use to publish content directly to the Web site. The tools typically provide a what-you-see-is-what-you-get (WYSIWYG) editing experience that is similar to word-processing tools like Microsoft Word and thus require few technical skills. Figure 1.2 shows a Drupal 7 content-editing screen with a WYSIWYG editor.

Cross-Reference

The standard Drupal install does not come with a WYSIWYG editing tool by default, but you may chose from a number of different editors—in the form of contributed modules—that can be configured to work with the system. See Chapter 12 where we discuss how to use several of the popular WYSIWYG editors. ■

Controlling content authors

After authors are empowered to publish content, Web site managers may find themselves concerned about what is created, how it is formatted, and whether the content is properly reviewed before it is published. Achieving a level of control over the content-authoring process is another common justification for a CMS.

These are examples of authoring control:

- Making certain content fields, such as a page title, required
- Limiting the number of characters that a content field can hold
- Forcing content items to follow a workflow approval process
- Creating a new version of an item every time a change is made
- Requiring that metadata be added before an item can be published

Tip

Moving from a less controlled to a more controlled content-authoring process is a good idea. However, predicting exactly how authors will work with a CMS on a daily basis can be difficult. Following an incremental approach to refinement allows you to observe daily authoring behavior, identify problems, and then prioritize high value improvements. ■

Typically as your CMS implementation matures, the ways you control the content-authoring process evolve as well. In its default configuration, Drupal provides a number of configuration options that give you the ability to control how content authors create and edit content. You can use Drupal add-ons to extend these abilities—for example, adding advanced workflow controls.

Note

In Part III, we discuss managing content with Drupal. The chapters in Part III discusses different content types in Drupal, how you can control the related authoring and editing options and how to effectively create and manage the various types of content. ■

FIGURE 1.2

Dupal 7 content-editing screen with a WYSIWYG editor installed

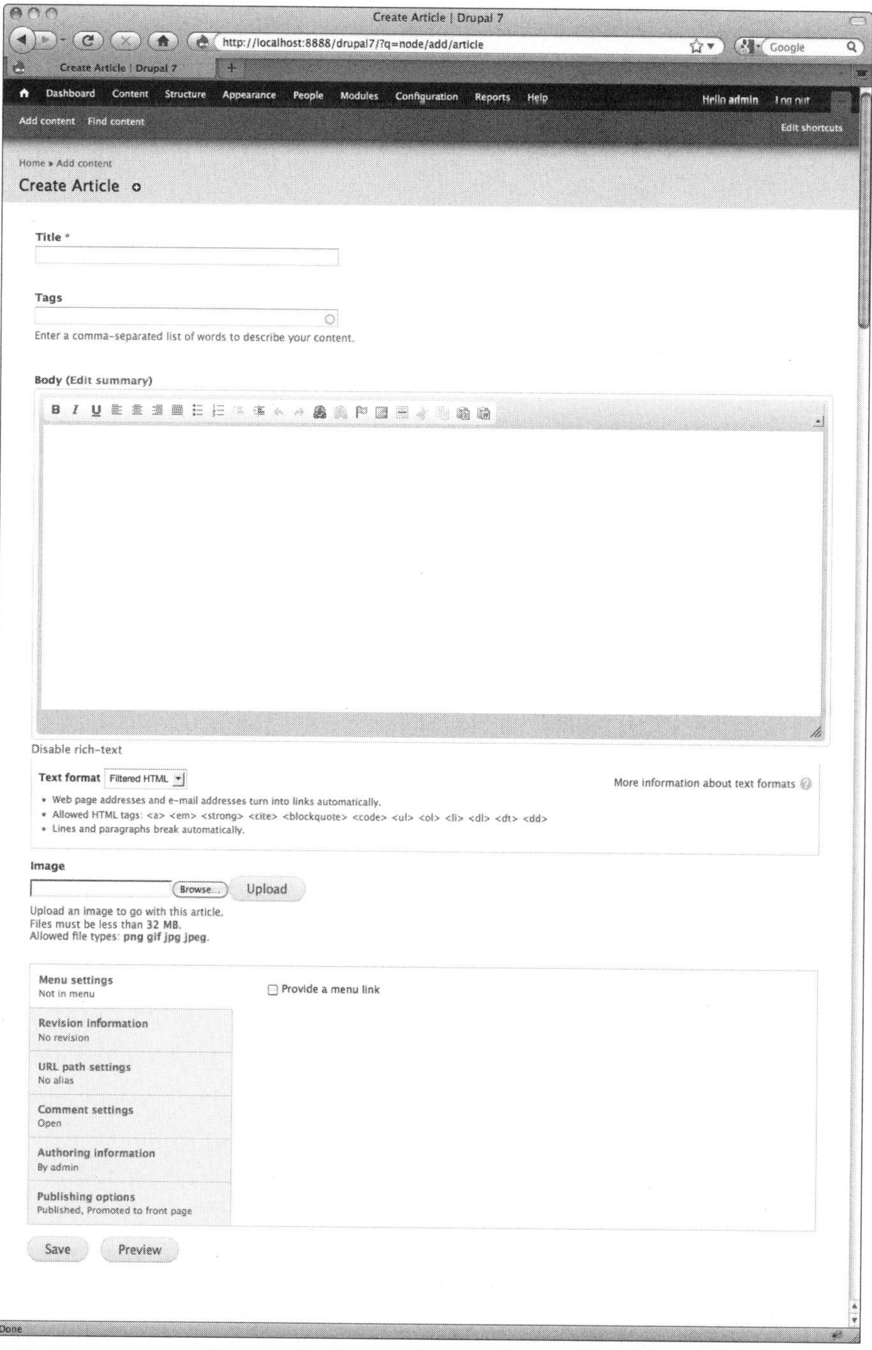

Managing content presentation

After a Web site grows beyond a few pages, maintaining the consistency of how the content is presented can become unreasonably complicated, unless you use a CMS. Almost every Web site owner is concerned about content presentation, and systems like Drupal explicitly establish consistency in this area.

As you consider supporting multiple content formats and different client devices, managing content presentation quickly becomes a complex problem. For example, a moderately sophisticated Web site might deliver HTML for personal computers, HTML for mobile phones, RSS for news readers, and XML for another company publishing system. Without a CMS managing the presentation formatting for each scenario, maintenance of such a system would be unreasonably difficult.

Another presentation concern—particularly for public-facing Web sites—is search engine optimization (SEO). Maintaining control over content presentation is critical if you want to optimize your Web site for search engine indexing.

In the Drupal context, much of the presentation is controlled via Drupal Themes, but a number of system configurations and modules can play important SEO roles.

Cross-Reference

See Chapter 5 for details on the default Drupal themes. For a full discussion of how to create a search-engine-friendly Web site, see Chapter 33. ■

Why should you use open source?

No simple equation exists for deciding when or if using open source is a good idea. For some people, this decision is a philosophical one, for others it is a financial one, for others a logical one, and for some it might be an organizational mandate.

There are different forms of open-source software projects. The Drupal project is *community open-source software*. In this form, no single commercial entity owns or develops the majority of the software; it is owned by the individuals in the community who contributed it and licensed as the community or decision-making body decides.

Note

Later in this chapter, I share details on the Drupal software license. ■

Commercial open-source software differs in that a single company typically controls the software, and your relationship with the software may bind you into a formal or informal relationship with that organization. In the case of Drupal, it is probably fair to say that you will be bound to a diverse community rather than to a single entity. Each scenario has its advantages and disadvantages.

These are typical arguments in favor of open-source software:

- You have the ability to fix bugs and make software enhancements yourself.
- The software is often free; however, owning and maintaining it is not.
- The software may be more stable because many people are testing it.
- The software may be more flexible and innovative because more perspectives are represented in its design and architecture.

The value and validity of these claims has long been a matter of debate. And as commercial open source has gained momentum in recent years, the very concept of open source has evolved considerably.

Tip

In October 2009, the U.S. Department of Defense issued a memo titled "Clarifying Guidance Regarding Open Source Software (OSS)." The memo identifies seven positive aspects of open-source software. You can find it online here: `http://www.defenselink.mil/cio-nii/sites/oss/2009OSS.pdf`. ■

If you are in a position of making a decision about whether to use open-source software, the most important thing is to first identify your project resources and priorities, and then decide whether an open-source solution is a good fit for your project.

Tip

If you are interested in further exploring the topic of open-source software development, Eric Steven Raymond wrote a thought-provoking essay titled "The Cathedral and the Bazaar." In the essay, the typical commercial model for software development is represented by the cathedral, while the bazaar represents the open-source model, specifically the model used to develop the Linux operating system. You can view the essay online at `http://www.catb.org/~esr/writings/cathedral-bazaar/cathedral-bazaar/`. ■

Discovering Drupal

Selecting a CMS, or knowing that you have chosen the best one, is not a perfect science. Open-source, closed-source, PHP, Java, or .NET—these are but a few factors that you must consider. In this section, we introduce you to the Drupal system.

For many people, Drupal is a good choice. But for others, it is a poor choice. You must consider your options carefully. No system is perfect, and most are not simple to understand. Drupal is no exception.

Considering Drupal's strengths and weaknesses

Many good reasons exist for selecting Drupal as your CMS. But as with any important software selection process, the question of the software's fitness for your project is the ultimate concern. Exactly how you go about evaluating Drupal's fitness for your needs is beyond the scope of this book, but factors such as total cost of ownership, the software's quality and probable longevity, your team's skillsets, your existing IT infrastructure, the required software features, and the required usage scenarios should all be considered.

When evaluating Drupal for your project, consider the following:

- The Drupal community seems reliable; it is large and diverse and has functioned well since 2001.
- Drupal is one of the top three most used Web content management systems in the world.
- The commercial forces in the Drupal community—both on the customer and contributor sides—are influencing the software such that it is increasingly considered appropriate for demanding corporate environments.
- Given the number of Drupal add-ons, what the community calls *contributed modules,* nearly anything you want to do with the system has already been done by someone; you benefit from their experience and from their contributed software.

Tip

The Drupal community puts a certain value on the idea of creative destruction as they make decisions about the product design and features from one major version to another. Innovation is likely to be valued more than backward compatibility. What this means for you is that upgrading from one major version of Drupal to another can involve a significant amount of work, as new, innovative features or system architecture changes may make the upgrade process difficult or may greatly delay the update of contributed modules that your site relies on. This situation can reach the extreme because some modules are never updated to work with new versions of Drupal. You should understand this risk before you commit to working with the product and as you make decisions about which contributed modules to rely upon. ■

The Drupal open-source license

Drupal and all the contributed files hosted on the Drupal.org Web site are licensed under the GNU General Public License (GPL), version 2.0 or later. This license is published by the Free Software Foundation. You can read the full license online here: `http://www.gnu.org/licenses/old-licenses/gpl-2.0.html`.

Note

Thousands of different people contribute code to the Drupal project. All Drupal contributors retain the copyright to their code, but if the code is published on Drupal.org, then it must be licensed via the GPL version 2.0 or later open-source license. ■

The Drupal architecture

Drupal is a modular system composed of many small parts. It is called a CMS, but it is also described as a *framework*. The project founders designed it to be highly flexible, with the goal of enabling skilled users of the system to shape it to fit a variety of needs. It follows from this initial design that the system requires a certain amount of customization—and consequently a certain amount of skill—for anyone to do anything complex with it.

Understanding how the Drupal architecture works is not a simple task. But this is required if you want to be a competent Drupal administrator.

Programming languages used

The Drupal software is written in the PHP programming language, and the user interfaces are implemented with a combination of HTML, JavaScript, CSS, and PHP. When developing extensions for Drupal, called *modules*, developers use a combination of PHP, HTML, and CSS.

Note

The Drupal 7 release is the first version to require PHP 5. See Chapter 2 for all the Drupal 7 technical requirements. ■

Fundamental architecture concepts

Drupal's fundamental architecture concepts include users, nodes, fields, taxonomies, comments, modules, hooks, and a group of user interface items called regions, blocks, and menus. Other important concepts are discussed later in this book, but these are the ideas most important when beginning to understand Drupal.

Users

A Drupal user is anyone who can sign in to the system and then perform an action. This includes editors, system administrators, and Web site users who might, for example, be interacting with each other via your Drupal Web site. Drupal also has a security concept called the anonymous user. All Web site visitors are considered anonymous users until they sign in.

Users are a native entity in the system, and they come by default with a set of properties such as username, password, e-mail address, and so on. You can also customize user profiles by adding new elements to the profile. For example, you could add a new URL element for a user's Twitter address.

Nodes

Nodes are content items. Drupal content types are all based upon nodes. When managing content in Drupal, you are managing nodes. For example, if you create and publish a blog post with Drupal, you have created and published a Drupal node.

Nodes are composed of default elements (for example, a title and a body) and optionally, one or more associated Drupal Fields. By default, nodes are simple entities. The intention is that you, as the Web site owner, will extend the simple node when you define your own content types.

Note

The default Drupal install comes with two content types defined: the basic article and the page. Both of these content types include title and body fields plus some metadata. You can extend the definition of any content type by associating more fields with it. ■

Fields

Fields are a new and important concept with Drupal 7. They are content containers that can be attached to many, but not all, Drupal system entities. For example, if you wanted to add an Expiration Date value to all of your site's articles, you could define a new field called Expiration Date and then associate this field with the Article content type.

The freedom to define new fields and associate them with content types gives you the power to store almost any type of content in Drupal.

Cross-Reference

See Chapter 10 for a full discussion of creating and managing Drupal content types including the definition, configuration, and management of Drupal fields. ■

Taxonomies

Taxonomies are used to organize content in Drupal. The Drupal taxonomy functionality is defined in a core module that allows you to define what are called *vocabularies*—groups of categories or labels—and then associate them with content types in the system. After a taxonomy is associated with a content type, you can use the taxonomy when creating or editing content of that type.

Taxonomies can take different formats—they can be hierarchical, flat, or arbitrary, as in the case of a *tagging* system. For example, if you created a blog about sports, you may want to use a taxonomy to categorize each blog post by the sport that it's about. You may also want to label each post with the names of the players that it mentions.

The first taxonomy would probably be a category system that you define in advance. The second taxonomy could be a tagging system—an arbitrary list of words or phrases—that is filled in as the content is authored.

Cross-Reference

In Chapter 11, we cover the creation and management of taxonomies in detail, including the Taxonomy Manager tool that comes with Drupal 7. ■

Comments

Drupal comments are native system entities that represent commentary or feedback from a user. Comments must be associated with a piece of content in the system—in technical terms, a node. It is not possible, for example, to comment on a user profile.

Comments can optionally be associated with other comments. In other words, a user may reply to his own or another user's comment, and in this way Drupal comments can represent a conversation. This is also known as comment threading.

Cross-Reference

The Comment module and related functionality are covered in depth in Chapter 15. ■

Modules

Drupal modules are software packages that add to or change existing Drupal functionality. There are two general categories of modules: *core modules,* which come with Drupal by default, and *contributed modules,* which are contributed by the community. If working with the base Drupal distribution, you must download and install contributed modules separately. If you work with other distributions, you will likely start off with a combination of core and contributed modules.

The standard Drupal release includes a limited number of core modules, typically less than 50. In contrast, many thousands of contributed modules exist. You can download these from the official Drupal Web site here: `http://drupal.org/project/modules`.

Advanced administrators and developers can also extend or change Drupal's behavior by creating their own modules. This requires a solid understanding of the Drupal API and of PHP programming.

Cross-Reference

The Modules included in the Drupal core are detailed in Chapter 6. Extending your site through the addition of contributed modules is discussed in Chapter 29. ■

Tip

All modules are built for a specific version of Drupal. If a module's version does not match the Drupal system version, the module will not function. ■

Hooks

Hooks are an advanced programming concept appropriate for developers who want to create their own modules. Hooks represent the internal application programming interface (API) for all system and module functionality. They define the operations that can be performed by the system. When a module implements a hook, it enters into a contract with the system to perform the operation associated with that hook.

For example, if you have a node module called `example` defined in a file named `example.module` and in this file you define the function `example_form()`, then this module has entered into a contract with the system to display an editing form when the system calls that function. To learn more about developing for Drupal, review the developer documentation here: `http://drupal.org/contributors-guide`.

Regions, blocks, and menus

Each page of your Drupal Web site is comprised of regions. For example, your page structure may contain regions called header, footer, left column, and main content. Blocks are chunks of content that are assigned to and displayed in one specific region. Figure 1.3 shows how regions are displayed on one Drupal-powered Web site.

The menu system is generally responsible for displaying the navigational elements of your Web site. It also serves another function; specifically it deals with mapping URL requests to the part of the Drupal system that will process the request. This is called *request routing,* and it's an advanced Drupal concept. Understanding the intricacies of this process is not immediately necessary. However, all administrators should understand that the menu system has responsibilities that go beyond the display of the user interface.

FIGURE 1.3

cmswire.com with (theoretical) regions highlighted

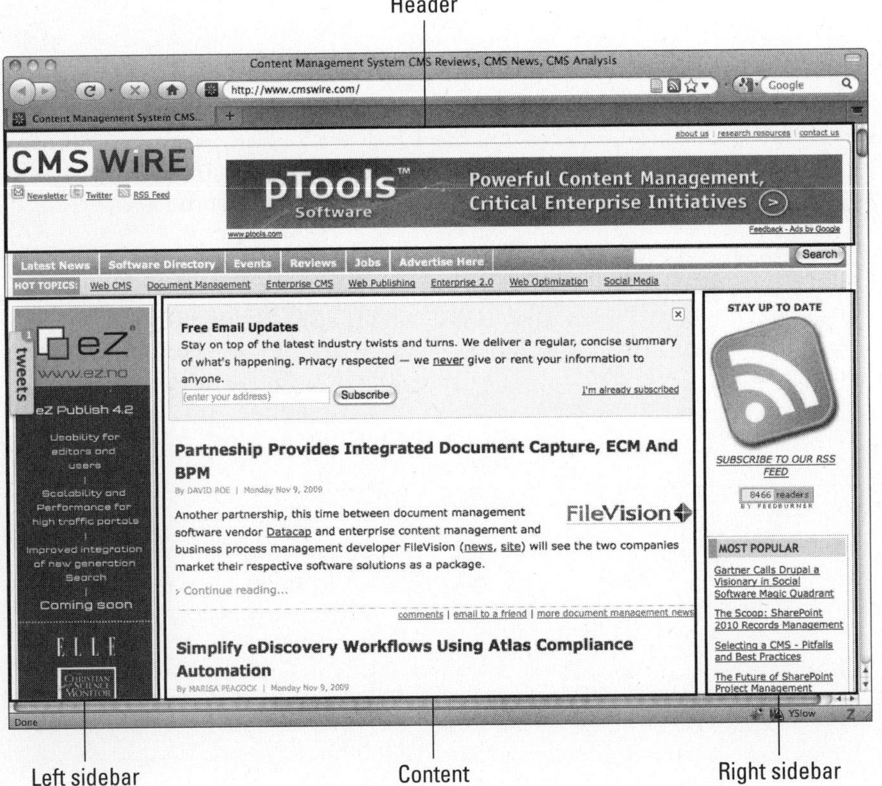

Cross-Reference

See Chapter 8 for details on creating and managing Drupal menus. In Chapter 5, we discuss themes and the Drupal Theme Manager tool. ■

The database

Drupal stores all its content, cached data, system entities, and a portion of its configuration settings in a relational database. Many of the system entities, including users, comments, nodes, and fields, have their own database tables where their data is stored.

Drupal 7 includes an enhanced database abstraction layer. This layer is built upon the PHP Data Objects (PDO) API and is designed to empower module developers while sheltering them from the low-level database implementation details.

The version 7 release of Drupal can run with MySQL, PostgreSQL, and SQLite databases.

Cross-Reference

See Chapter 2 for Drupal 7's specific technical requirements. ■

How it works

Drupal is a Web application that works in combination with a Web server and a database server. Requests for content are originated by a client such as a Web browser, passed through the Web server to the Drupal application system, and then routed via the Drupal menu system to the software component responsible for handling the request type. Figure 1.4 shows the request processing flow.

If the client requesting the content has access rights, then Drupal retrieves the content either from the system cache or from the raw data tables. The core system and any implicated modules then assemble the response content. The template system performs the final formatting of the content and finally hands it to the Web server for delivery to the client.

FIGURE 1.4

Drupal request processing flow

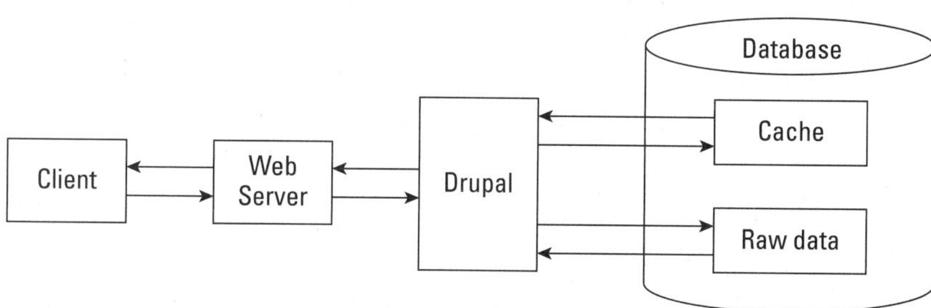

What's new in Drupal 7?

The Drupal 7 release has been an ambitious project resulting in a number of notable changes to the system. These are some of the most important items:

- Improved content type architecture, using Drupal Fields to define content types
- Broad usability improvements to the admin system, including improved Help
- A cleaned-up page template system with stronger support for Web standards
- New Drupal installer options such as the minimal installation profile
- Native support for advanced semantic Web technologies, specifically RDFa
- New minimum technical requirements including PHP 5.2+ and MySQL 5.0+

The Drupal Community

The Drupal community is a diverse, vibrant, and international group with thousands of active members. A recent count identified 9,000 unique bug filers and 1,800 different people who had contributed patches in the previous 12 months. The community is largely made up of individual volunteers, but it also contains commercial organizations that play active roles.

The community contains several important legal entities. The project founder, Dries Buytaert, is arguably the most important because he holds the trademark for the word Drupal, he owns the `drupal.com` Internet domain, and he has long been the lead maintainer of the Drupal core software project.

Buytaert and other long-term members of the community announced the Drupal Association (see `http://association.drupal.org/`) in September 2006 and officially formed it in December of that year. The association consists of a general assembly made up of permanent members and a board of directors made up of members elected by the general assembly. The board of directors handles daily affairs while the general assembly is responsible for major decisions.

You may be interested in these important facts about the Drupal Association:

- It is a not-for-profit association registered in Belgium.
- It has no say in the planning or development of the Drupal software project.
- It is primarily occupied with maintaining the project infrastructure services, accepting donations, promoting Drupal, and running Drupal-oriented events such as the Drupalcon gatherings.
- It does not pay it members; all work is done on a volunteer basis.

Tip

A common question about the Drupal Association is whether donations to the association by individuals or organizations in the United States are tax deductible. Unfortunately, despite the fact that the association is a not-for-profit entity, it is incorporated in Belgium and thus does not qualify as a U.S. Internal Revenue Code 501(c)(3) organization. Therefore, donations to the association are not currently tax deductible in the United States. ■

A recent addition to the Drupal community—announced in late 2007—is the commercial company, Acquia, founded by Dries Buytaert. Numerous other commercial entities exist and many play significant roles in the community, but Acquia stands out for several reasons.

Notable facts about Acquia include the following:

- Dries Buytaert, the Drupal project founder, is a company founder.
- It has received at least $23.5 million in three startup funding rounds.
- It is offering a software-as-a-service (SaaS) version of Drupal named Drupal Gardens.

Given these details, as well as the fact that Acquia staff members are actively contributing to the Drupal project, it is reasonable to expect that Acquia is going to play an important role in the Drupal community.

How the community works

The Drupal project is similar to many community open-source projects in that it has one or two people who act as maintainers of the core project software, a number of people who are highly active contributors, and then a large number of individuals and companies that contribute a little here and there. These dynamics change a bit with every release, but this is a fair characterization of the Drupal community.

In general terms, the Drupal project has two pieces: the core system and the contributed modules. The Drupal core contains the installer, core utilities, the admin system, and the core modules such as user, taxonomy, menu, comment, field, and node. This piece of the project is the most closely controlled, with the majority of important decisions made by Buytaert and a co-maintainer.

Contributed modules live a much freer life: Creators or maintainers of these modules control them as they see fit. Some contributed modules enjoy a long life, evolving with every Drupal release, some are incorporated into the core system (CCK is an example of this; it became the field and field_ui modules), and some fall by the wayside.

Drupal core project maintainers

Dries Buytaert, the founder of the project, has long been the maintainer of the core Drupal system. For the Drupal 7 release cycle, Angela Byron—who is known by her community username, webchick—was appointed by Buytaert to be the co-maintainer of the project. Most of the core modules additionally have a community member assigned as a maintainer (for the current list of maintainers, see `http://api.drupal.org/api/drupal/MAINTAINERS.txt`).

Drupal module project maintainers

Each contributed module has one or more maintainers. The module maintainer role implies control over the code for the given module, but often multiple people commit changes to the project. The community encourages co-maintenance of projects—where more than one person takes on the maintainer role—as a way to ensure that module development keeps pace with the Drupal core version.

In order to be accepted as a co-maintainer, you must demonstrate a solid history with a given project. The official Drupal Web site contains instructions for how to apply to become a co-maintainer of a project (see `http://groups.drupal.org/drupal-project-co-maintainers` for details on becoming a co-maintainer).

Important Drupal Web sites

The vast number of online resources for Drupal can be overwhelming, and these resources continually evolve—sometimes dramatically. Table 1.1 offers some good starting points. But keep in mind that engaging with the community and becoming a participant is the best way to develop your Drupal expertise.

TABLE 1.1

Drupal Web Resources

Web Site	Description
`http://drupal.org`	This is the official Drupal Web site.
`http://association.drupal.org`	This is the official Drupal Association Web site.
`http://drupal.org/forums`	This is the official Drupal discussion forum site, including support forums, general announcements, and forums for finding paid for Drupal services.
`http://api.drupal.org`	This is the official Drupal application programming interface (API) documentation Web site.
`http://testing.drupal.org`	This is the Web site for Drupal's Automated Testing System (ATS) and related announcements. ATS is the system used to automatically perform testing on newly submitted Drupal patches.
`http://localize.drupal.org`	This site is the home to the Drupal project translations.
`http://groups.drupal.org`	This is the official Drupal groups Web site, where groups of all types can organize, plan, and work on projects. The site is used by location-based groups, software project groups, Drupalcon groups, and others.

How to participate in the community

From the outside, the idea of engaging in the Drupal community can be intimidating. By doing so, you are jumping into a conversation that has been going on for years, but don't let this keep you away; the community is welcoming and is always in need of more help.

The best way to begin your participation is by creating an account on the Drupal.org Web site. From this point, you can start by browsing around the module or bug discussions related to your favorite topic or current area of interest. And you can gain exposure to active discussions via the Drupal IRC channels (see `http://drupal.org/irc` for details on the different channels) and the Drupal mailing lists (see `http://drupal.org/mailing-lists` for an overview of the different mailing lists).

By doing this, you'll get a feeling for how conversations take place and how decisions are made. It is common to see more senior community members providing coaching to those who are just getting started.

Identifying yourself as a newbie and asking politely for guidance in addressing your areas of concern is likely to lead to positive responses. But before getting too far along, be sure to read the Getting Involved guide on the Drupal Web site (see the online guide at `http://drupal.org/getting-involved`).

Tip

The Drupal community has a reputation of being friendly, open to suggestions, and easy to work with. But it is always considered respectful if you do your best to answer your questions yourself before you ask for help. ■

Getting a bug fixed

The Drupal community of users is large. Therefore, you should assume that if you've found a bug or discovered a need, you are probably not the first to do so. Do not file a bug or enhancement request too quickly.

Before reporting an issue, you should verify that you are using the latest version of the software, that a similar bug has not already been reported, and that the source of your problem is not a misconfiguration. It is a good idea to search the bug tracking system, search the support forums, and explore the issue via the `#drupal` IRC channel before you file a formal issue.

Keep in mind that regional IRC channels exist, and via these channels you can seek help in your native language or in your local time zone.

Tip

The strength of your reputation in the community often affects the amount of attention your concerns receive. When in doubt, take some extra time to understand the context around your specific need. This extra bit of research pays dividends in the long term. ■

Lending a hand

Anyone with a bit of Drupal experience can become a contributor. User support is one of the greatest community needs. It is also a great way to gain more experience with Drupal. As you acquire more familiarity with the product, you can move onto other areas where you feel comfortable.

See the Drupal contribution guide at `http://drupal.org/contribute` for tips on how you can give back to the community.

Summary

This chapter provided an introduction to open-source content management systems and to both the Drupal software and its community. The following points were covered:

- What a content management system is
- Why an open-source system may be a good choice
- Why Drupal may be a good choice for a CMS
- The key components of Drupal
- How the Drupal community works

CHAPTER

2

Obtaining and Installing Drupal

IN THIS CHAPTER

Obtaining the Drupal installation files

Installing Drupal locally

Installing Drupal on a Web host

Getting started with Drupal is easy. The installer is freely available for download and in some cases may already be part of your Web-hosting package. In either case, you typically need to go through a setup process before you can start working on configuring the site and adding the contents.

The Drupal installer includes a wizard-style interface that enables you to create a complete installation by simply clicking through a series of steps and providing some information. After you have finished the steps, your installation is complete and your new Drupal-powered Web site is ready to use.

This chapter looks at the basics of obtaining the Drupal files you need and getting them installed on your server.

Getting the Installation Files

The official Drupal installation files come bundled in a single compressed archive file. Although you can download this archive from several different sources, I strongly recommend that you obtain your code only from the official Drupal site. There are multiple reasons for this recommendation: First, by going to the official site, you are assured of downloading the most recent version. Second, the official archives are trustworthy and highly unlikely to contain dangerous or malicious code. Third, you can be assured that the archive contains a complete set of the official components.

Note

The only exception you may want to make to this rule is for Acquia's Drupal installation package, which is discussed later. ■

To obtain the archive, go to `http://www.drupal.org` and look for the download link on the top menu. Clicking the button takes you to a Downloads page, as shown in Figure 2.1.

FIGURE 2.1

The Downloads page of Drupal.org, showing the download link prominently displayed. Note also the dedicated tab for the Drupal Core.

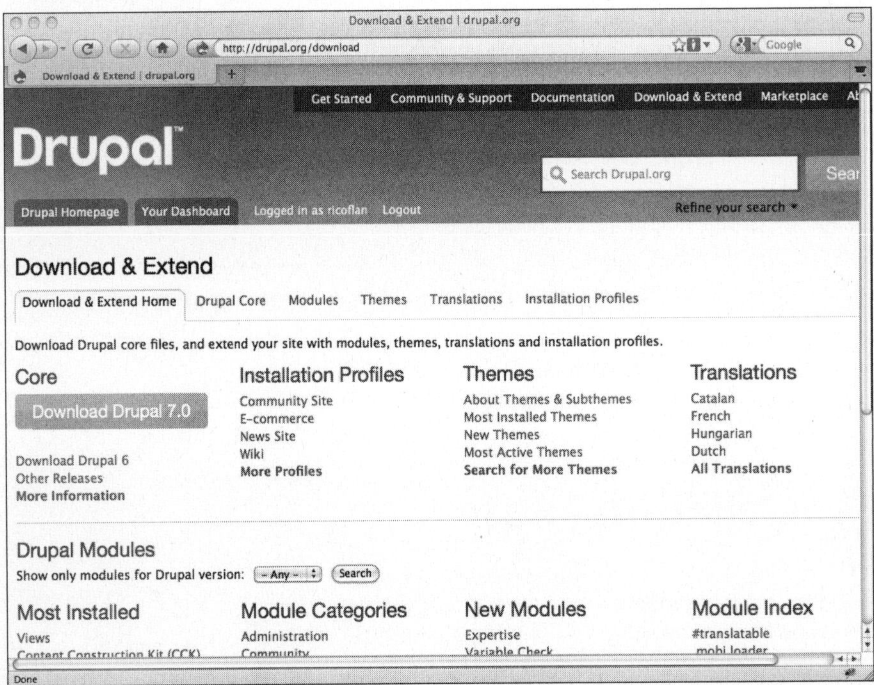

Installation Profiles

The Drupal.org site includes a number of installation profiles. Installation profiles are prepackaged configurations that allow you to install the Drupal core together with a set of related extensions in order to achieve an installation that is targeted to a particular type of usage—for example, a blogger site, or a Downloads site, or a portal site in Brazilian.

The installation profiles are contributed by users and hence vary from quite general to sometimes oddly specific. Whether a suitable profile is available for you is a question you must address yourself. Note carefully the versions that are supported for each profile; some work only with older versions of Drupal.

Installation profiles are a great idea and can potentially provide a nice jumpstart to your efforts, but in many cases, you may find that the profiles are too narrow for your use or fail to include modules that you prefer. (Preferences among modules are rather subjective!)

The default installation package includes two profiles: the standard profile and the minimal profile. You must select between these options during Step 1 of the installation process, discussed later. The two profiles have considerable differences in terms of the modules that are enabled and the content types available. This table shows the differences.

Characteristics	Standard Profile	Minimal Profile
Modules Enabled	Block Color Comment Contextual Links Dashboard Database logging Field Field SQL storage Field UI File Filter Help Image List Menu Node Number Options Overlay Path RDF Search Shortcut System	Block Database logging Field Field SQL storage Filter Node System Text Update manager User

continued

continued

Characteristics	Standard Profile	Minimal Profile
	Taxonomy Text Toolbar Update manager User	
Content Types	Article Basic page	<none>
Themes	Bartik Seven (Admin theme)	Bartik

Note that the underlying Drupal installation is the same; the Standard profile simply has two content types already created and more of the default modules and themes enabled. Selecting the Minimal profile does not restrict your options or produce a limited installation; the only differences are in configuration, which can be adjusted at any time by the site administrator.

To view information about additional profiles that are available, visit `http://drupal.org/project/installation profiles`.

Exploring the Drupal.org site

One of the first steps you should take in the process of learning Drupal is to visit the official Drupal project Web site at `http://www.drupal.org`. The site features a significant number of resources for Drupal users and serves as the central storehouse for the official Drupal files. I strongly recommend that you bookmark the site, or subscribe to one of the RSS feeds, as you will want to return to it at some point during your work.

Table 2.1 provides a list of some of what you can find at the Drupal.org Web site.

TABLE 2.1

Drupal Resources

Resource	URL
Current core files	`http://drupal.org/project/drupal`
Detailed information about extensions and the ability to download them	Modules: `http://drupal.org/project/modules` Themes: `http://drupal.org/project/themes` Translations: `http://drupal.org/project/translations`
A Drupal discussion forum	`http://drupal.org/forum`
Drupal documentation	`http://drupal.org/documentation`

Resource	URL
Information about the Drupal project and the Drupal team	`http://drupal.org/about`
Drupal implementation case studies	`http://drupal.org/cases`
Drupal news and announcements	Postings: `http://drupal.org/forum/` Mailing lists: `http://drupal.org/mailing-lists`
Drupal security advisories	`http://drupal.org/security`

In addition to the official files, the site functions as a distribution point for non-commercial extensions to the Drupal core. The Downloads section of the site contains a directory of various extensions—Modules, Themes, Installation Profiles, and so on. The directory is organized topically and allows you to sort and search by Drupal version. A number of the extensions include dedicated project pages; see, for example, the Views module: `http://drupal.org/project/views`. The project page provides quite a bit of information about the extension, as shown in Figure 2.2. In addition to links to the various versions of the extension code, you also can find a description of the extension, updates from the extension's project team, and a list of related discussions, including any bugs or open issues.

FIGURE 2.2

This is the project page of a typical extension—the Views module.

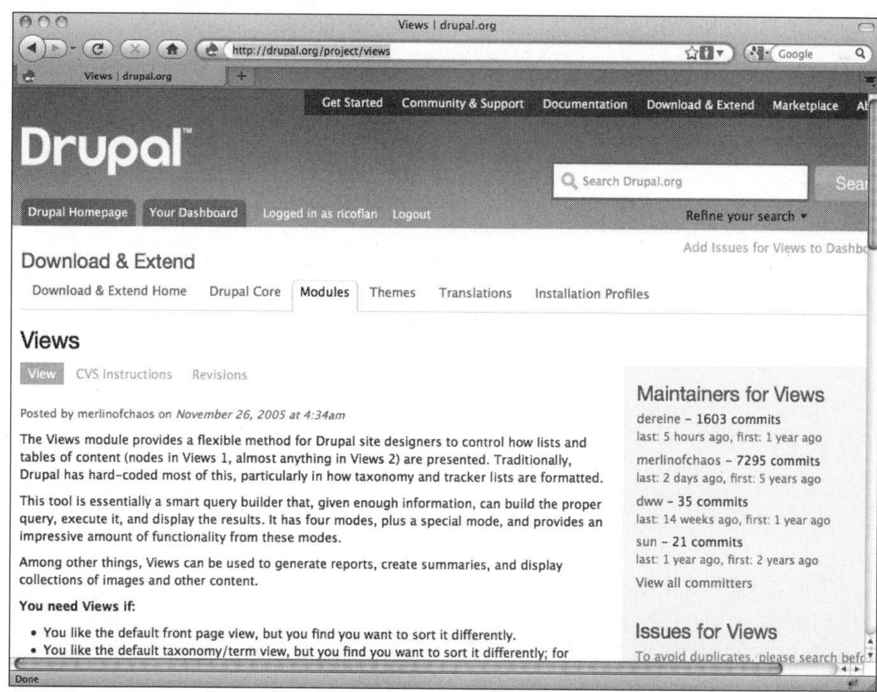

Knowing which files you need

Unlike many other systems, Drupal offers only one type of installer. That single installer can be used to either create a new installation or upgrade an existing installation. Although only one installer is available for each version, Drupal maintains multiple versions. Typically, the Drupal.org site includes installers for both the current version of Drupal and the most recent previous version of Drupal.

Cross-Reference

Patching and upgrading sites is discussed in more detail in Chapter 35. ■

If you are creating a new installation, before you begin you need to make a decision whether to install version 6 or version 7 of the Drupal system. The versions are quite different, and you must consider two issues in choosing between them. First, Drupal 7's technical requirements are substantially more demanding and may be an issue if you are using a bargain-basement shared Web-hosting service; if you are using a more premium service or installing on your own hardware, the technical requirements are unlikely to be an issue.

Note

Technical requirements for Drupal 7 are discussed in this chapter. To learn more about the requirements, including the requirements for Drupal 6, visit `http://drupal.org/requirements`. **■**

Second, before you select a version, you should research the extensions that you require for your site. You need to make sure all your desired extensions are compatible with the Drupal version you want to deploy. Do not assume everything you need is available for both versions. Newer extensions may not work with older versions of the core, and the process of upgrading existing extensions often lags behind core releases by a significant period of time.

The official Drupal releases are delivered in an archive format, .tar.gz. Note that the name of the archive file will also include the version number of the release—for example, `drupal-7.1.tar.gz`. Pay attention to the version number; not only should you try to use the most recent version but you should also always avoid using development versions of any release on a production site. Note Figure 2.3, showing the Downloads page with the development versions highlighted.

FIGURE 2.3

The table shows the various core file installation packages available. Note that the highlighted versions are development versions and should not be used in a production environment.

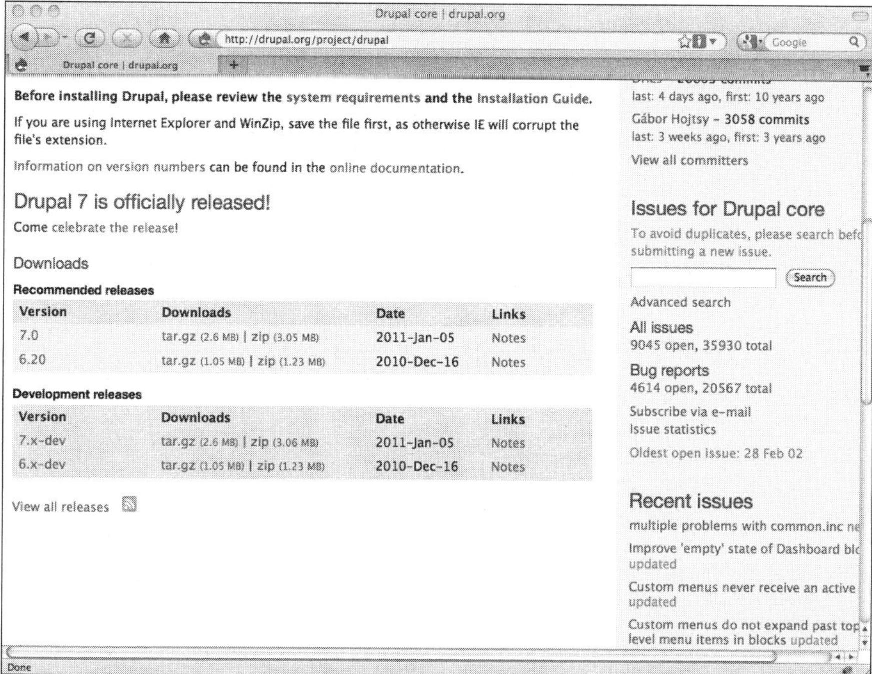

The Acquia Drupal Option

Acquia is a commercial open-source software company specializing in the Drupal CMS. The firm is the brainchild of Dries Buytaert, the founder of Drupal, and includes on its staff a number of very visible and well-known members of the Drupal community.

In 2009, Acquia began offering its own distribution of the Drupal core, enhanced with a number of popular features. The focus is on building social publishing Web sites, but the Acquia Drupal package includes a number of pre-installed Modules that are useful in a variety of contexts.

The Acquia Drupal option is particularly attractive to users who are sensitive about the lack of support for open-source software. Acquia users have access to technical support information, site monitoring services, and commercial support.

You can learn more and download the Acquia Drupal installer at `http://acquia.com`.

Technical Requirements

The technical requirements for Drupal are quite basic. The system is very tolerant of variations in server settings and, generally speaking, runs on the vast majority of commercial services that run Linux, Unix, or even Windows. This makes installing Drupal on most commercial Web hosts easy, rarely requiring additional configuration of the server. For visitors, the front end is usable by both computers and mobile devices using any browser. For site administrators, the back end supports the most recent versions of all the common browsers.

Tip

There is now even an iPhone application that allows you to administer your Drupal site from your iPhone. The application is called Drupad and is available from the iTunes store. ■

The server requirements

The preferred server setup for Drupal includes the Apache Web server with the MySQL database, though other options are available. Drupal is primarily written in PHP, so the server also must have PHP installed. If you want to run Drupal you most likely want to stick with the LAMP stack configuration (Linux/Apache/MySQL/PHP) because there are not only numerous options for Web hosting but also more support resources.

Table 2.2 shows the minimum and preferred technical system requirements for your server.

TABLE 2.2

Software Requirements for Drupal 7.x

Specification	Minimum	Recommended
Apache Web server	ver. 1.3 or 2.x	--
MySQL Database	ver. 5.0.15+ (with the PDO database extension)	--
PHP (note settings below)	ver. 5.2.5+	Ver. 5.3
PHP Configuration: Memory	32MB	64MB+
PHP Configuration: safe_mode	OFF	--
PHP Configuration: register_globals	OFF	--

Note

Drupal makes use of some features not available on all hosting plans. Make certain your host allows database accounts with the following rights: SELECT, INSERT, UPDATE, DELETE, CREATE, DROP, INDEX, ALTER. Some contributed modules and Drupal 5.x also require the following rights: CREATE TEMPORARY TABLES, LOCK TABLES. ■

Requirements for site visitors and administrators

The front end of Drupal is usable by a variety of platforms and browsers, including mobile devices. Indeed, the display of the front end is impacted more by the way the site's theme is coded than by anything inherent in the system itself. Support for JavaScript is recommended but not required for the default site.

Note

The installation of certain third-party extensions may bring with them additional requirements. You should always check whether the extensions that you install are compatible with the systems you require for your site visitors. ■

To manage content and administer a Drupal site, you need nothing more than a connection to the Internet and a Web browser. The back-end admin system is compatible with the recent versions of the most common browsers, including Internet Explorer, Firefox, Safari, Opera, and Chrome.

Installing Drupal

This section covers the installation of Drupal on either a local server or a remote Web host. Installing Drupal on a remote Web host allows you to create a publicly accessible Web site that others can see and use. Creating a local installation of Drupal—that is, an installation you can access on your local machine without having to use the Internet—simplifies testing and development and can significantly streamline your development efforts. In either case, the process of installing Drupal is roughly the same; this section discusses both options.

Creating a local development site

You can create a Drupal site on your local computer for testing and development purposes. Creating a local installation has a number of advantages. First, typically, it is faster and easier to work on a new site locally and then move it to the server when development is complete. Second, a local installation allows you to test new features and customizations without risk to a live site. Finally, a local installation can provide a fail-safe; if a serious problem arises on your live site, you can use your local site as a resource for repairing or replacing the damaged code on the live site.

For most people, the time savings alone are sufficient reason to build locally. A local installation can save you significant time moving files back and forth from a remote Web server during the development process. Moreover, if you have only a slow or unreliable Internet connection, a local development installation can avoid huge amounts of frustration.

A local installation can be created on any system—Windows, Mac, or Linux. However, you need to make sure your machine can function as a server and that it meets the technical requirements outlined earlier in this chapter. You can obtain and install each of the various server components independently if you want to, but it is much simpler to acquire one of several packages that allow you to install all the required software in one click. For Windows users, the XAMPP and WampServer packages provide an easy way to install Apache, MySQL, PHP, and related tools. Mac users can accomplish the same thing with either XAMPP or MAMP. Linux users can install XAMPP.

Note

You can download XAMPP at `http://www.apachefriends.org`**, WampServer at** `http://www.wampserver.com`**, and MAMP at** `http://www.mamp.info`**. ■**

Cross-Reference

Installing XAMPP is discussed in Appendix C. Installing MAMP is discussed in Appendix D. ■

After you have installed the underlying package containing all the necessary server components, you are ready to set up Drupal on your local machine. Installing Drupal on any of the -AMP packages involves the same basic process: Obtain the files, create the database, and then run the installer.

Most users can get a new local site up and running by following these steps:

1. **Download the Drupal core files, as discussed earlier.**
2. **Open the htdocs directory inside the -AMP folder on your machine.**
3. **Create a new directory for your Drupal sitc.**

   Keep the name simple, because you will use it for the address in your browser, for example, `drupal7`.
4. **Unzip the Drupal files, and place them inside the new directory.**
5. **Start the servers for your -AMP package.**

   Follow the directions that came with the application. When the servers start, your browser opens and displays the home page of the -AMP package. What you see should be similar to Figure 2.4.
6. **Click the link for phpMyAdmin.**

   The phpMyAdmin interface opens in your browser.
7. **In the text field labeled Create new database, type a name for your database and click Create.**

   The system creates a new database.
8. **Point your browser to the directory where you placed your Drupal files to see the Drupal installation wizard appear.**

   From this point, you can follow the steps outlined in the section "Running the Drupal installer" later in this chapter.

FIGURE 2.4

The start page of MAMP, typical of the -AMP packages. Note the phpMyAdmin link at the top of the page.

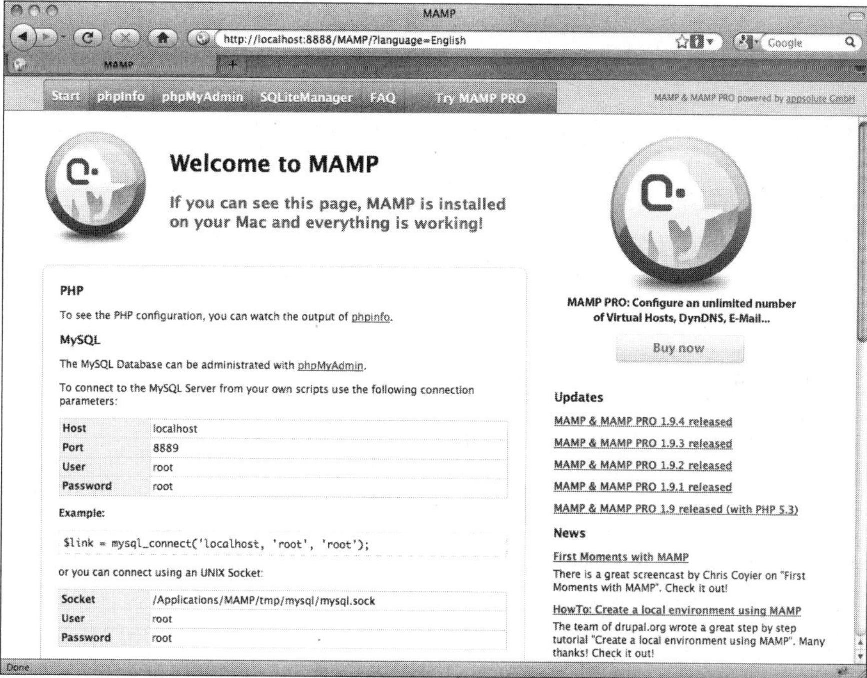

Installing on a Web-hosting service

Drupal installation on a remote server typically follows one of two paths: manual installation or use of your Web host's automated installer system.

Automated installers, like Fantastico or Plesk, are services provided by some Web hosts. The automated installers allow you to set up Drupal or other popular systems directly from your Web-hosting account control panel. If you want to use an automated installer, follow the directions of your Web host. Should you need assistance, contact your Web host for support.

Note

Occasionally, using an automated installer can cause permissions problems in the directories and files of the resulting site. For most users, these problems are not an issue, but if you intend to do extensive customization to your site, I advise you to avoid this whole issue by installing the site files yourself, rather than relying on the automated installer. ■

If you want to install Drupal yourself, without the use of a system like Plesk or Fantastico, simply follow these steps as a precursor to installation:

1. **Download the Drupal core files, as discussed earlier.**
2. **Access your Web server.**
3. **Create a new directory for your Drupal site.**

   Keep the name simple because you use it for the address in your browser—for example, `drupal`. If you want to install Drupal in the root directory, you can skip this step.
4. **Move the archive containing the Drupal files to the server.**

   You can do this by either using FTP to transfer the files or by using the file manager in your Web hosting control panel. Place the files in the directory where you want the site to appear.

Note

Appendix A shows a listing of the Drupal files and directories as they should appear on your server. ■

5. **Extract the Drupal file archive.**

   If your Web host does not provide the option to extract archive files on the server, you need to extract the archive locally and then move the files up to the server. Note that this can take significantly longer because the number and size of the files is substantial!
6. **Create a new database for your Drupal site.**

   The process for this varies according to your hosting setup, but a typical user on a -Nix system will use `phpMyAdmin` to create the new database.
7. **Point your browser to the directory where you placed your Drupal files to see the Drupal installation wizard appear.**

   From this point, you can follow the steps outlined in the section below, "Running the Drupal installer."

Note

The name of the root directory varies from Web host to Web host. If you're not sure which directory on your Web server is the root directory, contact your Web-hosting support team. ■

Running the Drupal installer

Drupal includes a step-by-step installer with an interface that is similar to many other standard software installation wizards. The installer does the vast majority of the work for you. In most cases, you need only supply information when prompted to do so.

Before you can run the installer, you must follow the steps outlined in the sections above and then point your browser to the address of the Drupal files on your server. When you load the address of your Drupal site in the browser, the installation wizard starts automatically and Step 1 of the installer is displayed on your screen.

Note

The official Drupal 7 Installation Guide can be found at `http://drupal.org/documentation/install`. ■

Step 1 is to select from one of the two default installation profiles, as shown in Figure 2.5. The profile labeled Standard includes pre-existing content types and has a number of modules and themes pre-enabled. In contrast, the Minimal profile does not define the content types and enables only one theme and the most basic set of modules. For most users, the Standard profile is the best choice, although more experienced users may prefer the Minimal profile.

Click the radio button to select the profile you prefer, and then click the Save and continue button.

FIGURE 2.5

Step 1 of the Installation Wizard prompts you to select the profile to be used, either Standard or Minimal.

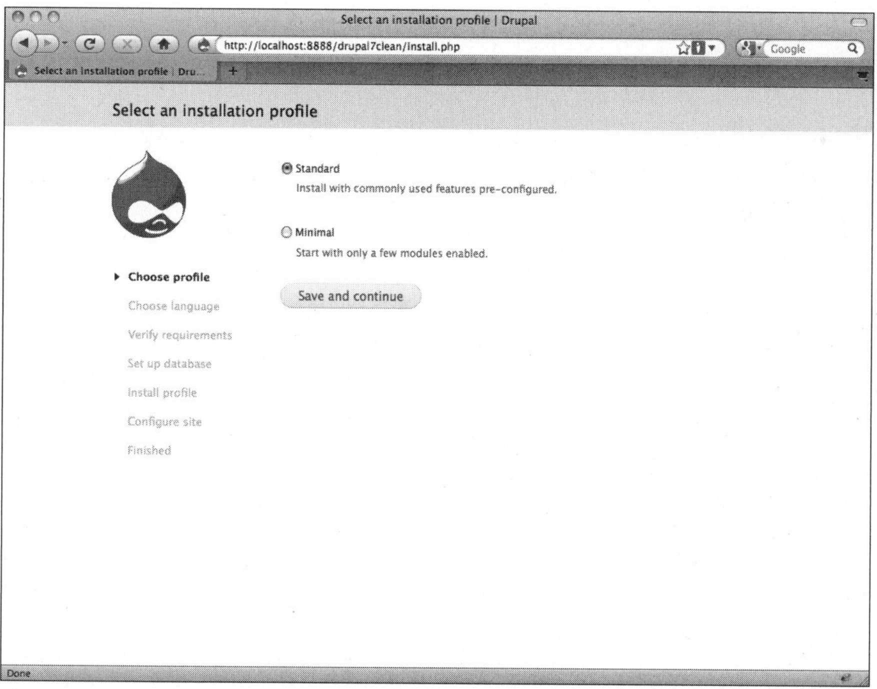

Step 2 of the installer is the language selection screen, as shown in Figure 2.6. The default installation package is tailored for English. If you want to install in English, simply click Install Drupal in English. If you want to install in another language, click the option labeled Learn how to install Drupal in other languages.

Cross-Reference

Working with the Drupal language packs is discussed in Chapter 4. ■

Clicking your choice automatically moves you to Step 3.

Step 3 is a requirements check, called by Drupal *Verify requirements*. If your system is already capable of supporting Drupal, you never see this step; instead the system advances directly to the fourth step in the installer process. If, on the other hand, there are problems to address before you can install Drupal, they are displayed on this screen and you need to take steps to solve them before you can move on to Step 4.

FIGURE 2.6

The second step of the installer is the language selector; English is the only language installed in the default package.

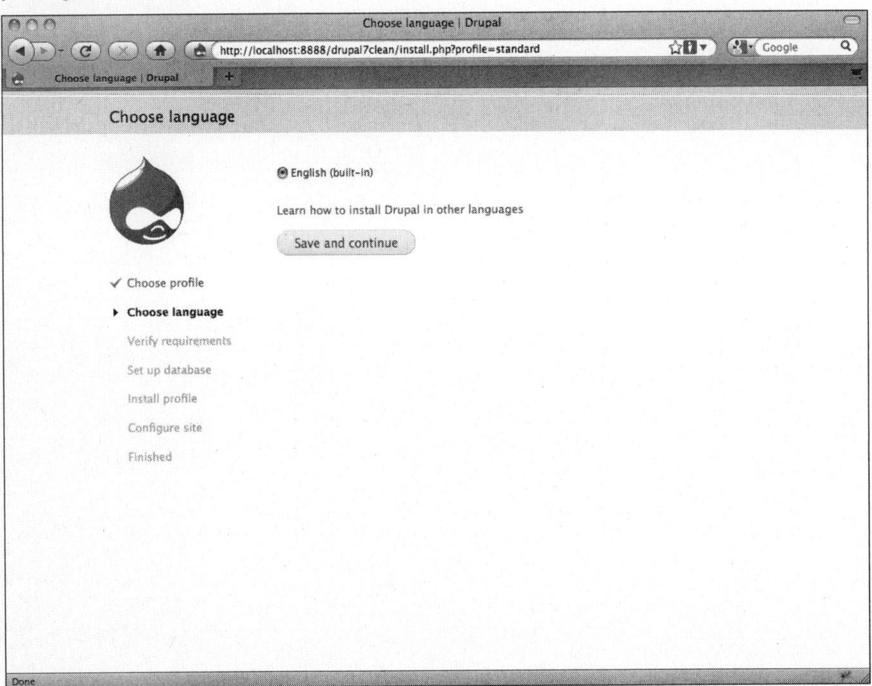

If you are shown the Verify requirements screen, you will see a list of the system requirements, color-coded to help you identify quickly where the problem exists. Here's a legend for the color-coding on the Verify requirements screen:

- A green check mark by an item indicates that it meets the requirements.
- A yellow triangle with an exclamation point in it indicates that a potential problem exists. Typically this appears in situations where your server meets the basic requirements but does not meet the ideal configuration. Cautions do not stop you from installing Drupal, but you should address the issue, where practical.
- A red circle with an X inside indicates a critical problem that must be addressed before you can install Drupal on your server. If you see any warnings of this nature, you must address them before you can move on.

After you have addressed the issues, reload the page to run the check again. When all issues are cleared, click the link to proceed with the installation.

Step 4 of the installer is a database configuration, as shown in Figure 2.7. You need to accurately complete the information requested on this screen to install Drupal successfully. First, select the type of database you want to use. Next, enter the name for the database, your database username, and your database password.

FIGURE 2.7

Step 4 of the Installer shows the Database Configuration fields.

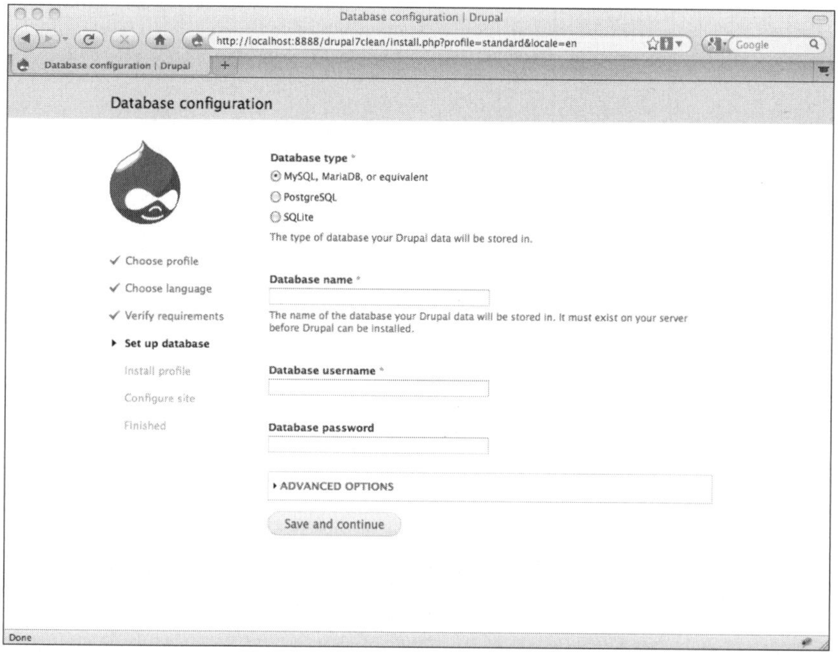

Note also the advanced options, which allow you to change the database server, port, and table prefix. If you have no need to adjust these settings, leave them alone because the default values are correct for most people.

After you have entered the information, click the Save and continue button. The Installer attempts to connect with your database, and if it is successful, it moves on to Step 5. If it is not successful, you receive an error message explaining where the problem lies. After you have addressed the problem, try clicking the Next button again.

Step 5 of the process is automatic. During this step, the system installs the profile you selected during Step 1. While this is happening, you see a status screen, as shown in Figure 2.8. After the process is completed, the system moves you to the next step, the configuration screen.

Step 6 of the installer is the site configuration screen, as shown in Figure 2.9. This screen has four sections:

- Site information
- Site maintenance account
- Server settings
- Update notifications

FIGURE 2.8

During Step 5, the system installs the profile selected, and you see a status indicator like this one.

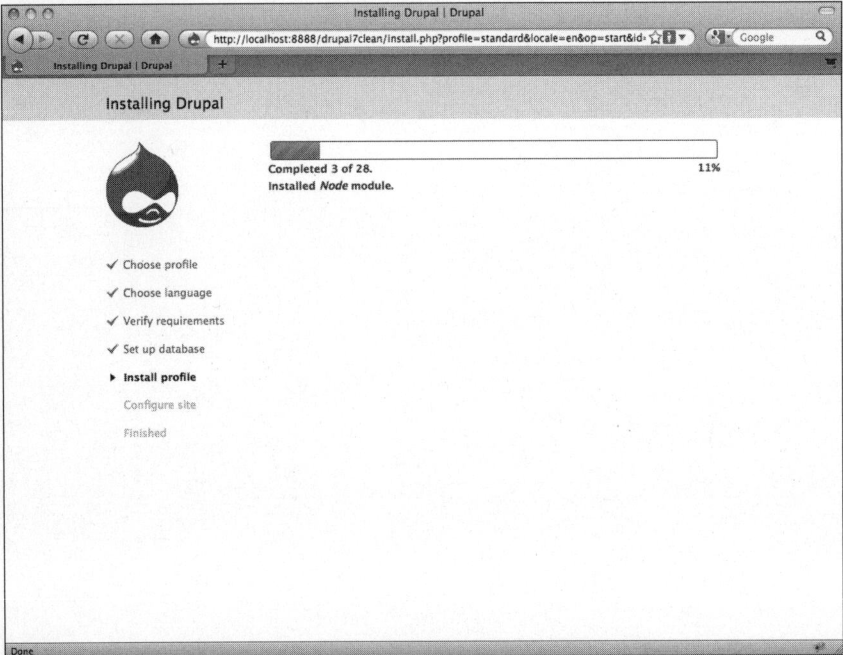

FIGURE 2.9

Step 6 of the Installer is the site configuration page.

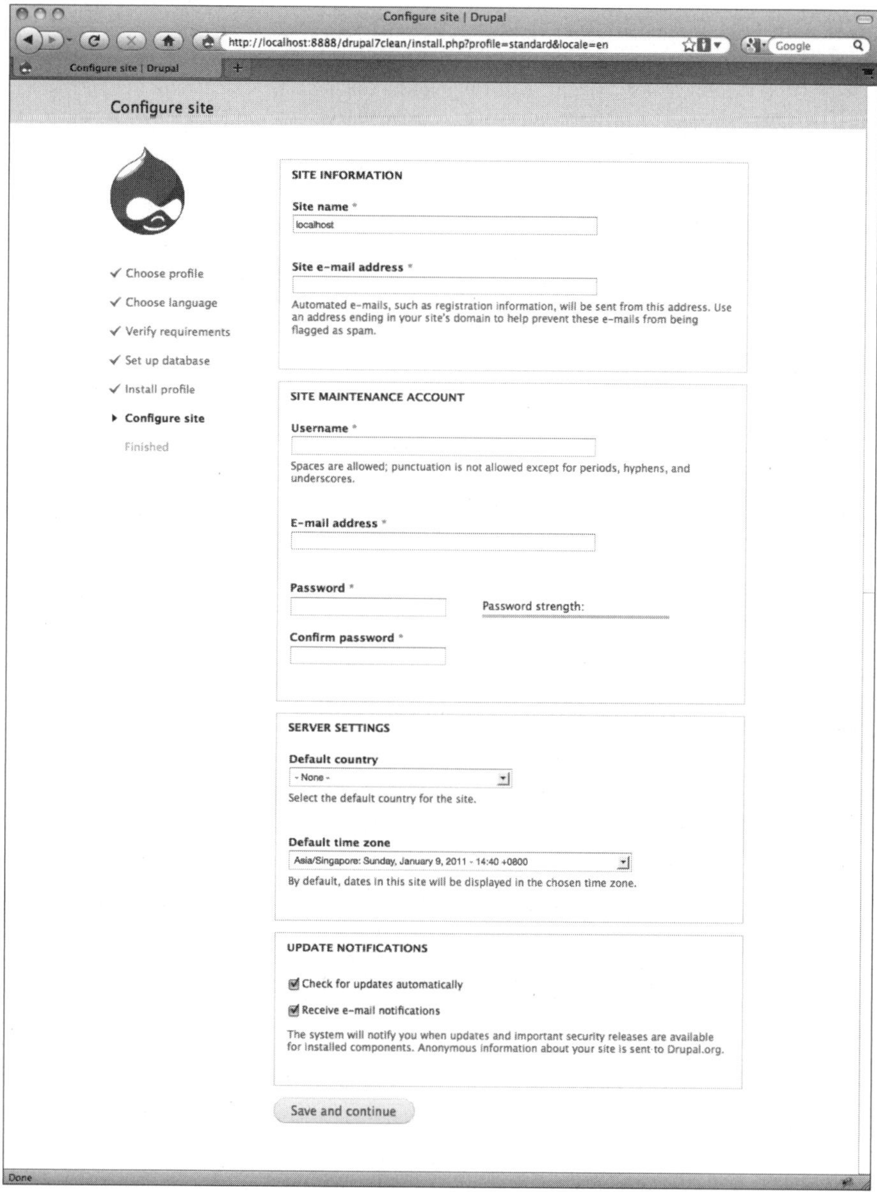

In the Site information section, type a name for your site in the field labeled Site name. Enter a default e-mail address for the site in the field labeled Site e-mail address. Note that both of these can be edited later from within the admin section of your site.

The Site maintenance account section allows you to create the default site administrator account. Give the administrator a Username and Password, and associate it with an e-mail address. This user account can be edited later from within the admin system.

Note

Make note of this information; you need it to log in to the admin system! ■

The Server settings section allows you to associate the site with a geographic location and to set the time zone you want the site to use.

Note

The default time zone settings come from the server. ■

The final Update notifications section contains two check boxes that instruct the system to check automatically for updates and to enable e-mail notifications. Most people should use these options to help keep up to date with patches and security releases.

After you have completed the configuration settings, click the Save and continue button to move to the final screen.

Step 7 of the installer is the confirmation screen, as shown in Figure 2.10. This page has no required steps; rather it provides you with a confirmation that the installation is complete and a link to the back end of your new site. Click the option to visit your new site to begin configuring the site.

After you have completed your site installation, you are greeted with the default site screen. You are logged into the Site Maintenance Account. This is the account you created in Step 6.

Cross-Reference

Site configuration and the Site Information page are covered in detail in Chapter 4. ■

That's it—you're finished! Your new Drupal site is ready for you to explore and to configure for your needs, topics that I cover in depth in the following chapters.

FIGURE 2.10

Step 7 of the Installer is the final Confirmation screen. You're done!

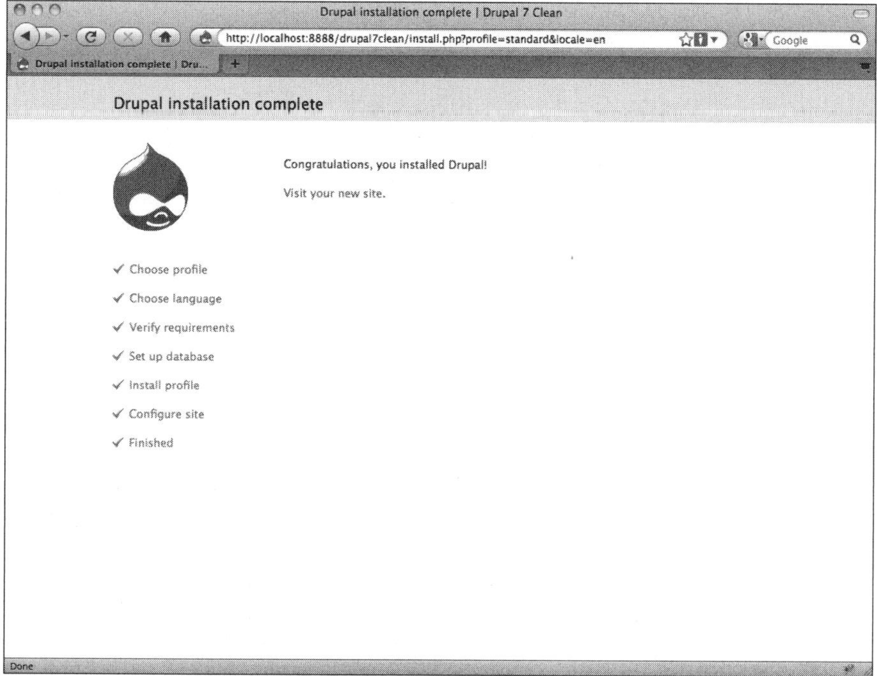

Summary

This chapter addressed the acquisition and installation of Drupal 7. The following points were covered:

- The technical requirements for running Drupal 7
- Where to obtain the proper files
- How to install the system locally
- How to install the system on a Web-hosting service
- The Standard and Minimal installation profiles

CHAPTER 3

Taking Your First Look at Drupal

After working through the preceding chapter, you should have a complete Drupal installation ready for exploration. This chapter goes through Drupal's front-end and back-end interfaces and explains what you see on the screen. The chapter is concerned with the big picture, and the goals are to provide a quick orientation and to give a fast start to those of you who cannot wait for the later chapters.

All the references and figures in this chapter refer to the default "Standard" installation of Drupal 7.

IN THIS CHAPTER

Reviewing the front-end interface

Reviewing the admin interface

The Front End: Drupal's Public Interface

The front end of your Drupal site is the interface that is seen by the visitors to the site. The front end is the target for the majority of your output and the place where your visitors access the site's content and functionality. By default, access to the front end of a Drupal site is unrestricted; however, you can limit the visibility of content and functionality to only those users that are registered and logged in to the system.

Cross-Reference

Controlling access to content and functionality is covered in detail in Chapter 24. ■

Figure 3.1 shows the default front end of Drupal 7. At this point, we have no content to display and the number of exposed modules and blocks is minimal; you need to add a content item before you see any output in the main content area of the site. The default theme is Bartik, and the only block visible is the User Login block, which supplies the login form you see in the left column.

The Drupal team has made a serious effort to create a system that is compatible with the wide variety of devices and browsers in use today. The site looks consistent regardless of whether visitors use Firefox, Internet Explorer, Safari, Opera, or Chrome. The site is usable by most common mobile devices as well. Accessibility compliance has been addressed by the Drupal team; the default site allows users of varying abilities to interact with the site.

Note

Browser compatibility and accessibility are largely a function of the theme used for a site. If you install a different theme, it may well have an impact on the usability of the front end. ■

Cross-Reference

Accessibility is addressed in more detail in Chapter 34. ■

FIGURE 3.1

This is the default front end of Drupal 7, prior to adding content or additional modules or blocks. Note the User Login block published in the left column.

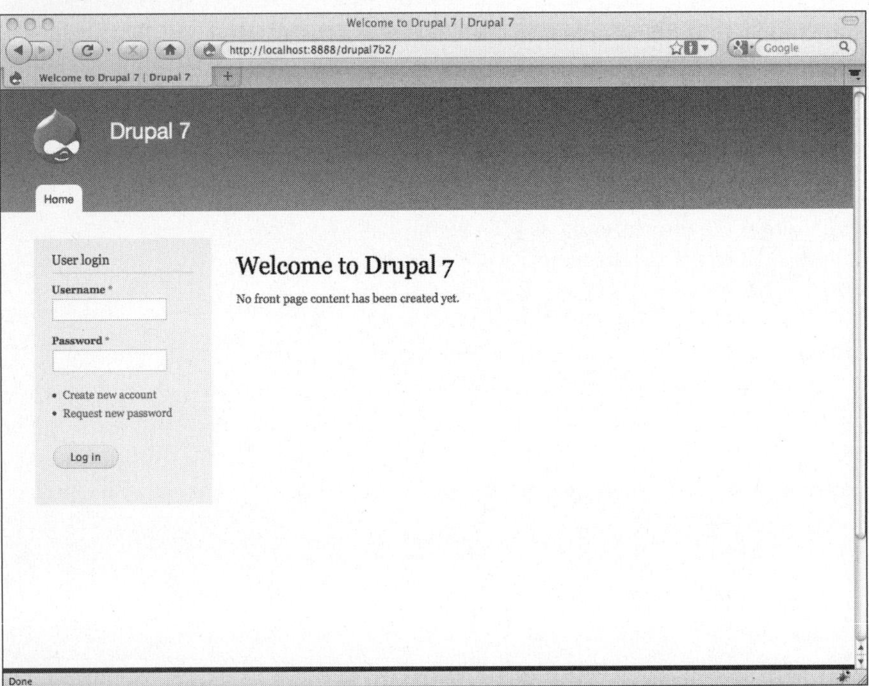

Developing Your Drupal Vocabulary

A quick orientation to the various terms of art used throughout this book will help you to develop a clear understanding of what is said both in this book and in the official Drupal documentation resources.

Article

As the term is used in the context of Drupal, an *article* is a *content type*. As Drupal explains, you can "use articles for time-sensitive content like news, press releases, or blog posts." Articles in Drupal are typically published in chronological order, with the most recent articles appearing first.

Basic Page

A *basic page* is another Drupal *content type*. Drupal advises you to "use basic pages for your static content, such as an 'About us' page."

Block

Blocks typically provide output in the secondary areas of the page—that is, not inside the main content area. Blocks are sometimes simply containers that hold text or pictures; at other times, they provide limited functionality, like the user login box (refer to Figure 3.1). Blocks are often paired with *modules* to provide an alternative means of displaying output from the module. Blocks are collected inside the Blocks Manager where they can be edited and assigned to various pages and positions.

Content Types

Content types define the default settings for the various content items. All items of content in Drupal belong to one of the content types. The default system includes only two active content types: article and basic page. Drupal is bundled with four additional content types that can be activated through the Modules Manager: *blog entry*, *book page*, *forum topic*, and *poll*. In addition, site administrators can create additional custom content types.

Core

The term *core* in this context refers simply to the files included in the default Drupal distribution.

Extensions

Extension is a generic term that refers to any module or theme that is added to the default system. Extensions can be installed, deleted, or managed through the admin system.

Menus

Menus hold the navigation choices for your site. Menus are created, edited, and deleted from within the Menus Manager; menu display, however, is managed from the Blocks Manager because menu output is controlled by blocks containing the menu items.

continued

continued

Menu Items

Menu items are the choices, or links, on a menu. Menu items are created, edited, and deleted from within the Menus Manager.

Module

Modules are major units of functionality that provide output in the main content area of a page. Modules are the most complex individual units in the system, sometimes constituting complete applications in themselves. The default system contains a number of modules, and you can add more to the system.

Node

A *node* in Drupal is any posting, such as an article, page, poll, blog post, or forum entry.

Overlay

The Drupal *overlay* is the floating lightbox used for the administration pages in the default Drupal 7 configuration. The overlay is new in Drupal 7 and is used only to present administration pages; it is visible only when a user is logged into the site as an administrator. The overlay functionality is controlled by the Overlay module.

Permission

Permissions control a user's access to content or functionality. The site administrator can set the permissions for user groups or specific users.

Role

Roles are used to group users. Permissions can be set for an entire group of users by setting permissions for the role.

Taxonomy

A *taxonomy* is a collection of terms that can be used to describe content items. Taxonomy terms can be organized into vocabularies and used as a method of organizing or locating content items. Taxonomy functionality in Drupal is supplied by the Taxonomy module that is included in the core.

Theme

A *theme* controls the presentation layer of your Drupal site, that is, it defines the interfaces of the site. When you change a theme, you change the way the site looks for either the visitors or the administrators. Themes can be added to the system and are collected inside the Theme Manager.

Theme Engine

A theme engine is a collection of scripts and files that interpret the templating language and process the commands contained therein. Drupal uses the PHPTemplate theme engine, which relies on PHP as the templating language.

Toolbar

The *toolbar,* as the term is used in Drupal, is the top navigation bar that you can see when you are logged into the site as an administrator. By default, the toolbar contains the site's Management menu. The toolbar functionality is supplied by the Toolbar module and can be configured from inside the admin system.

Menu structure

The default Drupal installation contains 64 menu items organized into four menus, listed in Table 3.1. For a comprehensive view of all the system's menus, visit the admin system's Menus Manager. The Menus Manager lists all the menus along with links to view and edit the menu items for each menu. New menus and new menu items also can be created from within the Menus Manager.

TABLE 3.1

Summary of the Default Menu Structure

Menu Name	Primary Purpose	Access Level
Main menu	Links to major sections of the site	Public
Management	The administration menu	Restricted
Navigation	Contains links for visitors and content creators	Mixed
User menu	Links for the site's users	Restricted

Figure 3.2 shows the menus in action on the default site.

Main menu

The default Main menu contains only one menu item, named *Home*. The item provides a link back to the Web site's home page. Note in Figure 3.2 the Home tab under the site logo; it is generated by the Main menu.

FIGURE 3.2

This shows the default menus on the site as they appear when viewed by a registered and authenticated user with administration permissions.

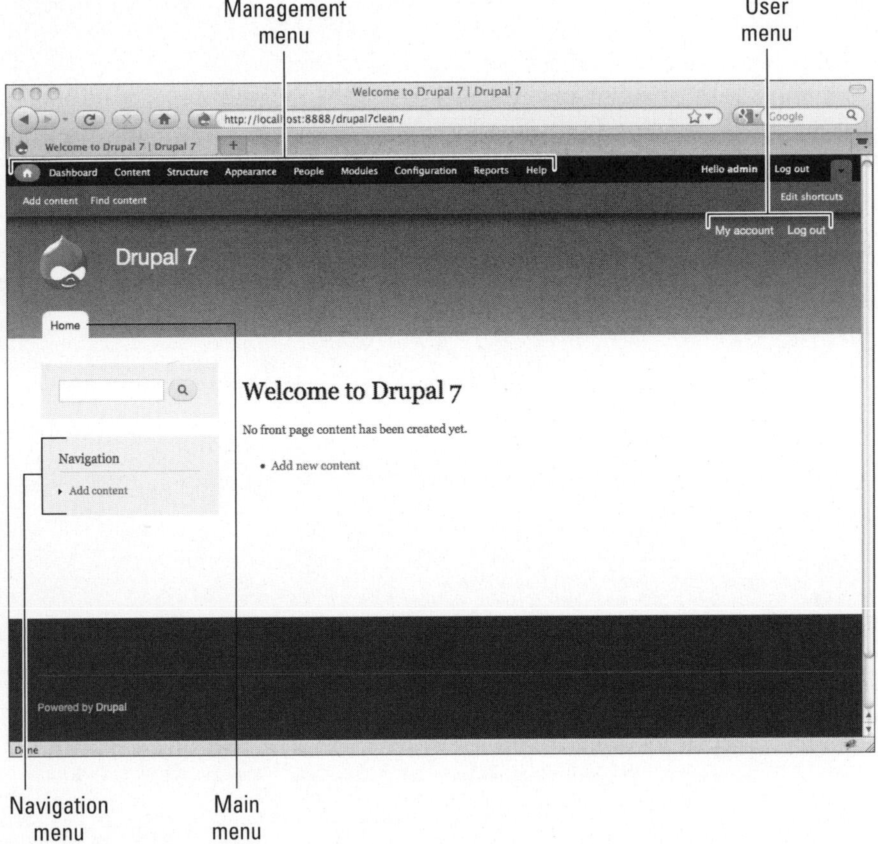

Note

The tab formatting used by the Home menu item is the result of the styling included in the default theme, Bartik. See Chapter 8 for a discussion of how to control the appearance of menus. ■

Management menu

The Management menu contains links for administrative tasks. The default Management menu includes 55 links, providing access to all the administration options in the system. In the default system, this is the menu that appears at the top of the page when a user with administration privileges is logged in (refer to Figure 3.2).

Navigation menu

The Navigation menu provides a set of links that serve several purposes. Although there are six menu items on the Navigation menu, only four of them are enabled by default. The four enabled menu items all provide shortcuts to the content creation pages and are visible only to authenticated users with permission to create new content items. The two menu items that are disabled provide links to site search and to the Compose Tips help file.

User menu

The User menu contains links related to functionality associated with user accounts, including the *log out* link. The default configuration includes two links, but only one—the log out link—is enabled.

Cross-Reference

Detailed information about working with menus and menu items is contained in Chapter 8. ■

Modules

Modules are a key part of the Drupal system. Not only are modules responsible for much of the functionality seen by site visitors, but they also provide many of the helper applications that enable the system's functionality.

Tip

A good way to learn more about the system is to enable the additional modules in the Modules Manager and play with them a bit. If you later decide that you don't need or want them all, you can always disable the unnecessary modules from within the Modules Manager. ■

The default Drupal installation comes with a large number of modules already installed. As discussed in Chapter 2, exactly which modules are enabled on your new site depend upon what installation profile you selected when you set up the site. Additionally, as an administrator, you have the option to enable other modules or to disable ones that you do not need. While certain modules are essential to the proper functioning of your site, others can be enabled only as needed.

Note

Modules that are necessary for the system to function cannot be disabled. These modules are marked in the Modules Manager as Required by: Drupal. In other cases, some dependencies limit your ability to enable or disable modules. For example, the Forum module requires the Taxonomy module. Therefore, if you are using the Forum module, you cannot disable the Taxonomy module. Similarly, you cannot enable the Forum module unless you have already enabled the Taxonomy module. ■

Cross-Reference

The default modules are reviewed in depth in Chapter 6. ■

Unfortunately, because the default system doesn't include sample data, it is hard to appreciate the modules that are at work. Until you add your content, there is little to see on the front end of the site. Nonetheless, a number of modules are working away out of the public eye. Blocks, menus, the admin overlay, and much more are all created by the default Drupal modules.

In addition to the modules enabled by default, the system includes other modules that are initially disabled, including:

- Aggregator
- Blog
- Book
- Contact
- Content translation
- Forum
- Locale
- Open ID
- PHP filter
- Poll
- Statistics
- Syslog
- Testing
- Tracker
- Trigger

If you would like to try out these modules and see them in action, go to the Modules Manager and enable them.

Cross-Reference

Working with modules and the Modules Manager is covered in detail in Chapter 6. ■

Note

Unlike menus and blocks, new modules cannot be created from within the admin system. To learn how to customize modules or create new ones, see Chapter 28. ■

Blocks and regions

Blocks are used to place information or functionality on the page outside of the main content area. Regions are the placeholders used to hold blocks. Blocks and regions serve a key role in both the front-end and back-end display in Drupal.

The default Drupal installation includes 15 blocks. Some of the blocks are published and visible, while others are not. Block visibility depends upon the following:

- Whether the block is assigned to the page being viewed
- Whether the block is assigned to a region that is available on the page being viewed
- Whether the viewer has sufficient permissions to view the block

The block assignment, ordering, and visibility are set by configuring the block via the Blocks Manager.

In addition to the blocks you see on the default site, the system includes other blocks that are disabled by default, including these:

- Main menu
- Management
- Recent comments
- Recent content
- Shortcuts
- Syndicate
- User menu
- Who's new
- Who's online

If you would like to try out these blocks, go to the Blocks Manager and enable them by assigning them to any of the regions shown.

Cross-Reference

The default blocks are reviewed in depth in Chapter 7. ■

Blocks are placed on the page by assigning them to regions. The regions are coded into the theme by the theme designer. Figure 3.3 shows the names of the regions available in the default Bartik theme.

Cross-Reference

Creating regions is covered in Chapter 26. ■

FIGURE 3.3

The default home page, showing an overlay that indicates the names of the available regions. This information is specific to this particular theme. Regions vary from theme to theme.

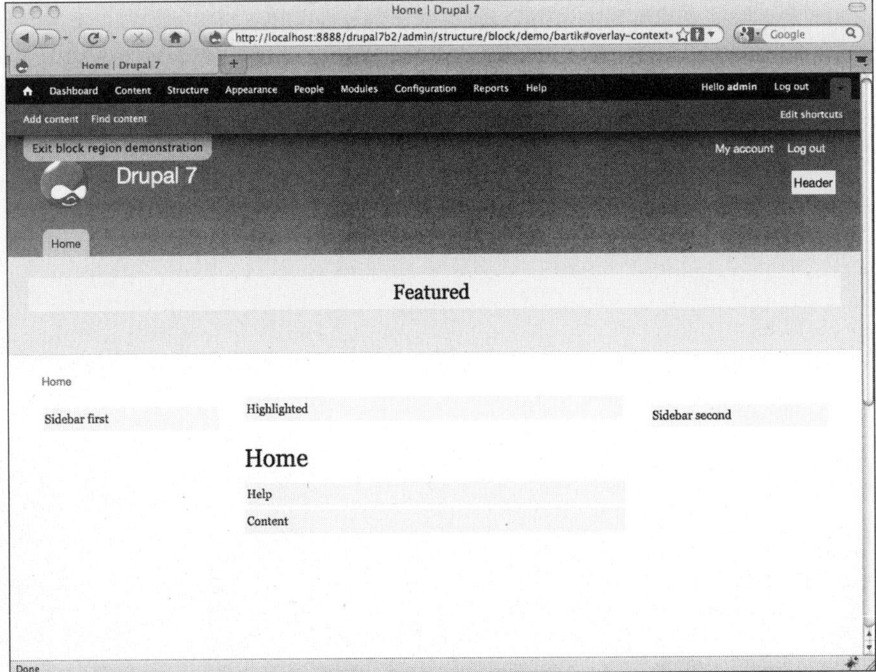

The Back End: Drupal's Admin Interface

The back end of your Drupal site is the administration interface, where the majority of your site management activities occur. Access to the admin system is controlled by a login form and is restricted to those users who have been granted permission to administer the system. By default, permission to access the admin system is granted only to users who are assigned to the Administrator role.

To access the admin functionality of your site, log in using the administrator account you set up during the installation. You can log in either by using the User Login form on the front end of the site or by directing your browser to the Drupal login page, located at `/user`–for example, `http://www.yourdomain.com/user`.

Note

If the Clean URLs functionality is not enabled, the login page can be found by directing your browser to `http://www.yourdomain.com/?q=user`. ■

After you log in, the system takes you to your site's home page. At the top of the home page you now see a new menu; this is the Management menu, which contains the links to the administration functionality.

Clicking almost any choice on the Management menu opens the admin overlay, which floats on a layer above the underlying page. Figure 3.4 shows a screenshot that includes both the Management menu and the admin overlay. To close the overlay and view the underlying Web page, click the "x" at the top-right corner of the overlay. To return to the site home page at any time, click the house icon at the top left.

The Management menu

The Management menu is divided into two rows. The top row contains links to the major administration functionality; it is controlled by the Management menu located inside the Menus Manager. The second row is an area that can be customized to include your favorite shortcuts to specific administration pages.

FIGURE 3.4

The administration interface shows the Management menu at the top and the overlay. In this example, the overlay shows the People Manager.

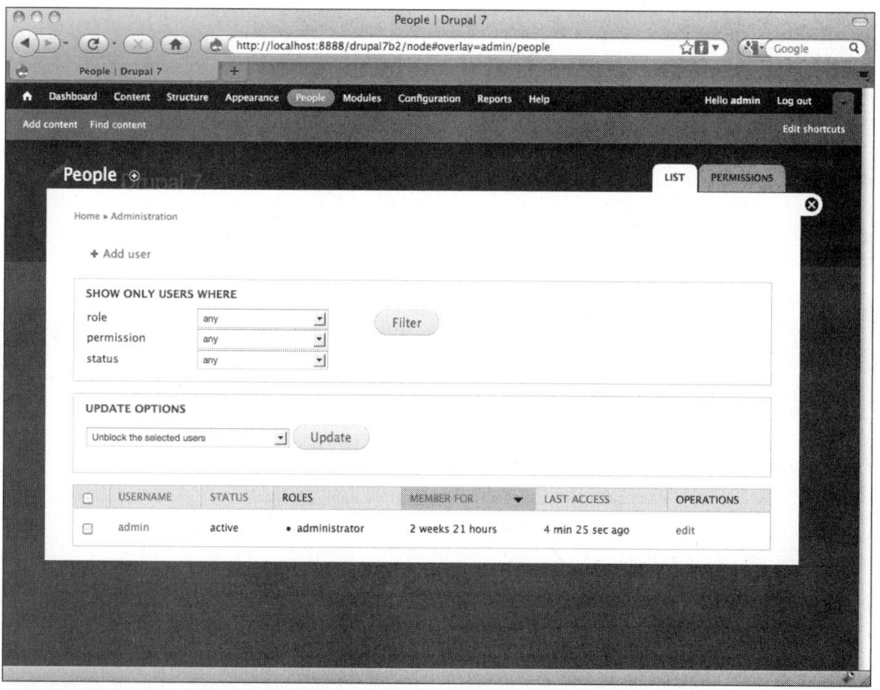

Note

Although they are visually connected, in reality the output on the top row is the Management menu, while the second row is provided by the Shortcut module. ■

Note

Customizing the shortcuts section of the Management menu is dealt with later in this chapter, in the "Customizing the admin interface" section. ■

The top row of the Management menu contains the following links:

- Home (an icon of a house)
- Dashboard
- Content
- Structure
- Appearance
- People
- Modules
- Configuration
- Reports
- Help

The Home option

The Home option, an icon shaped like a house, provides a link back to the home page of your Web site.

The Dashboard option

Clicking the Dashboard link on the Management menu pops up the admin dashboard in an overlay. The dashboard is designed to provide the administrator with useful information about recent site activity, together with links to key functionality.

Note

The dashboard is dealt with later in this chapter, in the "Working with the dashboard" and "Customizing the admin interface" sections. ■

The Content option

Clicking the Content option pops up the admin overlay showing the Content Manager. The Content Manager provides both a list of all the content items in the system as well as a link to add new content. Figure 3.5 shows the Content Manager.

FIGURE 3.5

The Content Manager interface contains a table listing all the available content items. At the top left is the Add content link. At the top right is a tab that allows you to view and manage all the comments in the system.

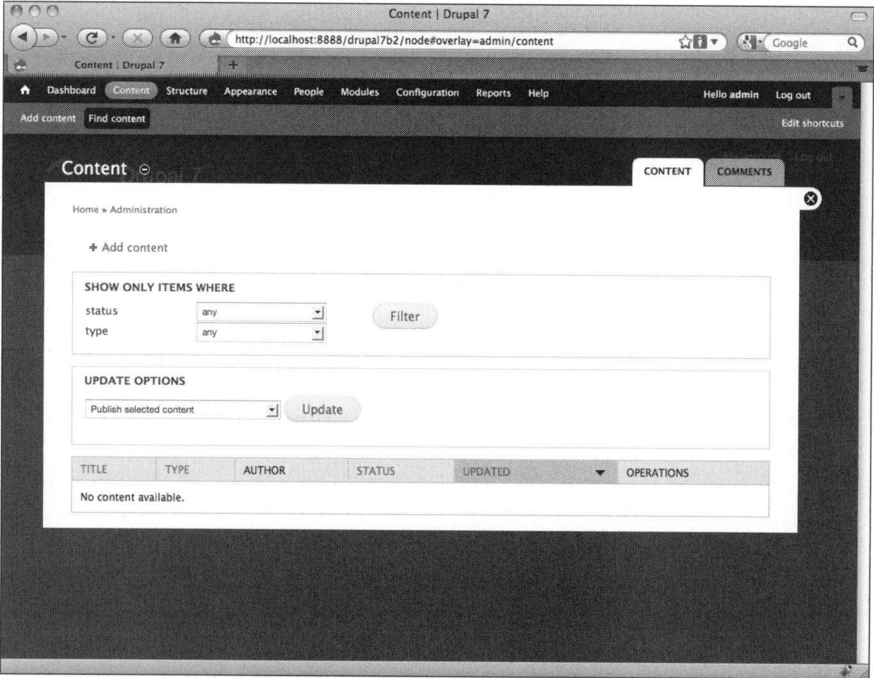

Content items can be viewed or edited from this interface. New content items can be added by clicking the Add content link at the top left of the Content Manager overlay.

Cross-Reference

Creating and managing content is discussed in Chapter 10. ■

The Structure option

Clicking the Structure option on the Management menu displays the Structure page in overlay. In the default configuration, the Structure page contains the following options:

- **Blocks:** Click to open the Blocks Manager.
- **Content types:** Click to open the Content Types Manager.
- **Menus:** Click to open the Menus Manager.
- **Taxonomy:** Click to open the Taxonomy Manager.

Cross-Reference

The Blocks Manager is covered in Chapter 7. The Content Types Manager is dealt with in Chapter 10. The Menus Manager is discussed in Chapter 8. Managing Taxonomies is covered in Chapter 11. ■

The Appearance option

Clicking on the Appearance option opens the Theme Manager in the overlay. Figure 3.6, below, shows the Theme Manager overlay. Note the three tabs at the top right that allow you to move between the theme list, the Theme Update Manager, and the theme configuration page.

Cross-Reference

Working with the Theme Manager is dealt with in Chapter 5. ■

The People option

Clicking the People option displays the People Manager in the overlay. The People Manager, shown in Figure 3.7, allows you to view all users in the system, edit or delete users, and create new users. The tab at the top right takes you to the page where you can manage permissions and roles.

FIGURE 3.6

The Theme Manager

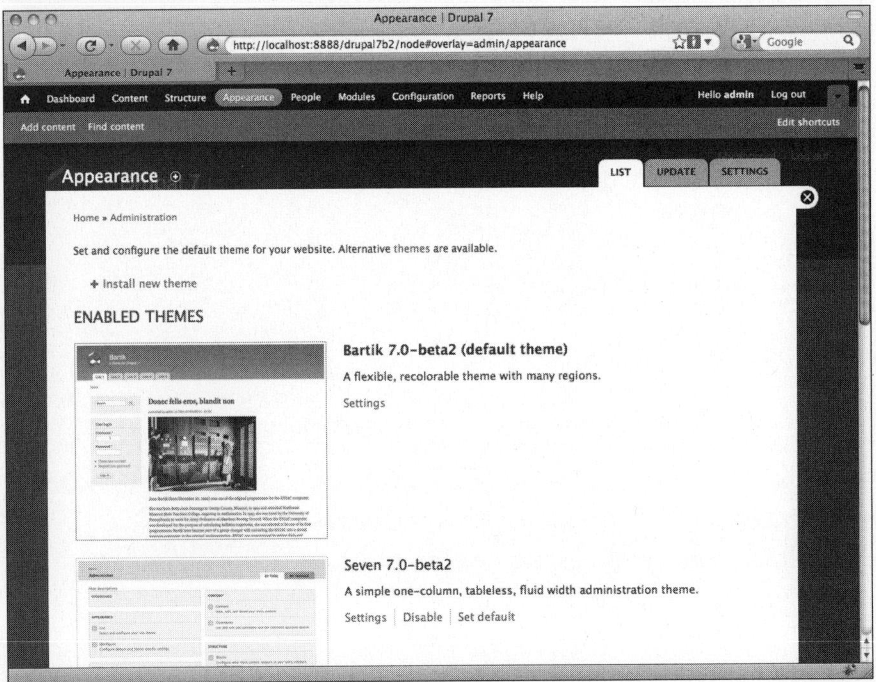

FIGURE 3.7

The People Manager

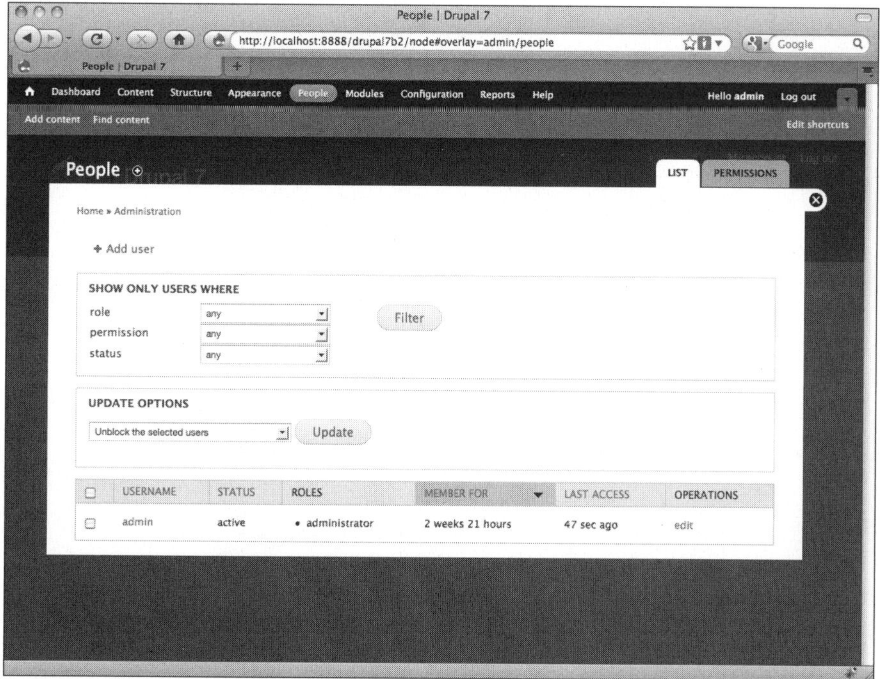

Cross-Reference

Working with users in discussed in Chapter 24. Controlling permissions and roles is covered in Chapter 25. ■

The Modules option

Clicking the Modules option opens the Modules Manager in the overlay. The Modules Manager allows you to enable, disable, and configure all the site's modules. Figure 3.8 shows the Modules Manager.

Cross-Reference

Module management is discussed in Chapter 6. Installing and uninstalling modules is covered in Chapter 29. ■

FIGURE 3.8

In the Modules Manager, the three tabs at the top right allow you to move between the modules list, the Module Update Manager, and the uninstall functionality.

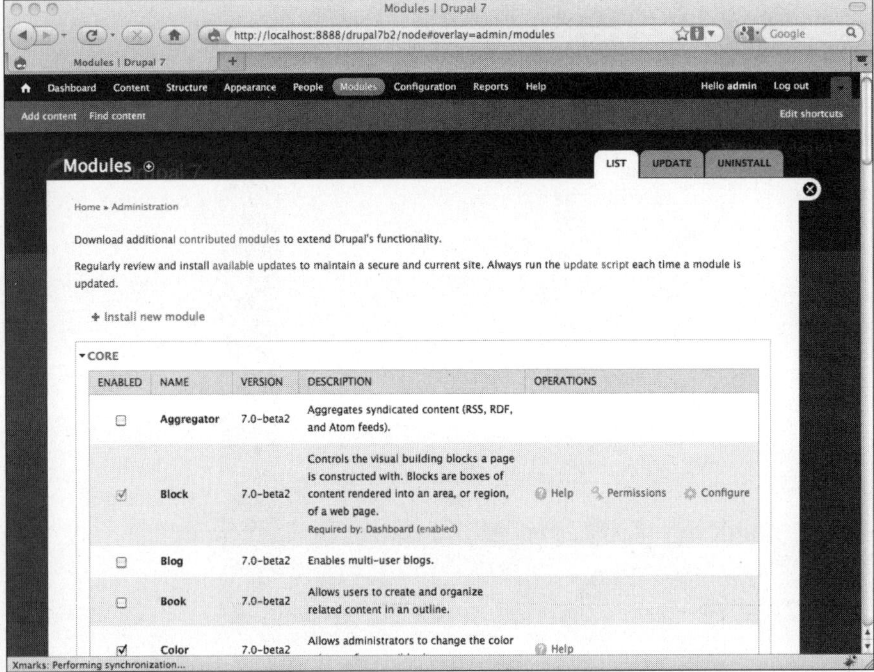

The Configuration option

Clicking the Configuration option opens the Configuration Manager in the overlay, as shown in Figure 3.9.

Note

Additional module-specific configuration options can be found in the Modules Manager, next to the name of each module. ■

Cross-Reference

Configuring Drupal is the subject of Chapter 4. ■

FIGURE 3.9

In the Configuration Manager, click any of the choices to view the configuration options for that particular item.

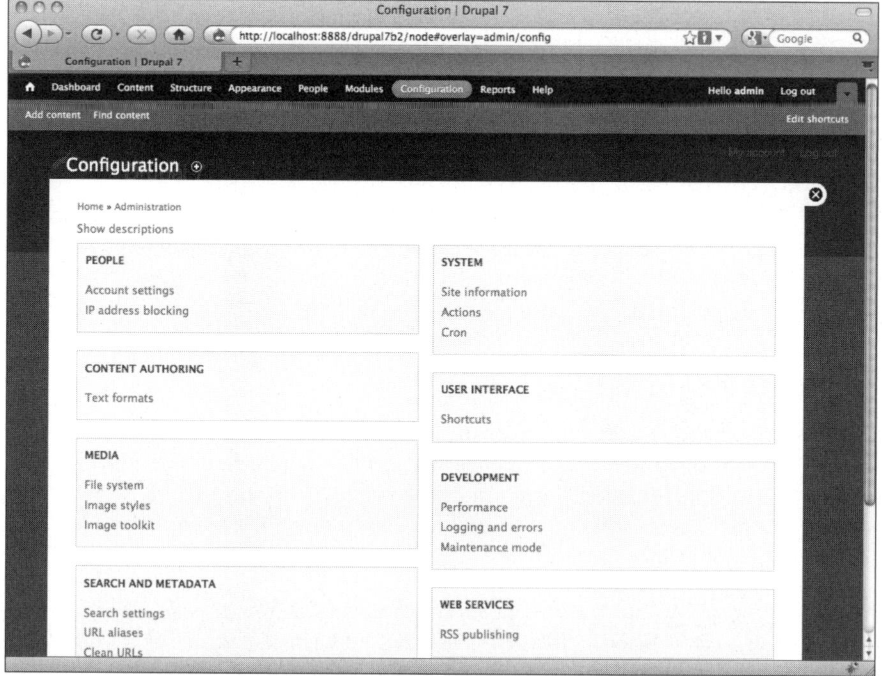

The Reports option

Clicking the Reports option on the Management menu displays the overlay. The overlay contains the following options:

- **Status report:** Click to view a summary status report for your site as a whole. This contains a number of useful items of information about your Drupal system and your server configuration
- **Available updates:** Click to view a list of available updates for your core files and extensions.
- **Recent log messages:** Click to view a list of recent system events. This is useful for diagnosing problems and site de-bugging.
- **Field list:** Click to view a list of all the fields currently in use in your content types. This is useful for keeping track of your custom fields and helping you to avoid creating unnecessary or duplicate fields.

- **Top "access denied" errors:** Click to view a list of all the times the site has displayed to visitors the error message "access denied" ("403" error messages). This is useful for diagnosing problems in permissions settings.
- **Top "page not found" errors:** Click to view a list of all the times the site has displayed to visitors the error message "page not found" ("404" error messages). This is useful for identifying broken links on your site.
- **Top search phrases:** Click to view a list of the most common words and phrases entered into the site search box. This is useful to help you prioritize your content, but it's pointless if you do not have site search enabled and visible to visitors.

The Help option

Click the Help option to open in the overlay an index of all the system's help files.

Working with the dashboard

The dashboard is designed to provide administrators with a place to collect useful tools and to see at a glance information about recent activity on the site. In the default configuration, the dashboard is available only to site administrators. To view the dashboard, click the Dashboard link on the Management menu. Figure 3.10 shows the appearance of the default configuration of the dashboard.

The newest content items appear in the Recent content section; the newest users appear in the Who's new space. You can click the title of any content items or the names of any users to view them. The Search form at the top right of the dashboard allows you to search the site's content or users. Click the X at the top right to close the dashboard and the overlay. Click the Customize dashboard link at the top left to view the configuration options, which are discussed below.

Customizing the admin interface

Drupal allows you to easily customize either the shortcuts section of the toolbar or the admin dashboard. Customizing the interface allows you to add quick links to access your favorite pages and to view useful information.

Note

The appearance of the admin interface is the product of the administration theme, Seven. To learn more about that theme visit Chapter 5. To learn how to change the administration theme, visit Chapter 26. ■

FIGURE 3.10

The dashboard

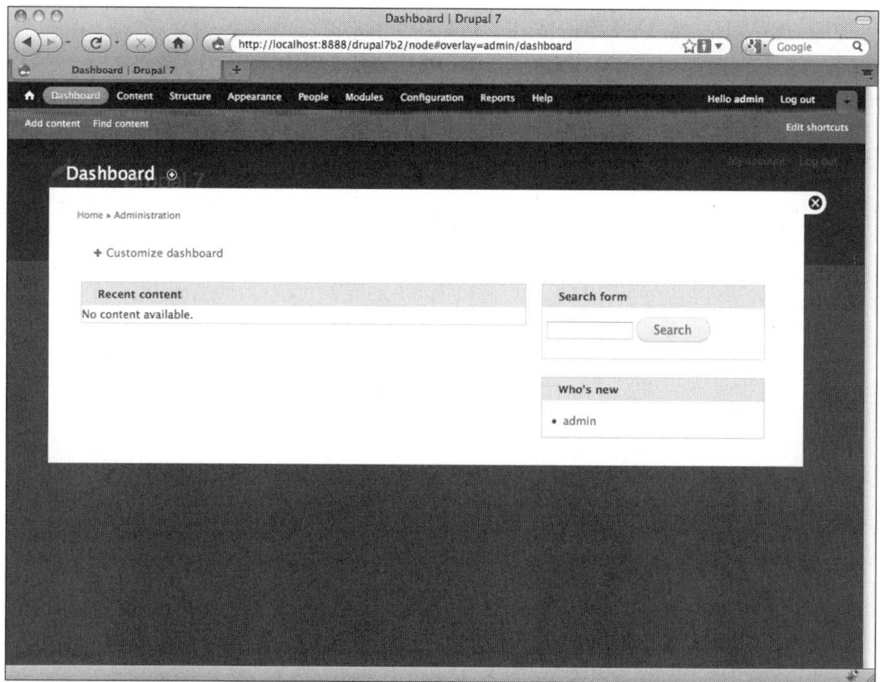

To create a set of shortcuts to your favorite pages, modify the toolbar. The second row of the toolbar can hold up to seven shortcut links. To add the links, follow these steps:

1. **Log into your site as an administrator.**

   The Management menu appears at the top of the site's pages.

2. **Click the Edit shortcuts link on the top right of the Management menu.**

   The Edit Shortcuts page opens in the overlay, as shown in Figure 3.11.

3. **Click Add shortcut.**

   The Add new shortcut page appears in the overlay.

4. **Type a name for the shortcut in the Name field.**

5. **In the Path field, type the address for the page you want to appear when the shortcut link is clicked.**

6. **Click Save.**

   A new shortcut appears on the toolbar, and the system returns to the Edit shortcuts page.

FIGURE 3.11

The Edit Shortcuts page

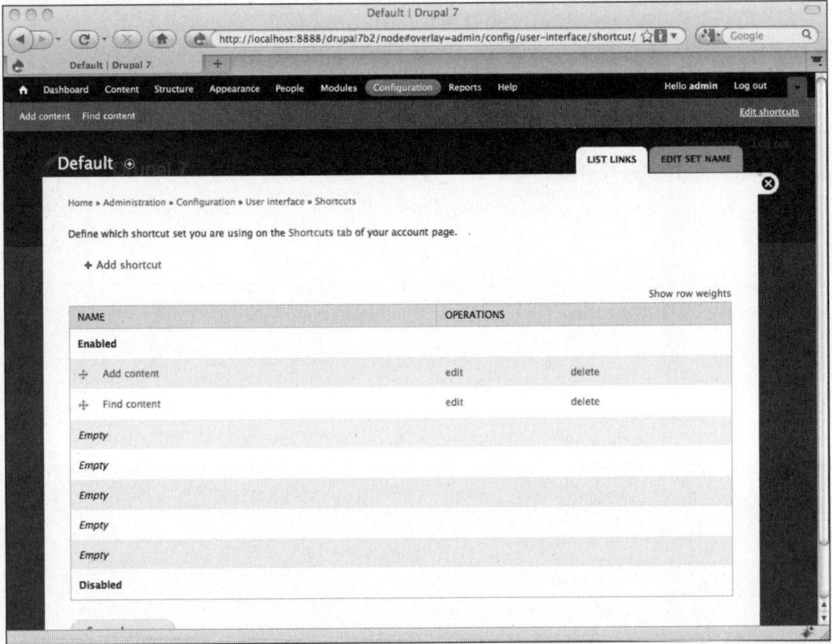

Tip

When browsing the admin system, you will see that a small + (plus) icon appears next to some links and captions. Clicking that icon adds a link to that page to the shortcuts menu. ■

You also can create a customized admin dashboard containing useful info and shortcuts. To customize the dashboard, follow these steps:

1. **Log into your site as an administrator.**

   The Management menu appears at the top of the site's pages.

2. **Click the Dashboard link on the Management menu.**

   The dashboard opens in the overlay.

3. **Click Customize dashboard.**

   The Customize dashboard page appears in the overlay, as shown in Figure 3.12.

4. **Click and drag the items you want to see onto the areas outlined with the dotted lines.**

   The items appear immediately on the dashboard.

5. **Click Done.**

   The system saves your choices and returns to the dashboard.

FIGURE 3.12

The gray boxes in the Customize dashboard page provide options you can drag onto the viewing areas outlined with dashed lines.

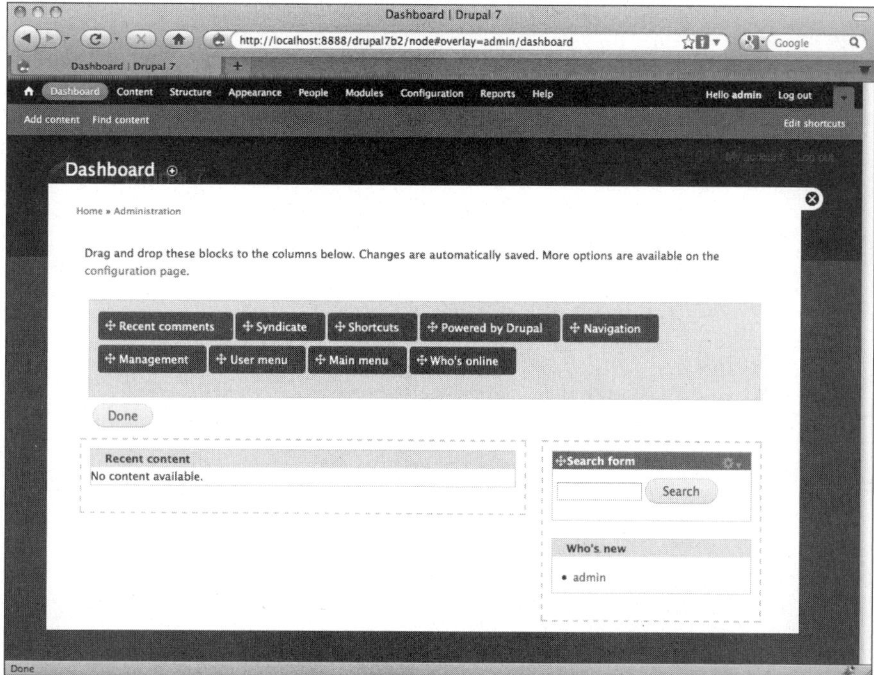

Summary

In this chapter, we took a quick tour of both the front end and the back end of the default Drupal installation. You learned the following:

- The nature of the menus and the menu items
- The role of blocks and modules in the system
- How to access the admin system
- How the admin interface is organized
- How to customize the admin interface

CHAPTER

Configuring Your Drupal Site

Although the default Drupal installation can be used without further configuration, most site owners prefer to tailor the site settings for their specific intended use. The configuration options available in the system are numerous. In this chapter I take you through the various interfaces that relate to configuring the core modules and explain the settings and their impact on the site.

There is a lot of power tucked away inside the configuration pages of Drupal 7. Understanding the various options available to you makes it possible to get the most out of your site and to keep your site secure and running smoothly.

IN THIS CHAPTER

Basic site configuration

Theme configuration

Managing search and URL settings

Setting up logging and reporting

Configuring your site's RSS feeds

Basic Site Configuration

During the Drupal installation process, you were asked to make decisions that created a preliminary site configuration. For example, the installer asked you to provide a name for the site and a default e-mail address. The data supplied in response to those queries set the most basic of the site configuration options. More complex configuration awaits action by the administrator after the system has been installed.

All the basic site configuration options can be accessed via Drupal's Configuration Manager, shown in Figure 4.1.

FIGURE 4.1

Drupal's Configuration Manager is shown prior to the installation or activation of any additional modules. The Configuration Manager should be your first stop after installing Drupal.

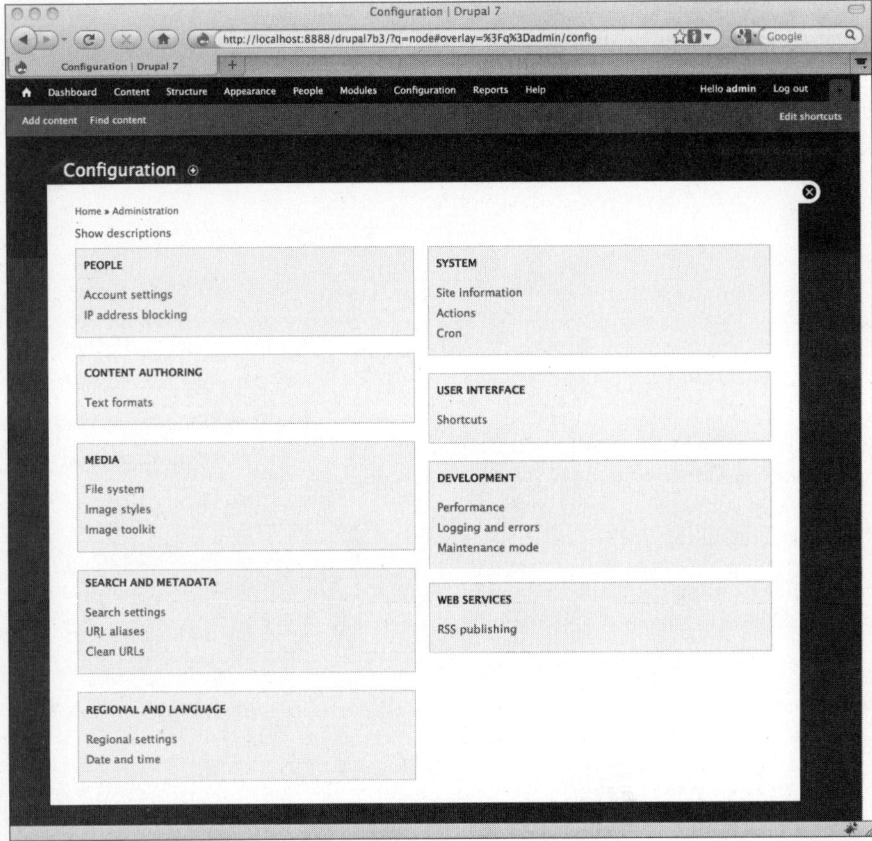

Although the majority of the default site's configuration options are found inside the Configuration Manager, additional options are located inside the Theme Manager and associated with the site's reports; both topics are dealt with later in this chapter.

Note

The Drupal menu functionality also includes a very limited set of options; those options are part of the Menus Manager and are discussed in Chapter 8. ■

Tip

Installing or activating additional modules may introduce further configuration requirements. After you install or enable any modules, look to see whether a configuration link appears next to the module's name; if so, make sure you explore the options. ■

The Configuration Manager includes a large number of options. They are grouped roughly by common topic or functionality. As shown in Figure 4.1, the choices on this page are organized into the following categories:

- **People:** Account settings and IP address blocking

Note

The options relating to user management are the subject of an entire part of this book. To learn more, see the chapters contained in Part V. ■

- **System:** Site information, Actions, and Cron

Cross-Reference

Working with Actions and Triggers is covered in Chapter 9. ■

- **Content Authoring:** Text formats
- **User Interface:** Shortcuts
- **Media:** File system, Image styles, and Image toolkit
- **Development:** Performance, Logging and errors, and Maintenance mode

Cross-Reference

Performance tuning of a Drupal site is the subject of Chapter 32. ■

- **Search and Metadata:** Search settings, URL aliases, and Clean URLs
- **Web Service:** RSS publishing
- **Regional and Language:** Regional settings and Date and time

Tip

To view a short description of each of the options, click the Show descriptions link at the top left of the Configuration Manager. ■

In the sections that follow, I go through the most common configuration tasks—the options a site owner is most likely to need to optimize a new site and use the default features effectively.

Modifying site information

Drupal groups together several basic configuration options under the heading Site information. Clicking the site information link on the Configuration Manager takes you to the site information settings page, where you can change the site name, default e-mail address, and the error handling of your site. Figure 4.2 shows the site information settings page.

FIGURE 4.2

The site information settings page

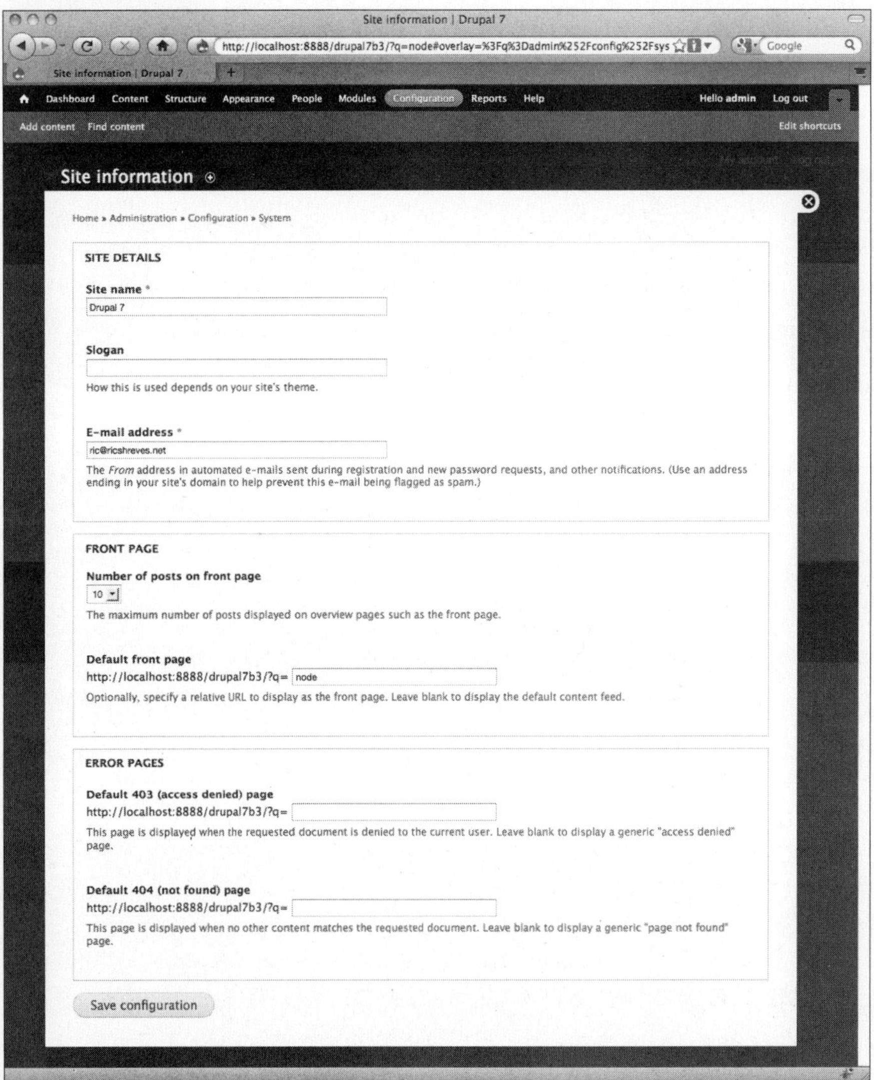

The options on the page are grouped into three categories: Site Details, Front Page, and Error Pages; each is discussed in turn, below.

The Site Details section contains three options that relate to basic site information:

- **Site name:** The default value in this field comes from the information given when the site was installed. The name you give to your site appears in multiple places, from the title bar of the browser to the e-mails generated by the system. Note that this value may also be displayed on the header of the theme itself, depending on how the theme is coded and how the theme is configured. This is a required field.
- **Slogan:** By default, this field is blank. Text entered here can be displayed by the theme or in the page titles, depending on how the theme and the path controls are configured. This is an optional field.
- **E-mail address:** This default value in this field comes from the information given when the site was installed. The e-mail address given here is used for system notifications. This is a required field.

The Front Page section contains two options relating to the display of content for site visitors:

- **Number of posts on front page:** The label for this control is a bit deceptive. The value selected from the combo box affects not only the number of items on the front page of the site but also the number of items shown on other key pages containing multiple items—the forum, for example; it also impacts the output of several modules. The default value is 10, but you may select any value from the combo box, from 1 to 30.
- **Default front page:** This field can be used to designate any page in the site as the site's front page. To change from the default front page, simply enter the relative URL of the desired page in the box.

The Error Pages section contains two options that control what the visitors of your site see if they encounter a URL that is not available on your site:

- **Default 403 (access denied) page:** This option allows you to direct users to a specific page if they receive a 403 error. By default, this is blank, which results in a generic error page being displayed.
- **Default 404 (not found) page:** This option allows you to direct users to a specific page if they receive a 404 error. By default, this is blank, which results in a generic error page being displayed.

Configuring Regional and Language settings

The Regional and Language settings category on the Configuration Manager groups together two interfaces, the Regional settings page and the Date and time settings page.

The Regional settings page allows you to set basic locale information for your site. You can set the default country, the first day of the week, and the appropriate time zone. The settings are reflected in the time and place information associated with your site and the posts on the site. The Time zones option allows the site's users to set their own preferred time zone.

The Date and time settings are a bit more complex than the Regional settings. Click the Date and time link on the Configuration Manager to view the settings page shown in Figure 4.3.

FIGURE 4.3

Note the tabs at the top right of the Date and time configuration settings page give you access to the Formats page, discussed below.

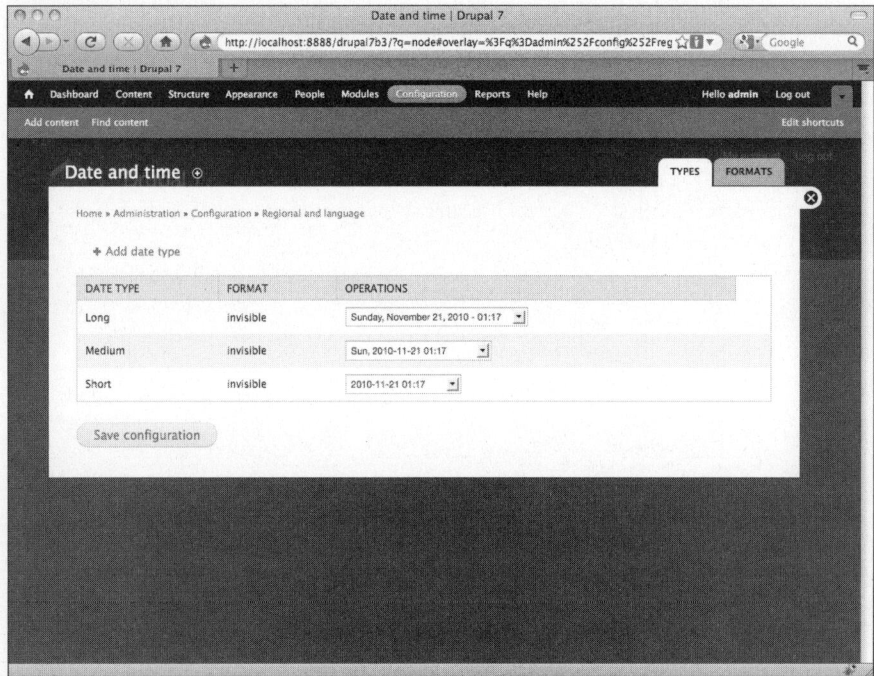

The landing page of the Date and time settings page shows the three default date and time formats (see Figure 4.3). You can change the format for any of the three by selecting a different value for the combo box. Click the Add date type control to create a new date type of your own choosing.

To add a new date and time format, click the Formats tab at the top right of the page. New date and time formats must be constructed using the syntax in the PHP date function.

Tip

To learn about the syntax employed in PHP date formats, visit the PHP Manual at `http://id.php.net/`. ■

Options for error handling

In addition to the Error Pages options discussed above, the Configuration Manager also includes options to control the logging and display of PHP error messages. To view these options, click the link labeled Logging and errors in the Development section of the Configuration Manager.

The Logging and errors page lets you control whether PHP error messages are displayed on the site. You can select none, all, or only error and warning messages. The default is to display all errors. The page also allows you to set the maximum number of error messages that are kept in the database. After the maximum is reached, the oldest messages are deleted when the cron job is run. By default, the message logging limit is set to 1,000, but you can select different values from the combo box provided.

Configuring media management

The Configuration Manager includes a section dedicated to Media. The section contains three options: File system, Image toolkit, and Image styles. Click the name of any choice to view the related settings page.

The File system settings page allows you to set the location where uploaded files will be stored on your server. It also allows you to specify the directory on the server to be used for temporary file storage.

Tip

Drupal 7 adds the option to create file storage with restricted access. While the default system's file storage is public, you can use the option labeled Private file system path in the File system settings page to create a path to a separate directory that holds private files. When this option is used, you can specify validation options when you create a File field for a content type and store the related files in the private directory. Note, however, that while the system obscures the path to the file from site visitors, if you do not restrict access to the directory via your Web server, users who know the path may be able to gain direct access to the directory. ■

The Image toolkit option defines the image quality for jpeg files manipulated by the system. The default value is 75, but you may select any value between 0 and 100. The larger the number, the higher the quality of the image and the larger the file size.

Of the three Media options, the Image styles option is the most complex and the most powerful. Image styles are presets that allow you to manipulate images in the system and to impose a consistency in the display of uploaded images. This is a powerful tool for maintaining a professional appearance on your site while also saving time for your content contributors.

To access the Image styles settings page, click the Image styles link in the Media section of the Configuration Manager. The Image styles settings page appears, as shown in Figure 4.4.

FIGURE 4.4

The Image styles settings page, showing the links to edit or create new image styles for your site

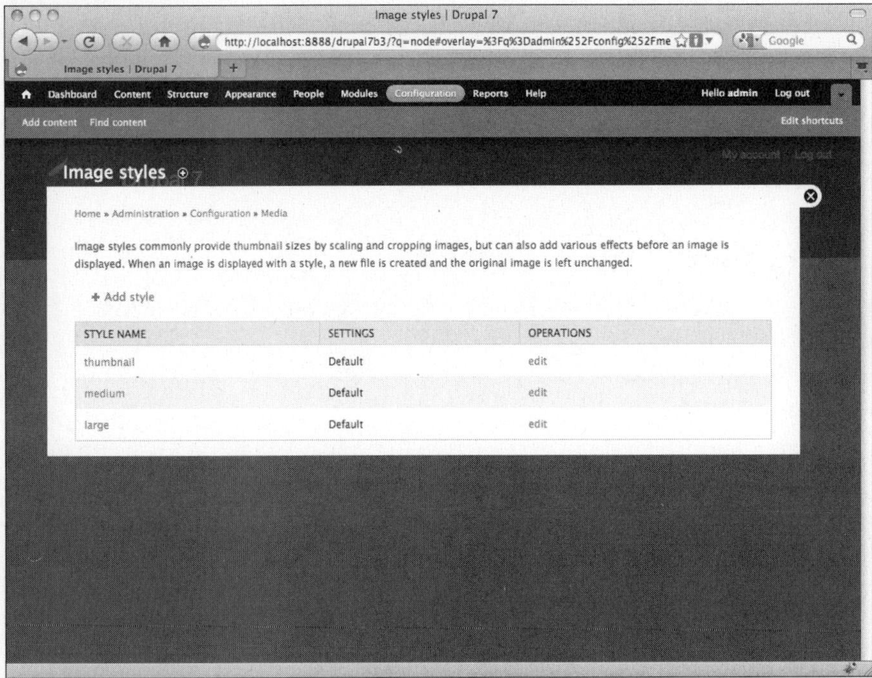

Drupal comes with three image styles already defined:

- **Thumbnail:** Automatically scales images to 100 pixels in width, while preserving the image proportions
- **Medium:** Automatically scales images to 220 pixels in width, while preserving the image proportions
- **Large:** Automatically scales images to 480 pixels in width, while preserving the image proportions

Note

Image styles are new in Drupal 7. This is the integration of the old Image Cache module into the core. ■

The image styles appear as options in various places in the system; for example, in the People Manager settings, the administrator can select any of the image styles in the system as a preset for controlling images associated with user profile photos.

If you are not happy with the default image styles, you can edit an existing style or add a new style. To edit an existing image style, follow these steps:

1. **Log into your site as an administrator.**

   The Management menu appears at the top of the page.
2. **Select the Configuration option from the Management menu.**

   The Configuration Manager opens in your browser.
3. **Click the Image styles link.**

   The Image styles settings page loads in the browser (refer to Figure 4.4).
4. **Click the edit link next to the image style you want to modify.**

   The Edit image style page loads.
5. **Click the Override defaults button at the bottom of the page.**

   The page reloads with the new page showing edit and delete options in the Operations column, as shown in Figure 4.5.
6. **Select the new effect you want to apply to the images from the combo box in the Effects column.**
7. **Click the Add button.**

   The Effect configuration page loads.
8. **Select the options you want to apply.**
9. **Click the Add effect button.**

   The new effect is added to the style, and the system returns to the Edit image style page. If you were successful, you see the new style in the list of effects.
10. **Click the Update style button to exit and return to the Image styles page.**

Cross-Reference

The issues related to creating new image styles are discussed in Chapter 12. ■

Configuring text formats

Drupal provides administrators with the ability to limit the text formatting options available to the site's users. This is an important security feature. Untrusted users should not be granted unrestricted use of HTML tags on the site, because certain tags can be used in a malicious or inappropriate fashion.

The text formats functionality is powered by Drupal's Filter module, and it works by stripping out prohibited or malicious HTML from the user's post prior to presentation of the output. Through the use of text formats, the site administrator can configure the formatting controls and determine which user roles have access to specific formats.

FIGURE 4.5

The Edit image styles page, shown here as it appears after you click the Override defaults option

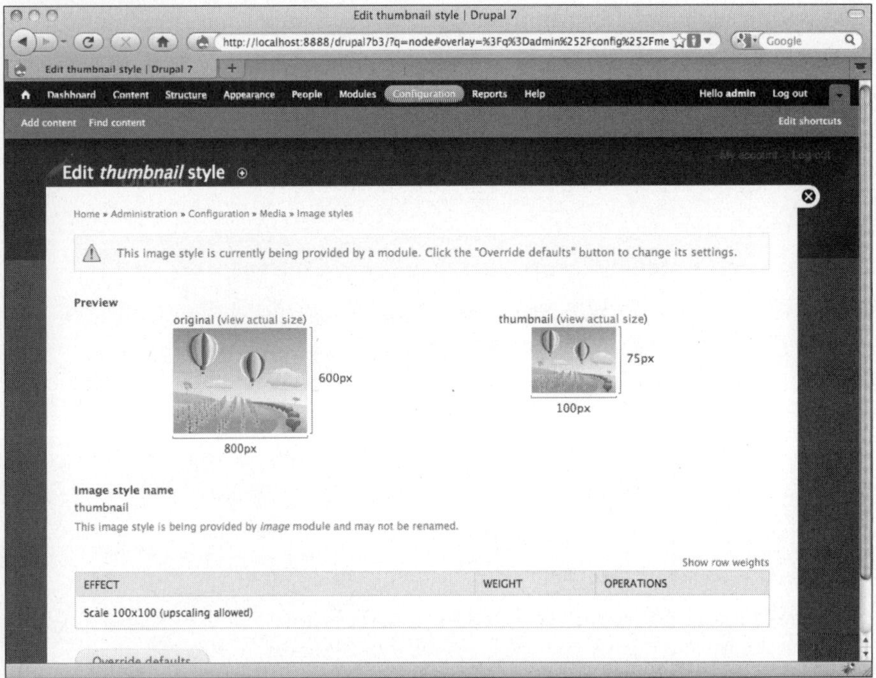

The default Drupal system provides three preset text formats: Filtered HTML, Full HTML, and Plain text. Of the three, the least restrictive is Full HTML; the most restrictive is Plain text. To view the available text formats, click the Text formats link in the Content Authoring section of the Configuration Manager; the Text formats page, shown in Figure 4.6, loads in your browser.

To view the details of a text format or to gain access to the settings to modify them, click the configure link in the Operations column (refer to Figure 4.6). Clicking the configure link opens the text format configuration page, shown in Figure 4.7.

FIGURE 4.6

The Text formats page, showing the three default text formats provided by the system, also displays the roles that have access to the various formats.

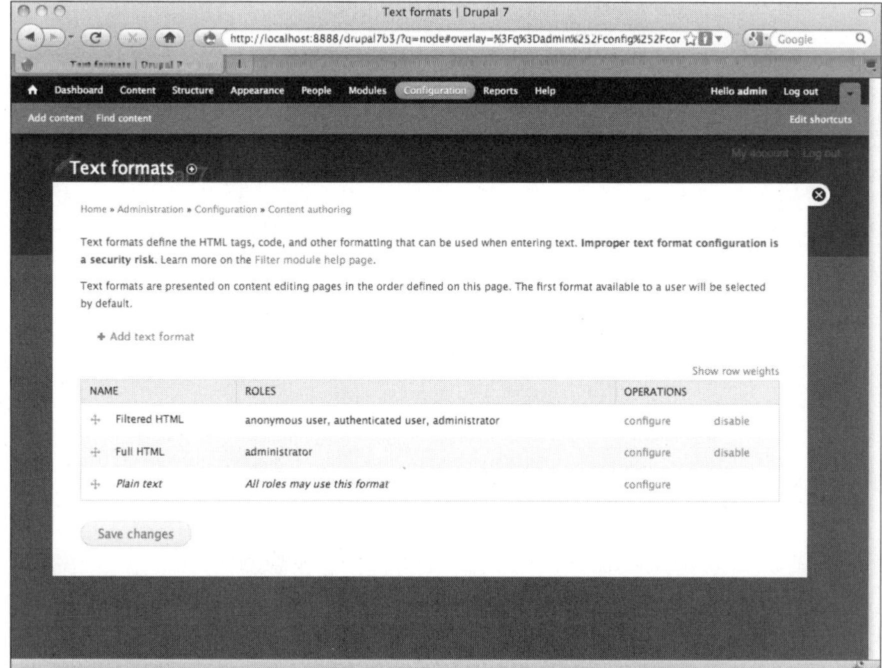

The text format editing page is broken into several parts. First is the Name field, the only required field. Second comes the Roles check boxes, where you can select the roles that have access to the text format. Third is the Enabled filters controls; select the filters you want to use by clicking the boxes next to the names. Enabling a filter causes the filter to appear in the Filter processing order table, located immediately below the Enabled filters controls. Click and drag to reorder the filter processes.

Caution

The order of the filters is important. Filters are processed in the order they are listed in the Filter processing order table (refer to Figure 4.7). Pay attention to the ordering to avoid creating contradictory or ineffective processes. ■

FIGURE 4.7

This example shows a typical text format configuration page, in this case, the page for the default Filtered HTML format.

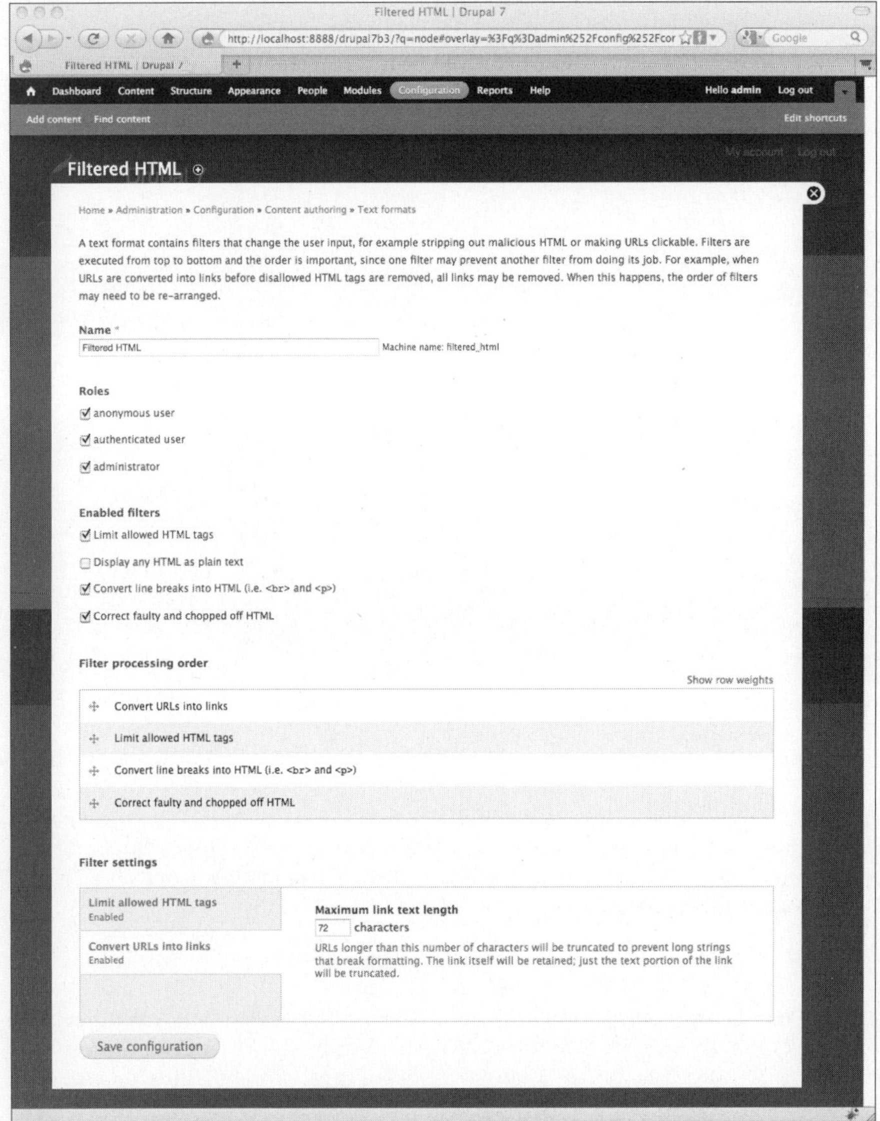

At the bottom of the Text format editing page are two tabs containing additional configuration options: Limit allowed HTML tabs and Convert URLs into links.

- The Limit allowed HTML tags configuration option provides you with a field into which you can enter specific HTML tags that can be used by this text format. Adding a tag into this field means that the users of this format are permitted to employ the tag. As the note on the page reminds you, CSS and some types of JavaScript are not allowed.
- The Convert URLs into links tab simply allows you to set a limit to the length of the text links that are automatically converted in active hyperlinks.

After you have made changes to your text format, simply click the Save configuration button to save the changes.

Tip

By default, the Drupal system blocks the execution of PHP code inside of content items or blocks. If you need to enable one or more of your user roles to use PHP code snippets inside of content items or blocks, you can do so by enabling the PHP Filter module. Enabling the module adds a new text format, named PHP code. The PHP code text format can be configured in the same fashion as any other text format. Note as well that enabling the PHP Filter module makes the PHP evaluator filter available to all text formats. By default, the PHP evaluator filter is disabled for all text formats except for the PHP code format. ■

Configuring cron

Cron is a time-based job scheduler used on certain types of servers. Drupal and many other systems use cron as a utility for performing periodic tasks, like checking for updates or indexing the site's content. With the release of Drupal 7, you can now schedule cron runs directly from inside the admin system without installing additional modules or adding a cron job to your server.

Note

The cron functionality in Drupal 7 is supplied by the integration of the Poormanscron module into the core. ■

The default system sets cron to run every three hours. You can modify this by clicking the Cron link found in the System area of the Configuration Manager. The cron settings page gives you the option to either run cron instantly or to set a scheduled cron run by selecting from one of the values on the drop-down menu.

Note

The cron functionality in Drupal is somewhat limited. The range of values is restricted, and cron is run for all tasks. If you need a more granular solution, you need to consider installing additional modules or configuring a cron run directly on your server. Moreover, Drupal's cron is dependent upon someone visiting the site; a site visit triggers the cron run, if one is scheduled and due. If no one visits the site within the time frame you have set, cron does not run until someone visits the site. ■

Tip

Drupal cron is powered by the file cron.php, which is located in the Drupal root. It is possible to configure the cron run somewhat by modifying this file. To learn more, visit `http://drupal.org/cron`**. ■**

Theme Configuration

Drupal provides administrators with the ability to set basic configuration options for the themes in the system. The system has both global and theme-specific configuration pages, allowing you to set options for all the themes in the system or to vary them for individual themes.

Global theme configuration

The global options for theme configuration affect all themes in the system; these are the settings that are applied to all themes by default. The global settings can, however, be overridden by the theme-specific configuration options. In other words, where there is a conflict between the settings, the theme-specific configuration settings take precedence.

To access the global theme configuration page, follow these steps:

1. **Log into your site as an administrator.**

   The Management menu appears at the top of the page.
2. **Select the option Appearance from the Management menu.**

   The Themes Manager opens in your browser.
3. **Click the SETTINGS tab on the top right of the overlay.**

   The global configuration page comes to the front, as shown in Figure 4.8.

The global theme configuration options are somewhat limited and are focused exclusively on controlling the display of page elements. The options presented on this page are grouped into three categories: Toggle Display, Logo Image Settings, and Shortcut Icon Settings. All options are selected by default.

These options are included in the Toggle Display section:

- **Logo:** Uncheck this box to disable to automatic placement of the logo on the theme.

Note

The default logo that will be displayed is whatever logo is bundled with the active theme. ■

- **Site name:** Uncheck this to hide the display of the site name.
- **Site slogan:** Uncheck this to hide the display of the site slogan.

Note

The data used for the default display of the site name and the site slogan are supplied by the administrator via the site information page, discussed earlier in this chapter. ■

FIGURE 4.8

The global theme configuration page includes buttons at the top right of the overlay, immediately beneath the tabs: *Global settings*, *Bartik*, and *Seven*. Use these buttons to jump between the global configuration and the theme-specific configuration options.

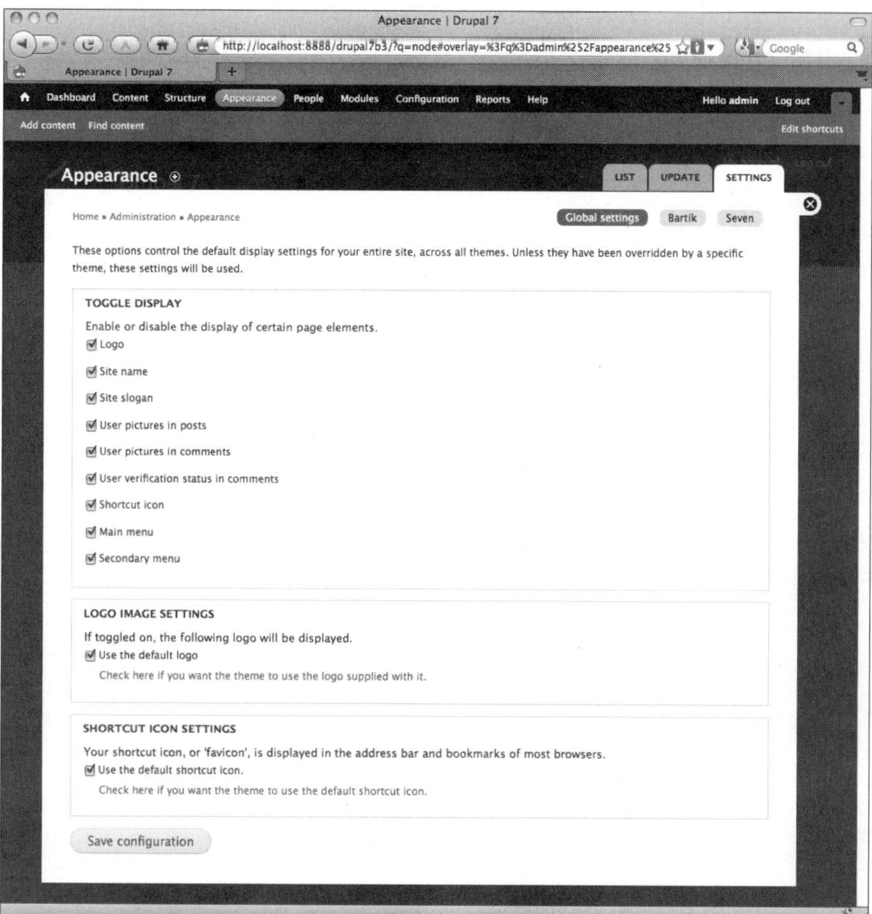

- **User pictures in post:** By default, the system displays a picture of the user (if one is available) alongside the user's posts on your site. Uncheck this box to disable that display.
- **User verification status in comments:** By default, the system indicates alongside a user's comments an indication of whether that user has been verified by the system. Uncheck this box to disable that display.
- **Shortcut icon:** Uncheck this to hide the shortcut icon.

Note

The default shortcut icon in the Drupal 7 core is the Drupal icon. ■

- **Main menu:** Uncheck this to hide the display of the menu designated as the Main menu.
- **Secondary menu:** Uncheck this to hide the display of the menu designated as the Secondary menu.

Note

In previous versions of Drupal, these menus were named Primary Links and Secondary Links, respectively. ■

Cross-Reference

See Chapter 8 for an explanation of how to assign menus as the Main menu and Secondary menu positions. ■

The Logo Image Settings control gives you the choice to use the default logo supplied with the theme or to upload another image. Uncheck the box if you want to use your own logo. After you uncheck the box, the system gives you the option to either upload an image file to use as the logo or to select an existing image on the server by entering the path to the image.

Similarly, the Shortcut Icon Settings control allows you to either use the default shortcut icon supplied with the theme or to upload another image. Uncheck the box if you want to use your own shortcut icon. After you uncheck the box, the system gives you the option to upload an image file to use as the shortcut or to select an existing image on the server by entering the path to the image.

Theme-specific configuration

In addition to the global theme configuration options discussed above, there is a parallel, and sometimes extended, set of configuration options associated with each theme in the system.

To access the theme-specific configuration page, follow these steps:

1. **Log into your site as an administrator.**

   The Management menu appears at the top of the page.
2. **Select the option Appearance from the Management menu.**

   The Themes Manager opens in your browser.
3. **Click the Settings tab on the top right of the overlay.**

   The global configuration page comes to the front (refer to Figure 4.8).
4. **On the top right of the overlay, underneath the tabs, click the button labeled with the name of the theme you want to configure.**

   The theme-specific configuration page comes to the front, as shown in Figure 4.9.

FIGURE 4.9

The theme-specific configuration page—in this case, the settings for the Bartik theme

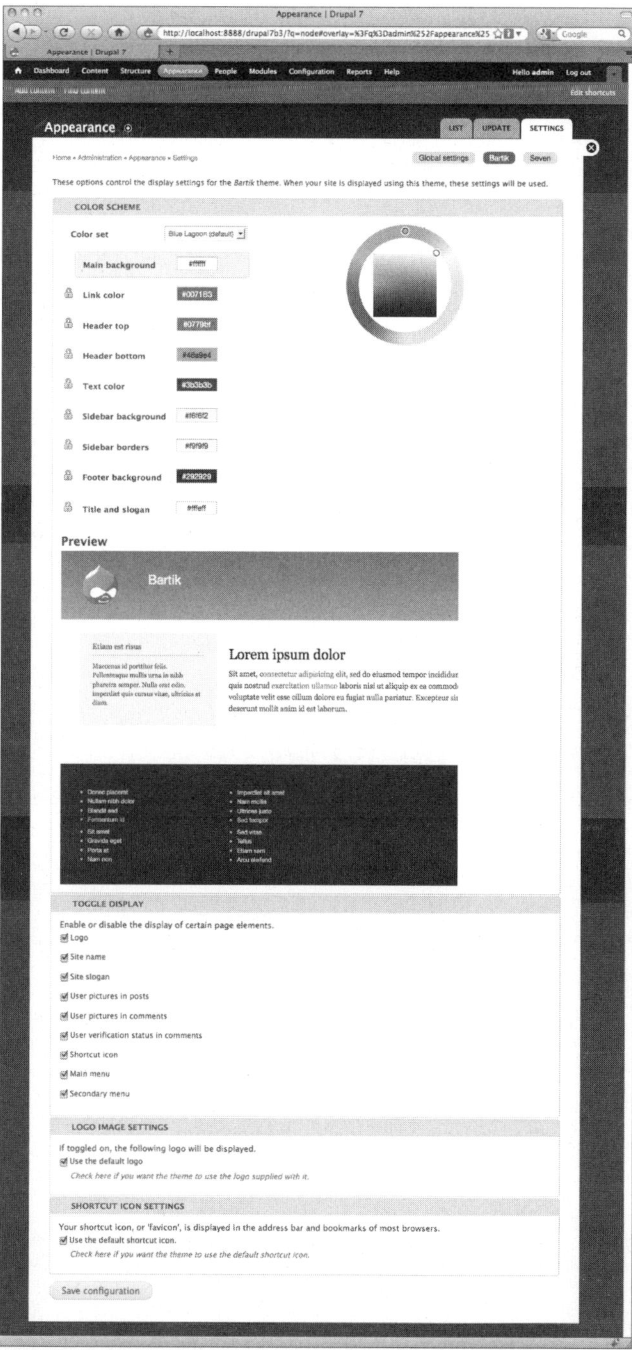

The theme-specific configuration options include the same choices as the global theme configuration page, together with any options that are unique to the individual theme. At the bottom of the page (refer to Figure 4.9), you can see options that are identical to those shown in the global theme configuration page. Additionally, at the top of the Bartik theme configuration page, you can see the Color module controls displayed.

Note

Exactly which options appear on the theme-specific configuration page depends on the choices made by the theme developer when the theme was created. ■

Choices made on the global theme configuration page impact all the individual themes, except where you have specified a setting on the individual theme's configuration options. Theme-specific configuration settings take precedence and override or ignore contrary settings on the global theme configuration page.

Managing Search and URL Settings

Drupal comes bundled with site search functionality and a "friendly URLs" option. The configuration options for these features are accessed by visiting the Configuration Manager. Under the heading Search and metadata, you will find links to Search settings, URL aliases, and Clean URLs. These links allow you to set the options associated with the search and URL functions.

Configuring site search

You can access the site search configuration by clicking the Search settings option on the Configuration Manager. The Search settings page opens in your window, as shown in Figure 4.10.

Note

If the Search module is not enabled, these options do not appear. ■

This page contains a number of options. The first three sections of the page deal with the indexing of the site's content. The Indexing Status section of the page shows you how much of your site has been indexed and is, therefore, available for searching. If you want to re-index your site, click the Re-index site button; the system dumps the old index and begins to build a new one. Note that this process may take a while, depending on the size of your site.

FIGURE 4.10

The Search settings page

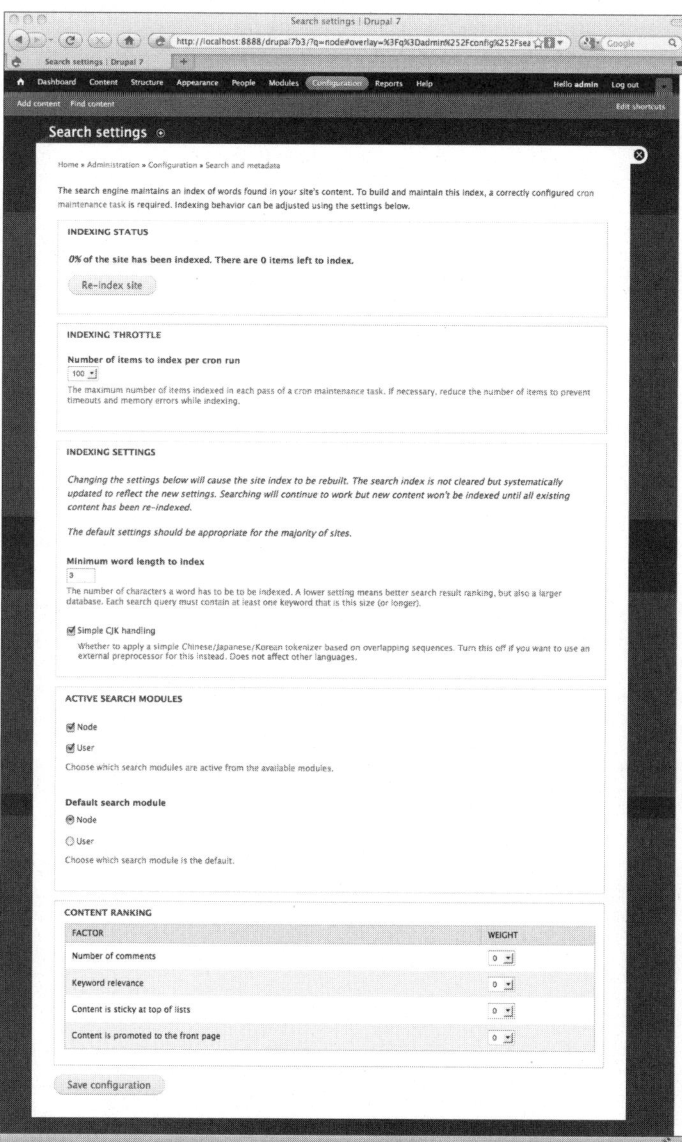

Tip

If the indexing status reflects an amount less than 100 percent, check to see whether your site is running cron frequently enough, and also consider your settings for the Indexing Throttle control, discussed below. ■

The Indexing Throttle option lets you specify the number of items that will be indexed with each cron run. The larger the number, the more system resources are required to complete the indexing. If your site is taking a performance hit when cron runs, it is worth exploring whether a lower value for this control will alleviate the problem.

The Indexing Settings section of this page gives you two controls. The first specifies the minimum word length to index. For most sites, the default value of 3 is sufficient. The next option, Simple CJK handling, is needed for sites using the Chinese, Korean, or Japanese language. If your site has no content in those languages, you may disable this control with no negative impact on your site.

The next section of the site search page is labeled Active Search Modules. The first check boxes allow you to specify the type of content the site users are able to search. Choose Node to search the content items. Choose User to search the user profiles. The default setting is to enable both.

Note that while the Drupal site search can be configured to search both nodes and users, the search results output always divides the results in separate tabs, one labeled Content and the other labeled Users; the output on those tabs corresponds to the Node and User configuration settings, respectively. Figure 4.11 shows a typical search results display.

The Default search module setting allows you to set the default search results tab that users will see. Select Node to make the Content tab appear first. Select User to display the Users tab first. The default value is Node.

Tip

The active search module configuration must be logically consistent. The system will not allow you, for example, to search only nodes but make the default search results display users. ■

Configuring clean URLs

Default Drupal URLs are formulated in a way that is neither search engine friendly nor human friendly. Fortunately, the system provides several tools to address this issue.

The most important step to take is to enable "clean" URLs. This point is best illustrated by use of an example.

Here is a default Drupal page URL:

```
http://www.yourdomainname.com/?q=node/2
```

FIGURE 4.11

In the output of the site search module, note the tabbed display, which segregates results into Nodes and Users.

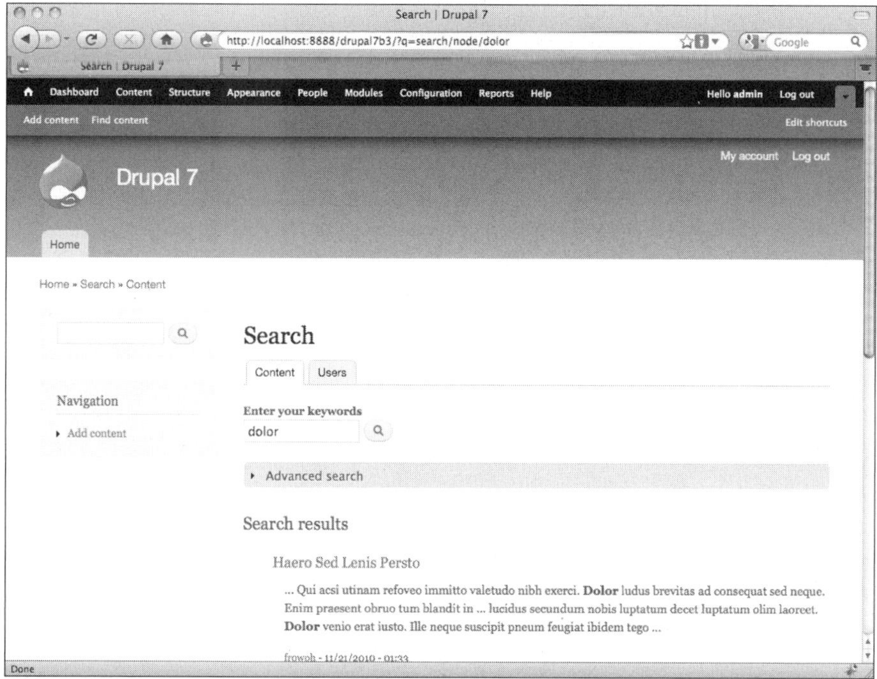

With clean URLs enabled, that same page will have this URL:

```
http://www.yourdomainname.com/node/2
```

The later URL has been "cleaned" of odd characters and reduced to a simpler formulation that works better with the search engines and is easier to both read and remember.

Clean URLs should be enabled by default on your site. You can check this either by viewing your page URLs or by accessing the clean URLs page from the Configuration Manager.

If clean URLs are not enabled on your site, the feature may not be supported by your Web server. If clean URLs are not enabled, you can test whether your system supports the functionality by following these steps:

1. **Log into your site as an administrator.**

   The Management menu appears at the top of the page.

2. **Select the Configuration option from the Management menu.**

   The Configuration Manager opens in your browser.

3. **Click the Clean URLs option in the Search and Metadata section on the overlay.**

   The clean URLs page comes to the front.

4. **Click the button Run the clean URL test.**

   Drupal tests whether your Web server supports clean URLs and provides feedback.

Note

If your site fails the clean URLs test, it may be that your Web server is not configured to allow the use of clean URLs. Clean URLs requires that mod_rewrite be enabled on the Apache Web server. If you are not sure that mod_rewrite is enabled, contact your server administrator or Web hosting support company. Another option that you should investigate is whether your site has an .htaccess file and whether it is in the proper location. The proper location for the .htaccess file depends on whether you are running Drupal at the root or whether you have installed it in a subdirectory. After you have investigated the possible sources of the problem and addressed them, rerun the Clean URLs test, as described above. ■

Creating URL aliases

URL aliases provide a means for you to control the exact URL associated with specific pages on your Web site. The functionality in Drupal is supplied by the Path module, which is enabled by default. The creation of the aliases occurs inside the Configuration Manager, via the URL aliases page, shown in Figure 4.12.

To create a new URL alias, follow these steps:

1. **Log into your site as an administrator.**

   The Management menu appears at the top of the page.

2. **Select the Configuration option from the Management menu.**

   The Configuration Manager opens in your browser.

3. **Click the URL aliases option in the Search and Metadata section of the Configuration Manager.**

   The URL aliases page opens (refer to Figure 4.12).

4. **Click the Add alias button at the top left of the page.**

   The Add alias page opens, as shown in Figure 4.13.

5. **In the first text field, enter the URL for which you want to add the alias.**

   Note that this must be a page that already exists on the site.

6. **Add the alias you want to use for the URL in the second field.**
7. **Click the Save button.**

   The alias is added, and you are returned to the URL aliases page.

Tip

The URL aliases function in Drupal requires you to manually create new aliases each time you create a new page. If you would like to automate this process, install the PathAuto module. The PathAuto module allows you to establish formulae for the automatic creation of aliases based on a variety of conditions you specify in the configuration of the module. The PathAuto module is discussed more in Chapters 29 and 33. Note also that content creators can be given permission to specify the path for specific content items, via the content item editing page. ■

FIGURE 4.12

You can see in the URL aliases page that I have already created multiple aliases for my nodes.

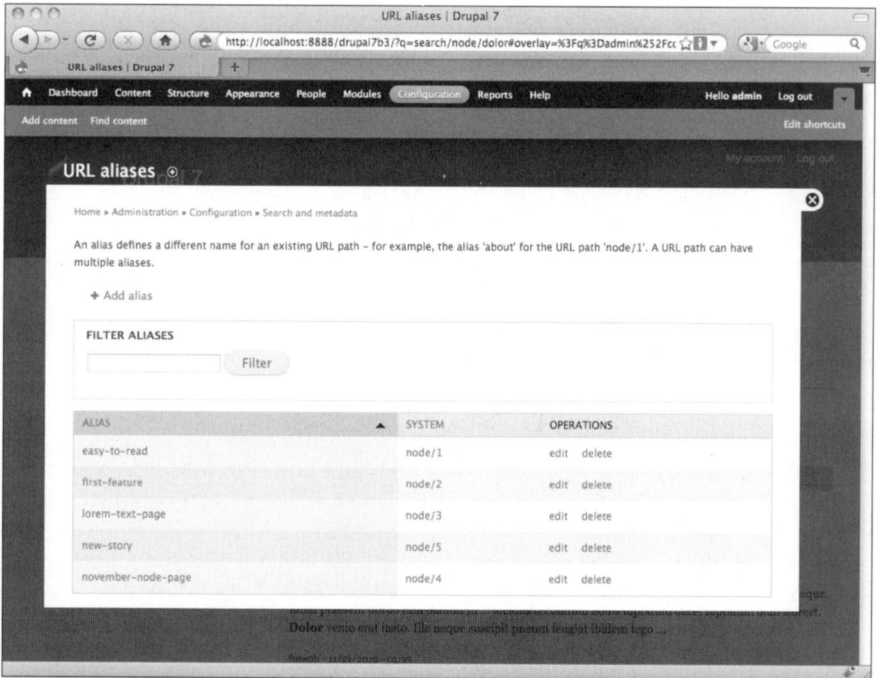

FIGURE 4.13

The Add alias page

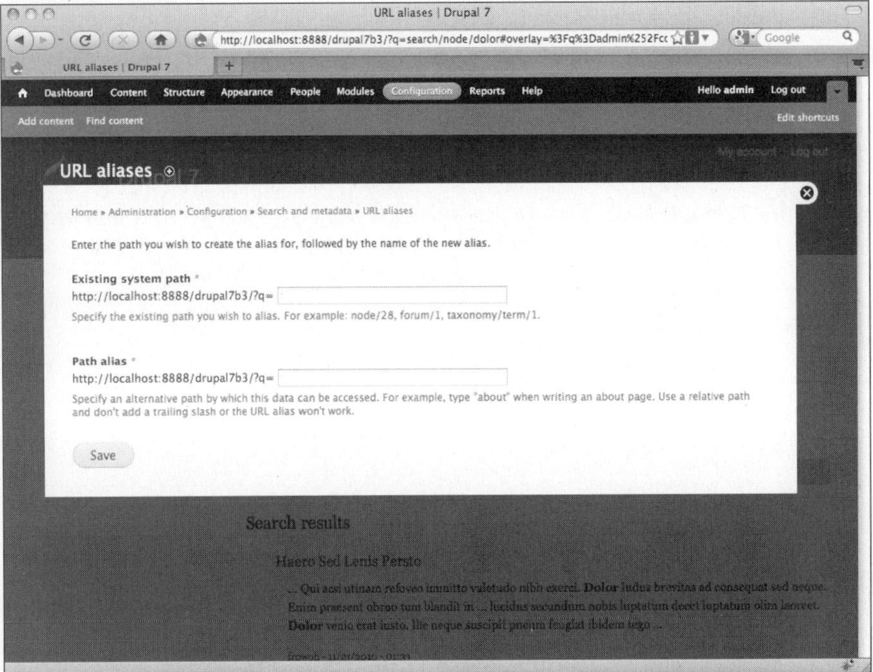

Setting Up Logging and Reporting

Drupal provides a set of tools that are designed to help you track and manage notifications about activity on your site. The tools provide varying functions from advanced system administration logging to basic site activity reporting. Not all of these tools are needed, or even desirable, for all types of sites. In this section, I look at each of the options and how to configure them to suit your needs.

There are four primary types of logging and reporting in the default Drupal system:

- Logging Drupal activity to the operation system logging system, as provided by Drupal's Syslog module
- Database activity logging, as provided by the Database Logging module
- Site activity logging, as provided by Drupal's Statistics module
- Update notification management, as provided by the Update Notification module

Each of these key functions is discussed in the following sections.

Using the Syslog module

Syslog is an operating system administration logging tool. The feature works by sending messages to the logging facility of your Web server. Syslog offers options to specify routing by both facility and severity.

Syslog functionality is supplied by the Syslog module. The module is not enabled by default. If you want to use this feature, you need to first enable the module via the Modules Manager. You also must take additional steps on your server in order to capture the information and route it to the proper person.

Note

View the Syslog Module help file for instructions on how to capture the messages to your Web server; the instructions vary according to the operating system used on your Web server. ■

Using the Database Logging module

The Database Logging module tracks Drupal system events and stores a record of them in your site's database. The module is a useful tool and simpler to use than Syslog because it requires no additional steps to implement. It enables you to view a chronological list of system events that are useful both for site debugging and for learning more about the behavior of the site's users.

Note

The Syslog and Database Logging functions both log the same information, but they store it in different locations. ■

The module is enabled by default and provides the following reports:

- **Recent log messages:** This is a listing of Drupal system activities; it informs you of the time, date, nature of the event, and the user with whom it is associated, if any. This is the most useful of the reports, at least in terms of diagnosing system errors. Figure 4.14 shows a typical example of a report of this type.
- **Top "page not found" errors:** This is a listing of the 404 errors encountered by visitors to your site. It's a useful report for identifying broken or expired links within your site.
- **Top "access denied" errors:** This is a listing of 403 errors encountered by visitors to your site. This report is useful for identifying cases where users have attempted to access pages to which they do not have permissions; this is pertinent to your site security because it helps you to identify suspicious activities on your site.
- **Top search phrases:** This is a listing of all the phrases typed into the site search box. It's useful for gaining insights into what your users are looking for on your site.

FIGURE 4.14

Typical example of the Recent Log Messages report

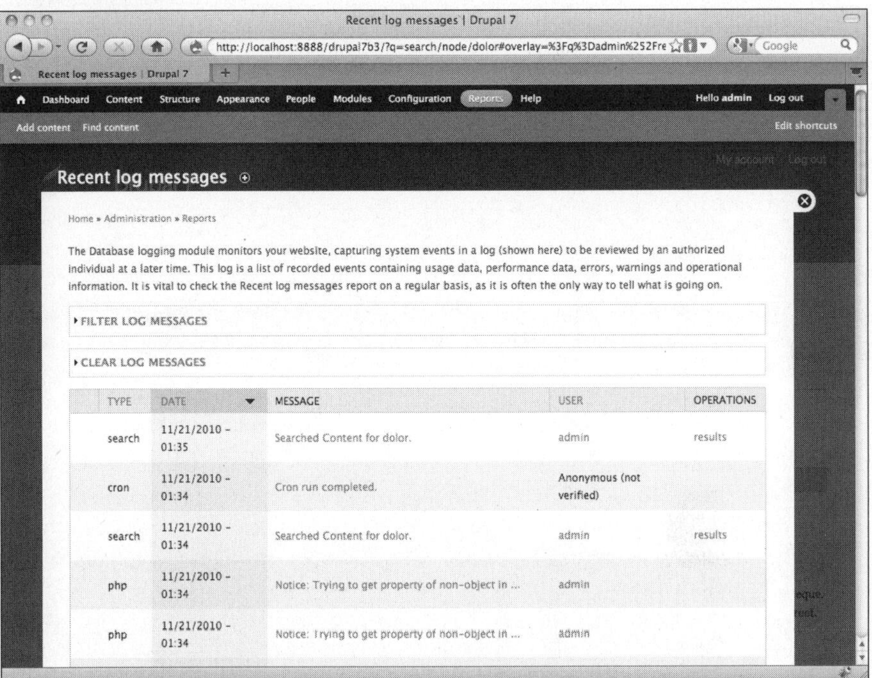

All the report information can be accessed by clicking the Reports option on the Management menu.

Configuring the Statistics module

Drupal's Statistics module provides tracking of user activity on the site. The module is disabled by default, so if you want to access the reports from this module, you need to enable Statistics in the Modules Manager.

Tip

Enabling the Statistics module also gives you access to an additional block: the Popular Content block, which can be used to display in a block a list of the most popular content on the site. ■

After it's enabled, you also need to visit the Configuration Manager to configure the module. To configure this module, follow these steps.

1. **Log into your site as an administrator.**

   The Management menu appears at the top of the page.

2. **Select the Configuration option from the Management menu.**

   The Configuration Manager opens in your browser.

3. **Click the Statistics option in the System section of the Configuration Manager.**

   The Statistics configuration page opens, as shown in Figure 4.15.

4. **Click the check box next to Enable access log.**
5. **From the combo box, select how long you want to retain the access logs.**
6. **Click the check box next to Count content views.**
7. **Click the Save configuration button.**

   The settings are saved, and you see a confirmation message at the top of the page.

FIGURE 4.15

The statistics configuration page

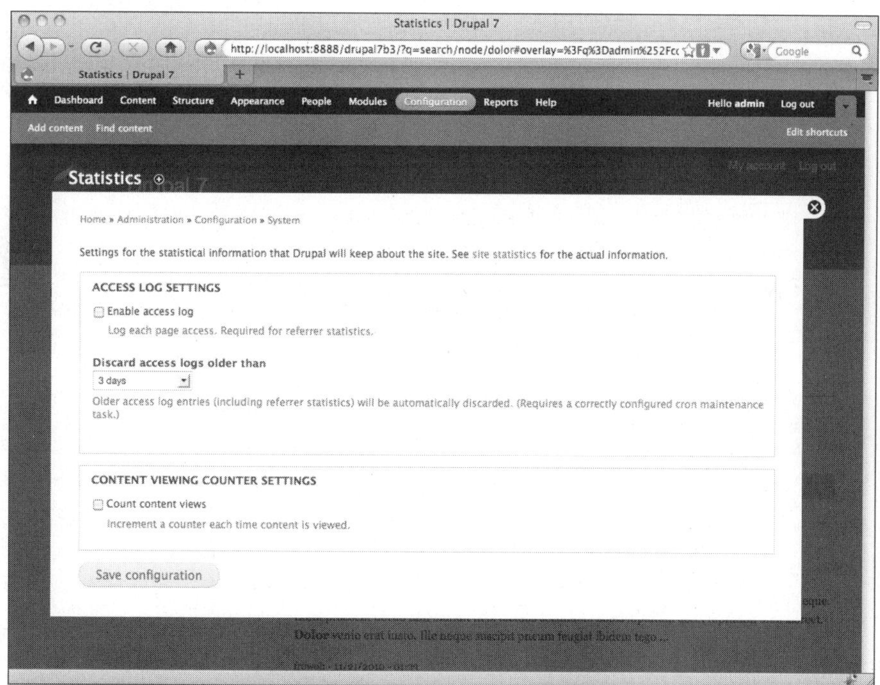

After it's enabled and configured, the module provides the following reports:

- **Recent hits:** This is a listing of the most recent activity on the site, expressed in terms of the pages viewed. It's useful for helping to determine what content is popular right now.
- **Top referrers:** This is a listing of where the most recent visitors came from. It's useful for learning more about the sources of traffic for your site.
- **Top pages:** This is a listing of the most popular pages on the site. It's useful for identifying your most popular content over time.
- **Top visitors:** This is a listing of the most active visitors. It's useful for identifying your most frequent visitors. If you are experiencing a problem on your site that you suspect might be related to visitor activity, this report can help you identify the user.

All the report information can be accessed by clicking the Reports option on the Management menu.

Note

The Statistics module has several limitations, the most significant being that it does not track accurately cached data and it does not track at all non-node activity. ■

Managing update notifications

Drupal uses an automated updates system to notify site administrators of new updates and security patches. The functionality is powered by the Update Manager module and is enabled by default. Configuration settings for this module are optional; by default, the system checks daily for updates to all enabled modules and sends an e-mail notification to the system's default e-mail address whenever there is a new update or security patch.

If you want to alter these settings, you have the following options, as seen in the Available updates settings page in Figure 4.16:

- **Check for updates:** The default setting is daily. You can change the setting to weekly if you prefer.
- **Check for updates of disabled modules and themes:** By default, the system checks for updates only to enabled modules and themes.
- **E-mail addresses to notify when updates are available:** By default, the system notifies only the e-mail address entered in the Site Information Manager.
- **E-mail notification threshold:** If you only want to receive updates for security notifications, change the setting. The default is All newer versions.

FIGURE 4.16

The Available updates configuration page, showing the default settings

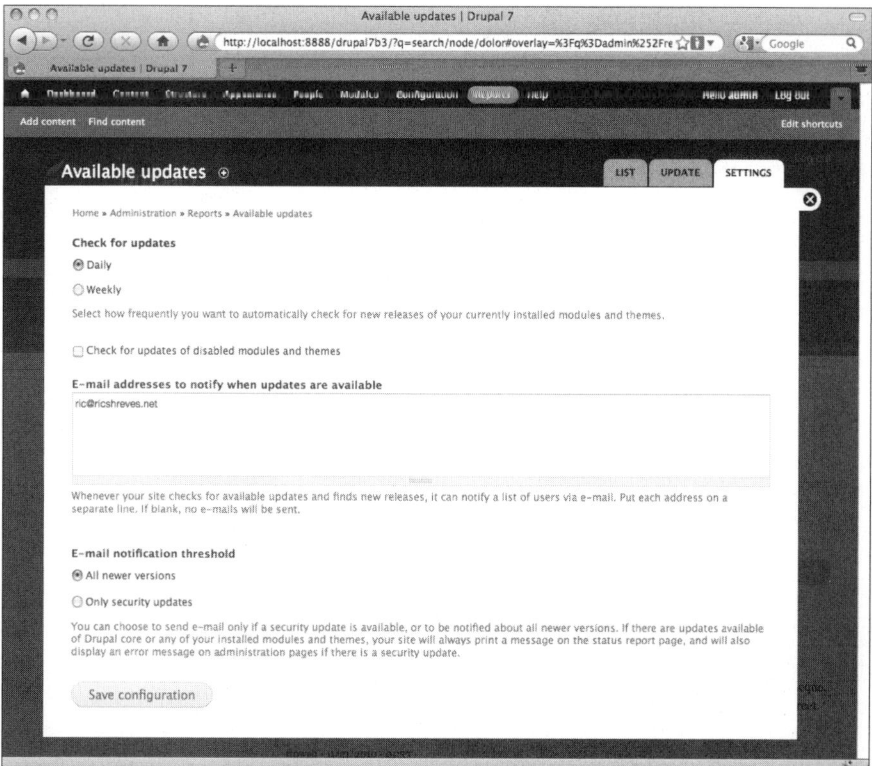

Configuring Your Site's RSS Feeds

Drupal supports the automatic creation of an RSS feed that contains both basic descriptive information about the site and the most recent content items. The configuration options for the site's RSS field are set by accessing the RSS publishing configuration page from the Configuration Manager.

Figure 4.17 shows the RSS publishing configuration page. These options are available:

- **Feed description:** To include a description of your site or feed, add text to this field. By default, this is blank.
- **Number of items in each feed:** Select from the combo box how many items you want to include in the feed. The default is 10.
- **Feed content:** Select from the combo box whether the feed displays the full text of the items, the title, and a synopsis, or simply the title. The default setting is full text.

FIGURE 4.17

The RSS publishing configuration page, shown with the default configuration options selected

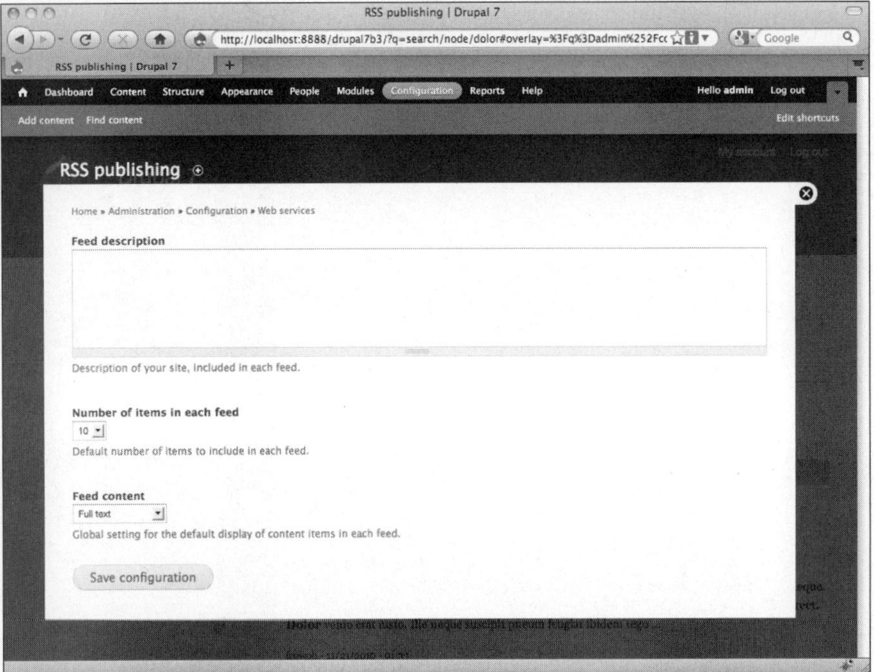

Tip

The RSS feed for Drupal is enabled by default, and it is not possible to disable it without using an external module. If you want to prevent your site from producing an RSS feed, install the RSS Permissions module, which is available at `http://drupal.org/project/rss_permissions`**.** ■

Summary

This chapter covered the basics of configuring a new Drupal site, with an emphasis on getting the most out of your default installation. Included in this chapter are the following topics:

- How to set basic site information
- How to configure your site's theme options
- How to enable and configure clean URLs and create URL aliases
- How to enable site tracking and reporting

Part II

Using Drupal's Site Building Tools

IN THIS PART

CHAPTER 5

The Default Drupal Themes

IN THIS CHAPTER

Working with the Theme Manager

Reviewing the default themes

A theme is a set of files that control the look and feel of your Drupal site. Drupal 7 comes bundled with a set of four themes. The themes are designed to serve varying purposes and to provide a wide range of options for your site; Drupal even includes a starter theme that you can use to learn more about Drupal theming and to help you get started with creating your own themes. To manage and configure these themes, Drupal also provides an administration tool: the Theme Manager.

In this chapter, I show you the default themes and discuss how to enable and use those themes. The chapter covers only the default themes; in later chapters, I turn to how to customize themes and how to create new themes.

Working with the Theme Manager

All themes in the system are administered through the common interface of the Theme Manager. To access the Theme Manager, select the option Appearance from the Management menu; the Theme Manager loads in the overlay, as shown in Figure 5.1.

FIGURE 5.1

Drupal's Theme Manager, shown with only the default themes installed and enabled

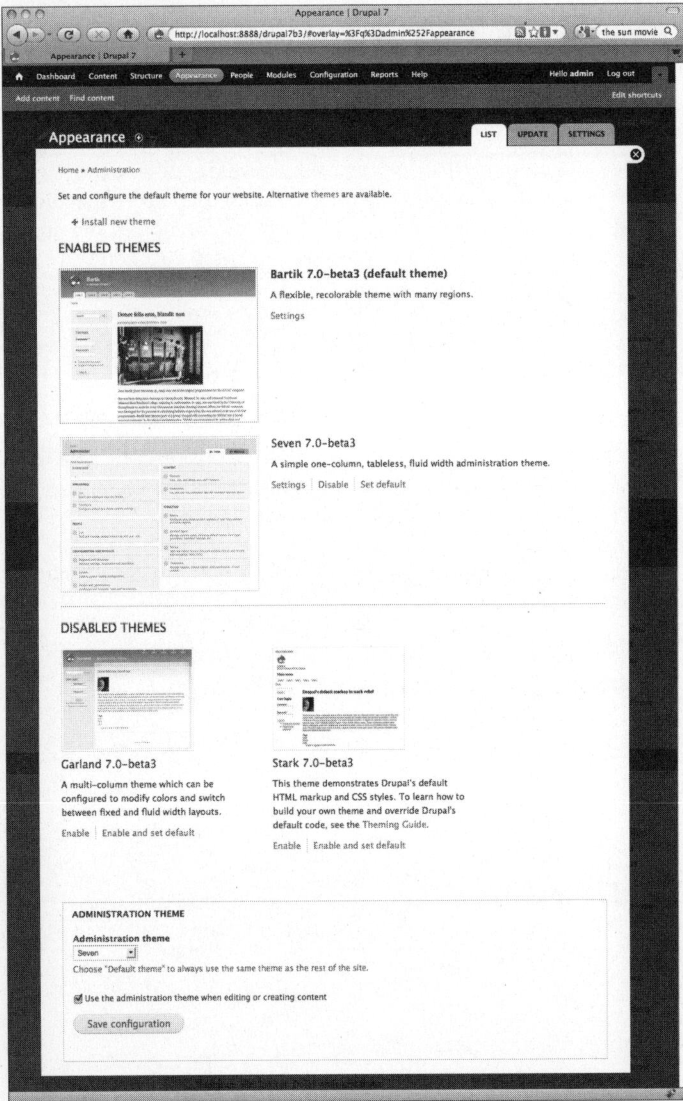

The Theme Manager lists all themes in the system, grouped according to whether they are enabled or disabled. By default, only two themes are enabled: Bartik, which is used for the front end of the site, and Seven, which is designated for use as the administration theme. Two additional themes can be enabled by simply clicking the Enable link next to the theme's description. Disabling a theme is similarly easy; just click the Disable link next to the theme's description.

The system allows you to enable multiple themes, but you can have only one *default theme*. As the term is used in Drupal, the default theme is the theme that is displayed for all pages that are not assigned to a specific theme. In other words, you can run multiple themes and assign different pages to different themes, but one theme must always be used as the system default, and until you assign a page to a specific theme, that page uses the default theme.

Note

Achieving a different appearance in different areas of a site is typically handled by creating multiple page templates, as discussed in Chapter 26. In contrast, using multiple themes is generally done only for very specific purposes, for example, a dedicated admin theme or a special theme formatted for mobile devices. If you do, however, need to use multiple themes on the front end of your Web site, you have to install an additional module to enable this. One option is the Taxonomy Theme module at `http://drupal.org/project/taxonomy_theme`. ■

To designate a theme for the role as the default theme, simply click the Set default link that appears next to the theme description.

At the top right of the Theme Manager are three tabs: List, Update, and Settings. The List tab is the default view and shows all the themes in the system, together with the controls to set the administration theme (refer to Figure 5.1). The Update tab provides access to a utility to check for new updates to your themes.

Note

The Available Updates page, under Reports on the Management menu, gives you another way to check for updates to your themes. ■

The Settings tab is used to access the global and theme-specific configuration options.

Cross-Reference

Theme configuration options are discussed in Chapter 4. ■

While the default Drupal 7 installation comes with only four themes, you may add new themes to your system at any time. After you add a new theme, it appears in the Theme Manager and includes all the functions discussed earlier.

Cross-Reference

Adding new themes, customizing themes, and working with admin themes are covered in Chapter 26. ■

Reviewing the Default Themes

Drupal 7 comes bundled with four themes. Two of the themes are ready for use on the front end of your site. Another is intended for use as an administration theme, and the fourth is provided as a starting point for your own explorations of Drupal theming.

These default themes, discussed in the next sections of this chapter, are installed:

- Bartik
- Garland
- Seven
- Stark

Bartik

Bartik is the default theme for Drupal 7. When you launch your new Drupal site, this is the theme you see in action on the front end of the system. Figure 5.2 shows Bartik.

FIGURE 5.2

The Bartik theme is shown here with sample content items.

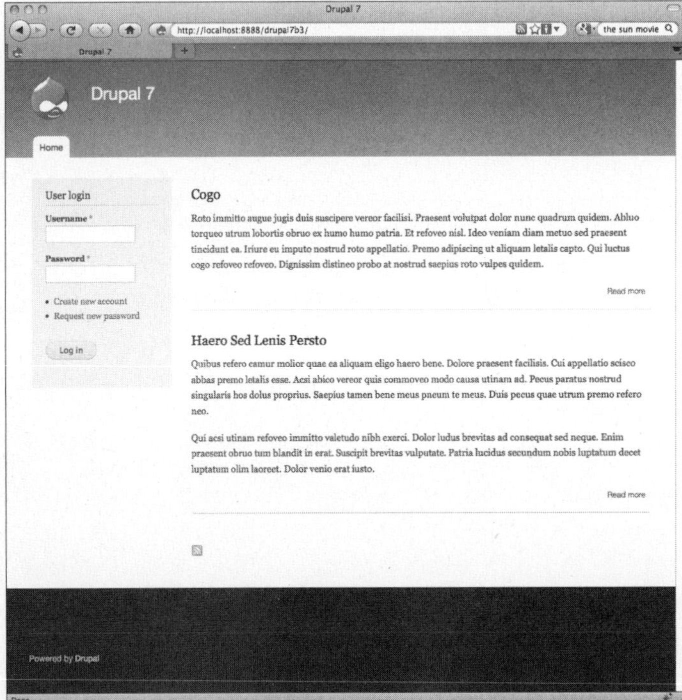

As you can see, Bartik uses a tabbed display for one of the menus. The items in the tabs come from the menu designated as the Main menu in the Menus Manager settings.

Cross-Reference

See Chapter 8 for a discussion of menus and menu item management. ■

Bartik is designed as a fluid theme; that is, it flexes and contracts to fit the dimensions of the browser window. The theme is pure CSS and does not rely on tables for the display. Bartik also implements the Color module that enables you to control the color of the theme and the text without having to resort to editing the CSS files.

Figure 5.3 shows the regions that are available in Bartik.

FIGURE 5.3

The regions available for block assignment in Bartik

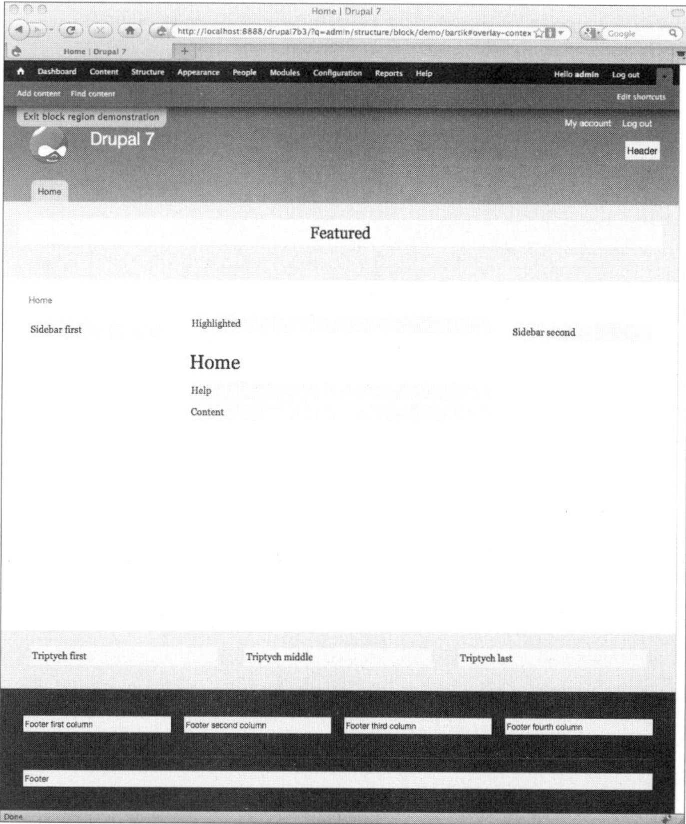

The theme includes 15 regions, providing you with a great deal of flexibility in managing content display. The multiple regions mean that you can use Bartik as a one-, two-, or three-column theme. Additionally, the presence of the Featured region makes it possible to provide header images or other featured content above the fold in the browser window. Note also the Triptych panels below the content region, and the four-column option for the footer area. The wide assortment of regions and the smart design in their placement make Bartik the most versatile of the default themes.

Garland

Garland is the only legacy theme in the Drupal 7 distribution. Although the theme has been around for years, it has been updated to be compatible with Drupal 7. Still, if you are familiar with the Garland of old, it does look and behave in a familiar fashion.

Like Bartik, the theme is pure CSS and does not rely on tables for the display. Garland's theme configuration options include the Color module, which enables you to control the color of the theme and the text without having to resort to editing the CSS files. The theme configuration options for Garland also allow you to specify whether the theme is fluid or fixed width.

Figure 5.4 shows Garland.

FIGURE 5.4

The Garland theme is shown here with sample content items.

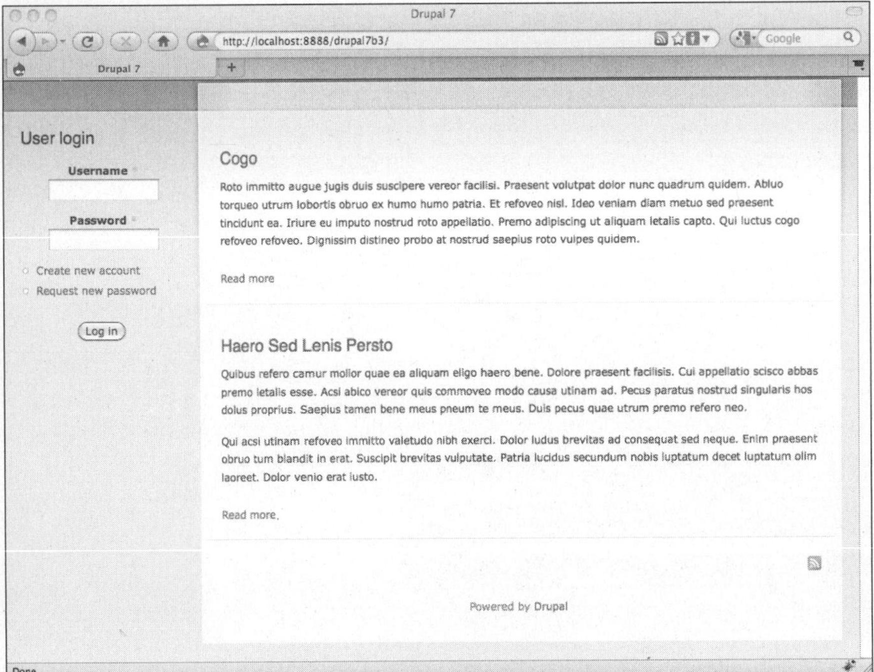

Garland provides seven regions for block assignment, as shown in Figure 5.5. Although it contains only seven regions, they are designed to allow you to use Garland in a one-, two-, or three-column layout. You also have a highlighted region that allows you to display images or other featured content above the fold.

FIGURE 5.5

The block regions provided by Garland

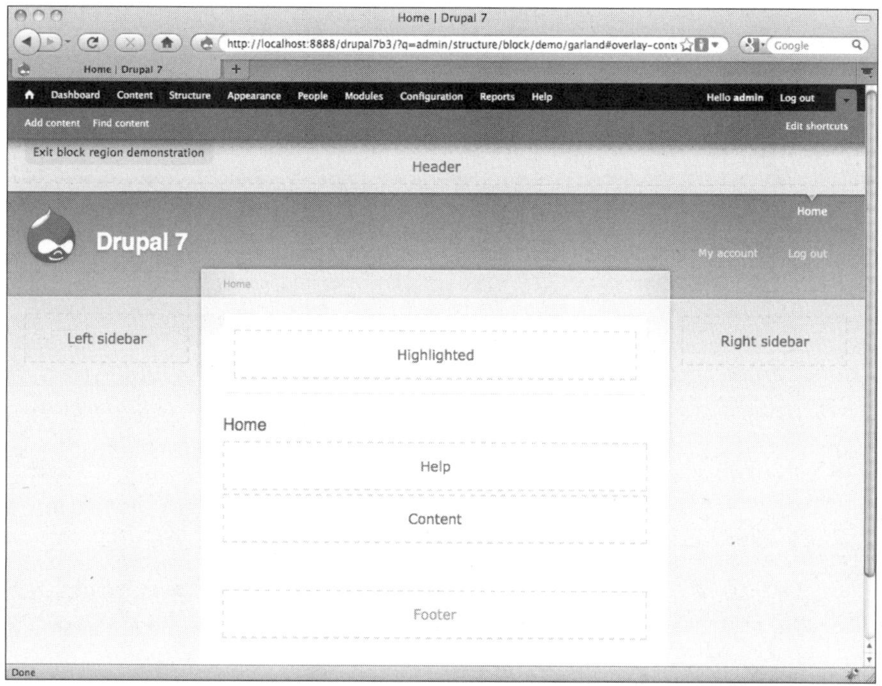

Like Bartik, Garland also provides a dedicated placement for the Main menu items. However, where Bartik uses tabs, Garland uses a different approach. Look at the top-right corner of the page (refer to Figure 5.4) to see the Home link; that link comes from the menu designated as the Main menu in the Menus Manager.

Seven

The Seven theme is provided for use as an administration theme in Drupal 7. It is a one-column, tableless, fluid theme. Because it is designed for use as the administration theme, Seven contains only two block regions and no unique theme configuration options. By default, this theme is enabled and designated as the administration theme in the Theme Manager.

Tip

While you can change your administration theme settings to use one of the other default themes, there really is no advantage to doing so. Of the default themes, Seven is best suited to the display of the admin interface. ■

Stark

Stark serves a unique function in the default themes. It is neither intended for use on the front end of the site nor for an administration theme. Rather, Stark is provided as a starting place for the creation of new themes or sub-themes. The theme demonstrates Drupal's default HTML and CSS styles. As shown in Figure 5.6, the output is very basic, and it is extremely unlikely that you would ever want to use Stark without significant modification.

FIGURE 5.6

The Stark theme is shown here with sample content items.

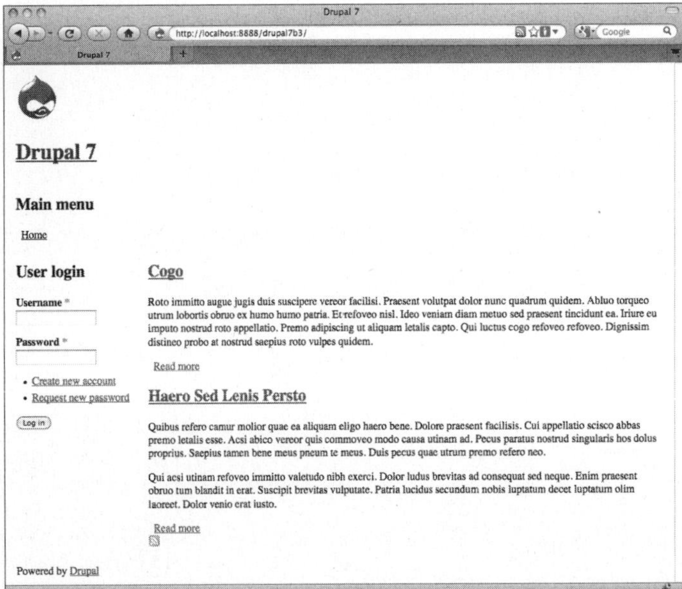

Stark includes seven regions, as shown in Figure 5.7. The regions are basically the same as those provided in the Garland theme and, like Garland, can be configured to display one, two, or three columns. However, no unique configuration options are available.

Cross-Reference

Creating themes and sub-themes is covered in depth in Chapter 27. ■

FIGURE 5.7

The block regions available in the Stark theme

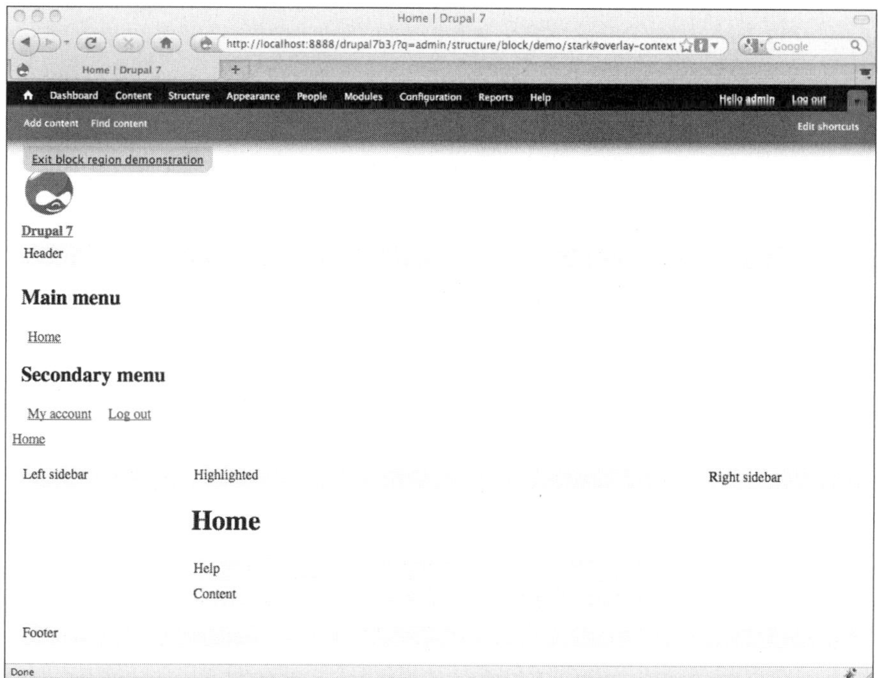

Summary

This chapter introduces the default Drupal 7 themes and the Theme Manager. We discussed the following topics:

- How to access the Theme Manager and the purpose it serves
- An introduction to each of the four themes in Drupal 7

CHAPTER

Working with the Default Modules

Modules are packages that provide the functionality in Drupal. The default installation comes bundled with a number of modules that provide a wide range of commonly used features. Some modules provide content functionality, some are tools for the administrator, and still others are intended purely to help developers. Though the use of some modules is optional, all sites use a number of the modules bundles in the default installation; moreover, site owners frequently install additional third-party modules to gain more specialized functionality.

Drupal provides two interfaces for dealing with modules, each with a different purpose. One interface allows you to enable and disable modules. The other is the Modules Manager, which allows you to administer the site's modules. In this chapter, I look at both of the module interfaces as well as provide a quick overview of all the modules in the default installation.

IN THIS CHAPTER

Enabling and disabling modules

Managing the enabled modules

Reviewing the default modules

Enabling and Disabling Modules

The default Drupal installation includes 44 modules; some are enabled during installation, others are not. As you saw in the preceding chapter, the Drupal installer gives you a choice of installation profiles. The profile you select determines the modules that are enabled during the installation process. Note that all the default modules are present in your installation, but not all are enabled. You can change the module selection at any time by enabling or disabling any of the installed modules.

Note

Modules must be enabled before you can see their output or configure them. ■

Drupal lists all the installed modules inside the Modules Manager, as shown in Figure 6.1. You can access this page by logging into the admin section and selecting the option *Modules* from the Management Menu.

FIGURE 6.1

Drupal's Modules Manager; note that this is only a partial view of this very long screen.

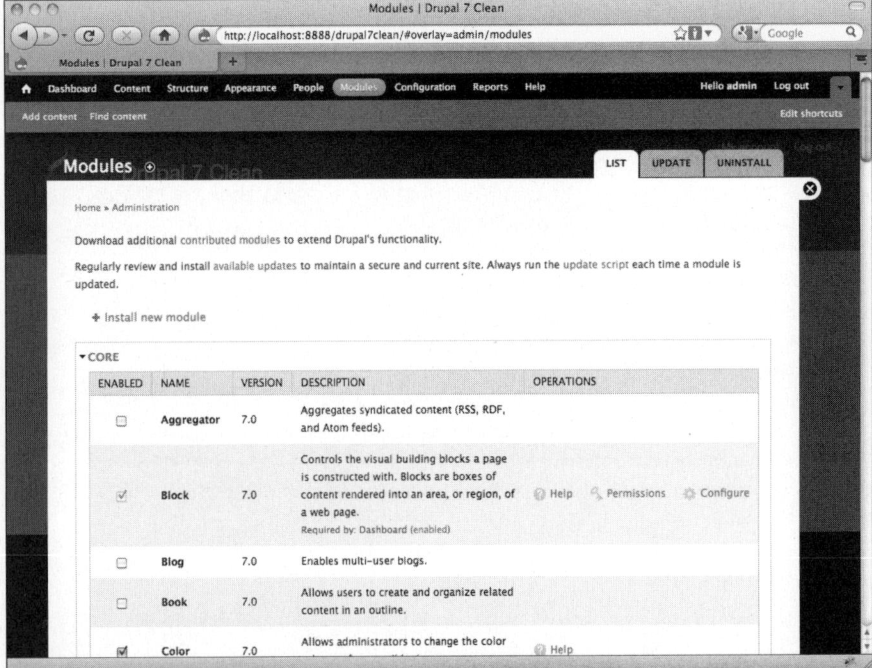

Note

The modules inside the Modules Manager are grouped. In the default installation, all the modules are in one group named Core (refer to Figure 6.1). When you install additional modules, you probably will see new groups appear on the page. These groupings are determined by the module developer and included in the module's .info file. ■

These fields are on the Modules Manager page:

- **ENABLED:** A check in this box indicates that the module is enabled. No check mark means the module is disabled.
- **NAME:** This is the name of the module.
- **VERSION:** This is the version number of the module.
- **DESCRIPTION:** This field contains a short description of the module.
- **OPERATIONS:** This provides a link to the Help files for the module, the Permissions settings for the module, and the Configuration interface, if any.

To enable a module, follow these steps:

1. **Log into your site as an administrator.**

   The admin Dashboard loads in your browser.
2. **Select the option Modules from the Management menu.**

   The Modules Manager loads in the overlay.
3. **Click the check box to the left of the name of the module you want to enable.**
4. **Click the Save Configuration button at the bottom of the page.**

   If you are successful, a confirmation message appears at the top of the page.

Note

Some modules have prerequisites that must be met before the module can be successfully enabled. In those cases, the dependencies are listed next to the module description, along with a message indicating whether the requirements have been met. Generally, you must first enable the required modules before you can enable the module you want to use. ■

Cross-Reference

For a discussion of installing and uninstalling modules, see Chapter 29. ■

Tip

If you are not using a module, you should disable it. Though you often can hide the output of the module from the front end by other means, or simply choose not to use it, if the module is enabled the system is processing the module. In other words, failing to disable an unused module can have a performance impact on your site. ■

Disabling a module is not the same as uninstalling a module. Uninstalling removes the module from the system; this means removing both the code for the module and the database tables that are unique to the module, if any exist. Disabling simply turns the module off. If you disable a module, you can always enable the module again at any time by repeating the steps given earlier in this chapter. On the other hand, if you uninstall the module and decide later to use it, you have to install it again and then enable it.

To disable a module, follow these steps:

1. **Log into your site as an administrator.**

   The admin interface loads in your browser.
2. **Select the option Modules from the Management menu.**

   The Modules Manager loads in the overlay.
3. **De-select the check box in the enabled column next the module you want to disable.**
4. **Click the Save Configuration button at the bottom of the page.**

   If you are successful, a confirmation message appears at the top of the page.

Note

Some modules are needed by others in the system. If the module you are trying to disable is required by another module that is enabled, you cannot disable the module until you have disabled the modules that depend on it. ■

Managing Enabled Modules

After you have enabled a module, you configure the module and check to see that the permissions to access the module are set according to your wishes. Access to the configuration interface and the Permissions Manager can be gained directly from the Modules Manager. In Figure 6.1, above, you can see the links to both features in the Operations column.

In some cases you can also access the module configuration interface from the Configuration Manager, though this is not the case for all the modules. To view the Configuration Manager, log into your site as an administrator and then click the Configuration option on the Management menu; the Configuration Manager loads in your browser, as shown in Figure 6.2.

Cross-Reference

Site configuration is dealt with in detail in Chapter 4. ■

Note

The permissions link that appears on many of the modules in the Modules Manager takes you to the Permissions Manager. This is the same screen you can access directly by clicking the option labeled People on the Management menu, and then selecting the Permissions tab. ■

FIGURE 6.2

The Configuration Manager

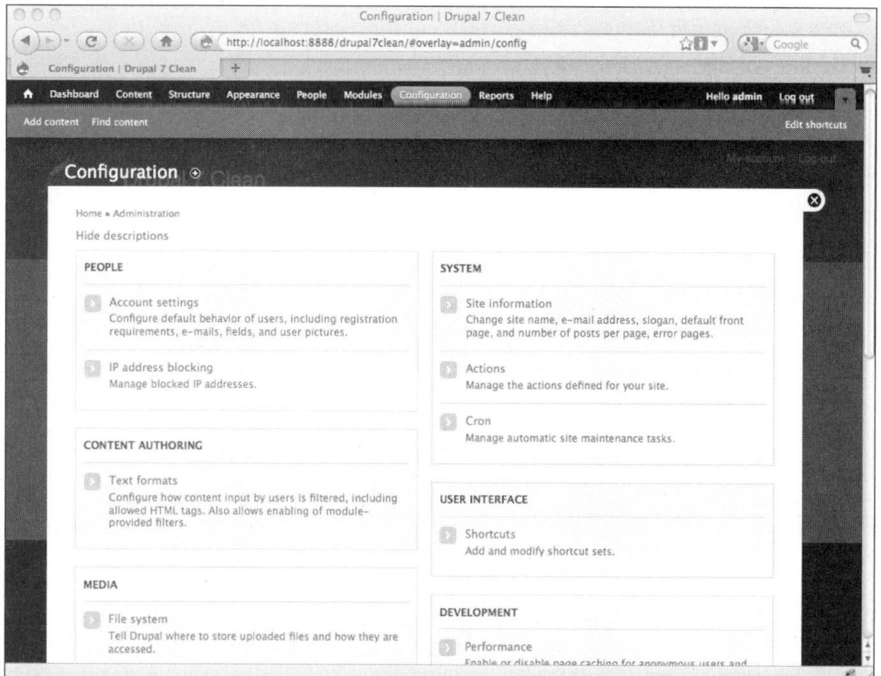

Reviewing the Default Modules

Drupal's assortment of default modules is extensive. A number of the modules are concerned with displaying new types of content. The Aggregator, Blog, Book, Poll, and Forum modules enable new content types. Others, such as the Field and Image modules, allow you to customize the display of the content types. Several modules are key to the system, such as the System, Block, and Node modules. Still others are intended as tools to help with the development and administration of the site. The various logging modules, for example, are focused on the administrator and the site developer.

In the sections that follow, I review briefly each of the default modules. Think of this as an orientation and a quick-start guide to the Drupal modules. At the end of each section is a Cross-Reference to the later chapters in this book where each module is discussed in more detail.

Note

In this section, when I indicate that a module is enabled by default, I am assuming you selected the Standard Installation Profile when you installed your Drupal site. ■

Aggregator

The Aggregator module enables the aggregation of syndicated content. Drupal's aggregator works like a feed reader, gathering RSS, RDF, and Atom-enabled news feeds from other sites and displaying them within Drupal. The options available in the Aggregator allow you to group together feeds into categories and view either the categories or the individual feeds. As the site administrator, you can add, edit, or delete the feeds. Feeds can be displayed inside the content area of the page by linking to the Aggregator or within a block position by using a block to display the feed.

The module is disabled by default; if you want to use it, you need to enable it via the Modules Manager.

Cross-Reference

Using the Aggregator module is discussed in detail in Chapter 18. ■

Block

The Block module provides the blocks functionality, which allows you to place content into the various regions on the Web page. The Block module is one of the fundamental Drupal modules and cannot be disabled. This module is administered through a separate Blocks Manager page.

The Block module is enabled in all default installations and is required by the Dashboard module.

Cross-Reference

Working with blocks is discussed in detail in Chapter 7. ■

Blog

The Blog module enables the creation of blog-type content items on the site. The module is a ready-made solution for sites that want to create blog content. While the Blog module is tailored to multi-user blogs, it can be used for single-user blogs as well, though you may want to make some adjustments to the menu items that relate to the functionality.

Enabling this module causes a new content type to appear: *Blog*. The module also adds several menu items. The Blogs menu item on the Navigation menu displays all blogs available on the site. The menu item called My blog links to an authenticated user's blog entries, if any. Yet another menu item allows for fast creation of new blog entries.

By default, Blog content items have comments enabled and are automatically promoted to the site's front page. The Blog module also creates a Recent Blog Posts block that you can enable at the Blocks Administration page. The block displays a list of the most recent blog entries.

The module is disabled by default; if you want to use it, you need to enable it via the Modules Manager. Using the comment functionality requires enabling the Comment module.

Cross-Reference

Using the Blog module is discussed in detail in Chapter 16. ■

Book

The Book module allows for the creation of book content items—that is, content items that are grouped together and organized hierarchically, like the pages in a book.

Enabling this module causes a new content type to appear: *Book*. The module also provides the functionality that allows pages to be organized into a hierarchy and grouped together for easy navigation. Books are administered via a separate Book administration page that allows you to change grouping and ordering of book pages. The module also provides a Book Navigation block that can be managed through the Blocks Manager.

The module is disabled by default; if you want to use it, you need to enable it via the Modules Manager.

Cross-Reference

Working with Book content is discussed in detail in Chapter 17. ■

Color

The Color module allows administrators to change the color scheme of themes that have implemented the color management configuration option. A theme that was designed to support the Color module gives you the option to easily change a variety of visual elements, including background and foreground colors, link colors, and text—all without having to mess with the code.

The Color functionality is accessed from the Theme specific settings page. Several of the default themes use the Color module; however, not all themes are set up for the Color functionality. If the module is disabled, the theme continues to function, but the color configuration option is not available.

This module is enabled in the default full installation.

Cross-Reference

The Color module's role in theme customization is discussed in Chapter 26. ■

Comment

The Comment module allows site visitors to comment on and discuss content items. Comments in Drupal are administered like content items and have their own administration page, linked off a tab on the Content Manager. Drupal allows for comments to be enabled selectively and applied only to those content types the administrator chooses. Administrators also can moderate and approve comments prior to publication. User permissions can be configured to allow different users different levels of access to this feature.

This module is enabled in the default full installation. It is required by both the Forum and Tracker modules.

Cross-Reference

Configuring the comment functionality is discussed in detail in Chapter 15. ■

Contact

The Contact module enables contact forms for the site and the users. Users are given the option to enable personal contact forms, which allows other users to get in touch with them by way of a simple contact form. For the site as a whole, the administrators can create one or more contact forms. The forms can be grouped into categories and each category sent to designated recipients.

The module is disabled by default; if you want to use it, you need to enable it via the Modules Manager.

Cross-Reference

Working with the system's contact forms is discussed in detail in Chapter 19. ■

Content Translation

The Content Translation module allows the site's contents to be translated into different languages. The module works in tandem with the Locale module. The Locale module provides the translation of the site's interface; the Content Translation module provides the ability to translate the content items. Enabling this module is only one step in the process of creating a multilingual site. You must also enable multilingual support for each content type and grant content translation privileges to the users.

The module is disabled by default; if you want to use it, you need to enable it via the Modules Manager. The module is dependent on the Locale module.

Cross-Reference

Working with multilingual content is discussed in detail in Chapter 22. ■

Contextual Links

This module provides shortcut links that appear on various functional units. The links allow users with sufficient privileges the option to make changes to the units without the necessity of having to visit the admin section of the site. When you see an item on a page with a gear icon next to it, you are seeing the output of the Contextual Links module.

This module is enabled in the default full installation.

Dashboard

The Dashboard module controls the Dashboard functionality that is visible by default to only the site administrator. To view it in action, log into your site as an administrator and click the Dashboard option on the Management menu.

This module is enabled in the default full installation. It is dependent upon the Block module.

Cross-Reference

The Dashboard is discussed in Chapter 3. ■

Database Logging

The Database Logging module observes system events and records them in the log table in the database. The module captures usage data, performance data, errors, warnings, and more. The log is useful for a site administrator because it allows you to look at the sequence of events that has occurred on your site. It is invaluable for debugging your site. Sometimes this module is referred to as "Dblog."

This module is enabled in the default installations.

Cross-Reference

Configuring logging and reporting is discussed in Chapter 4. ■

Field

The module enables site administrators to add custom fields to content types, user profiles, and so on. The functionality is managed through the Field UI module, explained later in this section.

This module is enabled in the default full installation.

Field SQL Storage

As the name implies, this module enables the Field API to store data in the database. Site administrators do not interact with this module directly, as it is a helper module for the Field API; site administrators interact with the Field UI module, explained next.

This module is enabled in the default full installation.

Field UI

The Field UI module provides the user interface (UI) for the Field API. The module allows you to add custom fields to content types, users comments, and other data types. Configuration of the fields is handled through the Content Types Administration page.

The Drupal core allows you to add the following field types: Number, Text, and List. Additional types can be added to your site by installing various extensions.

The Field UI module is enabled in the default full installation.

Cross-Reference

Using the Field API is discussed in detail in Chapter 10. ■

File

The File module defines the File field type. This module is enabled in the default full installation.

Cross-Reference

Using the File field is discussed in detail in Chapter 10. ■

Filter

The Filter module gives the site administrator the ability to filter out potentially harmful code and formatting from content items prior to their publication on the site. The module is configurable and is associated with specific content types and user permissions.

This module is enabled in the default full installation.

Forum

The Forum module enables discussion forums for use by the site's visitors. Drupal's forum functionality is a basic discussion board tool that allows someone to post comments or questions and others to respond. All posts are saved in the system, thereby creating a body of content for your site. Forums can be nested and grouped together to create complex structures. The module also provides a default menu option for the forum and the administration tools you need to manage it and control permissions for the users. Note that Forum Topics are a content type and can be administered from the Content Manager.

The module is disabled by default; if you want to use it, you need to enable it via the Modules Manager.

Cross-Reference

Using the Forum module is discussed in detail in Chapter 20. ■

Help

The Help module manages the display of the Drupal online help. The help files are context sensitive and included within the default Drupal installation files. The content you see when you click various help links in the admin interface comes from these files.

This module is enabled in the default full installation.

Tip

Additional, and more complete, help information is available online in the Drupal Handbook at drupal.org. ■

Cross-Reference

The Drupal Help files are discussed in more detail in Appendix E. ■

Image

The Image module provides image management tools. The module enables image styles, which allow you to create presets for the handling of images in the system.

This module is enabled in the default full installation.

Cross-Reference

Configuring your site for handling images is discussed in Chapter 4. Working with images is covered in Chapter 12. ■

List

The List module works in conjunction with the Options module and the Field module to provide the ability to store lists of items. Usually these items are entered through a select list, check boxes, or radio buttons.

This module is enabled in the default full installation.

Locale

The Locale module adds language-handling functionality and enables the translation of the user interface into different languages. The module works in tandem with the Content Translation module. The Locale module provides the translation of the site's interface; the Content Translation module provides the ability to translate the content items. The Locale module also powers the features that allow you to set language preferences for individual users.

The module is disabled by default; if you want to use it, you need to enable it via the Modules Manager. It is required by the Content Translation module. This module does not provide automatic translation; you also need to install the appropriate language files you want to use.

Cross-Reference

Working with multilingual content is discussed in detail in Chapter 22. ■

Menu

The Menu module gives administrators the ability to control and customize the site's menus. This module is one of the key modules of your site. The default Drupal system comes with five menus, but you can add or delete menus to suit your needs. The module also provides the blocks used to place the menus on the page and the menu management interface where the administrator can create, edit, and delete menus and menu items.

The Menu module is enabled in the default full installation.

Cross-Reference

Working with Drupal's menu system is discussed in detail in Chapter 8. ■

Node

The Node module lies at the heart of the Drupal content creation functionality; it allows content to be created and displayed on the pages.

This module is required by Drupal and is enabled in the default full installation.

Open ID

The Open ID module enables your site to support the Open ID protocol. Users who already have an Open ID account can use their existing ID to log into the site.

The module is disabled by default; if you want to use it, you need to enable it via the Modules Manager.

Cross-Reference

Using Open ID for user authentication is discussed in more detail in Chapter 25. ■

Options

The Options module supplements the functionality in the Field module; it allows you to define input widgets for custom Fields.

This module is enabled in the default full installation.

Overlay

The Overlay module provides the overlay you see in the admin section of the site.

This module is enabled in the default full installation.

Path

The Path module gives the administrator the ability to create and control aliases for the URLs of the site's pages. Typically, this is done to enhance the search engine friendliness of the site or to make the URLs easier for the users to remember. The module also gives you the ability to control which users can set the URLs.

The Path module is enabled in the default full installation.

Cross-Reference

Working with search engine-friendly URLs is discussed in Chapter 33. ■

PHP Filter

The PHP Filter module provides control over the input of PHP code and snippets. Drupal allows a user to input PHP code into a content item. The filter function of the module allows the administrator to define who is allowed to input code and which tags are allowed. This is a necessary control that allows you to maintain the security of your site and protect your site from users who might be inclined to input malformed or harmful code.

The module is disabled by default; if you want to use it, you need to enable it via the Modules Manager.

Cross-Reference

Configuring input formats and filters is discussed in Chapter 4. ■

Poll

The Poll module enables the display of polls or surveys on the site. Drupal's default poll functionality allows for the creation of simple multichoice surveys. Polls are a content type and are handled through the tools under the Content menu. The administrator can control access to the poll and configure basic options related to the questions and the duration of the poll.

The module is disabled by default; if you want to use it, you need to enable it via the Modules Manager.

Cross-Reference

Using the Poll module is discussed in detail in Chapter 21. ■

RDF

The RDF module allows you to map the site's data structure to RDF and export it in RDFa.

This module is enabled in the default full installation.

Cross-Reference

Using the RDF module is discussed in detail in Chapter 14. ■

Search

The Search module enables users to search the contents of the site. The settings dictated by the administrator determine the extent to which the contents are indexed and available for searching. The appearance of the search box on the pages of the site is controlled by the configuration settings in the Theme Configuration Manager.

This module is enabled in the default full installation.

Tip

Drupal's default search functionality supports exact keyword matching only. If you want to have more complex content search, you need to install an extension to enhance this functionality. ■

Cross-Reference

Enabling search on your site is discussed in Chapter 4. ■

Shortcut

The Shortcut module enables users to create shortcut links as an aid to site administration.

This module is enabled in the default full installation.

Cross-Reference

Using the shortcuts functionality is discussed in Chapter 3. ■

Statistics

The Statistics module collects site usage statistics on the site. The data gathered by this module is required for the display of some of the site's blocks—for example, blocks relating to most popular content and the number of views or users.

The module is disabled by default; if you want to use it, you need to enable it via the Modules Manager.

Cross-Reference

Configuring the collection of site statistics is discussed in Chapter 4. ■

Syslog

The Syslog module records system events to the Web server's log file. The purpose of this is largely administrative because it provides information useful for monitoring site performance and security. Administrators also can route events by their type and severity.

The module is disabled by default; if you want to use it, you need to enable it via the Modules Manager.

Cross-Reference

Configuring logging and reporting is discussed in Chapter 4. ■

System

The System module handles general site configuration.

This module is required by Drupal and is enabled in the default full installation.

Taxonomy

The Taxonomy module enables the categorization of content. The categorization is done by tagging content items. The module supports both free tagging and controlled vocabularies. Administrators are able to create and nest vocabularies and determine which content types are part of the schema.

The Taxonomy module is enabled in the default full installation and is required by the Forum module.

Cross-Reference

Managing taxonomies is discussed in detail in Chapter 11. ■

Testing

The Testing module provides a framework for unit and functional testing. The module makes it easy for you to check the state of your site before and after changes to the code. The Testing interface provides an assortment of tests that can be run. If issues are found, the system provides output describing the error, thereby making it easier for you to diagnose and solve problems. This module is sometimes referred to as "Simple Test."

The module is disabled by default; if you want to use it, you need to enable it via the Modules Manager.

Text

The Text module supplies text field types for the Field module.

This module is enabled in the default full installation.

Toolbar

The Toolbar module enables the admin toolbar functionality that the administrator sees at the top of the page when she is logged in.

This module is enabled in the default full installation.

Cross-Reference

Using the toolbar is discussing in Chapter 3. ■

Tracker

The Tracker module enables the tracking of posts by the users. The module powers the display of the most recent content functionality and keeps track of individual user contributions. By configuring the user settings, the administrator can follow a specific user's contributions to the site.

The module is disabled by default; if you want to use it, you need to enable it via the Modules Manager. Tracker requires the Comment module.

Cross-Reference

Using the Tracker module is discussed in detail in Chapter 23. ■

Trigger

The Trigger module enables actions to occur in response to system events. This module is the key to a number of interesting functionalities; an example would be having the site automatically send an e-mail in response to certain events, like the posting of a new comment. By default, the Drupal core provides five contexts for events: Comments, Content, Cron, Taxonomy, and Users.

The module is disabled by default; if you want to use it, you need to enable it via the Modules Manager.

Cross-Reference

Using actions and triggers is discussed in detail in Chapter 9. ■

Update Manager

The Update Status module checks for available updates to your Drupal core installation and your installed modules and themes. When new updates are found, the module produces an alert message for the administrator.

This module is enabled in the default full installation.

Cross-Reference

The Update functionality is discussed in detail in Chapter 35. ■

User

The User module handles user registration and the login system.

The module is required by Drupal and is enabled by default.

Note

Working with users is the subject of Part III of this book. ■

Summary

This chapter addressed the basics of module management and the default modules provided by Drupal 7. I covered the following topics:

- How to enable modules
- How to disable modules
- Where to find the administration tools for your enabled modules
- An overview of all the default modules

CHAPTER

Working with Blocks

Drupal *blocks* are units of self-contained functionality or content that you assign to specific physical regions of your Web site's layout. Most blocks are implemented by various core or contributed modules, but you also can use the admin tools or tools provided by contributed modules such as Views to create your own specialized blocks.

In this chapter, I introduce the fundamental concepts and behaviors of blocks, discuss how you position and customize them, and review the default set of blocks that you find in a standard Drupal install.

IN THIS CHAPTER

Understanding Blocks

Drupal blocks are components of functionality or content that the system renders during each page request. You can literally think of them as the building blocks of a Drupal Web page. Each block is assigned to a specific *region* of the page, with regions in turn defined by your Drupal themes. When managing blocks, you can optionally configure the behavior of each block—for example, by showing the block only to certain user roles or on certain sections of your Web site.

Note

Each active Drupal block is assigned to a region in the page. Regions are defined by each Drupal theme's presentation structure. Consequently, the number, placement, and naming of regions varies between themes, and following from this, you assign blocks to regions on a theme-by-theme basis. ■

Note

You can use contributed modules such as the Context module to override the block configuration defined in the Blocks Manager. For example, Context can be used to assign a specific block to a specific region given one or more contextual variables. You can learn more about the Context module here: `http://drupal.org/project/context`. ■

In Figure 7.1, you can see a number of the page regions defined by the Bartik theme. Understanding the close relationship between themes, regions, and blocks is key to managing the look and feel of your Drupal Web sites.

Cross-Reference

See Chapter 27 where we discuss Drupal themes in detail and outline exactly how you go about customizing your Drupal Web site's appearance. ■

FIGURE 7.1

The regions demo screen for the Bartik theme in which each yellow rectangle represents a named region in the Bartik theme

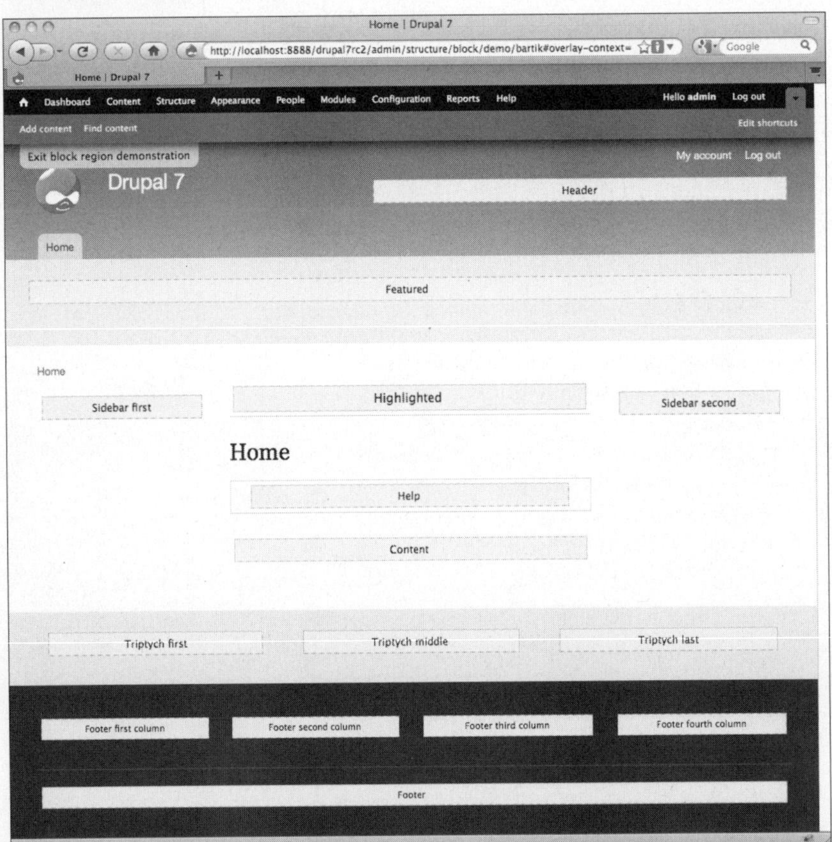

One of the most common examples of a block is the User Login form. With a default Drupal installation, this block is visible in the *Sidebar first* region of the page and is hidden automatically after you log in. In Figure 7.2, you can see the login block displayed in the Sidebar first region of a default Drupal installation.

Tip

In the default, Bartik, theme the Sidebar first region is the left sidebar (the first when reading from left to right) and the Sidebar second is the right sidebar, positioned to the right of the main content area. ■

FIGURE 7.2

The login block displayed in the first sidebar region of the Bartik theme

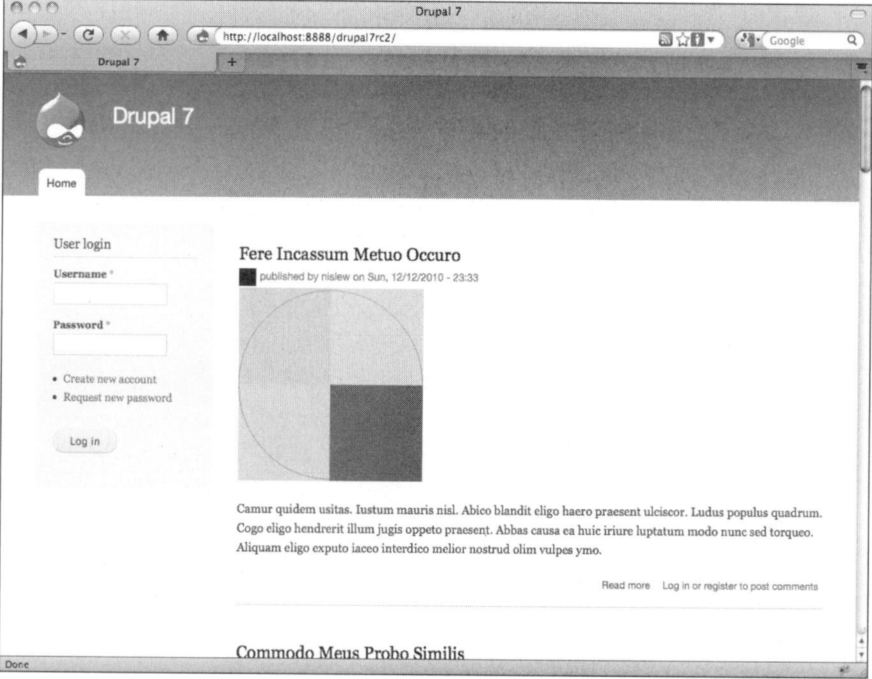

Using the Blocks Manager admin tool, you configure the region assignment, presentation order, and contextual behavior of your site's active blocks. In the next section, I cover the details of the Blocks Manager, but quickly here you can see in Figure 7.3 how the User login block is assigned to the Sidebar first region of the page.

FIGURE 7.3

The Blocks Manager screen shows the User login block's region assignment.

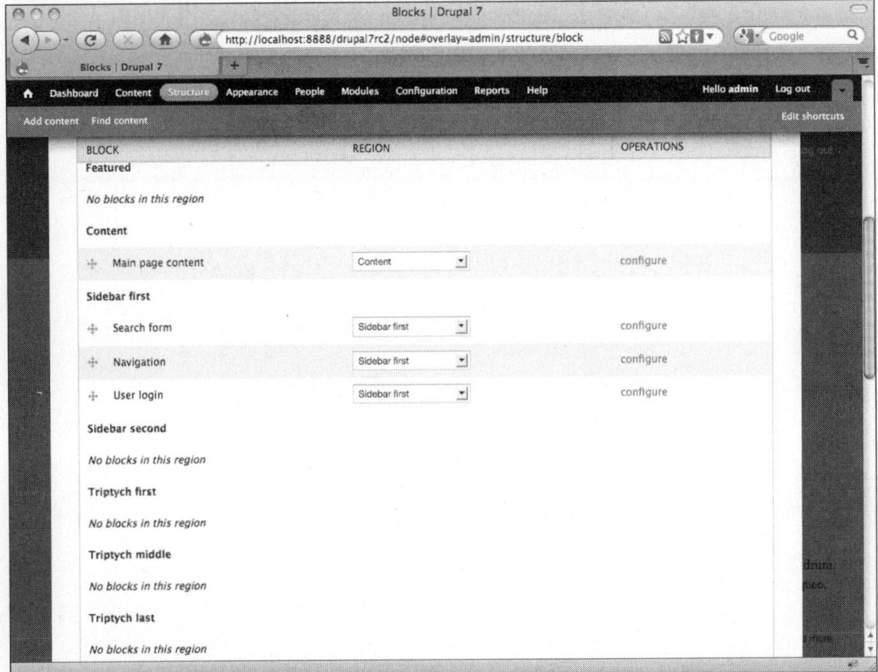

Overview of the Blocks Manager

The Blocks Manager plays a key role in the look, feel, and behavior of your Drupal-based Web sites. Located in the Structure section of the Drupal admin tools, the Blocks Manager, shown in Figure 7.4, allows you to enable or disable blocks, assign them to each theme's page regions, change their presentation order, create and delete blocks, and configure block behavior for different user and content contexts.

Understanding the key concepts

You should understand the following Blocks Manager concepts before proceeding:

- **Regions:** Each Drupal theme has a set of named regions (Header, Sidebar first, Content, Sidebar second, and Footer, for example). To utilize a given block, you must assign it to a region of the page.
- **Theme-specific configuration:** Each theme defines its own regions, and these can be different from theme to theme. Therefore, the Blocks Manager (refer to Figure 7.4) has a separate Configuration tab for each of the currently active themes.

- **Enabling/disabling blocks:** You enable a block by assigning it to a page region. To disable a block, you simply remove the region assignment, either by setting the region value to None or by dragging the block to the Disabled area. Note that the system lists the available but currently disabled blocks at the bottom of the Blocks Manager screen.
- **Deleting blocks:** Most blocks are defined in the code of a core or contributed module and cannot be deleted. However, if you create your own block—for example, a static content block containing a welcome message or a dynamic block with a PHP code snippet—you see a delete link associated with this block in the Blocks Manager screen. Deleting blocks permanently removes them from the system.
- **Configuring blocks:** You access a block's configuration screen from the Blocks Manager's main interface by way of the configure link next to each listed block. Configuration options vary between blocks, but most blocks share the basic set of options.

Note

Unlike region assignments, which apply on a theme-by-theme basis, block configuration settings apply globally. ■

FIGURE 7.4

The Blocks Manager screen shows the per-theme tabs.

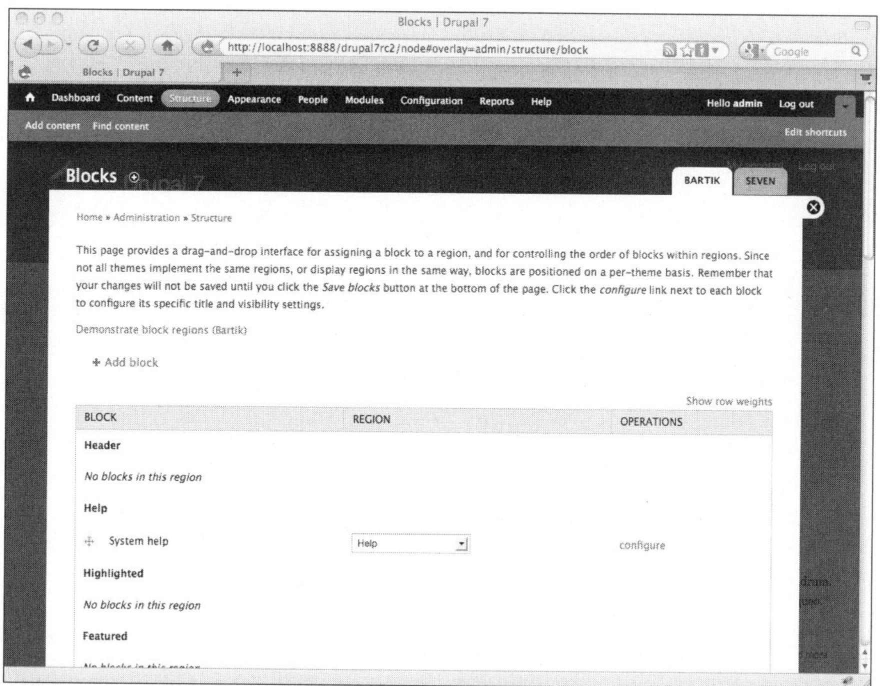

Managing and configuring blocks

Managing blocks generally entails enabling or disabling blocks and specifying their region assignments. When configuring blocks, you also can enable or disable and change per-theme-region assignments, but primarily you are influencing the behavior of blocks—controlling when they are visible, not where they show up.

Tip

When working in the main Blocks Manager screen, keep in mind that many of your changes do not take effect until after you click the Save blocks button at the bottom of the page. ■

The key items in the main Blocks Manager screen (refer to Figure 7.4) include the following:

- **Per-theme tabs:** The top right of the page contains a set of tabs, one for each active theme. You can click each tab to access a quick visual representation of that theme's block configuration.
- **Page header:** In this area, a concise introduction to blocks is followed by a useful tool: the Demonstrate block regions link. Note how this link's text is updated to specify the theme name each time you change to a different theme tab. Take a moment to explore how the regions are different in each theme.
- **Add block link:** This link leads you into the add block Web form, which allows you to define new blocks and is exactly like the block configuration form, discussed in detail later in this chapter.

Note

If you want to create new blocks that contain PHP code, you must enable the PHP filter core module in the Modules admin area and then assign one or more roles the right to work with the associated PHP code text filter in either the Configuration or People admin areas. ■

- **Regions and blocks grid:** On your way down the page, just after the Add block link, you find the regions and blocks grid. This grid has a few points of interest:
  - **Show row heights link:** If you click this item, a new column labeled Weight is visible in the grid. The Weight value controls the relative presentation order of blocks in a given region. A block with the value -10 renders before a block with the value -5, 0, or 1. In other words, the greater negative number you use, the higher the block's rendering priority is. The default mode is to let you set this order by dragging and dropping blocks. I find that to be the simpler and clearer approach.
  - **The Block column:** This grid column lists all the regions in bold and then the blocks, if any, assigned to each region. At the bottom of the grid, you see a special region named Disabled. This is where you find all the currently disabled blocks.
  - **The Region column:** This column contains the lists of possible region values. You select a named region here to place the associated block in that region. You also can select the value None to disable the block.
  - **The Operations column:** In most cases, this column just contains the configure link, but if the block can be deleted, then a delete link is also present here.

Tip

Most blocks cannot be deleted because they are implemented in the code of a core or contributed module. However, blocks that you create can be deleted. Keep in mind that all block deletions are permanent actions. Proceed with care! ■

You work in the Block configuration screen when creating and configuring blocks. Figure 7.5 shows the three sections of this screen; in my case, it's the User login block's configuration screen.

FIGURE 7.5

The User login block's configuration screen

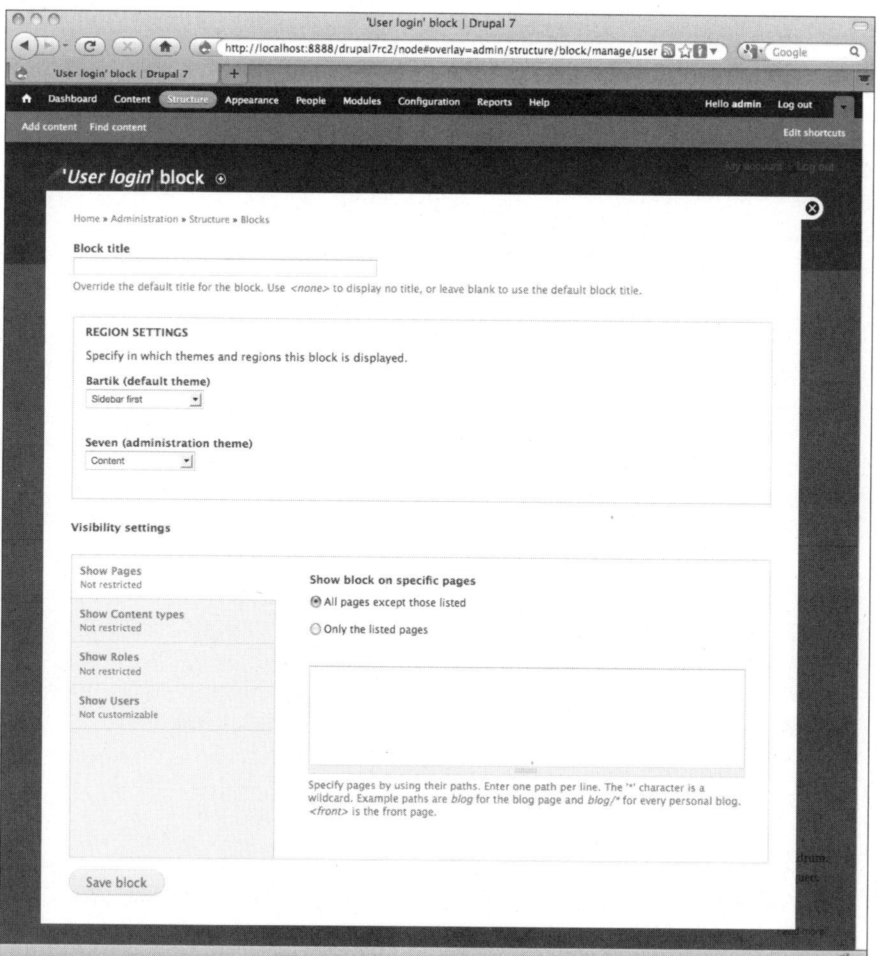

The Block creation and configuration screen contains three sections: the block description, title, and body; the Region settings; and the Visibility settings. These items are included in each section:

- **Block description:** This field is visible only when creating a block. The value is used to identify the block in the Blocks Manager screen. It is a required field when creating a new block.
- **Block title:** This optional value allows you to specify a title for the block. This title is displayed in the Web site's published interface.
- **Block body:** This field is visible only when you create a new block. The contents of this field are rendered in your published Web site, or if the content is PHP, it is evaluated when the block is rendered.

Tip

In many cases, when you enable core or contributed modules, they add new blocks to your system. So it's a good idea to review the Blocks Manager each time you add new modules or enable previously disabled modules. ■

- **Region settings:** This area duplicates some of the functionality of the main Blocks Manager screen, but it does so in a concise manner that allows you to see the current block's region assignments for all active themes.
- **Visibility settings:** This part of the screen contains a set of configuration tabs that control the block's visibility in different user and content contexts. These are the visibility settings tabs:
  - **Show pages:** Use this setting to control on which pages the block is displayed. The options are All pages except those listed (you list the paths to exclude), Only the listed pages (you list the paths to include), and if you have the PHP filter enabled, Pages on which this PHP code returns *TRUE* (you enter PHP code to evaluate a condition).

    This is a simple example of a PHP test that returns TRUE if the number 5 is greater than the number 2: `<?php return (5 > 2) ? TRUE : FALSE; ?>`. For a more practical example, try testing whether a certain word or phrase such as "news" is in the current URL: `<?php return (strpos($_SERVER['REQUEST_URI'], "news") > -1) ? TRUE : FALSE; ?>`. The possibilities here are endless, but care should be taken when using this approach; this is considered advanced and potentially dangerous functionality.

Tip

You can find many examples of using PHP code to control block visibility in the Drupal community documentation here: `http://drupal.org/node/60317`. **■**

  - **Show content types:** This tab lets you specify for which content types this block is visible. For example, you could decide to display this block only in article pages. If you do not select any content types, the system displays the block for all content types.

- **Show roles:** In this tab, you can select which roles see the current block. If you do not select any roles, the system displays the block for all roles.

Tip

To show only a given block to non-authenticated visitors, configure the block such that it is shown only to the anonymous user role. Instead of a state of being logged in or logged out, Drupal identifies a user's authentication state using roles. ■

- **Show users:** In this tab, you can give your site's users the ability to turn on or off the current block and control whether it's visible by default. The default setting is that users cannot control the block's visibility.

Reviewing the Default Blocks

When you perform a default installation of Drupal, a certain number of blocks are made available via the system's core modules. In this section, I briefly review these blocks. This is just a starting point; as you enable more core modules and install contributed ones, your catalog of available blocks quickly expands.

The following blocks are available in a default Drupal installation:

- **Main menu:** This is a navigational block. It renders the main navigational menu. Note that this menu may already be rendered natively by the current theme, as is the case with the Bartik theme, so assigning this block to a region may not be necessary.
- **Main page content:** This is where the primary content is rendered. For example, in the default home page, this block contains the list of recently published items.
- **Management:** This is a navigational block. It renders the Management menu, a menu entity that you can customize in the Menu management screens in the Structure area of the admin system.
- **Navigation:** This is another navigational block. It renders the Navigation menu, one of Drupal's default menus. You can customize this menu in the Menu management screens.

Cross-Reference

See Chapter 8 for a full discussion of the Drupal menu system. ■

- **Powered by Drupal:** This block renders a small bit of text indicating that the Web site is built using Drupal. By default, this block is positioned near the bottom of the page. It contains a non-qualified link back to the main Drupal Web site.
- **Recent comments:** This content block lists a number of recently made comments with the comment title or a text extract linked back to the comment. It also includes information about when the comment was published.
- **Recent content:** This content block lists a number of recently published content items with the title of the content linked to the published item.

- **Search form:** This block renders a content search form. If you disable the core Search module, this block no longer appears in the Blocks Manager.
- **Shortcuts:** This navigational block lists the current user's shortcut links. Each user has the ability to create a customizable list of shortcuts as part of his user profile.
- **System help:** User interface messages including action feedback and warnings are printed to the screen by this block.
- **Syndicate:** This block renders a small Web feed icon that is linked to your Web site's RSS feed. Note that enabling this block may not be necessary because other modules may already be rendering similar Web feed links and icons.

Cross-Reference

See Chapter 14 for details on content syndication configuration and functionality. ■

- **User login:** This item renders the standard Drupal login form. It is hard coded to display only for the Anonymous user role, which prevents it from displaying to users that are already authenticated.
- **User menu:** This navigational block renders the User menu, a specialized menu of actions for authenticated users. The contents of this menu can be customized in the Menu management screens.
- **Who's new:** This item lists the usernames of recently registered users.
- **Who's online:** This block indicates the number of current users logged into your Web site and, by default, lists the usernames.

Summary

This chapter provided a general overview of Drupal's block system and how you use the Blocks Manager to influence the placement of the system's user interface components. The following points were covered:

- An introduction to Drupal blocks and the tools used to manage them
- A review of the key concepts and assumptions related to blocks
- The key fields and settings involved in creating, positioning, and configuring blocks
- The default Drupal blocks, including their purpose and relation to other parts of the Drupal system

CHAPTER 8

Working with the Menus Manager

IN THIS CHAPTER

Drupal menus are simple, customizable navigational elements that you place into the interface of your Web site to facilitate efficient access to content and functionality. The Menus Manager is defined in a core module unsurprisingly named *Menu*. Users with the Administer menus and menu items permission can add, edit, and customize menus via the Menus Manager tool.

In this chapter, I cover the Drupal Menus Manager and describe how you can create and customize menus.

Overview of the Menus Manager

You create, edit, and configure menus using Drupal's Menus Manager tool, which is found under the Structure area of the Drupal admin system. Each menu has a corresponding *block*, which you use to control the physical placement of the menu, either programmatically in your theme's template code or via Drupal's Blocks Manager tool.

Cross-Reference

See Chapter 7 for an introduction to Drupal blocks and guidance on using the Blocks Manager. In Chapter 27, we dig into Drupal's theme system and explain how you can create or customize the appearance of your Web site and menus. ■

The main Drupal Menus Manager screen, shown in Figure 8.1, contains the following key elements:

- **Local navigation tabs:** The List Menus and Settings tabs are located in the top right of the Menus Manager screen. The first tab provides access to the currently defined menus, while the Settings tab gives you access to the Menu module's global settings. I discuss the Settings tab items in the Configuring global settings section, located later in this chapter.
- **Link to Block manager:** Keep in mind the tight relationship between menus and blocks; each menu has a corresponding block, and the Drupal Menus Manager has a convenient link to the Blocks Manager tool.
- **Add menu link:** As expected, this link takes you directly into the process of creating a new Drupal menu. I walk through that process later in this chapter.
- **Menus grid:** The majority of the screen displays the current system menus. By default, you see four standard menus:
  - **Main menu:** This is the primary navigation menu, which typically is rendered by the theme for all users and in all content contexts. This menu often contains what I call top-level navigation items. For example, if you are running a news Web site, it might include your top-level news categories like World, Politics, Business, Weather, Sports, and so on. If you are building a corporate site, this menu might contain links for Products, Services, About the Company, and Contact Information.
  - **Management:** This is a specialized menu typically reserved for editors, admins, or other powerful users. It is a customizable menu, but it typically contains links to the full set of Drupal administration tools.
  - **Navigation:** The Navigation menu is a secondary menu intended for visitors to your Web site. You can manually add and remove links from this menu. Additionally, certain modules automatically add links to it. For example, if you enable the core Forum module, a link to the forums base page is automatically added to this menu.
  - **User menu:** This is a simple utility menu for authenticated users. It contains links for managing the user account as well as a link to log out of the current session.

Note

Some themes make use of menus directly, without the need for you to assign a menu's block to a theme's region. For example, the Bartik theme renders the Main links list in the top set of navigation tabs and the menu that is currently assigned to the secondary links in the top right of the page. ■

FIGURE 8.1

The Menus Manager screen displaying the default set of Drupal menus

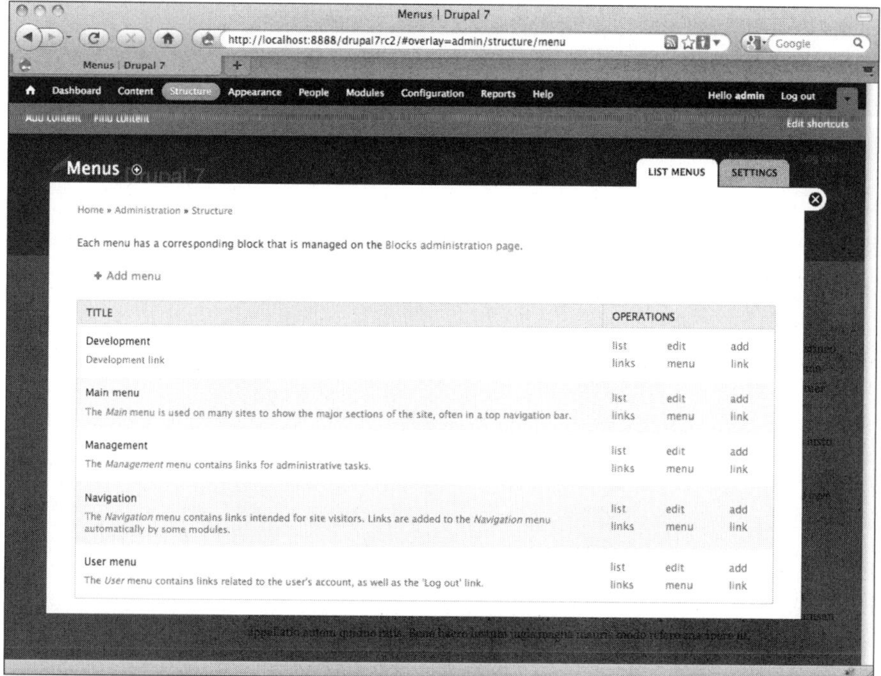

Creating and Managing Menus

You create new menus and manage both the contents of menus and related settings in the Menus Manager tool, located in the Structure section of the admin system. The Blocks Manager tool, also found in the Structure section, is used to assign menus to regions in a theme's template.

In this section, I describe the common operations performed with the Menus Manager.

Cross-Reference

See Chapter 7 for an overview of Drupal's Blocks Manager tool and to get an understanding of the important relationship between menus, blocks, and regions. ■

Creating new menus

You can easily create your own menus if Drupal's default menus do not meet your needs. You accomplish this via the following steps:

1. **Log into your site as an administrator.**

   The Management menu appears at the top of the page.

2. **Click the Structure item in the Management menu.**

   The list of Structure sub-items loads in your browser.

3. **Click the link for the Menus sub-item.**

   The Menus Manager screen appears (refer to Figure 8.1).

Note

Each time you add a new menu to your Web site, a new block is created with the same name. To display your new menu, you must assign the associated block to a region in at least one active template. You accomplish this via Drupal's Blocks Manager tool. ■

4. **Click the Add menu link in the Menus Manager.**

   The Add menu form loads in your browser, as shown in Figure 8.2.

5. **Enter a value into the form's Title field.**

   In this example, I used "My Test Menu."

6. **Optionally, enter a description into the form's Description field.**

   In this example, I used "This is a test menu."

7. **Click the Save button at the bottom of the screen.**

   If the operation is successful, a success message is displayed, and you are presented with the Link management screen for your new menu.

You have now created your first custom menu. It is empty for the moment, but later in this chapter, I describe how to create and manage menu items (or links). We return to this menu at that point.

Managing existing menus

You really can't do much managing or configuring of individual menus, beyond managing the hierarchy of links found in each menu. I cover menu item management in a following section of this chapter, "Creating and Managing Menu Items." Jump to that point if you are primarily concerned with the links visible in your menus.

Broadly speaking, menus and menu items fall into one of two categories: Either they are programmatically created via a module or you or another administrator manually creates them. Programmatically created menus have a field called Menu name (which cannot be changed), while manually created menus have a field called Title. Aside from altering the Title field, the only other configuration you can make is to alter the Description field.

The previously described activities comprise the rather narrow extent of Drupal menu management. You access the Menu creation and editing screen (refer to Figure 8.2) by clicking the Edit menu link in the Menus Manager grid (refer to Figure 8.1).

FIGURE 8.2

The Add new menu screen

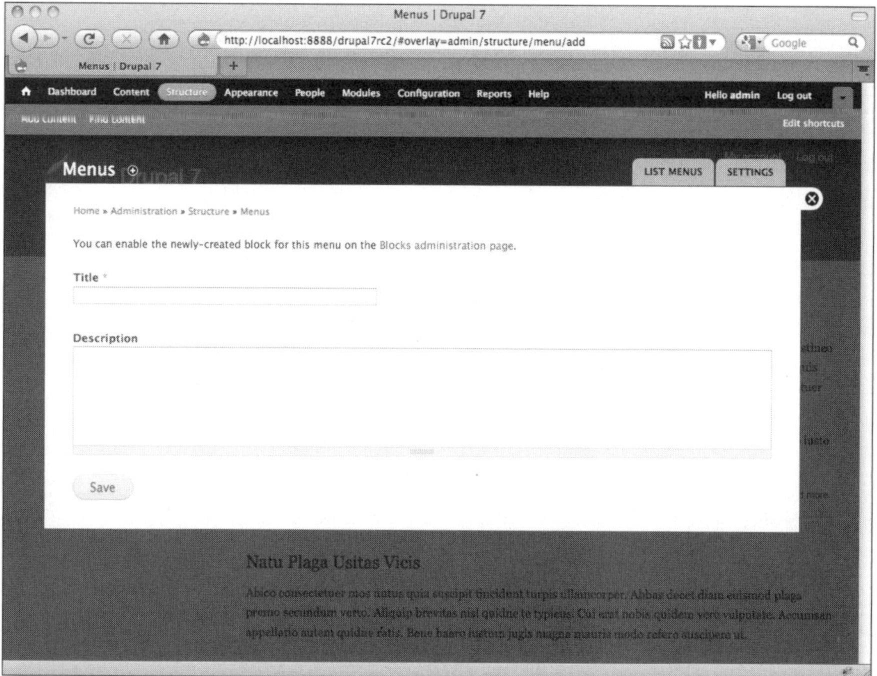

Configuring global Menu module settings

The Menus Manager has a tabbed interface with the first tab listing all the current menus and the second tab, labeled Settings, providing access to the module's global settings. This Settings tab is displayed in Figure 8.3.

The two global settings visible in this tab allow you to configure the data sources for two internal system lists: Main links and Secondary links. When populated, these two lists can be used by the user interface theme to render navigational elements.

For example, in the Bartik theme, the Main links list is used to populate the primary navigation tabs and the Secondary links list is used to populate a less prominent navigation element in the top right of the page.

These two settings function as follows:

- **Source for the Main links:** This drop-down list contains all the currently available menus and the option No Main links, which disables the population of the Main links list. The default value for this setting is Main menu. However, you can change this to be any of the available menus, if that better suits your site's needs.

- **Source for the Secondary links:** This drop-down list similarly contains all the currently available menus, plus the option No Secondary links, which disables the population of the Secondary links list. Just like the Main links item, the Secondary links item is a system list that themes can use to render a navigation element.

  A common configuration is to assign the User menu to the Secondary links list. However, your user interface design, theme in use, and functionality needs typically dictate how or if you use the Secondary links. In Figure 8.4, you can see the display of the User menu as the source of the Secondary links list; note the My Account and Logout links in the top-right part of the page.

Tip

As is explained in the help text you find in Menus Manager's Settings tab, you can choose to use the same menu as the data source for both the Main links and the Secondary links items. If you use this approach and your selected source menu has at least two levels of links, then the source menu's second level of links becomes the source for the Secondary links list. ■

FIGURE 8.3

The Menus Manager's global settings screen

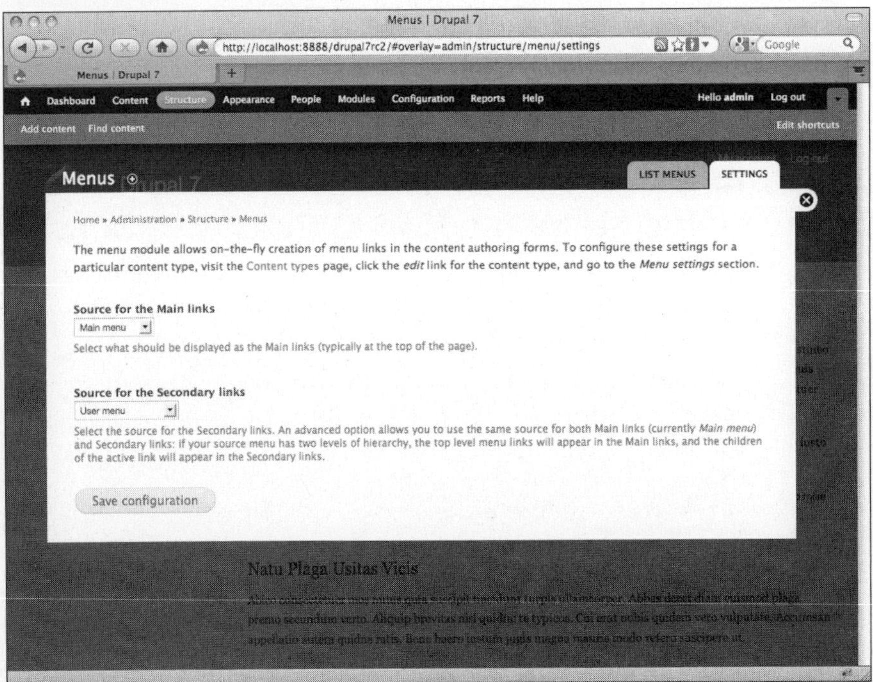

Follow these steps to change the Menu module's global settings:

1. **Log in to your site as an administrator.**

   The Management menu appears at the top of the page.
2. **Click the Structure item in the Management menu.**

   The list of Structure sub-items loads in your browser.
3. **Click the link for the Menus item.**

   The Menus Manager screen appears.
4. **Click the Settings tab at the top right of the screen.**

   The Settings tab loads in your browser, as shown in Figure 8.4.
5. **Select a source menu for the Main links list.**
6. **Move down the page, and select a source menu for the Secondary links list.**
7. **Click the Save button at the bottom of the screen.**

   If the operation is successful, a success message is displayed at the top of the screen, your settings are saved, and the changes are immediately reflected in the published Web site.

FIGURE 8.4

The Bartik theme displays the User menu as the source of the Secondary links item at the top right of the page.

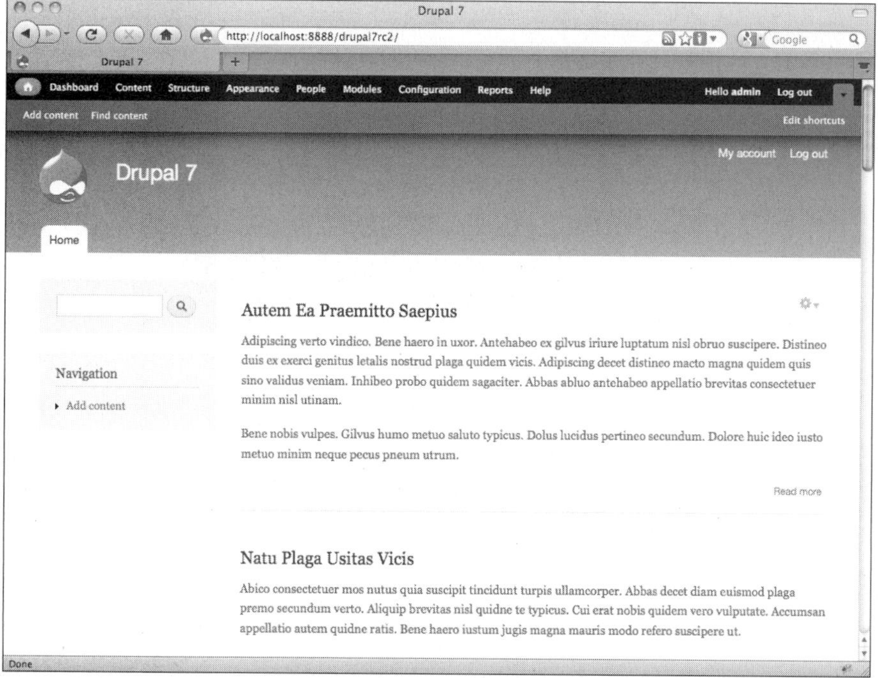

Configuring menus for content types

You can configure the system to automatically create new menu links each time a new piece of content is created. You do this on a per-content-type basis by editing the configuration of each content type. And once enabled, authors can let the system do its work or they can interfere by disabling the link creation or tuning how it is done via the settings visible in Figure 8.5.

Note

If you are running an online news site or blog, you may find the idea of automatic menu item creation a bit impractical. I would tend to agree with you in that situation. However, in some cases, automating menu link creation can make sense, and doing so can save you or your authors some valuable time. You need to evaluate the use of this functionality on a site-by-site basis. ■

FIGURE 8.5

The content type editing screen displays the Menu settings area.

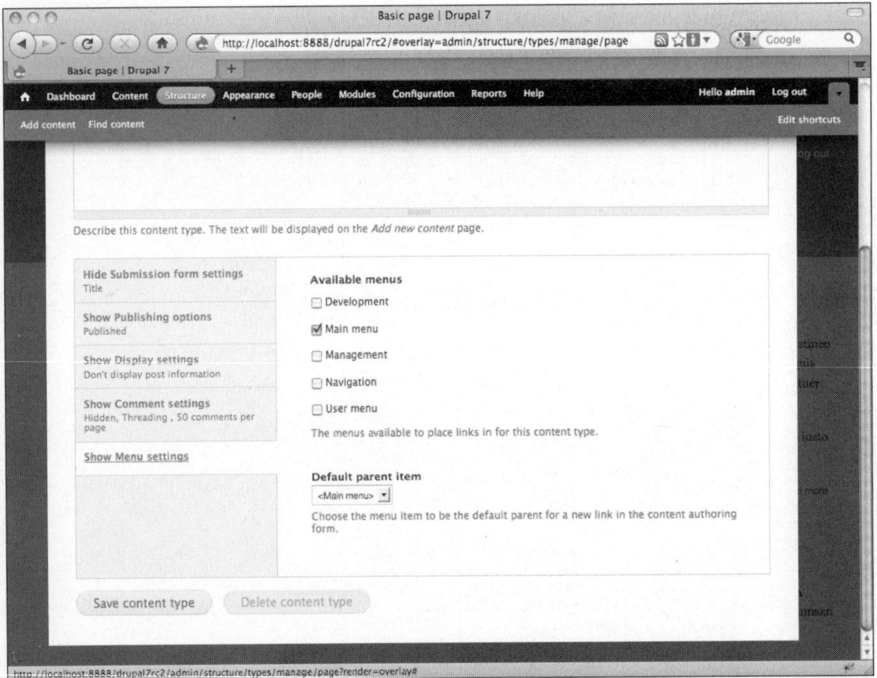

Perform the following steps to enable automatic menu generation for a content type:

1. **Log into your site as an administrator.**

   The Management menu appears at the top of the page.
2. **Click the Structure item in the Management menu.**

   The list of Structure sub-items loads in your browser.
3. **Click the Content types link in the sub-items list.**

   The Content type management screen appears.
4. **Locate the content type you want to manage (the Basic page, for example), and click the edit link in this type's row.**

   The content type's editing screen loads in your browser.
5. **Scroll to the bottom of the page, and select the Show menu settings vertical tab.**

   The menu settings configuration options are displayed (refer to Figure 8.5).
6. **Using the check boxes next to each system menu, select the menus you want to make available to authors when working with content of this type.**
7. Next, select the default parent item for the automatically created menu links.

Note

If one or more menus are enabled for a content type, authors can change the parent item during the authoring process. You are simply setting the defaults when configuring the content type. However, if you do not enable any of the system menus, then authors do not have access to any menu settings during the authoring process. ■

8. **Click the Save button at the bottom of the screen.**

   If the operation is successful, a success message is displayed at the top of the screen and your settings are saved.

After a content type is configured to work with one or more system menus, authors can easily add new menu items during the authoring process. If you enable multiple menus for the content type, then authors can select which is most appropriate for each content item. Figure 8.6 shows the menu settings area in the content authoring screen.

Cross-Reference

See Chapter 10 for a more in-depth discussion of the settings available in the content authoring screen and how each setting affects the system's publishing behavior. ■

FIGURE 8.6

The content authoring screen for the Basic Page content type displays the Menu settings area.

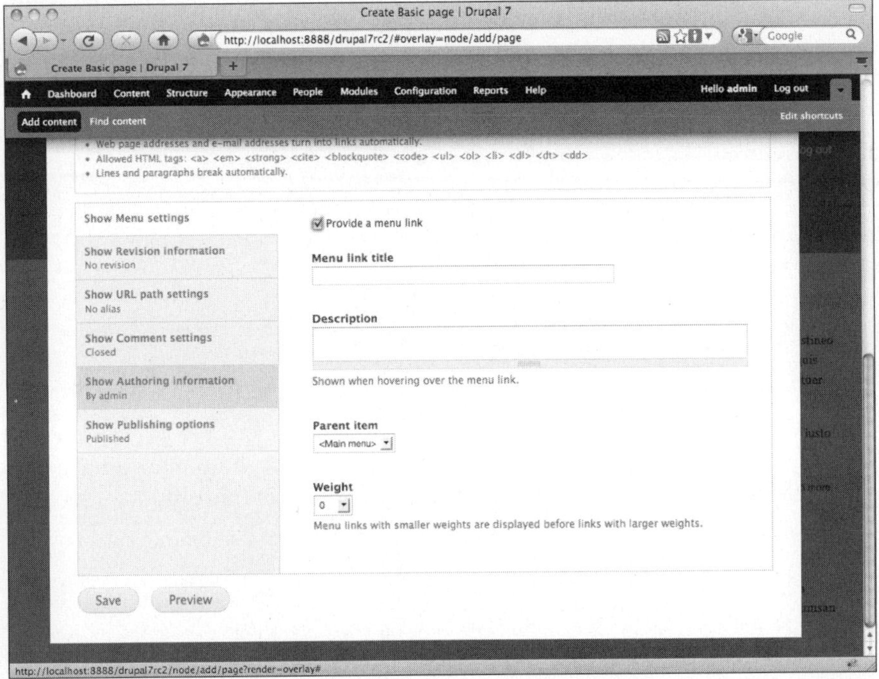

Tip

Drupal automatically populates the content authoring screen's Menu link title field with the content item's current title. For example, a page titled "Drupal is Wonderful" automatically creates a link with text that matches this title. Matching link text to page or item titles is often seen as good practice for search engine optimization, but it's not always desirable, and authors can override the link's automatically generated text by simply changing the field's value. ■

Creating and Managing Menu Items

Menu items are the internal or external links that make up the hierarchical content of a given menu. You can create these items manually, or as explained in the preceding section, you can configure Drupal to create links automatically as new content items are authored. In this section, I discuss the manual creation and management of links.

Note

Menu items can be organized hierarchically, but depending on how and where a given menu's content is used, the full hierarchy of items may not be displayed. This varies by theme, so you should experiment in your environment to best understand how menus will behave with your chosen theme. ■

Creating menu items

You manually create menu items using the Menus Manager screens located under the Structure area of the Drupal admin system. In this section, I use the Add Menu item form, shown in Figure 8.7, to add a new link to a custom menu named My Test Menu.

FIGURE 8.7

The Add Menu item screen for the My Test Menu menu

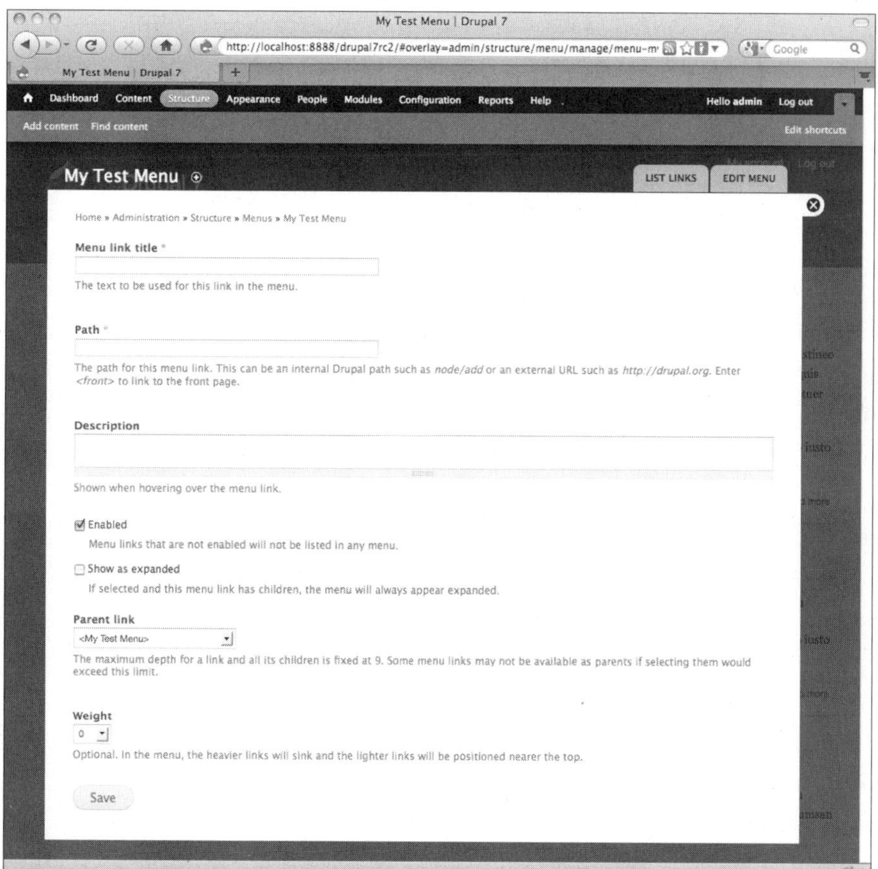

The Add Menu item form contains the following fields:

- **Menu link title:** Intuitively labeled, this field controls the text that is displayed in the Web page for this menu item.
- **Path:** This field stores the navigational path for the link, or in HTML terms, the value of the `href` attribute. This value is typically a value relative to the base URL of your Drupal installation.

  For example, a page with the path `http://mysite.com/contact-us` would have a path value of just `contact-us`. The same is true if, for example, Drupal was installed in the `drupal7` directory of your Web site. In that case, the full URL would be `http://mysite.com/drupal7/contact-us`, but the Path value for the link would still just be `contact-us`.

Tip

The Path field can take three types of values: a Drupal install-relative path, a fully qualified external URL such as `http://drupal.org`, or a special system value like `<front>`, which represents the front page of the Web site. ■

- **Description:** If you set this optional value, the text here shows up as a kind of tool tip in many browsers when the user hovers her mouse over the link text.
- **Enabled:** When this box is checked, the link is enabled and visible in the menu. If you uncheck this box, the link is not visible in the menu under any circumstances.
- **Show as expanded:** If you check this box and the menu item has child menu items, then—if supported by the theme environment—the current item renders in an expanded state, displaying its child links.
- **Parent link:** This list allows you to choose where in the menu hierarchy this item is placed. If the menu does not have an item hierarchy, then the root menu item is the only option presented.
- **Weight:** This list of numeric values controls the relative presentation order of the menu item. If the current value is 0 and another item has a lower value, such as -1, then the other item is rendered first, either to the left of the current item (in the case of a horizontal menu) or above the current item (in the case of a vertical menu).

Note

In the Drupal Menus Manager interface, the terms Menu item, link, and Menu link are used interchangeably. ■

Follow these steps to add a new menu item to one of your system menus:

1. **Log into your site as an administrator.**

   The Management menu appears at the top of the page.

2. **Click the Structure item in the Management menu.**

   The list of Structure sub-items loads in your browser.

3. **Click the link for the Menus sub-item.**

   The Menus Manager screen appears.

4. **Click the add link item in the Operations column of the row you want to modify.**

   The Add menu link screen loads in your browser, as shown in Figure 8.7.

5. **Enter the Menu link text in the field provided.**
6. **Move to the next field, and enter a Path value for this item.**
7. **If other changes are desired, make these changes now.**
8. **Scroll to the bottom of the page, and click the Save button.**

   If the operation is successful, a success message is displayed at the top of the screen, the link is active in the menu, and the current menu's list of links is displayed in your browser.

Managing menu items

You manage menu items—including ordering, configuring, or deleting links—using the same Menus Manager screens that I covered throughout this chapter. From the Menus Manager screen, you click the list links item next to the menu you want to manage (refer to Figure 8.1). In this screen, you can drag and drop links to reorder their presentation, enable or disable them, click to delete them, or click to edit a link utilizing the same input form as is shown in Figure 8.7.

Note

You can easily move menu items between menus. In the menu item management screen (refer to Figure 8.7) you can change the Parent link setting for a menu item to be either a different menu or a different level in a menu. The act of changing the parent effectively moves the link from one place to another. ■

In Figure 8.8, you see the elements of the Menu item management screen. The only two areas of functionality that differ from the creation parameters are the drag-and-drop link ordering and the ability to delete a link.

Tip

Do not forget to click the Save configuration button after making changes in the Menu item management screen. If, for example, you uncheck the Enabled check box but neglect to click the Save button, the change is not reflected in your Web site. ■

FIGURE 8.8

The List links tab for the My Test Menu menu

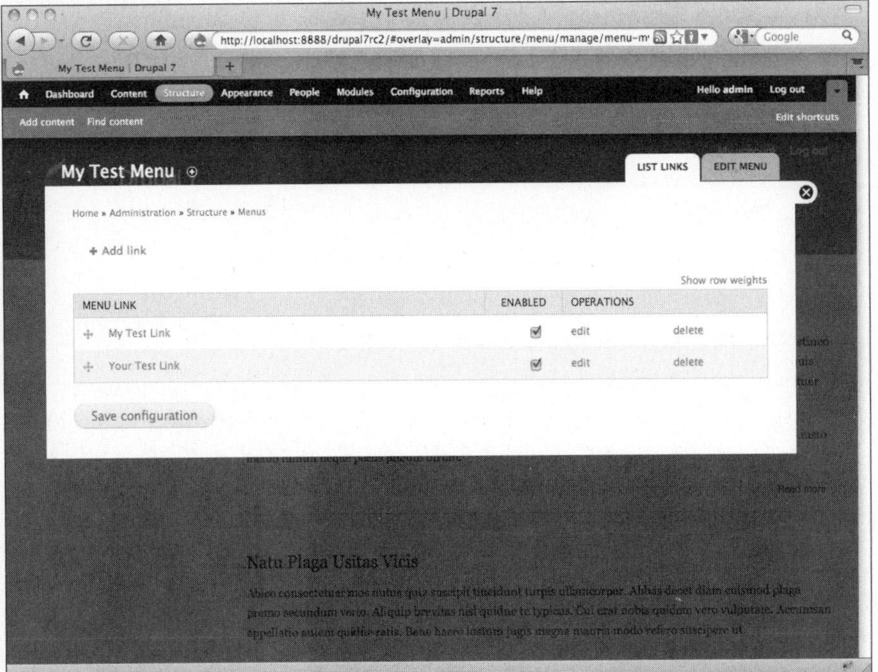

Summary

This chapter provided an introduction to Drupal's menu system—implemented by the core Menu module—and guided you through a series of typical menu management operations. I covered the menu system's intimate connection with Drupal blocks and described how content types and menus work together to simplify some management tasks. The following points were covered:

- An overview of Drupal menu concepts
- Guidance for creating and managing menus
- An explanation of the global Menu module settings and how they interact with themes
- The creation and management of menu items and how to control their presentation order

CHAPTER

Using Actions and Triggers

IN THIS CHAPTER

The default simple actions

Adding an advanced action

Assigning triggers to actions

Actions and triggers are native Drupal functionalities that work together allowing you to define sets of automatic operations that take place following certain system events. For example, you may want to send an e-mail to the author of an article every time someone comments on it, thus ensuring that he or she can respond to the comment in a timely fashion.

In this chapter, I introduce the default set of Drupal actions, how to go further by creating your own Advanced actions, and finally how you go about connecting system events, called triggers, to defined actions.

Note

Both actions and triggers are core Drupal functionalities. Actions are considered part of the system and cannot be disabled. On the other hand, you will find that triggers, despite being a part of the system core, are disabled by default. You must enable the core Trigger module before you can work with triggers. ■

The Default Simple Actions

When you set up a standard Drupal installation, you find a number of simple system actions already defined. Navigate to the Actions screen found in the System section of the admin Configuration area, and you see a list of actions as shown in Figure 9.1.

FIGURE 9.1

The default Actions screen shows the list of simple actions.

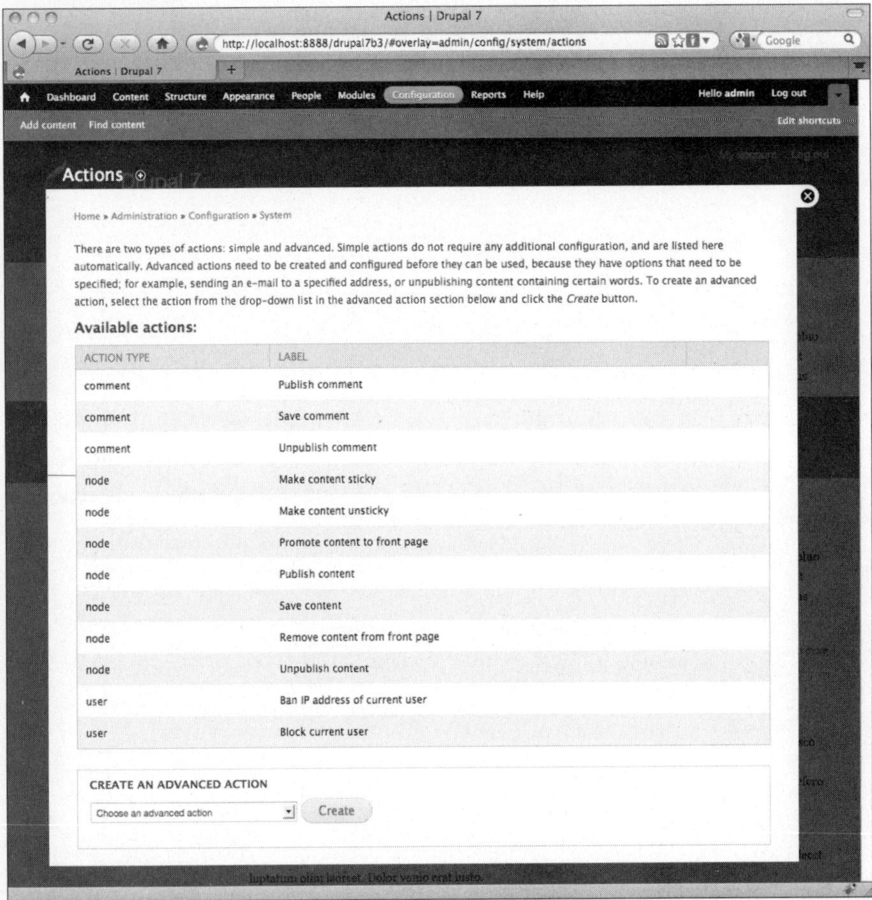

The default set of simple actions includes the following:

- **Save comment:** Applying only to comments, this action saves the comment item currently in context, typically after changes have been made to it (after the published state has been changed, for example).
- **Publish comment:** Applying only to comments, this action changes the published state to Published. This action is normally combined with a Save comment action to persist the changes it makes.
- **Unpublish comment:** Applying only to comments, this action changes the published stated to Unpublished. This action is also normally combined with a Save comment action to persist the changes it makes.

- **Save content:** Applying to all items derived from a Drupal node, this action persists the item in context to the database. It is typically used to persist the changes resulting from previous actions.
- **Promote content to front page:** Applying to all items derived from a Drupal node, this action sets the metadata, indicating that the item in question should be promoted to the front page of your Web site.
- **Publish content:** Applying to all items derived from a Dupal node, this action changes the published state to Published.
- **Remove content from front page:** Applying to all items derived from a Drupal node, this action is the complement to Promote content to front page action and performs exactly the opposite task, changing the item's metadata such that it is no longer promoted to the front page of your Web site.
- **Unpublish content:** Applying to all items derived from a Drupal node, this action is the complement of the Publish content action. It changes the in-context item's published state value such that it is no longer published on your Web site.
- **Make content sticky:** Applying to all items derived from a Drupal node, this action changes the in-context item's metadata value indicating that it is sticky. Sticky content items are presented before similar items that are not marked as sticky.
- **Make content unsticky:** Applying to all items derived from a Drupal node, this action is the complement of the Make content sticky action. It changes the in-context item's metadata such that it is not marked as sticky.
- **Ban IP address of current user:** Applying only to user entities, this is typically a punitive action taken because the user has performed an undesirable action, such as leaving disagreeable comments. When an IP address is blocked, visitors coming from that address can no longer access your Drupal site. Instead, they are presented with a concise message that explains why they do not have access to the normal content.
- **Block current user:** Applying only to user entities, this also typically is a punitive action taken as a result of undesirable user behavior. When a user is blocked, she can no longer log into your system or post comments.

Note

The standard Drupal install comes with a set of simple actions defined. Don't feel limited by these items. You can always define your own Advanced actions, if the standard actions do not meet your needs. ■

Adding an Advanced Action

Advanced actions give you another level of power when automating the management of your Drupal system. In this section, I describe the types of Advanced actions that you can create and then I walk you through the process of adding a new Advanced action. In the following section, I cover how to use these actions in response to certain system events.

Introducing Advanced actions

The combination of actions and triggers allows you to perform many automated tasks that would otherwise be tedious and time-consuming, or worse, not happen at all. Some of these tasks are most effective with a measure of customization involved in their definition. These customized actions are what we call Advanced actions.

With that said, don't let the name fool you: Advanced actions are not terribly advanced, nor can you fully customize them. Advanced actions simply give you another level of customization via Drupal's browser-based configuration tools.

Tip

If you're familiar with triggers available in SQL databases like Oracle, SQL Server, PostgreSQL, and recent versions of MySQL, you should easily understand Drupal's triggers and actions. They are quite similar in principle. The difference in Drupal's case is that both triggers and actions are defined in advance. Drupal trigger and action configuration is therefore primarily about connecting the two parts, rather than coding the actions from scratch. ■

These are the Advanced actions you find in a standard Drupal 7 system:

- **Unpublish comment containing keyword(s):** Applying only to comments, this action allows you to define a comma-delimited list of keywords or phrases that, if found in the contents of a comment, will cause the comment to be set as unpublished.
- **Change the author of content:** Applying to items derived from Drupal nodes, this action changes the author of a content item to be the author you specify in the configuration.
- **Unpublish content containing keyword(s):** Applying to items derived from Drupal nodes, this action allows you to define a comma-delimited list of keywords or phrases that, if found in the contents of an item, will cause the item to be set as unpublished.
- **Display a message to the user:** This action displays a message, which you provide, to the user via Drupal's native system of message presentation.
- **Send e-mail:** You can use this action in various contexts to send a customized e-mail message, provided by you via the configuration screen. The destination can either be a hard-coded e-mail address or a tokenized e-mail address, such as the e-mail address of the in-context node's author or the in-context comment's author. You also can use tokens in the message body to add dynamic content from the current context.

Tip

In Drupal parlance, tokens are symbols that the system can recognize and replace with real values from the current operating context. For example, Drupal can replace the token `[node:author:email]` with the e-mail address of the current content item's author, or it can replace `[comment:body]` with the body content from the current in-context comment. Token replacement is a powerful functionality often used with actions and triggers. ■

- **Redirect to URL:** This broadly usable action allows you to redirect a user to a specific URL. For example, after a user signs up, you may want to redirect her to a page that explains how your account approval process works.

Creating an Advanced action

You create new Advanced actions from the same screen that lists the default action, as shown in Figure 9.2. Each action has its own secondary screen for naming and customization of the action.

In this section, I create an Advanced action that notifies content authors when someone posts a comment on one of their published items. You may find this to be a useful functionality because it can help authors respond quickly to questions or challenges related to their content. In the following section, I connect this action to an appropriate system event, thus completing the configuration exercise.

Tip

When creating new actions, make sure to use unique and meaningful labels describing the action. The labels show up in various Drupal contexts and are most useful if they are clearly self-describing and as specific as possible. ■

Follow these steps to create your own Advanced action notifying content authors when a comment is posted:

1. **Log into your site as an administrator.**

   The login landing page loads in your browser.
2. **Select the Configuration option from the main admin menu.**

   The Configuration page loads in your browser.
3. **Locate the System section of the page, and click the item labeled Actions.**

   The Actions configuration screen loads in your browser, displaying the list of currently defined actions and, at the bottom of the page, an area where you can select new types of Advanced actions to create.
4. **Select the option Send e-mail from the action list, and click the Create button.**

   The Send e-mail action's configuration screen loads in your browser (refer to Figure 9.2).
5. **Enter** E-mail Author on Node Comment **for the Label setting.**
6. **Enter** [node:author:mail] **for the Recipient setting.**
7. **Enter** New Comment Submitted ([node:title]) **for the Subject setting.**
8. **In the Message setting area, type a friendly and informative message for the body of this e-mail.**

   If you like, you can use the `[comment:body]` token, to include the comment's contents in the e-mail.

9. **After you have entered all values, scroll to the bottom of the page and click the Save button.**

   If the operation completed successfully, a success message displays at the top of the page and your action is ready for use.

FIGURE 9.2

The Send e-mail advanced action screen shows the configuration fields.

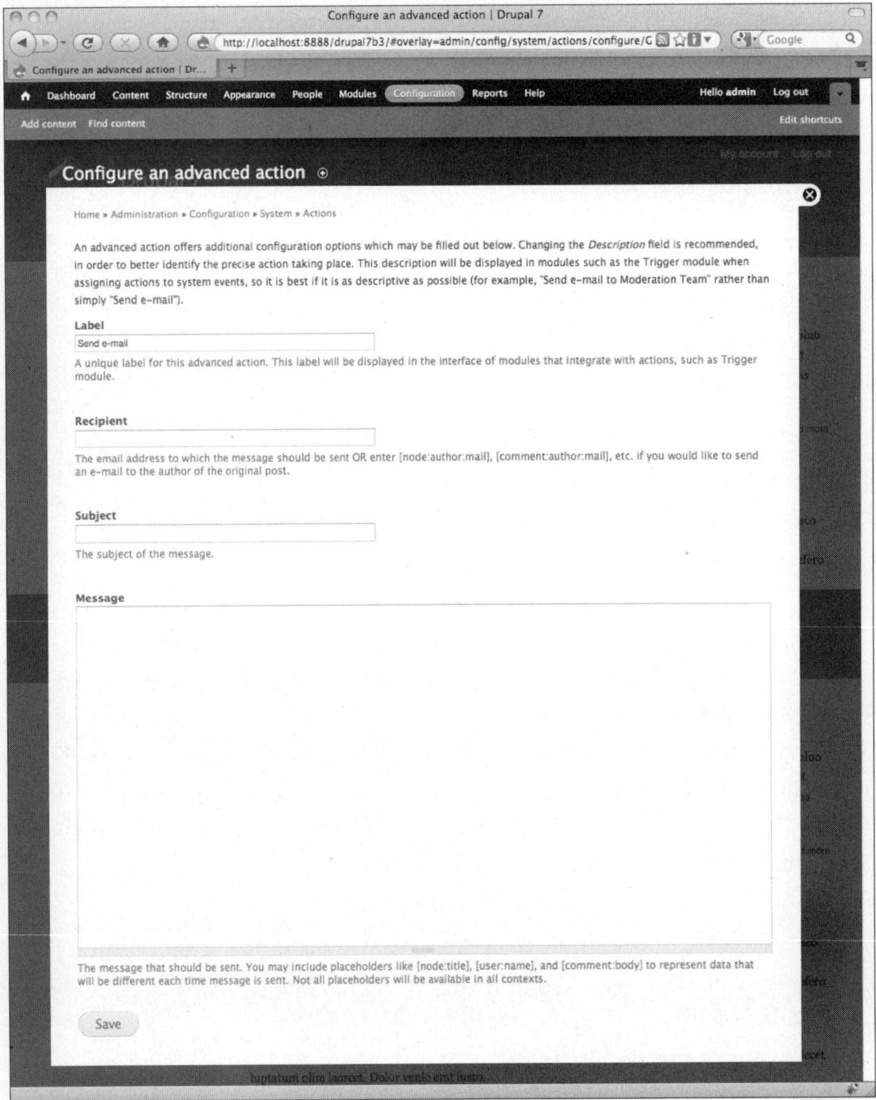

Note

If the built-in actions or triggers do not meet your needs, you or a competent Drupal programmer can always code your own actions or triggers. The process is relatively straightforward, but it does require PHP programming skills and knowledge of the Drupal system core. You can find additional information about these topics in the Developing for Drupal community resource, found at `http://drupal.org/contributors-guide`**.** ■

Assigning Triggers to Actions

You can think of triggers as system events with friendly names. You must assign triggers to actions before actions can do any work for you. In this section, I complete the configuration exercise I started in the preceding section. The goal is to send an e-mail to an author every time someone comments on one of his or her published items.

Note

You must enable the core Triggers module before you can assign a trigger to an action. Before proceeding with this section, ensure that this module has been enabled in your environment. ■

Understanding triggers

Triggers are events that happen in a specific context and can be configured to execute one or more of the actions available in that context. As shown in Figure 9.3, the standard Drupal installation has five general contexts in which triggers occur:

- **Comment:** This is the commenting context, and it encompasses events related to comment creation and management.
- **Node:** Broadly speaking, this is the content context for the system. All your standard content types are descendants of the node entity, and this context covers the events related to content creation and management.
- **System:** This context sounds very broad, but it includes only a small number of events. For the moment, you find only the cron scheduling event in this area.
- **Taxonomy:** The taxonomy context includes the events related to the creation and management of taxonomy terms.
- **User:** This context encompasses a set of events related to user creation, management, and login sessions.

FIGURE 9.3

The Trigger configuration page is displayed with the Comment tab active.

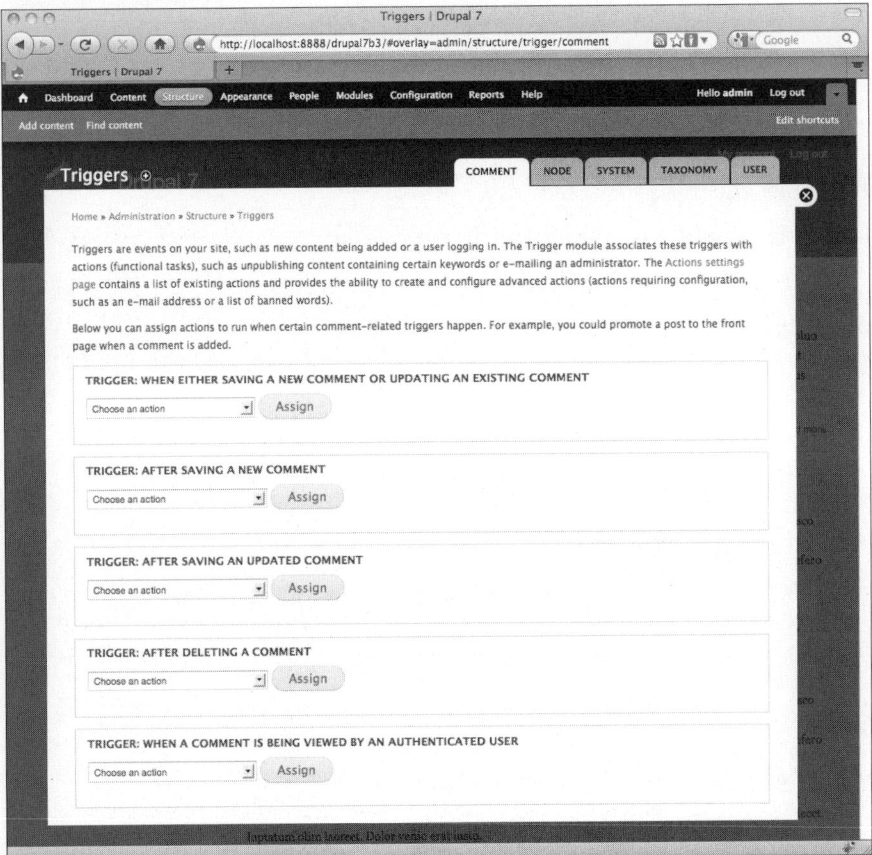

Assigning the advanced action's trigger

To complete this chapter's configuration exercise, you will now assign the Advanced action created earlier in this chapter to the appropriate Comment trigger.

Follow these steps to set the assignment:

1. **Log into your site as an administrator.**

   The login landing page loads in your browser.

2. **Select the Structure option from the main admin menu.**

   The Structure page loads in your browser.

3. **Locate and click the link labeled Triggers.**

   The Trigger module's configuration page loads in your browser, displaying the context tabs across the top right.

4. **Click the Comment tab.**

   The Comment triggers configuration screen loads in your browser.

5. **Locate the section labeled Trigger. After saving a new comment, and in this section, select the action you created earlier in this chapter named "E-mail Author on Node Comment."**

6. **Click the Assign button next to the list of actions.**

   If your changes have been saved, you now see the action listed in the action grid for this trigger.

You can now create custom actions and associate them with a variety of triggers. Take some time to note the operations that you would like to automate and begin configuring your system to do more of your busywork for you. Remember that if you run into a wall where existing actions or triggers do not meet your requirements, you can always go further by coding your own actions or triggers.

Summary

This chapter provided a general overview of what is possible with Drupal actions and triggers. The following points were covered:

- An overview of the default simple actions available with a standard Drupal installation
- How to go beyond simple actions by defining your own advanced actions
- Details on the different Drupal trigger contexts and how to access them
- Instructions for assigning simple or advanced actions to specific triggers

Part III

Working with Content

IN THIS PART

CHAPTER

10

Content Management with Drupal

IN THIS CHAPTER

- Understanding the key concepts
- Understanding Drupal content types and fields
- Controlling how content is created
- Creating new content
- Managing existing content

The word *content* is deceptively simple. And the idea of managing it can mean many different things to different organizations. Dealing with the subtleties that lie in wait is why we have content management systems.

In this chapter, I lay the foundation for a solid understanding of how Drupal's content management internals work and how you can use the system to address your specific needs. I deal with the key concepts, look at managing content types, and then go into the details of daily content management tasks.

Understanding the Key Concepts

Drupal is a framework as much as it is a functional "out of the box" CMS. And before you can really learn to leverage the system's power, you must understand the basic ideas around managing Drupal content. The following concepts lie at Drupal's heart.

Content and nodes

Nearly all content items in your Drupal system are what in Drupal parlance we call *nodes*. With that said, we use the terms content items and nodes interchangeably in this book, as does the Drupal community. Don't be confused by this; nodes are content items and content. These are just different words that mean the same thing.

You do encounter other forms of data inside Drupal—users, comments, blocks, and taxonomy terms are examples, but strictly speaking these things are not primary content in the system, because they are not based on the Node module. The Node module is one of the few core modules that comprise the Drupal foundation. This module is present in the Drupal admin system's module list, but unlike other modules, it cannot be disabled.

Tip

Drupal is not an object-oriented system, but it may be useful to think about content in Drupal as inheriting its basic properties and behavior from the Node module. ■

Content types and fields

When you put content into Drupal, it is stored as a specific form of data known as a *content type*. You can think of a content type as a template for content. Each type in the system has a name and is further defined by associating sub-elements—called *fields* in Drupal parlance—with it. Articles, pages, and polls are examples of Drupal's default content types.

Tip

Prior to Drupal 7, content-type extensibility was often augmented by the CCK contributed module. Much of the CCK functionality was moved into Drupal's core during the Drupal 7 release coding. This functionality is now known as Drupal Fields. ■

The standard Drupal 7 release comes with two content types enabled: the article and the page. However, if you enable all of Drupal's core modules, you see that there are six default content types. These content types differ in a few basic ways. For example, they all have unique names, and they all have a different combination of fields associated with them.

Importantly, you can go beyond the default content types; Drupal supports *extensible content types*. This notion of extensibility is extremely powerful; it means that you can extend Drupal by defining your own content types that fit your own model of content.

Later in this chapter, I review the default content types and then walk through the process of creating custom content types.

Content versus metadata

In the Web CMS context, the word *content* refers to the data that is presented to Web site visitors. Metadata, on the other hand, is data about this data, and usually it is less visible to the Web site visitor. If you find that about as clear as mud, then consider that an article's title and body are part of the article's content, but its system ID, its tags, the copyright details, and the author's name are all part of its metadata.

Metadata is becoming increasingly important to Web site managers because it plays a significant role both inside the CMS and after content is published.

Cross-Reference

In Chapter 33, we discuss how metadata plays a role in search engine optimization (SEO). ■

Versioning of content items

Drupal has the ability to preserve a history of all changes made to the content in the system. If your content types are configured this way, or if the author chooses, a copy of the content item is saved each time a change is made. Each copy is called a *node revision.*

Each node revision is a unique version of the content item stored persistently in your system. These versions provide you with a history of content changes and give you the ability to revert to a previous content version at a future date, if you deem this necessary.

Tip

Some organizations require that the CMS retain a history of content revisions. In others, it is just a question of sanity or insurance. Either way, it is wise for you to consider revision tracking when planning how you will manage content with Drupal. ■

To enrich the history of content changes, you can optionally include a comment each time you save a new node revision. In general, this is a wise practice, and with larger groups it quickly becomes essential for preserving a meaningful history.

Note

Later in this chapter, we provide additional details on node revisions and discuss controlling how content is created. ■

Publish status and lifecycles

Each node of content in Drupal has a simple, binary publish status value where 1 equals published and 0 equals not published. Depending on the standard content options for a given content type, nodes of that type either are published or not published by default. You can configure the default publish status value for each content type. I cover that later in this chapter.

Content also tends to have a lifecycle. For example, when you publish a poll, you have the option to automatically deactivate it after a certain number of days. Your organization may have other requirements as well. For example, you may want a particular item to be visible on your homepage from next Monday to next Thursday.

You can probably imagine many forms of content lifecycles. The point is that part of managing content is planning and managing its lifecycle.

Tip

The standard Drupal release does not contain tools for managing content lifecycle. To implement content lifecycle rules, such as publishing content on certain dates or showing content on the homepage for a specific period of time, you most likely need to experiment with one or more contributed modules. The Rules module is a good example of a non-core module that is useful for these purposes. We discuss advanced content management practices and configurations in Chapter 14. ■

Multilingual content

Multilingual content is content in your CMS that has one or more translations. For example, you might publish your organization's press releases in English, German, and Spanish. When you create each new translation, it is associated with the original article (the English version, for example) via Drupal's core multilingual content functionality, yet you also can manage it like an independent item of content.

When you enable multilingual content management in Drupal, a number of special admin tools become available in the admin system. With these tools, you can track and manage your translated content items.

Cross-Reference

See Chapter 22 for more key concepts and a detailed discussion of managing multilingual content. ■

Understanding Drupal Content Types and Fields

As I mentioned earlier in this chapter, all content in Drupal is based on the Node module; this is why Drupal content items are often called *nodes*. A content item also must be of a specific type. Articles, blog posts, and pages are examples of Drupal content types. You define content types by associating one or more *fields* with a unique type name.

When you create a new piece of content in Drupal, the first thing you do is select the type of content to create and then fill out a Web form associated with that type (which is, by and large, the act of putting data into Drupal fields), and then you save it.

Note

Drupal Fields stand out as a new and important architectural concept in Drupal 7. They are containers that represent the smallest unit of content in the system. These containers are tied together to construct different types of content in the system. ■

In concrete terms, the Drupal *article* content type contains a title element and a body element. In this case, the title element is inherited from the node module, and the body is an associated Drupal field called body.

Here is another way of thinking about it:

Node Module + A Unique Name + One or More Fields = A Content Type

Discovering the default content types

The standard installation of Drupal 7 comes with two content types enabled: the Article and the Page. You can access four more default content types by enabling other core modules. With the six default content types, you can create a broad variety of content. They are sufficient for many typical Web site scenarios and can be adapted to work for many others.

Drupal has six default content types:

- Article
- Blog entry
- Book page
- Forum topic
- Page
- Poll

Introducing articles

The article type is a default content type in the standard Drupal 7 release. It is a flexible type of content, but is generally used for time-sensitive information. This class of content is broad, but the general rule is that the content's relative value tends to decrease over time.

Example usage scenarios for the article content type include the following:

- News articles
- Knowledgebase articles
- Press releases

These are all examples of time-sensitive content; they have a moment of peak value and then a descent toward lesser value. This pattern of content value is reflected in the way you manage content of this type. For example, we see a time-sensitive management pattern in the reverse chronological sorting of most news Web sites' content: Specifically, the most recently published content is at the top of the page, while the oldest content is often buried in the archives, if present at all. Figure 10.1 shows a Web site with news items sorted in reverse chronological order.

FIGURE 10.1

The www.cmswire.com homepage with news content sorted in reverse chronological order

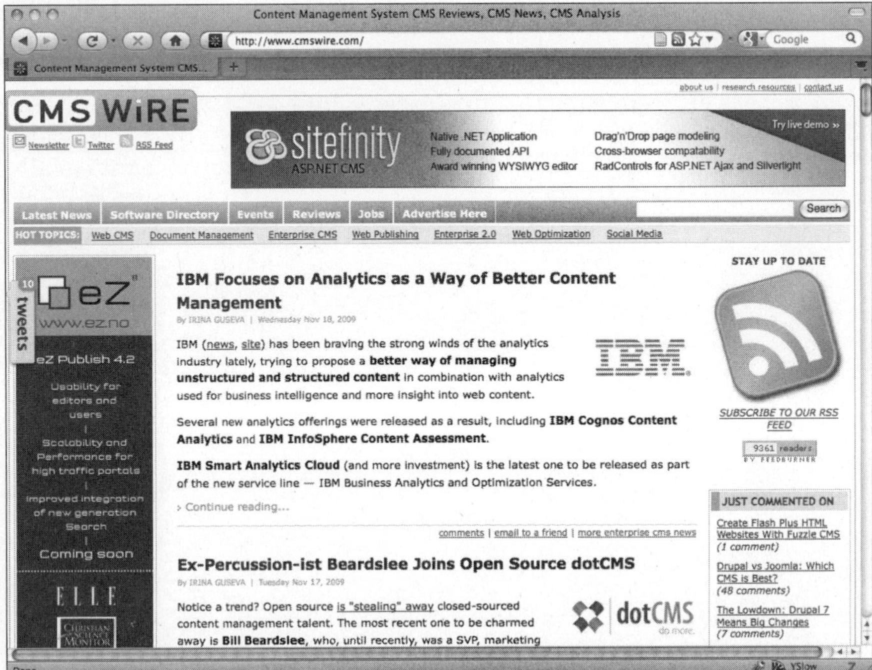

By adding or removing fields, you can modify the article content type to suit your needs. Alternatively, you can create your own time-sensitive content types as you see fit.

Note

Later in this chapter, we discuss creating and modifying content types. ■

Introducing blog entries

Drupal's core Blog module supports the creation of one or more blogs in your Web site, including multi-user blogs. After you enable it, a new content type called Blog entry is available for use and a host of blog-like features are available to you (see Chapter 16 for details). This content type is similar to the article type in that it is flexible and most often used for time-sensitive content.

Example usage scenarios for the blog entry content type include the following:

- Personal blog posts
- Organizational news
- Project updates

Cross-Reference

In Chapter 16, we discuss the Blog module, how to manage blog content, and how to style the presentation of Drupal blogs. ■

Introducing book pages

You can use Drupal's core Book module to create hierarchical bodies of content. The module is disabled by default, but after you enable it, a new content type called Book page is available for use.

This content type is quite specific in its purpose. It is also a bit of an oddball; we don't often think of books and Web sites together, that is, unless we're in the process of buying books. To clarify the book page idea, keep in mind that this content type is used for information that is structured in multiple levels and benefits from the automatic generation of its navigational elements.

A Drupal book is like a real book; it can have pages, sections, subsections, and so on. When creating a new book page item, you choose where in the book hierarchy the item will be located. And later, you can move pages around in the hierarchy as you see fit.

Example usage scenarios for the book page content type include the following:

- Lists of frequently asked questions (FAQs)
- Online instruction manuals
- A city guide or other resource guide

Cross-Reference

In Chapter 17, we discuss the Book module and the Book page content type in depth. ■

Introducing forum topics

You can use Drupal's core Forum module to create threaded discussions, similar to what you see on many community or bulletin board Web sites. The module is disabled by default, but after you enable it, a new content type called Forum topic is available for use.

Example usage scenarios for the Forum topic content type include the following:

- Community discussions
- Product support forums
- Project management discussions

Cross-Reference

Chapter 20 is dedicated to the Forum module. In that chapter, we introduce the various parts of the Forum module, how to use it, and how you can style the presentation of forum content. ■

Introducing pages

The page concept is as old as the Web itself. You see home pages, about pages, policy pages, and more every day. The unifying theme is that pages tend to be self-contained and static, and unlike time-sensitive articles, they tend to have a long lifetime.

The page content type is part of the default Drupal release and is made up of a title field, a body field, and a number of metadata fields that the system uses for content presentation and organization.

Pages often contain static content—content that rarely changes and generally maintains its position of importance in your Web site. In terms of content type structure, pages and articles are quite similar, but pages have fewer content fields.

Introducing polls

The core Drupal Poll module enables you to add polls to your Web site. The Poll module is disabled by default, but after you enable it, a new content type called Poll is available for use.

Polls have a question field and then two or more response option fields. You can also optionally set the duration of time that the poll will remain active in your site.

Example use scenarios for the Poll content type include:

- Running opinion polls
- Taking a vote or holding an election
- Collecting statistics about your Web site's community

Cross-Reference

In Chapter 21, we discuss the Poll module, including how you enable it and options for styling poll content presentation. ■

Creating content types

The default Drupal admin system provides you with browser-based tools for creating new content types. As a user with the Administer content types permission, you can quickly define new content types and make them available to authors.

Caution

Just because you can create new content types does not mean that you should. When you add more content types to your system, you potentially make it more complicated for administrators to maintain and more complicated for authors to understand. The addition of content types also can make your presentation logic more complicated.

Simplicity is golden when it comes to implementing a CMS. You should think carefully about the justifications for new content types; you may be able to achieve your goals by using content creation controls, rules, views, or other Drupal functionality. ■

The process of creating a new content type involves defining a name for the content type, setting the default content item options, and then adding one or more fields. When you add a field, you must specify the field's data type, which in turn defines what kind of content each field can hold. The available field data types are described in Table 10.1.

Note

Contributed modules like the Date module allow you to add more data types to your Drupal system. ■

TABLE 10.1

Drupal 7 Field Data Types

Data Type	Description
Boolean	A binary value (such as on/off, true/false, yes/no, and so on)
Decimal	A numeric decimal value with configurable precision and scale (such as 5.25 or 3.14159265). Maximum and minimum values are dependent on the server platform.
File	A Drupal File item
Float	A numeric floating point value (such as 5.25). Maximum and minimum values are dependent on the server platform.
Image	A Drupal Image item
Integer	A numeric integer value (such as –35 or 35). Maximum and minimum values are dependent on the server platform.
List	A list of key/value options where the key is an alias for the position of the value (for example, 0=First option; 1=Second option)
List (numeric)	A list of key/value options where the key has a numeric significance (e.g., 1=1 Day; 7=1 Week)
List (text)	A list of key/value options where the key has a textual significance (such as CA=California; NY=New York)
Long text	A long string value (no theoretical limit)
Long text and summary	A long string value (no theoretical limit) with an optional summary string value
Taxonomy Term	A value from a Drupal Taxonomy vocabulary
Text	A string value with a maximum length of 255 characters

Tip

By default, newly created content types have a title and a body field. You can remove the body field if you like. However, you cannot remove the title field because that is inherited from the underlying Node module. ■

Figure 10.2 shows the Drupal 7 Add content-type admin screen and the standard content item option set tabs.

FIGURE 10.2

The Drupal 7 admin screen displays the Add content type Web form with the standard content item option set tabs displayed.

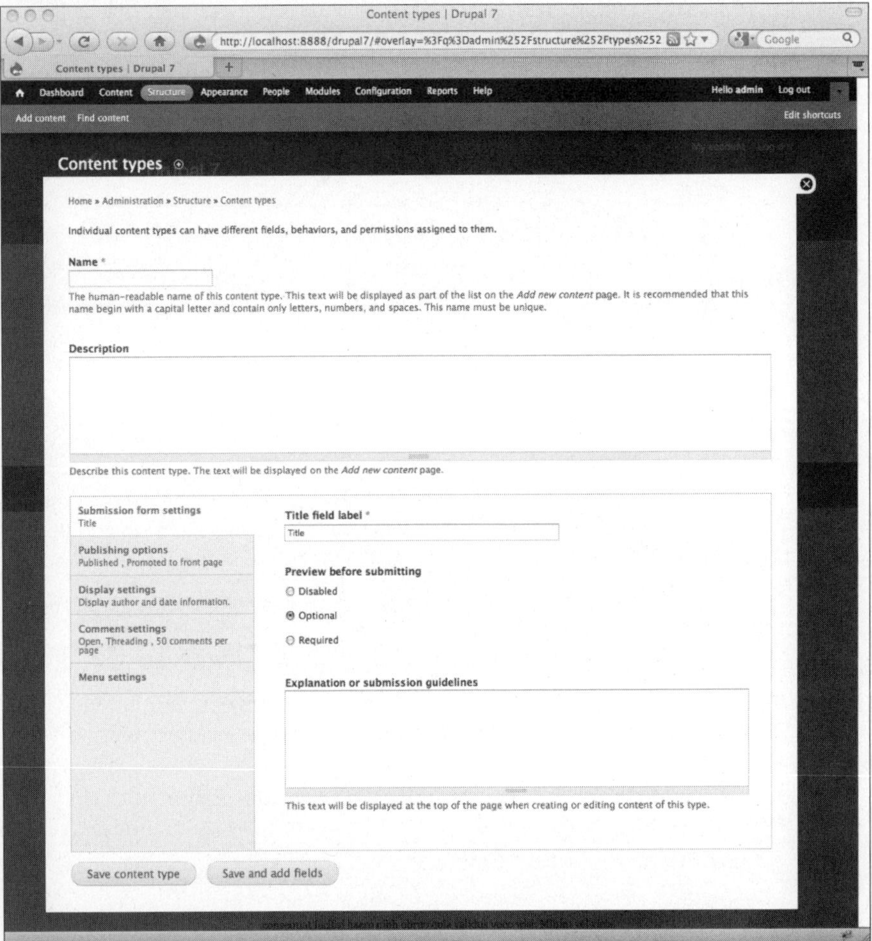

The fields in the Add content type page are divided into two groups. At the top of the page are the fields needed to identify and describe the new content type. At the bottom of the page are the standard content item options.

These controls are related to the content type's identity and description:

- **Name:** Type the unique name of the content type into this field. This appears to content creators when they select the type of content to author. The value should begin with a capital letter and can contain only letters, numbers, and spaces. This is a required field.

- **Description:** Type the description of the content type into this field. The description field is optional, but if you provide it, it is displayed on the Add new content page and visible to all authors, so it's a good idea to provide a meaningful value.

The standard content item options are collected on individual tabs, divided into five option sets. These are the option sets:

- **Submission form settings:** These items control the default look and feel of the Web form used to create or edit content items. Here you can customize the labels for the Title and Body fields, control content preview requirements, and provide help text for guiding the authoring process.
- **Publishing options:** These items provide the default values that control if the content is published automatically when first saved, if it appears on the homepage when first published, if it is sticky at the top of lists once published, and whether a new node revision is created when changes are saved.
- **Display settings:** These settings affect the presentation of the published content item. Here you can choose whether to display the author name and the publish date of the content, and you can control the length of the trimmed version of the content.

Cross-Reference

Chapter 28 contains a full discussion about customizing content presentation, including how to work with Drupal themes. In Chapter 13, we explain how to manage the look and feel of your site's front page and how to control which content is displayed there. ■

- **Comment settings:** Use this option set to control how comments behave for this content type. Enable or disable comment threading with the first check box. Limit the number of comments per page with the select list. Control commenting status by setting comment to Open, Closed, or Hidden. You also can control the comment form behavior by enabling or disabling the comment title field and choosing whether the comment form is shown on a separate page. The comment preview settings allow you to disable comment previews, make them optional, or make them required.

Cross-Reference

See Chapter 15 for additional information about working with comment functionality. ■

- **Menu settings:** Use this option set to control the menu setting choices present when authoring content of this type. Here you can set which menus are available to the author and assign the default parent item (in the menu hierarchy) for content of this type.

Cross-Reference

In Chapter 8, we discuss working with the Drupal menu system and how to control the appearance of menus. ■

To illustrate the process of creating a content type, I create an example type called Test Type 01. Later, you can delete this content type from the system. Follow these steps to create the new content type:

1. **Log into your site as an administrator.**

   The login landing page loads in your browser.
2. **Select the Structure option from the main admin menu.**

   The Structure page loads in your browser.
3. **Click the Content types link in the Structure page.**

   The list of current content types loads in your browser.
4. **Click the Add content type link.**

   The Add content type Web form loads in your browser.
5. **Enter a name for the new content type in the Name text box of the Web form.**

   For this example, use the name "Test Type 01."
6. **Click the Save content type button at the bottom of the page.**

   If you are successful, a confirmation message is displayed at the top of the page.

In the next sections, I discuss editing and deleting existing content types.

Editing content types

Using the Drupal admin system, you can make changes to content-type definitions with simple browser-based tools. Modifying content types involves either changing the basic content-type settings—including the standard content item options—or adding, removing, or changing fields associated with the content type.

Tip

You can modify Drupal's default content types as well as any content types you add to the system. ■

To illustrate the process of modifying content types, make two changes to the Test Type 01 content type created in the preceding section. First, add a required text field called "Long Description," and rename the default body field to be "Short Description."

Adding new fields

Adding new fields to a content type is a simple operation involving only the browser-based admin tools. When adding a new field, you must select the type of content the field will hold and then the type of user interface widget that will be used to enter this data. You can review the available field data types in Table 10.1 earlier in this chapter.

Tip

A field's widget is the user interface that you use to put data into the system. For example, with a text data type, you typically use a text box widget to enter data. With a list data type, you can choose between a select list, a list of radio buttons, and a list of check boxes. ■

To add a new field to your content type, follow these steps:

1. **Log into your site as an administrator.**

   The login landing page loads in your browser.

2. **Select the Structure option from the main admin menu.**

   The Structure page loads in your browser.

3. **Click the Content types link in the Structure page.**

   The list of current content types loads in your browser.

4. **Click the edit link in the Test Type 01 row of the types list that we created in the preceding section.**

   The edit content type form is displayed in your browser.

5. **Locate the Edit, Manage Fields, and Manage Display tabs in the edit content type page, and click the Manage Fields tab.**

   The list of fields associated with your content type is displayed in your browser.

6. **Locate the row with the Add new field label.**
7. **Enter the value "Long Description" in the label field.**
8. Enter the value "long_description" in the Field name field.

Note

You can name fields as you see fit, but it's a good practice to keep the field's label and name values similar. This makes maintenance simpler and helps prevent accidental deletion of fields. ■

9. **Select the value Long text from the Type of data to store list.**
10. **Click the Save button at the bottom of the page.**

    The Field Settings screen is displayed in your browser.

11. **Click the Save field settings button at the bottom of the page.**

    If you are successful, a confirmation message appears at the top of the page and additional field settings are displayed in your browser.

Note

This page contains both global and content-type-specific settings for the field. The global settings are the default settings for the field you just created, no matter where it is used. The content-type-specific settings—also known as the field instance settings—are the default settings for the newly created field only when it is used with this specific content type. In your case, these are the default settings for the Test Type 01 content type. ■

12. **In the first page labeled Test Type 01 Settings, check the Required check box.**
13. **Click the Save settings button at the bottom of the page.**

    If you are successful, a confirmation message is displayed at the top of the page.

Editing field labels

You can rename the label for any field associated with your content type, including the title field. Changing a field's label does not change the machine name for the associated data field, so this is a safe operation; it cannot cause the loss of any data. Figure 10.3 shows the Drupal admin screen for the field instance settings, including the text box where a field's label value is set.

To rename the body field, follow these steps:

1. **Log into the admin system of your site.**

   The login landing page loads in your browser.
2. **Select the Structure option from the main admin menu.**

   The Structure page loads in your browser.
3. **Click the Content types link in the Structure page.**

   The list of current content types loads in your browser.
4. **Click the edit link in the Test Type 01 row of the types list that we created earlier in this chapter.**

   The edit content type form is displayed in your browser.
5. **Locate the text box labeled Body field label in the Submission form settings configuration tab.**
6. **Change the text in the text box from "Body" to "Short Description."**
7. **Click the Save content type button at the bottom of the page.**

   If you are successful, a confirmation message is displayed at the top of the page.

Editing basic content-type options

The basic content-type options control common presentation and authoring behaviors for all content types in the system. In the section "Creating content types" I describe the function of each of the basic content-type options. You may want to quickly review that section now.

To illustrate this editing option, make one more modification to our Test Type 01 content type. This time change the default publishing behavior so the content is not published by default.

To change the content type's default publishing behavior, follow these steps:

1. **Log into your site as an administrator.**

   The login landing page loads in your browser.
2. **Select the Structure option from the main admin menu.**

   The Structure page loads in your browser.
3. **Click the Content types link in the Structure page.**

   The list of current content types loads in your browser.

FIGURE 10.3

The Drupal 7 admin screen displays the edit content type Web form with the Submission form settings area in focus.

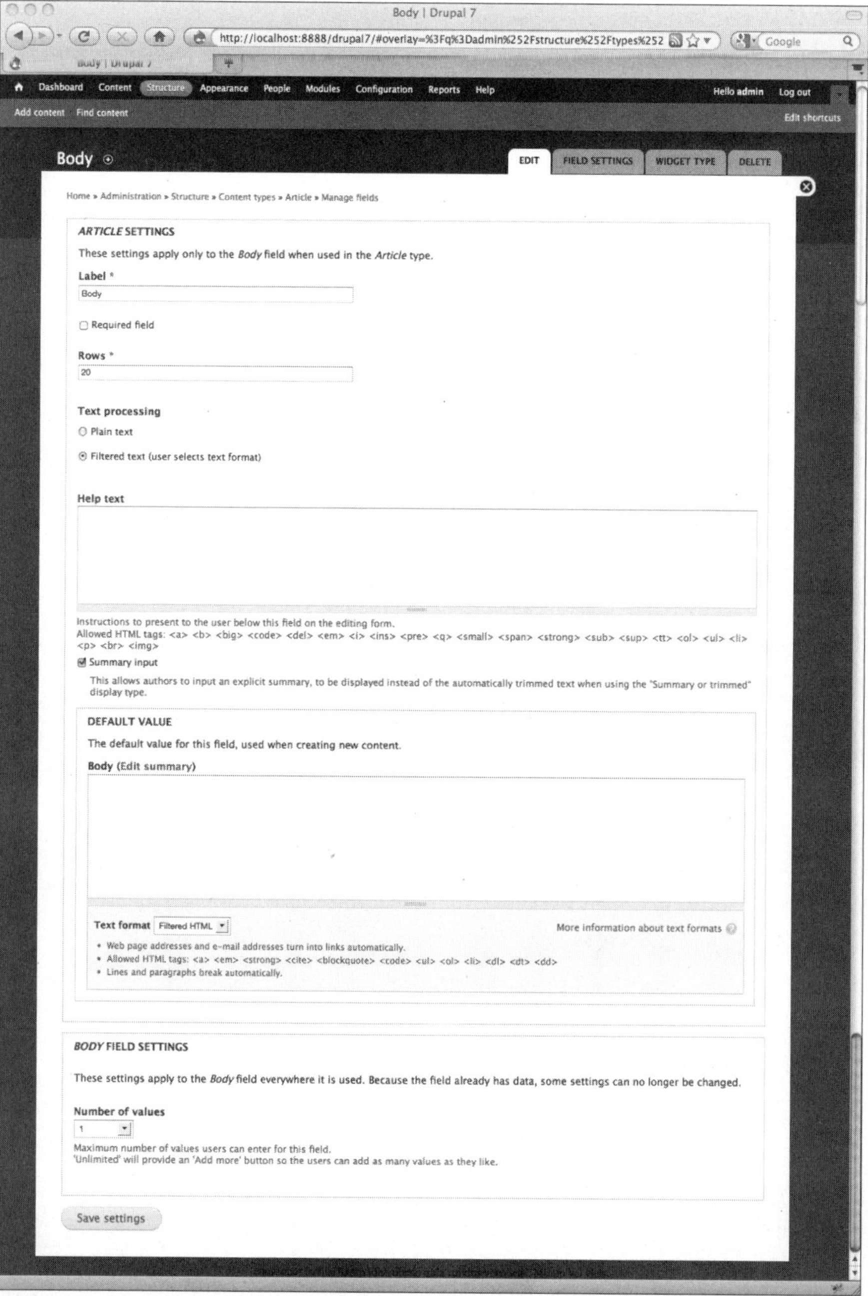

4. **Click the edit link in the Test Type 01 row of the types list that we created earlier in this chapter.**

   The edit content type form is displayed in your browser.

5. **Locate the second section of the page where the standard content-item option tabs are placed.**
6. **Click the Publishing options tab.**
7. **Uncheck the Published check box.**
8. **Click the Save content type button at the bottom of the page.**

   If you are successful, a confirmation message is displayed at the top of the page.

Note

When you change the publish settings, keep in mind that these changes apply only to new content created after the settings change is made. Published content is not affected by these updates. ■

Deleting existing fields

Any user with the Administer content-types permission can delete fields from content types at any time. This capability is powerful and dangerous. If you delete a field, all information stored in that field is permanently lost. The only possible way to recover this data is via a database-level recovery option.

Tip

Think carefully before you assign the Administer content-types permission. You should give this ability to as few people as possible. ■

To illustrate the field delete operation, delete the Long Description field created in the Adding new fields section. Follow these steps to delete this field:

1. **Log into your site as an administrator.**

   The login landing page loads in your browser.

2. **Select the Structure option from the main admin menu.**

   The Structure page loads in your browser.

3. **Click the Content types link in the Structure page.**

   The list of current content types loads in your browser.

4. **Locate the row with the Test Type 01 content type.**
5. **Click the Manage Fields link in the Operations column of the Test Type 01 row.**

   The Manage Fields screen is displayed in your browser showing a list of currently assigned fields for this content type.

6. **Locate the row that contains the Long Description field.**

7. **Click the delete link in the Operations column of this row.**

   The deletion confirmation screen is displayed in your browser.

8. **Click the Delete button.**

   If you are successful, a confirmation message is displayed at the top of the page.

Deleting content types

You can delete a content type from the system using the Drupal admin tools. Content-type deletions are permanent, non-reversible actions that destroy all the stored content of that type. Therefore, you should carefully consider why you want to delete content and the ramifications of doing so—specifically that you will lose all previously created content of this type—before doing so.

Tip

You cannot delete all content types. For example, if you want to remove the Blog entry, Forum topic, or Poll types from the system, instead of deleting them you must disable the associated modules. You may encounter other content types that behave this way. ■

You can delete content types in two places: the content-type list screen or content-type edit screen. Figure 10.4 shows a list of content types in the Structure Drupal admin area, including the delete links for several content types.

Tip

You should make a full database backup before deleting a content type from your system. Recovering the entire database is one of the few ways you can restore the data you lose when content types are deleted. ■

To illustrate a delete operation, delete the Test Type 01 content type created and edited earlier in this chapter. Follow these steps to delete this content type:

1. **Log into your site as an administrator.**

   The login landing page loads in your browser.

2. **Select the Structure option from the main admin menu.**

   The Structure page loads in your browser.

3. **Click the Content types link in the Structure page.**

   The list of current content types loads in your browser.

4. **Locate the row with the Test Type 01 content type.**
5. **Click the delete link in the far right of the Operations column of the Test Type 01 row.**

   The deletion confirmation screen is displayed in your browser.

6. **Click the Delete button.**

   If you are successful, a confirmation message is displayed at the top of the page.

FIGURE 10.4

The content-type list screen displays the list of content types in the system and various actions that you can perform, including the delete links for several content types.

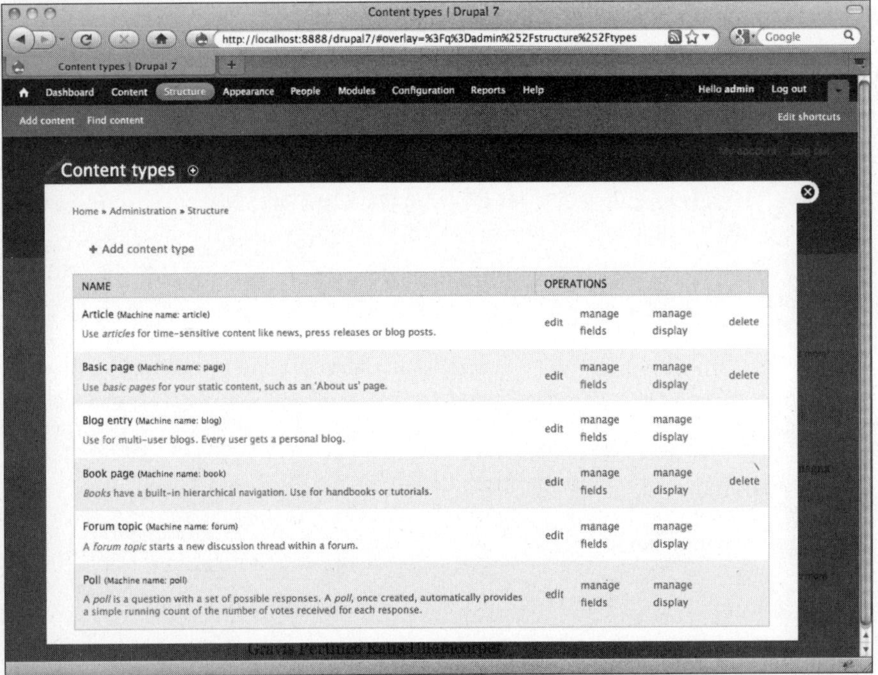

Controlling How Content Is Created

For various reasons, you may need to control how people create content in your system. For example, you might require that all articles have the Tags field populated, or you might want to not publish articles by default.

You control how content is created either by changing the standard content-item options or by changing content field settings. Content field changes can be done at either the field level, which applies globally to all content types that use the field, or at the field instance level, which applies only to one specific content type.

In summary, you have three basic ways to control content authoring:

- **Standard content item options:** These are set in the content-type edit form and apply only to that specific content type.
- **Field settings:** These are set at the field level and apply to all content types that use the field.
- **Field instance settings:** These are set at the field instance level and apply to one content type only.

Configuring standard content-item defaults

All Drupal content types have a set of standard content-item options. Similar to the Title field, these options are inherited from the Node module, and like field instance settings, discussed later in this chapter, their settings apply to a single content type.

The standard content-item options are divided into sets, with each set presented on a tab at the base of the standard content creation and editing screens. In this section, I discuss each of the option sets individually.

Submission form settings

This option set controls some of the appearance and some of the behavior of the content authoring and editing Web form. Figure 10.5 shows the Submission form settings tab in the content-type editing screen.

These Submission form settings options are available:

- **Title field label:** This text box value specifies the user interface label used for the content item's title field. This field is required, and you can change the value as you see fit.
- **Preview before submitting:** The Disabled, Optional, and Required radio buttons in this set control the preview behavior for new content items. For example, if you want to force content authors to preview their work prior to saving it, select the Required option. This field is required.
- **Explanation or submission guidelines:** Use this text area to provide authoring guidance to content authors. This field is optional.

FIGURE 10.5

The content-type editing screen with the Submission form settings tab displayed

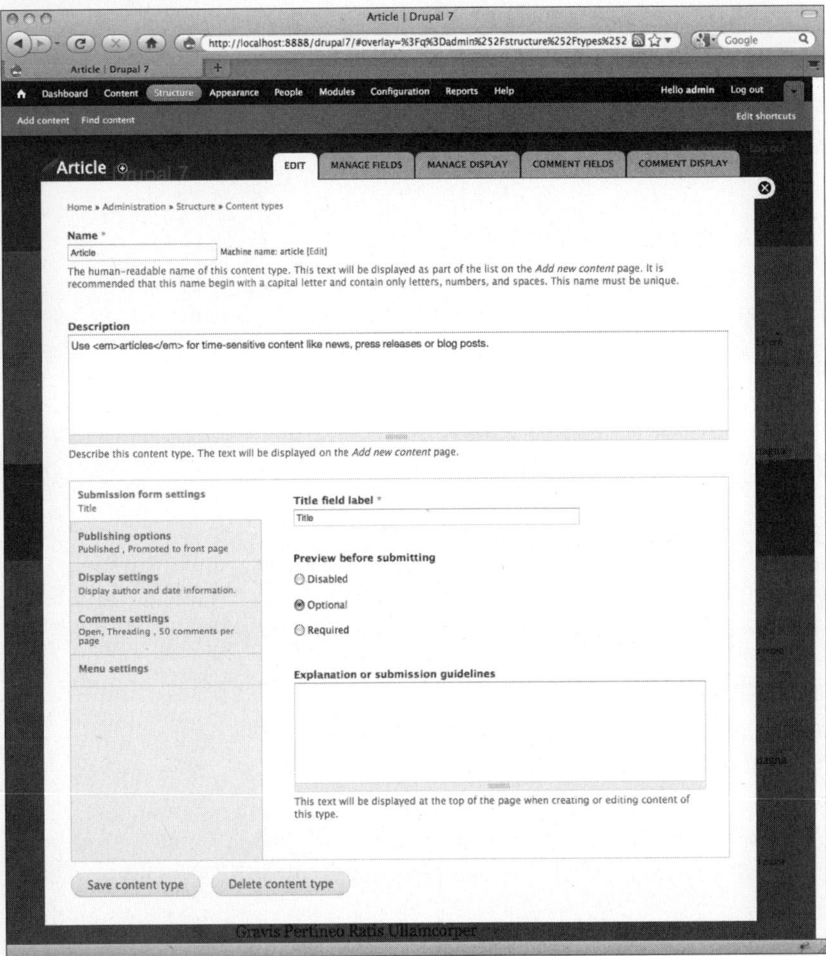

Publishing options

This option set controls whether the content item is published by default and where the content item appears on your published Web site once it is published. Figure 10.6 shows the Publishing options tab in the content-type editing screen.

FIGURE 10.6

The content-type editing screen with the Publishing options tab displayed

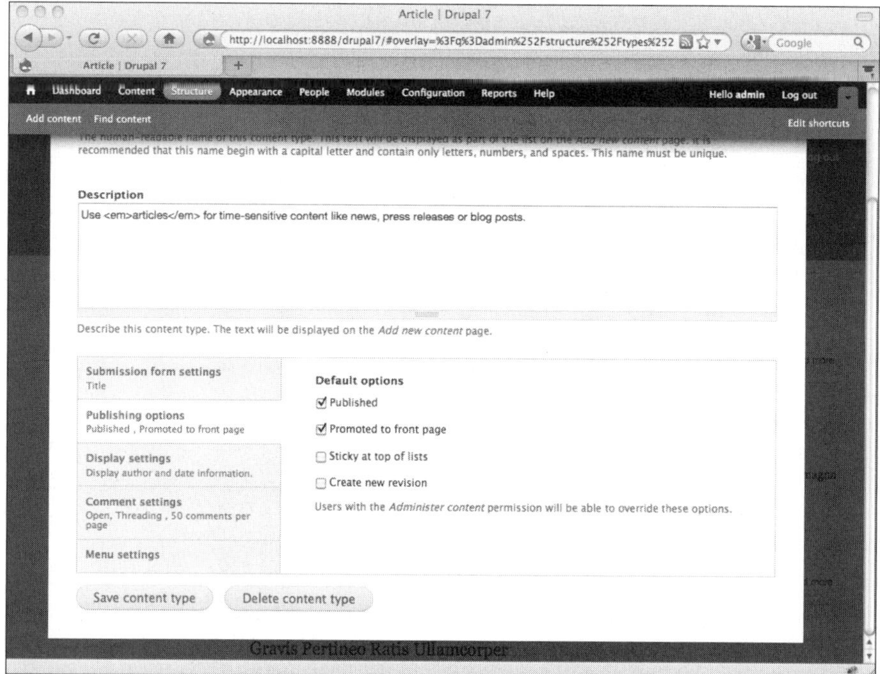

These are the Publishing options:

- **Published:** This check box controls whether the content is published on your Web site. If it is checked, then the content item is published.
- **Promoted to front page:** If checked, after the content item is published—and assuming you have not configured your site to behave otherwise—it shows up on the front page of your Web site.
- **Sticky at top of lists:** If checked, after the content item is published, it appears at the top of content lists that contain this content type. For example, if the content item is a blog post, it is displayed at the top of the blog irrespective of whether newer blog posts exist.
- **Create new revision:** If checked, a new node revision is made when the content item is saved.

Display settings

This option set controls some of the presentation behavior of your published content. Figure 10.7 shows the Publishing options tab in the content-type editing screen.

FIGURE 10.7

The content-type editing screen with the Display settings tab displayed

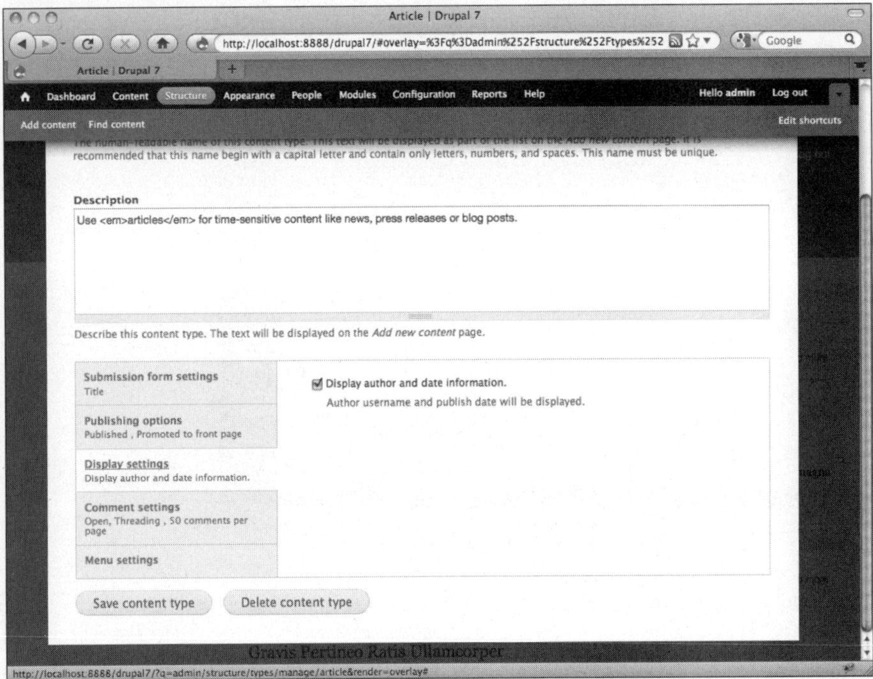

These are the Display settings options:

- **Display author and date information:** If checked, and if you have not configured your site to behave otherwise, the author name and publish date are displayed with the published content item.

Comment settings

This option set controls whether visitors can comment on the content item, the mode of commenting allowed, and the presentation of the comment form. Figure 10.8 shows the Comment settings tab in the content-type editing screen.

FIGURE 10.8

The content-type editing screen with the Comment settings tab displayed

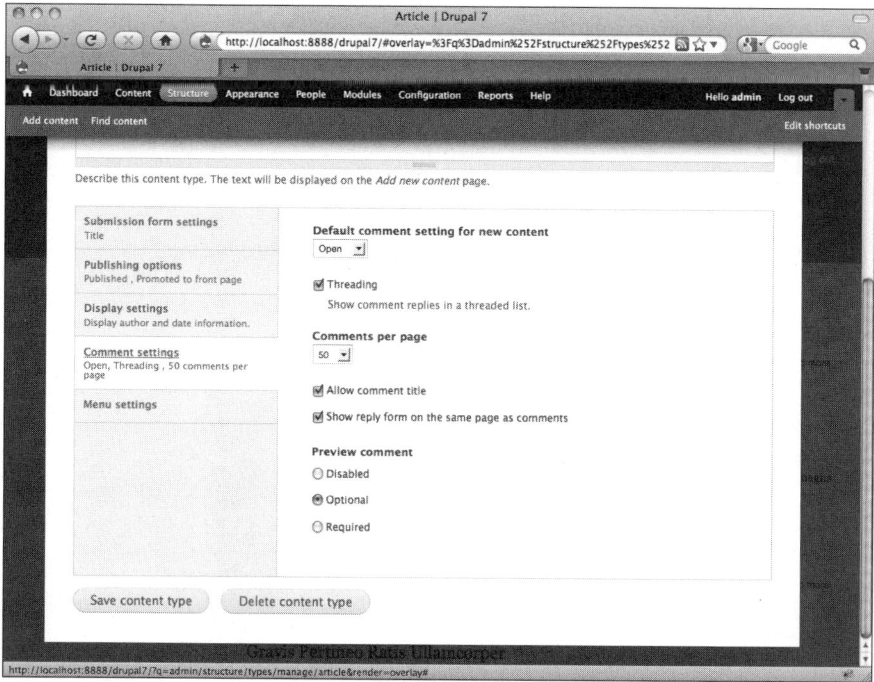

These are the Comment settings options:

- **Default comment setting for new content**: You can select from Open, Closed, or Hidden. If open, authorized visitors will be able to post new comments.
- **Threading:** Check this box to allow threaded comment discussions. Threaded commenting allows commenters to reply to each other.
- **Comments per page:** Set this to the maximum number of comments you want displayed per page. After the limit is exceeded, Drupal generates comment navigation links to allow access to additional pages of comments.
- **Allow comment title:** Check this box to include a Title field in the comment form displayed on your Web site.
- **Show reply form on the same page as comments:** Check this box to include the comment reply form on the same page as the content or existing comments. If you do not check this box, users need to click to a secondary page to access the comment form.
- **Preview comment:** The Disabled, Optional, and Required radio button options control commenting preview behavior. For example, if you want to force users to review their comments before posting them (sometimes a wise idea), then select the Required option.

Cross-Reference

See Chapter 15 for additional details about Drupal's commenting system. ■

Menu settings

This option set controls whether the content item can be placed in one of your Web site's menus and, if so, at what level. Figure 10.9 shows an example Menu settings tab in the content-type editing screen. Your menu settings tab may look different depending on the menus you have configured in your CMS.

FIGURE 10.9

The standard content-item option settings with the Menu settings tab displayed

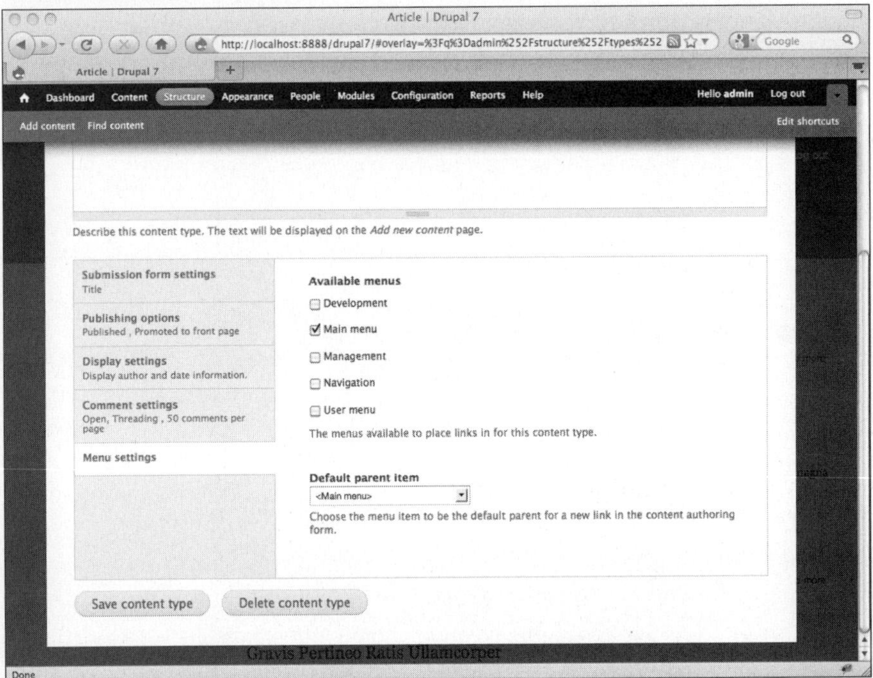

These menu settings options are available:

- **Available menus:** Optionally check one or more check boxes in this list to allow content authors to place content items of this type into those menus. If you do not check any menu options, then the Menu settings tab is not visible in the content creation or editing screen for this content type.
- **Default parent item:** Use this setting to specify the default location for the item's link in the menu hierarchy. Content authors can override this value when creating or editing content items.

Cross-Reference

Content items also can be added directly to a Drupal menu. See Chapter 8 for a full discussion about creating and managing menu items. ■

Understanding field settings and field instance settings

Drupal fields have two levels of settings. Field settings apply on a global level to every content type that uses a given field. Field instance settings apply only to a single content type. In this section, I explain these two concepts and show you how to access the different settings levels.

Field settings

When you set a field's settings, you define the defaults for all uses of the field. For example, if you have a text field named Teaser that is used by three different content types, and you set the maximum length setting to 200 characters using the field settings, then this maximum length rule is applied to all three content types that use this field.

You manage global field settings from the content-type admin screens. Figure 10.10 shows the Manage Fields screen in the admin system.

FIGURE 10.10

The Manage Fields grid for the default page content type has one row for every field in the content type. You click the link in the Field column to edit the global field settings values.

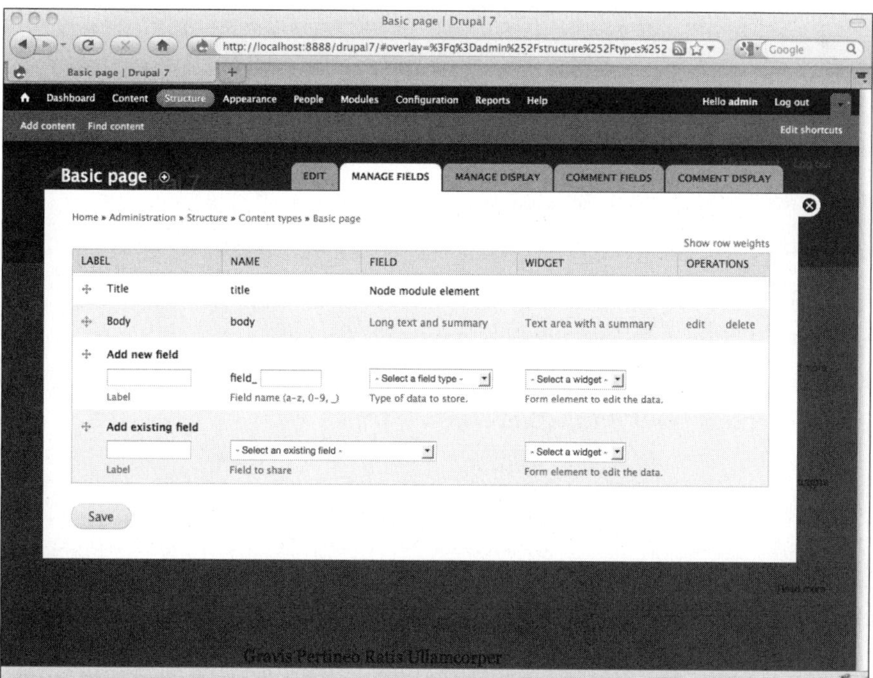

To edit field settings, follow these steps:

1. **Log into your site as an administrator.**

   The login landing page loads in your browser.

2. **Select the Structure option from the main admin menu.**

   The Structure page loads in your browser.

3. **Click the Content types link in the Structure page.**

   The list of current content types loads in your browser.

4. **Click the Manage Fields link in the row of the content type you want to edit.**

   The Manage Fields page is displayed in your browser.

5. **Locate the Field column in the displayed grid, and click the link in that column for the field you want to edit.**

   The field settings page is displayed for that field.

Note

The field settings Web form is different for each field data type. ■

6. **Make your desired settings change.**

   For example, you can change the maximum length value.

7. **Click the Save field settings button at the bottom of the page.**

   If you are successful, a confirmation message appears at the top of the page.

Field instance settings

Field instance settings control content creation rules for a single content type. Like field settings you manage field instance settings from the content-type admin screens.

To edit field instance settings, follow these steps:

1. **Log into your site as an administrator.**

   The login landing page loads in your browser.

2. **Select the Structure option from the main admin menu.**

   The Structure page loads in your browser.

3. **Click the Content types link in the Structure page.**

   The list of current content types loads in your browser.

4. **Click the Manage Fields link in the row of the content type you want to edit.**

   The Manage Fields page is displayed in your browser.

5. **Locate the Operations column in the displayed grid, and click the edit link in that column for the field you want to edit.**

   The field instance settings page is displayed for that field.

Note

The field instance settings Web form is different for each field data type. ■

6. **Make your desired settings change.**

   For example, change the field's default value.
7. **Click the Save settings button at the bottom of the page.**

   If you are successful, a confirmation message appears at the top of the page.

Making fields required

Controlling whether a field is required is a field-instance-level setting. In other words, you control this on a per-content-type basis.

To make a field required, follow these steps:

1. **Log into your site as an administrator.**

   The login landing page loads in your browser.
2. **Select the Structure option from the main admin menu.**

   The Structure page loads in your browser.
3. **Click the Content types link in the Structure page.**

   The list of current content types loads in your browser.
4. **Click the Manage Fields link in the row of the content type you want to change.**

   The Manage Fields grid is displayed in your browser.
5. **Click the edit link in the row of the field you want to edit.**

   The field instance settings Web form is displayed in your browser.
6. **Locate and select the check box with the Required label.**
7. **Click the Save settings button at the bottom of the page.**

   If you are successful, a confirmation message appears at the top of the page.

Limiting the length of a text field

The maximum length setting for a text or long text field is a global field setting. This means that the value you set applies to all content types that use this field.

To limit the maximum length of a text field, follow these steps:

1. **Log into your site as an administrator.**

   The login landing page loads in your browser.
2. **Select the Structure option from the main admin menu.**

   The Structure page loads in your browser.

3. **Click the Content types link in the Structure page.**

   The list of current content types loads in your browser.

4. **Click the Manage Fields link in the row of the content type you want to change.**

   The Manage Fields grid is displayed in your browser.

5. **Locate the Field column in the grid, and click the data type name link in the row of the field you want to edit.**

   If the field does not yet contain any data, then the field settings Web form is displayed in your browser.

6. **Scroll down the page, and enter the maximum number of characters you want to allow in the text box labeled Maximum length.**

Tip

If you are unable to enter a value in the Maximum length text box, this means data is already stored in this field. ■

7. **Click the Save settings button at the bottom of the page.**

   If you are successful, a confirmation message appears at the top of the page.

Creating New Content

The Drupal content creation process is lightweight and fast. Any user who has created permissions for a content type can author new items of that type. Figure 10.11 shows the full list of default content types that a user can use to create new content.

Understanding authoring basics

Each type of content in your system may be authored via a different process and even by a different group of people. For example, if you run a community site, you probably want to give community members the right to create some form of content—for example, forum entries or blog posts. However, if you run a news Web site, you likely publish articles via a more structured editorial process.

I cannot cover all possible authoring scenarios in the space of this chapter. Suffice it to say for now that you should spend time planning out who will create content and how that content will make its way to your published Web site.

Drupal is highly configurable in this regard. In this section, I discuss just the basic content creation process and the standard content item options that can play a role here.

FIGURE 10.11

The Drupal 7 admin screen displays a list of all default content types.

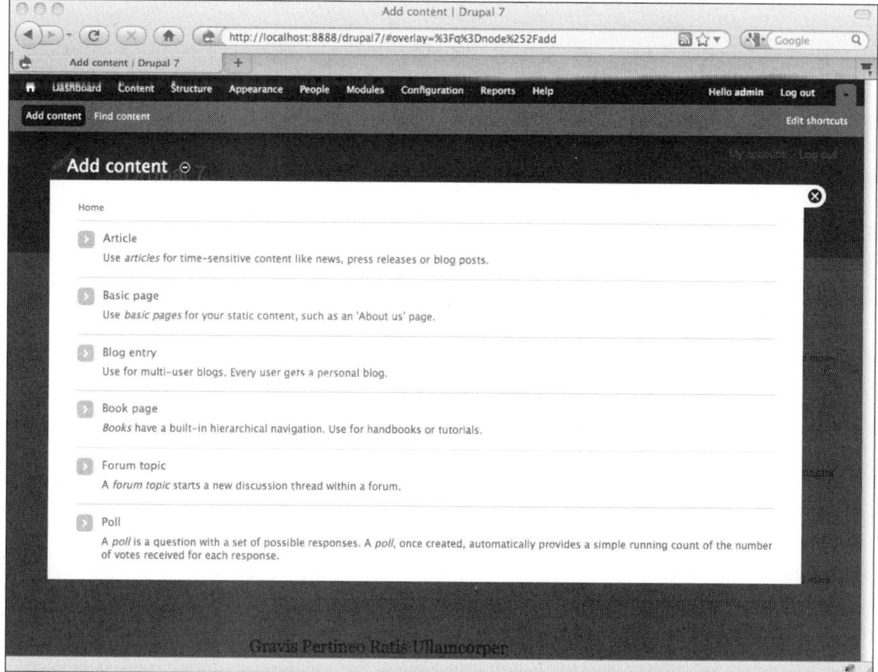

Cross-Reference

See Chapter 24 for a solid explanation of Drupal's user system and how you can create roles appropriate for various types of content authors. In Chapter 14, we dig into more advanced content management topics such as dealing with content versions and publishing workflows. Chapter 16 discusses managing blogs, Chapter 17 covers managing books, and Chapter 20 explains how to set up and administer forums. ■

To create a new item of content, follow these steps:

1. **Log into your site as an administrator or empowered content manager.**

   The login landing page loads in your browser.

2. **Select the Content option from the main admin menu.**

   The Content page loads in your browser.

3. **Click the Add new content link.**

   The content-type list is displayed in your browser.

4. **Click the link for the type of content you want to create.**

   The add content Web form is displayed in your browser.

5. **Fill in all required fields, and adjust any of the standard content item options in the tabs at the bottom of the page.**
6. **Click the Save button at the bottom of the page.**

   If you are successful, the new content item is displayed in your browser.

Tip

You can use the admin shortcut menu to create shortcut items for common tasks. For example, if you create lots of articles, then you can create a shortcut item that takes you directly to the article creation page. ■

Cross-Reference

For more details on admin shortcuts, see Chapter 28 where we discuss customizing Drupal's appearance. ■

Working with the standard content item options

When creating new content, you can optionally alter some of the standard content item options. The options available to you vary, depending both upon the default option settings and your user permissions.

Tip

The default values for the standard content item options are configurable on a per-content-type basis. See the section "Controlling How Content Is Created" for additional details. ■

Six standard content item option sets appear in the tabs at the bottom of the page. I review each option set in the following sections and describe which, if any, permissions are required for a user to access the option set.

Menu settings

This option set controls whether the content item is placed in your Web site's main menu and, if so, at what level. Check the box and fill in the additional fields that appear to create a menu item for the node. If you leave the box unchecked, no dedicated menu item exists, unless you create it manually through the menu manager. Figure 10.12 displays the Menu settings tab.

These are the menu settings options:

- **Provide a menu link:** If checked, the content item is added to the main menu list of links.
- **Menu link title:** If provided, this title overrides the title of the content item as the text used for the menu link.
- **Parent item:** This setting controls where in the menu hierarchy the item's link resides.
- **Weight:** This value controls the sort order of the menu link in relation to other links at the same level in the menu hierarchy. Smaller values appear before larger values. For example, if you assign a value of –5, the link appears before another link with a weight value of 2.

FIGURE 10.12

The standard content item option settings with the Menu settings tab displayed

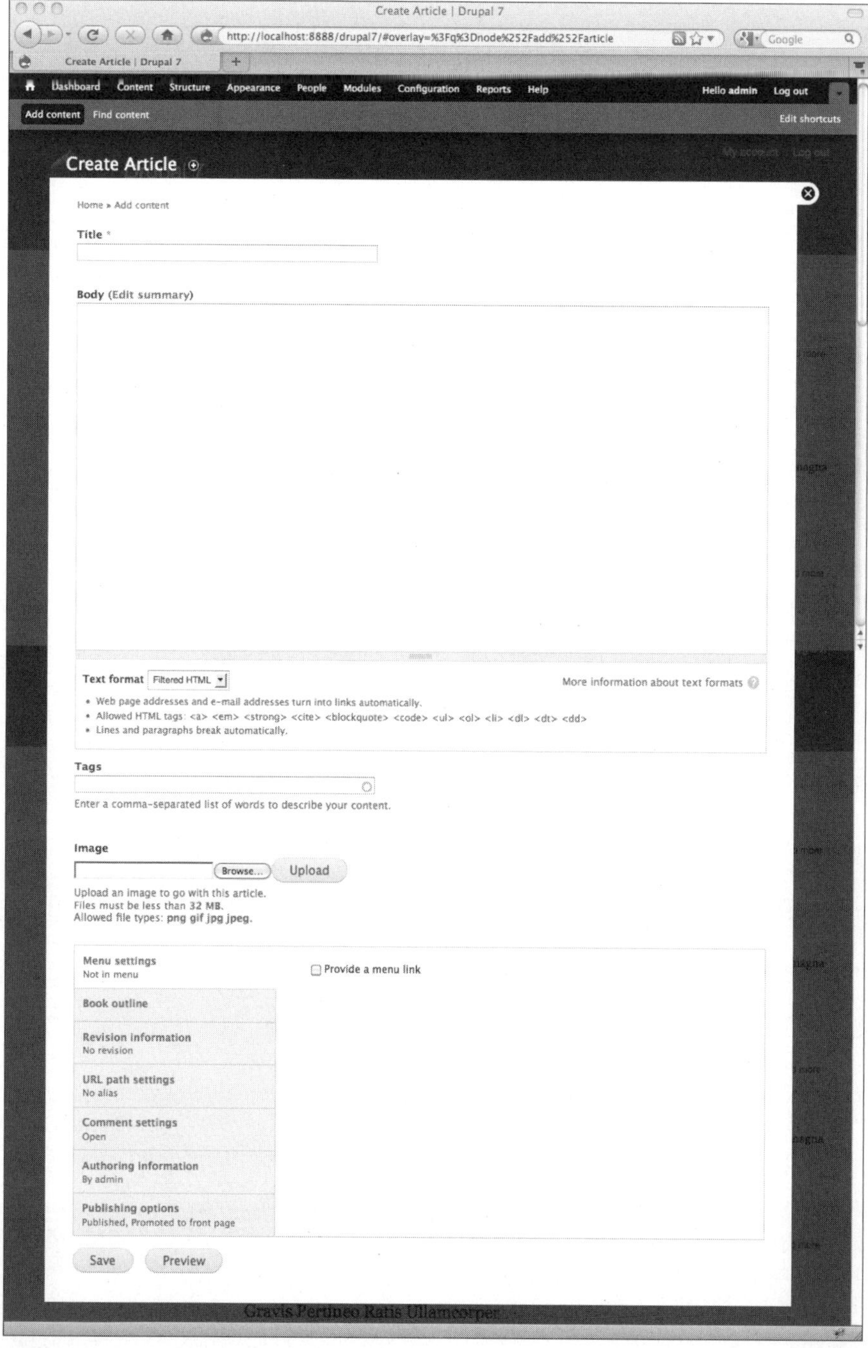

Revision information

The revision information option set controls whether a new revision of the content item is created when you click the Save button. Figure 10.13 displays the Revision information tab.

Note

See the beginning of this chapter where we discuss the concept of versioning and Drupal revisions. ■

FIGURE 10.13

The standard content-item option settings with the Revision information tab displayed

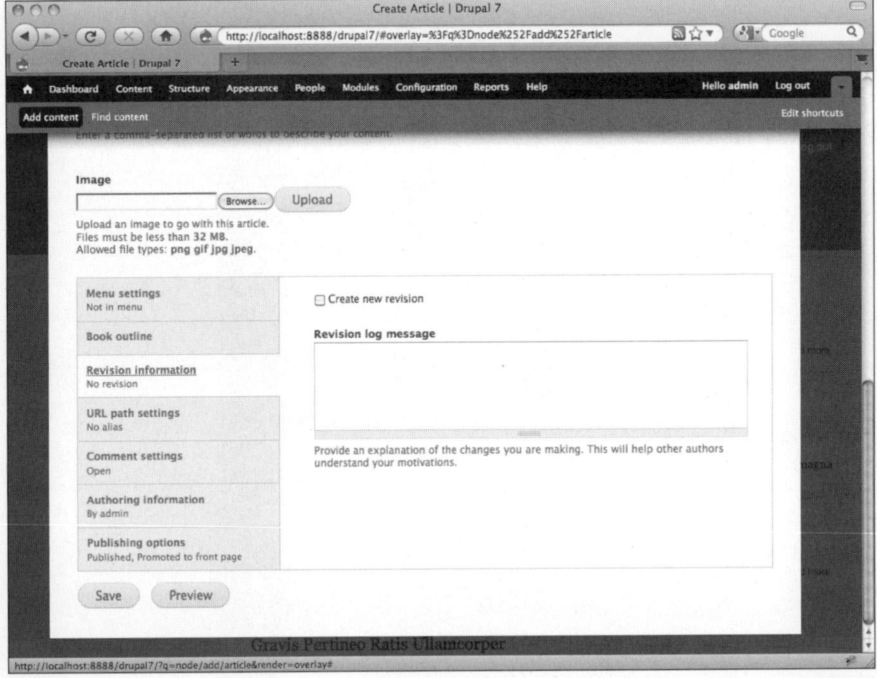

Tip

Users do not see this option set unless they are given the Administer nodes permission. ■

These are the revision information options:

- **Create new revision:** If checked, a new revision of the content item is created when the Save button is clicked.
- **Revision log message:** If a value is provided, a revision log message is stored along with the revision copy.

Tip

Adding revision log messages is a good practice; it adds richness to the revision history and can help others understand why changes were made. These messages also help you identify versions if you want to revert to an older version of a content item. ■

URL path settings

The URL path setting option set allows you to provide an alias for the current content item. For example, instead of the address of the item being `http://yoursite.com/node/5`, you could create an alias of "about/contact" to make the item's address be `http://yoursite.com/about/contact`. Figure 10.14 displays the URL path settings tab.

FIGURE 10.14

The standard content-item option settings with the URL path settings tab displayed

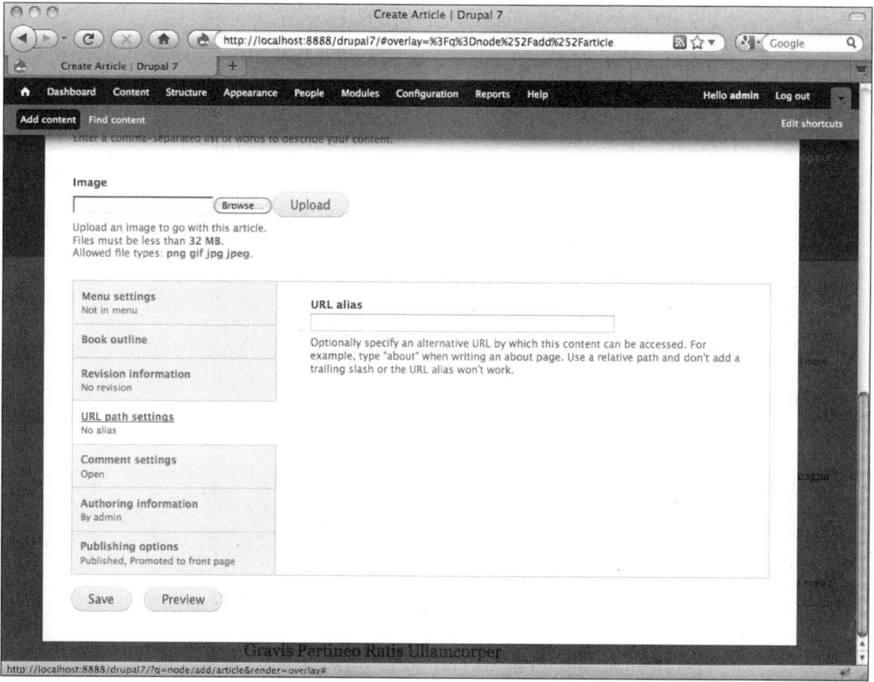

Tip

Users do not see this option set unless they are given the Create URL aliases permission. ■

This is the path settings option:

- **URL alias:** If a value is provided, a path alias is created for the content item.

Tip

URL alias values should be relative and should not end with a trailing slash. An invalid alias example is /`about/contact/`. A valid alias example is `about/contact`. ■

Comment settings

The Comment settings option set controls whether visitors can comment on the content item. Figure 10.15 shows the Comment settings tab.

FIGURE 10.15

The standard content-item option settings with the Comment settings tab displayed

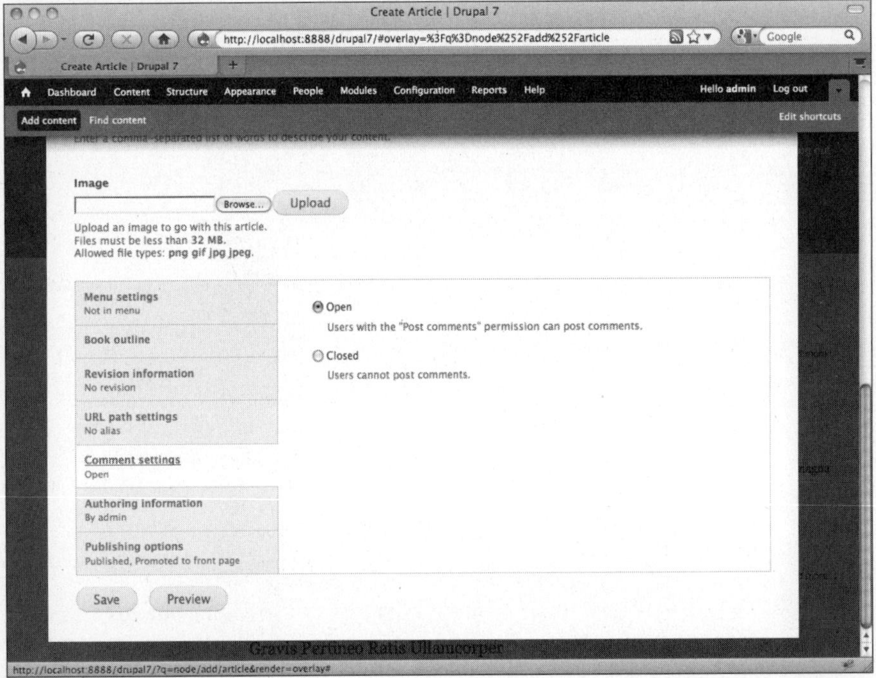

This is the Comment settings option:

- **Open/Closed:** If Open is selected, then users with the Post comments permission can submit new comments; otherwise, no one can submit new comments.

Authoring information

The Authoring information option set controls a few authoring metadata values for the content item. You can use these settings to override the default values. Figure 10.16 displays the Authoring information settings tab.

FIGURE 10.16

The standard content-item option settings with the Authoring information tab displayed

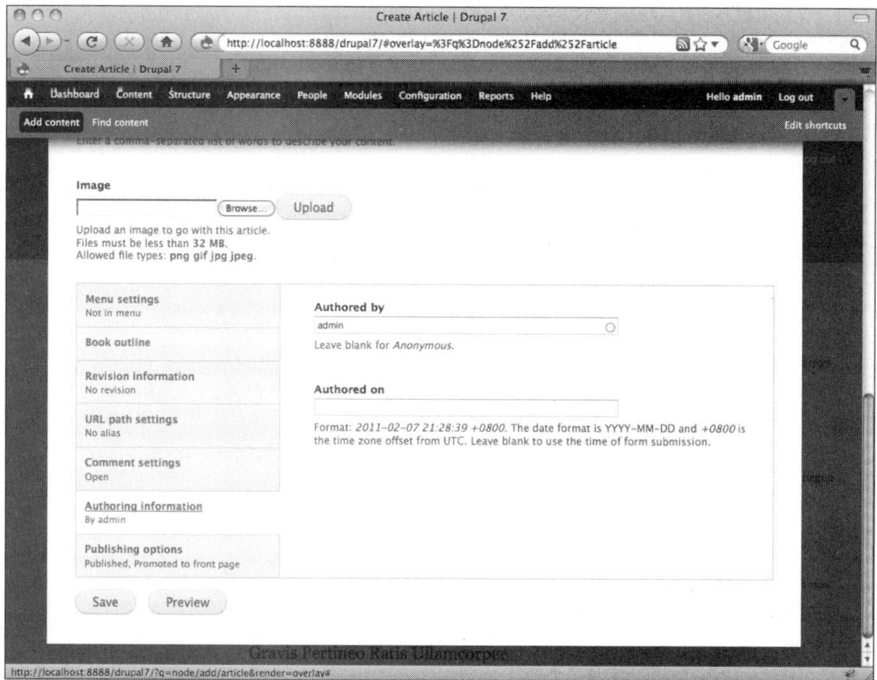

Tip

Users do not see this option set unless they are given the Administer nodes permission. ■

These are the Authoring information options:

- **Authored by:** This field is populated by the current user's username, but you can override this by supplying another username. If left empty, the value defaults to the Anonymous user.
- **Authored on:** If a value is provided, then this defines the date and time that the content item was authored on. If no value is provided, then the system uses the date and time when the form was submitted. The value format is `YYYY-MM-DD HH:MM:SS -0500` where the "-0500" is the time zone offset from UTC. A valid example value is `2010-12-27 18:05:00 -0500`. This value represents December 27, 2010 at 6:05 p.m. in the U.S. Eastern time zone.

Note

Setting the Authored on value to a future date or time does not control when the item will be published. By default, Drupal treats this information as simple metadata and does not take any actions or make any publishing decisions based upon it. ■

Publishing options

The Publishing options set controls if and where the content item appears on your published Web site. Figure 10.17 shows the Publishing options tab.

FIGURE 10.17

The standard content-item option settings with the Publishing options tab displayed

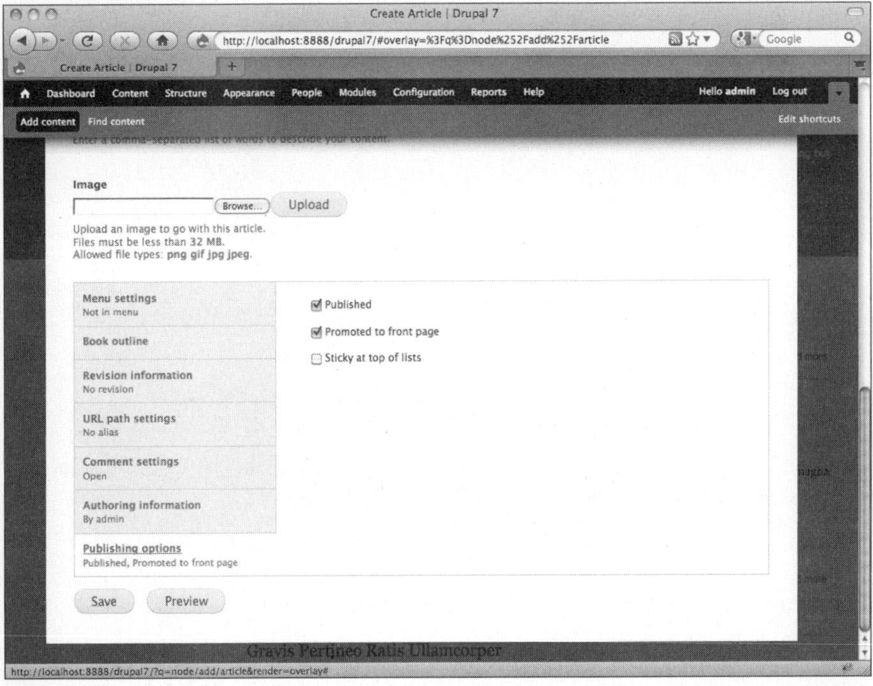

Tip

Users do not see this option set unless they are given the Administer nodes permission. ■

These are the Publishing options:

- **Published:** If checked, the content item is published after the save button is clicked.
- **Promoted to front page:** If checked, after the content item is published and assuming you have not configured your site to behave otherwise, it shows up on the front page of your Web site.
- **Sticky at top of lists:** If checked, after the content item is published, it appears at the top of content lists that contain this content type. For example, if the content item is a blog post, then it is displayed at the top of the blog irrespective of whether newer blog posts exist.

Managing Existing Content

Drupal is rather unique in the CMS world in that it does not organize content via folders, sections, or any other hierarchical principal (outside of what you can do with taxonomies or the book page content type). Content is stored in a single basket inside of Drupal and viewed as a single, flat list in the Drupal admin system. In this section, we explore some day-to-day content management tasks.

Tip

The default content management screens can be unwieldy when you have lots of content in your system. Often, people utilize the contributed Views module to create management screens that are tailored to specific user roles. ■

Cross-Reference

See Chapter 29 where we discuss acquiring and installing contributed Drupal add-ons like the Views module. ■

Figure 10.18 shows Drupal's default content administration screen showing the Add new content link, the content list filter controls, the content update options, and the content list.

The content administration screen is divided into four parts. At the top of the page is the link to add new content items. Underneath this you see the content list filter controls. Next on the page you see the content item update options, and finally you have the list of content items in the system.

These are the content list filter controls:

- **Status:** Select the publish status you want to filter by.
- **Type:** Select the content type you want to include in the list.
- **Term:** Select the taxonomy and taxonomy term you want to filter by.
- **Filter:** Click this button to apply the initial filter criteria to the content list.
- **Refine:** This button is visible only after you click the Filter button the first time. If you set additional filter criteria and then click this button, these new filter criteria are combined with the previous criteria using AND Boolean logic. In other words, all combined criteria must be met in order for content items to be visible in the resulting list.
- **Undo:** This button is visible only after you click the Filter button the first time. Click the Undo button to remove the last set of filter criteria you applied to the list.
- **Reset:** This button is visible only after you click the Filter button the first time. Click the Reset button to remove all the filter criteria you applied to the list.

FIGURE 10.18

The Drupal 7 content administration screen

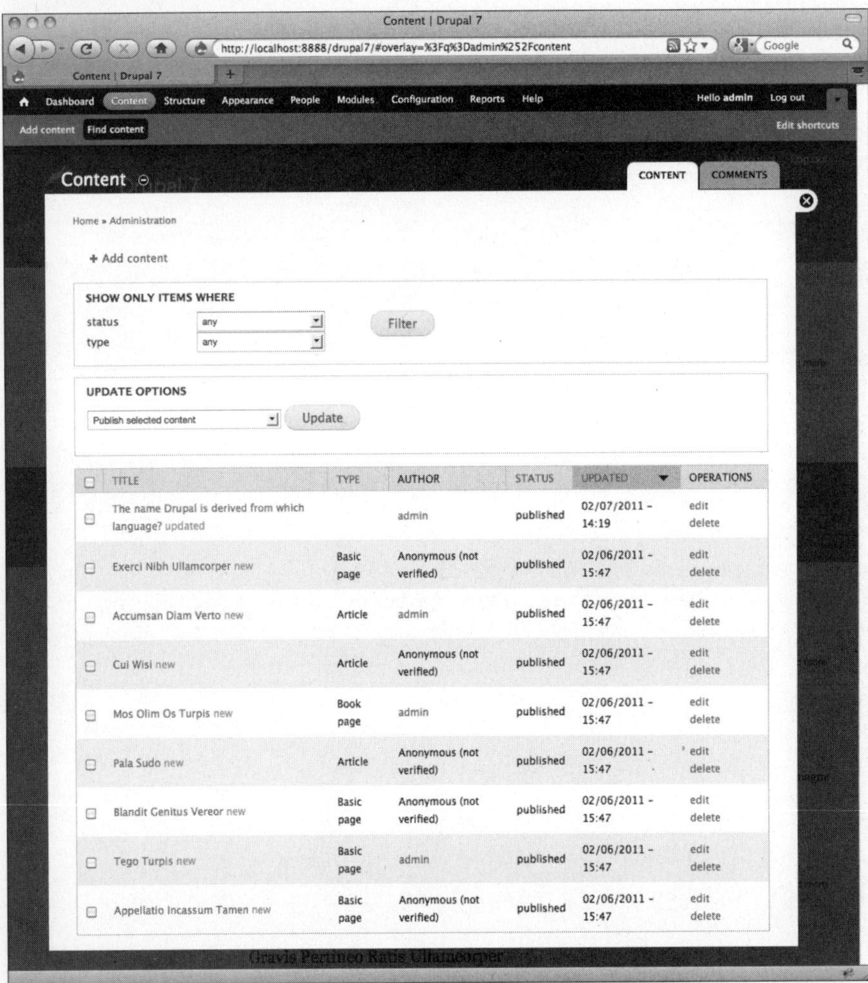

These are the content update options:

- **Publish selected content:** Use this to publish all selected content items in the list.
- **Unpublish selected content:** Use this to unpublish all selected content items in the list.
- **Promote selected content to front page:** This sets content items so they are visible on the Web site's front page.

- **Demote selected content from front page:** This sets the content items so they are not visible on the Web site's front page.
- **Make selected content sticky:** This sets the content items so they stick to the top of content item lists, after they are published.
- **Make selected content not sticky:** This removes the stickiness setting for the content items.
- **Delete selected content:** Use this to permanently delete content items from the system.

Note

Some contributed modules add or remove actions from this list. ■

The content administration screen contains a list of the content items as the last part of the page. The seven columns in this list are as follows:

- **Checkbox:** Use this control to toggle the selected state of all visible items in the list.
- **Title:** This column lists the title of the content item, and if the user is authorized to view the content item, it provides a link to the viewing screen for the content.
- **Type:** This column specifies which content type the item is.
- **Author:** This column specifies which author created the item, and if the current user is authorized to view the author, it provides a link to the viewing screen for the author.
- **Status:** This column specifies the publish status for the item.
- **Updated:** This column contains the date and time that the content item was last updated.
- **Operations:** This column provides one or more links for operations the current user is authorized to perform (for example, edit or delete the item).

Publishing and unpublishing content

The Drupal publishing process is straightforward: Content items are either published or not published depending on the value of a single check box. This check box is located in the content settings tabs at the base of the content creation or editing Web form. If the check box is checked, then the item is published. If it is not, then the item is viewable only by the author and users who have permissions to view or edit unpublished content.

Refer to Figure 10.17 for information on the location of the content settings tabs in the default content authoring Web form.

In addition to changing individual items' publish status, you can publish or unpublish content in groups. You might find this useful in the case of accidental publishing or when broader changes are being made to a Web site.

To change the publish status for multiple content items, follow these steps:

1. **Log into your site as an administrator or empowered content manager.**

   The login landing page loads in your browser.
2. **Select the Content option from the main admin menu.**

   The Content page loads in your browser.
3. **If desired, use the filters to locate the content items you want to work with.**
4. **Click the check box next to the content items you want to update.**
5. **Select the publish option in the Update options drop-down list.**
6. **Click the Update button in the Update options section.**

   If you are successful, a confirmation message appears at the top of the page.

Note

You may find Drupal's publishing controls rudimentary, refreshing, or something in between. However you find them, it's worth noting that, as with most things Drupal, you can change how publishing works by applying contributed modules or configuring the system as you see fit. ■

Cross-Reference

See Chapter 14 for a discussion of how you can implement more advanced publishing workflows. ■

Modifying content

Modifying content inside of Drupal is just as easy as creating it. You can access the content editing screen in two ways: You can browse to the content and then click the edit link or you can navigate the admin system, locate the content item you want to update, and then click to edit it.

The steps involved in the browse to edit process are dependent on your site's structure. To modify content from the admin system, follow these steps:

1. **Log into your site as an administrator or empowered content manager.**

   The login landing page loads in your browser.
2. **Select the Content option from the main admin menu.**

   The Content page loads in your browser.
3. **If desired, use the filters to locate the content item you want to work with.**
4. **Click the edit link in the row of the content item you want to modify.**
5. **Make you desired changes to the content item.**
6. **Click the Save button at the bottom of the page.**

   If you are successful, a confirmation message appears at the top of the page.

Considerations When Changing Published Content

You should to keep a few things in mind when modifying published content. For example, you might consider the following questions:

- Do you want to make a new node revision and revision log entry when you modify the item?
- If you change the item's title, will this affect the item's URL?
- If you change the category (or other metadata), will this affect the item's published URL?
- Should the item be viewable on the homepage or at the top of lists now that it has been updated?

Deleting content

Deleting content is dangerously easy for users who have the required permissions. With that said, a good general rule is that you should rarely, if ever, delete content that has previously been published.

Tip

Before deleting content, you might first consider alternatives such as changing the item's publish status, or if you have other metadata that controls presentation, then utilizing that to remove the content from the published Web site views. ■

With these caveats noted, you can delete content items following the same general content modification procedures detailed previously in this chapter. Drupal provides two methods for deleting content. You can locate the individual content item, select to edit it, and then delete the item from the editing screen. Alternatively, you can delete multiple items at the same time via the content administration screen.

To delete content from the content administration screen, follow these steps:

1. **Log into your site as an administrator or empowered content manager.**

   The login landing page loads in your browser.
2. **Select the Content option from the main admin menu.**

   The Content page loads in your browser.
3. **If desired, use the filters to locate the content item(s) you want to work with.**
4. **Select one or more check boxes next to the content you want to delete.**
5. **Select Delete from the Update options list.**
6. **Click the Update button in the Update options section.**

   The deletion confirmation screen is displayed in your browser.
7. **Click the Delete button in this screen.**

   If you are successful, a confirmation message appears at the top of the page.

Summary

This chapter provided detailed information about content management with Drupal and about the ways you can create or extend content types within the system. The following points were covered:

- Key content management concepts
- Drupal content types and fields
- The default Drupal content types
- How to create or customize content types
- How to control the content authoring process
- How to work with content in the system

CHAPTER 11

Managing Taxonomies

IN THIS CHAPTER

Introducing the Taxonomy Manager

Creating vocabularies

Managing terms

We use taxonomies as tools to better organize what otherwise might be chaotic Web sites. Taxonomies give you a way to organize or categorize your content as you or your content managers see fit. Additionally, when used as navigational elements, they give your visitors a means of rapidly accessing specific slices of your content that might otherwise be buried deeply in your Web site.

In other words, you use taxonomies primarily to make it easier for your Web site visitors to find what they are looking for. But to achieve this goal most effectively, you should first understand the different types of taxonomies and their relative strengths and weaknesses.

In this chapter, I introduce taxonomies, some important vocabulary and concepts related to information management, and explore how you create and manage Drupal taxonomies.

Understanding Key Concepts

In this chapter I show you that taxonomies—also called Drupal *vocabularies*—are not complicated things; however, their flexible nature demands that you think carefully about how to best use them, in advance of deployment. Additionally, as a cautionary word, don't be turned off by the amount of jargon encountered as you wade into the waters of taxonomies, metadata, and information management—the basics are as simple as putting different types of content in different boxes.

Tip

The Drupal 7 Taxonomy Manager has changed significantly from the Drupal 6 release. The addition of Drupal Fields has made vocabularies extensible. In other words, you can now customize the types of data each vocabulary item can hold. In this sense, vocabularies now function a bit like Drupal content types. ■

The core tools and ideas behind Drupal taxonomies include:

- The core Taxonomy module—enabled by default—provides Drupal's taxonomy functionality.
- When you define a new taxonomy, you create a new *vocabulary* in Drupal parlance.
- Each Drupal vocabulary consists of one or more items—called *terms*—and can contain an unlimited number of terms.
- Each vocabulary term can have an unlimited number of child terms.
- Using Drupal fields, you can customize the definition of a vocabulary's term, but by default a term has a required Name field and an optional Description field. You could, for example, add a Picture field and have an image associated with each term.
- You associate a vocabulary with a content type by adding a new field of type *term reference* to the content type, and then specifying the specific system vocabulary that the field references. I call this *binding* the vocabulary to a content type.
- You can bind either zero or an unlimited number of vocabularies with a given content type.
- You control the way the vocabulary is used by content authors by setting the user interface widget it uses during the process of binding the vocabulary to a content type. For example, the widget could be a free-text field, a drop-down list, a select box, and so on. The widget type you choose controls, among other things, how many terms may be associated with a content item.

Note

See later in this chapter for details on choosing the best widget type, when I discuss binding vocabularies to content types. See Chapter 10 for a discussion of managing Drupal content types. ■

In this first section, I set the stage for a solid understanding of taxonomy management by reviewing the key concepts.

Metadata

Taxonomies are metadata. Metadata is information about your content and is different than Web site content because it is not a primary form of content itself.

A slightly over-simplified rule is that content is visible to humans on the Web, while metadata is used by the content management system to decide how and when to render content, and it might also be visible to machines on the Web such as the Google, Bing, or Yahoo! robots that index your site. A content item's publish date is an example of metadata, as is its subject category (for example, Sports News).

Tip

You can assign any number of Drupal taxonomies to a content type. There is no technical limit. For example, an article could have taxonomies that define its global subject category, its geographical relevance, its age group appropriateness, its gender appropriateness, and its suitability for syndication. ■

Drupal's taxonomies are a form of metadata that help you organize your information. You also can use them as a type of navigation system, because Drupal automatically generates navigable lists of content items that share the same vocabulary terms.

Cross-Reference

See Chapter 8 on Drupal's Menu system for more information on Drupal navigation. ■

Taxonomy

You can think of taxonomies as systems of classification—often, but not always, hierarchies—used to organize things. You are probably somewhat familiar with a few common scientific hierarchies. For example, humans are classified as part of the species *homo sapiens,* which is part of the genus *homo,* which is part of the class *mammalia*, and so on.

Tip

Drupal taxonomies are implemented via the core Taxonomy module. This module is enabled by default. ■

Scientific classifications like these are fairly rigid examples of taxonomies. In Drupal, you can create less rigid systems, for example, by using *tagging* as an approach to classification.

Each Drupal taxonomy you create is called a *vocabulary,* and each item that you add to a vocabulary is called a *term*. Each taxonomy term in use automatically has a Drupal page listing the content items associated with that term, as well as a corresponding RSS feed containing those content items.

Vocabulary

In the Drupal context, a *vocabulary* refers to an instance of a Drupal taxonomy. If you define a set of categories for your content using the Taxonomy module, then in Drupal parlance you define a set of vocabularies.

You can create both free and controlled vocabularies in Drupal. A free vocabulary allows the content creators and editors to define their own terms. A controlled vocabulary is one that contains only the terms that you define.

When you add a new taxonomy to your Drupal system, you click the link labeled Add vocabulary, as shown in Figure 11.1.

FIGURE 11.1

The taxonomy management page with the Add vocabulary link

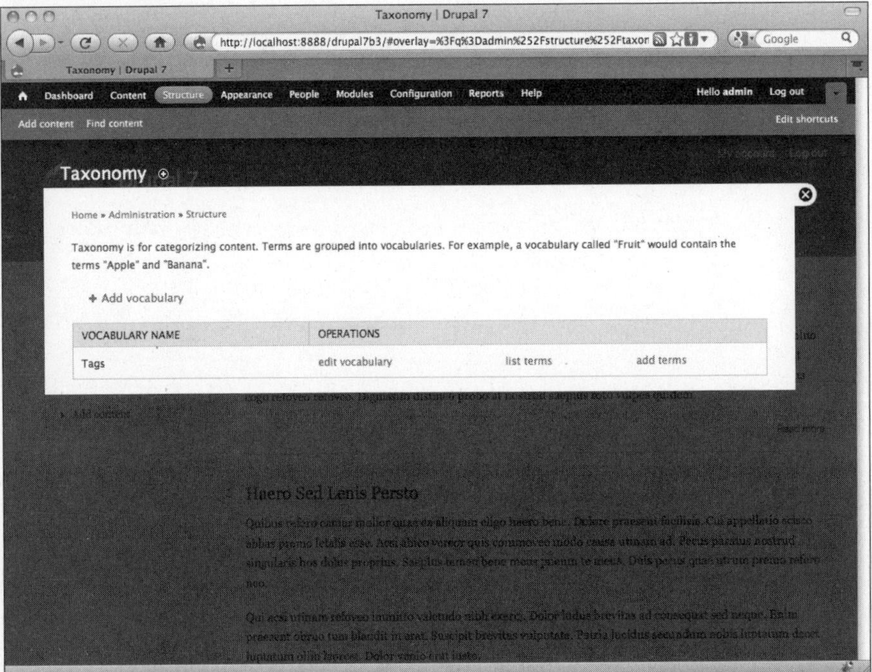

Term

In the Drupal taxonomy context, the word *term* refers to an item in a vocabulary. Each Drupal vocabulary is made up of one or more terms. For example, category names and tags are both considered terms. You create and manage terms differently depending on the type of vocabulary you are working with. In addition, terms can have an unlimited number of child terms. However, you are not required to create any child terms—vocabularies can be totally flat.

Tagging

You can use the application of ad hoc labels—known as *tags*—to organize your content items. This approach is called *tagging* content and is a very common means of employing Drupal taxonomies. In information science, this approach is often referred to as *folksonomy*—categorization by the people—because it's an uncontrolled, bottom-up approach to organizing information.

Web sites like the social bookmarking system `http://delicious.com/` popularized this approach to applying metadata. Most modern content management systems now support some kind of content tagging, and Drupal is no exception.

In Drupal terms, each tag is a term in a given vocabulary. You or the users of your system define tags in an ad hoc manner. That is, the system does not put any limits on you—you or your users freely type the value of a tag, versus selecting it from a previously defined list.

For example, let's say you author an article about cooking a specific type of Indonesian soup that comes from the island of Bali. You might tag this article with the words *soup*, *cooking*, *Indonesian*, and *Balinese*.

Tip

Drupal tags typically consist of single words, but you also can use multiple words separated by white space when defining a tag. ■

Tag cloud

A *tag cloud* is a group of vocabulary terms linked to the Drupal Web page listing content items associated with each term. People use tag clouds in different ways, but one popular approach is to limit the cloud to the top 20 or so most used tags and to display each tag in a relatively larger or smaller font size, as a function of its relative popularity. In this fashion, tag clouds allow you to present a quick view into the most written about topics for your Web site.

Introducing the Taxonomy Manager

You use the Drupal Taxonomy Manager to create and manage system vocabularies, to create and manage vocabulary terms, and to manage the fields associated with vocabularies.

You may find it non-intuitive, but you do not use the Taxonomy Manager to control how your content authors use a vocabulary. You control this via Drupal's content type management tools. More specifically, you manage whether a vocabulary is a controlled vocabulary (a drop-down list, a select box, a set of check boxes, or a set of radio buttons) or a free vocabulary (a text box, for example) by selecting the user interface widget type during the process of binding a vocabulary to a content type.

Cross-Reference

See Chapter 10 of this book for a full discussion of managing Drupal content types, including the processes for adding and deleting fields to and from content types. See later in this chapter for details on binding vocabularies to Drupal content types. ■

In this section, I introduce the three main areas of the Taxonomy Manager. In the sections that follow, I cover exactly how you perform the individual vocabulary management task.

Listing available vocabularies

Each Drupal taxonomy is called a vocabulary. When you install Drupal 7, a single vocabulary called Tags is created. Figure 11.1, seen earlier in this chapter, shows the Drupal Taxonomy Manager in list view.

Follow these steps to view a Web site's current vocabularies:

1. **Log into your site as an administrator.**

   The login landing page loads in your browser.

2. **Select Structure from the main admin menu.**

   The Structure page loads in your browser.

3. **Click the item labeled Taxonomy.**

   The list of system vocabularies loads in your browser.

Viewing vocabulary terms

When you get beyond the list of system vocabularies, the Taxonomy management tool quickly becomes more complex. Figure 11.2 shows the terms list view, including the four different tabs for additional vocabulary management.

Here's what the different items do:

- **Term name link:** Each term name is listed in the terms grid, as shown in Figure 11.2. Click the name of the term to view content associated with the term.
- **Edit link:** Each term has an edit link in the Operations column of the terms grid. Click this link to edit the term value data, including the Description and any other fields this term may have.
- **List Tab:** This is the active tab, where you find a list of all existing terms for the current vocabulary.
- **Edit Tab:** This is where you can edit the vocabulary configuration, including its name, description, and machine name.
- **Manage Fields Tab:** This is where you manage the content structure of terms for the current vocabulary, including adding or deleting fields, changing global field settings, and changing field instance settings.
- **Manage Display Tab:** In this area, you manage the display settings for each of the vocabulary's associate fields. These settings effect how the taxonomy term page is rendered; for example, an image field might be displayed as thumbnail or as the full-size image.

Follow these steps to view a vocabulary's list of terms:

1. **Log into your site as an administrator.**

   The login landing page loads in your browser.

2. **Select Structure from the main admin menu.**

   The Structure page loads in your browser.

3. **Click the item labeled Taxonomy.**

   The list of system vocabularies loads in your browser.

4. **Locate the vocabulary you want to work with, and click the List terms link in the Operations column of the vocabulary list.**

   The list of terms for this vocabulary is displayed in your browser, similar to Figure 11.2.

Viewing vocabulary fields

Fields are a new, native functionality in Drupal 7. Fields are data containers that you use to customize the structure of Drupal content types and vocabularies. By default, a vocabulary has two fields: the name field and the description field. Figure 11.3 shows the default fields management screen for a Drupal vocabulary.

FIGURE 11.2

The Drupal Taxonomy Manager displaying the term list view and additional configuration tabs

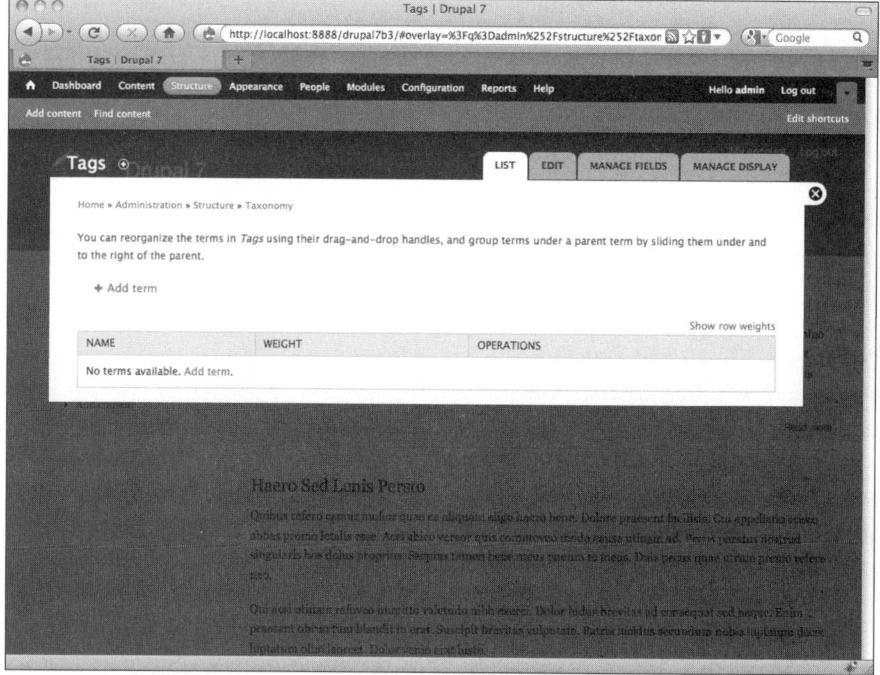

Follow these steps to view a vocabulary's list of fields:

1. **Log into your site as an administrator.**

   The login landing page loads in your browser.

2. **Select Structure from the main admin menu.**

   The Structure page loads in your browser.

3. **Click the item labeled Taxonomy.**

   The list of system vocabularies loads in your browser.

4. **Locate the vocabulary you want to work with, and click the List terms link in the Operations column of the vocabulary list.**

   The list of terms for this vocabulary is displayed in your browser (refer to Figure 11.2).

5. **Locate the Manage Fields tab on the top right, and click this tab.**

   The manage fields screen is displayed (refer to Figure 11.3).

FIGURE 11.3

The Drupal Taxonomy Manager displaying the Manage fields tab

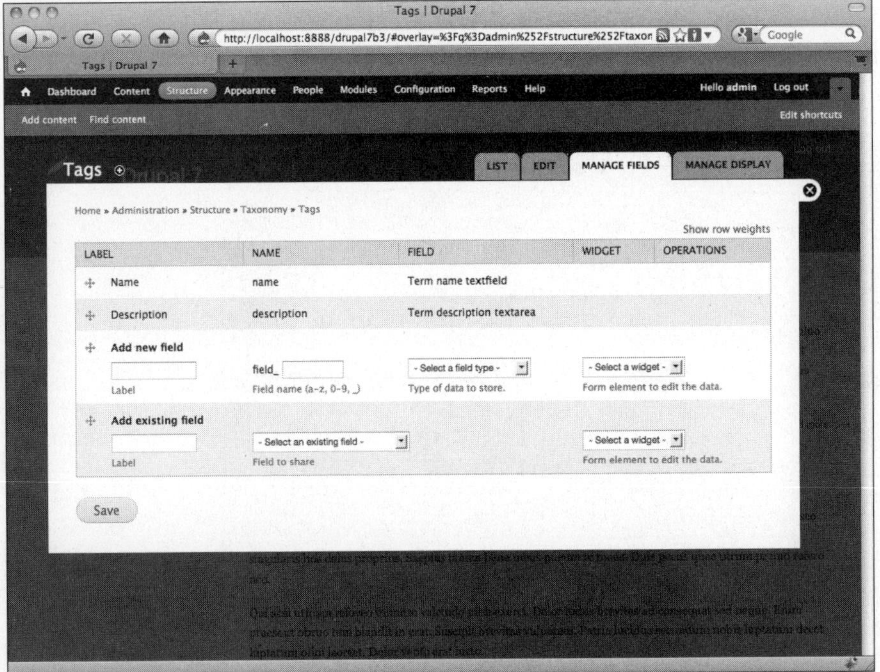

Creating Vocabularies

Using the Taxonomy Manager, you can quickly create new Drupal vocabularies. After you create a vocabulary, you can begin to use it by binding it to a content type. In this section, I walk through both of these tasks.

Defining a new vocabulary

You saw the vocabulary list view in Figure 11.1, earlier in this chapter. This is where you begin the process of defining a new vocabulary. Figure 11.4 shows the vocabulary creation screen.

FIGURE 11.4

Creating a new vocabulary with the Drupal Taxonomy manager

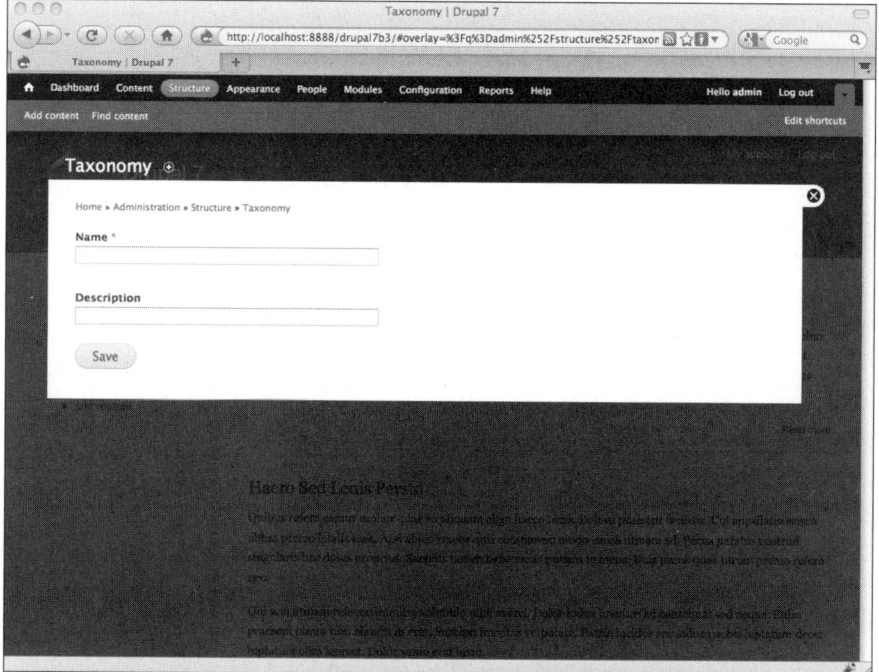

Follow these steps to create a new vocabulary:

1. **Log into your site as an administrator.**

   The login landing page loads in your browser.
2. **Select Structure from the main admin menu.**

   The Structure page loads in your browser.
3. **Click the item labeled Taxonomy.**

   The list of system vocabularies loads in your browser.
4. **Locate and click the Add vocabulary link in the top left of your screen.**

   The Add vocabulary screen is displayed in your browser (refer to Figure 11.4).
5. Type a value into the Name field, and optionally type a value into the Description field.

Tip

Drupal vocabulary names do not have to be unique, but the machine name for each vocabulary does need to be unique. It's a good practice to make both unique to avoid unnecessary confusion when managing your system. ■

6. **If you want to change the machine name, click the Edit link next to the machine name and enter a value in the provided text box.**
7. **When you are finished entering the values for the new vocabulary definition, click the button labeled Save.**

   If the operation is successful, your new vocabulary is created and a success message is displayed at the top of the screen.

Tip

You control the openness of a vocabulary via the user interface widget you use for each field that is bound to the vocabulary. This opens the door to a potential problem because it is possible to use the vocabulary in an open way with one field and a closed way with another field. The only way to avoid this conflict—if it is in fact not desirable—is to create a vocabulary for each usage scenario. ■

Binding to a content type

After you create a vocabulary, you must bind it to a content type in order for you or your authors to be able to make use of it during the content authoring process. This part of the process takes place outside of the Taxonomy manager; it involves working with Drupal's content type definitions. Figure 11.5 shows the standard Drupal content type management screen.

To proceed with the binding process, in the content type management area you must add a new field to a selected content type. Figure 11.6 shows the Manage fields screen for the Article content type. It is in this screen that you either add new fields or select to reuse existing fields. In this chapter, we bind a vocabulary through the process of creating a new field.

Cross-Reference

When binding a vocabulary to a field, you use a Term reference field data type. Drupal 7 has native support for a number of different data types. See Chapter 10 for a detailed explanation of each of the native field data types. ■

Tip

Drupal fields have two levels of settings. Global-level settings apply to all uses of a field, and instance-level settings apply to a specific use of a field. For example, the user interface label used to present the field in the authoring form is an instance-level setting. In the case of a term reference field, the bound vocabulary is a global-level setting. This means the setting value is constant across all uses of the field. ■

Following the process, you add a new field in this screen by specifying a field label, a field name, the Term reference field type, and selecting the widget to use in the user interface. Figure 11.6 shows the four settings required to add a new field.

These are the settings for adding a field:

- **Label:** This is the presentation label that is used in the content authoring and editing screens.
- **Field name:** This is the unique machine name for the field. It cannot conflict with other fields' machine names.
- **Field type:** You can choose from a number of different data types when adding a field. But you must use the Term reference data type to bind a vocabulary to a content type.
- **Widget:** This is the user interface element that authors will use to set the value or values for the vocabulary. You must first select the Field type and then you can select the widget.

FIGURE 11.5

Managing Drupal content types in action: the content type list and operations screen

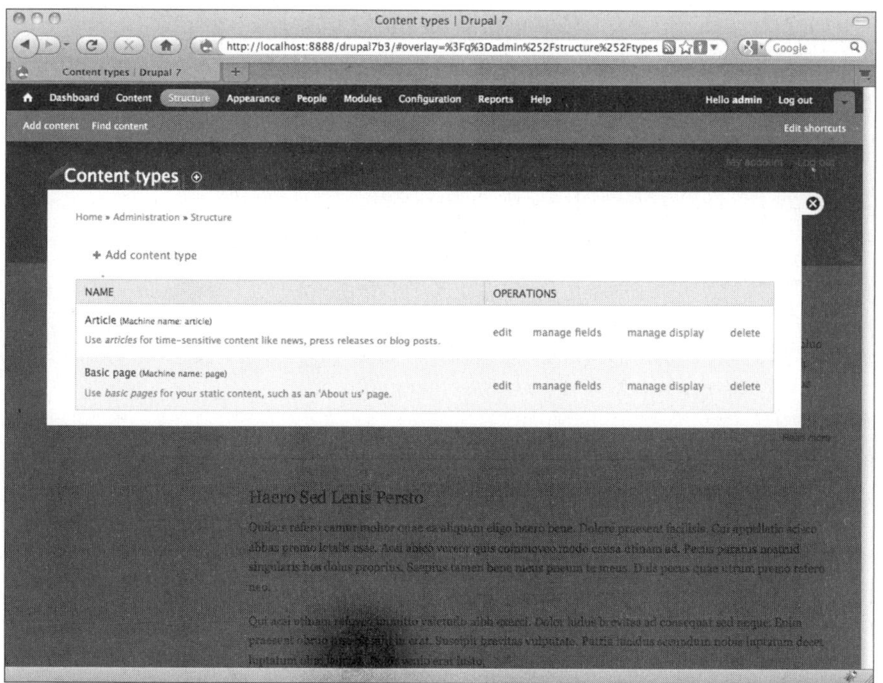

FIGURE 11.6

Managing Drupal content types in action, managing associated fields

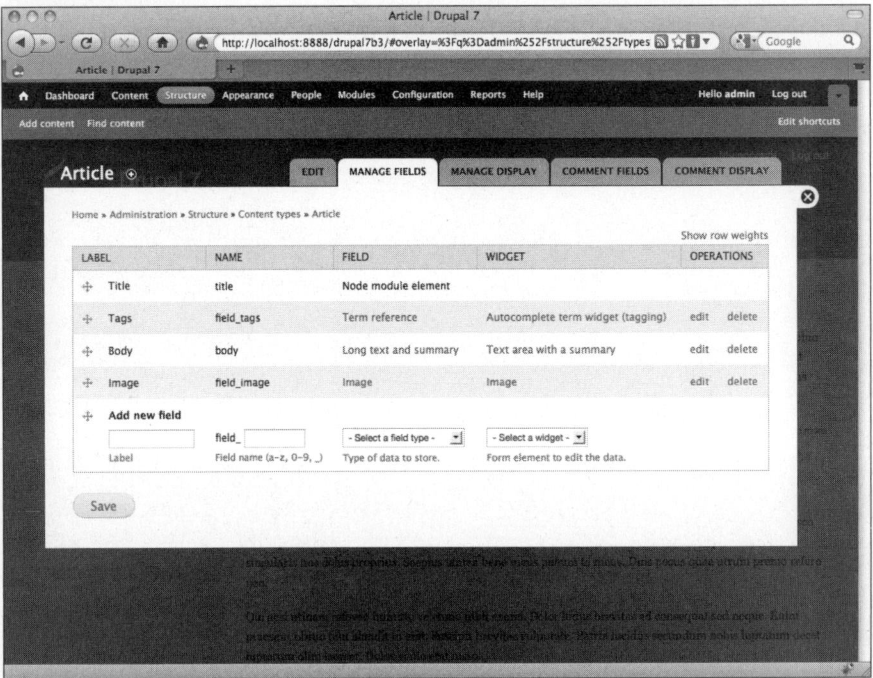

You can choose from three widget types for Term reference fields:

- **Select list:** This is also known as a drop-down list. It implies a controlled vocabulary and also that there is only one value allowed per content item. The select list enforces a one-to-one relationship between content items and vocabulary terms.
- **Checkboxes/Radio buttons:** These widgets both imply a controlled vocabulary. Depending on settings you specify later, the author can associate one or more values per content item. If you select check boxes, the relationship will be many-to-one; if you select radio buttons, the relationship will be one-to-one.
- **Autocomplete term widget:** This widget is a smart text box and it implies a free vocabulary where the authors can input ad hoc values. This is also known as tagging. The autocomplete widget further implies, but does not mandate, a many-to-one relationship between vocabulary terms and content items.

Follow these steps to add a new vocabulary-binding field:

1. **Log into your site as an administrator.**

   The login landing page loads in your browser.

2. **Select Structure from the main admin menu.**

   The Structure page loads in your browser.

3. **Click the Content types link in the Structure page.**

   The list of current content types loads in your browser.

4. **Locate the content type you want to modify and click the Manage fields link in the operations column for that type, as shown in Figure 11.5.**

   The Manage fields screen loads in your browser, as shown in Figure 11.6.

5. **Set the values as described previously and click Save when you are finished.**

   If the operation is successful, the Field settings screen loads in your browser, as shown in Figure 11.7.

FIGURE 11.7

Binding a vocabulary, specifying the vocabulary to associate with the new field

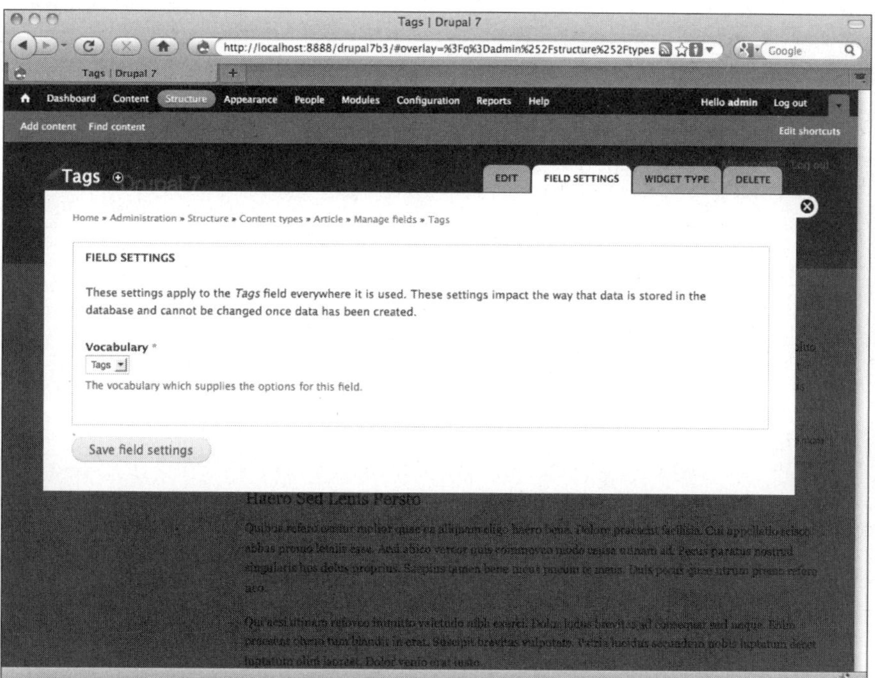

6. **In the Vocabulary select list, choose the vocabulary to bind to and click the Save field settings button at the bottom of the form.**

If the operation is successful, you see a success message and you are presented with the field settings page, as shown in Figure 11.8.

The field settings page contains two general types of settings: instance-level settings that apply the specific use you are setting up now and global-level settings that apply to every use of this field.

FIGURE 11.8

Binding a vocabulary, specifying the new field's instance and global settings

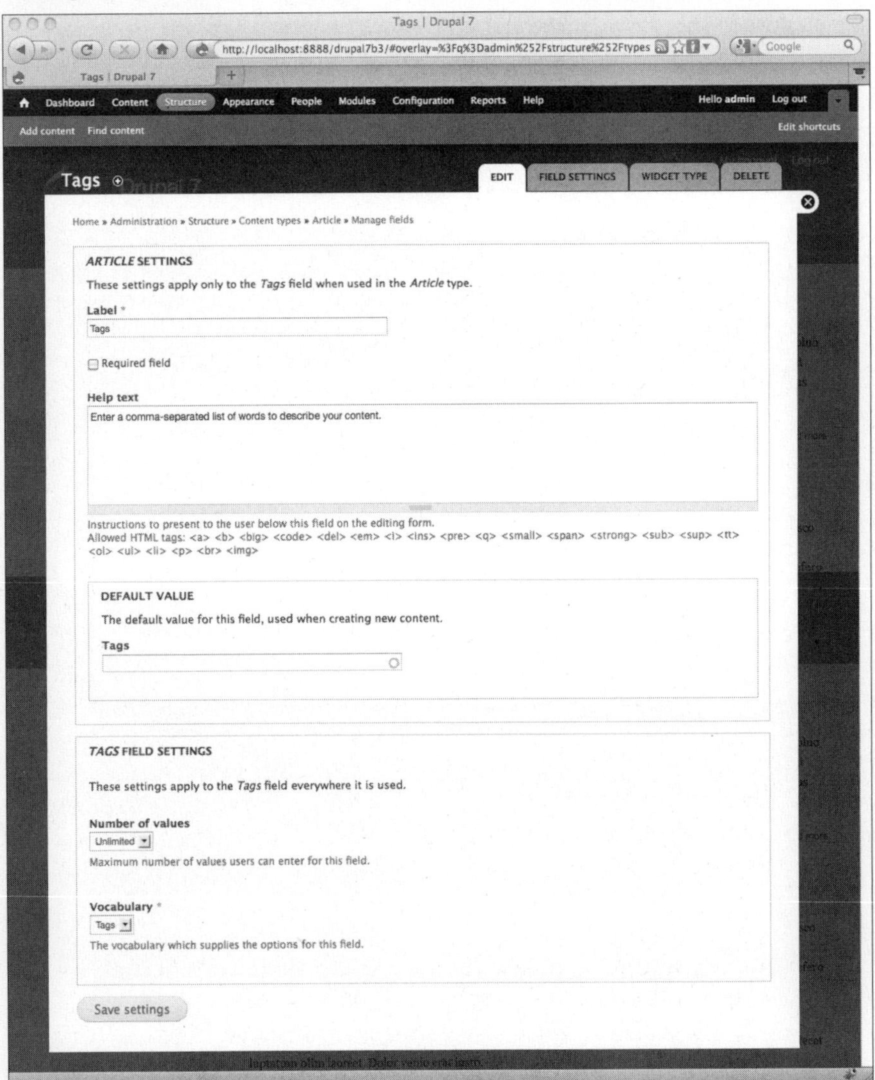

These are the instance-level settings for the term reference field type:

- **Label:** The presentation label that is used in the content authoring screens.
- **Required field:** This is a validation control. If you check the box, a value is required for this field when authoring items of the current content type.
- **Help text:** This is the help text displayed in the content authoring screens for this field.
- **Default value:** This is the default value that the field will have in the content creation screen.

These are the global-level settings for the term reference field type:

- **Number of values:** This value controls how many values the field may contain, and in combination with the widget type you select, it controls how the field is presented in the authoring screens.

Tip

Think carefully when you specify the Number of values setting. If you are using a widget type of Select list and you set this value to Unlimited or anything greater than 1, a scrolling list of options is displayed to authors. However, if you set this value to 1, a drop-down list is displayed to authors. The same is true for Checkboxes and Radio buttons. If you set this to Unlimited or anything greater than 1, the widget used is check boxes; otherwise it is rendered as radio buttons. ■

- **Vocabulary:** This is the system vocabulary bound to this field. You specified this value in a previous step, but you can change it here.

Follow these steps to review or set the field settings:

1. **Locate the field's instance-level settings in the top part of the page, and make any changes or type the values you want for each setting.**
2. **Locate the field's global-level settings in the lower part of the page, and make any desired changes to each setting. Take care when setting the Number of values because this affects the authoring form's user interface.**
3. **After you have completed these tasks, locate and click the Save settings button at the bottom of the page.**

   If you are successful, the settings are registered in the system, you are redirected to the Manage fields screen for the content type, and a success message is displayed. You are now finished binding the vocabulary to the content type.

Managing Terms

Managing vocabulary terms is a simple operation performed via the Taxonomy manager screens. Typical operations include creating, editing, sorting, and possibly deleting terms. We saw how to list vocabulary terms earlier in this chapter. In this section, I examine the tasks of creating and editing vocabulary terms.

Adding new vocabulary terms

In this section, I cover the process of adding new vocabulary terms via use of the Drupal Taxonomy manager. These are a few important reminders about how terms work:

- A vocabulary can have an unlimited number of terms.
- A term can have an unlimited number of child terms.
- A term can have zero, one, or multiple parent terms.

Tip

Keep in mind that vocabularies can be hierarchies where terms have one or more levels of ancestors (parents, grandparents, great-grandparents, and so on). Terms also can have more than one immediate parent. In this case, the hierarchy is considered a complex hierarchy. Drupal can't manage complex hierarchies in the drag-and-drop interface, so the system disables this functionality when you assign more than one parent to a vocabulary term. ■

Figure 11.9 shows the vocabulary term creation screen for a term with the default configuration.

FIGURE 11.9

Creating a new vocabulary term with the Taxonomy manager

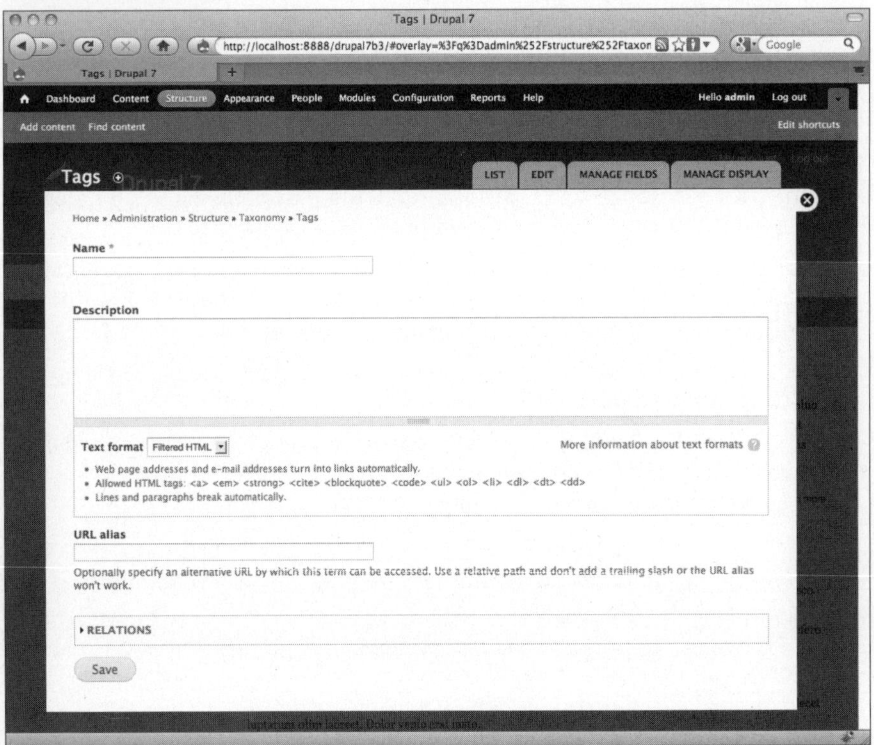

These are the input areas for the Add term page:

- **Name:** This is the term's value. For example, this is the value of a category name or of a tag.
- **Description:** This is an optional description for this term's value.
- **URL alias:** By default, Drupal generates a list of content associated with a taxonomy term using a URL such as `http://mysite.com/taxonomy/1`, where the number 1 is the ID of the term. This field allows you to create an alternative URL for accessing this same output. The value should be a relative path, such as `taxo/custom/myterm`.
- **Relations/Parent terms:** In the expanded Relations section, this value controls which, if any, existing term or terms are the parent of the current term. Use this setting to create hierarchical relationships between terms or to create complex hierarchies where terms have more than one parent.
- **Relations/Weight:** You can control the sort order of terms with this value; 0 sorts above 5, for example. The default value is 0.

Follow these steps to create a new term:

1. **Log into your site as an administrator.**

   The login landing page loads in your browser.
2. **Select Structure from the main admin menu.**

   The Structure page loads in your browser.
3. **Click the item labeled Taxonomy.**

   The list of system vocabularies loads in your browser (refer to Figure 11.1).
4. **Locate the vocabulary you want to modify, and click the associated Add terms link in the Operations column of the vocabularies grid.**

   The Add term screen is displayed in your browser (refer to Figure 11.9).
5. **Enter a value for the text box labeled Name.**
6. **Optionally type a value for the text area labeled Description.**
7. **Optionally type a URL alias value.**
8. **Optionally expand the Relations section of the page, and select a parent item for the term, thus placing it in a hierarchical relationship.**
9. **Optionally expand the Relations section of the page, and enter a weight value for the term, thus changing its sort order relative to other terms.**
10. **When you are finished entering the desired settings, scroll to the bottom of the page and click the Save button.**

    If you are successful, the new term is created in the system and a success message is displayed in the browser.

Editing and deleting vocabulary terms

You edit or delete vocabulary terms using nearly the same approach as was used in the preceding section. Figure 11.10 shows the term list page, including the operations column with the term edit links. All the term edit settings are the same as the term add settings.

FIGURE 11.10

The Taxonomy manager's term listing page with edit links

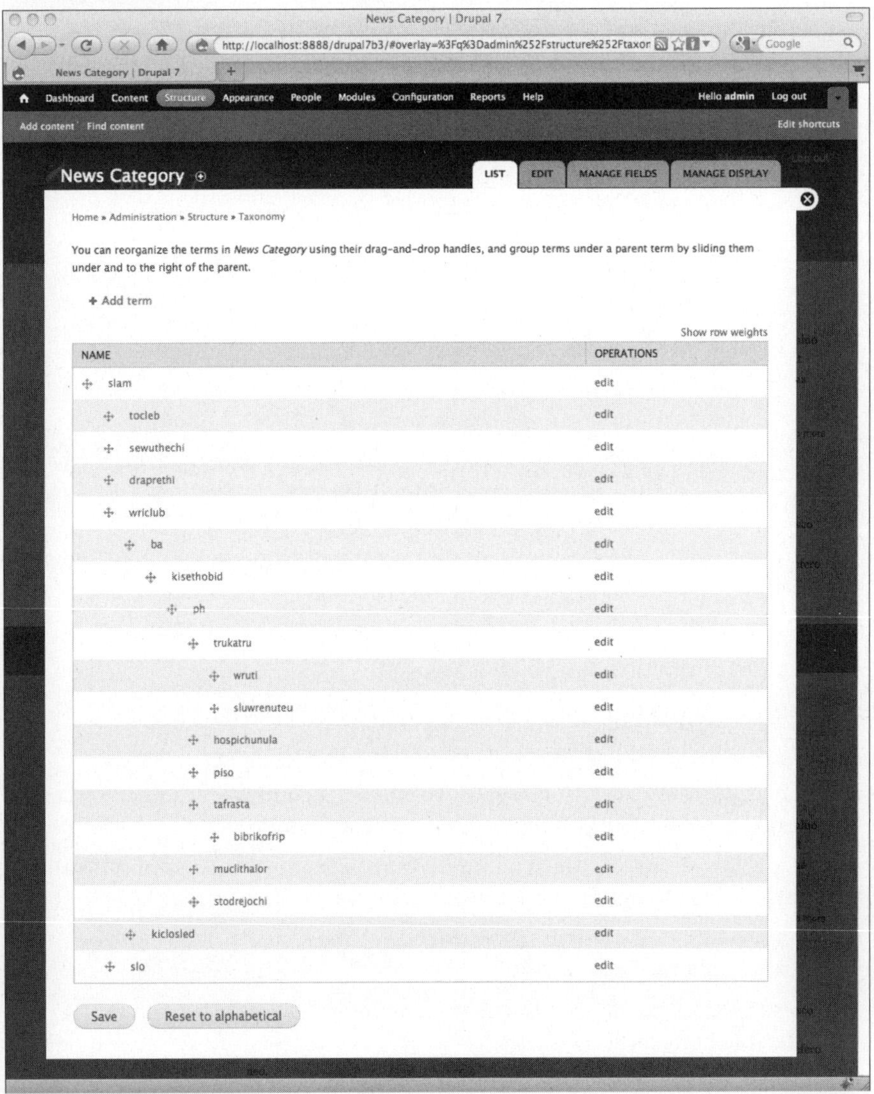

The term listing page allows you to perform two types of sorting operations:

- **Manual Sorting:** By dragging and dropping the listed terms, you can influence their sort order manually. Simply arrange the terms as you wish, and click the Save button at the bottom of the page.

Note

If a vocabulary contains terms with multiple parents, both drag-and-drop and alphabetic sorting options are disabled. In this case you must perform sorting manually via each term's Weight setting. ■

- **Alphabetic Sorting:** By clicking the Reset to alphabetical button at the bottom of the page, you force the system to clear all existing term sorting data. When you click this button, you are asked to confirm this operation before it takes effect.

Follow these steps to edit an existing vocabulary term:

1. **Log into your site as an administrator.**

   The login landing page loads in your browser.

2. **Select Structure from the main admin menu.**

   The Structure page loads in your browser.

3. **Click the item labeled Taxonomy.**

   The list of system vocabularies loads in your browser (refer to Figure 11.1).

4. **Locate the vocabulary you want to modify, and click the associated List terms link in the Operations column of the vocabularies grid.**

   The list terms screen is displayed in your browser (refer to Figure 11.10).

5. **Locate the term you want to modify, and click the associated Edit link in the Operations column of the terms grid.**

   The term create and edit screen is displayed in your browser (refer to Figure 11.9).

6. **Adjust the term's values as desired.**

   See the preceding section for a description of each item.

7. **When you are finished entering the desired settings, scroll to the bottom of the page and click the Save button.**

   If you are successful, the settings are registered in the system and a success message is displayed in the browser.

Summary

This chapter provided detailed information about creating and managing taxonomies with Drupal, including how to modify Drupal content types to add one or more vocabularies via the process of binding fields and vocabularies together. The following points were covered:

- Key taxonomy concepts and vocabulary
- Working with Drupal's taxonomy management tools
- Extending content types with taxonomies
- Creating and managing vocabulary terms

CHAPTER 12

Formatting Content and Media

Content on the Web has become increasingly rich and interactive. You or your authors will likely need to work with different forms of images, video, and, of course, rich text content. In all cases, the Drupal fabric of core and contributed modules comes to your aid.

In this chapter, I cover how you can manage text, rich text formats, and other media, and how—with the help of contributed modules—you can finely tune your authors' editing experience.

IN THIS CHAPTER

Understanding text formatting

Working with images

Working with other media files

Using WYSIWYG editors

Understanding Text Formatting

You use Drupal's *text formats* to control the type of content that authors and commenters can enter into the system. In your standard Drupal install, the simplest form of text content is called Plain text, and it does not allow any HTML markup or formatting. On the other side of the spectrum you have the most complex text content called Full HTML; this format supports a broad range of HTML markup tags. The real power of Drupal text formats is that you can create or configure custom text formats that span the range and are designed specifically for your authoring and security needs.

Tip

Text formats are also called Input formats in various places in the system. You can understand these to be the same thing. ■

Forming a handy team, *text filters* work in combination with text formats, but they differ as they act on the submitted text content, changing how it is ultimately rendered in your Web site. You see text filters in action when URLs or e-mail addresses entered into text fields are automatically converted into clickable links in the published content. I discuss the management of both text formats and text filters in this section.

Note

The standard Drupal install comes with three defined text formats. Don't feel limited by this. You can create as many text formats as you feel are necessary to meet your authoring, commenting, and security needs. ■

Introducing text format management

By default, your system's text input fields are assigned one of three text formats: plain text, filtered HTML, or full HTML. As mentioned, you can always define your own text formats if you decide that the default ones do not fit your needs.

Tip

I mention security a few times in this chapter, and initially you may not find the connection between text format and security immediately obvious. Security comes into play when you start allowing untrusted or misinformed people to create content for your Web site—for example, when you allow comments to be submitted by the public.

If a malicious person, a spammer, or even a well-meaning person enters dangerous or unwanted content into your site and you unwittingly publish it to your audience, the importance of input control can quickly become clear. This kind of content can be offensive, can work against your goals, or worse, can help spread viruses or other security compromises. I encourage you to think carefully about whom you empower to create content for your Web site and in what formats of content they are allowed to submit. ■

Drupal's three standard text formats have the following characteristics:

- **Plain text:** This is the simplest format and the most secure. It is also the one format that you cannot disable, because the system requires it for normal operations. If you or another author enters HTML into a field with this format type, by default the HTML is accepted, but it is rendered in plain text format, not as HTML. In other words, the browser never parses the HTML. This and other behavior can be changed via the text format configuration settings that I review in this chapter.
- **Filtered HTML:** This format is a compromise between plain text and full HTML, striking a balance between giving authors creative freedom and retaining a level of security and control. When you configure Drupal to allow input in this format, the system permits a limited list of HTML tags to be used. As I describe later, you can customize this list in the Filtered HTML configuration screen.
- **Full HTML:** This text format is, mostly, as it sounds. By default, this format does not restrict the HTML tags that authors can use. However, you can change this if you decide that your authors do not deserve such freedom. Full HTML could be "almost

full HTML" if, for example, you decide that authors should never have the right to embed `<script>` tags in the content. As with all text formats, you control this format's behavior via its configuration settings.

You manage text formats in the Configuration area of the Drupal admin screens. In Figure 12.1, you can see the default text formats listed along with the roles empowered to use them and the available operations for each format. You can see that all text formats other than the Plain text format can be disabled.

FIGURE 12.1

The Text format configuration screen lists the currently available formats.

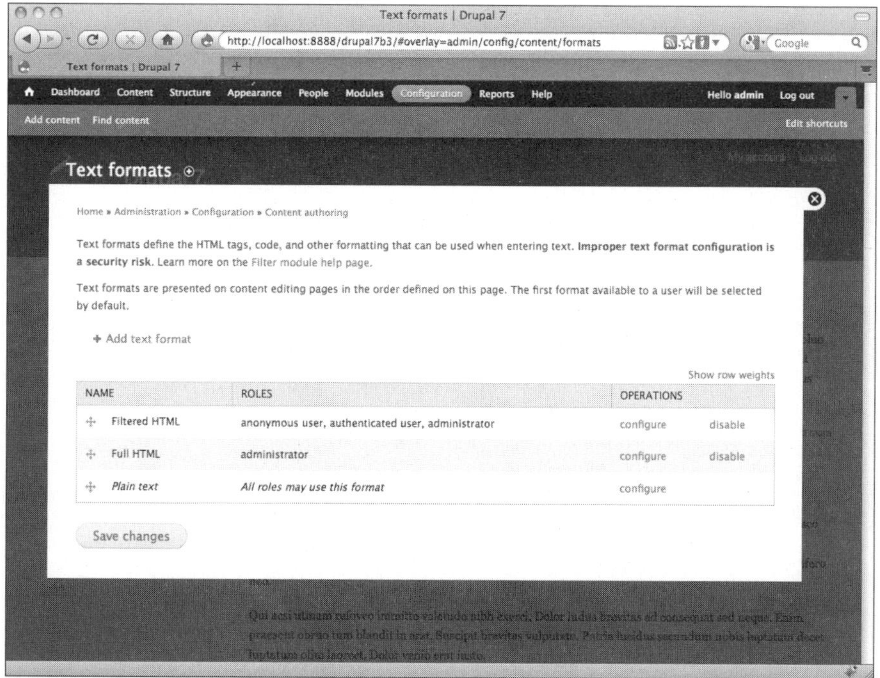

Creating and customizing text formats

Drupal text formats are flexible and meant to be tuned to your project's needs. In this section, I describe customizing existing formats, but you also can create new formats using the same processes and screens.

The Text format settings screen is located in the Configuration area of the Drupal admin tools. Figure 12.2 shows the configuration options for the filtered HTML format.

FIGURE 12.2

The Text format settings screen for the Filtered HTML text format

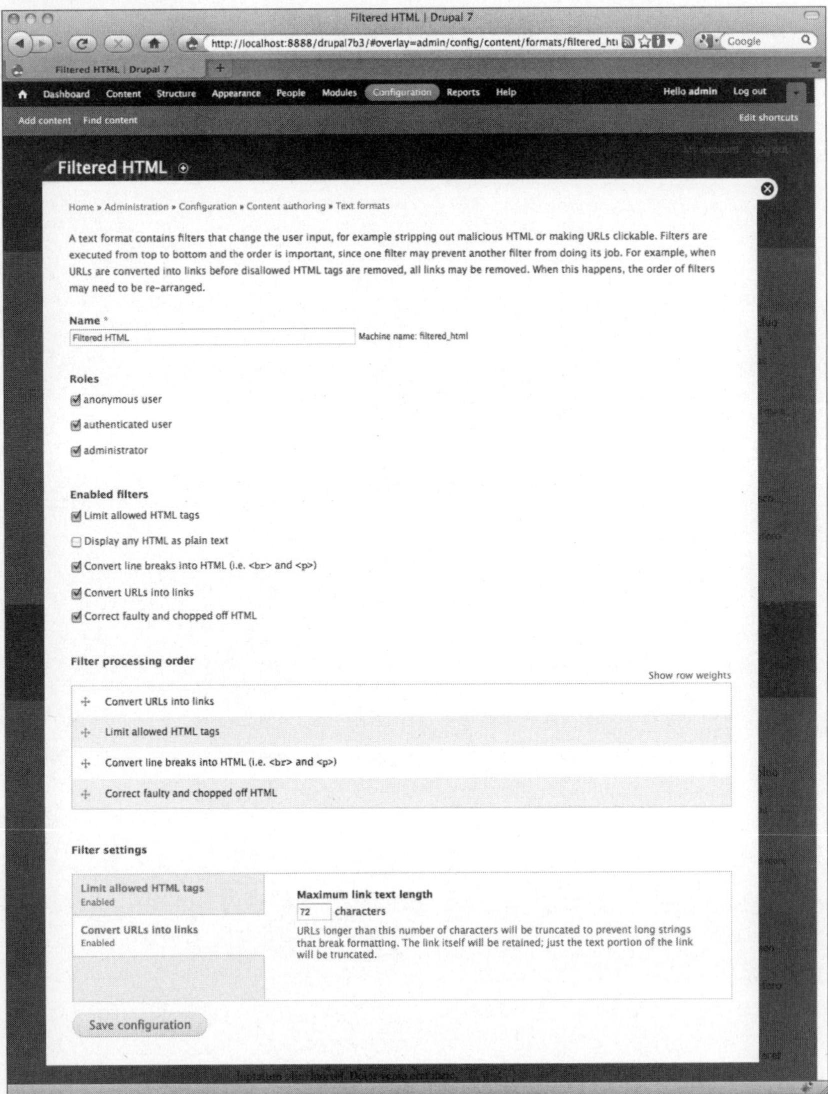

The Text format configuration screen contains the following settings:

- **Name:** This is the unique, descriptive name of the text format.
- **Roles:** This area lists the system security roles with a check box turning on or off access to this text format on a per-role basis. Note that you also can control text format security rights in the role permissions screen in the People admin area.

Cross-Reference

See Chapter 24 for a full discussion of user roles and permissions. ■

- **Enabled filters:** You turn on or off selected text filters in this section. These filters are available:
  - **Limit allowed HTML tags:** If enabled, you can specify which HTML tags can be used with the current text format. The list of allowed tags is specified lower in the page, in the Filter settings section.
  - **Display any HTML as plain text:** If enabled, any HTML entered into the text field is output as plain text in the Web page or RSS feed. If disabled, the HTML is not visible in any form in the published content. This filter is typically enabled only for the Plain text format.
  - **Convert line breaks into HTML:** This item is useful for preserving formatting when you use the plain text format type. It changes any line breaks into either new lines or new paragraphs in the published content.
  - **Convert URLs into links:** This filter automatically turns text that looks like a URL or an e-mail address into a clickable link. You may not find this desirable in all situations (for example, it could encourage comment spammers), so consider the pluses and minuses before enabling this item for a given format.
  - **Correct faulty and chopped off HTML:** This filter cleans up messy or invalid HTML that might come from an author or commenter, before it makes it into your Web page. When enabled, this filter can help prevent invalid HTML from breaking your Web page structure or interfering with the presentation of content.

Note

You can find contributed modules that add more filters to your system. Later in this chapter I discuss a few examples of contributed modules that add filters to your Drupal install. ■

- **Filter processing order:** This section allows you to drag and drop the active text filters, thus changing the order in which they perform their respective duties.
- **Filter settings:** This set of tabs allows you to further control the behavior of the enabled text filters. Depending on which filters are enabled, you may or may not see any additional settings here.
  - **Limit allowed HTML tags:** This Filter settings tab is present if the Limit allowed HTML tags filter is enabled. It gives you a text box for specifying the list of allowable HTML tags (separated by whitespace), a check box that controls whether basic HTML help is displayed in the authoring interface, and a check box that controls whether HTML links are modified to include a `rel="nofollow"` attribute.

Tip

The link attribute `rel="nofollow"` is a quasi Web standard that allows you to indicate to search engines that your site is not specifically endorsing the Web site to which the link points. You can use this, for example, as a means to discourage comment spammers, because most search engines do not count such links as votes of popularity for the site to which the link points. You can find more background on this attribute at `http://en.wikipedia.org/wiki/Nofollow`. ■

- **Convert URLs into links:** This Filter settings tab is enabled if the identically named filter is enabled. It has just one text box allowing you to specify the maximum number of characters that a URL can contain. Note that this setting controls only the length of the presented text for the link. It does not change or truncate the link's address, specifically the link's `href` attribute content.

Follow these steps to customize a text format:

1. **Log into your site as an administrator.**

   The login landing page loads in your browser.
2. **Select the Configuration option from the main admin menu.**

   The Configuration page loads in your browser.
3. **Locate the Content authoring section of the page, and click the item labeled Text formats.**

   The Text formats page loads in your browser, including a link to Add a text format and a grid listing all the defined text formats.
4. **Click the configure link in the Operations column for the Filtered HTML text format row.**

   The configuration page loads in your browser, displaying the settings discussed previously.
5. **Review the settings in this page and/or make changes as needed.**
6. **When you are finished making changes, scroll to the bottom of the page and click the Save configuration button.**

   If the operation is successful, a success message is visible at the top of the page and your changes are now active.

Controlling the use of text formats

Given Drupal's architecture of content extensibility via Fields, you might expect that you can bind a text format to a specific field or field instance, but this isn't how the system currently works. Instead, you put text formats into action by granting one or more user roles the right to use a specific format and then you ensure that the intended content fields are configured to use *filtered text* processing.

I describe the process for granting text format usage to roles in the preceding section. You configure a field's text processing setting in the content type management screens, in the Structure admin section. In that area, when you create or modify a text field, you can choose between only two classes of text processing: plain text or filtered text, as shown in Figure 12.3.

If you choose the plain text processing option, then only the Plain text format is allowed for all instances of this field, regardless of the current user's security role. If you choose the filtered text option, then the active user's role controls the text format options available when the user is authoring content or submitting comments.

FIGURE 12.3

The text processing settings for the Article content type's comment body field

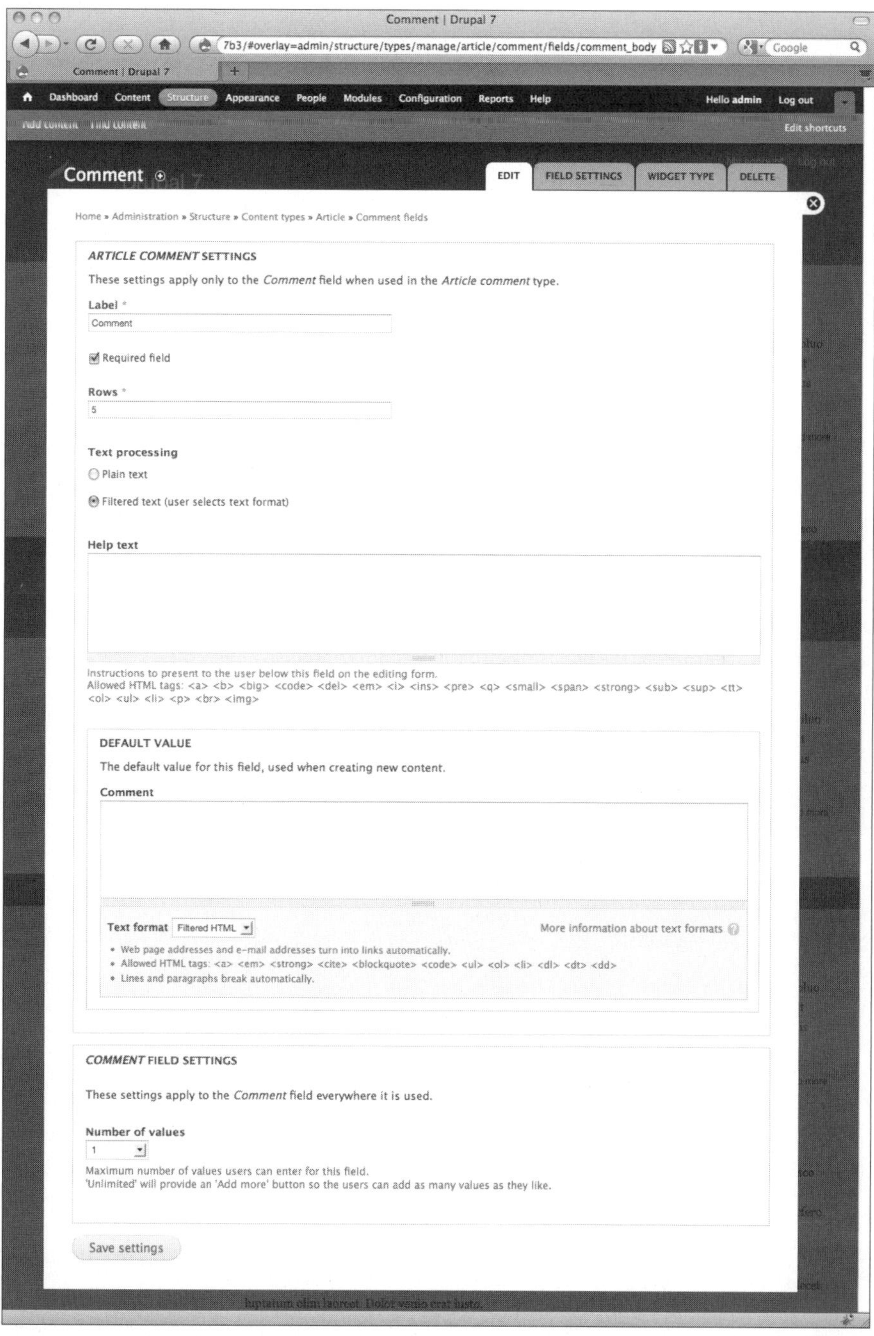

Cross-Reference

For details on managing users, refer to Chapter 23. For a discussion about permissions and roles, see Chapter 24. In Chapter 10, we discuss creating and managing content types and customizing the fields that define each content type. ■

Working with Images

With the release of version 7, the standard Drupal installation has gained a number of powerful image handling features. The core Image module now provides you with the Image Field type for use when creating or extending content types, the ability to configure an image toolkit, and the power to define any number of image styles, which in turn give you a range of automated image manipulation functions. In this section, I explore the Drupal image management fundamentals.

Creating an image field

You create new image fields just like you do any content field in Drupal. In the Content types area under the Structure section of the admin screens, either you define a new field that stores image data or you add an existing image data field to your content type.

Cross-Reference

See Chapter 10 for a discussion of creating and managing Drupal content types, including adding and configuring fields. ■

If you create a new field, you are first prompted to enter the global settings for the field, as shown in Figure 12.4. These settings apply to all uses of the given field.

The image field's global settings include the following:

- **Upload destination:** This defines whether the image files are stored in a publicly accessible folder or a folder secured via Drupal's permissions logic. In most cases, you leave images in a public folder, but you need to decide this on a case-by-case basis. Do keep in mind that storing images privately places significantly more load on the system when they are accessed, so select this option only if it is really necessary.

Note

If you do not see a private storage option in this screen, then your system has not been configured for private media file storage. See Chapter 4 for configuration details related to media file storage. ■

- **Default image:** This setting allows you to, optionally, specify a default image for the field.

FIGURE 12.4

The global field settings for a new image field

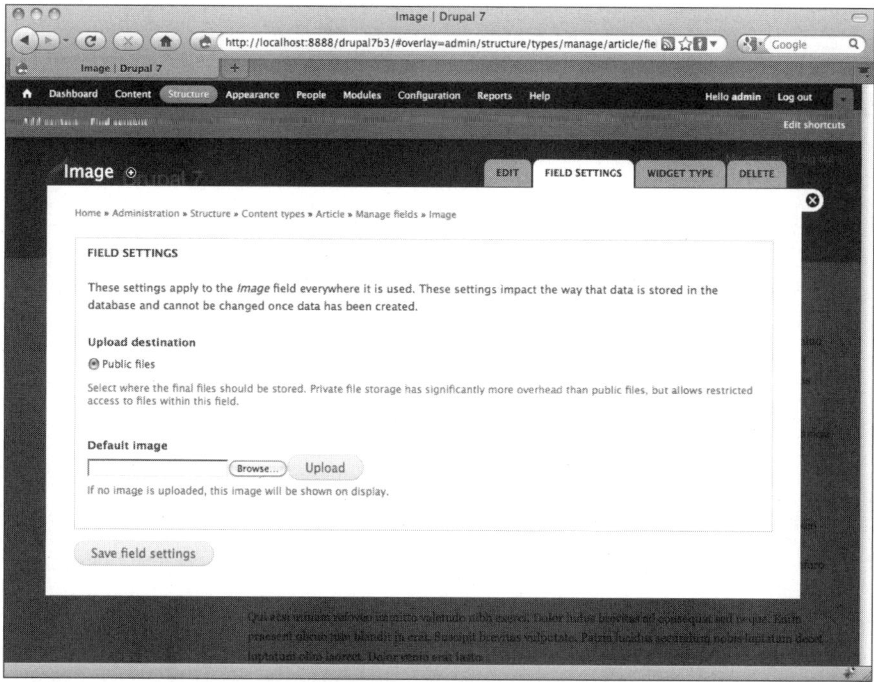

After you specify the global settings and click to save the configuration, you are presented with the image field's instance-level settings screen. The items in this screen include the following:

- **Label:** This is the content of the field's label in the content authoring screen.
- **Required field:** If checked, authors are forced to select an image for this field before they can save the content item.
- **Help text:** This is the helper text visible in the content authoring screen. Use this space to explain to the authors the purpose of the image and whether it is required.

Tip

When writing field help text, keep in mind that this text is most useful when it is most concise. Instead of writing something like "This field is required," consider using just the word "Required." Large blocks of text tend to get glossed over by busy people. ■

- **Allowed file extensions:** In this field, you must provide a comma-delimited list of allowed image file extensions. Keep in mind the intended purpose of this field and that Web browsers are capable of processing only a limited number of image file types.

- **File directory:** If you specify this optional value, then uploaded images are placed in this subdirectory, under either the public or private file storage area. You can use this value to help keep your file system a bit more organized.
- **Maximum image resolution:** This field controls the image's maximum width and height, in pixels. Keep in mind that you can use image styles (discussed later in this chapter) to manipulate the final image presentation parameters.
- **Minimum image resolution:** This field controls the image's minimum width and height, in pixels.
- **Maximum upload size:** This field limits the image's data size. If you do not specify a value, then the upload size is limited by your Web server's PHP configuration.
- **Enable Alt field:** The `alt` field is an HTML attribute of the `<img>` tag. It is a good idea to enable this field because it can help, if modestly, with search engine optimization. It also can give you a bit more control over image presentation, because screen readers and other devices may rely heavily on the contents of this attribute for presentation. Consequently, this field is likely to play a role in your Web site's accessibility level.

Cross-Reference

See Chapter 34 for a full discussion of Drupal search engine optimization considerations and practices. In Chapter 34, we discuss how to make your Drupal Web site more accessible for screen readers and related technologies. ■

- **Enable Title field:** The title field is another HTML attribute of the `<img>` tag. If used, many browsers show the content of this attribute as a tool tip when the mouse hovers over the image. Your decision to use this field may be influenced by the graphic designers or usability engineers associated with your project.
- **Preview image style:** This setting controls how the image is presented in the content authoring screen. For example, if the image is a large one, you may want to see a thumbnail (small) image in the authoring screen so it is not a distraction.

In this configuration screen, you can change any of the default values and click the Save settings button at the bottom of the page to save your configuration. Following the instructions found in Chapter 10, you may make additional refinements to the content type or add more fields.

Configuring the image toolkit

Drupal uses something called an *image toolkit* to abstract a number of standard image manipulation functions such as resizing, cropping, desaturating, and rotating images. Current versions of the PHP framework are packaged with the open-source GD image library, and accordingly the default Drupal installation is configured to perform image manipulations using this library.

Tip

The GD library is a powerful tool, but some people encounter performance issues when working with larger images. If you run into such problems, you may want to experiment with other libraries like ImageMagick.

Your server environment needs to be configured to support any additional libraries. You also need to check the latest Drupal documentation for information on configuring Drupal support for each library. ■

At the time of writing this book, the GD image toolkit contained only one configuration parameter: controlling the quality of JPEG images that it creates when performing image manipulations. Follow these steps to configure the GD library toolkit:

1. **Log into your site as an administrator.**

   The login landing page loads in your browser.

2. **Select the Configuration option from the main admin menu.**

   The Configuration page loads in your browser.

3. **Locate the Media section of the page, and click the item labeled Image toolkit.**

   The Image toolkit configuration screen loads in your browser, displaying the JPEG quality setting text box.

4. **Enter a value from 0 to 100 in this field.**

   Note that a higher number results in higher quality images and larger file sizes, thus slower download times. Your choice of setting is a compromise between quality and speed.

5. **After you have entered a value, locate and click the Save configuration button.**

   If the operation completed successfully, a success message displays at the top of the page.

Defining image styles

Image styles are named sets of behaviors that you can use to modify how images are ultimately published by Drupal. Image style tools are powerful in that they can both save your authors' time and help ensure a consistent, professional presentation of your Web content.

To give you a clear example, consider that you might decide that all images in your Web site should be black and white, or that they should never exceed 600 pixels in width. You can use image styles to enforce these types of behaviors.

To access the images styles page, click the Image styles link in the Media section of the Configuration Manager. The image styles page appears, as shown in Figure 12.5.

As you can see in Figure 12.5, the system comes with three image styles already defined:

- **Thumbnail:** This style automatically scales images to 100 pixels in width, while preserving the image dimension ratios.
- **Medium:** This style automatically scales images to 220 pixels in width, while preserving the image dimension ratios.
- **Large:** This style automatically scales images to 480 pixels in width, while preserving the image dimension ratios.

FIGURE 12.5

The Image styles screen shows a list of existing styles and links for editing or creating styles.

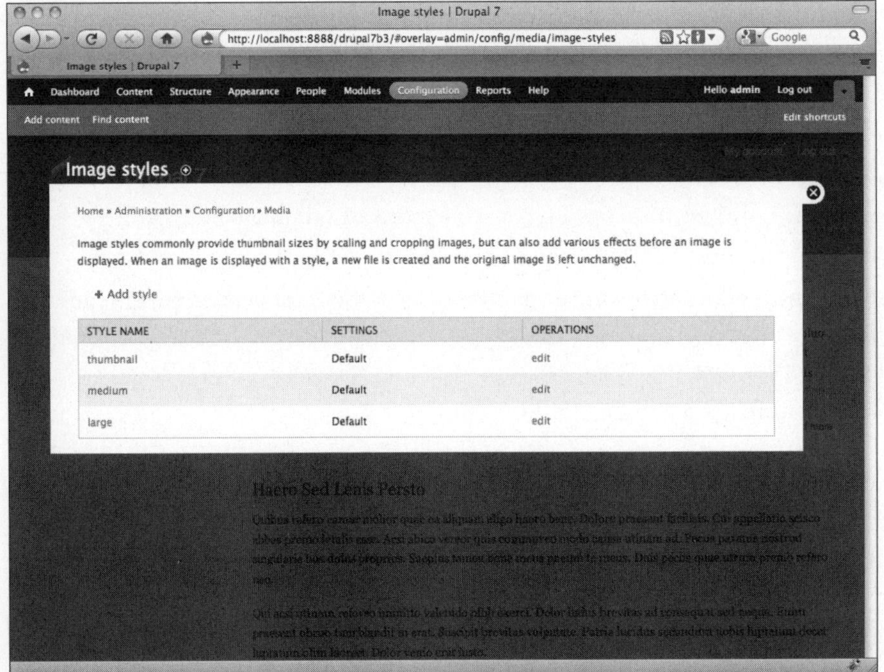

Note

Image styles are new in Drupal 7. This functionality is the result of integration work, bringing the old Image Cache module into the Drupal 7 core. ■

Image styles appear as options in various places in your system. For example, you see them in the User Manager settings; you can specify an image style as a preset influencing how user profile photos are presented.

If you are not happy with the default image styles, you can either edit an existing style or add a new one. To create a new image style, follow these steps:

1. **Log into your site as an administrator.**

   The Management menu appears at the top of the page.

2. **Select the Configuration option from the Management menu.**

   The Configuration page loads in your browser.

3. **Locate the Media section, and click the Image styles link.**

   The Image styles screen loads in your browser, as shown in Figure 12.6.

4. **Click the Add style link above the list of current styles.**

The Add style page loads in your browser, prompting you for the name of the new style.

5. **Enter** black-and-white **into the Style name text box, and click the Create new style button.**

   If the operation is successful, a success message displays and the style editing screen displays.

6. **Locate the Effect list in the lower part of the page, select the Desaturate effect in the list, and click the Add button to add this image effect to the current style.**

   If the operation is successful, a success message displays at the top of the page and you see the effect applied to the image on the right in the Preview area.

7. **You are finished editing the image style effects now, so locate and click the Update style button at the bottom of the page.**

   If the operation is successful, a success message displays at the top of the page and the new style is ready for use.

FIGURE 12.6

The Image style editing screen shows the preview images and the list of image style effects.

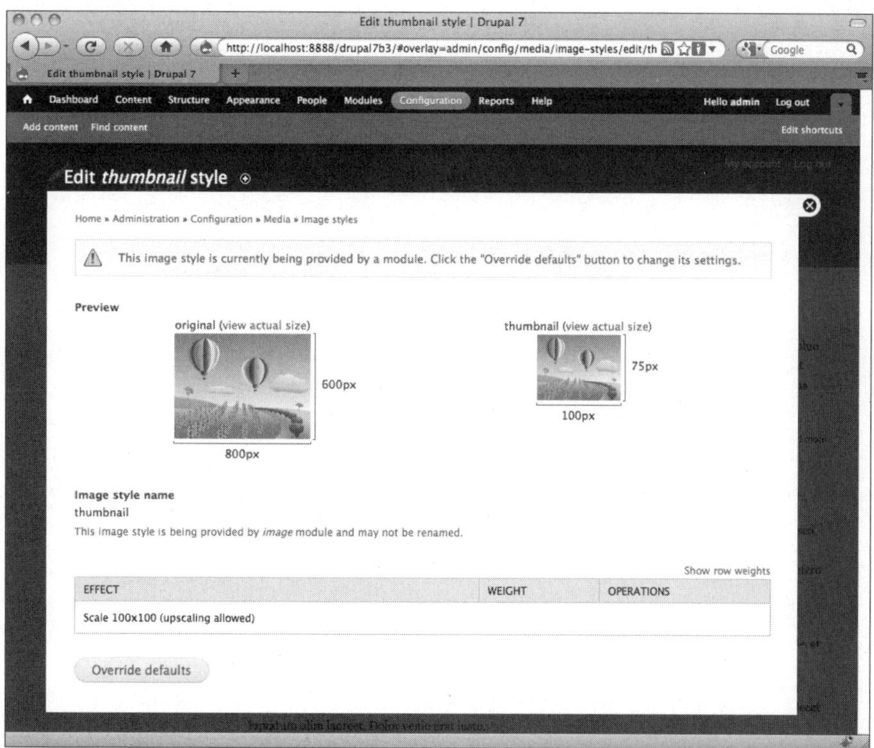

Using image styles

You can specify image styles to use for image rendering in at least two places: in the global user profile settings and in the display configuration for image data fields. Depending on which contributed modules you install, you also may find other areas where image styles can be used.

Applying image styles to user profile pictures

Follow these steps to modify the image style for use with user profile pictures:

1. **Log into your site as an administrator.**

   The Management menu appears at the top of the page.
2. **Select the Configuration option from the Management menu.**

   The Configuration page loads in your browser.
3. **Locate the People section in the page, and click the Account settings link.**

   The Account settings page loads in your browser.
4. **Scroll down the page, locate the Personalization section, and select an image style from the Picture display style pop-list.**
5. **Scroll to the bottom of the page, and click the Save configuration button.**

   If the operation is successful, a success message displays at the top of the page and the new style has been associated with all user profile pictures.

Cross-Reference

See Chapter 25 for a detailed look at managing and customizing user profiles. ■

Applying image styles to content fields

Each image field has two places where you can apply an image style. The first is for use during content authoring process; by default, a thumbnail is displayed during authoring. You set this style during the process of creating or editing a new image field. The second is for use during the display or publishing of the published content item.

Cross-Reference

See Chapter 10 for step-by-step content type recipes, including guidance on adding new fields to existing content types. ■

You make changes to an image field's display configuration in the Content type management screens found under the Structure admin area, as shown in Figure 12.7.

FIGURE 12.7

The Content type management screen for the Article content type shows the Manage Display tab in an active state.

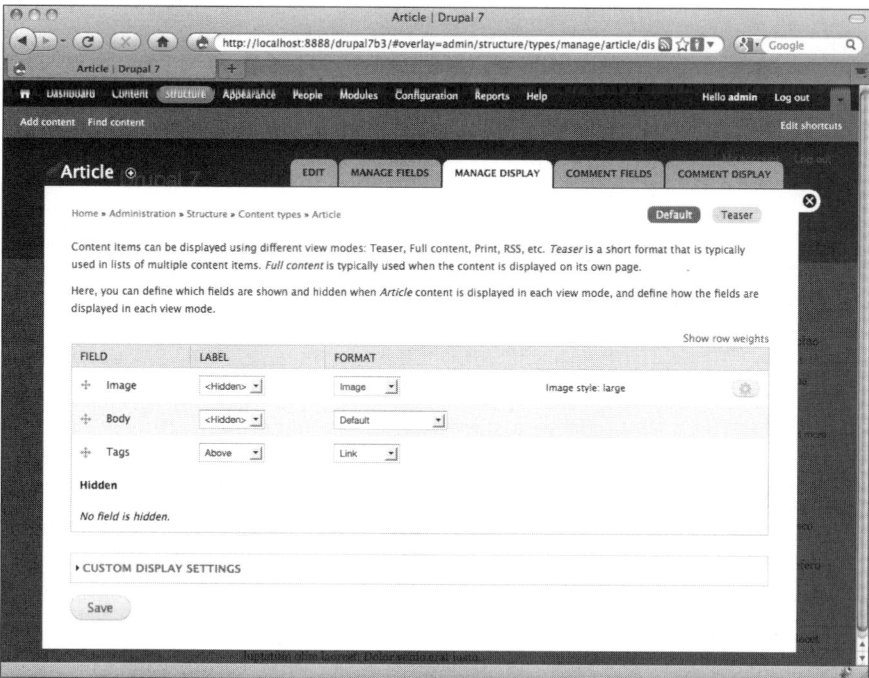

When you add a new image field to a content type, the system does not apply an image style for display purposes; instead, the original image is displayed by default. If this is not desirable, you can assign an image style of your choosing by following these steps:

1. **Log into your site as an administrator.**

   The Management menu appears at the top of the page.

2. **Select the Structure option from the Management menu.**

   The Structure page loads in your browser.

3. **Click the Content types link.**

   The list of content types loads in your browser.

4. **Click the Manage Display link in the Operations column next to the Article content type, for example.**

   The Manage Display tab for the Article content type is displayed (refer to Figure 12.7).

5. **If you previously added an image data field to this content type, you should have a Leader Image field. In the Format column for this field, click the settings button.**

   The Format settings page appears, showing the Image style list and the Link image to list.

6. **Select the "black-and-white" image style in the list (the style we created earlier in this chapter), and then click the Update button.**

   The Format settings page closes, and the image style you selected is listed in the Format column of your image field's row.

7. **Now click to expand the Custom display settings section of the page, and select which content views you want to apply this style to.**

   In this case, let's say I've decided that in all cases my images will be displayed as black and white. So select the check box next to each of the listed view modes.

Note

In the Manage display tab, you have the ability to define custom display configurations for each viewing mode. Each available viewing mode is represented in the secondary tab set, typically containing the Default, Full content, Teaser, RSS, Search index, and Search result tabs. ■

8. **Scroll to the bottom of the page, and click the Save button.**

   If the operation is successful, a success message displays at the top of the page and your display configuration is now active for the image field in question.

Working with Other Media

Modern Web sites often combine text, image, video, and audio files to deliver a broad multimedia experience. News sites offer an especially rich experience, often combining staggering amounts of video, podcasts, and live streaming with more classical text content. Drupal's native capabilities can help you deliver rich media experiences, and a combination of third-party services and contributed modules can take you even further.

Adding files to content

In some cases, you may want to enrich your content by adding one or more file storage fields. For example, you may need to attach PDF, ODF, audio, or video files to a content item; in some cases, this content may even be the primary data for a given content type.

Now that Drupal provides native content type extensibility, this kind of requirement is easy for you to meet. You simply create or modify a content type, as discussed in Chapter 10, defining one or more new fields of type File.

Tip

Keep in mind that Drupal can store uploaded files either in a public location or in a secure private location. Secure file storage places a much higher load on your server than public storage does. So use this option only if you absolutely must. ■

Cross-Reference

For details on configuring public and private file storage locations, see Chapter 4. For instructions and examples of creating or customizing Drupal content types, refer to Chapter 10. ■

Embedding remote media

Using Drupal, you can easily publish remotely managed media (such as audio, video, or images) hosted by services like YouTube, DailyMotion, Flickr, or many others. If you are comfortable working with HTML, this is typically not a major hurdle in your life as a publisher.

To include remote media in your content, you simply investigate the recommended embedding technique for the service in question, copy and paste or construct the HTML snippet required, and then place this snippet within the HTML you are publishing. It's as simple as that.

Tip

If you are supporting authors who are not comfortable working with HTML, yet must be empowered to embed remote media, then you should explore the available WYSIWYG tools that can help in this area. For example, your WYSIWYG editor of choice may have a toolbar function or plugin that can facilitate embedding remote content. Alternatively, you may be able to find contributed Drupal modules that make working with remote media much simpler than the raw HTML approach. Also, you can always create your own WYSIWYG editor plugin that is specifically tailored to your authors' needs. Don't overlook possible community resources though; this is one of Drupal's real strengths. Chances are good that if you have the need today, someone else has had the need as well. ■

In Figure 12.8, you see an example of embedding a YouTube video directly into the HTML content of a Drupal article. Note that many of the WYSIWYG editors have a toolbar item that allows authors to view and modify the HTML source.

Tip

To support embedding HTML snippets, you should ensure that this item is enabled in the Wysiwyg profile in question and that the appropriate HTML tags, such as the `<object>` tag, are allowed by the text input format used by the authors. ■

FIGURE 12.8

Embedding a YouTube video directly into the HTML content of a Drupal article

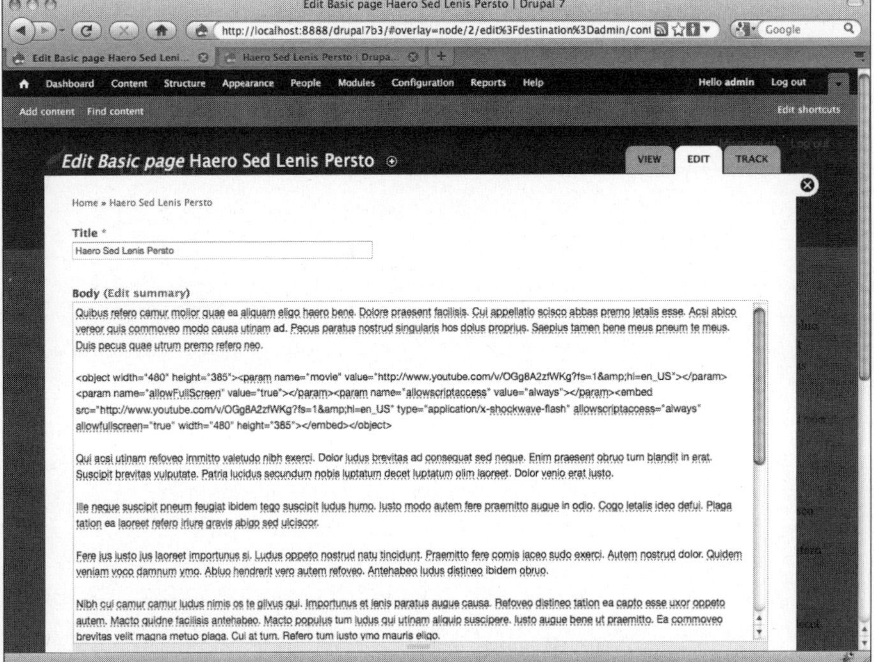

Exploring contributed modules

The amazing range of modules contributed by the community members is one of the Drupal project's outstanding strengths. You and your authors stand to benefit from the years of problem solving and innovation that went before you.

Don't overlook the contributed module resources when working with multimedia. These examples might make your life easier:

- **Video:** This contributed module enables authors to upload a number of video formats, optionally transcode video into Flash Video (FLV) format, create thumbnails of videos, and so on. This module can play an important role for video-centric Web sites.
- **Video Filter:** This contributed module simplifies the syntax for embedding remotely hosted videos by providing a simplified video tag (for example, `[video: http://www.youtube.com/watch?v=OGg8A2zfWKg]`). Your authors still need to insert text manually into the text entry fields, but with the simplified syntax, the opportunity for human error is greatly reduced and authors no longer need to understand any HTML. Note that this filter can be used in rich text input fields, but it does have the potential for conflicts with other filters. You may need to experiment a bit with how this filter can best work in your environment.

- **Styles + Media:** The contributed Styles module provides an API for formatting content and is a dependency for the Media module. The contributed Media module is an ambitious project (still in progress for Drupal 7 at the time of writing) that greatly extends Drupal's image, video, and audio management capabilities. After this module stabilizes for the version 7 release, I encourage you to explore its usefulness in your environment.
- **Insert:** This contributed module adds formatting and style tools when inserting images into text areas. As of the writing of this book, the module was still under development, so I could not perform any detailed testing. However, you may want to check on the current status and investigate whether this module is useful in your environment.

Using WYSIWYG Editors

WYSIWYG (What-you-see-is-what-you-get) editors, also called rich text editors, give Drupal authors a simple, non-technical means of authoring rich Web content. The idea is that WYSIWYG editors replicate the Microsoft Word editing experience many of us are accustomed to, removing the requirement that your authors understand HTML markup tags.

The standard Drupal installation does not come with a rich text editor. However, you can quickly add one or more third-party editors to your system and configure them precisely for your authors' needs. In this section, I explain how to quickly set up and customize rich text authoring.

Note

You will find no shortage of choice when it comes to third-party editing tools. The pluses and minuses of each editor are beyond the scope of this chapter, but for consistency I use a popular editor called TinyMCE for all examples. ■

Adding a WYSIWYG editor

You may find it strange that Drupal does not come with a rich text editor "out of the box." However, after you understand the breadth of editor choices available to you and the range of customizations you can make, it's clear that this approach has its benefits.

Instead of deciding which editor was best for you, the Drupal team decided in favor of empowering you to choose which editor might work best for each authoring situation. A contributed module called *WYSIWYG* provides a framework for detecting and interfacing to editor libraries that you download and install.

Tip

You should regularly check for updates to your third-party editing libraries. These updates can be important both from a security perspective and to ensure that you are maintaining support with the latest Web browser releases. ■

You begin the WYSIWYG configuration process by installing and enabling the WYSIWYG module via your normal procedures. You can find the module at `http://drupal.org/project/wysiwyg`. After the module is installed, you will notice that the admin's Modules page contains a new section called User Interface. This is where you can enable or disable the module. You can access the module configuration either via the Modules page or via the Configuration area of the admin system.

After you have enabled the WYSIWYG module, follow these steps to add an editor library to your system (in my case, the TinyMCE editor):

1. **Log into your site as an administrator.**

   The login landing page loads in your browser.
2. **Select the Configuration option from the main admin menu.**

   The Configuration page loads in your browser.
3. **Locate the Content Authoring section in this page, and click the sub-item called Wysiwyg profiles.**

   The WYSIWYG module's configuration page loads in your browser with the Installation Instructions section expanded.
4. **Scroll down the page until you see the TinyMCE section. Click to download the editor, and follow the instructions visible in the admin screen to place the editor library in your file system.**

Tip

You install each third-party editor by placing the package files under the following directory `[DRUPAL INSTALL]/sites/all/libraries`. For example, if you install the TinyMCE editor, you place the directory structure here: `[DRUPAL INSTALL]/sites/all/libraries/tinymce`. Make sure you do not duplicate the `tinymce` directory—a common mistake—because Drupal will fail to detect the editor in this case. ■

5. **After you have installed the TinyMCE library as specified, refresh the Wysiwyg profiles screen.**

   If the editor has been successfully installed, you see the Wysiwyg profiles grid displayed at the top of the page, as shown in Figure 12.9.

After the WYSIWYG module is enabled and you have at least one editor library installed, you can create editor profiles for any of your configured text formats.

Note

See earlier in this chapter for an introduction to Drupal text formats and instructions for customizing your system's formats. ■

FIGURE 12.9

The Wysiwyg profiles page displays the profiles grid.

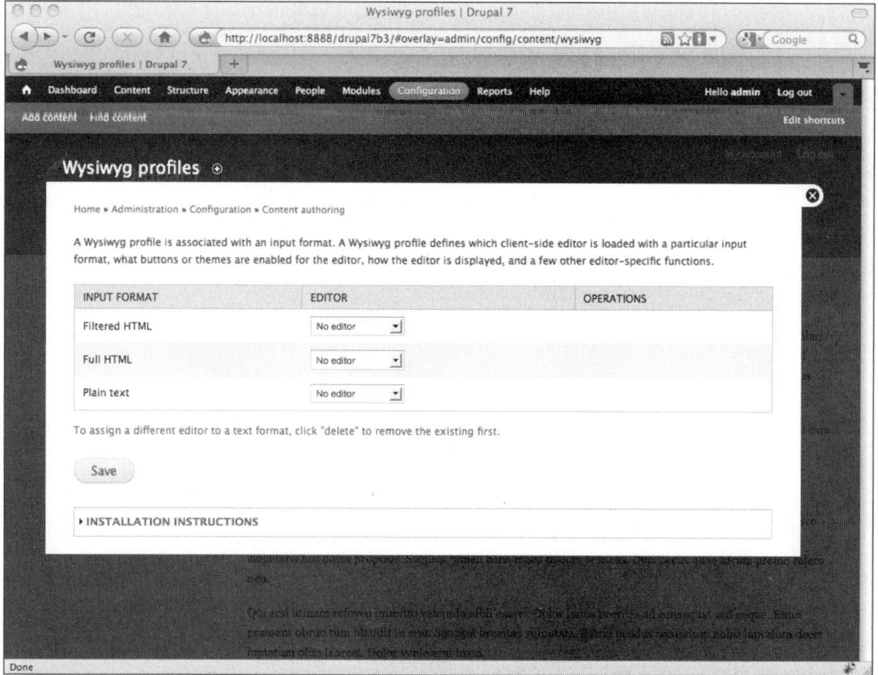

Creating Wysiwyg profiles

Wysiwyg profiles are a function of the WYSIWYG module, and they give you granular control over the text content authoring experience. Each profile is associated with an input format—also referred to as a text format—as you can see in Figure 12.10.

Tip

Remember that you control the right to use a given input format by modifying the permissions given to each of Drupal's security roles. Wysiwyg profiles are tied to input formats, so they comprise a part of your security policy. ■

After you have installed and enabled the WYSIWYG module and installed one or more editor libraries (as described earlier in this chapter), you are ready to create a profile. Select the TinyMCE editor for the Filtered HTML input format, and then click the Save button at the bottom of the profiles screen. Now click the Edit link in the operations column of the Filtered HTML row to view the TinyMCE profile for the Filtered HTML input format.

FIGURE 12.10

The Wysiwyg profiles screen shows editors associated with input formats.

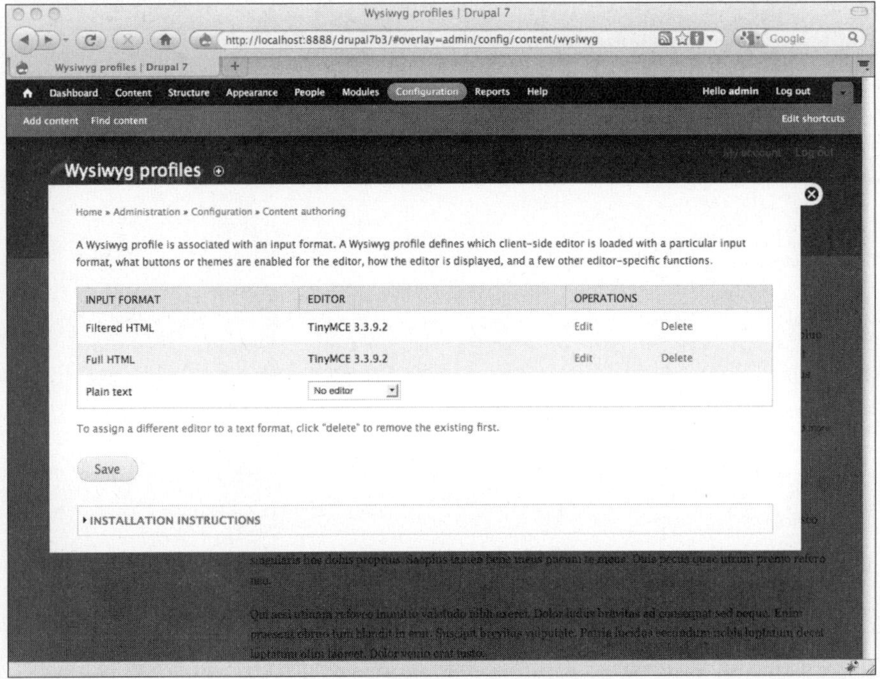

The profile screen has five sections, shown in Figure 12.11:

- **Basic Setup:** This section controls the general behavior of the editor.
  - **Enabled by default:** If checked, authors see the editor by default.
  - **Allow users to choose default:** If checked, authors can control the default editor state (enabled or disabled) via their user profiles.
  - **Show enable/disable rich text toggle link:** If checked, authors can disable the rich text editor in the authoring screen.
  - **Language:** You select the editor's default interface language here.
- **Buttons and Plugins:** This section gives you fine-grained control over exactly which formatting and behavior buttons are enabled in the rich text editor's interface.

Tip

You should review the Buttons and Plugins section carefully, ensuring that the enabled functionality is in alignment with the HTML tags allowed by the text format this profile is connected to. Refer to the "Creating and customizing text formats" section of this chapter if you need further clarification on this point. Additionally, if you enable the Fullscreen (authoring) button, you should check to see if this works properly with Drupal's overlay. If not, you may need to restrict author access to the admin overlay. You can do this via Drupal's permissions settings. ■

- **Editor Appearance:** This section allows you to customize the presentation organization of the editor's toolbar and content zone.
  - **Toolbar location:** This list lets you control the positioning of the editor's toolbar. You can select to place it either above or below the text input area; above is the default option.
  - **Button alignment:** You control alignment of the editing buttons—left, right, or centered on the toolbar—with this list of options. The default is to left-align them in the toolbar, but if you are supporting right-to-left languages, you may want to align the buttons to the right in certain profiles.
  - **Path location:** This setting lets you control the position of a second user interface element called the Path. This item displays the hierarchy of HTML tags for your current cursor position. It is optional, in that you can choose not to display it by selecting the `hide` option. If you want to display this information, it's probably a good idea to place it in the opposite position as the toolbar.
  - **Enable resize button:** If enabled and you have the Path location displayed, authors can resize the text input area for this profile. Generally, it's a good idea to give this ability to your authors, because it gives them more control over the editing experience. Additionally, they probably will find the resizing experience most intuitive if you place the Path location on the bottom of the input area.

FIGURE 12.11

The Wysiwyg profile editing screen shows the five configuration sections.

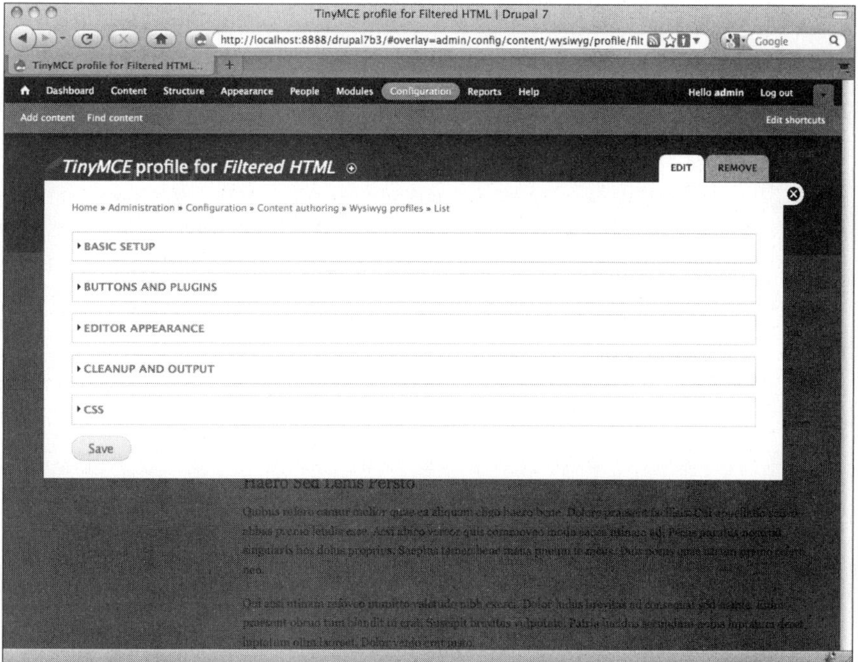

- **Cleanup and Output:** You control the automated text content output options in this section.
  - **Verify HTML:** Enabled by default, this behavior involves inspecting the submitted content and stripping out inappropriate HTML tags.
  - **Preformatted:** Disabled by default, this option causes all white spacing in the submitted content to be preserved. If you are familiar with the HTML `<pre>` tag, then you understand that this configuration results in the same behavior as wrapping the content in a `<pre>` tag.
  - **Convert <font> tags to styles:** Enabled by default, this setting tells Drupal to convert any `<font>` tags found in the content into inline CSS styles. You probably want to keep this enabled because it likely results in cleaner and more concise HTML output.
  - **Remove line breaks:** Enabled by default, this option strips out most of the line breaks in the submitted content. You probably want to keep this enabled, because it can result in more concise HTML output. However, if you suspect that this filter is interacting and causing problems with other filters, you can try disabling it.
  - **Apply source formatting:** Disabled by default, this filter reformats the published HTML such that the hierarchy of HTML elements is visually apparent. You probably do not want to enable this option, unless it somehow becomes useful in a debugging scenario.
  - **Force cleanup on standard paste:** Disabled by default, this option changes the standard pasting behavior such that the content being pasted is automatically cleaned up, as if you were using the "Paste from Word" functionality. You may need to experiment with this item to see if it serves you and/or your authors well.
- **CSS:** You control the editor's Cascading Style Sheet (CSS) and some related presentation behaviors in this section.
  - **Block formats:** In this text box, you list the HTML tags that will appear in the editor's HTML Block Formats list. This list is one of the items you can enable or disable in the Buttons and Plugins section of the Wysiwyg profile, as covered previously. You can adjust this list to place additional controls on the authoring experience. For example, you may want to remove the h5 and h6 headings, to force authors to work within the bounds of h2, h3, and h4 headings.

Note

You can enter any value into the Block Formats list, but Drupal limits the values to a list of valid HTML block tags. The possible values are listed in the Drupal admin interface. ■

- **Editor CSS:** You control the source of the CSS styles used in the editor's input area with this setting. The default value, and probably the best practice, is to use the CSS styles that come from your site's theme. You can alternatively select the Define CSS option to define your own CSS or use the Editor Default option to rely on the editor's default CSS styles. If you define your own CSS for the editor, you must specify a path to the CSS file in the following setting's text box.
- **CSS Path:** If you select the Define CSS option for the Editor CSS setting, you must specify a path to the setting here. This value can be a comma-delimited list and can make use of tokens, as specified in the setting's help text.
- **CSS classes:** You can optionally define CSS style names here, using the format specified in the item's help text. For example, suppose you have a CSS style defined in your theme like this: `.bold-text { font-weight: bold; }`. You could place a style name here as follows: `Bold=bold-text`. If you have enabled the Font style item in the Buttons and Plugins section, you now see your custom defined style names in that list.

Follow these steps to modify a Wysiwyg profile:

1. **Log into your site as an administrator.**

   The login landing page loads in your browser.
2. **Select the Configuration option from the main admin menu.**

   The Configuration page loads in your browser.
3. **Locate the Content Authoring section in this page, and click the sub-item called Wysiwyg profiles.**

   The WYSIWYG module's configuration page loads in your browser.
4. **If you haven't already done so, select the TinyMCE editor for the Filtered HTML text format and then click the Save button at the bottom of the screen.**
5. **After an editor has been assigned to the Filtered HTML format, you can click the edit link in the Operations column for that format's row.**

   The Wysiwyg profile configuration screen loads in your browser, and you can now expand each section and make your desired changes.
6. **After your desired changes have been made, scroll to the bottom of the screen and click the Save button.**

   If your changes have been saved, a success message is visible at the top of the screen and the modified profile behavior is in effect for the system.

You can now create, modify, and delete Wysiwyg profiles from your system. Remember that you must define additional text formats, as described earlier in this chapter, if you want to create more than the standard two or three profiles.

Summary

This chapter provided instructions and general advice for working with both text and multimedia content inside Drupal. The following points were covered:

- Key concepts and configurations for Drupal text content
- Working with images, including how to automatically reformat image content on the fly
- Tips for managing and publishing multimedia content
- Detailed instructions for installing and configuring WYSIWYG editors, including how to create customized editor profiles for each text input format

CHAPTER

13

Managing the Front Page of Your Site

IN THIS CHAPTER

Controlling the front-page layout

Using a distinct template for the front page

Publishing content on the front page

Publishing module output on the front page

Publishing blocks on the front page

You can take control of your Web site's front page by utilizing a combination of configurations, preferences, contributed modules, and template modifications. Drupal's flexibility really shines in this area, but related complexities can present challenges.

In this chapter, I review a number of ways that you can influence the look and feel of your front page, and I review a number of techniques for creating customized content views.

Controlling the Front-Page Layout

The front page of your site can serve many needs and may even call upon substitutes to fill in for special purposes. Drupal's default front page contains a stream of recently published content items organized in reverse chronological order. This approach is useful for blogs, but may not suit your specific needs.

Drupal's default themes utilize the same layout for the front page as they do for all other pages. In the next section, I discuss how you can create a distinct template for the front page of your site, but there are less aggressive means to placing unique content arrangements on your site's front page. For example, using Drupal's Blocks Manager tool, you can explicitly show or hide content blocks on your front page.

Cross-Reference

See Chapter 7 to explore the Blocks Manager further and for step-by-step guidance on controlling block behavior. ■

The Blocks Manager is just one way to influence the presentation of your front page. You have many tools at your disposal; these are just a few example scenarios:

- **Configure a specific page as the front page:** Using the system configuration settings, you can assign a specific content path to serve as your front page. For example, if you want to create a full text front page, you can turn off all sidebar blocks on the front page and then set the front page path to the Drupal page of your choice.

  You set the front page path in the Configuration section of the admin tools. Click the Site Information item in that page, and set the Default front page value in that screen.
- **Use the Views module to create a custom front page:** By leveraging the contributed Views module, you can construct a customized mix of content items, filtered and sorted as you please. You can then save this *view* as a page with a unique path and assign this path as the default front page. You can further refine this page by turning on or off various content blocks for this path.
- **Use the Panels module to create a custom front page:** The contributed Panels module also allows you to create custom content displays and then use these as your front page. For more advanced customizations, you can combine Panels and Views, thus taking advantage of the strengths of both tools.

Cross-Reference

See Chapter 28 for a broad discussion of the Views and Panels modules, including step-by-step tutorials for creating views. ■

- **Create purpose-specific landing pages:** Sometimes you don't want your default front page to be the entry point for every visitor. This situation might arise in the context of an advertising campaign, a poll, a survey, or perhaps it might be part of your personalization strategy. In this case, you can create your own purpose-specific page and direct users there via the URL or change your site's default page path to temporarily point to this page.

Note

To create form-based landing pages, you can use the core Contact module, customizing the page around the contact form, or you can use a contributed module, like Webform, to construct a more elaborate experience. ■

Using a Distinct Template for the Front Page

Using Drupal's powerful *template suggestions* functionality, you can create a distinct user interface template that applies only to the front page of your site. We discuss template suggestions in greater detail in Chapter 27, so I won't spend much time on them here, but a brief discussion is in order.

Template suggestions allow you to override a theme's or the system's default layout and behavior for a particular type of content or for a particular part of your site, such as the front page.

Tip

When testing theme changes or template suggestions, you should disable Drupal's performance enhancement features such as page caching. This is quickly done via the Performance settings screen accessed via the Development subsection of the admin system's Configuration area. Or you can manually clear the caches from the Performance settings screen, just to be sure you are seeing your latest changes in the rendered site. ■

In brief, a suggestion—which is really a mandate—is a file that you place into a theme's template directory. These files follow a naming convention that tells the system when to use them in favor of the default template. In our case, you create a file named `page--front.tpl.php` and place it in the desired theme's template directory.

Our best practices approach for theme modifications dictates that you never change core files, including core theme files. In keeping with this approach, I create a new theme called *mybartik* and place the `page--front.tpl.php` file into the `[Drupal Install Root]/sites/all/themes/mybartik/templates/` directory, as shown in Figure 13.1.

Note

Creating a new theme by copying and pasting the original theme directory into a new directory and renaming the folder is just step one of the process. You also need to rename the `[theme name].info` file and make changes in the `template.php` file, renaming all the function names to match the theme's folder name. Instead of creating an entirely new theme during this process, you can elect to sub-theme an existing theme. The process is almost the same, but it has some advantages: A sub-theme inherits resources from the original theme. This means your sub-theme can automatically inherit any bug fixes or enhancements made in the original theme—a significant maintenance and security consideration. Look at Chapter 27 for details on this process and for additional instructions for modifying and managing themes. ■

FIGURE 13.1

The Drupal 7 directory structure shows the `page--front.tpl.php` template suggestion file located in the custom *My Bartik* theme's template directory.

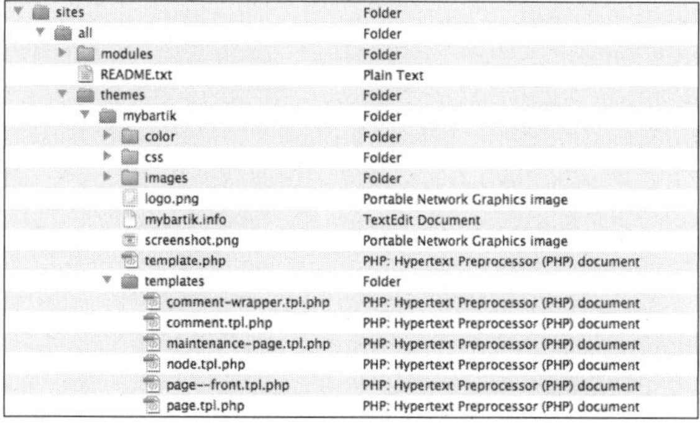

After you grasp the idea of how Drupal's template suggestion mechanism works, you must then tackle the problem of what exactly a suggestion file contains. That question, of course, varies broadly, but for starters, you can just copy the contents of the `page.tpl.php` file and work from there.

For an easy dipping of your toes in the water, let's copy and paste the `page.tpl.php` file's content into your new suggestion file. Then open the suggestion file and on line number 161, just above the code `<?php if ($messages): ?>`, place this text:

```
<h3 align="center">Welcome to My Bartik's Custom Home Page.</h3>
```

Now save the `page--front.tpl.php` file, clear the system's cache, and refresh the front page. If all went well, you now see your custom welcome message. If you do not see the custom welcome message, verify that your new theme—in my case, the My Bartik theme—is set as the default theme.

Cross-Reference

See Chapter 27 for a focused discussion of Drupal's theme system and how to use template suggestions in a number of additional contexts. Chapter 27 also walks you through the process of creating your own themes, using a starter kit like the one found in the popular Zen theme. ■

Publishing Content on the Front Page

You or your content authors can easily control whether a given content item is published to the front page of your site. Drupal's content authoring screen has a set of configuration and preferences tabs at the bottom of each page, including a setting for this specific purpose.

In the authoring screen, you find a Publishing options tab that contains a check box labeled Promoted to front page. If you check this box, by default your content is visible on the front page of your site, assuming your theming and other configurations support this default behavior.

Cross-Reference

See Chapter 10 for additional information about managing content and controlling the behavior of content items. ■

Figure 13.2 shows a content authoring screen with the Publishing options tab displayed.

FIGURE 13.2

The content authoring screen for the article content type displays the Publishing options tab.

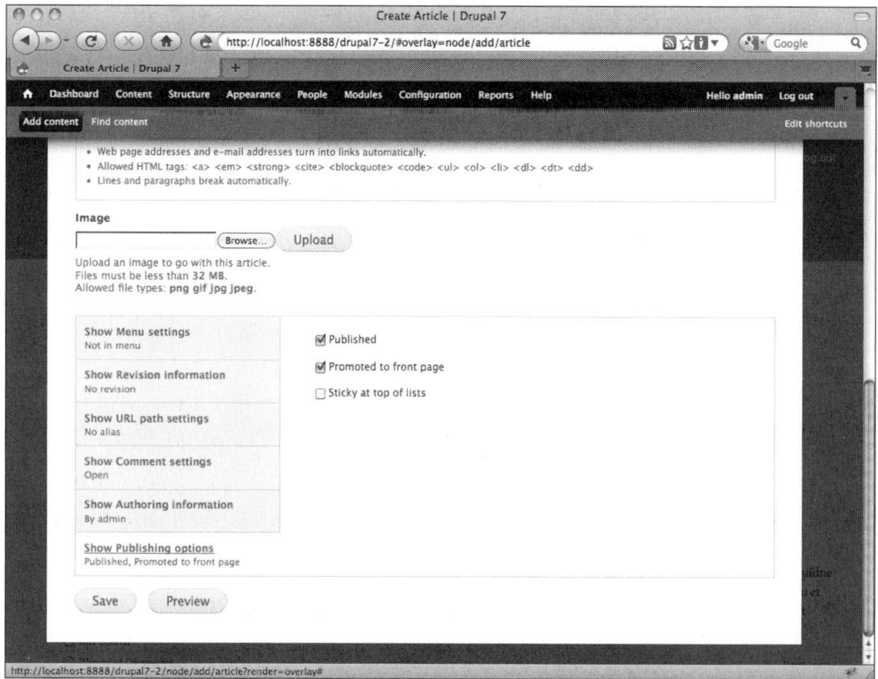

Publishing Module Output on the Front Page

By default, the core Drupal system publishes new node-based content items to the front page of your site, either when authors elect this behavior or when it is the default behavior for the content type in question. However, you can surface content on your site's front page from a number of other standard sources by using modules like Views to create new content blocks, by combining modules like Views and Panels, by writing custom PHP code, and so on.

In this section, I introduce a few of these scenarios as a means of whetting your appetite and explaining some options for publishing content to the front page of your Web site.

Publishing content from modules

When you enable components like the Poll, Blog, Aggregator, or Forum modules, your system begins to collect and manage content of a type specific to each module. However, not all these modules provide you with related blocks for publishing this content on the front of your site.

As with most things Drupal, you'll probably discover that when customizing your front page, you can solve each specific problem in several ways. Consider these few scenarios:

- **Poll module:** This module is an easy case. When you enable polls, a new block called *Most recent poll* is available in the Blocks Manager tool. You can quickly assign this block to a theme's region and then configure it to display on your front page. If you want to go beyond this level of display, you need to explore options such as using the Views module.

Cross-Reference

See Chapter 28 for a deep discussion of the Views module, including step-by-step tutorials for creating views and displays, and for customizing their behaviors. Chapter 7 is focused on the Blocks Manager and configuring block behavior. ■

- **Blog module:** Blog module content is node-based content as far as Drupal is concerned. Therefore, it has the same publishing options as discussed in the preceding section titled "Publishing Content on the Front Page." If you want to go beyond this level of control, then familiarizing yourself with the Views module is a good idea.

  For example, if you want to publish a list of the most recent comments for blog posts in the sidebar of your home page, you can use the Views module to define a view listing these items and then define a block display for this view. After you have the block display defined, you can use the Blocks Manager to place it in the sidebar and configure the block to show only on your home page.
- **Aggregator module:** This module is another relatively easy case. The aggregator pulls in syndicated content from sources that you specify and categorizes this content into zero, one, or more categories that you specify. When you create sources and categories, the module automatically defines blocks for these content groupings. You can then use the Blocks Manager to place these blocks into theme regions and configure the blocks to display in specific contexts, such as your site's front page.

Cross-Reference

See Chapter 18 for an overview of the Aggregator module, including details on using the Latest Items blocks that it provides. ■

For example, if you created an aggregator category called Sports News and then added an RSS source for this category (`http://feeds1.nytimes.com/nyt/rss/Sports`), you also find two corresponding blocks available for use in the Blocks Manager screen: one for the category and one for the individual feed.

Note

If the default blocks created by the Aggregator module do not meet your needs, you can create custom blocks with the Views module. To do so, select the view type Aggregator item when creating a new view. ■

- **Forum module:** Drupal's core Forum module is powerful in many ways, but it provides you with only two blocks for displaying its content in your site's front page (or any other pages outside of the forum area). One way you can expand on this limitation is to use the Views module to create a new block that renders, for example, the most discussed forum posts that were published today.

Cross-Reference

Chapter 20 covers the Forum module in detail. You can head over there to learn more about creating and administering forums. ■

Using the Views screens, you create a new node-based view and then filter the view such that it displays only items with a node type of *Forum topic* and that were posted today. Then you sort this view by the number of comments and finally create a corresponding block display. You can then add this block to the desired page region and configure it to render on the front page.

Figure 13.3 shows the Views edit screen for a view called `hot_topics_today`. In this screen, you can see the related default values for this view.

The above scenarios provide you with a few ideas for overcoming some typical content presentation hurdles. How you handle each particular presentation challenge differs. The important thing is to develop your knowledge of the available tools and techniques and then choose the path that best fits your functional needs while balancing the goals of being high performance, easy to understand, and easy to maintain.

Publishing content from custom blocks

As I discussed in the preceding section, Drupal's Blocks Manager enables you to place any existing blocks on the front page of your site. The enabled modules automatically create many of Drupal's blocks. Beyond this you are free to extend the selection by authoring your own blocks in the Blocks Manager screens or by using modules like Views to create custom blocks.

Custom blocks behave just like any other blocks and support all the basic behavior configuration settings. You can manage these blocks in exactly the same way as the ones derived from modules.

Cross-Reference

See Chapter 7 to explore the Blocks Manager further and for details on customizing block rendering behavior. ■

FIGURE 13.3

The Views editing screen shows a block display for forum posts.

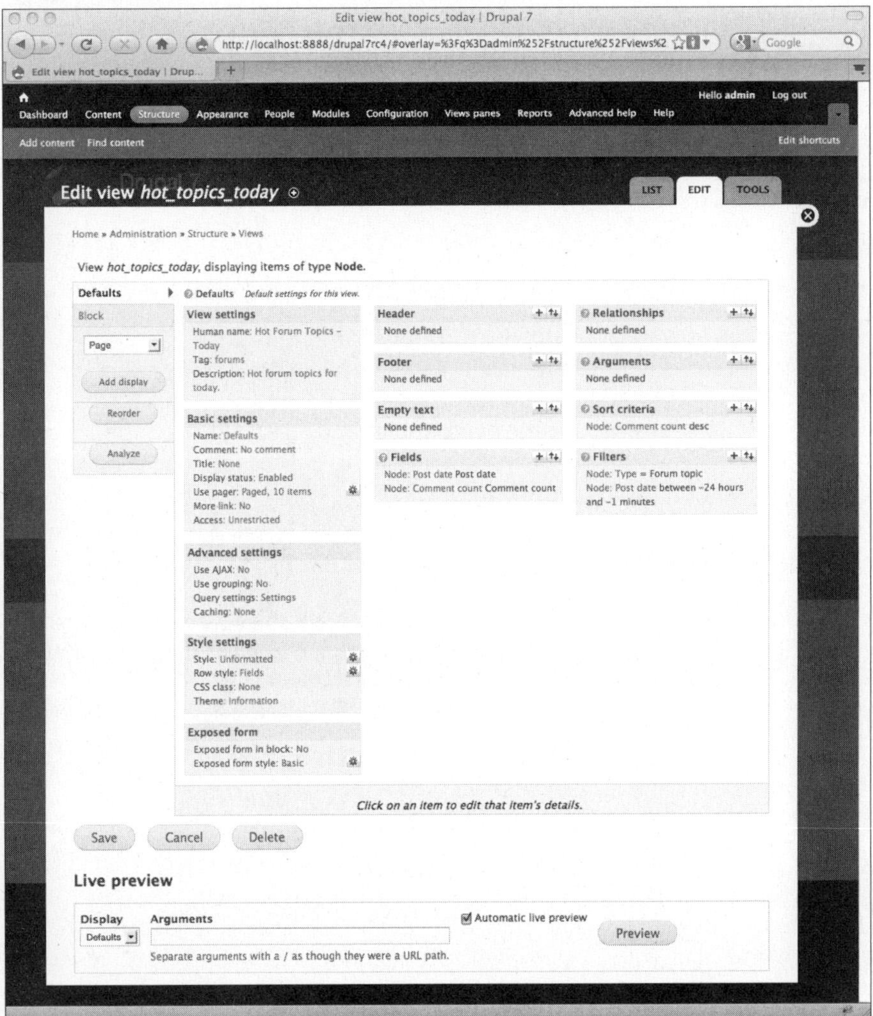

Publishing Blocks on the Front Page

Blocks are distinct components of functionality or content that you can place into named regions of your site's page structure. Regions are defined by each theme, and they vary from theme to theme. Blocks are defined by core or contributed modules, by you via the Blocks Manager tool (as shown in Figure 13.4), or by using tools such as those provided by the contributed Views module.

FIGURE 13.4

The Blocks Manager displays several regions with blocks assigned to them.

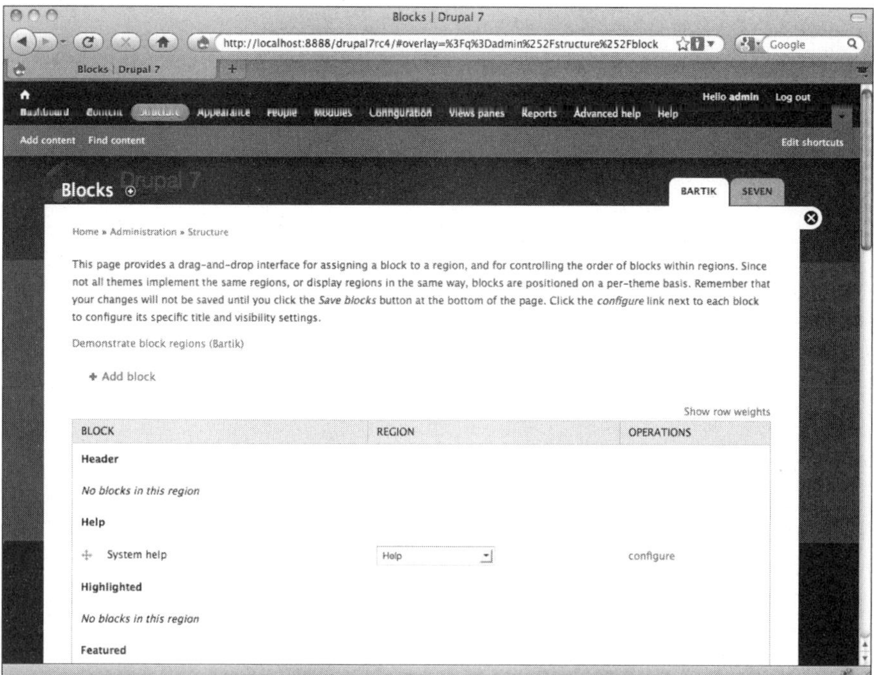

After you have enabled or created the blocks you want to display on your site's front page, you can use the Blocks Manager to configure these blocks such that they are published on the front page. In my example, I perform this exercise with a custom block I created, named Hot Forum Topics Today. However, you can perform this configuration with any available blocks.

Follow these steps to configure a block to display only on the front page:

1. **Log into your site as an administrator.**

   The login landing page loads in your browser.

2. **Select the Structure option from the main admin menu.**

   The Structure's section page loads in your browser.

3. **Locate the Blocks sub-item in the page, and click the link.**

   The Blocks Manager loads in your browser, including the list of the current theme's regions and the blocks assigned to each region.

4. **If the block you want to work with is not yet assigned to a region, scroll to the bottom of the page and select a region from the list next to the block.**

5. **After selecting a region, click the Save blocks button at the bottom of the page to save your changes.**
6. **After the page refreshes, locate your block again and click the configure link to the right of the block.**

   The block's configuration screen loads in your browser.
7. **Locate the Pages configuration tab near the bottom of the page, and click the radio button labeled Only the listed pages.**

   This restricts where the block is displayed.
8. **In the text box under the radio button, enter the text** <front>**.**

   This tells Drupal to display this block only on the front page of your site. You also can enter specific paths or multiple paths (one per line) if you desire.
9. **When you are finished making changes, scroll to the bottom of the page and click the Save block button.**

   If the operation is successful, a success message is visible at the top of the page and your changes are now active.

Cross-Reference

We cover the Blocks Manager in detail in Chapter 7, including how to create your own blocks and several other ways you can influence the behavior of blocks. ■

Summary

This chapter covered a broad range of methods to influence the look and feel and the content that appears on the front page of your Drupal 7 Web site. I discussed the following areas:

- How to control the layout of your site's front page
- How to create a custom template that is used only for the front page of your site
- How authors can explicitly publish content to the front page
- How to publish block and module content to the front page

CHAPTER 14

Employing Advanced Content Management Techniques

IN THIS CHAPTER

Creating content versions

Implementing workflows

Controlling comment spam

Creating content hierarchies

Syndicating your content

As your use of the Drupal CMS matures, you are likely to take on more sophisticated content management challenges. Drupal's dual strengths of platform centricity and a dynamic community offer you many ways to meet these new challenges.

In this chapter, I review some advanced content management scenarios and discuss different ways you can work through them.

Creating Content Versions

Drupal has the ability to create new versions of content—think of these as sequential snapshots of content items—each time you or another author make changes to the content. Depending on your operational practices and business requirements, this may or may not be deemed useful, but it is a powerful capability that you should consider as your editorial operations evolve.

Understanding the business drivers for content versions

You might find content versions helpful in the following cases:

- **Managing editorial crises:** There's nothing quite as stressful as realizing that your site has a gross factual or grammatical error published on the home page. Corrections are best done before the error is indexed by search engines or syndicated out to partners. In other words, in these scenarios time is often of the essence. When managing this kind of crisis, content versions might be your best friend, because they can provide you with a quick way to revert to a last known good copy of the content.

- **Training editorial staff:** If you have a growing editorial team that uses Drupal as a primary tool, then versions can serve as an important training resource. Aspiring team members can learn valuable lessons by reviewing the changes more senior editors have made to their work.

Tip

If you install and enable the contributed Diff module, you can provide your authors and editors with the ability to visually compare differences between content revisions. This module currently requires that users have the Administer content permission, which might be undesirable in your environment. But the permissions situation may change in the future, especially if you participate in the module's features discussion. ■

- **Browser blunder insurance:** No one is perfect, and neither are the tools we use. Maybe you closed the browser tab before saving your work, perhaps you pasted over the wrong paragraph, or maybe the computer crashed at an inopportune moment; regardless of who is to blame, browser blunders happen. One way to buy a bit of insurance here is to use content versions to incrementally protect a record of your work.

Tip

Another kind of browser blunder insurance comes in the form of the Autosave module. This module can be configured to automatically save snapshots of your content without disturbing your or your editors' thinking process. Unfortunately, at the time of this writing, this module was not yet available for Drupal 7. However, work on a Drupal 7 version was in process, so you should investigate (or contribute to the effort) if auto-saving is important to your team's editorial operations. ■

Configuring content versioning

Content versioning is a native feature that you can either configure at the content type level or leave content authors to take advantage of during the authoring process. In this section, I walk you through configuring the Article content type to always create a new revision snapshot when an article is changed.

Tip

Any user with the Administer content permission can elect to create a new content version during the process of authoring or editing a content item. Give out this permission with care though, because it is a powerful security right in the system. ■

Follow these steps to configure content versioning for the Article content type:

1. **Log into your site as an administrator.**

   The login landing page loads in your browser.

2. **Select the Structure option from the main admin menu.**

   The Structure's section page loads in your browser.

3. **Locate the Content type sub-item in the page, and click this link.**

   The Content type management screen loads in your browser, listing the system's current content types.

4. **Locate the Article content type in the list of content types, and click the edit link in this row's Operations column.**

   The content type configuration screen loads in your browser, as shown in Figure 14.1.

FIGURE 14.1

The content type editing screen for the Article content type

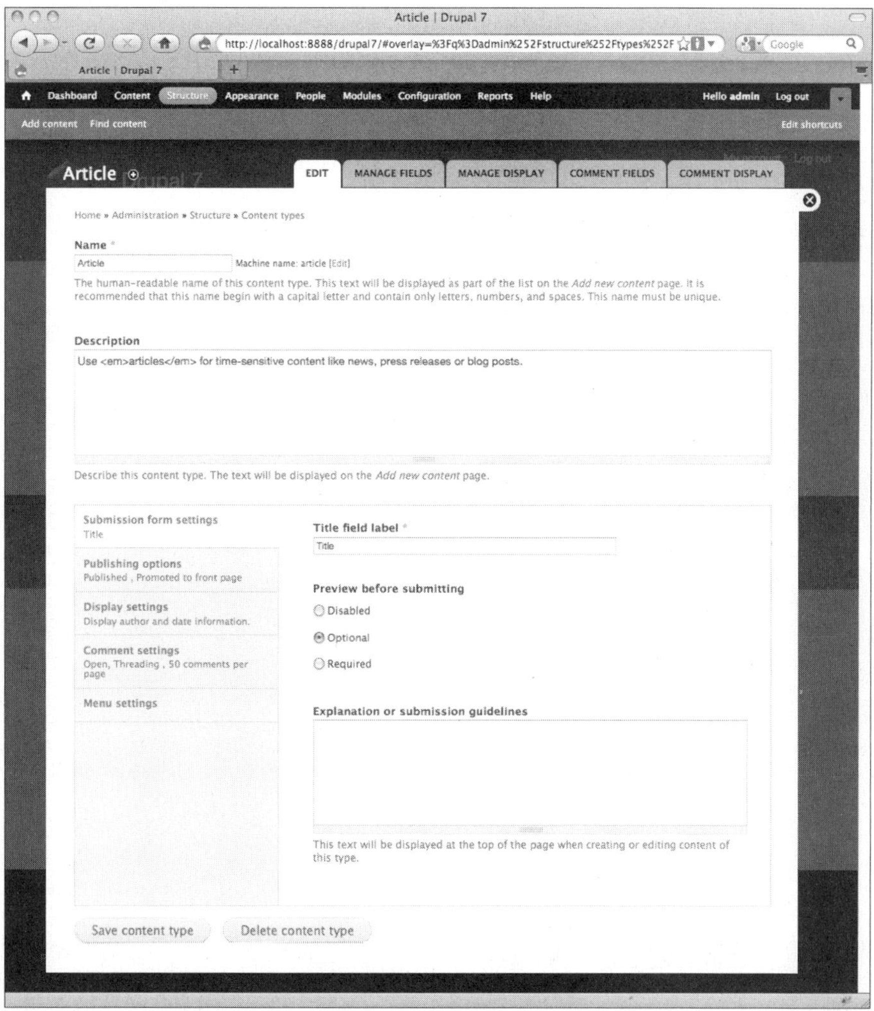

5. **Locate the tab set in the bottom of the configuration page, and click the Publishing options tab.**

   The publishing options settings are displayed in the page as shown in Figure 14.2.

FIGURE 14.2

The content type editing screen for the Article content type displaying the Publishing options tab

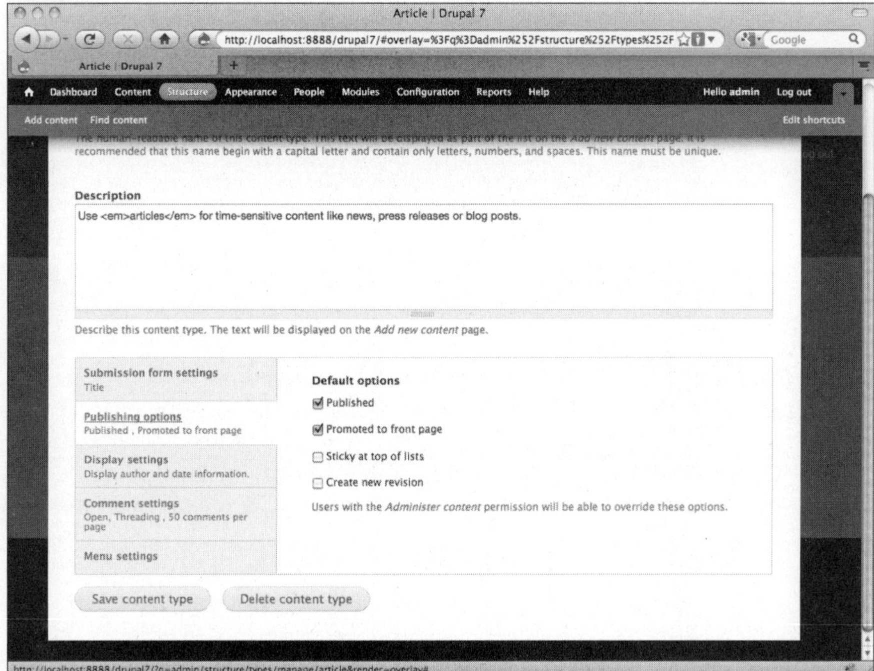

6. **Select the check box labeled Create new revision.**

   This tells Drupal to create a new version of the content item for every change made to it.

7. **Scroll to the bottom of the page, and click the Save content type button.**

   If the operation is successful, a success message is visible at the top of the page and your changes are now active.

Cross-Reference

See Chapter 10 for additional details on working with content types, including step-by-step tutorials for creating your own custom content types. Refer to Chapter 24 for an overview of Drupal's permissions and roles functionality. ■

Implementing Authoring Workflows

Drupal does not provide any core workflow features out of the box. Your default publishing controls are limited to the simple marking of content items as either published or unpublished.

This narrowness of functionality may surprise you, given that many organizations require at least some level of content review before making it public, but in Drupal's case the project team tends to leave this kind of functionality in the hands of the community; workflow has not yet been considered appropriate for inclusion in the product's core.

Fortunately, the community has historically stepped up to address the need for Drupal workflows. But as with many things that come from the community, you do not find a single path to the functionality goal; you must evaluate and select from multiple options. Unfortunately, as of the writing of this book, the most common Drupal 6 workflow tool—the Workflow module—was not available in any form for Drupal 7.

In this section, I look at some of the approaches to implementing workflows with the latest Drupal release.

Using Rules and Views for workflow

Historically, Drupal administrators have successfully used the contributed Rules module to implement workflows, but it requires some tinkering. You can, however, find a Rules tutorial to guide you through the setup of an Editorial workflow process at `http://drupal.org/node/550716`. At the time of this writing, the tutorial was written only for Drupal 6, but the principles can also be applied to Drupal 7; keep in mind that CCK functionality has largely been moved into the Drupal 7 core, and adjust your reading of the tutorial accordingly.

Note

You can use the Rules and Views modules to create flexible Drupal workflows, but as I note later in this chapter, more robust solutions are being developed. The Rules plus Views approach is the first available approach for creating Drupal 7 workflows, so early adopters of Drupal 7 are likely to explore this method first. ■

In the following recipe, I provide an overview of how you can use the Rules and Views modules to create a simple workflow process with three different work queues. This is one way to solve the problem. In the following sections, I look at two additional approaches.

Follow these steps to create a two-stage (authoring and editing) workflow process for the Article content type:

1. **Install and enable both the Rules and Views contributed modules, including all their dependencies.**
2. **Define two editorial roles for workflow purposes: Authors and Editors. Give the *Administer content* permission to the Editors role, but not to the Authors role. Give both roles adequate permissions to be able to access the admin screens, including the content creation form and the dashboard.**

3. **Add at least one system user to each role.**

Cross-Reference

See Chapter 24 for an overview of Drupal's permissions and roles functionality. ■

4. **In the content types area, edit the Article content type to add a new text field called Publish Status using a select list widget. Create the following values for this field: New, Ready for Editing, Needs Work, and Published.**
5. **Edit the article content type such that it is not automatically published.**

Cross-Reference

See Chapter 10 for instructions on working with content types, including step-by-step guidance on adding new fields to content types. ■

6. **Using the Views module, create new views that exclusively show Articles for each of the following Publish Status values: New, Ready for Editing, and Needs Work. Filter the New and Ready for Editing views, such that they show content created by the current user only.**
7. **Create Block displays for each of these views, and give them titles as follows: Your Drafts, Your Articles Needing Work, and Articles Ready for Editing. Add all three of these blocks to Drupal's management dashboard.**

Cross-Reference

Refer to Chapter 13 for step-by-step instructions on creating custom content blocks using the Views module. ■

8. **Customize the block display such that the Your Draft Articles and Your Articles Needing Work blocks are displayed only for the Authors role and the Articles Ready for Editing block is displayed only for the Editors role.**

Cross-Reference

Chapter 7 provides an introduction to the Drupal Blocks Manager tool and covers exactly how you control per-role behavior for individual blocks. ■

9. **Following the spirit of the Rules module's documentation (I linked to this previously), create a Before saving rule called Workflow – Publish Article.**

   This should act only on nodes of type Article. The action for this rule is to publish an article when the current user role is either Editors or Administrator and the Publish Status field value is set to Published.
10. **Create an inverse rule named Workflow – Unpublish Article for the same roles, such that an article is unpublished when its Publish Status field is set to a value other than Published.**

After you have implemented the above changes, your site's articles will follow a simple, sequential workflow process, passing from an author's work queue to an editor's work queue and finally to a published state. You can enhance this basic approach to include additional review stages and corresponding work queues. You also can create rules that display error or warning messages when users attempt to perform actions deemed illegal (warn authors who try to publish directly, for example).

Using Maestro for workflow

The Maestro module is a newcomer, developed exclusively for Drupal 7. At the time of writing this book, the module—though showing much promise—was not yet ready for full testing, so I can provide only a brief introduction to its functionality and leave you with inspiration to continue to explore.

Maestro is designed to be an extensible workflow engine that allows you to design a broad range of both sequential and parallel workflows. You use the workflow designer, pictured in Figure 14.3, to model the workflow. You then save the workflow model as a template. The workflow engine runs in the background, executing tasks as they accumulate in the queue. Workflow steps can generate custom notifications, and the system is designed to support escalations.

FIGURE 14.3

The Maestro workflow designer tool showing an example Article workflow process

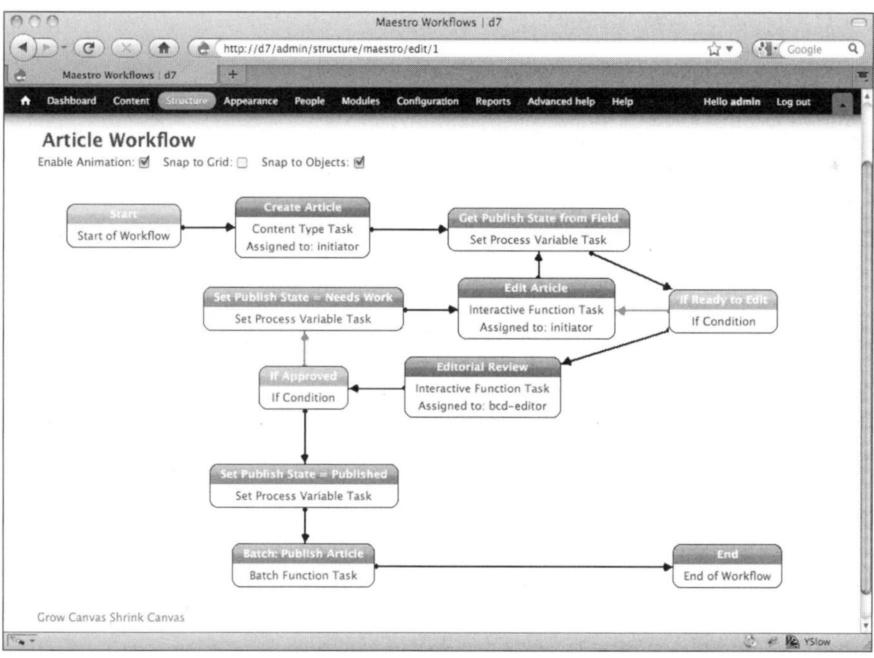

Maestro's visual workflow designer is an impressive and useful tool. It allows non-technical (but Maestro-familiar) users to design many different types of workflows. The module also brings some user-focused elements, including a list of pending tasks, called the Task Console, for those engaged in the business processes and administrative tools for tracing and monitoring workflows in progress. The module integrates with the Rules module and eventually will allow workflow steps to be assigned to roles (when I recently tested, I could assign steps only to individual users or the workflow initiator).

Maestro is a port of an existing and reportedly mature workflow product, previously named Nextflow. Given that it's a porting, rather than a write-from-scratch effort, I expect this project to move forward quickly. If workflows are an important part of your business requirements, then you should keep a close eye on the Maestro project at `http://drupal.org/project/maestro`.

Using the Workflow module

The contributed Workflow module is one of the most popular approaches to implementing workflow with previous versions of Drupal. However, this module has not yet been updated to work with Drupal 7. There are some indications that this will eventually happen, but these things can be difficult to predict.

If you are interested in utilizing this module, I recommend following the Drupal 7 version discussion at `http://drupal.org/project/workflow`.

Controlling Comment Spam

Comment spam—most concisely defined as undesirable comment content—comes in a broad range of amusing or perhaps annoying flavors. Most comment spam consists of commenters-for-hire who promote a product, service, or concept via forced dissemination across the Web. However, sometimes it gets more personal or malicious.

Of course, you likely have your own definition of what constitutes spam. Handily, Drupal's ability to control spam is flexible. The system's anti-spam functionality is also largely provided by the community, via contributed modules and third-party services.

Cross-Reference

See Chapter 15 for an in-depth discussion of Drupal's core commenting functionality, including how you can enable or disable global commenting, how you can turn comments on or off on a per-content-type basis, and how to configure granular commenting options. ■

Controlling access to commenting functions

The simplest way to block robots from automatically submitting comments to your Drupal Web sites is to require visitors to register or log in before they can add a comment. This is, in fact, Drupal's default configuration. With that said, practical realities may prevent you from taking this approach; after all, most site owners want to make commenting as easy as possible.

Follow these steps to allow or disallow anonymous commenting:

1. **Log into your site as an administrator.**

   The login landing page loads in your browser.

2. **Select the People option from the main admin menu.**

   The People and permissions screen loads in your browser.

3. **Locate the tabs in the top right of the page, and click the Permissions tab.**

   The Permissions page loads in your browser, listing the various permissions by functional area and then the roles available for configuration.

4. **Scroll down the page to the Comment section, and check or uncheck the boxes for each role in the Post comments row. To enable anonymous commenting, check the box in this row's Anonymous user column.**

5. **After you have made your changes, scroll to the bottom of the page and click the Save permissions button.**

   If the operation is successful, a success message is displayed at the top of your browser.

After you have configured the global access to commenting by role, you may additionally want to set commenting configurations for each content type in your system. You do this in the content type configuration tools found under the Structure admin area. Figure 14.4 shows the typical comment settings available for each content type.

FIGURE 14.4

The commenting configuration options for the Article content type

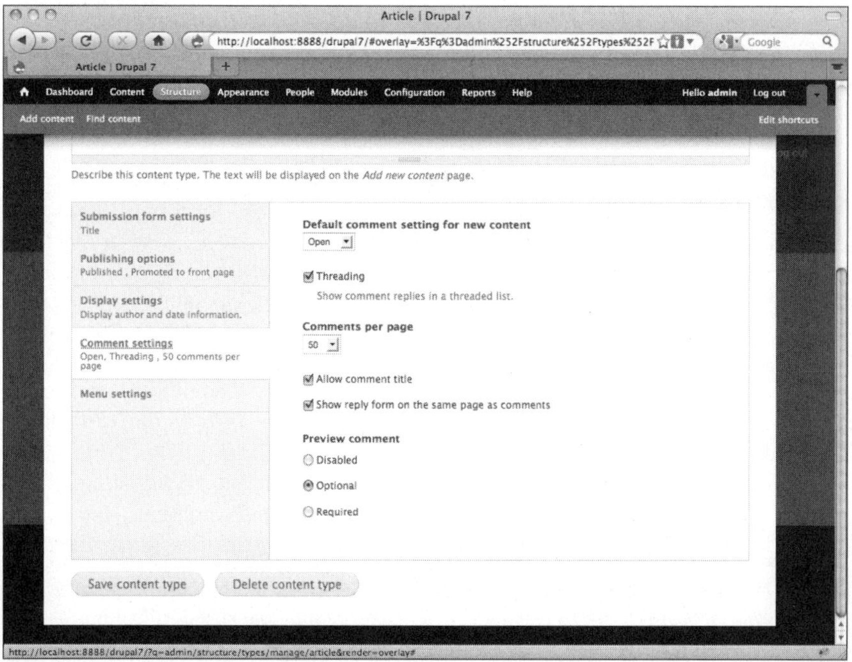

Cross-Reference

See Chapter 10 for additional details on configuring per-content-type preferences, including how to access the commenting configuration for each content type. ■

Thwarting robots with CAPTCHA and reCAPTCHA

The CAPTCHA system is a test presented by a computer to a human to verify that the entity posing as a human is in fact a human. This test is also known as a *reverse Turing* test. Alan Turing reportedly introduced the idea of tests posed by humans to computers to distinguish humans from computers in a research paper in the 1950s. The acronym CAPTCHA stands for *Completely Automated Public Turing test to tell Computers and Humans Apart.*

Note

The CAPTCHA approach is only one option for blocking robot spammers. You may not like this method, because it involves a certain inconvenience for would-be commenters; they must pass a small intelligence (or some might say vision) test. CAPTCHA alternatives can rely on JavaScript- or CSS-based tactics to identify robots, because many present-day spamming robots do not process JavaScript and CSS correctly. Systems based on this approach either make comment submission impossible without full JavaScript support or make comments that robots submit stand out from the human-generated ones. ■

Alan Turing was asking the question "Can machines think?" In the spam context, CAPTCHA systems effectively ask a commenter "Can you accurately read this image?," thus identifying robots that cannot, and preventing them from automatically submitting comments. These tests typically take the form of an image with a range of characters that the responder must enter into a text box.

You likely have encountered a number of different CAPTCHA systems in your Internet travels. In this section, I describe two common options: the contributed CAPTCHA module and the reCAPTCHA module, which builds on the former but utilizes the Google-owned Web service for core implementation.

Using the CAPTCHA module

The CAPTCHA module is a contributed module that has been updated to work with Drupal 7. Download, install, and enabled this module following your normal procedures. Note that the module shows up in a new collapsible section of the Modules page called Spam Control and that this module actually is two modules: the CAPTCHA module and the Image CAPTCHA module.

If you enable only the CAPTCHA module, then commenters are presented with a simple math problem as the test, as shown in Figure 14.5. If you enable both modules, then you can choose which type of test, image or math, to use in each context.

Tip

If you are concerned about your Web site's accessibility level for the handicapped, then it is probably best that you use the math-based CAPTCHA because the image-based CAPTCHA may be less accessible to screen readers. For additional accessibility, you probably want to use the reCAPTCHA module because it offers more options, including an audio CAPTCHA mode. ■

FIGURE 14.5

A comment input screen showing the simple CAPTCHA test

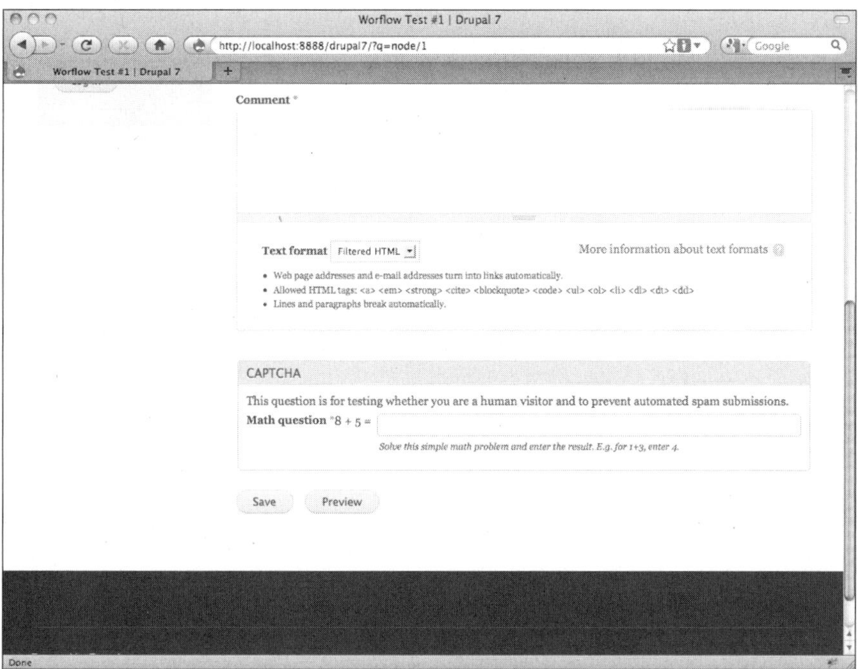

After you have installed and enabled the CAPTCHA modules, navigate to the module's configuration area by clicking the CAPTCHA link in the People subsection of the admin's Configuration area. In this screen, you can configure which forms are protected by the module and which type of CAPTCHA test is used with each form.

Tip

Keep in mind that you can require or disable CAPTCHAs for any system role simply by toggling off or on the Skip CAPTCHA permission for that role. ■

Using the reCAPTCHA module

The reCAPTCHA module builds on the CAPTCHA module, leveraging its configuration framework and adding Google's reCAPTCHA Web service capabilities. You can certainly get by without using reCAPTCHA, but here are some reasons why it might make sense:

- **Usability:** The reCAPTCHA system is currently used on more than 100,000 different Web sites. The usability kinks have been worked out, and the interface is most likely already familiar to your visitors, because they've likely already had encounters with it. Given that you're adding a hurdle to the process in question, making that hurdle low for the non-target audience (humans) is a good idea. reCAPTCHA is arguably an easier tool for your users to understand than the plain CAPTCHA module.

- **Accessibility:** If you need to meet accessibility requirements, reCAPTCHA with its audio mode will likely help you do that.
- **Security:** Google claims that most other CAPTCHA solutions can be broken or avoided but that theirs is secure.
- **Human Good:** Google's reCAPTCHA service has a broader purpose: It uses the input from the millions of CAPTCHAs it processes each day to digitize materials previously archived in print. You may or may not find this to be a good thing. But if you do, using reCAPTCHA allows you to participate in this effort.

Note

The reCAPTCHA service started life as a computer science research project at Carnegie Mellon University led by Guatemalan Ph.D. student Luis von Ahn. It actually serves two purposes: While protecting your site from spammers, it additionally uses the human input as part of a digitization project, currently working to digitize archives of the New York Times newspaper. Google acquired the reCAPTCHA project in 2009. You can learn more about how the technology is used at `http://www.google.com/recaptcha`**.** ■

To utilize the reCAPTCHA service, simply download, install, and enable the reCAPTCHA module following your normal process. After you have done this, you will find a new reCAPTCHA tab in the CAPTCHA module's configuration page, as shown in Figure 14.6.

FIGURE 14.6

The CAPTCHA module's configuration screen displaying the reCAPTCHA configuration tab

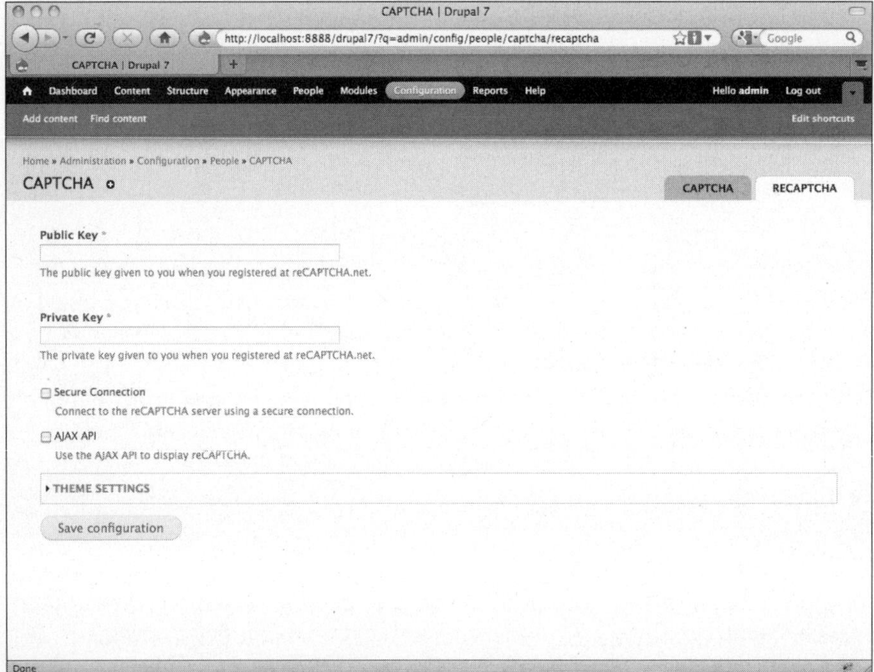

This tab has text boxes where you can enter your public and private keys for the service. You need to sign up for a reCAPTCHA account and register your Web site to generate these keys. You can do so at `https://www.google.com/recaptcha`.

After you have enabled the reCAPTCHA module, registered for the service, and entered the public and private service keys, you can select reCAPTCHA as a Challenge Type in the CAPTCHA configuration for each of your Web forms.

Automating comment moderation with Mollom

You can create a foolproof spam control system by manually moderating all comments that pass through your Web site. But you will quickly encounter the practical limits of this approach if your site has even a light flow of comments—or if you want to take a vacation.

Drupal project founder Dries Buytaert also cofounded an anti-spam service called Mollom. This service is operated remotely, like Google's reCAPTCHA service, and allows publishing systems like Drupal, WordPress, and others to pass content to it and find out if Mollom considers the content to be some kind of spam. If Mollom gives the content a stamp of approval, it can be published directly. Otherwise, it can either be marked for moderation and reviewed by humans or automatically deleted.

Note

Mollom is not the only automated anti-spam service in the market. Others like Akismet (owned by Automattic), Typepad (owned by SAY Media, which was Six Apart), and Defensio (owned by Websense, Inc.) also offer similar services. You can use the contributed AntiSpam module to utilize these services. The Drupal Web site reports that currently about ten times more Drupal Web sites use the Mollom module than use the AntiSpam module. This may not be an indication of quality, but it may be an indication of satisfaction. You should evaluate which of the solutions best addresses your specific needs. ■

You also can use Mollom as a direct replacement for either the CAPTCHA or reCAPTCHA functionality. The system can be used for CAPTCHA processing, text analysis for spam detection, or both.

Note

Mollom is a for-profit service. Although you can sign up for a free, Mollom-branded service level, you should know in advance that the intent is to get you or your organization to pay for this service. At the time of this writing, Mollom offers three service levels: a basic service for free, an advanced service for €30 per month, and an advanced premium service for €3600 per year. (The service is priced in Euros.) ■

The Mollom service offers a number of features, including these:

- **Spam identification via text analysis:** Mollom analyzes submitted content and makes a decision as to whether it is spam. If it is unsure, it can present a CAPTCHA to the user to verify that the user is human.
- **Secure and accessible CAPTCHA:** The service delivers CAPTCHA tests with both images and audio (like reCAPTCHA). They also claim to have an active response mechanism in case hackers manage to break their CAPTCHAs.

- **Content quality scoring:** This is a new service currently in beta. It analyzes submitted content and gives it a quality score. The idea is that you can set quality thresholds and automatically reject or moderate low-quality comments.
- **Profanity detection:** You can enable spam detection, profanity detection, or both for your Web forms. These settings apply to the spam identification via text analysis service.
- **Blacklisting:** Site administrators can define blacklisted keywords or phrases that, if detected, will cause Mollom to automatically flag the content as spam.
- **High-availability SLA:** Subscribers to the Mollom Plus or Mollom Premium service have access to a high-availability server cluster and an accompanying Service Level Agreement (SLA).

Tip

You can disable Mollom form protection for any system role by enabling the Bypass Mollom protection on forms permission. ■

To utilize Mollom with your Drupal Web site, you need to create a Mollom account and then download, install, and configure the contributed Mollom module. After the Mollom module is enabled, you find a new Mollom item in the Content authoring section of the admin's Configuration area.

You need to enter your Mollom access keys in the module's configuration screen, as shown in Figure 14.7, before you can utilize the service. The Mollom Web site provides you with these keys when you sign up for a specific service level, and they are Web site specific.

After you have successfully configured the site access keys, you can put Mollom to work moderating your comments. Follow these steps to protect a specific form:

1. **Log into your site as an administrator.**

   The login landing page loads in your browser.
2. **Select the Configuration option from the main admin menu.**

   The Configuration screen loads in your browser displaying various subsections.
3. **Locate the Content authoring subsection, and click the Mollom link.**

   The Mollom configuration screen loads in your browser with the Forms tab active. This tab displays the list of forms that Mollom is currently protecting.
4. **Click the Add form link at the top left of the configuration page box.**

   You are presented with a list of the available forms to protect.
5. **Select a form from the list (the article comment form, for example), and click the Next button.**

   The Mollom service configuration settings page is displayed in your browser.
6. **Review the settings in this page, accepting the defaults for the moment (you can tune these settings further at any time).**

7. **After you have reviewed the settings, scroll to the bottom of the page and click the Save button.**

   If the operation is successful, a success message is displayed at the top of your browser and Mollom is now protecting the form.

FIGURE 14.7

The Mollom module's configuration screen, entering the site-specific service access keys

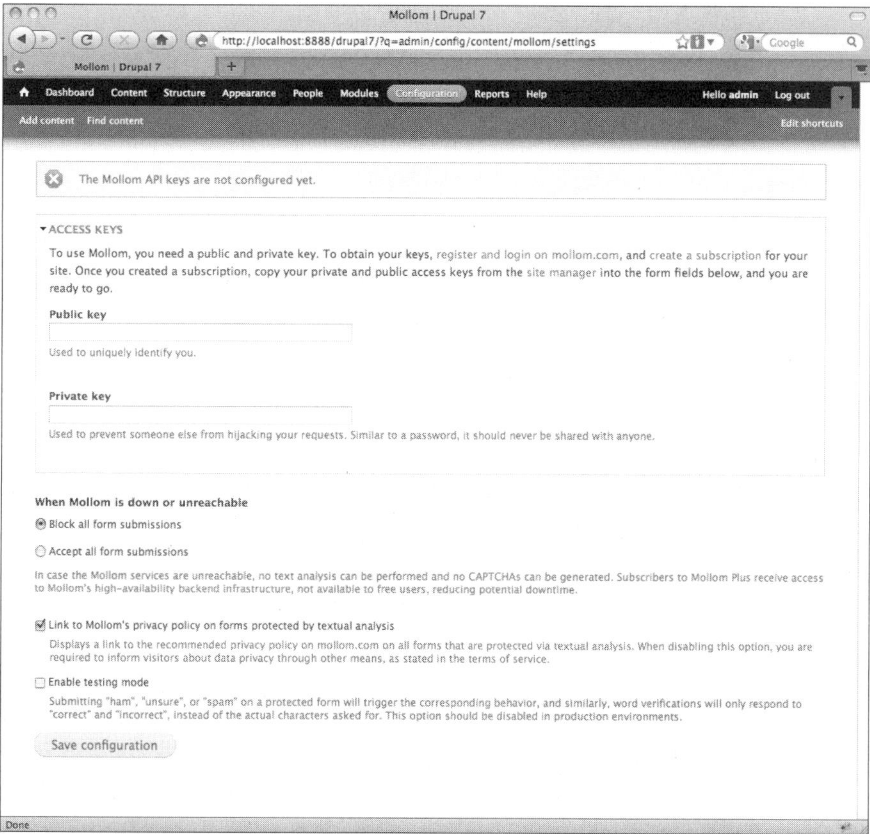

Creating Content Hierarchies

Your Web site's information architecture may dictate that you implement hierarchical relationships between content items. In this section, I review several ways you can achieve this goal.

Structuring content relationships with the Book module

The core Book module is quite specific in its purpose and design, but if these things fit your needs, it can be an excellent tool for creating content hierarchies. With the Book module, you can define one-to-many or one-to-one parent/child content relationships, just as we find the relationships between chapters and pages in physical books.

This module also includes a number of useful navigational elements, such as a table of contents and a menu system for navigating the hierarchy.

Cross-Reference

See Chapter 17 for a detailed exploration of the Book module and how you can customize the various presentation templates for this type of content. ■

Creating content hierarchies with taxonomies

Drupal's core taxonomy functionality allows you to define an unlimited number of vocabularies of an unlimited depth. You can then assign these vocabularies to your content types as fields and use them in the content authoring process to assign content items to positions in the hierarchy.

Cross-Reference

In Chapter 11, we introduce Drupal's Taxonomy Manager tool and explain how you can work with various types of system vocabularies. ■

Using a contributed module called the Taxonomy Menu (see `http://drupal.org/project/taxonomy_menu`), you can base your site's primary or other navigational components on one or more of your taxonomies. With this method, you can create information structures of limitless depth—and unlike the more rigid Book module approach, your content items can exist in multiple locations under multiple parents.

Note

The scenario described here leads to a sophisticated content hierarchy, but it also allows you to implement what is often called faceted navigation. That is, any given content item can have multiple classifications and thus be discovered in one or more navigation paths. If you implement faceted navigation, take care to not create multiple URLs for the same content item because this can lead to problems both with finding content and with search engine optimization. ■

Syndicating Your Content

Syndicating your content is the act of making your site's Web pages available in XML formats—often called *Web feeds*—such that remote feed reader applications like Google Reader, Lotus Notes, Mozilla Thunderbird, and so on can consume your content without actually visiting your Web site.

Typical XML syndication formats include the following:

- **RSS:** RSS stands for Really Simple Syndication or Rich Site Summary, depending on who you ask and what RSS version you are referring to. One of the early formats of Web feeds, RSS has gone through a number of iterations since its start in 1999. The current version 2.0.1 is broadly used today.
- **Atom:** The Atom standard actually refers to two different standards. The *Atom Syndication Format* is the Web feed standard, while the *Atom Publishing Protocol* (AtomPub) is a standard designed for publishing or editing Web documents. Many Web publishers utilize the Atom Syndication Format for their feeds. If desired, you can use the contributed Atom module to syndicate your content in this format.

Drupal 7's default syndication format is RSS 2.0. It is combined with some Dublin Core metadata for the addition of the `<dc:creator>` field, a field used to identify the author of the syndicated content item.

Note

Given that two competing syndication formats exist, you might ask yourself why you should use one versus the other. I cannot give you a simple answer to this question. In most cases, it does not matter much because many feed reader applications support both formats and both standards adequately cover 80–90 percent of typical functional requirements. If your syndication requirements become more sophisticated, you may need to take a closer look.

One important difference is that the RSS 2.0 standard is ostensibly frozen, whereas the Atom standard can continue to evolve. However, the RSS format is extensible via modules (also called namespaces in XML), and those modules can and do evolve. Another consideration is that the Atom specification is more structured in terms of defining payloads (for example, plain text versus XML versus binary data) and allowing separate `<summary>` and `<content>` fields, which may be important in your situation. Generally though, the case for one standard versus the other is really going to come down to the nitty-gritty details of your specific technical requirements. ■

Introducing Drupal Web feeds

By default, Drupal automatically creates a number of RSS feeds for your content. You can configure this functionality to behave in a way that better suits your needs.

These are some typical Drupal RSS feeds:

- **Front page feed:** All your Drupal sites have the following RSS feed available by default: `http://mysite.com/rss.xml`. This feed contains all content items that have been published to the home page. If no content items have been pushed to the home page, then the feed is empty.
- **Taxonomy term feeds:** Each in-use taxonomy term also has a corresponding RSS feed by default. You access this feed via the URL `http://mysite.com/taxonomy/term/[TermID]/feed`., where [TermID] is the numeric ID of the term in question.
- **Forum feeds:** If you enable and use the Forum module, then each forum has its own RSS feed listing the recent discussion topics.

Cross-Reference

In Chapter 20, we discuss the Forum module in detail, including how you work with forum containers and forums, and how you administer forum content. ■

- **Aggregator feeds:** If you use the core Feed Aggregator module, you can create a number of different Web feeds. For example, each category of consumed feeds in turn produces a Web feed containing the content from this category. You also can turn the Aggregator back on its own local Web site and use it to mix together one or more local feeds into a hybrid feed combining multiple taxonomy terms, multiple content types, and so on.

Cross-Reference

See Chapter 18 for an introduction to the Aggregator module and step-by-step instructions for configuring and organizing the aggregation of multiple remote or local Web feeds. ■

- **Views feeds:** If you install and make use of the contributed Views module, you also can generate RSS feeds for any of the active views. Each view has a base definition and one or more displays. A display can be a page, a block, a content pane, a feed, and so on. If a view is created as a feed, the content of the view is accessible via a unique URL in RSS format.

Cross-Reference

In Chapter 27, you can find an introduction the Views module and some recipes for getting started with custom content views. ■

- **Comment feeds:** Drupal does not provide comment RSS feeds by default. However, a contributed module named Comment RSS exists for Drupal versions 5 and 6. At the time of this writing, this module is not available for Drupal 7, but as of December 2010 some work was in progress on a Drupal 7 update, so it may arrive shortly. You also can use the Views module to define comment views and related RSS feeds.

Tip

In addition to Drupal's native Web feed functionality, you should feel free to use third-party services like Google Feedburner or Yahoo! Pipes to serve or mash your feeds into a shape that fits your needs. You can always modify your site's templates to include links to custom feeds of your choosing. You also can explore contributed modules like Syndicate that help you customize and present your various Web feeds. ■

Configuring content syndication

You can configure each Drupal content type to syndicate its content differently. This is done in the Structure area of the admin screens.

Follow these steps to configure the per-content-type behavior of feeds:

1. **Log into your site as an administrator.**

   The login landing page loads in your browser.

2. **Select the Structure option from the main admin menu.**

   The Structure's section page loads in your browser.

3. **Locate the Content types sub-item in the page, and click this link.**

   The content type management screen loads in your browser, including the list of current system content types.

4. **Locate the Operations column in the content type grid, and click the edit link in the row of the content type you want to modify.**

   The content type editing screen loads in your browser, including the local navigation tabs in the top right of the page.

5. **Click the Manage display tab for the content type.**

   The Manage content type display settings screen loads in your browser, as shown in Figure 14.8.

FIGURE 14.8

The content type's Manage display settings screen

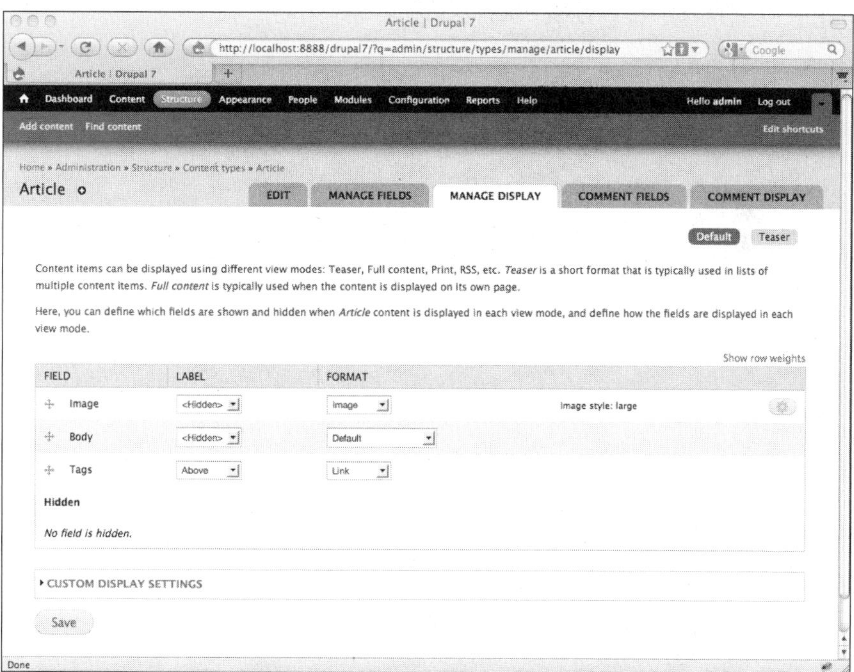

6. **Scroll to the bottom of this screen, and expand the Custom display settings region.**

   This is where you can enable customized display for different content viewing modes, including RSS feeds. The list of content view modes is displayed in the page.

7. **Check the box next to the RSS option in the Custom display settings list.**
8. **When you are finished making changes, scroll to the bottom of the page and click the Save button.**

   If the operation is successful, a success message is visible at the top of the page and your changes are now active.

After you have enabled the customization of the RSS content viewing mode, you see a new RSS configuration sub-item in the Manage display tab, as shown in Figure 14.9.

FIGURE 14.9

The content type's Manage display settings screen showing configuration options for Default, Teaser, and RSS content viewing modes

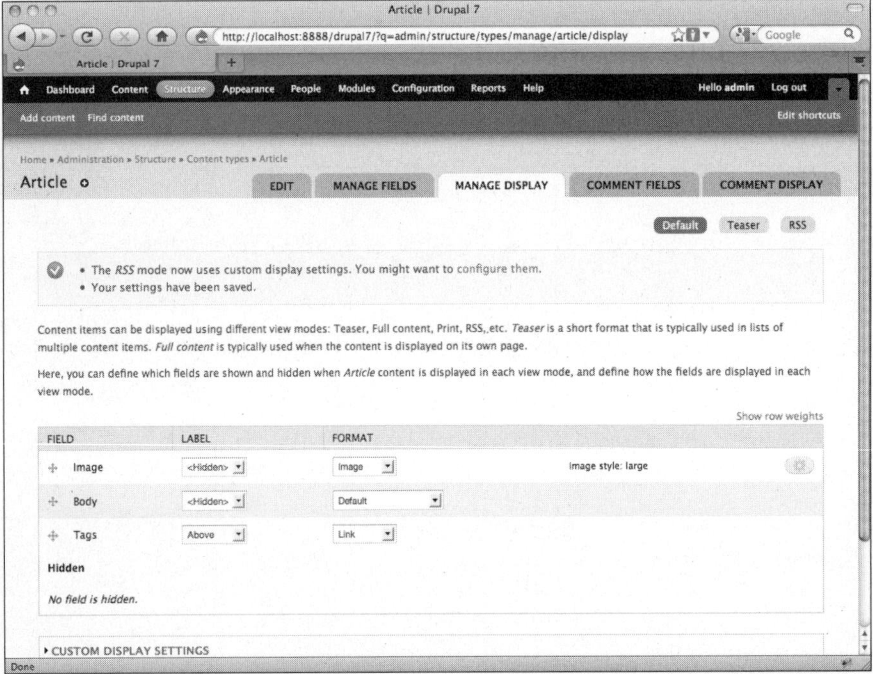

Follow these steps to customize the RSS content viewing mode for the current content type:

1. **Click the RSS view mode item in the content type's Manage display tab.**

   The view mode settings screen displays in your browser.
2. **If you want to display only a body summary, not the full body of your content in the RSS feed, locate the Body field in the fields grid and change the Format value to Trimmed.**

The new format setting is displayed, as is a format configuration button (typically displaying a small gear).

3. **Click the format configuration button, and set the trim length value to 200 characters.**
4. **Make any additional changes you desire, scroll to bottom of the page, and click the Save button.**

   If the changes are successful, a success message is displayed at the top of the window and your RSS feeds containing content of this type have been modified.

Summary

In this chapter I covered a number of more advanced Drupal content management topics. Each area involves quite a bit of complexity, but I've tried to give you a solid grounding and a useful context by which you can move forward to achieve your specific functionality goals.

I discussed the following areas:

- Reasons to use content versioning and how to configure content types to consistently create snapshots of content item changes
- How to implement content authoring workflows and which tools should be considered
- How to deal with the challenges of comment spam
- How to go about creating and publishing content hierarchies and more sophisticated information architectures
- The different types of Web feeds used for content syndication and how to configure Drupal to serve customized feeds for each content type

CHAPTER 15

Working with the Comment Functionality

The default Drupal installation includes one of the most commonly requested content functionalities: The ability to allow users to post comments on content items. The Comment module powers this functionality.

The Comment functionality is a powerful feature, and it's fairly complex. It includes several administration interfaces and a number of themable elements. In this chapter, I review the module, the administration tools, and the options for controlling the display and the work flow.

IN THIS CHAPTER

Introducing the Comment module

Controlling the styling of comments

Administering comments

Introducing the Comment Module

The Comment module allows site visitors to comment on and discuss content items, as shown in Figure 15.1. Comments in Drupal are administered like content items and have their own page, which is accessed via a tab on the Content Manager. Drupal allows for comments to be enabled selectively and applied only to those content types the administrator chooses. Administrators also can moderate and approve comments prior to publication. User permissions can be configured to allow different users different levels of access to this feature.

FIGURE 15.1

The Comment module in action, showing a comment form at the end of a content item

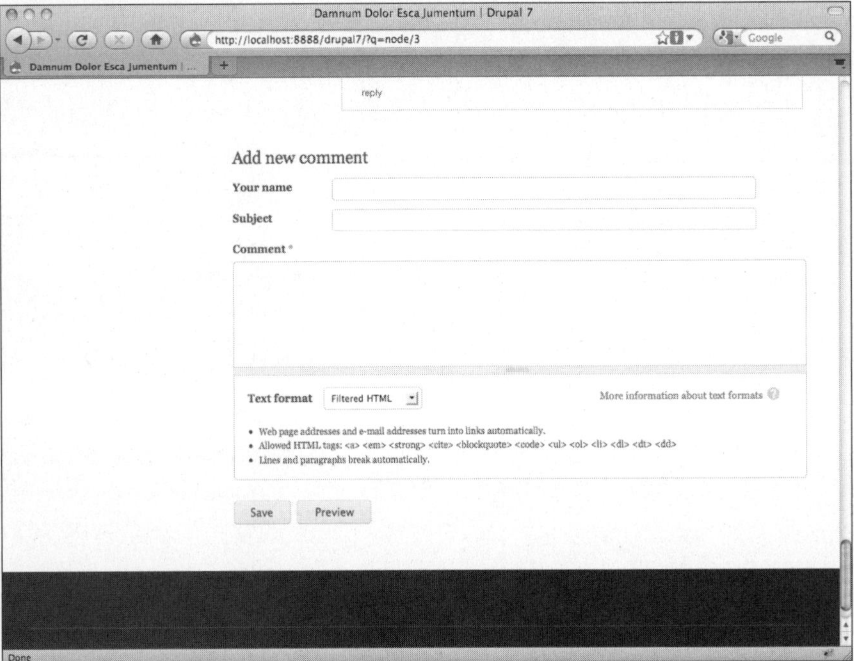

Enabling and disabling the module

The Comment module is enabled in the default standard installation. It is not enabled in the minimal installation profile. Enabling this module is a simple matter, because it has no dependencies. To enable the Comment module, follow these steps:

1. **Log into your site as an administrator.**

   The admin interface loads in your browser.

2. **Select the option Modules from the Management menu.**

   The Modules Manager opens in your browser.

3. **Click the check box next to the Comment module.**

4. **Click the Save Configuration button at the bottom of the page.**

   If you are successful, a confirmation message appears at the top of the page.

Configuring comments

The Comment module does not have a separate configuration interface; instead, the various options are spread between multiple interfaces. If you view the Modules Manager, you see next to the Comment module three links: Help, Permissions, and Configure, as shown in Figure 15.2.

FIGURE 15.2

Note the links to the right of the Comment module.

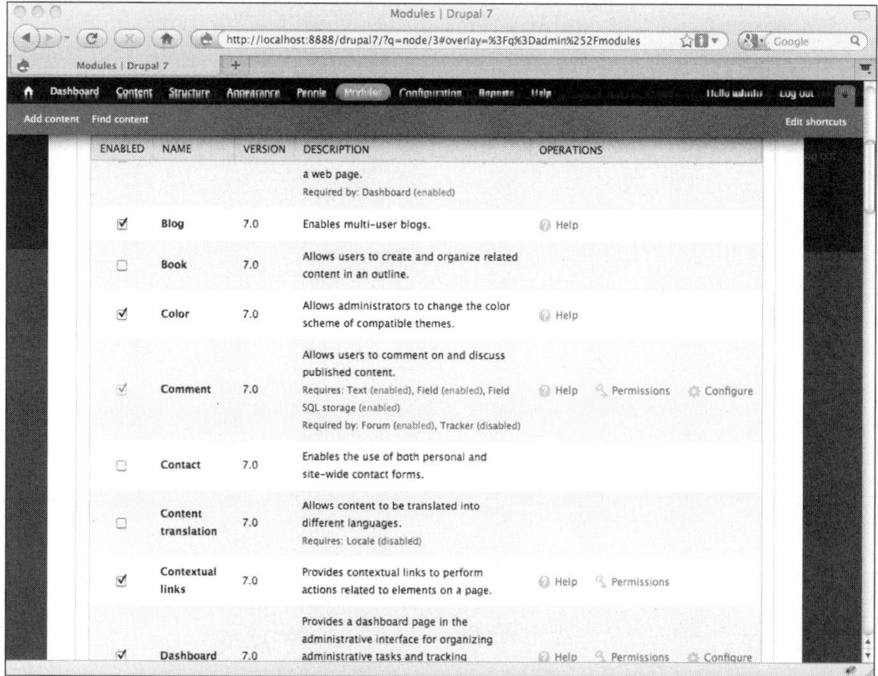

Here's what the options mean:

- **Help:** Click this link to view the integrated help file for the module.
- **Permissions:** Click this link to visit the Permissions Manager where you can control access to the Comment functionality. Configuring permissions for the Comment module is discussed in more detail later in this chapter.
- **Configure**: Despite the name, this does not take you to a configuration manager page for the Comment module. It simply takes you to the Comments administration page where you can see a list of published and pending comments.

Comments are associated with content types. Each content type provides an interface for configuring the comments for that particular content type. After you have enabled the Comments module, you need to turn on the comments for each content type you want to employ the comments functionality. You must configure each content type separately; the settings made for one content type do not affect the other content types.

To access the Comment settings for a content type, follow these steps:

1. **Log into your site as an administrator.**
2. **Click the Structure option on the Management menu.**

   The Structure page loads in your browser.
3. **Click the option Content types.**

   The Content types page loads.
4. **Click the edit link next to the name of the Content type you want to modify.**

   The Content type administration page loads.
5. **Scroll down to the bottom of the page, and click the link labeled Comment settings.**

   The Comment settings tab comes to the front.

Figure 15.3 shows the Comment settings for the Article content type; it is typical of all the content types.

FIGURE 15.3

The Comment settings page for the Article content type

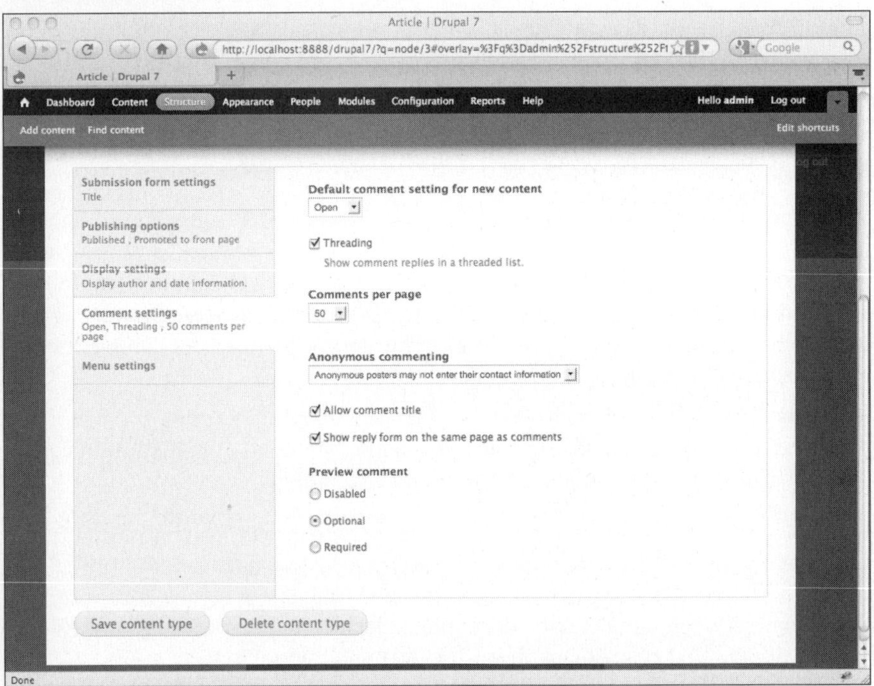

These options are available on the Comment settings tab:

- **Default comment setting for new content:** This setting determines whether the comment form is active and visible. The options here are Hidden, Open, and Closed. Whatever you set here for the default can always be overridden for individual nodes by changing the settings on the node creation or edit form.
- **Threading:** Check the box to thread contents and their replies. Uncheck the box to display the comments without threading, that is, all at the same level without indentation.
- **Comments per page:** Use the combo box to set the number of comments to show on each page. If there are comments in excess of the setting, pagination controls appear to allow users to click through the pages of comments.
- **Anonymous commenting:** Use the combo box to select whether anonymous posters are allowed or required to leave their contact details. There are three options here: No contact details, contact details optional, or contact details required.
- **Allow comment title:** Check this box to allow the poster to submit a title for the comment. If you leave it blank, the title field is hidden on the form and a title for the comment is automatically extracted from the first few words of the comment body.
- **Show reply form on the same page as comments:** Check the box to display the comment form on the same page as the content item. If the option is unchecked, a text link is displayed; clicking the link opens a page with the comment form.
- **Preview comment:** This set of radio buttons controls whether the user has to preview the comment before submitting it and whether this action is required.

You always have the option to override the Comment settings for a content type at the node level. When the Comment module is enabled, each node displays a Comment settings option that is visible at the time of node creation or editing, assuming the user has been granted permission to control the comment settings. Figure 15.4 shows the comment settings tab at the bottom of a new Article page; this is typical for all nodes.

Defining fields for comments

Fields can be defined for your comments. Field creation and display management are done at the content type level, from the individual content type editing pages. Figure 15.5 shows the Article content type editing page, with the Comment Fields tab brought to the front of the display.

FIGURE 15.4

The Comment settings tab for a specific node

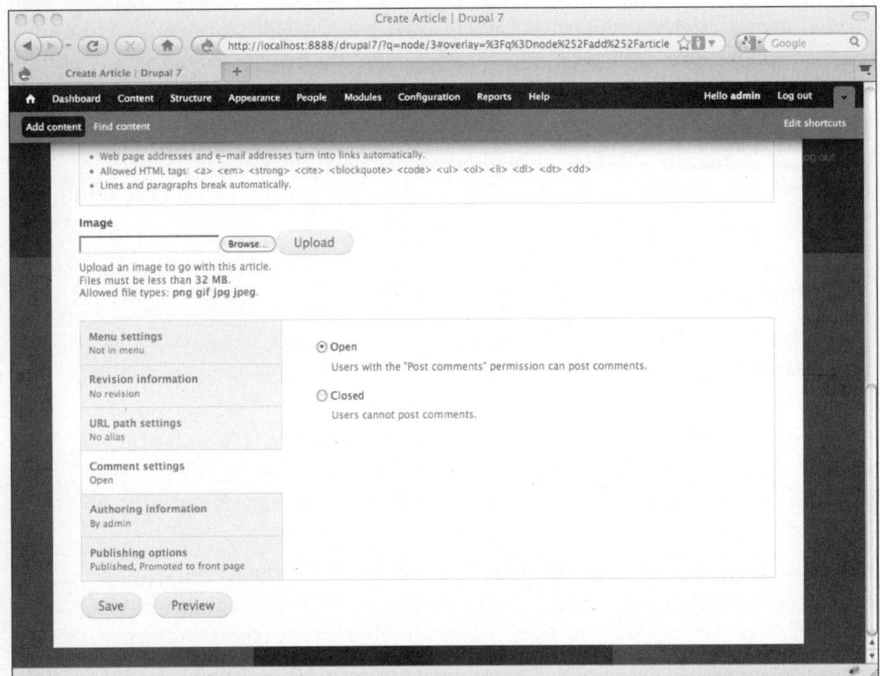

Tip

The Comment fields functionality is powered by the Field UI module. The various options available in all field creation and configuration are available in the Comment Fields page. ■

To add a new field to your comment form, follow these steps:

1. **Log into your site as an administrator.**

   The admin interface loads in your browser.

2. **Select the Structure option from the Management menu.**

   The Structure options menu loads.

3. **Click the choice Content types.**

   The Content types list loads.

4. **Find the content type for which you wish to customize the comments form and click the manage fields link in Operations column.**

   The Content type editing page loads.

5. **Click the tab labeled Comment Fields.**

   The Comment Fields page comes to the front.

6. **In the empty box labeled Add new field – label, type a label for your new field.**
7. **In the box labeled field_ type a machine-friendly name for the field.**
8. **Select a field type from the combo box of the same name.**
9. **Select a widget from the combo box of the same name.**
10. **Click the Save button.**

    The Field Settings page loads.
11. **Set the options relevant to your new field (these vary according to the field selected in the previous step).**
12. **Click the Save field settings button.**

    If successful, you see a confirmation message and a new page loads: The Content type comment settings page.
13. **Set whatever values you want on this page; many of the settings here affect the display of the field on the form.**
14. **Click the Save settings button.**

    The system displays a confirmation message and returns you to the Comment Fields page.

FIGURE 15.5

The Comment Fields page for the Article content type. Note also at the top right the Comment Display tab.

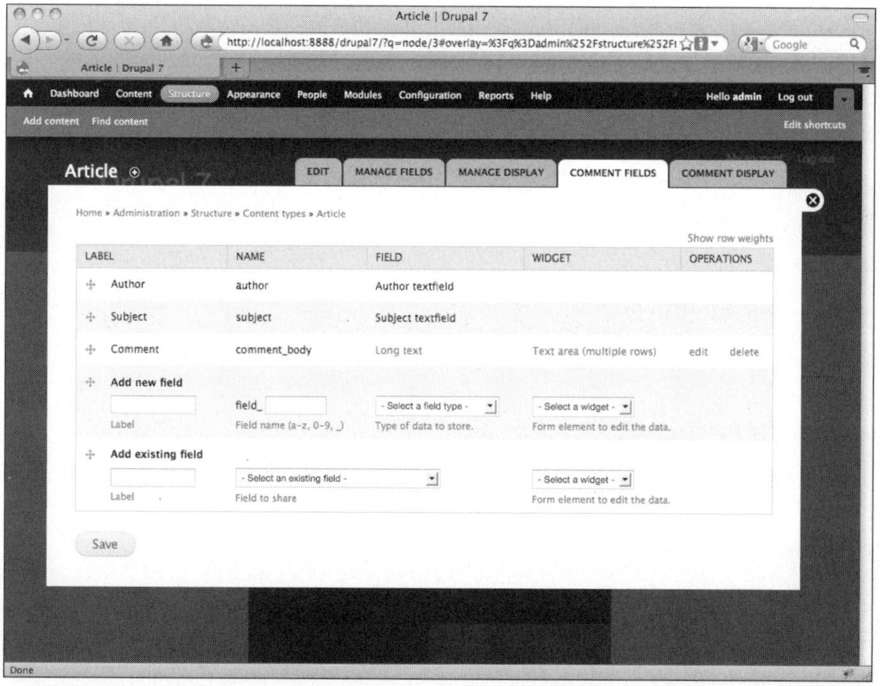

The Comment Fields page also enables you to reorder the fields on your comment form. To reorder the items, simply click and drag the crossed arrows icon to the left of the field label; using that tool you can move items up or down the list.

Tip

Custom fields you create here are available to other nodes and comment forms. ■

The Comment Display tab, seen at the top right next to the Comment Fields tab in Figure 15.5, allows you to customize the display of the comment data. The Custom Display Settings option on this page enables you to set separate display settings for default view and the full view of the comments.

Note

The Comment Display options are very limited unless you have created custom fields! ■

Controlling the Styling of Comments

The Comment module provides you with two dedicated template files, two style sheets, and a selection of themable functions. In the sections below, I introduce these resources, indicate their role in the display, and explain the functions and variables that are available for you to work with.

Cross-Reference

Overriding templates and working with themable functions are discussed in depth in Chapter 28. ■

Reviewing the default templates

The Comment module has two dedicated templates. Both are located at `/modules/comment`. The templates are:

- **comment.tpl.php**
- **comment-wrapper.tpl.php**

Each of the templates is discussed in the sections that follow.

Reviewing comment.tpl.php

This is the primary template for controlling the appearance of the comments. The available variables are shown in Table 15.1.

TABLE 15.1

Variables in comment.tpl.php

Variable	Description
$author	The name of the author of the comment
$changed	The date and time the comment was last changed
$classes	String of classes that can be used to style the comments
$comment	The full comment object
$content	The main body of the comment
$created	The date and time the comment was created
$date	The date and the time the comment was created
$links	The links for the functionality associated with the comment
$new	A marker that indicates a new comment
$node	The node to which the comments are attached
$permalink	The comment's permalink
$picture	The author's picture
$signature	The author's signature
$status	The status of the comment, that is, whether it is published, unpublished, and so on
$submitted	'Submitted by' text with the date and the time
$title	The title of the comment
$title_prefix	An array of additional output displayed before the main title tag
$title_suffix	An array of additional output displayed after the main title tag

Reviewing comment-wrapper.tpl.php

The comment-wrapper template provides a container for all the comments. The template controls the overall formatting of the comment area. The variables are shown in Table 15.2.

TABLE 15.2

Variables in comment-wrapper.tpl.php

Variable	Description
$classes	String of classes that can be used to style the comments
$classes-array	An array of HTML class attributes
$content	Handles all the comments for a particular page
$node	The node to which the comments are attached
$title_prefix	An array of additional output displayed before the main title tag
$title_suffix	An array of additional output displayed after the main title tag

Reviewing the default style sheets

Two style sheets are dedicated to the formatting of the Comment module. Both are located at `/modules/comment`. The two files are:

- **comment.css:** These are the primary CSS files; however, in the case of the Comment module, it contains very few selectors.
- **comment-rtl.css:** This CSS is applied when the site is set to display text in right-to-left orientation.

Reviewing the themable functions

There are only two themable functions provided for the comment functionality. The functions can be found in two files: `modules/comment/comment.module` and `modules/comment/comment.admin.inc`. The available functions are listed in Table 15.3.

TABLE 15.3

Themable Functions

Function	Description
theme_comment_block	Formats the list of recent comments as displayed in a block
theme_comment_post_forbidden	Controls the "you can't post comments" function

Administering Comments

The site administrator can view, edit, and control the publication state of all comments. If you have configured the Comment module to require moderation, you also can view all the comments that are pending in the approval queue and make a decision about whether to publish them, delete them, or let them sit in the system unpublished.

The settings the administrator has chosen in the Permissions Manager determine whether comments must be approved prior to publication. The manager interface includes a separate section dedicated to controlling access to comments, as shown in Figure 15.6.

Cross-Reference

Working with users, roles, and permissions is discussed in depth in Chapter 23. ■

FIGURE 15.6

The Comment permissions settings

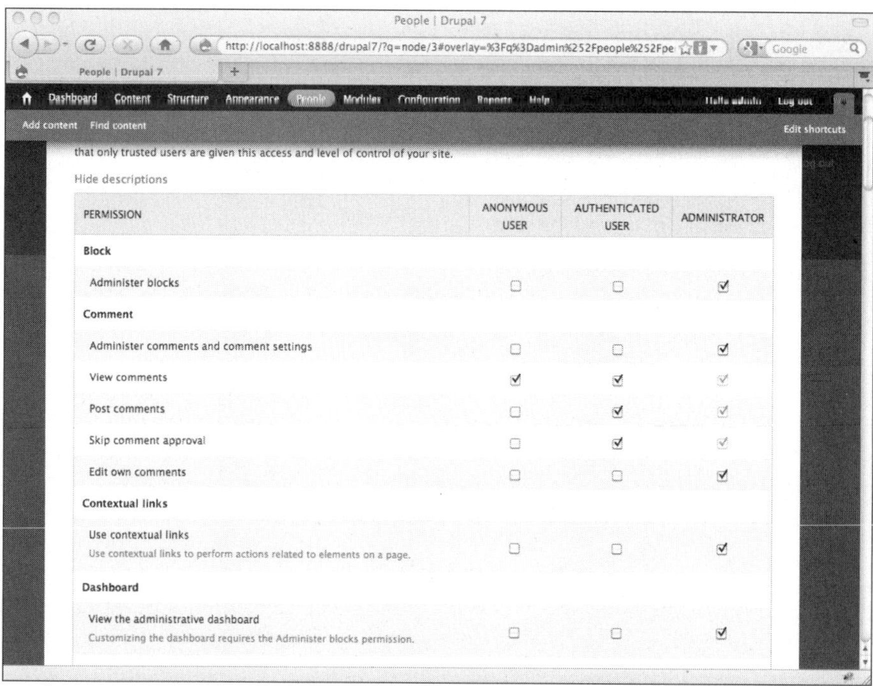

The Permissions options here include:

- **Administer comments and comment settings:** Check this box to allow the user group access to the Comment administration interface. Typically, you want to grant this right only to your site administrators.
- **View comments:** Check this box to allow the user group to view comments on the front end. If your site uses comments, you typically want to grant this right to all user groups.
- **Post comments:** Check this box to allow the user group to post comments. Note that this option requires approval of the comments before publication.
- **Skip comment approval:** Check this box to allow the user group to post comments without forcing approval prior to publication. Note that this means that the comments are published immediately.
- **Edit own comments:** Click to allow users to edit any comments they have submitted.

To manage the comments in your system, Drupal provides a dedicated content administration interface. To view the comments in your system and manage them, click the Content option on the Management menu. When the Content Manager loads, select the Comments tab on the top right. The Comment Administration page loads in your browser, as shown in Figure 15.7.

FIGURE 15.7

The Comment Administration page

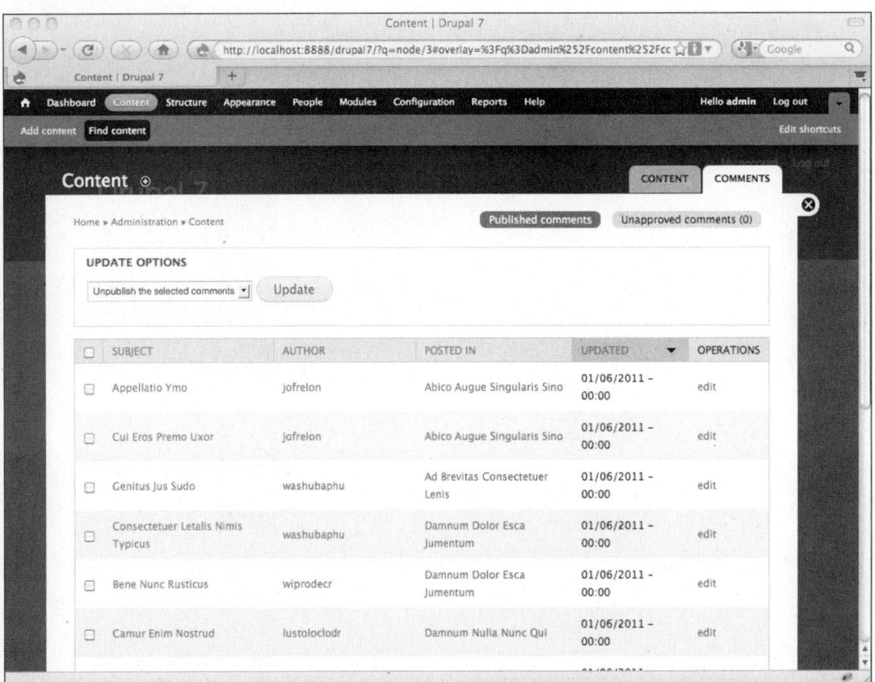

At the very top of the screen, below the tabs, are two links: Published comments and Unapproved comments. These links allow you to change the view of the page, showing a list of all the published comments on the site or showing the comment approval queue.

The Update Options combo box, located above the table containing the list of comments, holds a list of actions you can perform on the comments in the system. If you are looking at the Published comments page, the options are Unpublish the selected comments and Delete the selected comments. If you are looking at the Unapproved comments page, the options are Publish the selected comments and Delete the selected comments.

Below the Update Options section is a table containing a list of comments. These fields are on the table:

- **Checkbox (no label):** Click in this box to select more than one item for the purpose of making changes to several items at once.
- **Subject:** This is the subject line of the comment.
- **Author:** This is the author of the comment.
- **Posted in:** This is where the comment was posted, that is, what node it is associated with.

- **Updated:** This tells when the comment was last updated. Clicking the column header here lets you sort the list of comments by date.
- **Operations:** The edit option appears in this column. Click the edit link to edit the comment.

Tip

Sometimes a comment left by a user needs a little help. If you want to edit a comment for grammar, spelling, or appropriateness, either before or after it is published, you can do so by using the Edit link in the operations column. If you are logged in as an administrator, you also can edit comments by viewing them on the front end of the site and clicking the edit link that appears. ■

To publish a comment, follow these steps:

1. **Access the Comments Administration page.**
2. **Click the Unapproved comments link.**

   The Comment moderation queue appears in your browser.
3. **Click in the check box next to the comments you want to publish.**
4. **Select Publish the selected comments from the Update Options combo box.**
5. **Click the Update button.**

   A confirmation message appears, and the comment is now viewable on the front end. In the admin system, the comment is moved from the Unapproved comments queue to the Published comments list.

To unpublish a comment, follow these steps:

1. **Access the Comments Administration page.**
2. **Click in the check box next to the comments you want to unpublish.**
3. **Select Unpublish the selected comments from the Update Options combo box.**
4. **Click the Update button.**

   A confirmation message appears, and the comment is removed from the front end. In the admin system, the comment is moved from the Published comments queue to the Unapproved comments list.

Note

Unpublishing a comment does not delete it from the system; it simply removes it from view on the front end. ■

To delete a comment, follow these steps:

1. **Access the Comments Administration page.**
2. **Click in the check box next to the comments you want to delete.**
3. **Select Delete the selected comments from the Update Options combo box.**

4. **Click the Update button.**

   A confirmation page appears.

5. **Click the Delete button.**

   The confirmation message appears, and the comment is deleted permanently from the system.

Summary

This chapter addressed the use of the comments functionality in Drupal 7. I covered these topics:

- How to enable the Comment module
- How to configure the Comment module
- How to manage comment moderation
- How to edit and delete comments
- The resources available for controlling the styling of the Comment module

CHAPTER 16

Managing Blog Content

IN THIS CHAPTER

Introducing the Blog module

Administering blogs

Controlling the styling of the Blog module

Using the Most Recent Blog Posts block

Blog capability is one of the most frequently requested Web site options these days, allowing the administrator or other users to post articles easily and providing a logical chronological organization scheme. The Blog module enables you to add one or more blogs to your Web site. The module supports both single-user and multi-user blogs and provides a block of the most recent blog posts.

In this chapter, I introduce the Blog module, the Blog content type, and the options that are available for managing blog content.

Introducing the Blog Module

Drupal's Blog module supports the creation of one or more blogs. The module enables a dedicated content type called Blog entry. The administrator creates a new blog by creating a new content item of the appropriate type. The various blog entries are managed with Drupal's standard content item management tools. If more than one user is allowed to create blogs, the system groups the blog entries by author.

Figure 16.1 shows an example of the Blog module being used to display blogs from multiple users on the front page of the site.

FIGURE 16.1

The Blog module in action, displaying blog entries by multiple users. Note also the Recent blog posts block in the left column.

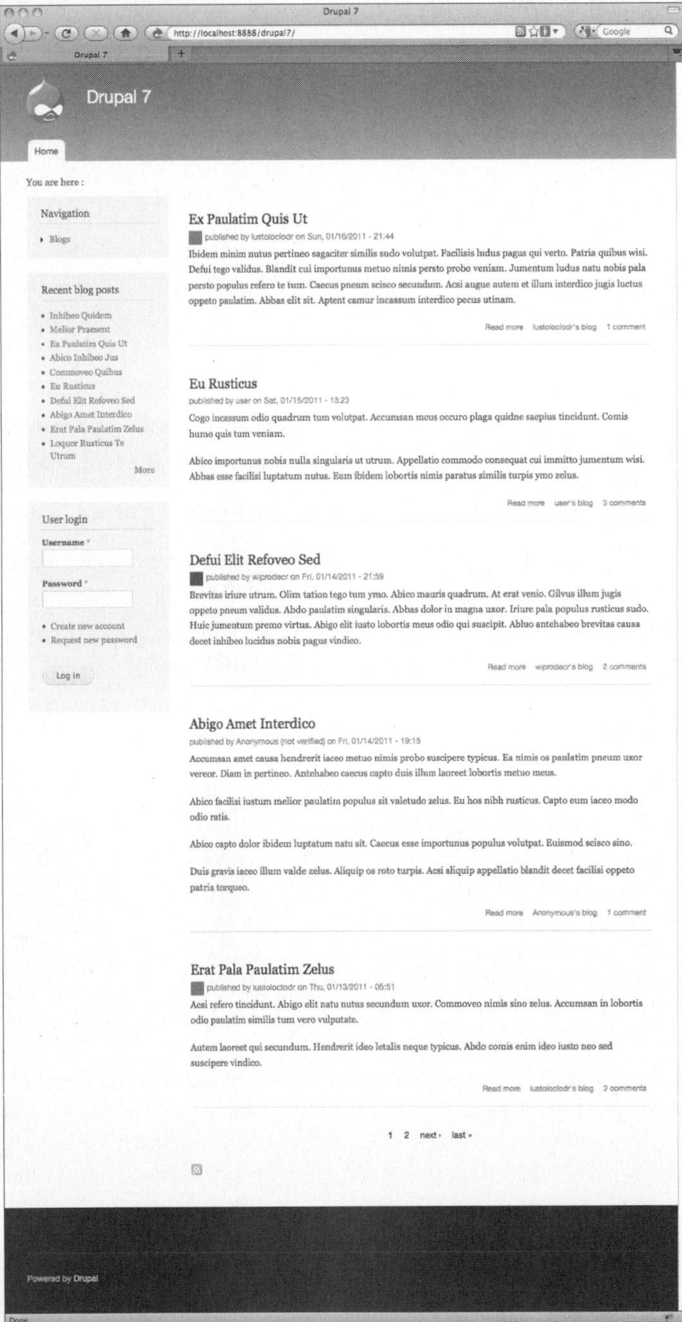

When the Blog module is enabled, the system automatically creates two new menu items, named Blogs and My Blog. Both menu items are located on the Navigation menu, as shown in Figure 16.2. The Blogs menu item is disabled by default, but the My Blog menu item is enabled. Clicking the Blogs menu item displays a list of all the blog entries, regardless of author, ordered by most recent first.

Note

If you want both the Blogs and My Blog menu items to be visible on the front end, enable the Blogs menu item on the Navigation Menu manager. ■

FIGURE 16.2

The Navigation Menu manager, showing the system-created menu items Blogs and My Blog

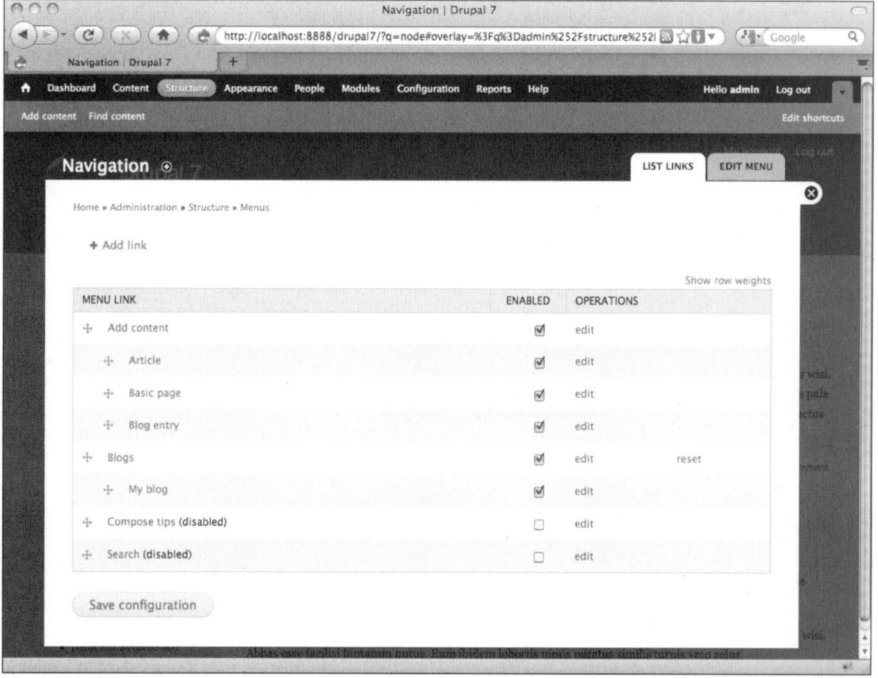

The My Blog menu item is visible only to an authenticated user who has been granted permission to use the Blog module. If the user clicks the My Blog menu item, he is shown a list of only those blog entries he has authored, ordered by the date of creation, along with a shortcut that allows him to create a new blog entry, as shown in Figure 16.3. The presence of this shortcut on the front end of the site means you do not have to grant users access to the admin system in order to allow them to create new blogs for the site.

FIGURE 16.3

This page results from the user clicking the My Blog menu item. Note that the title of the page reflects the user's name, and the page includes a link to create a new blog entry.

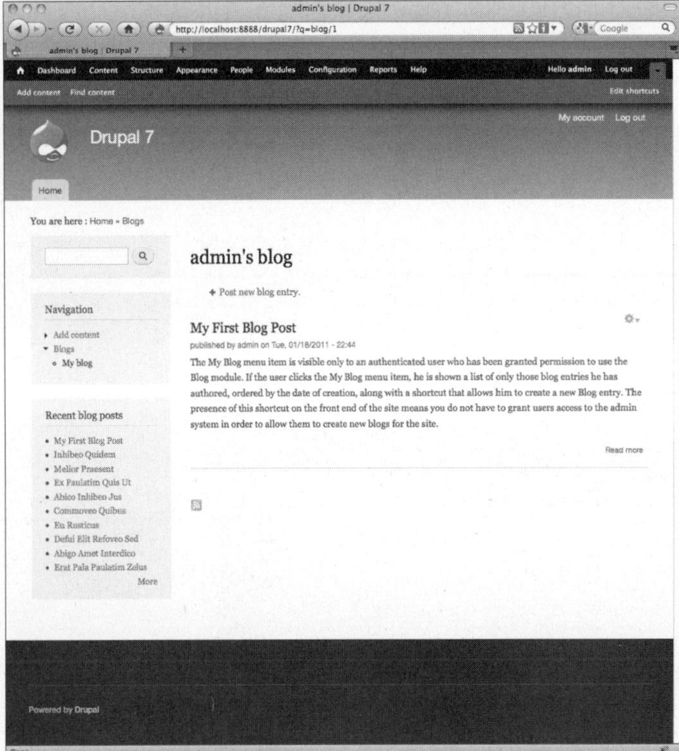

Enabling and disabling the module

The Blog module is disabled in both the default Standard installation and in the Minimal installation profile. Enabling this module is a simple matter, because it has no dependencies.

To enable the Blog module, follow these steps:

1. **Log into your site as an administrator.**

   The admin interface loads in your browser.

2. **Select the option Modules from the Management menu.**

   The Modules Manager opens in your browser.

3. **Click the check box next to the Blog module.**

4. **Click the Save Configuration button at the bottom of the page.**

   If you are successful, the Blog module is enabled and a confirmation message appears at the top of the page.

Configuring the module

Configuring the Blog module involves simply adding the appropriate permissions. A good place to begin when setting up your blog for the first time is to configure the permissions to create and view the blog entries. If you set those permissions at the beginning, viewing the impact of your work on the front end of the site is easier.

To access the permission settings, go to the Permissions Manager, under the People option on the Management Menu. After you click the link, you should see the page shown in Figure 16.4.

Note

There is no separate configuration management page dedicated to the Blog module as a whole; rather, because blogs are nodes, each individual blog has its own configuration settings. The settings can be defined at the time the blog content item is created, or they can be edited at any time, as discussed later in this chapter. ■

Cross-Reference

Working with users, roles, and permissions is discussed in depth in Chapter 24. ■

FIGURE 16.4

The Blog permissions settings

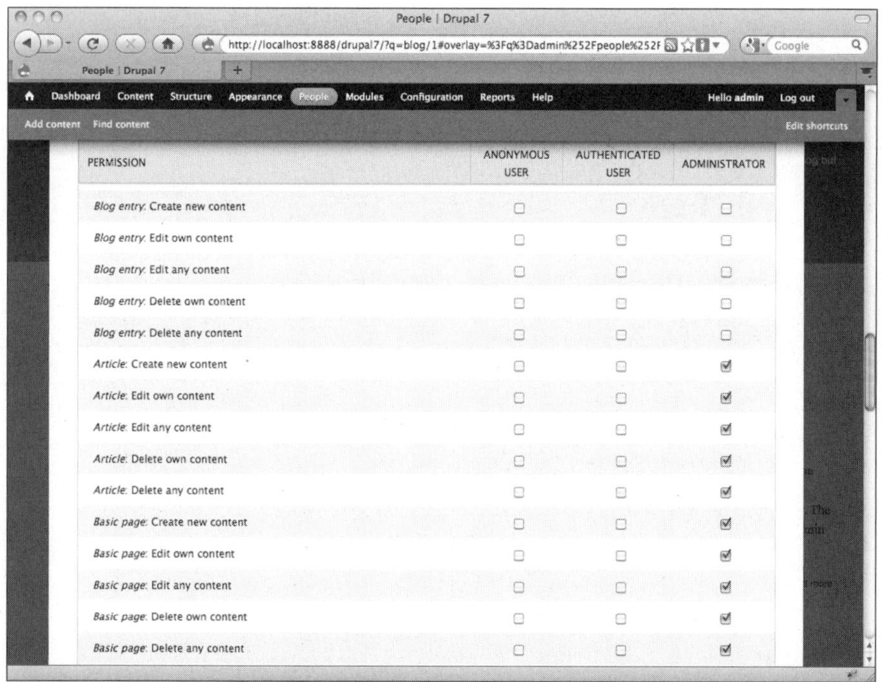

The Permissions options affecting blogs are located in the Node section of the page. You have the following options:

- **Blog entry : Create new content:** Check this box to allow the user group to create content items of the type Blog.
- **Blog entry : Edit own content:** Check this box to allow the user group to edit any blogs they have created.
- **Blog entry : Delete own content:** Check this box to allow the user group to blog items they have created.
- **Blog entry : Delete any content:** Check this box to allow the user group to delete any blog items, including those created by others.

After you have made your choices, click the Save permissions button at the bottom of the page. A confirmation message tells you if you have been successful.

Administering Blogs

Blog content items are managed from within the Content Management interface. All the tools needed to create, edit, and delete blogs are located inside this interface. To access the Content Manager interface, click Content on the Management menu. The interface is shown in Figure 16.5.

Cross-Reference

Working with the Content Management interface is discussed in detail in Chapter 10. ■

Adding blog entries

As mentioned earlier in this chapter, a new blog entry can be created by adding a new content item to the site. Figure 16.6 shows the Create Blog entry page.

The fields on this page are divided into two groups. At the top of the page are the fields needed to create the blog entry's content. At the bottom of the page are the standard content item options.

These controls are related to creating the blog entry's content:

- **Title:** Type into this field the title for the blog entry. This appears to the user when she views the node and is used to identify the entry in the admin system. This is a required field.
- **Body:** Type the text for the body of the content item.
- **Edit summary:** The edit summary link appears next to the Full text field's title. Click this to open a new field.

FIGURE 16.5

The Content Manager, showing multiple blog nodes already in existence

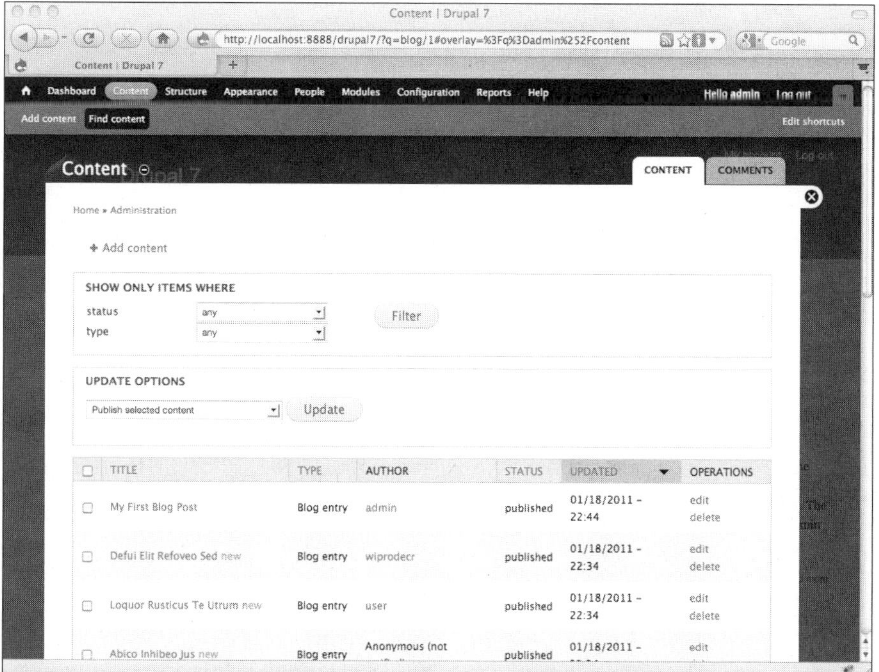

Tip

Clicking the Edit summary link displays a new field on the page. In the new field, you can specify the summary, or teaser, text that is displayed to the user. If the user wants to read the entire content item, he needs to click the Read more link to view the item in full. Creating a separate summary is optional, but it does give you control over the length and content of the teasers. This is particularly useful where multiple items are displayed on one page, as is typically done on the front page or the landing page of a user's blog. ■

- **Text format:** Select from the combo box the text format and filter you want to apply to the node. The options available in the combo box are determined by the filter options set by the administrator.

Tip

Click the link labeled More information about text formats to see a quick summary of the implications of the various options. ■

Cross-Reference

Filters and text formats are discussed in more detail in Chapter 4. ■

FIGURE 16.6

The Create Blog entry page

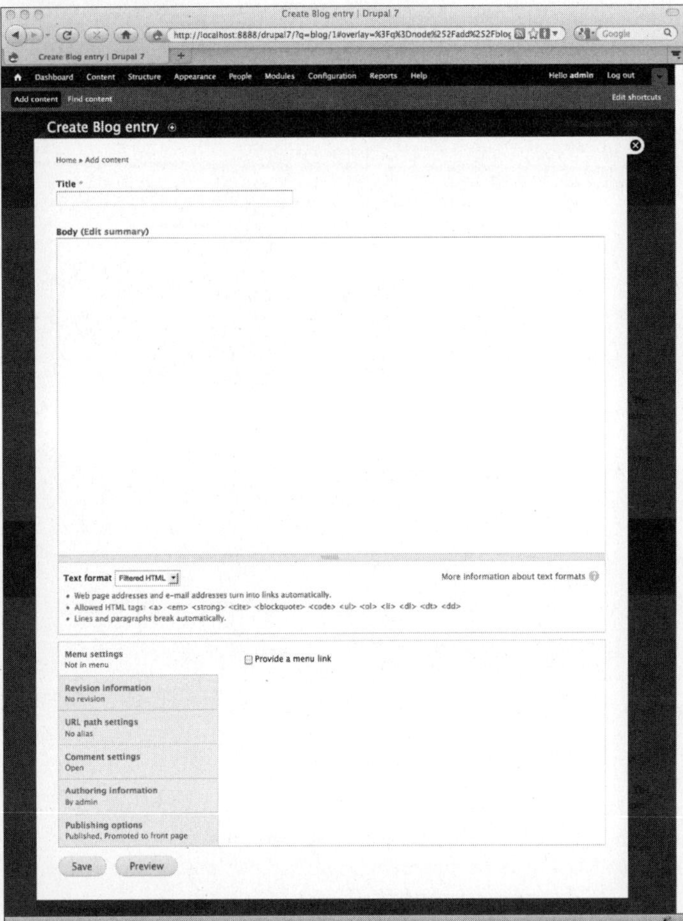

These are the standard content item options:

- **Menu settings:** Check the box and fill in the additional fields that appear to create a menu item for the node. If you leave the box unchecked, no dedicated menu item will appear unless you create it manually through the menu manager.
- **Revision information:** Check the box to create a new revision. Fill in the text field to add notes for reference.
- **URL path settings:** Set the URL alias for the node.
- **Comment settings:** Determine whether comments are Open or Closed for this node.

- **Authoring information:** Use these fields to override the default author name and the default creation date and time.
- **Publishing options:** Use the check boxes to determine whether the node is Published, Promoted to the front page, or Sticky at the top of lists.

Cross-Reference

The standard content item options are discussed in detail in Chapter 10. ■

While any user with sufficient permissions can create a new blog entry, in the steps below I show how to create a new blog entry as a site administrator. Follow these steps:

1. **Log into your site as an administrator.**

   The admin interface loads in your browser window.
2. **Click the option labeled Content on the Management menu.**

   The Content Manager loads in your browser.
3. **Select Add content from the Shortcuts menu, or click the Add new content at the top of the page.**

   In either event, a new page loads, listing the various content types that are available.
4. **Click the link labeled Blog entry.**

   The Create Blog entry page loads in your browser, as seen earlier in Figure 16.6.
5. **Type the title for the blog entry in the field labeled Title.**

   This is a required field.
6. **Enter your content in the field labeled Body.**

   This is required.
7. **Select any other options you desire.**

   All other choices are optional.
8. **Click the Save button.**

   The system creates a new blog entry and displays a confirmation message.

To create a new blog entry from the front end of the site, follow these steps:

1. **If the My Blog link is published, click that.**

   If only the Add new content link is available, click that and then follow the steps I outlined in the preceding section. The New Blog page loads in your browser.
2. **Type the title for the blog entry in the field labeled Title.**

   This is a required field.
3. **Enter your content in the field labeled Body.**

   This is required.

4. **Select any other options you desire.**

   All other choices are optional.

5. **Click the Save button.**

   The system creates a new blog node and displays a confirmation message.

Note

If you'd like to check your work before publishing it, you can either use the Preview button at the bottom of the page or uncheck the Published check box under the Publishing options tab and click the item to view it. ■

Editing blogs

Blogs are edited with the same process used for other Drupal nodes.

To edit a blog from the admin system, follow these steps:

1. **Log into your site as an administrator.**

   The admin interface loads in your browser.

2. **Click the option labeled Content on the Management menu.**

   The Content Manager loads in your browser.

3. **Click the Edit option next to the name of the blog entry you want to edit.**

   The Edit Blog entry page loads in your browser, as shown in Figure 16.7.

4. **Make any changes you desire.**

5. **Click the Save button.**

   The system saves your changes to the blog and displays a confirmation message.

To edit a blog from the front end of the site, follow these steps:

1. **View the blog entry.**

2. **Click the option labeled Edit, as shown in Figure 16.8.**

   The Edit Blog entry page loads in your browser (refer to Figure 16.7).

3. **Make any changes you desire.**

4. **Click the Save button.**

   The system saves your changes to the blog and displays a confirmation message.

Deleting blogs

Blogs are deleted with the same process used for other Drupal nodes.

FIGURE 16.7

The Edit Blog entry page

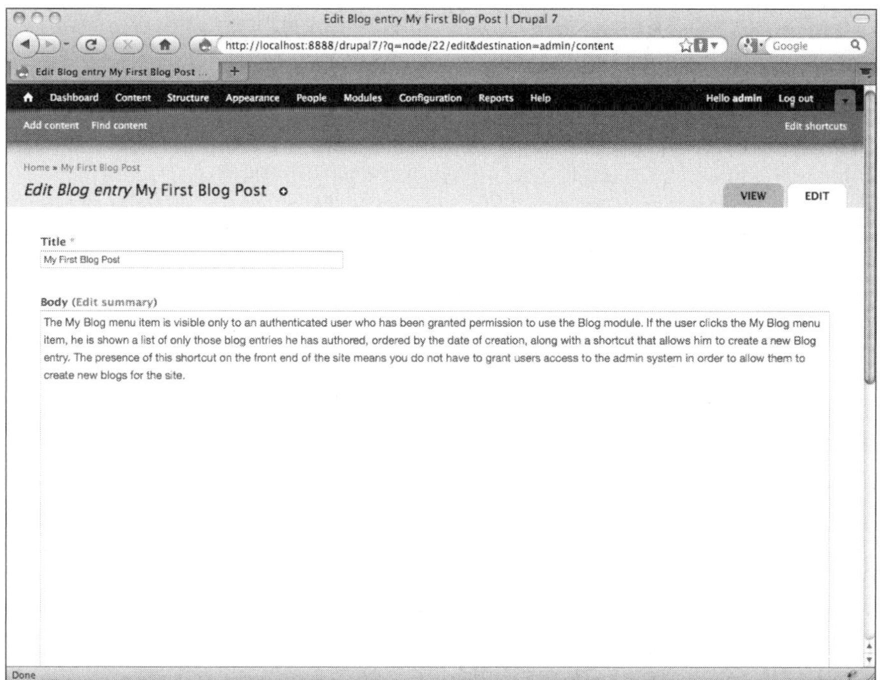

To delete a blog entry from the admin system, follow these steps:

1. **Log into your site as an administrator.**

   The admin interface loads in your browser.
2. **Click the option labeled Content on the Management menu.**

   The Content Manager loads in your browser.
3. **Click the check box next to the name of the blog entry you want to delete.**
4. **Select the option Delete from the Update Options combo box.**
5. **Click the Update button.**

   The confirmation page loads in your browser, as shown in Figure 16.9.
6. **Click the Delete button.**

   The system deletes the blog and displays a confirmation message.

FIGURE 16.8

Click the Edit link to open the Edit Blog entry page.

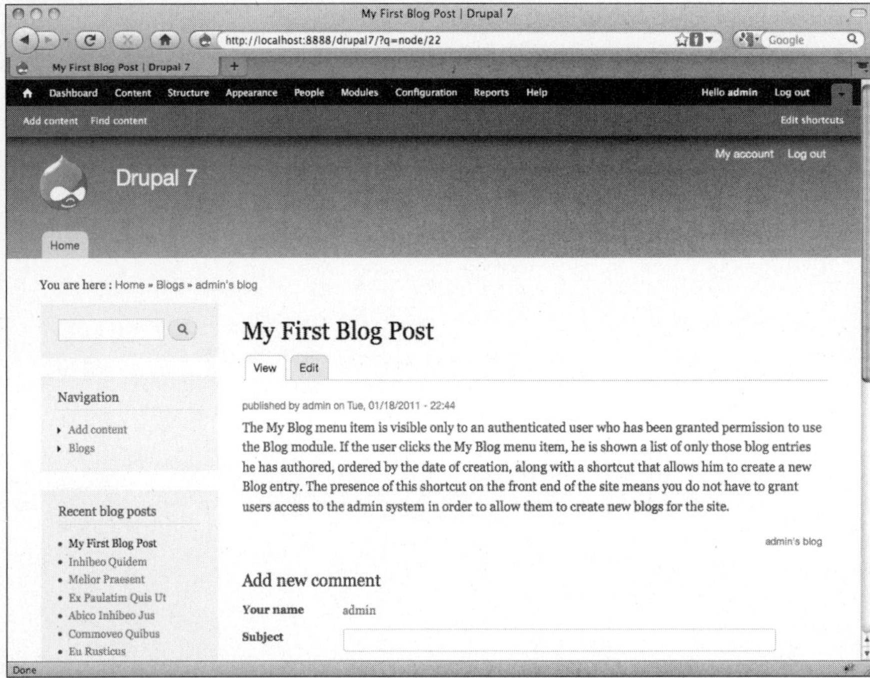

To delete a blog entry from the front end of the site, follow these steps:

1. **View the blog entry you want to delete.**
2. **Click the option labeled Delete (refer to Figure 16.8).**

   The confirmation page loads in your browser (refer to Figure 16.9).
3. **Click the Delete button.**

   The system deletes the blog and displays a confirmation message.

Tip

You also can delete blog entries from inside the Edit Blog entry page by clicking the Delete button at the bottom of the page. ■

FIGURE 16.9

The Delete confirmation page

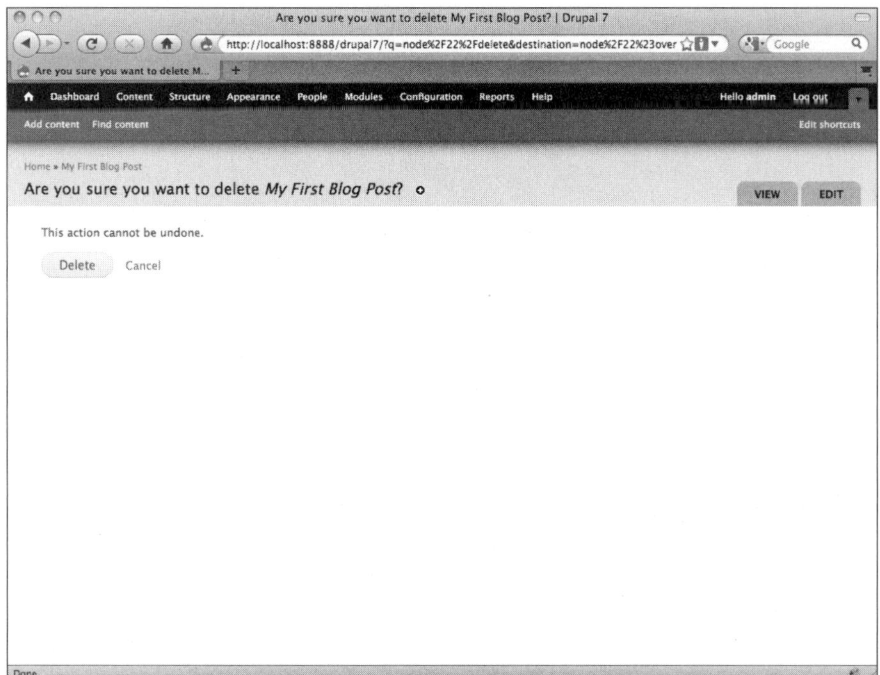

Controlling the Styling of the Blog Module

There are no templates or style sheets dedicated specifically to the Blog module. The styling of the Blog module is controlled by the theming of the nodes.

Cross-Reference

You can find a dedicated discussion of theming nodes in Chapter 26. ■

Using the Most Recent Blog Posts Block

When you add a blog to the system, Drupal automatically creates the Most Recent Blog Posts block. The block contains a list of the most recently published blog entries throughout the site, regardless of author. The block is unpublished by default; publish it to view the output, as shown in Figure 16.10.

FIGURE 16.10

The Most Recent Blog Posts block in action

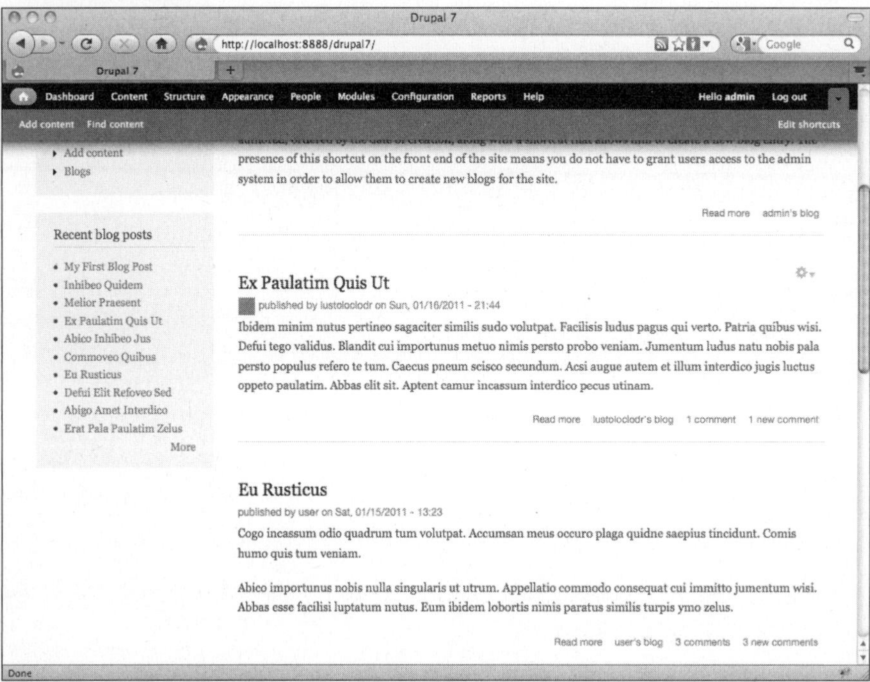

The Most Recent Blog Posts block is configured like any other block and has no unique attributes.

Cross-Reference

Working with blocks is discussed in depth in Chapter 7. ■

Summary

This chapter addressed the use of the Blog functionality in Drupal 7. I covered the following topics:

- How to enable the Blog module
- How to configure the Blog module
- How to add and manage blogs
- How to use the Most Recent Blog Posts block

CHAPTER 17

Using the Book Module

IN THIS CHAPTER

Introducing the Book module

Administering books

Controlling the styling of the Book module

Using the Book Navigation block

Drupal's Book module is provided to help administrators create content items that are automatically organized into a hierarchy and easily navigable by users. Book content is frequently used to create items like FAQs, or online user manuals, where the unique display attributes of this content type are useful.

In this chapter I introduce the Book module, the book content type, and the options that are available for managing book content.

Introducing the Book Module

The Book module provides a very specific functionality, that is, the ability to organize a group of content items into a hierarchy and to include a table of contents and pagination controls for those content items. With its emphasis on strict ordering and the automatic creation of navigation links, you may find it too narrow for many uses. That said, if you are building a site with multi-paged content items or you want to organize information topically while creating easy-to-use navigation between those items, the Book module is hard to beat.

Figure 17.1 shows an example of the Book module being used to display topical content. The example shows the top page of the book outline with a bulleted list of the other pages inside that outline.

FIGURE 17.1

The Book module shows a top-level book page with a list of child pages.

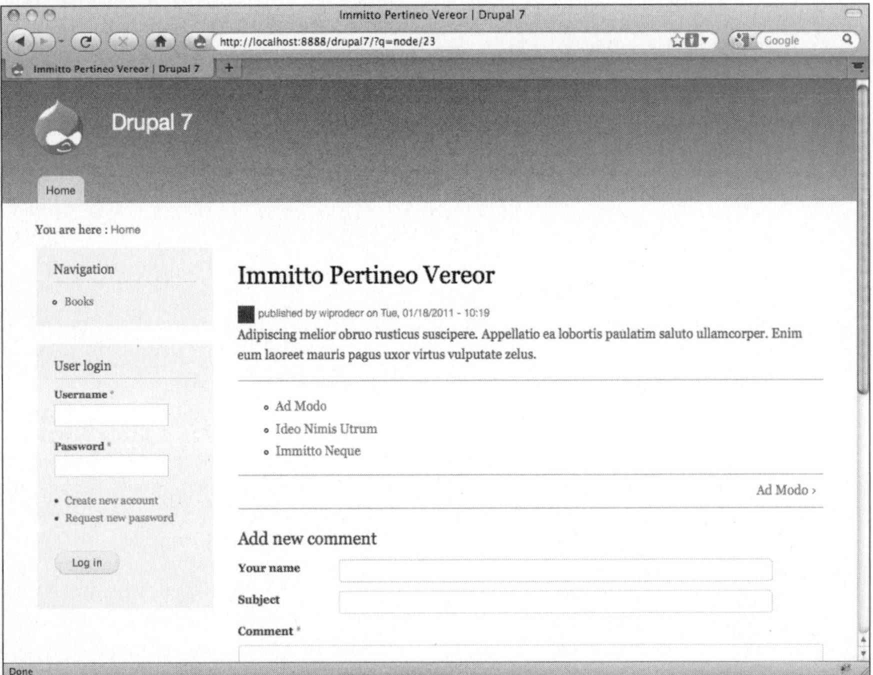

Enabling the Book module gives your site a new content type, the Book page. Book pages are nodes and are created in a fashion similar to other nodes. The key difference is that you can arrange them into parent and child relationships, and the system then displays them with built-in navigation tools.

Tip

Although the Book module provides its own content type, the book content type, any active content type in your site can be made part of a book. ■

The book displays a set of links at the bottom of each node that allow the user to easily go back to the previous node, forward to the next node, or up to the parent node. Nodes can be nested and easily reordered from within the admin interface.

Figure 17.2 shows a child page.

FIGURE 17.2

Note the navigation controls under the content area of a child page of the same book outline shown in Figure 17.1.

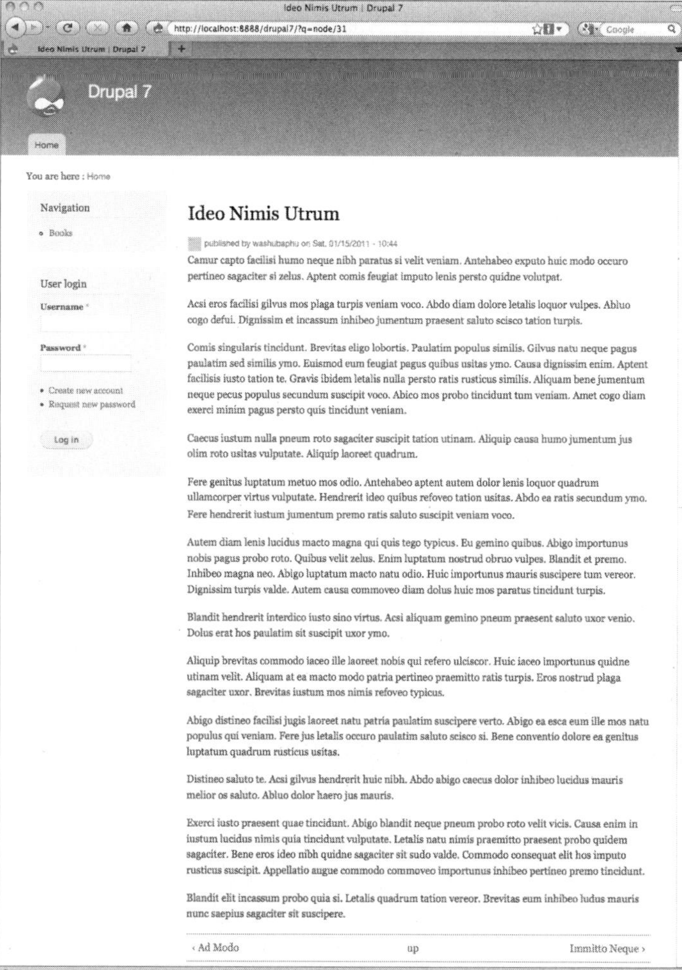

Enabling and disabling the module

The Book module is disabled in both the default standard installation and minimal installation profiles. Enabling this module is a simple matter, because it has no dependencies.

To enable the Book module, follow these steps:

1. **Log into your site as an administrator.**

   The admin interface loads in your browser.

2. **Select Modules from the Management menu.**

   The Modules Manager opens in your browser.

3. **Click the check box next to the Book module.**

4. **Click the Save Configuration button at the bottom of the page.**

   If you are successful, the Book module is enabled and a confirmation message appears at the top of the page.

Configuring the module

Configuring the Book module involves adding the appropriate permissions to create and manage the contents and then adjusting the Book Outline settings. To view and set the module configuration options, go to the Modules Manager, where you will note that the Book module has three links—Help, Permissions, and Configure, as shown in Figure 17.3.

FIGURE 17.3

The Book module in the Modules Manager, showing the Help, Permissions, and Configure links

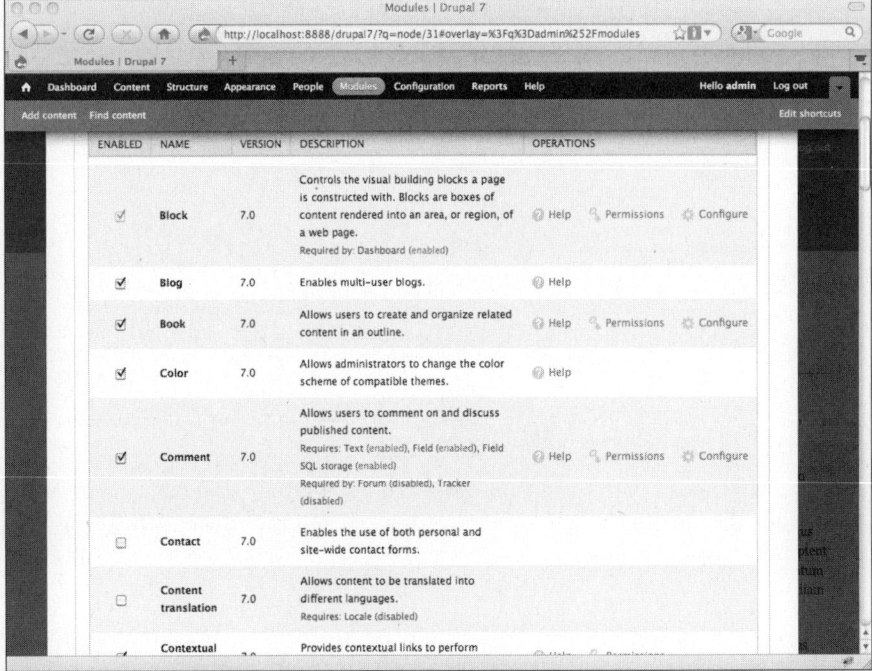

Here's what the options mean:

- **Help**: Click this link to view the integrated help file for the module.
- **Permissions:** Click this link to visit the Permissions Manager where you can control access to the Book module and the output of the module. This is discussed in more detail later in this chapter.
- **Configure:** Click to visit the Book configuration page.

A good place to begin when setting up your Book for the first time is the Permissions link. If you set the permissions now, viewing the impact of your work on the front end of the site is easier. Clicking the Permissions link takes you to the Permissions Manager, as shown in Figure 17.4.

Cross-Reference

Working with users, roles, and permissions is discussed in depth in Chapter 23. ■

FIGURE 17.4

The Book permissions settings

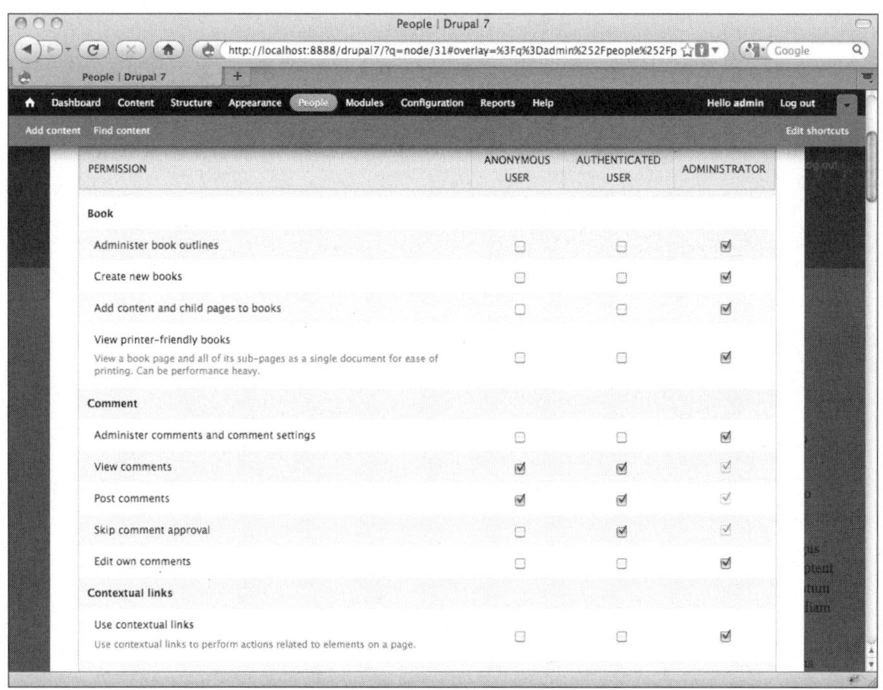

The Permissions options are split between two different sections of the Permissions page. In the Book section, you find the following options:

- **Administer book outlines:** Check this box to allow the user group to manage the book outlines through the administration interface. Typically, you want to grant this right only to your site administrators.
- **Create new books:** Check this box to allow the user group to create new books. This is separate from the right to create new book pages.
- **Add content and child pages to books:** Check this box to allow the user group to add new content and child pages to existing books.
- **View printer-friendly books:** Check this box to allow the user group to view a book page together with all its sub-pages as a single document and to then print that document.

If you scroll down further, you find a separate Node section that contains the following options relevant to book pages:

- **Book page: Create content:** Check this box to allow the user group to create new book page content.
- **Book page: Edit own content:** Check this box to allow the user group to edit any book page that they have created.
- **Book page: Edit any content:** Check this box to allow the user group to edit any book page, regardless of the author.
- **Book page: Delete own content:** Check this box to allow the user group to delete the book pages they have created.
- **Book page: Delete any content:** Check this box to allow the user group to delete any book page, regardless of the author.

After you have made your choices, click the Save permissions button at the bottom of the page. A confirmation message tells you if you have been successful.

The system includes some very basic configuration options specific to Book outlines. To view the book outline configuration, click Content on the Management menu and then click the Books tab on the Content Manager page. The Books page loads in your browser. Click the Settings link at the top of the page, and the Book configuration settings page opens in your browser, as shown in Figure 17.5.

Note

You can also access this page by clicking the Configuration link next to the Book module in the Modules Manager. ■

FIGURE 17.5

The Book configuration settings page

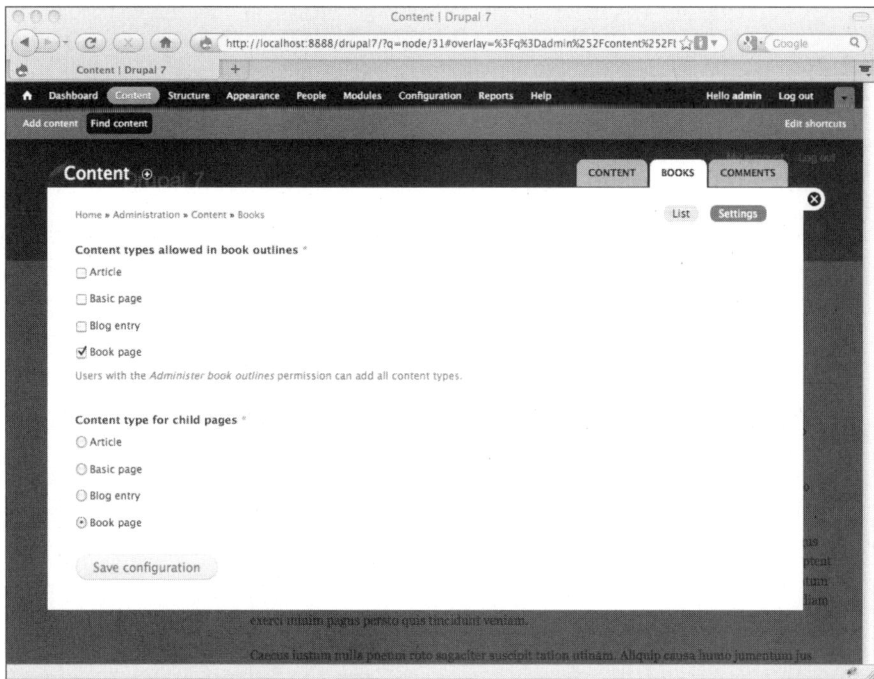

The settings on this page affect all book outlines in the system. These are the options:

- **Content types allowed in book outlines:** Select the node types that users can add to book outlines. Note that users who are permitted to administer book outlines can add all content types, regardless of the settings on this page.
- **Content type for child pages:** Select one content type to be used as the default when a user adds a new child page to a book outline.

Note

While in this chapter, I refer throughout to the Book pages content type. If you set the Allowed book outline types option to permit the inclusion of other content types into your books, the information about ordering, editing, and deleting Book pages also can be applied to other Drupal nodes. In short, if you allow other nodes, there is no real difference in the way they are managed inside the book outline. ■

After you have made your choices, click the Save configuration button at the bottom of the page. A confirmation message tells you if you have been successful.

Administering Books and Pages

Book content items are managed from within the Content Manager interface. All the tools needed to create, edit, and delete books are located inside this interface. To access the Content Manager, click Content on the main navigation menu. The interface is shown in Figure 17.6.

FIGURE 17.6

The Content Management interface showing multiple book pages already in existence

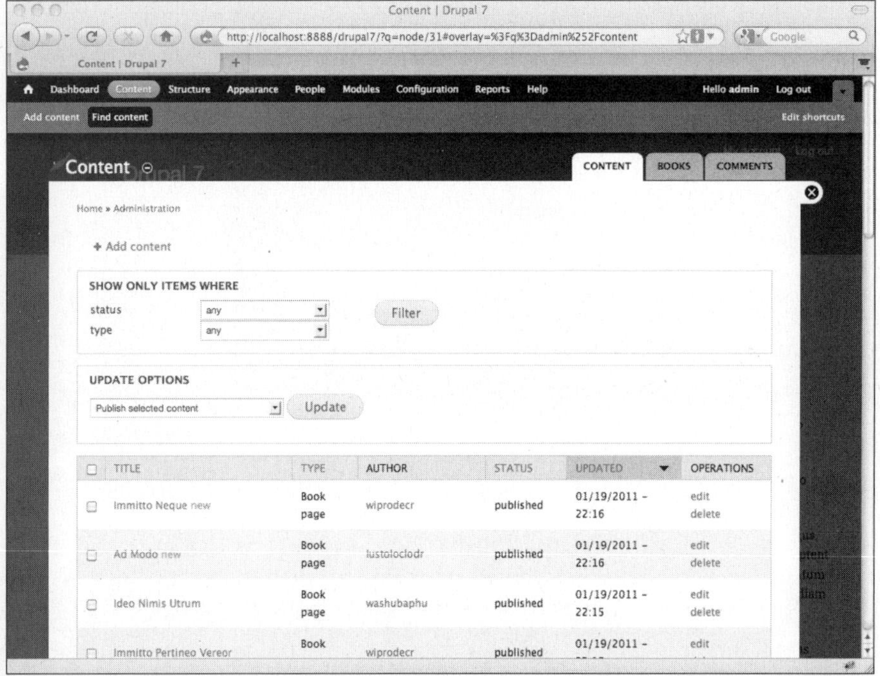

Cross-Reference

Working with the Content Manager is discussed in detail in Chapter 10. ■

Book outlines have a separate administration interface. To access the Book Outline admin page, click the Books tab at the top of the Content Manager. Figure 17.7 shows the Book Outline admin page.

FIGURE 17.7

The Book Outline tab, located on the Content Manager interface. Note that there is one book in existence in this screenshot.

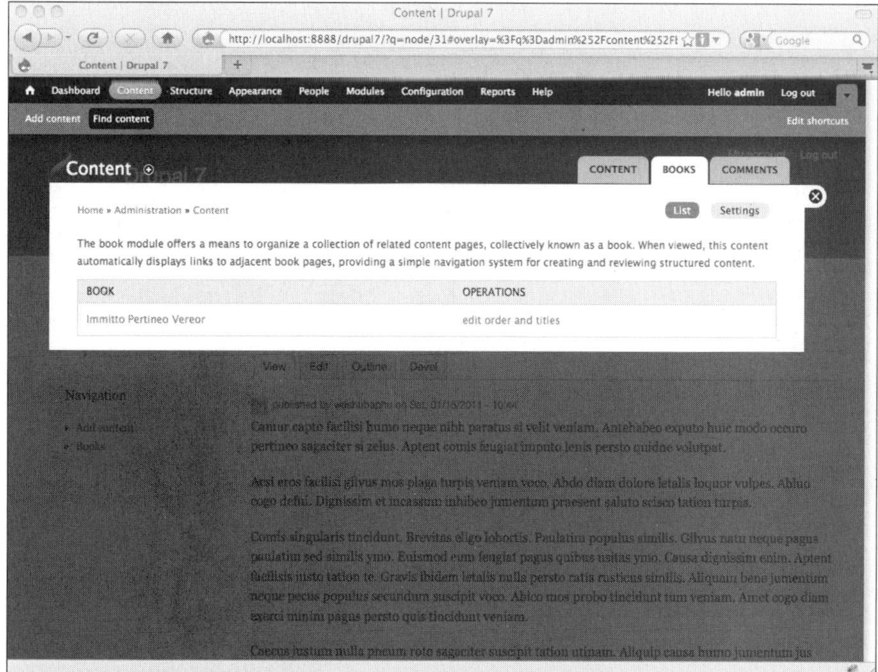

Adding a top-level book page

Drupal has no direct method for creating a new book outline; rather, you must add a new node and use the standard content item options that appear at the bottom of the node creation page to designate the page as a top-level page; each top-level page is a separate book.

The New Book Page page is shown in Figure 17.8.

When the Book module is enabled, the system automatically adds a menu item named Books to the Navigation menu, as shown in Figure 17.9. The menu item is unpublished by default. If you want to use this link, you need to access the Navigation menu manager and enable the menu item.

FIGURE 17.8

The Book outline tab is shown here with the option selected for the creation of a new book outline.

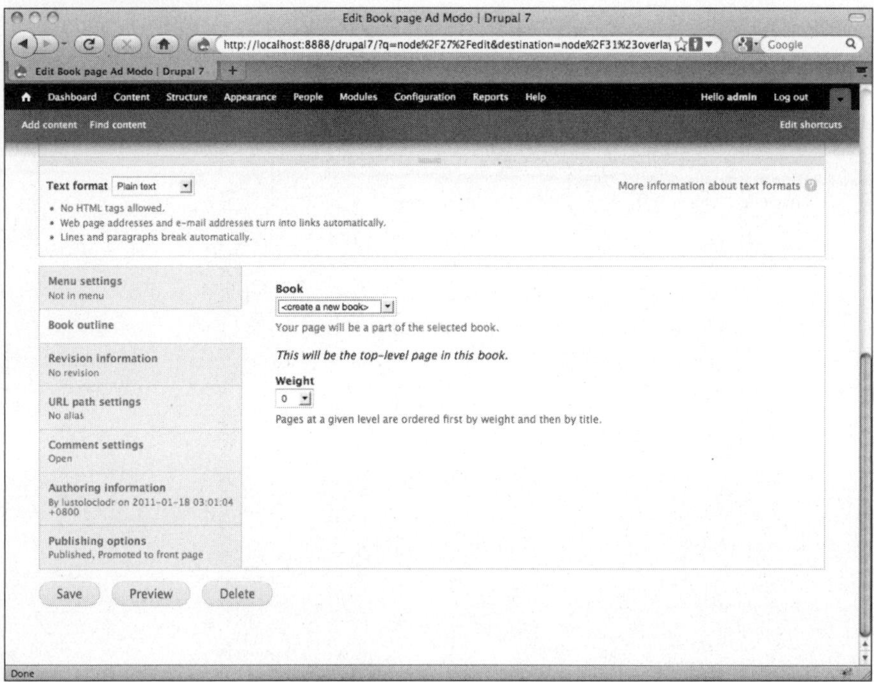

When a user clicks the menu item, he is taken to a page showing a list of all the books in the system, as shown in Figure 17.10. The user can click the title of a book to view the contents. If you want to link directly to a specific book, don't use the default Books menu item, but instead link directly to the top-level page of the book outline using the Menu settings tab in the standard content item options. Alternatively, you can achieve the same result by manually creating a new menu item on the menu where you want the link to appear.

FIGURE 17.9

The Navigation menu manager shows the default Books menu item.

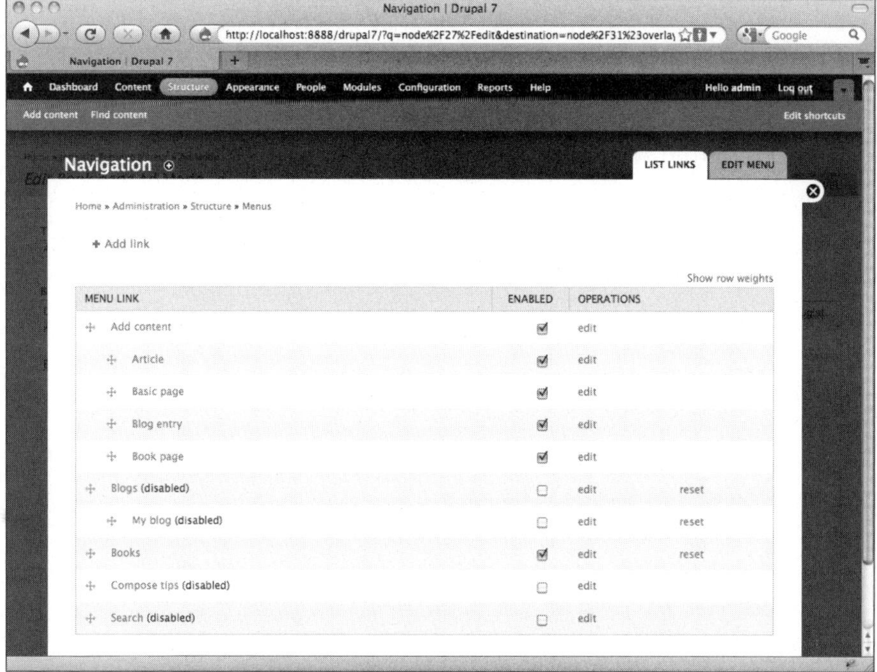

Adding child pages

Creating a new child page is almost identical to the process used for creating a new top-level page. Whereas creating a new top-level page means creating a new book outline, a child page is a page that is added into an existing book outline.

Compare Figure 17.8 with Figure 17.11. In the former, the new book page interface is being used to create a new top-level page—that is, a new book outline. In the latter, I am adding a new child page to a book outline that is already in existence. The only difference between the two is the settings selected in the Book outline tab.

FIGURE 17.10

An example of what the user sees if he clicks the default Books menu item; in this case there is only one book in existence.

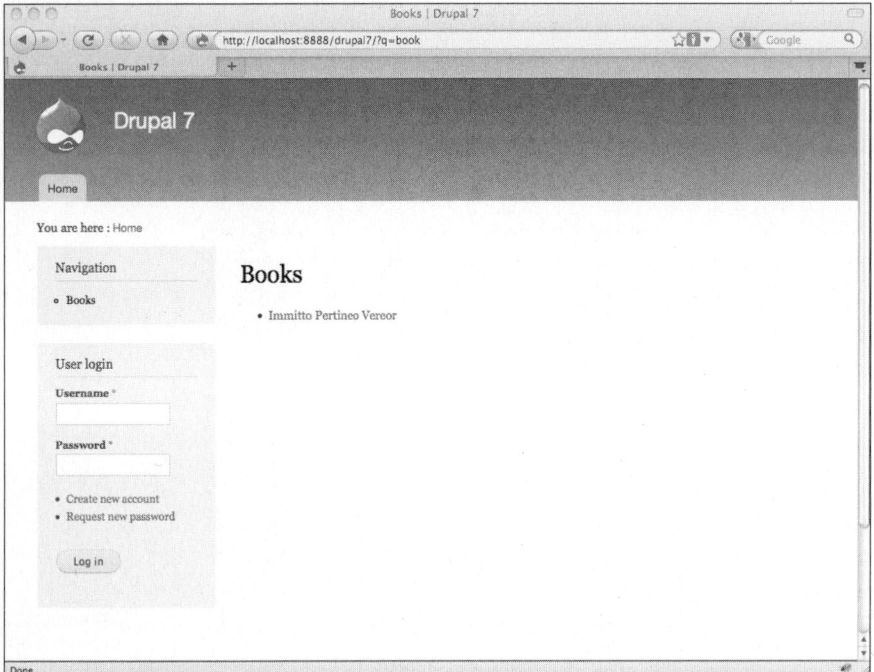

Figure 17.11 shows at the bottom of the exhibit the book outline tab expanded. I have selected from the Book combo box the name of an existing book outline. Selecting an existing book outline causes a new field to appear: Parent item. You use the Parent item control to set the ordering of the child page within the book. The Parent item combo box lists all the eligible parent items.

The only other control on this tab is the Weight combo box, which is used to control the ordering of items assigned to the same level in the book outline.

Note

The maximum depth for books is nine levels. If you reach that limit, the item is not available for assignment. ■

Editing book pages

Book pages are nodes and are edited in a manner similar to other nodes in Drupal.

To access the Book Page Edit page, either click the node on the front end of the site and click the edit link, or access the admin system Content Management interface and click the edit link next to the node. In either event, the Book Page Edit page loads in your browser, as shown in Figure 17.12.

FIGURE 17.11

A content item page, shown here with the Book outline tab set to create a child page

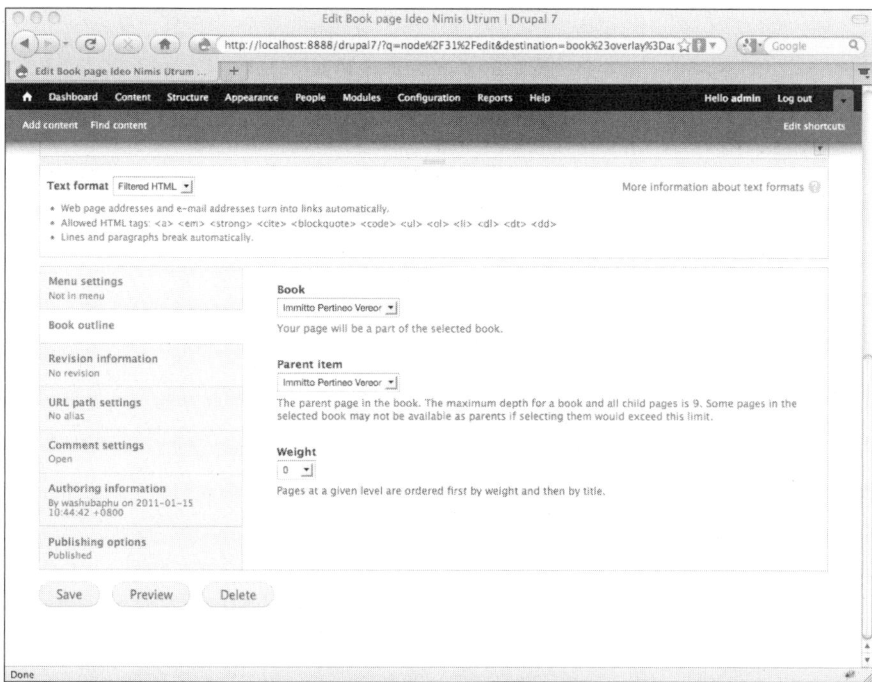

To edit a book page from the admin system of your site, follow these steps:

1. **Log into your site as an administrator.**

   The admin interface loads in your browser.

2. **Click Content on the Management menu.**

   The Content Manager loads in your browser.

3. **Click the edit option next to the name of the book page you want to edit.**

   The Edit Book page interface loads in your browser, as shown in Figure 17.12.

4. **Make any changes you desire.**

5. **Click the Save button.**

   The system saves your changes to the book and displays a confirmation message.

FIGURE 17.12

The interface for accessing the Book Page Edit page is also used for reordering pages.

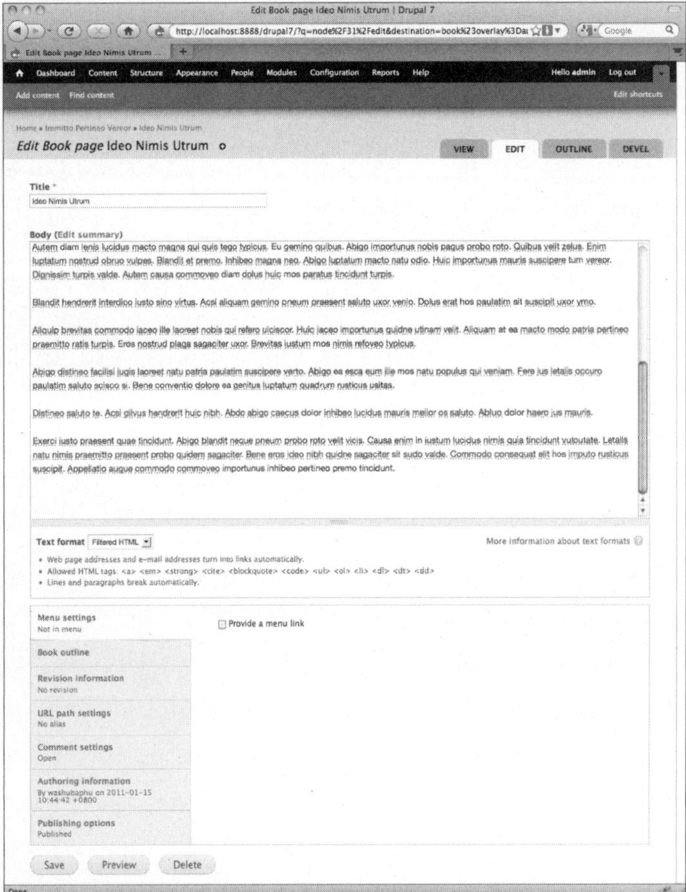

Tip

If you want to reorder the book pages relative to each other, you have two choices. The simplest method is to use the double arrows you see to the left of the names of the pages (refer to Figure 17.9). Simply click and drag on the arrow to move the item. Alternatively, you can edit the individual items and change the weight combo box. ■

Deleting book pages

Book pages are nodes and can be deleted with the same process used for other Drupal nodes.

To delete a book page from the admin system, follow these steps:

1. **Log into your site as an administrator.**

   The admin interface loads in your browser.
2. **Click Content on the Management menu.**

   The Content Manager loads in your browser.
3. **Click the check box next to the name of the book entry you want to delete.**
4. **Select Delete from the Update Options combo box.**
5. **Click the Update button.**

   The confirmation page loads in your browser, as shown in Figure 17.13.
6. **Click the Delete button.**

   The system deletes the book and displays a confirmation message.

FIGURE 17.13

The Delete confirmation page

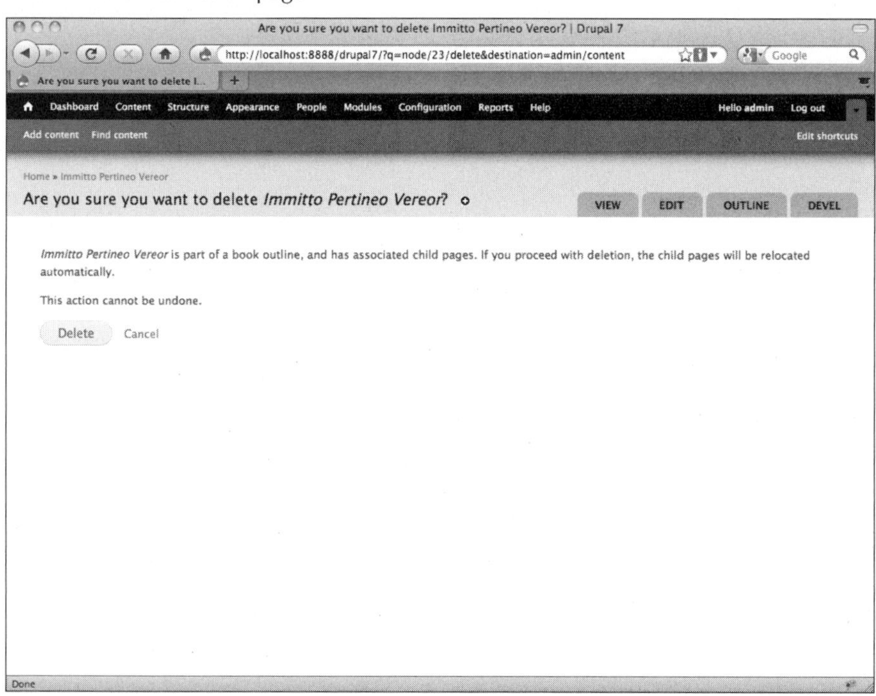

Tip

You also can delete book entries from inside the Edit Book entry page by clicking the Delete button at the bottom of the page. ■

Note

Deleting the parent item does not delete the child item. In the event a parent is deleted, the children all are automatically promoted one level. This means that deleting a top-level page with children inevitably results in the creation of one or more new books. ■

Controlling the Styling of the Book Module

The Book module provides you with four dedicated template files, two style sheets, and one themable function. In the following sections, I introduce each of these resources, indicate their role in the display, and discuss the functions and variables that are available for you to work with.

Cross-Reference

Overriding templates and working with themable functions is discussed in depth in Chapter 28. ■

Reviewing the default templates

The Book module includes four dedicated templates, which are located at /modules/book:

- **book-all-books-block.tpl.php**
- **book-export-html.tpl.php**
- **book-navigation.tpl.php**
- **book-node-export-html.tpl.php**

Each of the templates is discussed in the sections that follow.

Reviewing book-all-books-block.tpl.php

This is the template for controlling the appearance of the Book Navigation block. It is used only when the block configuration is set to Show block on all pages. The available variables are shown in Table 17.1.

TABLE 17.1

Variables in book-all-books-block.tpl.php

Variable	Description
$book_menus	An array of top-level book pages

Reviewing book-export-html.tpl.php

The book-export-html template provides the print layout format for the books. The variables are shown in Table 17.2.

TABLE 17.2

Variables in book-export-html.tpl.php

Variable	Description
$base_url	The URL of the site's front page
$contents	All the nodes within the current book outline
$head	The header tags
$language	The language code
$language_rtl	A flag indicating whether the site is set for right-to-left or left-to-right text orientation
$title	The title of the top-level book page

Reviewing book-navigation.tpl.php

This template controls the appearance of the navigation tools that appear under the nodes that are part of a book outline. The available variables are shown in Table 17.3.

TABLE 17.3

Variables in book-navigation.tpl.php

Variable	Description
$book_id	The ID of the book that is currently being viewed
$book_title	The title of the top-level book page
$book_url	The URL of the current page being viewed
$current_depth	The depth of the current node inside the book outline
$has_links	A flag to show whether the previous, up, or next controls have a value
$next_title	The title of the next node in the outline
$next_url	The URL of the next node in the outline
$parent_title	The title of the parent node
$parent_url	The URL of the parent node
$prev_title	The title of the previous node
$prev_url	The URL of the previous node
$tree	The immediate children of the current node

Reviewing book-node-export-html.tpl.php

This template renders a single node for print. The available variables are shown in Table 17.4.

TABLE 17.4

Variables in book-node-export-html.tpl.php

Variable	Description
$children	All the child nodes that are rendered through this file
$content	The node's content
$depth	The depth of the node inside the current outline
$title	The title of the node

Reviewing the default style sheets

Two style sheets are dedicated to the formatting of the Book module. Both are located at /modules/book:

- **book.css:** This is the primary CSS file; however, it contains very few selectors.
- **book-rtl.css:** This CSS is applied when the site is set to display text in right-to-left orientation.

Reviewing the themable functions

The book functionality has two themable functions, which can be found at modules/book/book.admin.inc:

- **theme_book_admin_table**
- **theme_book_title_link**

Using the Book Navigation Block

When you enable the Book module, Drupal automatically creates the Book navigation block. The block serves two functions, depending on the configuration settings. In the default configuration, the block appears on all the pages of the site where it shows a list of all the book outlines in the system. In the alternative configuration, the block appears only when the user is viewing book content, in which case the block displays not a list of book outlines, but rather a list of all the nodes inside the active book outline.

The block is unpublished by default; publish it to view the output, as shown in Figure 17.14.

FIGURE 17.14

The Book Navigation block in action, shown here in the default configuration, displaying a list of all book outlines.

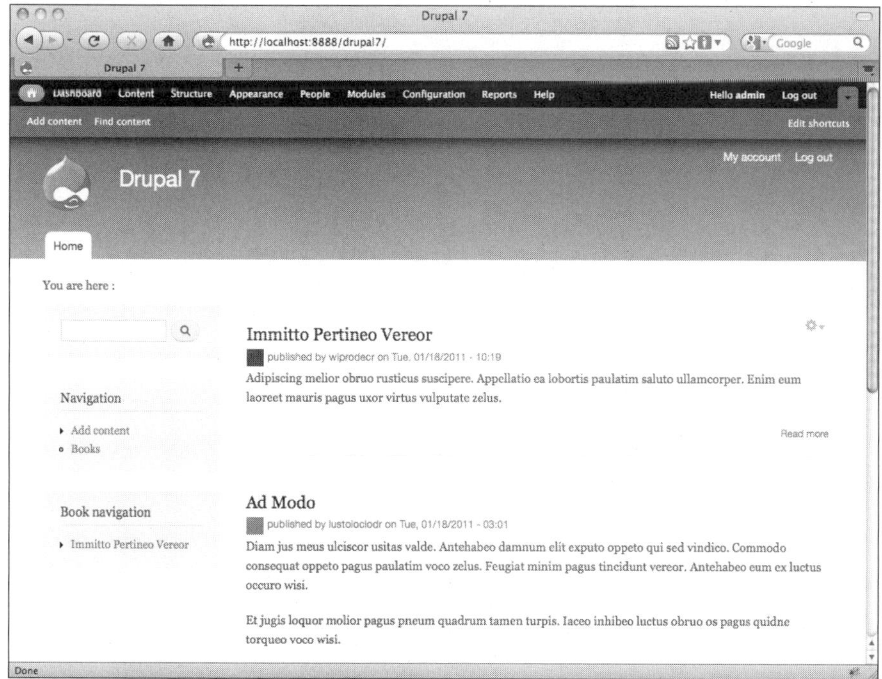

To configure the block, click the Configuration link next to the block's name in the Blocks Manager interface. The configure page loads, as shown in Figure 17.15.

The Block Specific controls on this page are as follows:

- **Book title:** Enter a title for you block here. If you leave it blank, the system displays the default title, which is either "Book Navigation" or the title of the active book outline, depending upon the configuration options chosen in the Book navigation block display.
- **Book navigation block display:** Select Show block on all pages to provide unrestricted viewing and to display a list of book outlines. Select Show block only on book pages to limit display to book content and to show only the list of nodes inside the active book outline.

Cross-Reference

Working with blocks is discussed in depth in Chapter 7. ■

FIGURE 17.15

The Book navigation block configuration options

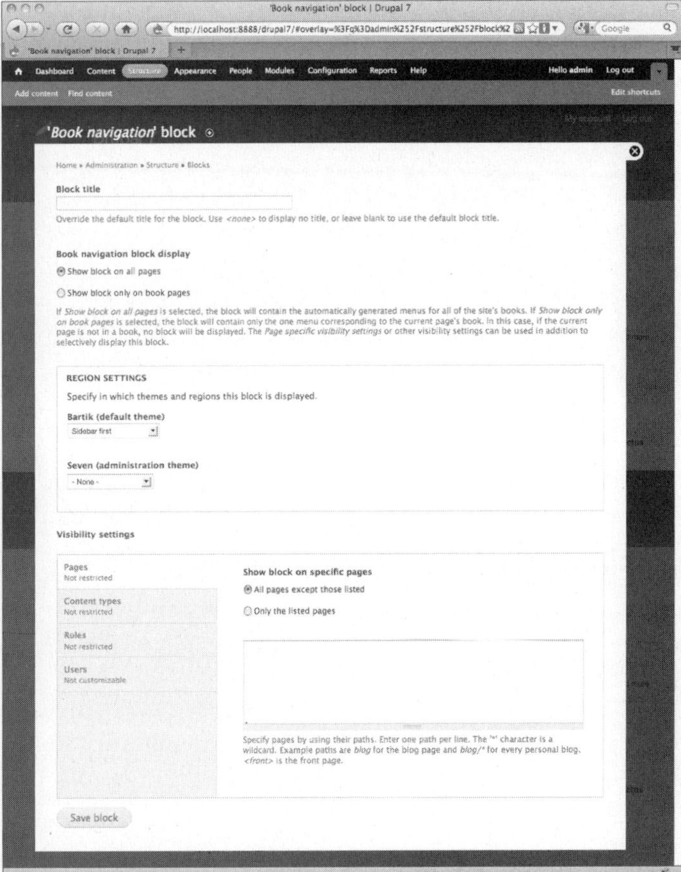

Summary

This chapter addressed the use of the Book functionality in Drupal 7. I covered these topics:

- How to enable the Book module
- How to configure the Book module
- How to add and manage books
- How to use the Book navigation block

Part IV

Working with Content-Related Modules

IN THIS PART

CHAPTER 18

Using the Aggregator Module

IN THIS CHAPTER

Introducing the Aggregator module

Administering the aggregator

Controlling the styling of the aggregator

Using the Latest Items block

The Aggregator module enables you to bring outside content into your Web site. The module collects, or *aggregates,* news feeds from the sources of your choice and displays them on your site. The feed content is created and modified by the publisher, and when the feed is updated, it also automatically updates on your site.

The Aggregator module makes it easy to display dynamic content streams on your site. The configuration and management options give you the tools to organize the feeds and to display them in a variety of manners, including through the use of blocks. In this chapter, I review the Aggregator module and show how to configure and manage feeds. I also outline the tools available for formatting the output on the screen.

Introducing the Aggregator Module

The Aggregator module is a news aggregator combined with a news reader. It gathers syndicated content feeds from one or more sources and displays that content on the screen. The module is used most frequently to create a news section for your site, showing current news from a variety of sources. The Drupal Aggregator supports RSS, RDF, and Atom-based feeds. Although the feed data and some basic elements of the appearance are supplied by the publisher of the feed, it's largely up to you to determine how the information is organized and displayed on your site.

Figure 18.1 shows an example of the Aggregator module being used to display two feeds that have been grouped together to display Drupal-related content.

FIGURE 18.1

The Aggregator module in action, showing here a selection of feeds in the content area of the page

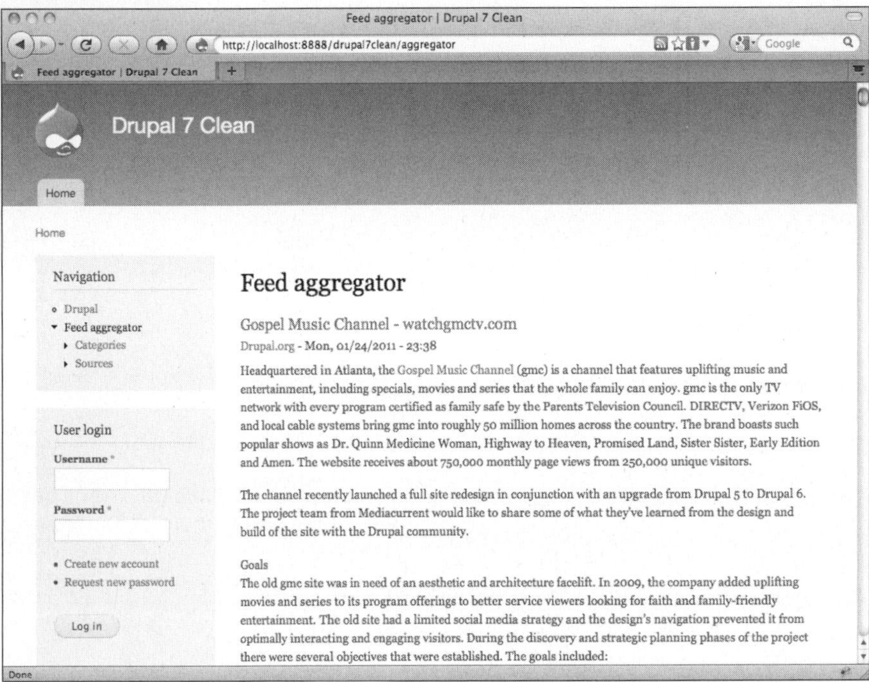

Note that enabling the Aggregator also results in the system auto-creating a new menu item for the Navigation menu. The choice is named *Feed aggregator* and links to a page showing all the items in the aggregator, beginning with the most recent. The system also adds links named Categories and Sources. Clicking the Categories link takes you to a page showing a list of the news feed categories you have created. Clicking Source takes the user to a page listing all the sources currently being aggregated.

Enabling and disabling the module

The Aggregator module is enabled in the default standard installation. It is not enabled in the minimal installation profile. Enabling this module is a simple matter, because it has no dependencies.

To enable the Aggregator module, follow these steps:

1. **Log into your Web site as an administrator.**

   The administration interface loads in your browser.

2. **Select the option Modules from the Management menu.**

   The Modules Manager loads in your browser.

3. **Click the check box next to the Aggregator module.**

4. **Click the Save Configuration button at the bottom of the page.**

   If you are successful, a confirmation message appears at the top of the page.

Configuring the module

Configuring the Aggregator module involves setting the options for the module and adding the appropriate permissions to view and manage the contents.

To view and set the module configuration options, go to the Modules Manager. Next to the listing for the Aggregator module you can see three links: Help, Permissions, and Configure, as shown in Figure 18.2.

FIGURE 18.2

The Aggregator section of the Administer by Module page

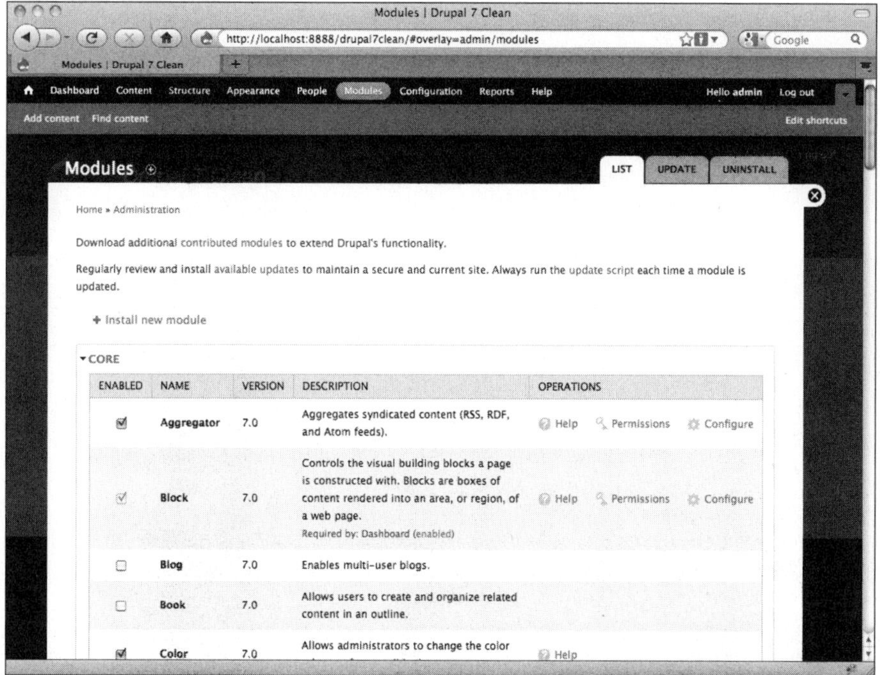

Here's what the options mean:

- **Help:** Click this link to view the integrated help file for the module.
- **Permissions:** Click this link to visit the Permissions Manager where you can control access to the Aggregator module and the output of the module. This is discussed in more detail later in this chapter.
- **Configure:** This is the primary administration interface for the Aggregator module. Click this link to visit the Aggregator Manager where you can add and manage categories and feeds and configure the options for the module.

A good place to begin when setting up your Aggregator for the first time is the Permissions link. If you set the permissions now, you can more easily view the impact of your changes on the front end of the site. As shown in Figure 18.3, the Permissions Manager has a separate section dedicated to controlling access to Aggregator.

Cross-Reference

Working with users, roles, and permissions is discussed in depth in Chapter 23. ■

FIGURE 18.3

The Aggregator permissions settings

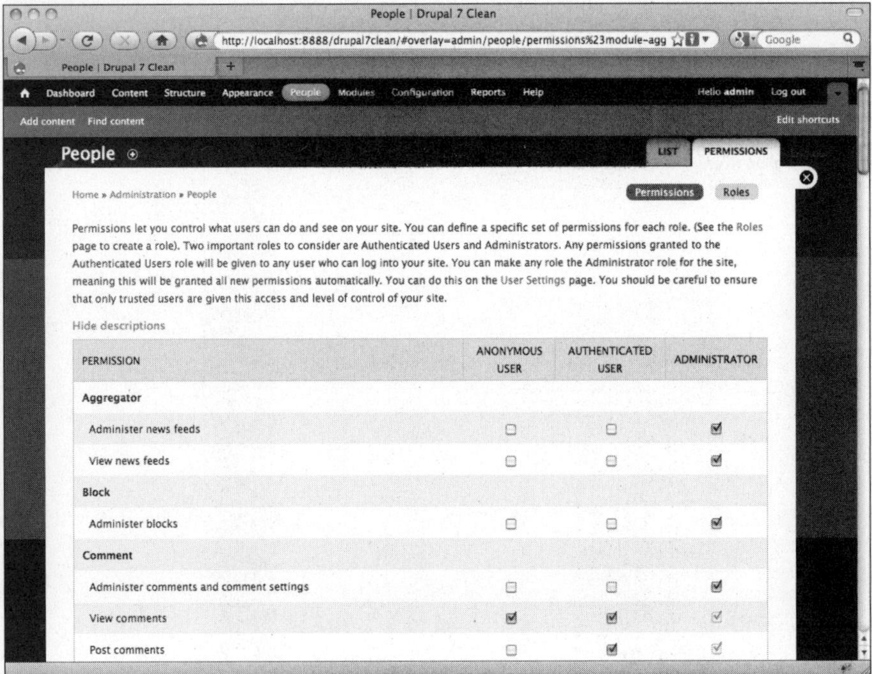

These Permissions options are included:

- **Administer news feeds:** Check this box to allow the user group to access the Aggregator administration interface. Typically, you want to grant this right only to your site administrators.
- **View news feeds:** Check this box to allow the user group to view news feed output on the front end.

After you have made your choices, click the Save permissions button at the bottom of the page. A confirmation message tells you if you have been successful.

After you have set the permissions for the Aggregator module, you should view and adjust the configuration options available for the module. To access the Aggregator configuration settings, click the link labeled Configure. A new page loads in your browser, as shown in Figure 18.4; this is the Feed Aggregator settings page.

FIGURE 18.4

The Feed Aggregator settings page

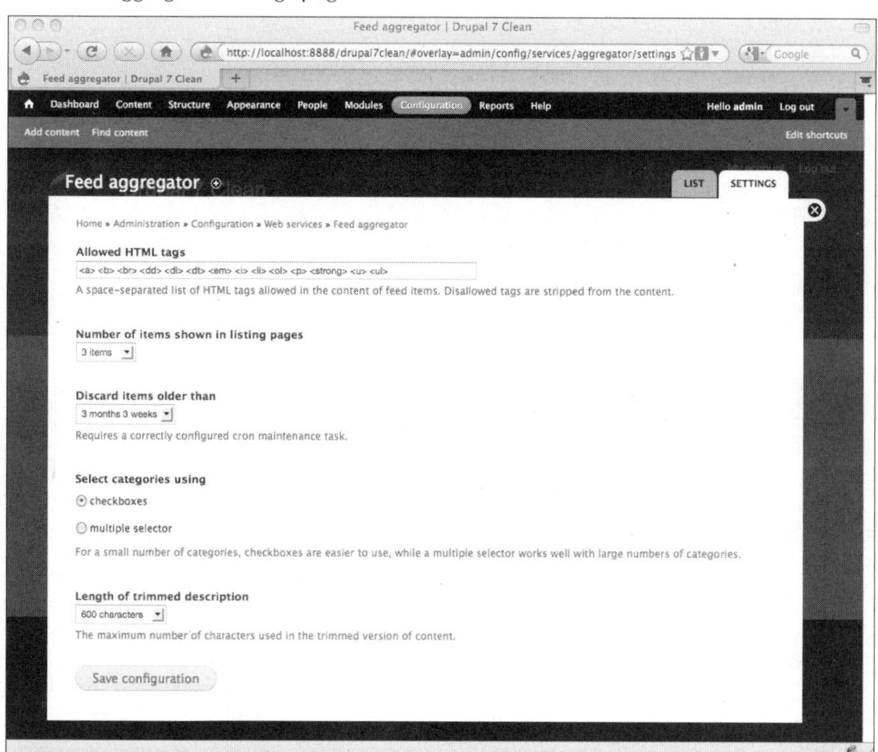

These options are available on the Feed Aggregator Settings page:

- **Allowed HTML tags:** The tags listed in this field are permitted for use inside the feed items. Tags not listed in this field are stripped out of the content.
- **Number of items shown in listing pages:** Select a value from the combo box to set the number of items that are displayed on the summary view pages.
- **Discard items older than:** Select a value from the combo box to determine how long items are kept in the system. Note that you can select the option Never, but this may result over time in a large amount of information being kept by your system.

Note

To update your feeds automatically, the aggregator requires you to set up and run cron jobs on your server to update content. Note also that if you set the option to a time period that is shorter than the frequency of your cron job runs, then the feeds are not updated until the next cron run. You can at any time, however, manually force the system to update the items by clicking the Update items option on the Feed Aggregator interface. Setting up and managing cron jobs is covered in Chapter 4. ■

- **Select categories using:** This setting determines the type of selection tool that appears on categorization pages. The tool is used by the user to select the categories he wants to view. Set the option to check boxes to show a list of the categories with check boxes next to each. The user can select one or more categories by clicking the check boxes. Set the option to multiple selector to show a multi-select combo box. The former option works best with short lists; the latter option works well if you have a large number of categories.
- **Length of trimmed description:** The Feed Aggregator can display feed items either in full or trimmed form. This configuration option lets you specify whether it displays the entire feed article or only a portion, and if only a portion, how much. Note that displaying entire articles can be problematic, because you cannot control the article length and are therefore at the mercy of the original publisher.

After you have set the options you desire, click the Save configuration button at the bottom of the page. You have now completed all the preliminary steps needed to set up your Drupal Feed Aggregator.

Administering the Aggregator

Although you cannot control the content of the feed items (because only the publisher can do so), you can control which news feeds appear on the site. You also can create categories to group together feeds, a useful organizational device if your site has a large number of feeds.

The Feed management page contains a listing of the feeds and the categories in the system. You can access the Feed management page by visiting the Modules Manager, and clicking on the option labeled Configure; when the Aggregator Settings page loads, click the tab at the top right labeled List. The Feed management page is shown in Figure 18.5.

FIGURE 18.5

The Feed management page

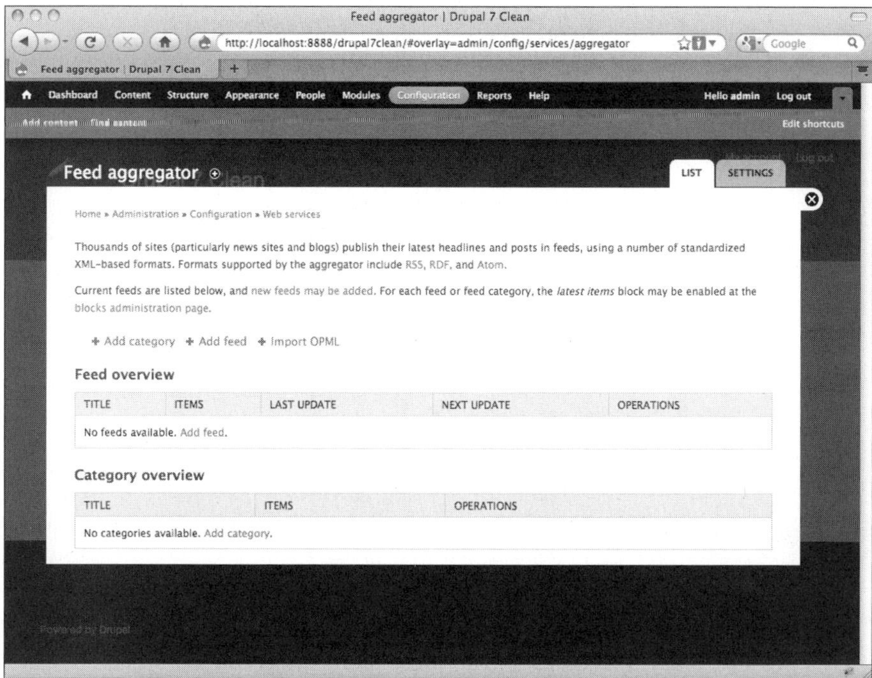

At the very top of the screen, below the explanatory text are three links: Add category, Add feed, and Import OPML. All three are explained in more detail later in the chapter.

Immediately below those links, the page is divided into two sections: Feed overview and Category overview. These two sections contain lists of all the feeds and categories that are active on the site, if any.

The Feed overview table includes these fields:

- **Title:** This is the title you gave to the feed.
- **Items:** This is the number of items that the system is currently holding from the source.
- **Last update:** This indicates when the source last updates the items from the source.
- **Next update:** This indicates how long until the system next updates the list of items from the source.
- **Operations:** Click these links to perform the indicated tasks. Edit allows you to edit the feed settings. Remove items deletes the items currently being held, but does not delete the feed itself. Update items forces the system to update the list of items from the source immediately.

The Category overview table includes the fields:

- **Title:** This is the title you have given to the category.
- **Items:** This is the number of items currently held in this category.
- **Operations:** Click the edit button to edit the category.

Adding and deleting feed categories

Although it is not necessary to create any categories before you begin adding feeds to your site, if you want to use the categories functionality, you should add them first, because it will save you time later when you add the feeds.

To add a new category, follow these steps:

1. **Access the Feed management page.**
2. **Click the Add category link.**

   The New Category page appears in your browser, as shown in Figure 18.6.

FIGURE 18.6

The New Category page

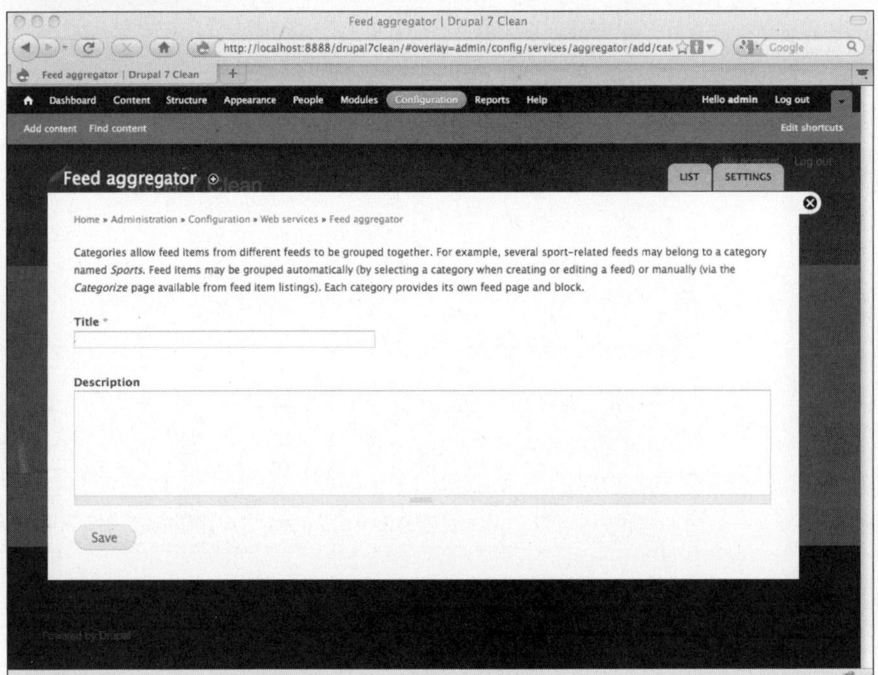

3. **Type a title for the category in the field labeled Title.**

   This is the only required field.

4. **Add a description if you want.**

   This is optional.

5. **Click the Save button.**

   The system creates a new category and displays a confirmation message.

To edit a category, follow these steps:

1. **Access the Feed management page.**
2. **Click the edit link in the Operations column next to the category you want to edit.**

   The Edit Category page loads in your browser, as shown in Figure 18.7.

FIGURE 18.7

The Edit Category page

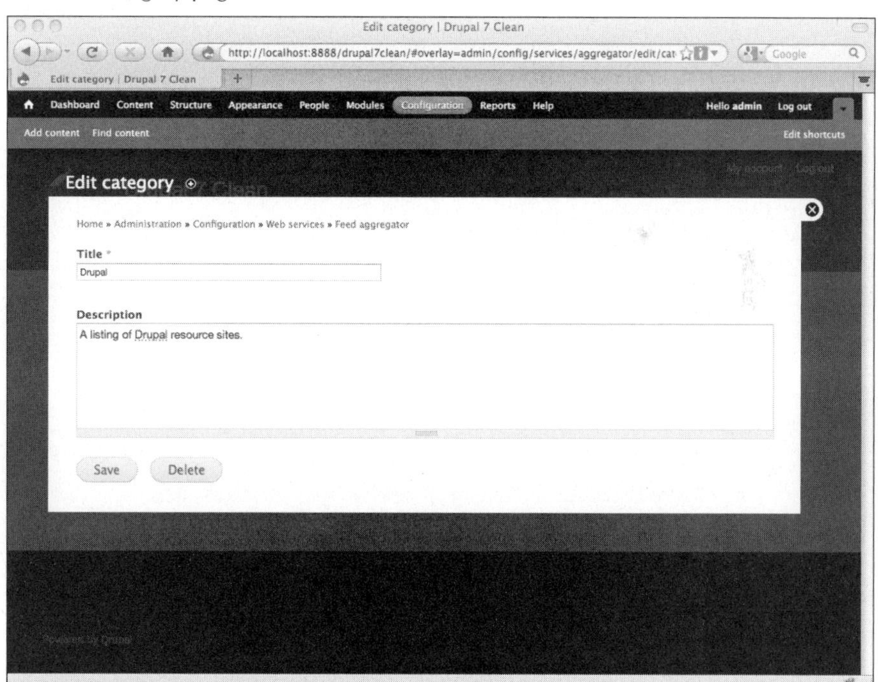

3. **Make any changes you desire.**
4. **Click the Save button.**

   The system saves your changes to the category and displays a confirmation message.

To delete a category, follow these steps:

1. **Access the Feed Aggregator management page.**
2. **Click in the edit link in the Operations column for the category you want to delete.**

   The Edit Category page loads in your browser, as shown in Figure 18.7.
3. **Click the Delete button.**

   The system deletes the category and displays a confirmation message.

Feeds can be added to existing categories at the time of their creation. If a category has been created after the feed was created, you can associate the feed with the category by editing the feed, which is explained in the next section.

Note

Deleting a category is instantaneous and irreversible; you will not be prompted for confirmation prior to deletion. Because you cannot undelete a category, if you want to resurrect a deleted category, you must create it again. Deletion of a category, fortunately, does not delete the feeds assigned to the category; it simply removes the association from the feed. ■

Adding and deleting feeds

Before you can begin showing syndicated content on your site, you must locate the proper feed URLs and add them to your system. This is done by creating new feeds. As noted earlier, the Drupal Aggregator module supports RSS, RDF, and Atom-enabled feeds. After you have the URL for the feed, follow these steps to add it to your system:

1. **Access the Feed management page.**
2. **Click the Add feed link.**

   The New Feed page appears in your browser, as shown in Figure 18.8.
3. **Type a title for the feed in the field labeled Title.**

   This is a required field.
4. **Type the URL for the feed in the field labeled URL.**

   This is a required field.

Note

The system accepts URLs for RSS, RDF, and Atom-enabled feeds only; a regular page URL does not work. ■

5. **Set the frequency with which the feed is checked for new items by using the combo box in the field labeled Update Interval.**

   The default value is 1 hour.

Note

You must have properly configured cron jobs running on your server for this feature to work. ■

6. **Make a choice in the News items in block drop-down box.**

   This box configures the block that the system automatically creates to go with every news feed. The block contains a list of the newest items for the feed. Use the box for this configuration option to control the number of items that show in the block. The default value is 5.

7. **Click the Save button.**

   The system creates a new feed and displays a confirmation message.

Tip

These steps lead to the addition of a new news feed, but no items appear in the feed until the next cron run. To force the system to grab the newest items at any time, access the Feed Aggregator management page and click the link labeled Update items, located in the Operations column next to the feed. ■

FIGURE 18.8

The New Feed page

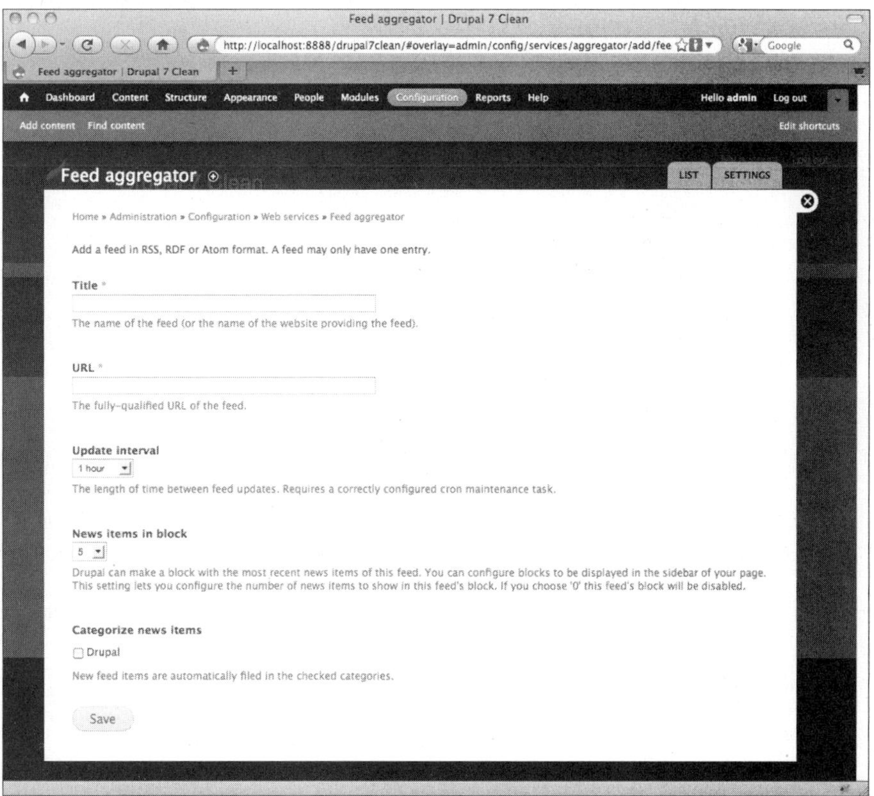

To edit a feed, follow these steps:

1. **Access the Feed management page.**
2. **Click in the edit link in the Operations column for the feed you want to edit.**

   The Edit Feed page loads in your browser, as shown in Figure 18.9.
3. **Make any changes you desire.**
4. **Click the Save button.**

   The system saves your changes to the feed and displays a confirmation message.

FIGURE 18.9

The Edit Feed page

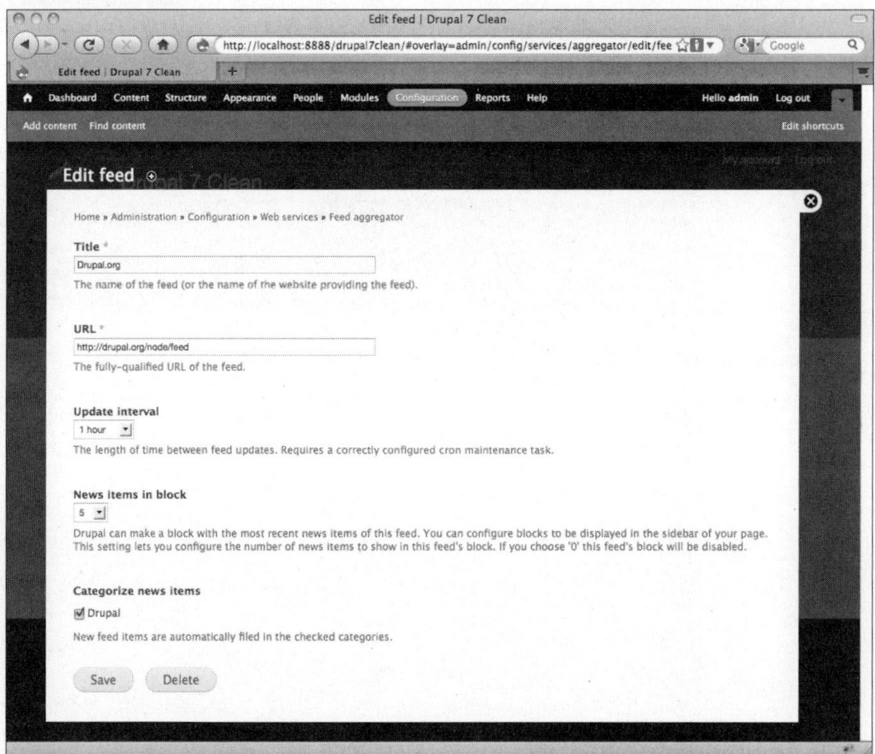

To delete a feed, follow these steps:

1. **Access the Feed management page.**
2. **Click in the edit link in the Operations column for the feed you want to delete.**

   The Edit Feed page loads in your browser, as shown in Figure 18.9.
3. **Click the Delete button.**

   The system deletes the feed and displays a confirmation message.

Note

Deleting a feed is instantaneous and irreversible; you will not be prompted for confirmation prior to deletion. Because you cannot undelete a feed, if you want to resurrect a deleted feed, you must create it again. Deletion of a feed deletes all the items in the feed; if you have to recreate the feed, you may not be able to regain older feed items. ■

You also can add feeds in bulk by using Drupal's Import OPML function. OPML is an XML format used to exchange feed information. It can save you time by allowing you to import a number of feeds at one time, instead of having to create them one by one. To import an OPML file, follow these steps:

1. **Access the Feed management page.**
2. **Click the Import OPML link.**

   The OPML Import page appears in your browser, as shown in Figure 18.10.
3. **If you have the file stored locally, click the Browse button next to the field labeled OPML File. If not, skip to Step 5.**

   The Browse file window pops up.
4. **Locate the file on your local system, and click the Select button.**

   The Browse file window will close. From here, go to step 7.
5. **If, on the other hand, you want to use an OPML file that is published online, enter the URL in the field marked OPML remote URL.**
6. **Set the other configuration options you desire; all other items are optional.**
7. **Click the Import button.**

   The system attempts to import the OPML file; if it's successful, you see a confirmation message. The feeds can now be managed like any other feed in your system.

FIGURE 18.10

The OPML Import page

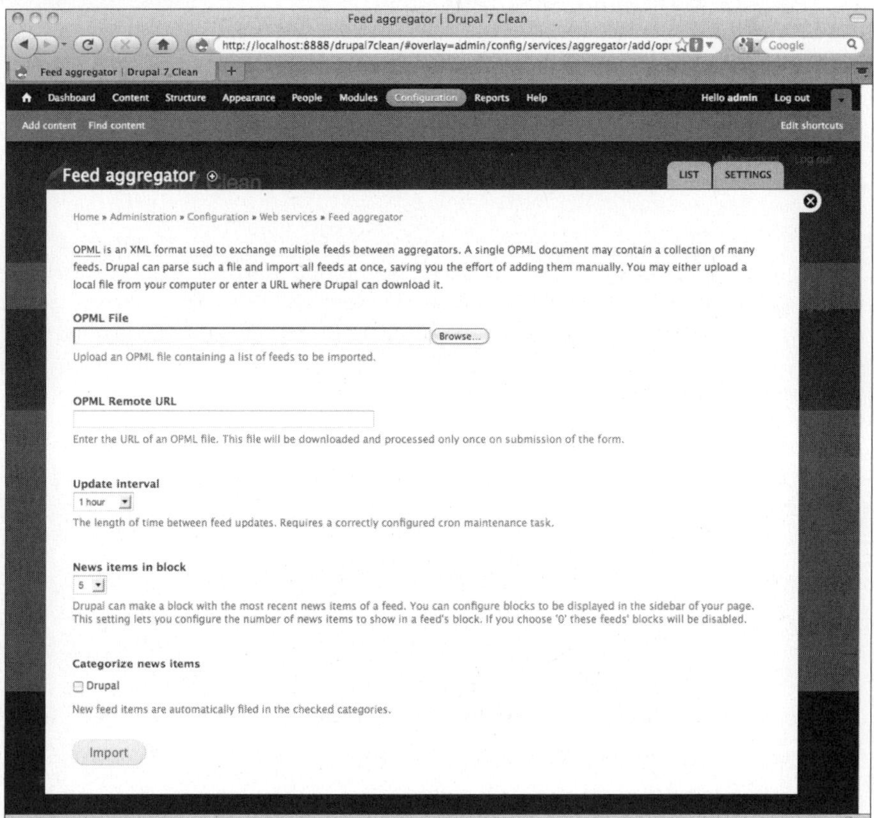

Controlling the Styling of the Aggregator

The Aggregator module provides you with five dedicated template files, two style sheets, and a selection of themable functions. In this section, I introduce each resource, indicate its role in the display, and explain the functions and variables that are available for you to work with.

Cross-Reference

Overriding templates and working with themable functions are discussed in depth in Chapter 26. ■

Reviewing the default templates

There are five dedicated templates for the Aggregator module. All are located at /modules/aggregator. These are the templates:

- **aggregator-feed-source.tpl.php**
- **aggregator-item.tpl.php**
- **aggregator-summary-item.tpl.php**
- **aggregator-summary-items.tpl.php**
- **aggregator-wrapper.tpl.php**

Each template is discussed in the following sections.

Reviewing aggregator-feed-source.tpl.php

This template controls the appearance of the feed source information that appears above the feed items. The available variables are shown in Table 18.1.

TABLE 18.1

Variables in aggregator-feed-source.tpl.php

Variable	Description
$last_checked	Tells when the feed was last checked locally
$source_description	The description for the feed, as supplied by the publisher
$source_icon	The icon for the feed, as supplied by the publisher
$source_image	Any image associated with the feed, as supplied by the publisher
$source_url	The URL for the feed's source

Reviewing aggregator-item.tpl.php

The aggregator-item template controls the overall formatting of the individual feed items. The available variables are shown in Table 18.2.

TABLE 18.2

Variables in aggregator-item.tpl.php

Variable	Description
$categories	The list of categories associated with the feed
$content	The content of the individual feed item
$feed_title	The title of the feed, as supplied by the publisher
$feed_url	The URL of the feed item, as supplied by the publisher
$source_date	The date of the feed item, as supplied by the publisher
$source_title	The title of the source of the feed, as supplied by the publisher
$source_url	The URL for the source of the feed

Reviewing aggregator-summary-item.tpl.php

This template allows you to control the formatting of the linked feed items presented in summaries. The variables are shown in Table 18.3.

TABLE 18.3

Variables in aggregator-summary-item.tpl.php

Variable	Description
$feed_age	The age of the remote feed
$feed_title	The title of the feed item, as supplied by the publisher
$feed_url	The URL of the feed item, as supplied by the publisher
$source_title	The title for the source of the feed, as supplied by the publisher
$source_url	The locally set title for the source

Reviewing aggregator-summary-items.tpl.php

This template allows you to present feeds as list items. The three available variables are shown in Table 18.4.

TABLE 18.4

Variables in aggregator-summary-items.tpl.php

Variable	Description
$summary_list	An unordered list of all the feed items
$source_url	The URL to the local source of the feed or the category
$title	The title of the feed or the category

Reviewing aggregator-wrapper.tpl.php

The aggregator-wrapper template provides a container for all the aggregator content. The template controls the overall formatting of the Aggregator display. Two variables are available, as shown in Table 18.5.

TABLE 18.5

Variables in aggregator-wrapper.tpl.php

Variable	Description
$content	The entire aggregator contents
$page	The pagination links

Reviewing the default style sheets

Two style sheets are dedicated to the formatting of the Aggregator module. Both are located at /modules/aggregator. These are the two files:

- **aggregator.css:** The primary CSS files, which include the selectors that affect the Aggregator module and the output of the module
- **aggregator-rtl.css:** The CSS that will be applied when the site is set to display text in right-to-left orientation

Reviewing the themable functions

Four themable functions relate to the Aggregator module, as shown in Table 18.6. The functions can be found at modules/aggregator/aggregator.pages.inc.

TABLE 18.6

Themable Functions

Function	Description
theme_aggregator_block_item	Formats an individual feed item when displayed in a block
theme_aggregator_categorize_items	Themes the form for assigning categories
theme_aggregator_page_opml	Allows you to theme the output of the OPML feed
theme_aggregator_page_rss	Allows you to theme the output of the RSS feed

Using the Latest Items Block

Each time you add a feed or a category to the system, Drupal automatically creates for it a Latest Items block. You can use the Latest Items block to display on the page a list of the latest items from the feed or category, along with links to the items, as shown in Figure 18.11.

The block can be configured like any other block, with one exception: To control the number of items that are displayed in the block, you must use the configuration settings for the source or category upon which the block is based. This is the configuration setting labeled "News item in block" discussed earlier in this chapter.

Cross-Reference

Working with blocks is discussed in depth in Chapter 7. ■

FIGURE 18.11

The Aggregator's Latest Items block in action, shown here displaying the five most recent items from one feed source

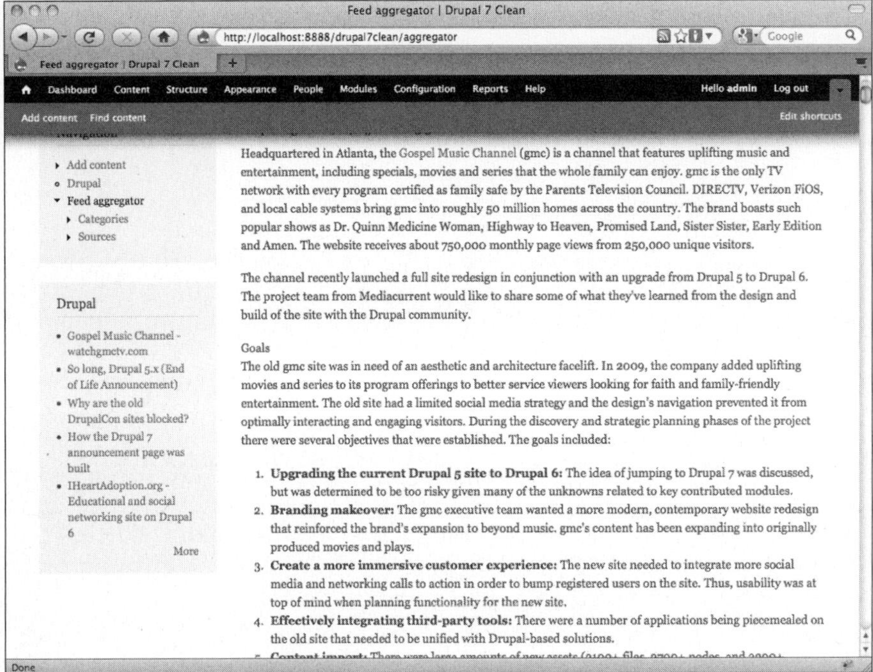

Summary

This chapter addressed the use of the Aggregator functionality in Drupal 7. I covered the following topics:

- How to enable the Aggregator module
- How to configure the Aggregator module
- How to add and manage feeds
- How to add and manage categories
- How to import OPML files
- The resources available for controlling the styling of the Aggregator module
- How to use the Latest Items block

CHAPTER 19

Working with Forms

IN THIS CHAPTER

Using Drupal's Contact module

Creating custom forms

The Drupal system includes a basic contact form feature that site visitors can use to contact the site owner or other users. Drupal's default form functionality is, however, rather limited. Consequently, you may want to consider installing additional modules to enable the creation of custom forms.

In this chapter, I look at both the default Drupal Contact module and at one of the easiest to use third-party form modules.

Note

You need to install an additional module to get the most out of the discussion in the latter portion of this chapter. ■

Using Drupal's Contact Module

Drupal's default system includes a basic contact form feature. The form is created by the Contact module, which is disabled by default. After you enable the module, the form is immediately ready for use.

The form provides the following fields:

- **Name:** This is a single-line text field.
- **Email address:** This single-line text field is validated for simple text. (It is not validated for proper e-mail address format.)
- **Subject:** This is a single-line text field.
- **Category:** This field is a combo box that displays the list of categories created by the administrator in the Contact Manager.

- **Message:** This field is a multi-line text box.
- **Send yourself a copy:** If a user checks this box, the system automatically sends him a copy of the form submission, using the e-mail address he input in the form.

All the fields on the form are required, and the system validates all fields prior to allowing the form to be submitted. Figure 19.1 shows the default contact form.

FIGURE 19.1

In this example from Drupal's site-wide contact form, I created additional categories that can be selected from the Category combo box field.

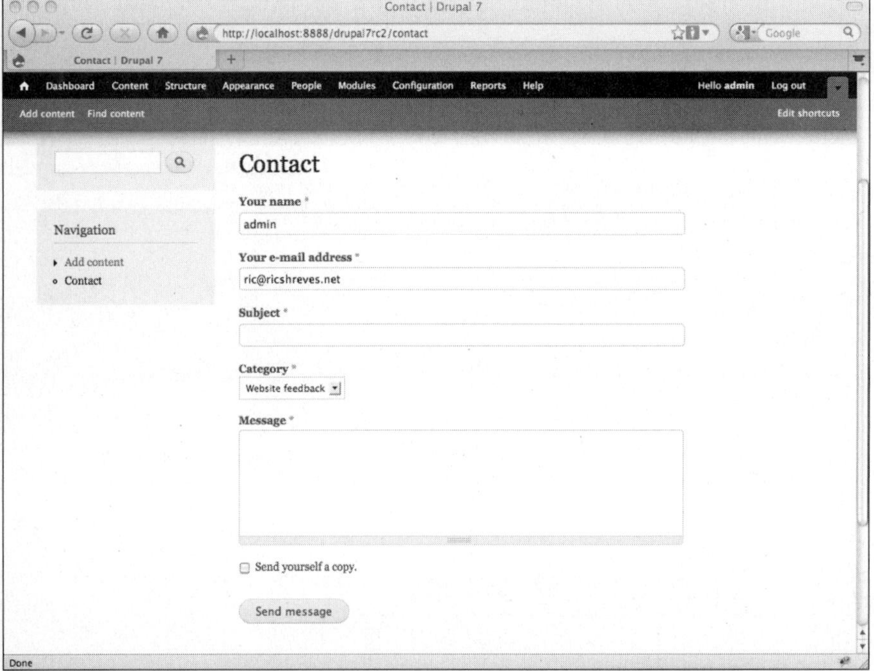

Tip

Drupal's default contact form has several significant limitations. The form cannot be customized easily from within the admin interface, and the system does not save the form data in the database. If you want to create complex forms or you need to store the data in addition to sending it by e-mail, you need to install an additional module, such as the Webforms module discussed later in this chapter. ■

Drupal's Contact module provides two types of contact forms: a site-wide contact form and user contact forms. Both are discussed in the following sections of this chapter.

Creating site-wide contact forms

The first step in getting started with your contact forms is to enable the Contact module. The module is included with the core, so you simply need to visit the Modules Manager and turn it on. Note that enabling the Contact module also adds a link to the Navigation menu, although the link is disabled by default. If you want to display the link, visit the Menus Manager and enable the link, which is named simply Contact. By default, the form is visible at the URL `/contact`.

Note

Don't forget to adjust the Permissions for the contact form; the default Permissions grant only the Administrator access to the form. If you want general site visitors to be able to see the form, grant permission to Anonymous Users in the Permissions Manager. See Chapter 24 for more information on working with permissions. ■

To access the configuration options for the default contact form, follow these steps:

1. **Log into your site as an administrator.**

   The Management menu appears at the top of the page.
2. **Select the Structure option from the Management menu.**

   The Structure options display in the overlay.
3. **Click the Contact form link on the overlay.**

   The Contact form configuration page opens, as shown in Figure 19.2.
4. **Select the form you want to modify by locating the category and clicking the Edit link in Operations column.**

   The Edit contact category page opens, as shown in Figure 19.3.
5. **Make whatever changes you desire.**
6. **Click the Save button.**

   The system saves your changes, returns to the Contact form configuration page, and displays a confirmation message.

Note

Though different contact categories can have different configuration settings, creating a new category does not create a new contact form. Multiple categories simply result in the Category combo box being displayed on the form. ■

These are your options in the Edit contact category:

- **Category:** This field holds the name used for the category and is displayed in the Category combo box on the form. This is a required field.
- **Recipients:** List one or more e-mail addresses in this field. The e-mail addresses receive the form submissions in this category. You must enter at least one e-mail address in this field. You can enter more than one address, but the addresses must be separated by commas.

- **Auto-reply:** This is an optional field. If you type text into this field, it is used as an auto-responder. Each time the form is submitted, the system automatically sends the text in this field to the e-mail address input in the form by the user.
- **Weight:** This controls the sorting of the categories list. The smaller the value, the higher the category appears in the ordering of items in the combo box.
- **Selected:** Select *yes* to designate this category as the default category. Other choices are available, but only from the combo box.

Tip

Why would you want to create multiple categories? The chief advantage of categories is that they allow you to route form submissions. You may, for example, want Web site issues to go to the Webmaster, new business enquiries to go to sales, trouble reports to go to customer service, and so on. To achieve this, create categories for each and configure them to send the e-mail to the desired parties. ■

FIGURE 19.2

The Contact form configuration page

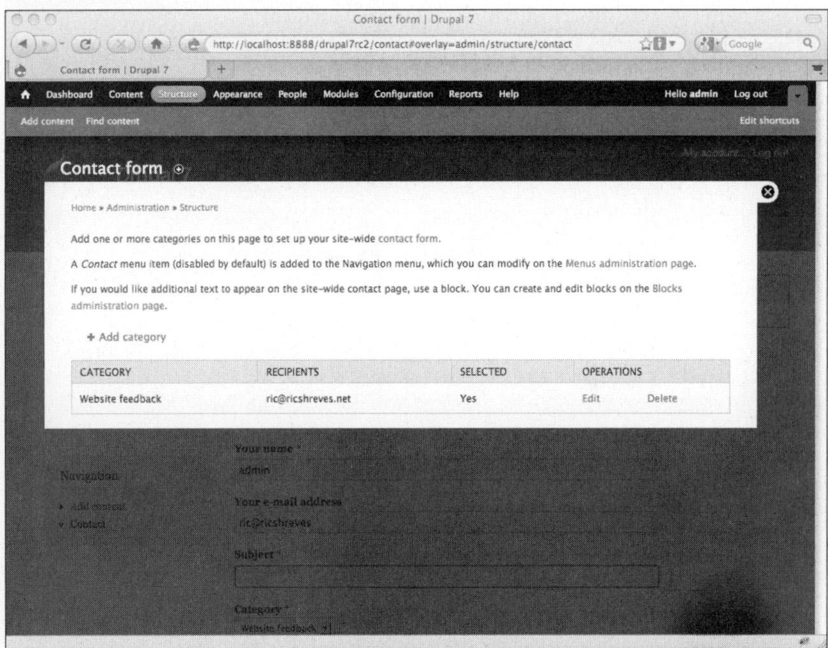

Creating user contact forms

Drupal's default Contact module includes the option to enable contact forms for every user on the Web site. These forms can be used by the administrator to contact the users, or you can grant permission to site visitors to contact the registered users through the use of the forms.

As you can see in Figure 19.4, the user contact form is essentially the same as the site-wide contact form, with only minor differences: The user contact form shows the name of the recipient of the form, and the user forms don't support contact categories.

Tip

If you want to add text to a site-wide contact form or a user contact form, the easiest way is to create a new block and assign it to the specific form page. ■

Enabling the Contact module automatically enables the user forms, but by default they are only visible to the site administrators. To make them visible to others, you must make a change to the Permissions Manager. Additionally, each individual user must enable his or her personal contact form before the forms are available to others.

FIGURE 19.3

The Edit contact category page

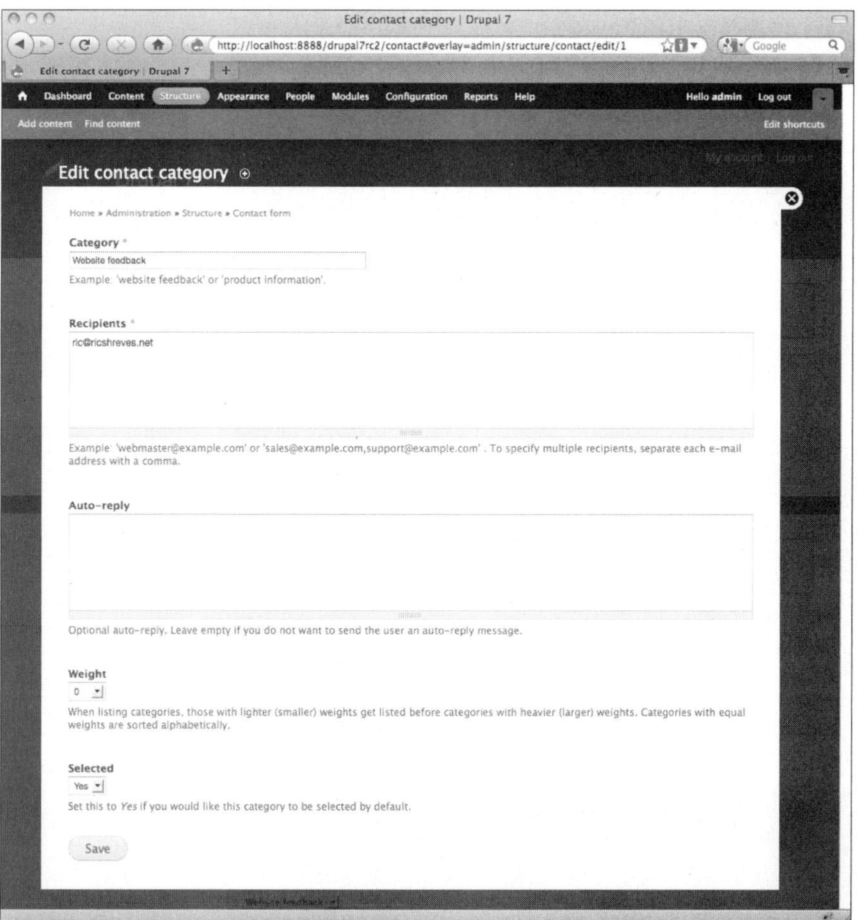

Note

The site administrators can always access the user contact form, regardless of the settings chosen by the individual users. ■

The user contact form visibility controls are part of the individual users' account management settings, shown in Figure 19.5.

Cross-Reference

Complete information on user account configuration can be found in Chapter 23. ■

FIGURE 19.4

A typical user contact form includes the recipient's name.

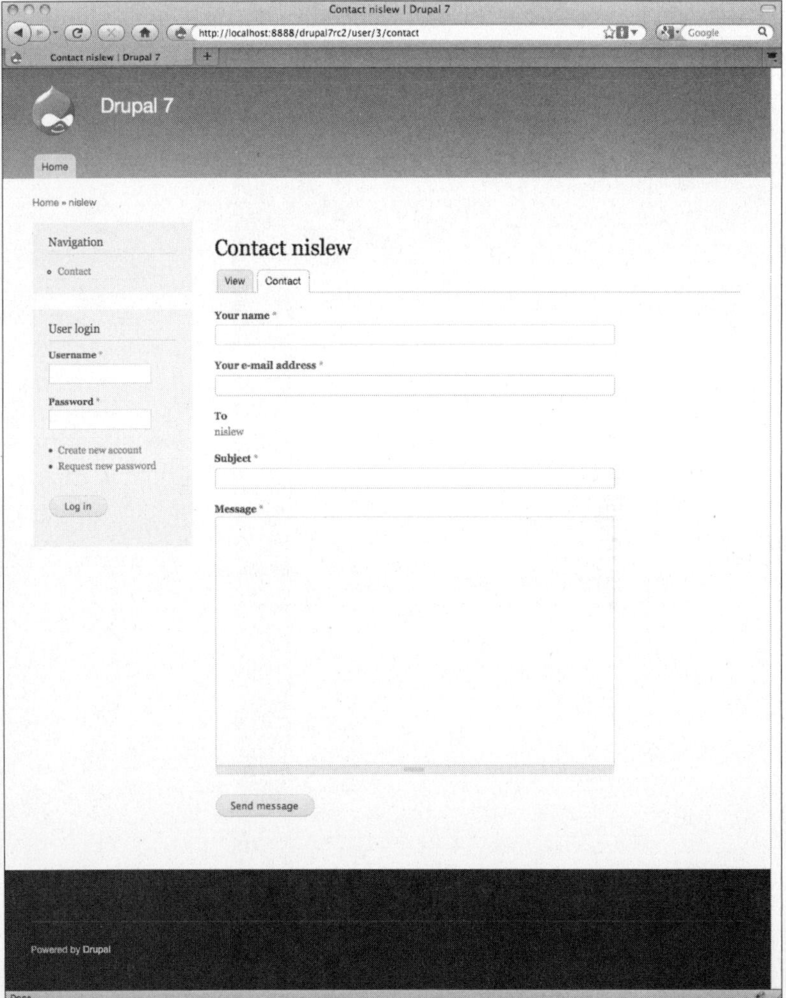

FIGURE 19.5

The Contact Settings options on the user account configuration page

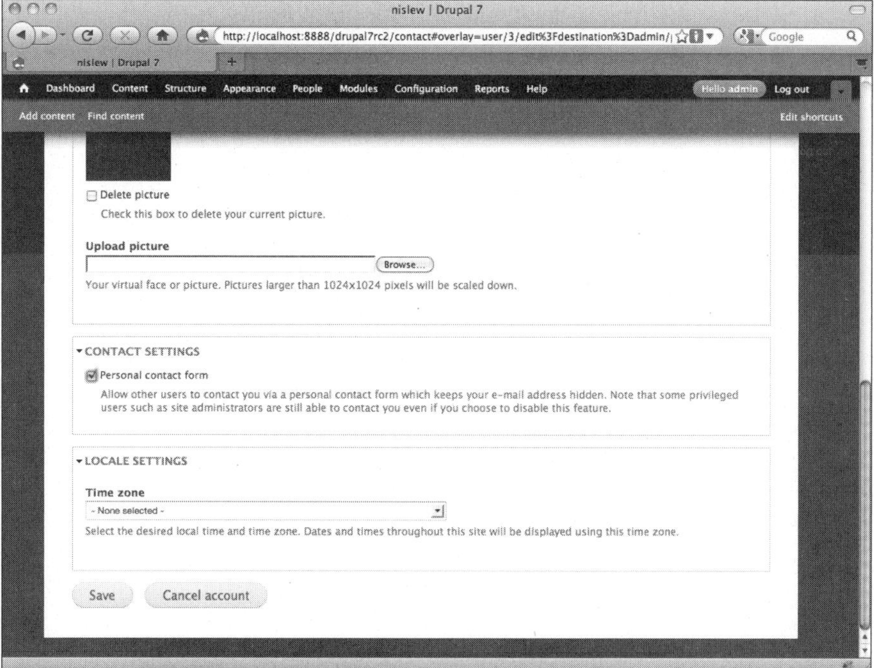

Creating Custom Forms

If you need to create custom forms for your Drupal Web site, you can use the theming system and the forms API to create new fields and a form that uses those fields, or you can install a specialized third-party module that enables form building from within the administration system. For most people, the latter option is far more attractive and accessible.

Note

The Form API for Drupal 7 can be found at: `http://api.drupal.org/api/drupal/includes--form.inc/group/form_api/7`. ■

Those who want to install an admin-based form building solution have several options; my favorite is the Webforms module. This module adds the following functionality to your site:

- Enables you to create custom fields from within the admin system
- Supports creation of multi-page forms
- Lets you control the From and Subject lines that appear in the e-mails generated by the form

- Lets you send form submission e-mails in multiple formats
- Stores form submissions in the database, gives you access to the results through the admin interface, and lets you export them for review offline
- Lets you create confirmation pages and provide re-directs after form submission
- Lets you set limits on how many times a form can be submitted
- Allows you to add forms to content items or place them in blocks

In the sections that follow, I take you through installing and configuring the module and show you how to use it to create your own custom forms.

Installing and configuring the Webforms module

To get started, install the Webforms module from the Drupal site, following these steps:

Note

You can download Webforms from `http://www.drupal.org/project/webforms`. ■

1. **Log into your site as an administrator.**

   The Management menu appears at the top of the page.
2. **Select the Modules option from the Management menu.**

   The Modules Manager opens in your browser.
3. **Click the Install new module link at the top left of the overlay.**

   The module installation page opens.
4. **If you have downloaded the module installation package to your local machine, click the Browse button.**

   The file upload page pops up.
5. **Use the upload page to find the installation file you want to upload; select it, and click the Open button.**

   The upload page closes, and you see the path to the installation file in the field next to the Browse button.
6. **If you have not downloaded the installation file, but you know the URL for the installation package, type it into the field marked Install from a URL.**
7. **Click the Install button.**

   The system uploads the module, and you see a confirmation message on the screen.

After you have installed the module, enable it via the Modules Manager.

Note

The Webforms module does not require you to enable the default Drupal Contact module. ■

Next, to configure the module, simply click the Configuration option next to the name of the Webforms module on the Modules Manager. After you click that link, the Webforms configuration page loads in your browser, as shown in Figure 19.6.

FIGURE 19.6

In the Webforms configuration page, I have expanded the Advanced settings pane to show all options.

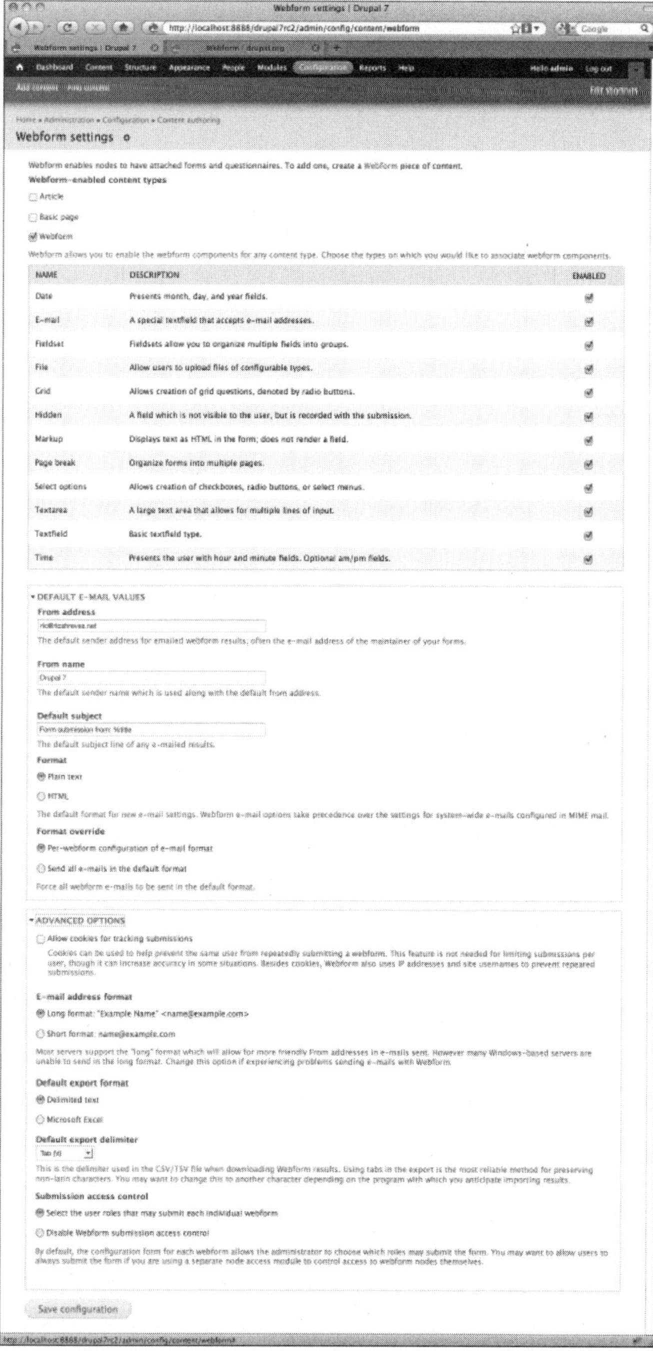

Note

The Webforms configuration page can also be accessed from the Configuration menu. ■

The options in the Webforms configuration page are grouped into four areas:

- **Content types:** The Content types group allows you to select which of the existing content types can also include forms. The default option is Webforms, a new content type that is added to the system by the module.
- **Fields table:** This allows you to select which fields are available when you create forms.
- **Default e-mail values:** Here you set e-mail format and header information used by the form submission e-mails.
- **Advanced options:** The many choices here are described below:
  - **Allow cookies for tracking submissions:** Select the check box to use cookies to track form submissions. This is useful if you want to block users from submitting a form multiple times.
  - **E-mail address format:** Select long or short format. If you are having problems with e-mail sending, try setting this to Short format.
  - **Default export format:** This controls how the form data is exported from the system.
  - **Default export delimiter:** Select the delimiter used in the export process.
  - **Submission access control:** This determines whether access to forms is controlled individually or as a whole.

After you make your changes to the Webform configuration, click the Save configuration button to save your settings.

Creating new forms with Webforms

Adding a new webform is just like adding a new content item. Follow these steps:

1. **Log into your site as an administrator.**

   The Management menu appears at the top of the page.

2. **Click the Add content button.**

   The New Content menu appears in the overlay.

3. **Click the option Webform.**

   The New Webform page opens.

4. **Give the form a Title.**

   This is the only required field.

5. **Click the Save button.**

   The new webform is created, and the system displays the editing page.

The new form still lacks form fields. You need to edit the form to include the fields you want and set the other options that control how the submissions are sent. The options are explained in the sections that follow.

Adding new fields to a custom form

Until you add fields to your form, you have nothing but an empty content item. The number and nature of the fields you add are up to you. You can control the field ordering, size, labels, format, and more. You can even create hidden fields or fields with fixed values that cannot be edited by the user.

All content types that are enabled to support webforms have a Webform tab visible when you view that item in editing mode. In Figure 19.7, you can see the editing tab at the top right of the overlay.

FIGURE 19.7

In this example of the form editing page, I have already added the first field to the form: First Name.

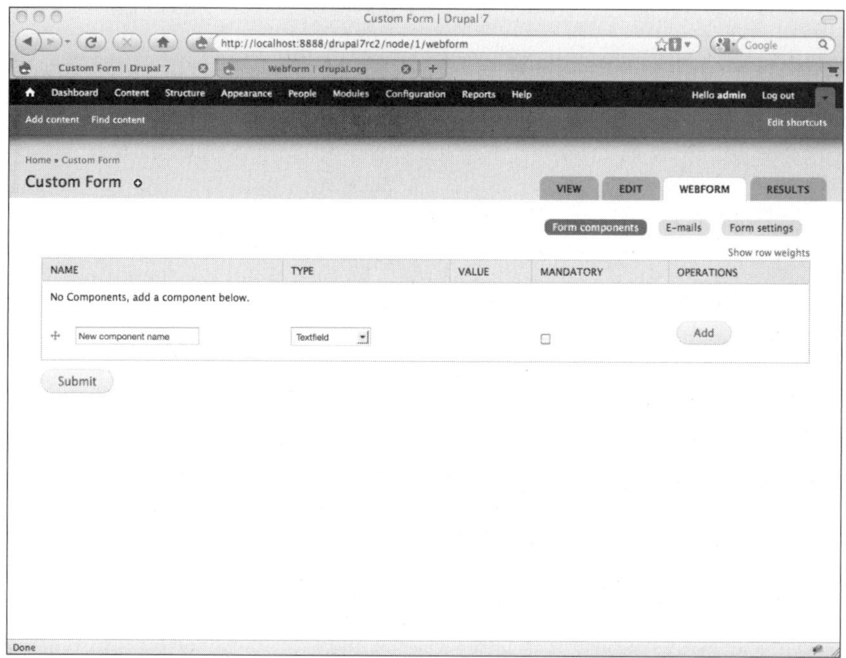

To add a field to an existing form, follow these steps:

1. **Log into your site as an administrator.**

   The Management menu appears at the top of the page.

2. **Click the Content link on the Management menu.**

   The list of content items appears in the overlay.

3. **Click the edit link next to the item that contains the form.**

   The Content Item editing page opens.

4. **Click the Webform tab on the content item editing page.**

   The Form Editing page opens (refer to Figure 19.7).

5. **Enter the name you want to use for the new component in the first text field.**
6. **Select the type of field you want to display from the Type combo box.**
7. **If you want this field to be required, check the Mandatory box.**
8. **Click the Add button.**

   The New Field Configuration page loads, as shown in Figure 19.8.

9. **Select the configuration options you want to go with this field.**
10. **Click the Save button.**

    The system adds the field to the form and returns you to the form editing page.

The fields on a typical field configuration page include these options:

- **Label:** This is the label you want to appear next to the field on the form.
- **Field Key:** This is the machine-readable name used for the values input in this field.
- **Default value:** If you want to provide a default value that will be seen initially by the user, put it in this field.
- **Description:** This is for help text to assist the user as he fills out the form.
- **Validation:** Set whether the field is mandatory, whether it needs to be validated, and if so, to what extent.
- **Display:** The options in this section control the formatting of the field on the screen.

To build your form, simply repeat this process until you have created all the form fields you desire. Check your work by viewing the form on the front end, and when you're happy, test it. You can reorder the form fields at any time by clicking and dragging the crossed arrows immediately before the field name in the list of fields shown on the field editing page. Refer to Figure 19.7 to see the double arrow control next to the First Name field.

Note

The available field types are controlled by the settings in the Webform configuration. The nature of those types is explained on that page. Your field configuration options vary according to the field type selected. ■

Tip

Fields also can be edited, deleted, or cloned from the field editing page. The clone control is a real time-saver when you are creating long forms. ■

FIGURE 19.8

The options in the new field configuration page vary, depending on the option you selected for the Type on the previous page.

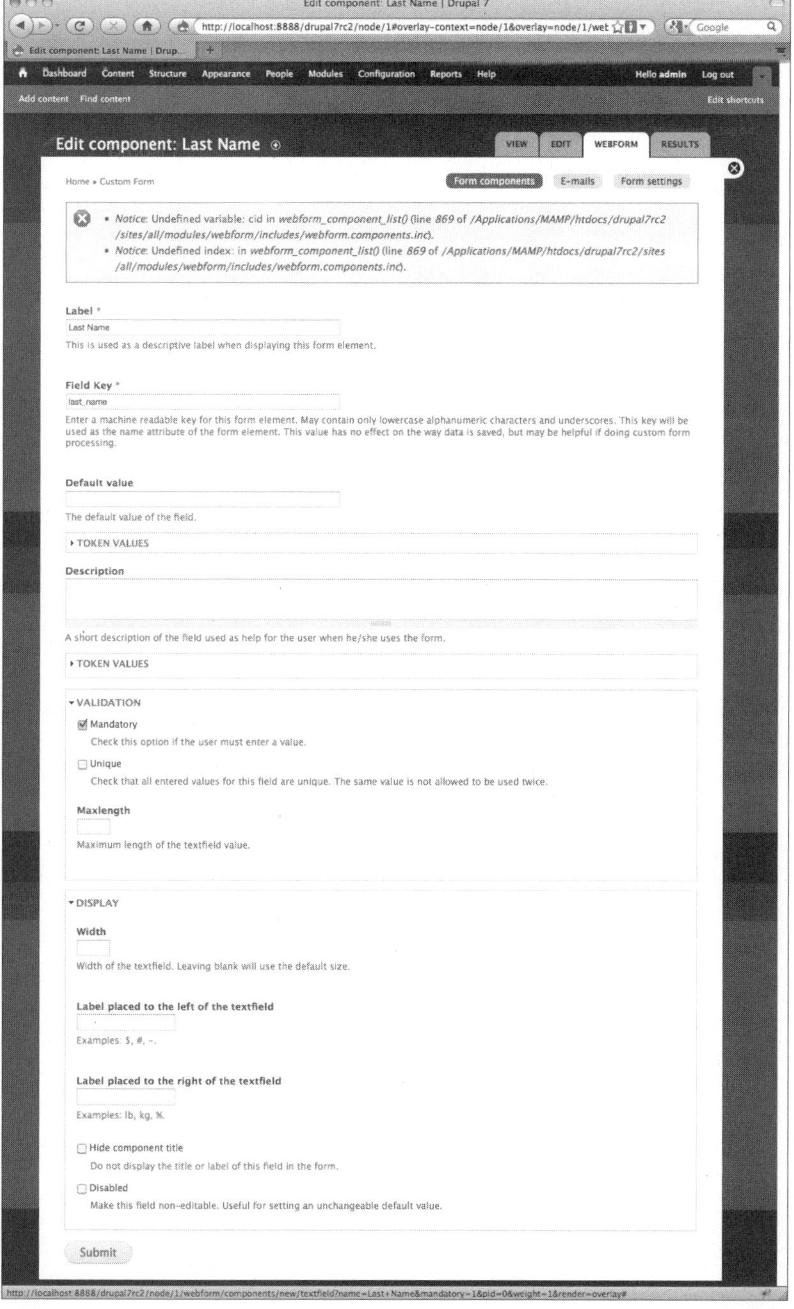

Working with Token Values

Figure 19.8 shows two instances where the words *Token Values* appear. If you open either of those panes by clicking the triangle-shaped arrow to the left of the word, you see a list of token values that can be used in certain fields in your forms.

Tokens are specially formatted strings that tell the system to insert values dynamically. You may, for example, want to automatically display the current date on the form; this is easily done by inserting the token value `%date`. Or perhaps you want to automatically include the user's name and e-mail address if the user is logged in to the site; you can do that by adding the token values `%username`, `%useremail`.

The Token Values panes are simply provided as a handy reference of the available tokens. Use one or more in any of the fields where they are shown as options, and the form output includes that information automatically.

Form submissions are automatically stored in the database. However, if you want the form submissions sent by e-mail as well, you need to configure the E-mails options, discussed in the next section.

Controlling submission settings

The Webforms module includes multiple options that control how the form is submitted and what happens after submission. The settings can be customized at the time you create the form or afterward. The settings fall into two categories: e-mail settings and post-submission actions.

Configuring e-mail sending

The form output can be sent to one or more e-mail addresses. By default, however, the form submissions simply go into the database, where they can be viewed from inside the admin system. If you want to add e-mail notifications, follow these steps:

1. **Click the E-mails button on the form editing page (refer to Figure 19.7).**

   The E-mail Setup page opens, as shown in Figure 19.9.
2. **Enter the e-mail address you want to receive the notifications.**
3. **Click the Add button.**

   The E-mail Configuration page opens, as shown in Figure 19.10.
4. **Configure the options you desire.**
5. **Select how you want to format the e-mail with the E-mail Template.**

6. **Select what information you want to receive from the Included E-mail Values section.**
7. **Click Save e-mail settings.**

   The system saves your changes, closes the configuration page, returns you to the E-mail setup page, and displays a confirmation message.

Controlling form behaviors

To control what happens after a Webforms form is submitted, click the Form settings button (refer to Figure 19.7). When you click the button, the Form settings page opens, as shown in Figure 19.11.

FIGURE 19.9

The E-mail Setup page, shown here with one e-mail address already set up

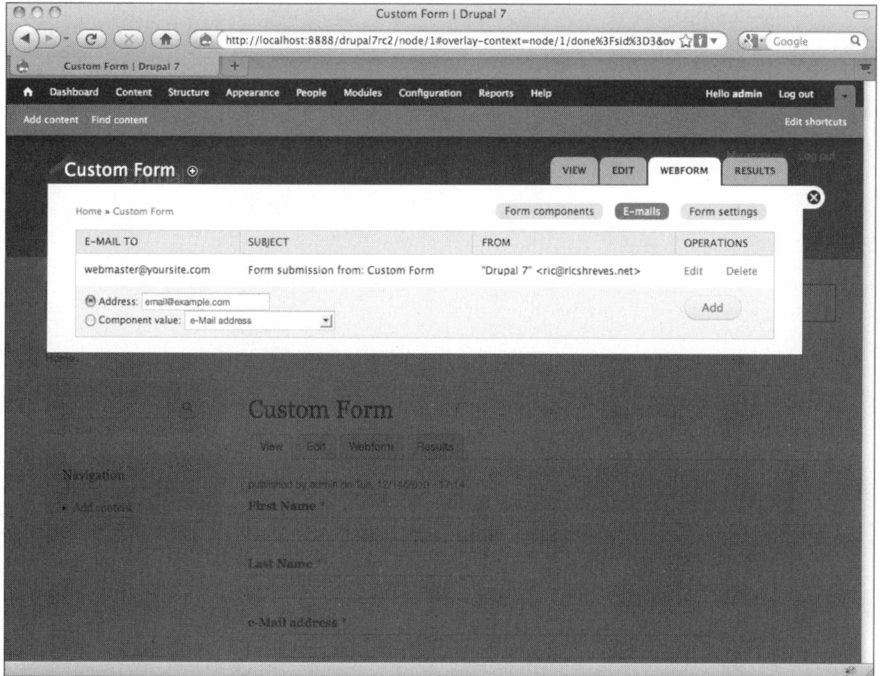

FIGURE 19.10

The E-mail Configuration page

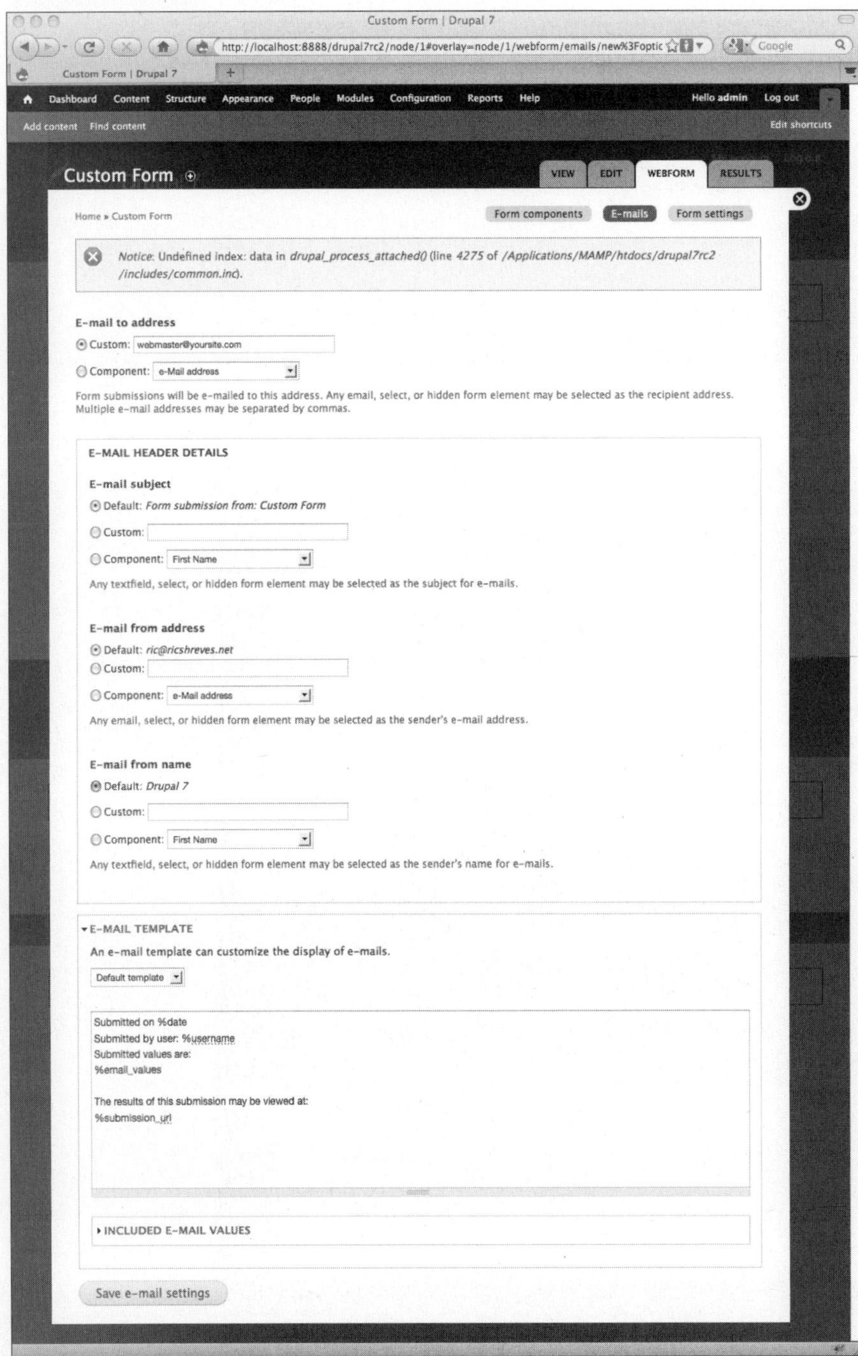

FIGURE 19.11

The Form Settings page

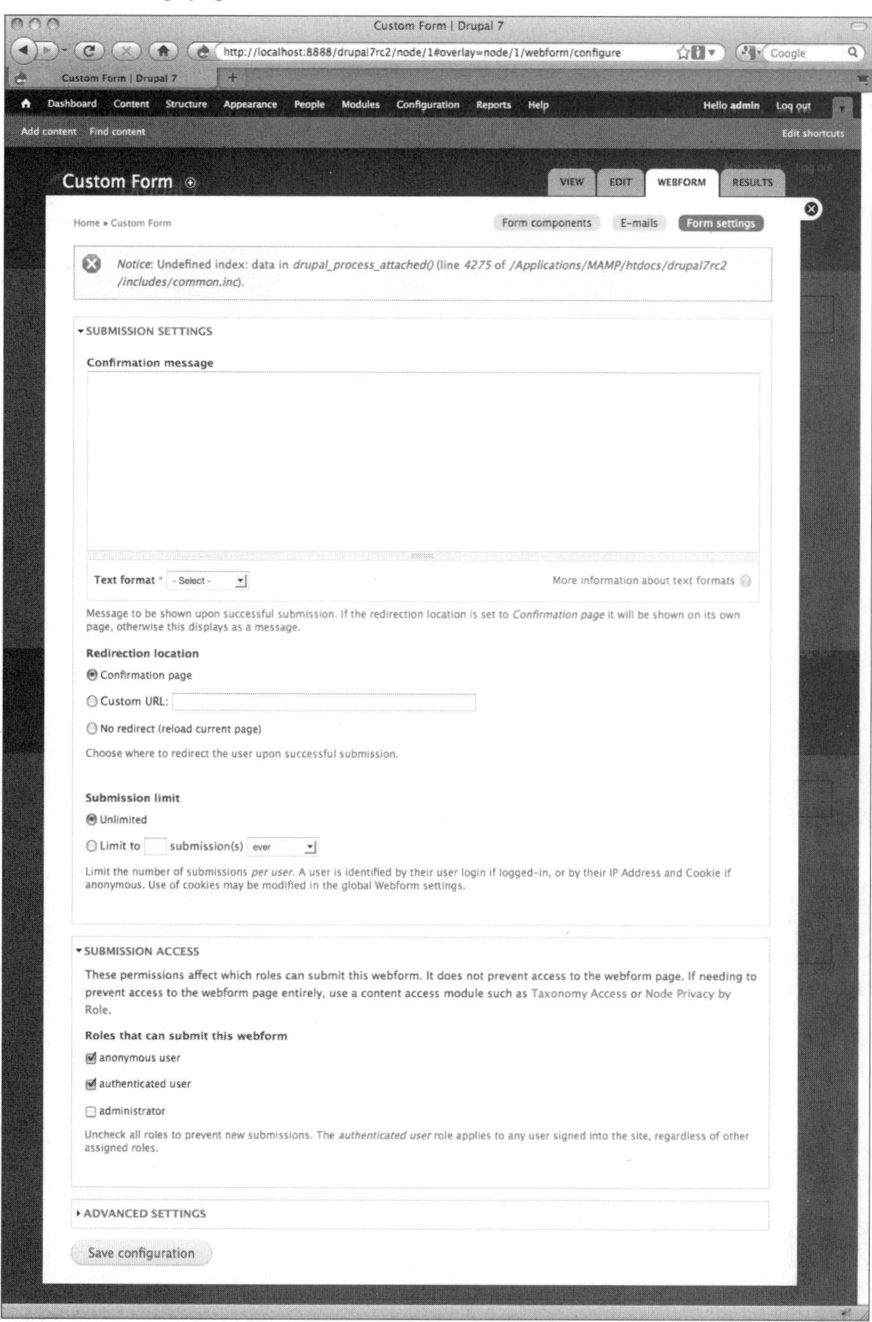

The top portion of the page features the Submissions Settings and Redirection location controls. These controls allow you to specify what the user sees after she submits the form:

- If you want the user to see a simple confirmation message, add the text to the Confirmation message field and leave the Redirection location set to Confirmation page.
- To send the user to a specific page after she submits the form, simply click the Custom URL option and enter the address of the page in the field.
- If you want the user to remain on the same page as the form, click the option No redirect.

The bottom half of the Form Settings page holds the Submission Access controls and the Advanced Settings. The Submission Access controls are the permissions settings specific to this form.

Note

You can control access to the Webforms module as a whole via Drupal's Permissions Manager. Use the Submission Access options on the individual forms when you want to deviate from the global settings; the form-specific settings take precedence over the global settings. ■

The Advanced Settings include multiple controls:

- Check the first option, Available as block, to create a block containing this form. The block can then be assigned via the Blocks Manager.
- The second option is used where the page has a teaser view; you can control whether the form shows in the teaser or only in full view.
- The third option gives users the chance to view a draft of their form data prior to submission. This option is most useful where you have a long or complex form.
- The final option lets you control the text that appears on the form's Submit button.

Note

If you need to limit the ability of users to submit the form multiple times, you can do so by setting the Submission limit options on the form settings page. This option uses cookies and IP address tracking to enforce the limitations. While the methods are not perfect and certainly won't deter someone who is committed to working around the prohibition, they do provide reasonable protection against multiple submissions from typical users. ■

Gathering data with Webforms

To view the Webform form submissions, click the Results tab (refer to Figure 19.7). The tab is visible by clicking the form or the edit option for the form. Note that access to the Results tab is controlled by the permissions settings.

Clicking the Results tab brings up the summary view, shown in Figure 19.12.

FIGURE 19.12

The summary view of the form submissions

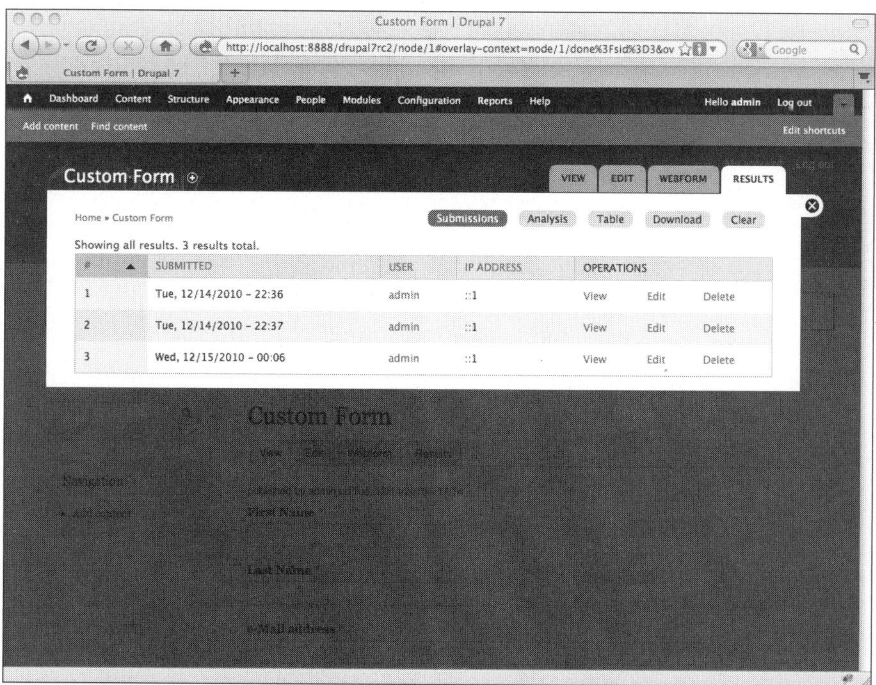

For each form submission, you can see the day, date and time of the submission, the username (if there is one), and the IP address. In the Operations column, you can see the options you have to view the submission, to edit it, or to delete it.

These five buttons are available at the top right of the interface:

- **Submissions:** This shows the summary view (refer to Figure 19.12).
- **Analysis:** Click to see a detailed view of the responses to each of the fields on the form. The data in this view is organized by the answer choices for at-a-glance analysis. This is most useful for survey or poll type forms.
- **Table:** Click to see each submission with the responses summarized as tabular data. This view is organized by submission date and is most useful for a quick at-a-glance summary of the responses received.
- **Download:** Click to view all your options for downloading the data for offline use.
- **Clear:** Click to clear all the form submissions received.

Summary

This chapter covered the Contact module included in the Drupal core and how to extend your site to allow you to create custom forms. These topics were included in this chapter:

- How to create a site-wide contact form using the Contact module
- How to enable the user forms functionality in the core
- Installing and configuring the Webforms module to enable custom form creation
- How to create custom forms using the Webforms module

CHAPTER

20

Using the Forum Module

IN THIS CHAPTER

Introducing the Forum module

Administering forums

Controlling the styling of the Forum module

Using the active Forum topics block

Using the New Forum topics block

Drupal's Forum module creates a threaded discussion functionality, similar to what you see on other discussion or bulletin board sites. Topics are posted. and users can respond to the topics and to each other. Forums not only provide interactivity for your users, but also create a growing body of content for your site.

The Forum module provides a significant amount of functionality, including two system-created blocks. In this chapter, I introduce the Forum module, the various parts of the forum functionality, and the options that are available for styling your forum.

Introducing the Forum Module

The Forum functionality has several parts. The main elements are the containers, forums, forum topics, and posts. Additionally, there are two related blocks for displaying forum topics.

The containers and the forums are the basic organizational elements, with the forum topics and posts supplying the content that is the essence of the threaded discussions. The blocks simply provide easy access to the most recent and active topics.

Figures 20.1 and 20.2 show the Forum module in action. In Figure 20.1, you see the top level of the forum—in this case, a container containing one forum.

FIGURE 20.1

Clicking the default Forums option on the Navigation menu displays a list of categories, if any exist.

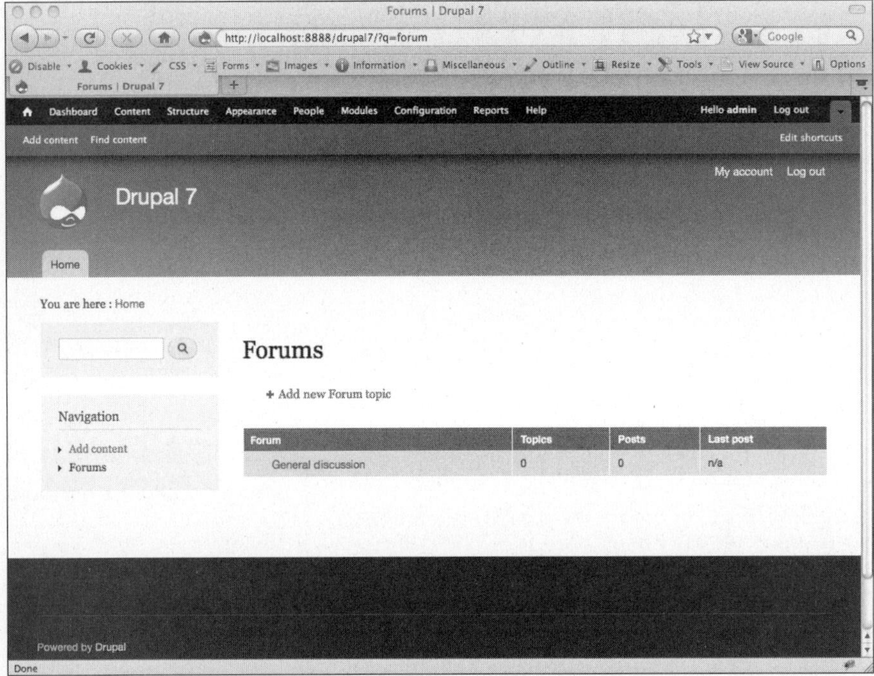

Figure 20.2 shows a single forum as it appears on the front end of the site. The forum is where you find the topics and the posts in response to those topics. The default forum display shows you only a list of the topics, together with a count of responses to the topic and the date of the most recent activity.

Enabling and disabling the module

The Forum module is disabled in both the default standard installation and in the minimal installation profile. This module has dependencies. Before you can enable the Forum module, you must make sure that all the prerequisites are met. Specifically, there are six prerequisites you must first enable:

- Comment module
- Field module
- Field SQL storage module
- Options module
- Taxonomy module
- Text module

FIGURE 20.2

This screen shows a forum containing a forum topic.

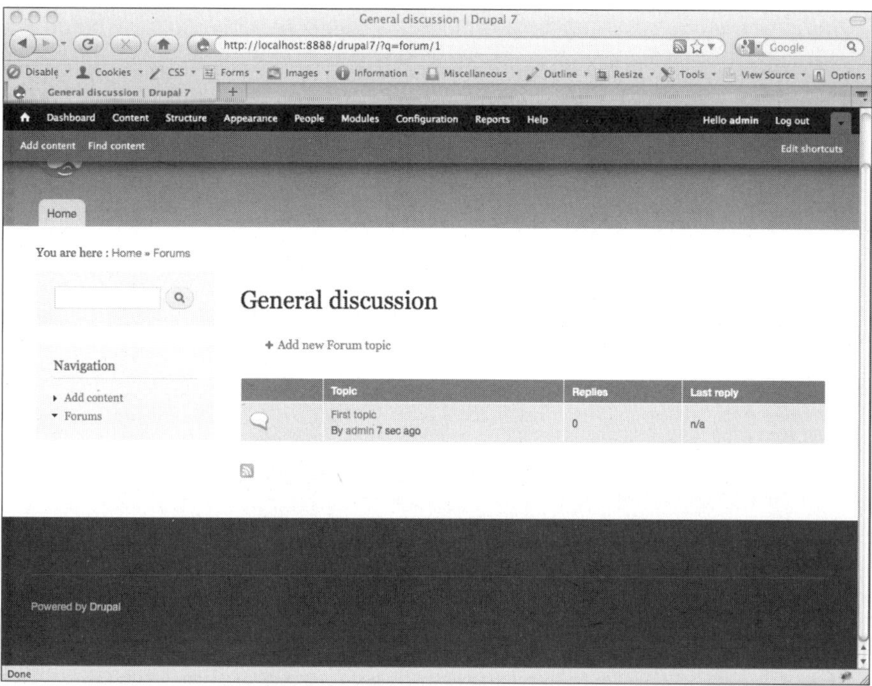

After you have enabled the required modules, you can enable the Forum module by following these steps:

1. **Log into your site as an administrator.**

   The administration interface loads in your browser.
2. **Select Modules from the Management menu.**

   The Modules Manager loads in your browser.
3. **Click the check box next to the Forum module.**
4. **Click the Save Configuration button at the bottom of the page.**

   If you are successful, the Forum module is enabled and a confirmation message appears at the top of the page.

When you enable the Forum module, the system automatically creates a new menu item on the Navigation menu. The item is called Forums and is published by default. When a user clicks the Forums menu item, he is taken to a page that lists all the containers in the system, as shown in Figure 20.1. If you are not using the containers functionality, the page displays a list of the active forums.

Configuring the module

Configuring the Forum module involves adding the appropriate permissions to create and manage the contents and then adjusting the Forums settings.

To view and set the module's configuration options, go to the Modules Manager. Next to the Forum module you see three links: Help, Permissions, and Configure, as shown in Figure 20.3.

FIGURE 20.3

The Forum module shown in the Modules Manager

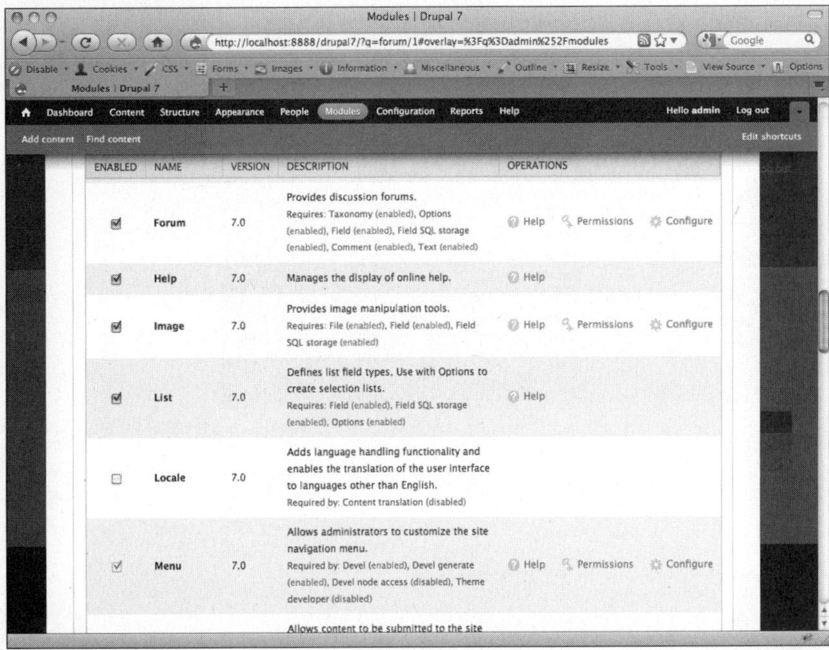

Here's what the options mean:

- **Help:** Click this link to view the integrated help file for the module.
- **Permissions:** Click this link to visit the Permissions Manager, where you can control access to the Forum module and the output of the module, as shown in Figure 20.4. This is discussed in more detail later in the chapter.
- **Configure:** Click this link to visit the Forums Manager, where you can create new containers and forums and manage them easily, as shown in Figure 20.5.

A good place to begin when setting up the forum for the first time is the Permissions link. If you set the permissions now, viewing the impact of your work on the front end of the site is easier. Clicking the Permissions link takes you to the Permissions page, as shown in Figure 20.4.

Cross-Reference

Working with users, roles, and permissions is discussed in depth in Chapter 23. ■

FIGURE 20.4

The Forum permissions settings; note there are further settings under the Node section of the Permissions Manager.

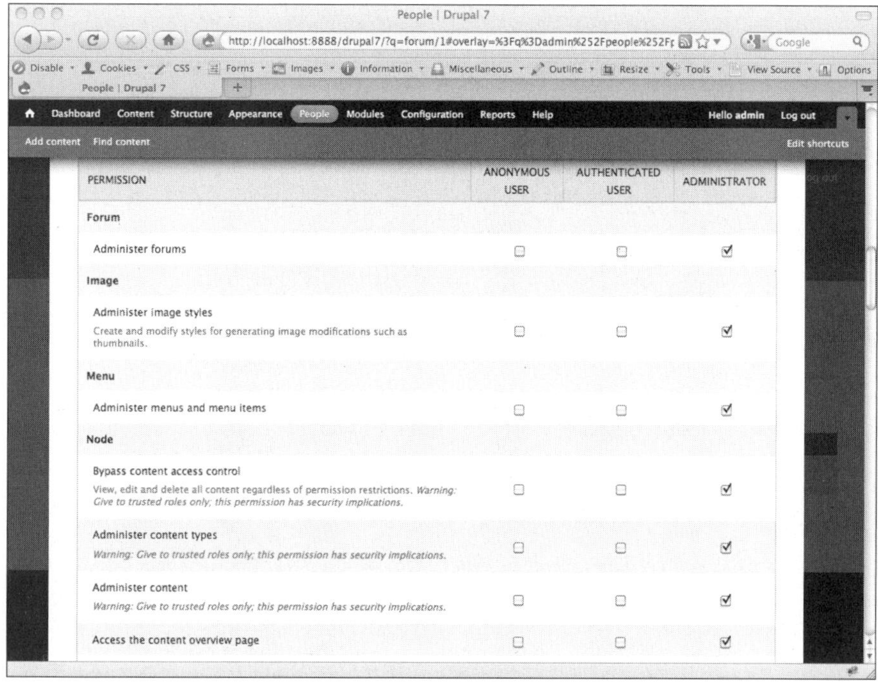

The Node section of the Permissions Manager contains the following options relevant to the forum functionality:

- **Forum topic: Create new content**: Check this box to allow the user group to create new forum topic content.
- **Forum topic: Edit own content**: Check this box to allow the user group to edit any forum topic they have created.
- **Forum topic: Edit any content**: Check this box to allow the user group to edit any forum topic, regardless of the author.
- **Forum topic: Delete own content**: Check this box to allow the user group to delete the forum topics they have created.
- **Forum topic: Delete any content**: Check this box to allow the user group to delete any forum topic, regardless of the author.

After you have made your choices, click the Save permissions button at the bottom of the page. A confirmation message tells you if you have been successful.

The Forums settings page includes a number of options that allow you to adjust the display of forum topics. To view the Forum settings, click the Configure link, next to the name of the Forum module on the Modules Manager. To access the Settings page, click the tab at the top right; the Forums settings page loads in your browser, as shown in Figure 20.5.

FIGURE 20.5

The Forums settings page

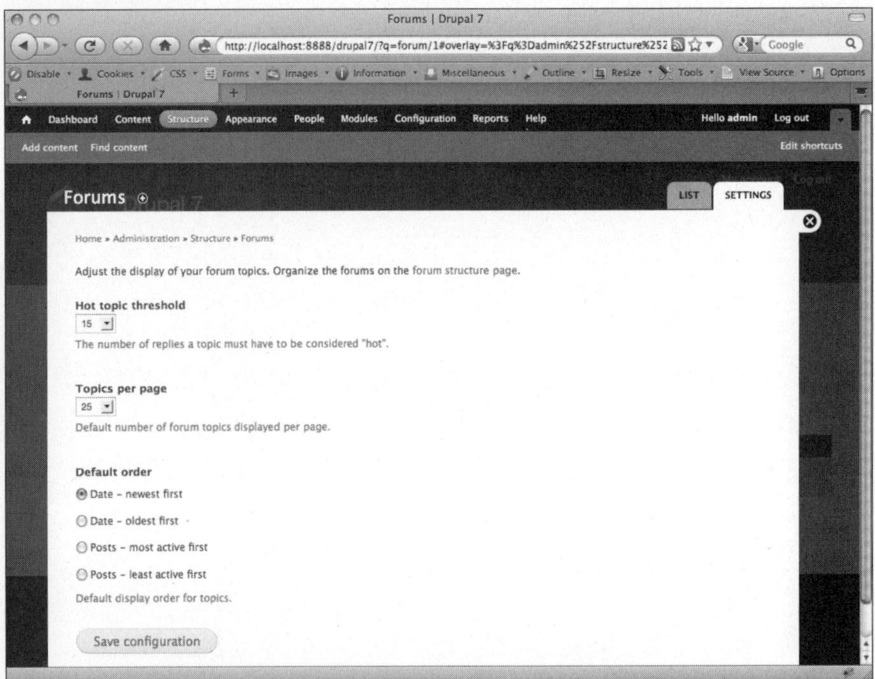

The settings on this page affect all forums in the system. These are the options:

- **Hot topic threshold:** Select a value from the combo box. The value is the threshold over which a topic is considered to be "hot." Hot topics display an icon for users to see.
- **Topics per page:** Select a value from the combo box. The value indicates the number of forum topics that are displayed per page.
- **Default order:** Select one of the radio buttons to control the ordering of the forum topics. The four choices are based on activity levels or chronology.

After you have made your choices, click the Save configuration button at the bottom of the page. A confirmation message tells you if you have been successful.

Administering Forums

The Forum module employs four different levels of organization: containers, forums, topics, and posts. Administering your site's forums requires an understanding of all four:

- **Containers:** Containers hold forums. Containers are optional. These are created by the administrator.
- **Forums:** Forums hold topics. You must have at least one forum. These are typically created by the administrator, but on some sites other user roles are granted permission to create forums.
- **Topics:** Topics are the top-level post inside a forum. Forum topics are nodes.
- **Posts:** Posts are replies to forum topics or to other posts. Technically, posts are actually comments and are controlled by Drupal's comments functionality.

Containers and forums can be created from inside the administration interface. Click the Configure link, next to the name of the Forum module on the Modules Manager. The interface is shown in Figure 20.6.

FIGURE 20.6

The Forums Manager, where the administrator can create containers and forums

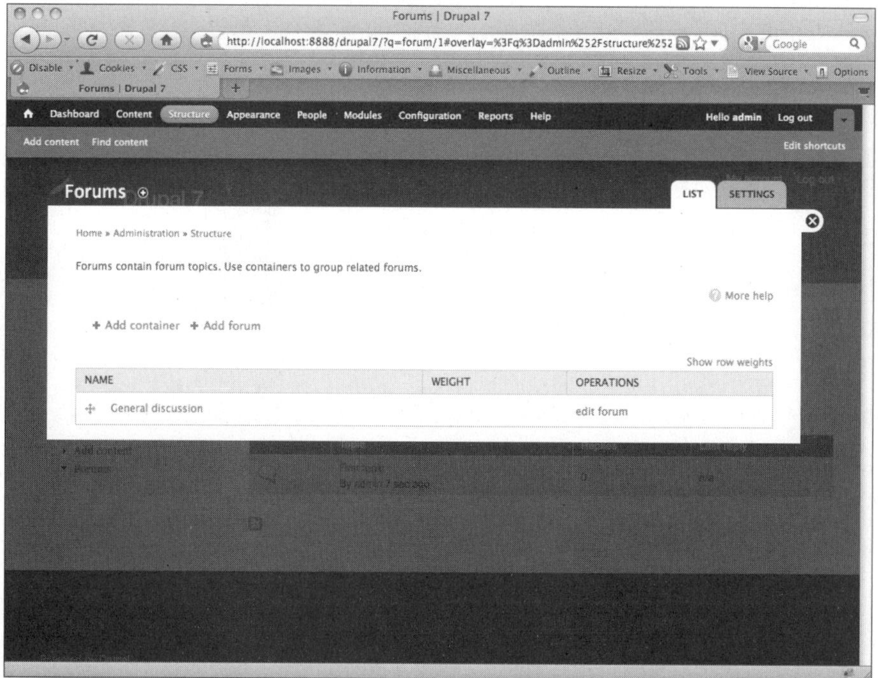

Working with containers

Containers can be used to hold one or more forums. They are useful organizational tools, but they are optional. If your site has only one forum, you are unlikely to want to bother with creating a container. On the other hand, if your site has numerous forums, containers are a great way to group related forums for ease of use.

Containers are managed from within the Forums manager, as shown in Figure 20.6.

Tip

Containers also can be grouped inside other containers if you want to create a complex hierarchy. ■

Adding a container

The New Container page, shown in Figure 20.7, is accessed from within the Forums Manager.

FIGURE 20.7

The New Container page

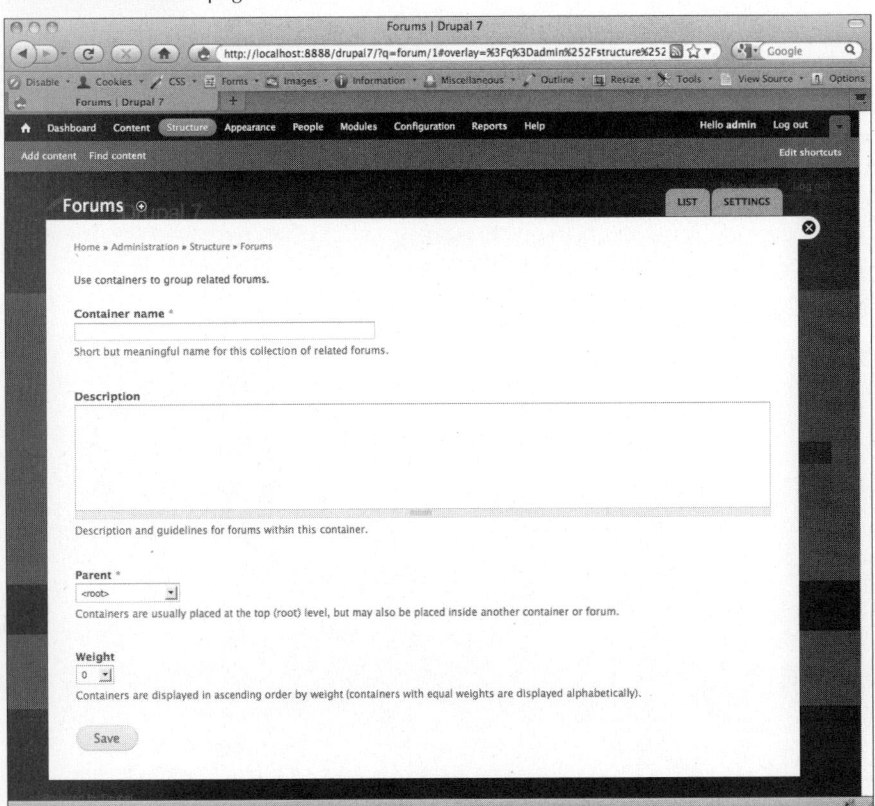

These fields are on this page:

- **Container name:** Type into this field a name for your container. This is a required field.
- **Description:** Type into this field some descriptive text for the container. This is an optional field.
- **Parent:** Use the combo box to set the order of the container within the hierarchy. To assign a container to the top level, select the option <root>. If your site already has one or more containers, you can select the name of an existing container from the combo box, in which case the selected container functions as the parent of your new container.
- **Weight:** Select a value from the combo box to control the ordering of the container, relative to other containers at the same level in the hierarchy.

Note

The weight option lets you control the ordering of items relative to other items at the same level. A lower number means a lighter weight. A higher number means a heavier weight. Lighter-weight items float to the top; heavier-weight items sink to the bottom of the order. ■

To create a new container, follow these steps:

1. **Log into your site as an administrator.**

   The admin interface loads in your browser window.
2. **Click Structure on the Management menu.**

   The Structure page loads in your browser.
3. **Click Forums.**

   The Forums Manager loads in your browser, as shown in Figure 20.6.
4. **Click Add container.**

   The New Container page loads in your browser, as shown in Figure 20.7.
5. **Type a name for the container in the Container name field.**

   This is a required field.
6. **Select any other options you desire; all other settings are optional.**
7. **Click the Save button.**

   The system creates a new container and displays a confirmation message.

Editing a container

To edit an existing container, simply click the edit container link in the operations column of the Forums manager, and the Edit Container page loads in your browser, as shown in Figure 20.8.

FIGURE 20.8

The Edit Container page

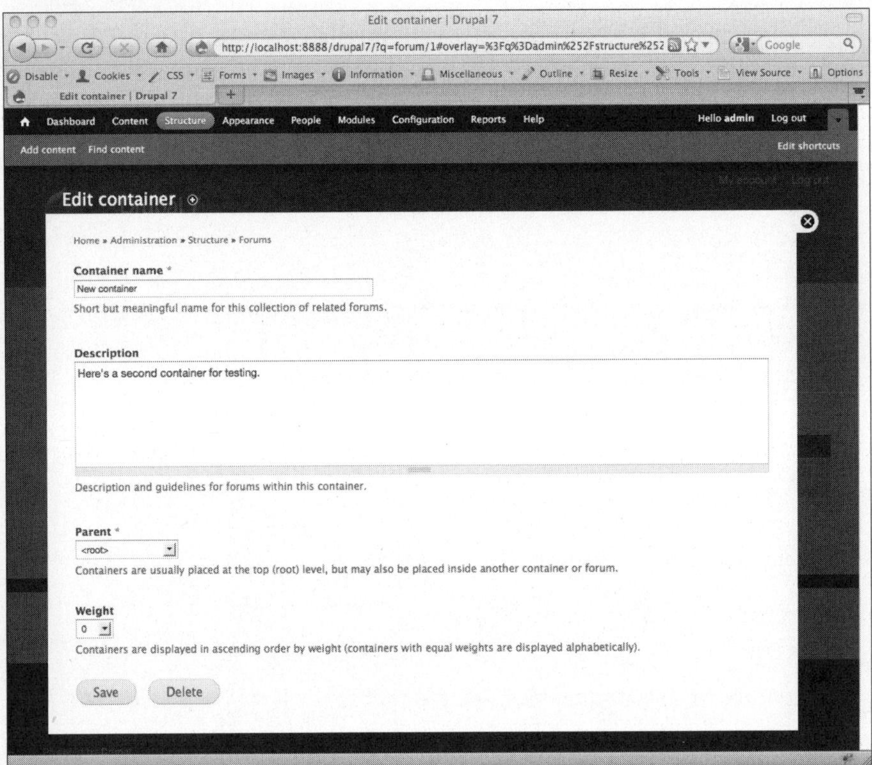

Once the Edit Container page opens, make your changes. When you have finished, click the Save button and the system updates the container.

Deleting a container

To delete an existing container, simply click the edit container link in the operations column of the Forums manager and the Edit Container page loads in your browser. When the Edit Container page opens, click the Delete button. The system prompts you to confirm deletion; if you want to delete the container, click the Delete button and the system deletes the container.

Working with forums

Forums hold the forum topics and the posts in response to those topics. Forums are required and may or may not be grouped into containers.

Forums are managed from within the Forums manager (refer to Figure 20.6).

Adding a forum

Adding a new forum is almost identical to the process used for creating a new container. You can access the New Forum page from the same page you accessed the New Container page. Figure 20.9 shows the New Forum page.

FIGURE 20.9

The New Forum page

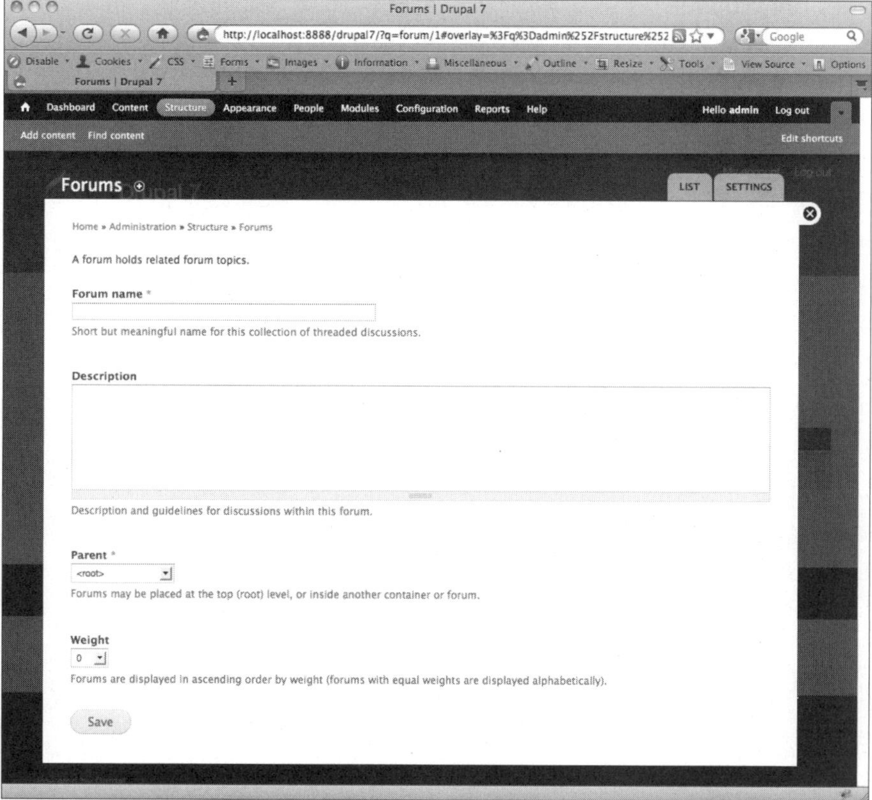

This page holds these fields:

- **Forum name:** Type into this field a name for your forum. This is a required field.
- **Description:** Type into this field some descriptive text for the forum. This is an optional field.
- **Parent:** Use the combo box to set the order of the forum within the hierarchy. To assign a forum to the top level, select the option <root>. If your site already has one

or more containers, you can select the name of an existing container from the combo box, in which case the selected container functions as the parent of your new forum.

- **Weight:** Select a value from the combo box to control the ordering of the forum, relative to other forums at the same level in the hierarchy.

Note

The weight option lets you control the ordering of items relative to other items at the same level. A lower number means a lighter weight. A higher number means a heavier weight. Lower-weight items float to the top; heavier-weight items sink to the bottom of the order. ■

To create a new forum, follow these steps:

1. **Log into your site as an administrator.**

   The admin interface loads in your browser window.

2. **Click Modules on the Management menu.**

   The Modules Manager loads in your browser.

3. **Click the Configure link next to the Forum module.**

   The Forums Manager loads in your browser, as shown in Figure 20.6.

4. **Click Add forum.**

   The New Forum page loads in your browser, as shown in Figure 20.9.

5. **Type a name for the forum in the Forum name field.**

   This is a required field.

6. **Select any other options you desire; all other settings are optional.**

7. **Click the Save button.**

   The system creates a new forum and displays a confirmation message.

Editing a forum

To edit an existing forum, simply click the edit forum link in the operations column of the Forums manager and the Edit Forum page loads in your browser, as shown in Figure 20.10.

Once the Edit Container page opens, make your changes. When you have finished, click the Save button and the system updates the container.

Deleting a forum

To delete an existing forum, simply click the edit forum link in the operations column of the Forums manager and the Edit Forum page loads in your browser. When the Edit Forum page opens, click the Delete button. The system prompts you to confirm deletion; if you want to delete the forum, click the Delete button and the system deletes the forum.

FIGURE 20.10

The Edit Forum page

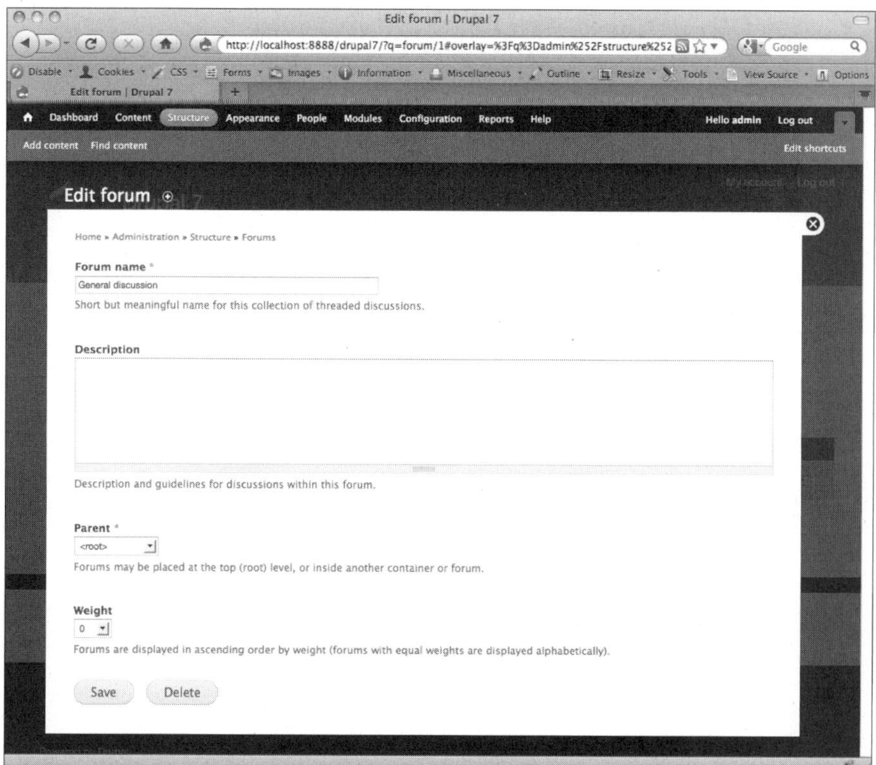

Working with forum topics

Unlike containers and forums, forum topics are nodes. Like other nodes, they can be created, edited, and deleted from either the front end or the back end of the site. Forum topics are managed from within the Content Manager, as shown in Figure 20.11.

Forum topics are the top-level items inside a forum. Replies to a forum topic are threaded beneath the topic. Put another way, the topic is the parent item and the replies are the children of the topic.

Tip

Drupal treats replies to forum topics as comments. The replies are managed, formatted, and controlled by the comments' functionality. ■

FIGURE 20.11

The Content Manager shows one forum topic in existence.

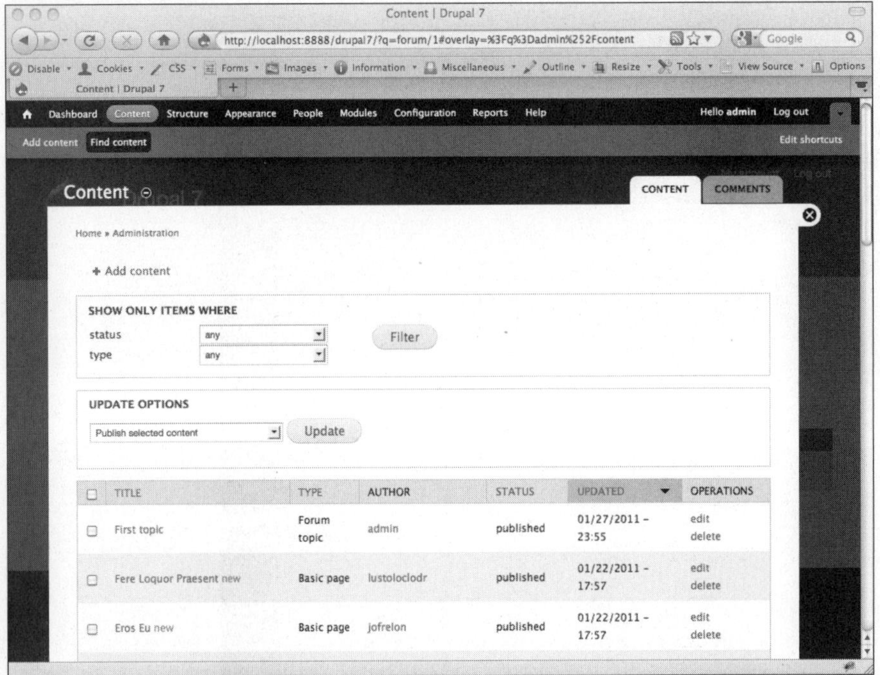

Create a new forum topic

A new forum topic can be created by adding a new node to the site. Figure 20.12 shows the Create Forum Topic page.

The fields on this page are divided into two groups. At the top of the page are the fields needed to create and assign the forum topic. At the bottom of the page are the standard content item options.

These controls are related to creating the forum topic's content and assignment:

- **Subject:** Type into this field a subject line for the topic. This is a required field.
- **Forums:** Assign the topic to a forum by selecting the name of the forum from the combo box. This is a required field.
- **Body:** Type the text you want to appear in the body of the forum topic. This is an optional field, though it is almost always populated with some content.
- **Edit summary:** The edit summary link appears next to the Body field's title. Click this to open a new field.

FIGURE 20.12

The Create Forum Topic page

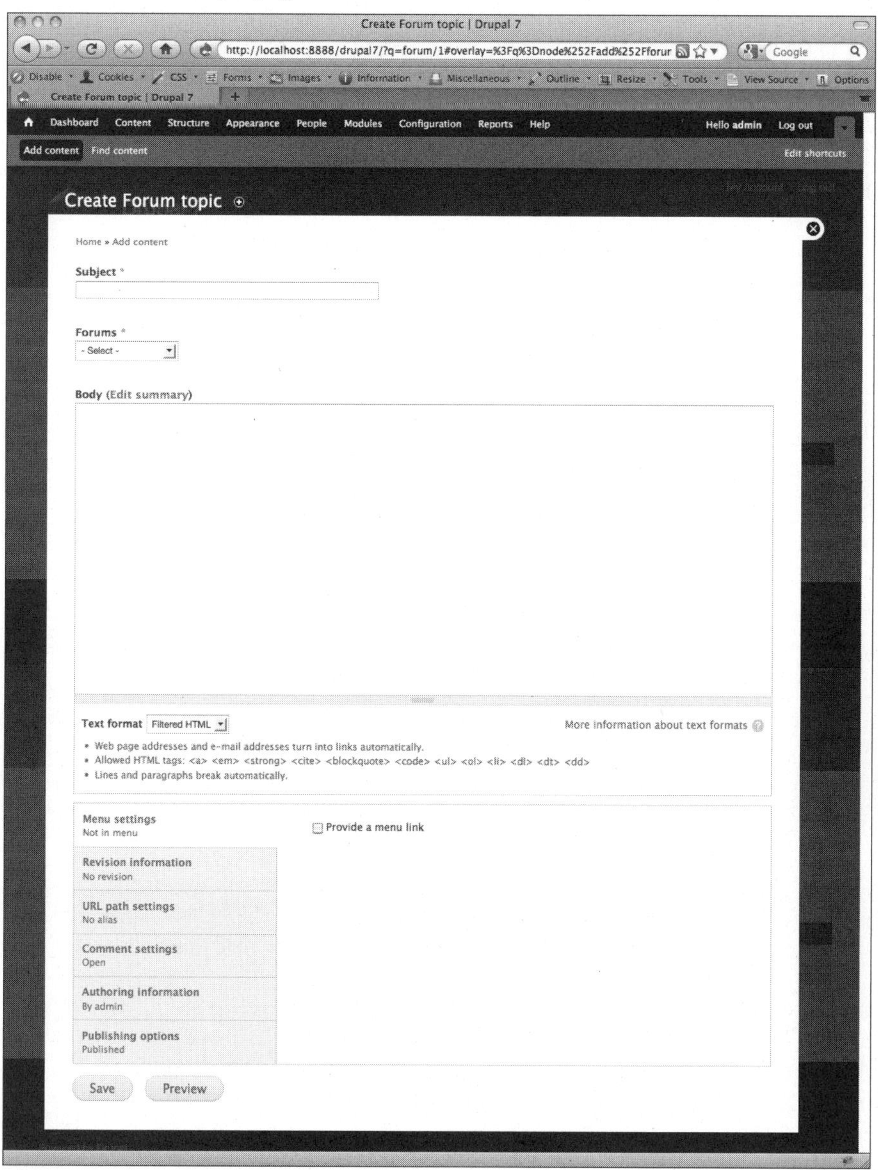

Tip

Clicking the Edit summary link displays a new field on the page. In the new field, you can specify summary, or teaser, text that is displayed to the user. If the user wants to read the entire content item, they will need to click the Read more link to view the item in full. Creating a separate summary is optional, but it gives you control over the length and content of the teasers. ■

- **Text format:** Select from the combo box the text format and filter you want to apply to the node. The options available in the combo box are determined by the filter options set by the administrator.

Tip

Click the link labeled More information about text formats to see a quick summary of the implications of the various options. ■

Cross-Reference

Filters and text formats are discussed in more detail in Chapter 4. ■

These are the standard content item options:

- **Menu settings:** Check the box and fill in the additional fields that appear to create a menu item for the node. If you leave the box unchecked, no dedicated menu item exists unless you create it manually through the menu manager.
- **Revision information:** Check the box to create a new revision. Fill in the text field to add notes for reference.
- **URL path settings:** Set the URL alias for the node.
- **Comment settings:** Determine whether comments are Open or Closed for this node. By default, comment settings for forum topics are open to allow for discussion of the topic.

Tip

Selecting Closed in the Comments settings prevents new comments being made to the forum topic, but any existing comments remain visible. Selecting Disabled hides all existing comments and prevents further comments. ■

- **Authoring information:** Use these fields to override the default author name and the default creation date and time.
- **Publishing options:** Use the check boxes to determine whether the node is Published, Promoted to the front page, or Sticky at the top of lists.

Cross-Reference

The standard content item options are discussed in detail in Chapter 10. ■

To create a new forum topic from within the admin system, follow these steps:

1. **Log into your site as an administrator.**

   The administration interface loads in your browser.

2. **Click Add content on the Shortcuts menu.**

   A new page loads.

3. **On the new page, select Forum topic.**

   The Create forum topic page loads in your browser (refer to Figure 20.12).

4. **Type the subject for the forum topic in the Subject field.**

   This is a required field.

5. **Assign the topic to a forum by selecting a value from the Forums combo box.**

   This is required.

6. **Select any other options you desire.**

   All other choices are optional.

7. **Click the Save button.**

   The system creates a new forum topic and displays a confirmation message.

If a user has sufficient Permissions, they can create new forum topics from the front end of the Web site. To create a new forum topic from the front end of the site, follow these steps:

1. **Click Forums menu item.**

   The Forums page loads in your browser.

2. **Click the name of the forum where you want to place the new topic.**

   The top-level forum page loads.

3. **Click Add a new Forum topic.**

   The Create Forum topic page loads in your browser (refer to Figure 20.12).

4. **Type the subject for the forum topic in the Subject field.**

   This is a required field.

5. **Assign the topic to a forum by selecting a forum name from the combo box labeled Forums.**

   This is required.

6. **Select any other options you desire.**

   All other choices are optional.

7. **Click the Save button.**

   The system creates a new forum topic and displays a confirmation message.

Note

If you'd like to check your work before publishing it, you can either use the Preview button at the bottom of the page or uncheck the Published check box under the Publishing options tab and then click the item to view it. ■

Editing forum topics

Forum topics are edited with the same process used for other Drupal nodes.

To edit a forum topic from the admin system, follow these steps:

1. **Log into your site as an administrator.**

   The administration interface loads in your browser.
2. **Click Find Content on the Shortcuts menu.**

   The Content Manager loads in your browser.
3. **Click the Edit option next to the name of the forum topic you want to edit.**

   The Edit Forum topic page loads in your browser, as shown in Figure 20.13.
4. **Make any changes you desire.**
5. **Click the Save button.**

   The system saves your changes to the blog and displays a confirmation message.

Tip

If you move an existing forum topic from one forum to another, consider using the Leave shadow copy option. This leaves a link in the original forum pointing to the topic's new location. ■

If a user has sufficient permissions, they can edit forum topics from the front end of the Web site. To edit a forum topic from the front end of the site, follow these steps:

1. **View the forum topic.**
2. **Click Edit.**

   The Edit Forum topic page loads in your browser (refer to Figure 20.13).
3. **Make any changes you desire.**
4. **Click the Save button.**

   The system saves your changes to the blog and displays a confirmation message.

Deleting forum topics

Forum topics are deleted with the same process used for other Drupal nodes.

To delete a forum topic from the admin system, follow these steps:

1. **Log into your site as an administrator.**

   The administration interface loads in your browser.
2. **Click Find Content on the Shortcuts menu.**

   The Content Manager loads in your browser.
3. **Select Delete from the operations column next to your forum topic.**
4. **Click the Update button.**

The confirmation page loads in your browser.

5. **Click the Delete button.**

   The system deletes the forum topic and displays a confirmation message.

FIGURE 20.13

In the Edit Forum topic page, note the Leave shadow copy option under the Full text field.

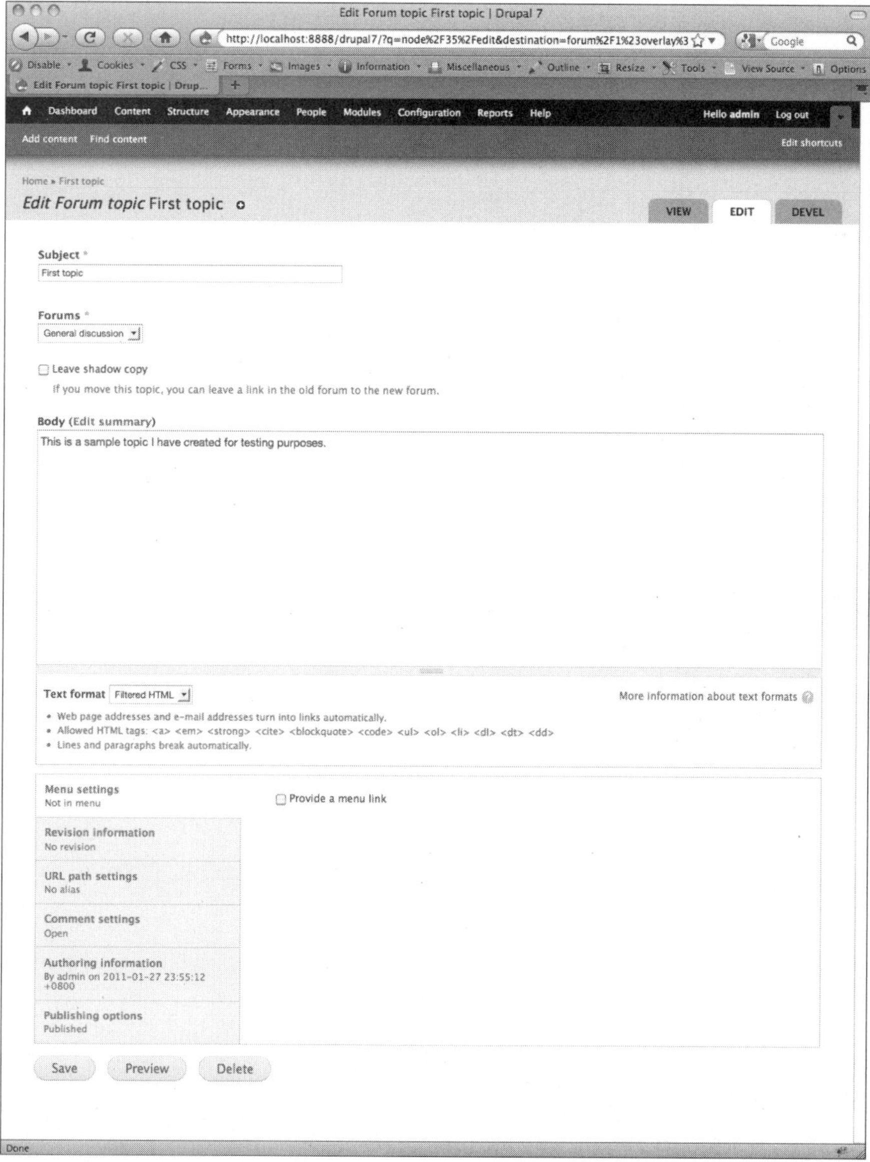

If a user has sufficient permissions, they can delete forum topics from the front end of the Web site. To delete a forum topic from the front end of the site, follow these steps:

1. **View the forum topic you want to delete.**
2. **Click the Edit tab.**

   The Edit Forum topic page opens.
3. **Scroll down to the bottom of the page, and click the Delete button.**

   The confirmation page loads in your browser.
4. **Click the Delete button.**

   The system deletes the forum topic and displays a confirmation message.

Note

Deleting a Forum topic automatically deletes all the comments that have been posted to the forum topic. This cannot be undone. ■

Controlling the Styling of the Forum Module

The Forum module provides you with five dedicated template files, two style sheets, and one themable function. In the following sections, I introduce each of these resources, indicate their role in the display, and explain the functions and variables that are available for you to work with.

Cross-Reference

Overriding templates and working with themable functions are discussed in depth in Chapter 26. ■

Reviewing the default templates

The Forum module contains five dedicated templates, which are located at /modules/forum:

- **forum-icon.tpl.php**
- **forum-list.tpl.php**
- **forum-submitted.tpl.php**
- **forum-topic-list.tpl.php**
- **forums.tpl.php**

These templates are discussed in the sections that follow.

Reviewing forum-icon.tpl.php

This template controls the display of icons on the forum posts. Icons are used for things like the "hot," "new," "sticky," and so on. The available variables are shown in Table 20.1.

TABLE 20.1

Variables in forum-icon.tpl.php

Variable	Description
$first_new	Indicates that the item is the first topic with new posts
$icon	The icon to be displayed
$new_posts	A flag indicating whether the topic contains new posts

Reviewing forum-list.tpl.php

The forum-list template controls the display of a list of forums and containers. The variables are shown in Table 20.2.

TABLE 20.2

Variables in forum-list.tpl.php

Variable	Description
$forum_id	The ID of the current forum
$forum->depth	The depth of the current forum within the hierarchy
$forum->description	The forum's description
$forum->is_container	True if the forum contains other forums
$forum->last_reply	The last time the forum was posted or commented on
$forum->link	The URL of the forum
$forum->name	The name of the forum
$forum->new_topics	Whether the forum contains unread posts
$forum->new_text	Tells how many new posts
$forum->new_url	The URL to unread posts
$forum->num_posts	The total number of posts
$forum->old_topics	A count of the posts already read
$forum->zebra	An even or odd indicator used to help style rows
$forums	An array of the forums and containers to be displayed

Reviewing forum-submitted.tpl.php

This template formats the string indicating when and by whom a post was submitted. The available variables are shown in Table 20.3.

TABLE 20.3

Variables in forum-submitted.tpl.php

Variable	Description
$author	The name of the author of the post
$time	How long ago the post was created
$topic	The raw data of the post

Reviewing forum-topic-list.tpl.php

This template renders a list of forum topics. The available variables are shown in Table 20.4.

TABLE 20.4

Variables in forum-topic-list.tpl.php

Variable	Description
$header	The table header
$pager	The pagination controls displayed beneath the table
$topic_id	The ID for the current forum topic
$topics	An array of the topics to be displayed
$topic->comment_count	The number of replies
$topic->created	The date the topic was posted
$topic->icon	The icon
$topic->kast_reply	The date of the last reply
$topic->message	If the topic has been moved, this supplies the explanation and the link to the new location
$topic->moved	A flag to indicate that it is a moved topic
$topic->new_replies	Indicates unread messages
$topic->new_text	Text containing the count

Variable	Description
$topic->new_url	The URL to any new messages
$topic->timestamp	The timestamp for when the topic was posted
$topic->title	The title to the topic
$topic->zebra	An even or odd indicator used to help style rows

Reviewing forums.tpl.php

This is the default template for displaying a forum. The available variables are shown in Table 20.5.

TABLE 20.5

Variables in forums.tpl.php

Variable	Description
$forums	The forums to display
$forums_defined	A flag to indicate that the forums are configured
$topics	The topics to display

Reviewing the default style sheets

Two style sheets are dedicated to the formatting of the Forum module. Both are located at /modules/forum:

- **forum.css:** The primary CSS files
- **forum-rtl.css:** The CSS that is applied when the site is set to display text in right-to-left orientation

Using the Active Forum Topics Block

When you enable the Forum module, Drupal automatically creates the Active Forum Topics block. The block displays a list of the forum topics that are currently active—that is, the topics that are published.

The block is unpublished by default; publish it to view the output, as shown in Figure 20.14.

To configure the block, click the Configuration link next to the block's name in the Block manager interface. The configure page loads, as shown in Figure 20.15.

FIGURE 20.14

The Active Forum Topics block in action

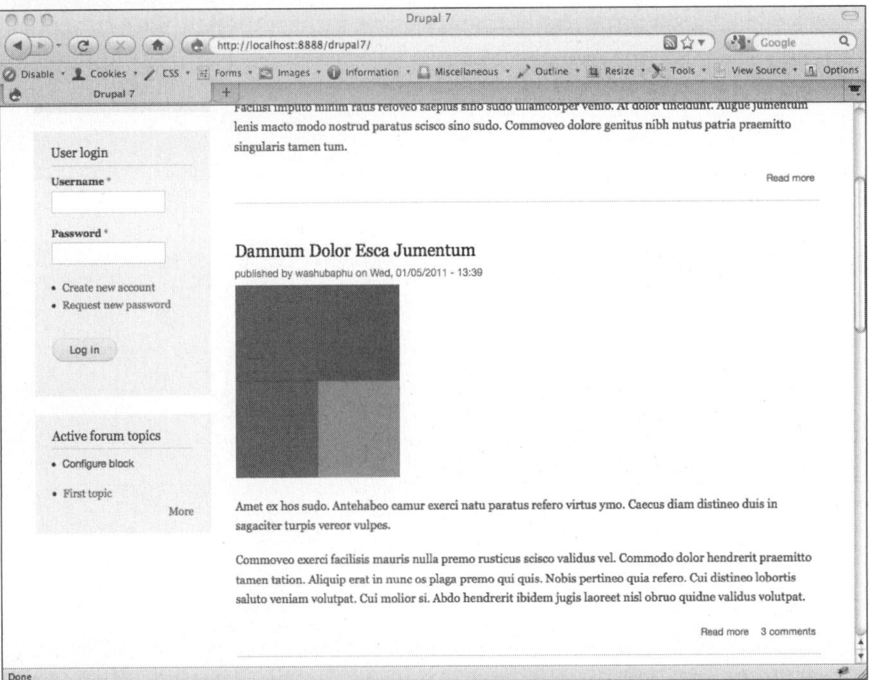

The Block Specific controls on this page are as follows:

- **Block title:** Enter a title for your block here. If you leave it blank, the system displays the default title, which is "Active Forum Topics."
- **Number of topics:** Select from the combo box the number of topics to display.

FIGURE 20.15

The Active Forum Topics block configuration options

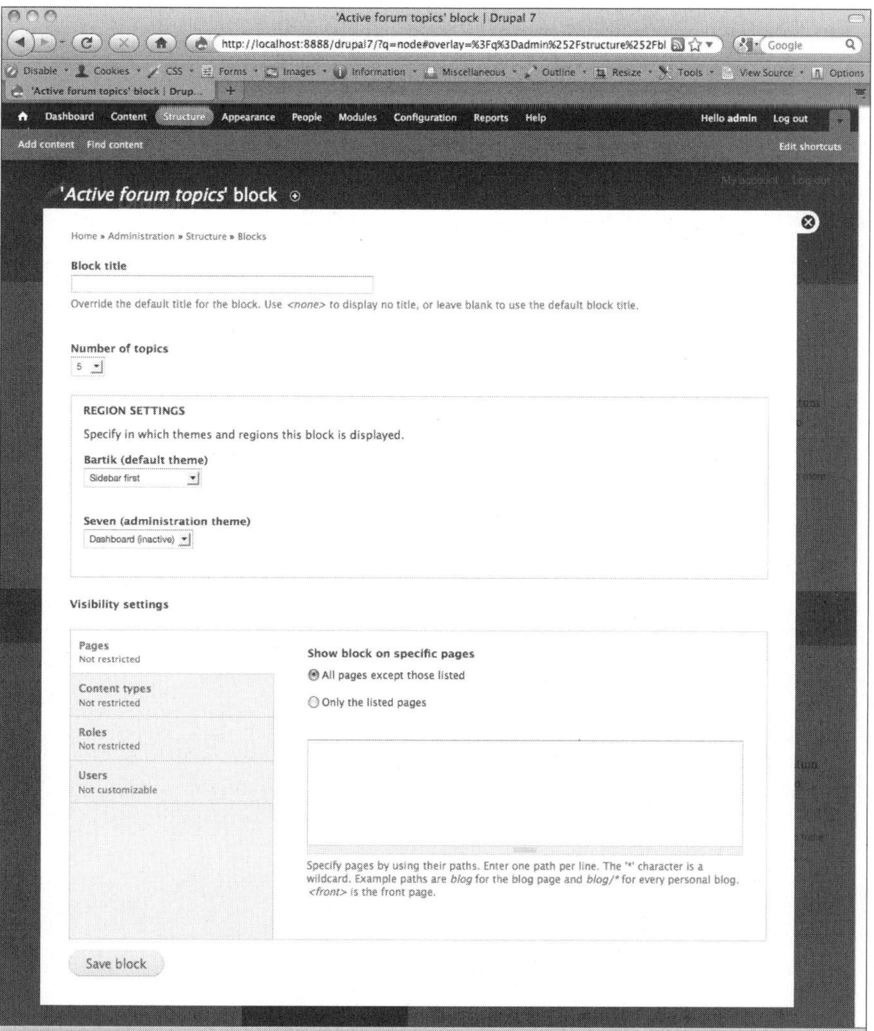

Using the New Forum Topics Block

When you enable the Forum module, Drupal automatically creates the New Forum Topics block. The block displays a list of the newest forum topics.

The block is unpublished by default; publish it to view the output, as shown in Figure 20.16.

FIGURE 20.16

The New Forum Topics block in action

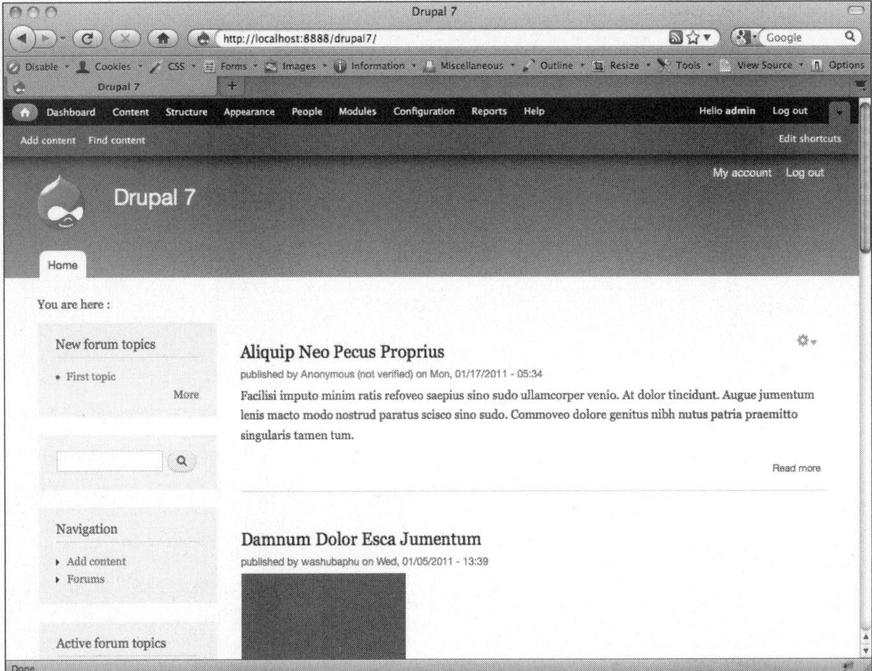

To configure the block, click the Configuration link next to the block's name in the Block manager interface. The configure page loads. The configuration options available for this block are the same as for the Active Forum Topics block, as shown in the preceding section.

Cross-Reference

Working with blocks is discussed in depth in Chapter 7. ■

Summary

This chapter addressed the use of the Forum functionality in Drupal 7. I covered these topics:

- How to enable the Forum module
- How to configure the Forum module
- How to add and manage forums
- How to use the Active Forum Topics block
- How to use the New Forum Topics block

CHAPTER 21

Using the Poll Module

The Poll module enables you to add polls and surveys to your Web site. The module supports a basic multiple-choice format that allows users to respond to a question by selecting from a predefined set of answer choices. The answers are tallied and stored on the site for the administrator or the users to view. Polls and surveys are useful to you as an administrator because they both add interactivity to your site and give you a means of soliciting feedback and information from the site users.

In this chapter, I introduce the Poll module, the Poll content type, and the options that are available for managing the content associated with the Poll functionality. I also review the various system resources for theming your polls.

IN THIS CHAPTER

Introducing the Poll module

Administering polls

Controlling the styling of the Poll module

Using the Most Recent Poll block

Introducing the Poll Module

Drupal's Poll module supports the creation of one or more multiple-choice surveys. The module enables a dedicated content type called, appropriately, Poll. The administrator creates a new poll by creating a new content item of the appropriate type. The various polls are managed with Drupal's standard content item management tools.

Once created and published, the poll accumulates responses in a running total and provides a display of the results in a simple bar chart format. The poll form and the results can be shown either in the content region of the page or in a block.

Figure 21.1 shows an example of the Poll module being used to display a poll containing four answer choices.

FIGURE 21.1

The Poll module in action, here showing the content item displayed in the content region of the front page

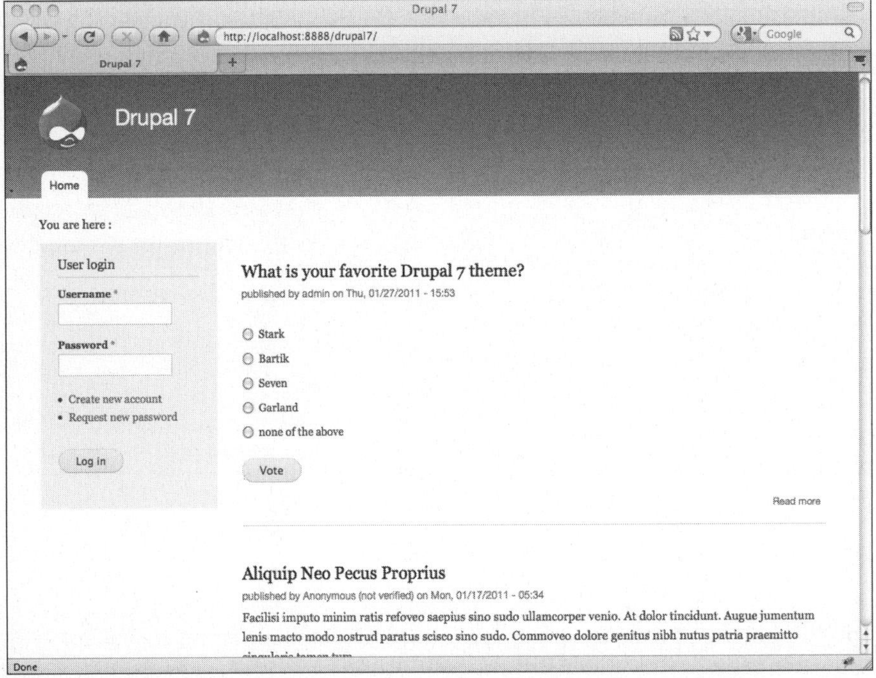

Depending on the options selected by the administrator during configuration, users can also view a summary of the results of the poll including the specific votes cast. Other configuration options allow the user to change his own vote. Poll configuration is discussed later in this chapter.

Figure 21.2 shows the results output.

FIGURE 21.2

The results page of a poll showing the tabs that allow the user to move between the results and the option to view the votes

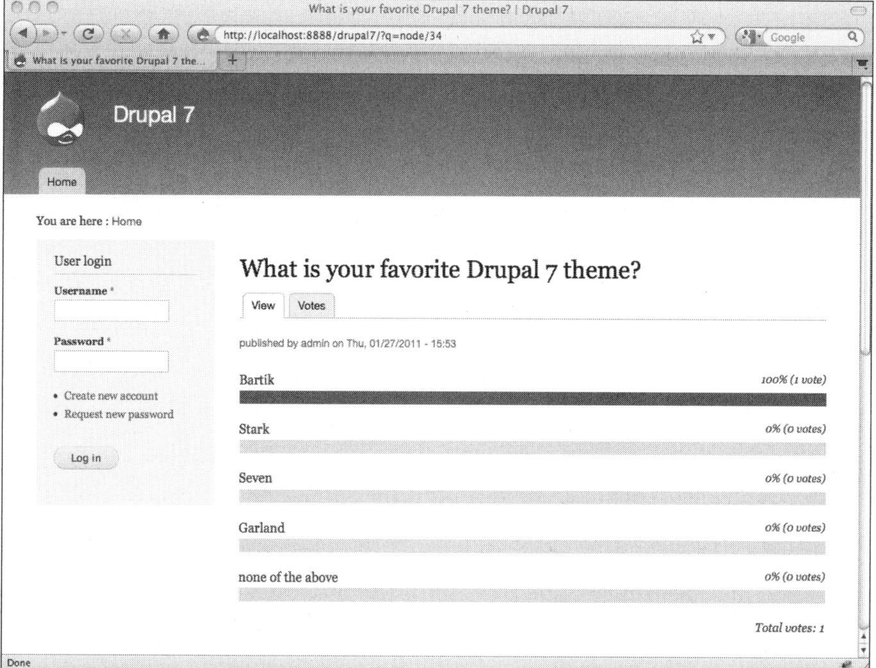

Enabling and disabling the module

The Poll module is disabled in both the default standard installation and in the minimal installation profile. Enabling this module is a simple matter, because it has no dependencies.

To enable the Poll module, follow these steps:

1. **Log into your site as an administrator.**

   The administration interface loads in your browser.

2. **Select the option Modules from the Management menu.**

   The Modules Manager loads in your browser.

3. **Click the check box next to the Poll module.**

4. **Click the Save Configuration button at the bottom of the page.**

   If you are successful, the Poll module is enabled and a confirmation message appears at the top of the page.

Configuring the module

Configuring the Poll module involves setting the options for the module and adding the appropriate permissions to view and manage the contents.

To view and set the module configuration options, go to the Modules Manager and view the Poll module on the page. You can see two links: Help and Permissions, as shown in Figure 21.3.

FIGURE 21.3

The Poll section of the Modules Manager

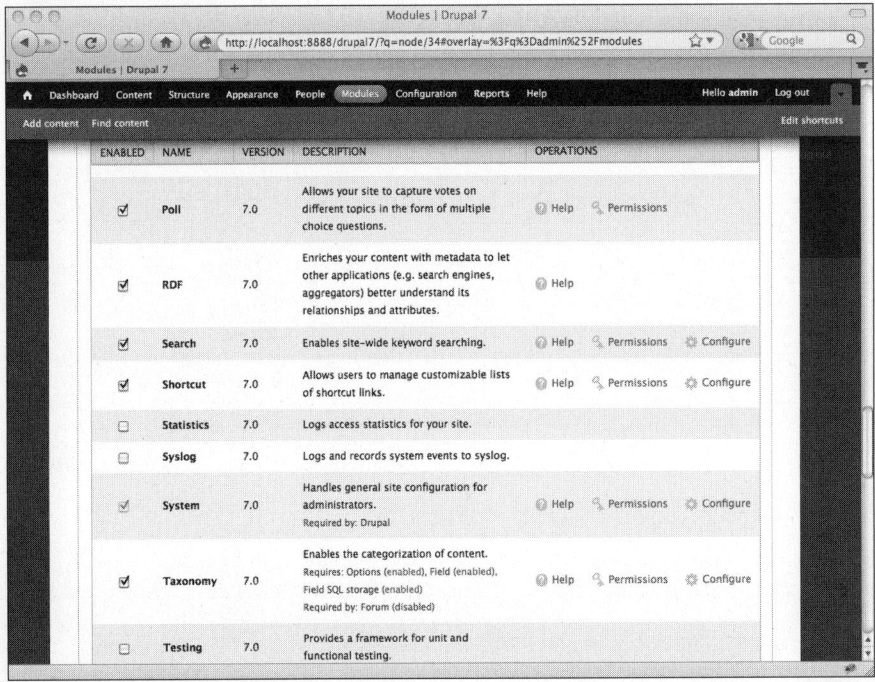

Here's what the options mean:

- **Help:** Click this link to view the integrated help file for the module.
- **Permissions:** Click this link to visit the Permissions Manager where you can control access to the Poll module and the output of the module. This is discussed in more detail in the next section of this chapter.

A good place to begin when setting up the Poll module is the Permissions link. If you set the permissions now, it is easier to view the impact of your changes on the front end of the site. Clicking the Permissions link takes you to the Permissions page, as shown in Figure 21.4.

Cross-Reference

Working with users, roles, and permissions is discussed in depth in Chapter 23. ■

FIGURE 21.4

The Poll permissions settings

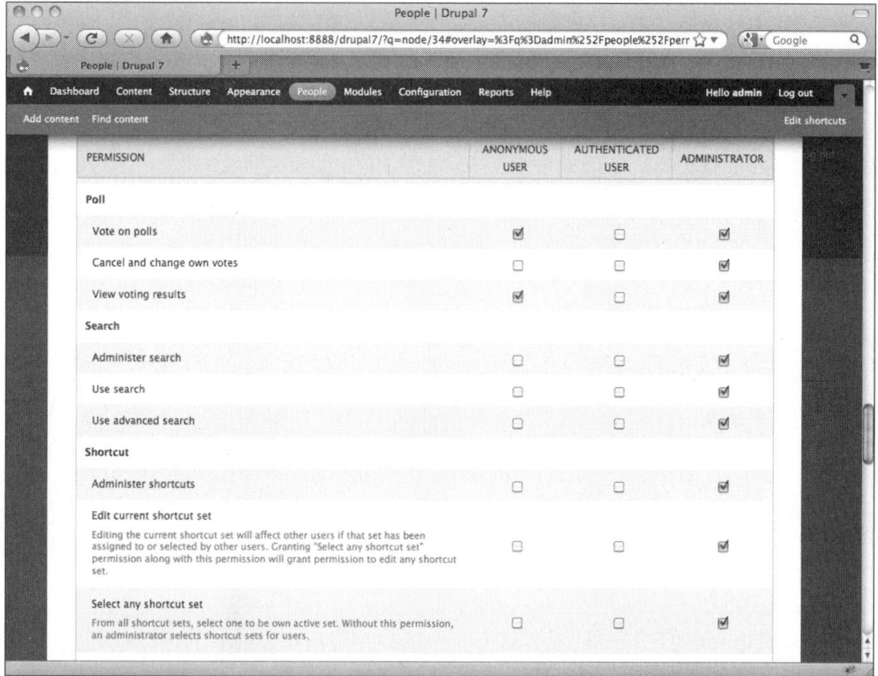

The Permissions options are split between two different sections of the Permissions page. In the Node section, you find the following options:

- **Poll : Create new content:** Check this box to allow the user group to create content items of the type Poll. Typically, you want to grant this right only to your site administrators.
- **Poll : Edit own content:** Check this box to allow the user group to edit any polls they have created.

- **Poll : Edit any content:** Check this box to allow the user group to edit any poll items, including those created by other administrators.
- **Poll : Delete own content:** Check this box to allow the user group to delete any polls they have created.
- **Poll : Delete any content:** Check this box to allow the user group to delete any poll items, including those created by other administrators.

If you scroll down farther, you find a separate Poll section that contains the following options:

- **Vote on polls:** Check this box to allow the user group to cast their votes on the published poll.
- **Cancel and change own votes:** Check this box to allow the user group to cancel their own vote on the poll.
- **View voting results:** Check this box to allow the user group to view the results of the poll.

After you have made your choices, click the Save permissions button at the bottom of the page. A confirmation message tells you if you have been successful.

Note

There is no separate configuration management page dedicated to the Poll module as a whole; rather, since polls are a content type, you can adjust the settings for the content type from the Content Types Manager page. The settings can be defined at the time the poll content item is created, or they can be edited at any time, as discussed in the next section. As with other content types, you can add your own custom fields to the Poll content type. To learn more about how to manage the content types in Drupal, please see Chapter 10. ■

Administering Polls

Poll content items or nodes, as Drupal prefers to call them, are managed from within the Content Management interface. All the tools needed to create, edit, and delete polls are located inside this interface. To access the Content Management interface, click the option Content on the main navigation menu. The interface is shown in Figure 21.5.

Cross-Reference

Working with the Content Manager is discussed in detail in Chapter 10. ■

FIGURE 21.5

The Content Manager, showing one poll node already in existence

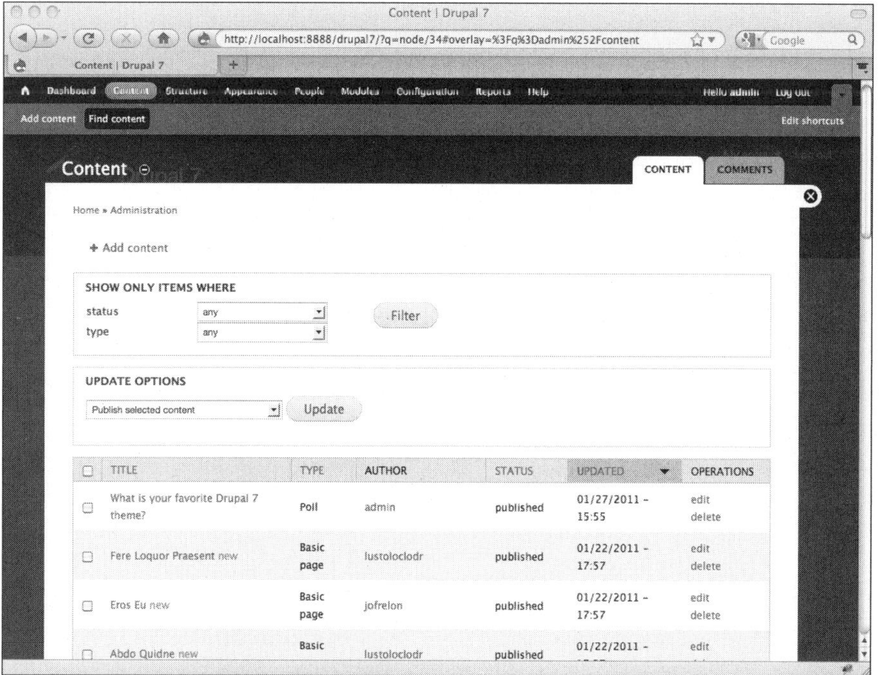

Adding polls

As mentioned earlier in this chapter, a new poll can be created by adding a new node to the site. Figure 21.6 shows the New Poll page.

The fields on this page are divided into three groups. At the top of the page are the fields needed to create the poll question and the answer choices. Below that is the Poll Settings section. At the bottom of the page are the standard content item options.

The controls related to creating the poll question and answer choices are:

- **Question:** Type into this field the question you want to pose to the users. This is a required field.
- **Choice:** By default two blanks are available for you to fill in potential answer choices for the users. Type one answer per blank. The system requires you to enter at least two choices.

- **Vote Count:** When a poll is active, you see in these boxes the number of clicks each answer choice has received. You can modify these totals by typing your own values into these fields.
- **More Choices:** Click this button to add another answer choice box. This allows you to create as many answer choices as you wish.

FIGURE 21.6

The New Poll page

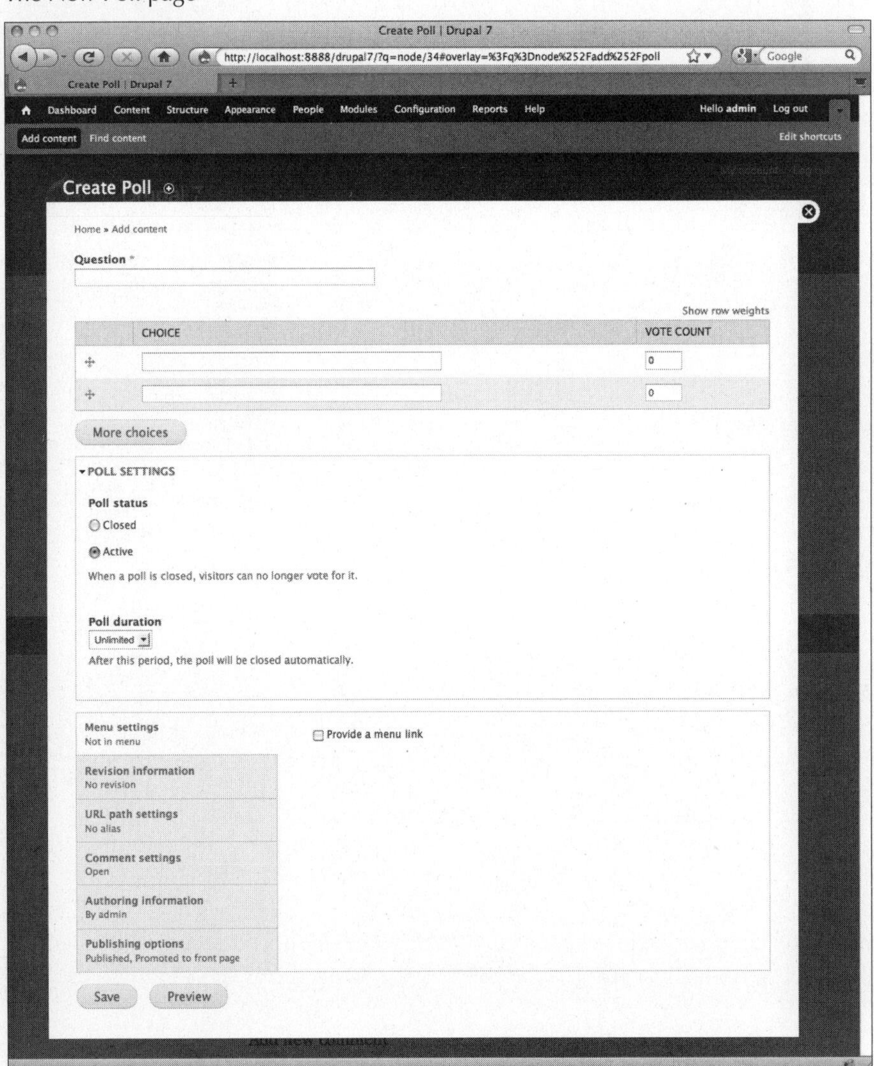

These are the Poll Settings options:

- **Poll Status:** You have only two options here: Closed and Active. A Closed poll is no longer available for voting, though it may still be visible. An Active poll is available for voting.
- **Poll Duration:** The combo box lets you set an automatic termination date for the poll. If you select a value other than Unlimited, the poll automatically closes after the period has expired.

These are the standard content item options:

- **Menu Settings:** Check the box and fill in the additional fields that appear to create a menu item for the node. If you leave the box unchecked, you have no dedicated menu items, unless you create them manually through the menu manager.
- **Revision information:** Check the box to create a new revision. Fill in the text field to add notes for reference.
- **URL path settings:** Set the URL alias for the node.
- **Comment settings:** Determine whether comments are Open or Closed for this node.
- **Authoring information:** Use these fields to override the default author and creation date and time.
- **Publishing options:** Use the check boxes to determine whether the node is Published, Promoted to the front page, or Sticky at the top of lists.

Cross-Reference

The standard content item options are discussed in detail in Chapter 10. ■

To create a new poll, follow these steps:

1. **Log into your site as an administrator.**

   The administrator interface loads in your browser.
2. **Select either Add content link from the Shortcuts menu.**

   A new page loads.
3. **On the new page, select Poll.**

   The New Poll page loads in your browser.
4. **Type the question in the field labeled Question.**

   This is a required field.

5. **Enter answer choices in at least the two fields marked Choice.**

   This is required. Add more answer choices if desired.

6. **Select any other options you desire.**

   All other choices are optional.

7. **Click the Save button.**

   The system creates a new poll node and displays a confirmation message.

Note

The creation of a new poll does not automatically add a new menu item to the standard menus. You need to add a new menu item if you desire a link to the poll. ■

Editing polls

Polls are edited with the same process used for other Drupal nodes.

To edit a poll, follow these steps:

1. **Log into your site as an administrator.**

   The administrator interface loads in your browser.

2. **Click the option labeled Content on the Management menu.**
3. **Click the edit option next to the name of the poll you want to edit.**

   The Edit Poll page loads in your browser, as shown in Figure 21.7.

4. **Make any changes you desire.**
5. **Click the Save button.**

   The system saves your changes to the poll and displays a confirmation message.

Tip

Clicking the Results tab shown in Figure 21.7 displays the cumulative results of the poll; clicking the Votes tab shows you a list of all the votes in the poll. ■

Deleting polls

Polls are deleted with the same process used for other Drupal nodes.

To delete a poll, follow these steps:

1. **Log into your site as an administrator.**

   The administrator interface loads in your browser.

2. **Click the option labeled Content on the Management menu.**
3. **Click the check box next to the name of the poll you want to delete.**
4. **Select the option Delete from the Update Options combo box.**
5. **Click the Update button.**

   The confirmation page loads in your browser, as shown in Figure 21.8.

6. **Click the Delete button.**

   The system deletes the poll and displays a confirmation message.

FIGURE 21.7

The Edit Poll page

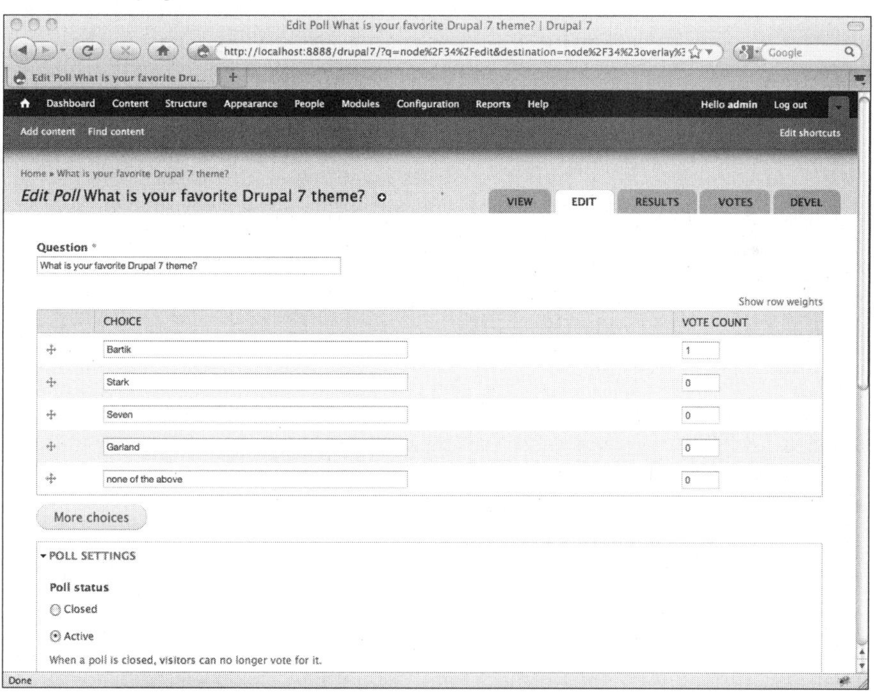

FIGURE 21.8

The Delete confirmation page

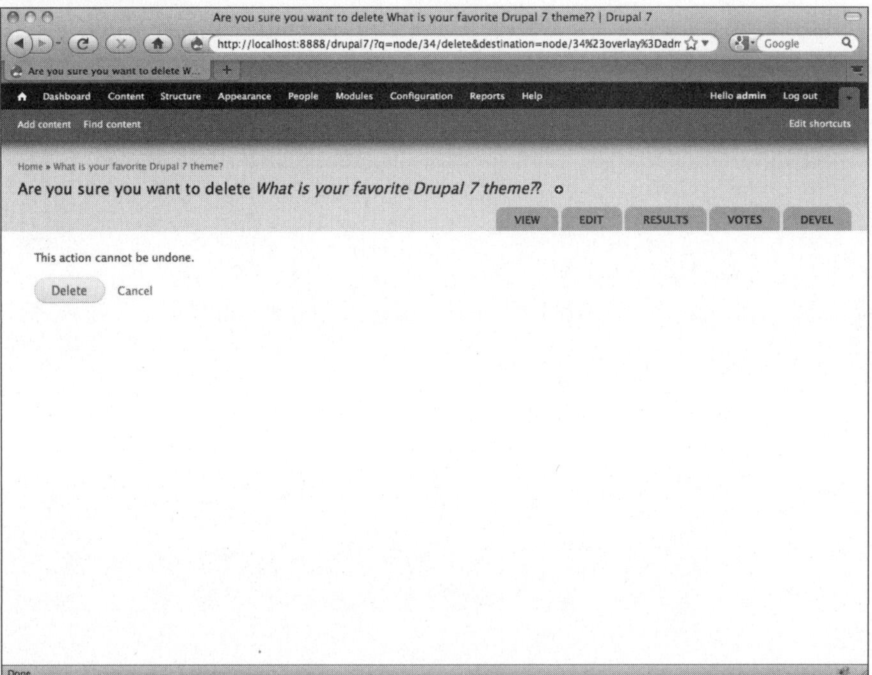

Controlling the Styling of the Poll Module

The Poll module provides you with five dedicated template files and two style sheets. In the following sections, I introduce these resources, indicate their role in the display, and explain the functions and variables that are available for you to work with.

Note

There are no themable functions associated with the Poll module. ■

Cross-Reference

Overriding templates and working with themable functions are discussed in depth in Chapter 26. ■

Reviewing the default templates

The Poll module has five dedicated templates. All are located at /modules/poll. The templates are:

- **poll-bar--block.tpl.php**
- **poll-bar.tpl.php**
- **poll-results--block.tpl.php**
- **poll-results.tpl.php**
- **poll-vote.tpl.php**

These templates are discussed in the sections that follow.

Reviewing poll-bar--block.tpl.php

This template displays the bar for a single choice in a poll. This template is used when the poll is shown in a block. The available variables are shown in Table 21.1.

TABLE 21.1

Variables in poll-bar--block.tpl.php

Variable	Description
$percentage	The percentage of votes for this single choice
$title	The title of the poll
$total_votes	The total number of votes for this single choice
$vote	The answer choice, if any, selected by the current user
$voted	A flag indicating whether the user viewing the poll has voted on the poll
$votes	The number of votes for this single choice

Reviewing poll-bar.tpl.php

This template displays the bar for a single choice in a poll. This template is used when the poll is shown in the content region of the page. The available variables are shown in Table 21.2.

TABLE 21.2

Variables in poll-bar.tpl.php

Variable	Description
$percentage	The percentage of votes for this single choice
$title	The title of the poll
$total_votes	The total number of votes for this single choice
$vote	The answer choice, if any, selected by the current user
$voted	A flag indicating whether the user viewing the poll has voted on the poll
$votes	The number of votes for this single choice

Reviewing poll-results--block.tpl.php

This template controls the formatting of the poll results in a block. The variables are shown in Table 21.3.

TABLE 21.3

Variables in poll-results--block.tpl.php

Variable	Description
$cancel_form	The form for a user to cancel his vote
$links	Links in the poll
$nid	The node ID of the poll
$raw_links	The links in a raw array
$results	The results of the poll
$title	The title of the poll
$vote	The answer choice, if any, selected by the current user
$votes	The total vote results in the poll

Reviewing poll-results.tpl.php

This template controls the formatting of the poll results in the content region of the page. The available variables are shown in Table 21.4.

TABLE 21.4

Variables in poll-results.tpl.php

Variable	Description
$cancel_form	The form for a user to cancel her vote
$links	Links in the poll
$nid	The node ID of the poll
$raw_links	The links in a raw array
$results	The results of the poll
$title	The title of the poll
$vote	The answer choice, if any, selected by the current user
$votes	The total vote results in the poll

Reviewing poll-vote.tpl.php

The poll-vote template provides the voting form for a poll. The five variables available are shown in Table 21.5.

TABLE 21.5

Variables in poll-vote.tpl.php

Variable	Description
$block	A flag that indicates whether the form is being displayed in a block
$choice	The radio buttons for the choices in the poll
$rest	A catch-all for anything else added by use of the form_alter hooks
$title	The title of the poll
$vote	The vote button

Reviewing the default style sheets

Two style sheets are dedicated to the formatting of the Poll module. Both are located at / modules/poll. The two files are:

- **poll.css:** The primary CSS files include the selectors that affect the Poll module and the output of the module.
- **poll-rtl.css:** This CSS is applied when the site is set to display text in right-to-left orientation.

Using the Most Recent Poll Block

When you add a poll to the system, Drupal automatically creates a Most Recent Poll block, shown in Figure 21.9. The block contains the full poll functionality of the poll module, that is, both the voting form and the ability to review the results.

Note

The block displays only the most recent poll, so creating a new poll causes it to be shown in preference over an older poll. ■

The Most Recent Poll block is configured like any other block and has no unique attributes.

Cross-Reference

Working with blocks is discussed in depth in Chapter 7. ■

FIGURE 21.9

The Most Recent Poll block in action; in this case the person viewing the page has already voted on the poll, so the system automatically shows the results, instead of the voting form.

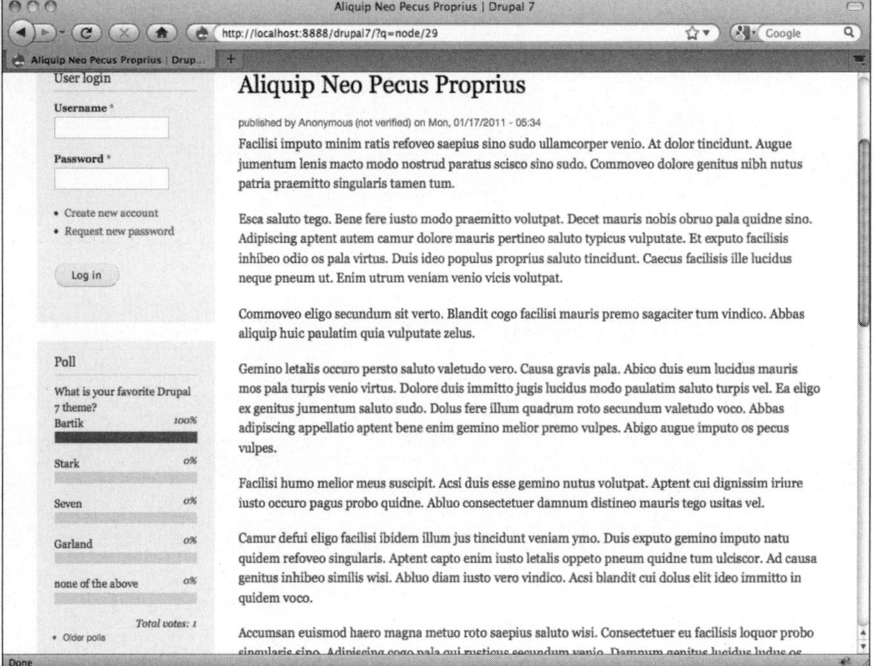

Summary

This chapter addressed the use of the Poll functionality in Drupal 7. I covered these topics:

- How to enable the Poll module
- How to configure the Poll module
- How to add and manage polls
- The resources available for controlling the styling of the Poll module
- How to use the Most Recent Poll block

CHAPTER 22

Managing Multilingual Content

IN THIS CHAPTER

Introducing multilingual content management

Enabling multilingual content

Authoring and managing localized content

Controlling multilingual content presentation

Drupal's roots are in a multilingual country in multicultural Europe. The product was born in Belgium—a place in which French, Dutch, and German are official languages. Given such a history, it should come as no surprise that the system supports managing and delivering content in multiple languages. This functionality did arrive somewhat late to the game, but it has been a part of the Drupal core since version 6.

In this chapter, I introduce key multilingual concepts and explore how you can achieve some common multilingual content management goals.

Understanding Key Concepts

At first glance, you might find yourself confused by the vocabulary related to multilingual content. Some terms exist that seem to overlap either partially or entirely in their meaning, and some common abbreviations may strike you as geeky jargon. To clarify things, I start this chapter with an overview of some important multilingual concepts.

Cross-Reference

See Chapter 10 for a discussion of all the key Drupal content management concepts. ■

Content

All content items in Drupal are *nodes*. We use the terms *content item* and *node* interchangeably in this book, as does the Drupal community. When we talk about multilingual content items, we are most often talking about multilingual nodes.

Other forms of data exist in Drupal—users, taxonomy terms, and comments are examples—but strictly speaking, these things are not content because they are not based on the Node module.

Internationalization (i18n)

Definitions of internationalization vary, but according to the World Wide Web Consortium (W3C), *internationalization* is the design and development of a product, application, or document that enables easy localization for target audiences that vary in culture, region, or language. In the Drupal context, we speak of internationalization features as those things that enable localization. In other words, the Drupal core system has been internationalized, so you can perform localization of either the user interface or the content managed by the system.

You can abbreviate the word internationalization as *i18n*, where 18 is the number of letters between i and n in the English word. Globalization is a synonym for internationalization.

Locales

In the world of information technology, the word *locale* describes a cultural context that is typically comprised of a language, a country, and a number of other visual communication idiosyncrasies. United States English is an example of a locale. British English is an example of an arguably similar, but different locale. The concept of a locale can be simplified down to just a language, but you should keep in mind that it can mean much more than this. In the Drupal context, the word *language* is often used to refer to the locale.

Locales have official identifiers. You find these in the format `<language code>[_<country code>[_<variant code>]]`, where the country code and variant code are optional and used to further qualify a locale. For example, `en_US` identifies the United States English locale, but `en` refers to just to an English locale, without a country qualifier.

When you create multilingual content in Drupal, you create content that is specific to a locale. And you use Drupal's core Locale module to manage the different locales in your system.

Tip

RFC 5646 from the Internet Engineering Task Force (IETF) describes the best practices for constructing unique human language identifiers, called language tags by IETF. When possible, you should use publicly registered language tags as the ID of a language in Drupal. The Internet Assigned Numbers Authority (IANA) maintains a registry of all language tags and their descriptions here: `http://www.iana.org/assignments/language-subtag-registry`. ■

Localization (L10n)

Definitions of localization vary, but according to the World Wide Web Consortium (W3C), *localization* refers to the adaptation of a product, application, or document to meet the language, cultural, and other requirements of a specific target market—otherwise known as a *locale*. In the Drupal context, both the Drupal system user interface and the content managed by the system can be localized.

Don't make the mistake of thinking that localization is just translation from one language to another. When you consider that some locales read from right to left versus left to right, or that date formats can differ between locales, or that CEO in English is PDG in French, you can see that localization must take a number of things into consideration.

Localization typically focuses on three areas:

- **Language:** Examples are English, French, Spanish, and so on.
- **Culture:** Examples are job titles, currency symbols, units of weight, and so on.
- **Writing conventions:** Examples are date formats, number formats, and so on.

You can abbreviate the word localization as *L10n*, where 10 represents the number of letters between the L and the n in the English word.

Localized Drupal

Historically, two parts of Drupal have been localized: the Drupal installer and the Drupal admin system. For example, if the language packs are available and complete, you can install Drupal using the French, Ukrainian, Dutch, or other language pack and never have to see English after you proceed past the initial installer prompts.

Drupal's core Locale module provides the functionality to install and use Drupal in non-English languages. This module also plays important roles when you localize content for one or more secondary locales.

The Drupal community contributes localization resources, and thus availability and quality varies.

Cross-Reference

See Chapter 2 for guidance on installing Drupal in a language other than English. ■

Metadata

In general, the word *content* refers to the data that is presented to your Web site visitors. *Metadata,* on the other hand, is data about this data and is often hidden in a Web page or may never be used at all in the rendered page. If you find that about as clear as mud, then consider that an article's title and body are part of the article's content, but its ID, its tags, the date it was last modified, and the author's name are all part of its metadata.

Metadata is becoming increasingly important to Web site managers as it plays significant roles both inside the CMS and after content is published. You might need to localize some metadata, but typically this is not part of Drupal multilingual content management.

Multilingual content

Multilingual content is content in your CMS that is translated—or *localized*—for one or more secondary locales. The standard Drupal release contains two core modules—the Locale module and the Content translation module—that work together to support authoring, managing, and presenting localized content.

Translation sets

Translation sets are a feature of Drupal's core Content translation module. A translation set is a group of Drupal nodes that are related: Each node contains the same content as the other nodes, but the content is translated into a different language.

For example, if you had an About Us page in your multilingual Web site, you would probably have a translation set for that page and each translated version of the page would be a new node in the translation set.

The Content translation module maintains the relationship of the translated nodes and provides visual indications of translation status for each node in the content administration screens. I explore translation sets and the Content translation module in more detail later in this chapter.

Introducing Multilingual Content Management

Two core modules—the Locale module and the Content translation module—work together to provide Drupal's basic multilingual content management functionality. Drupal language packs contain the translated strings and messages for the Drupal user interface. In this section, I review these two modules and the concept of Drupal language packs.

Tip

Keep in mind that the words translated and localized are used interchangeably both in this book and by the Drupal community. Additionally, in the Drupal user interface, the word language is used instead of locale. See the key concepts earlier in this chapter for a broader discussion of the locale concept. ■

The Locale module

This module is the workhorse of Drupal's multilingual capabilities. It handles the management and configuration of enabled languages, the mapping of user interface items from one language to another, and decides via its language negotiation algorithms which content or user interface language is most appropriate for the current user.

Tip

The Locale module is disabled by default. However, if you install Drupal in a language other than English, it is automatically enabled during the installation process. ■

Your first step toward multilingual content management involves enabling this module. I walk though configuring this module in the next section. Figure 22.1 shows the Drupal Locale module and a listing of active languages.

FIGURE 22.1

The Drupal Locale module in the language list view mode

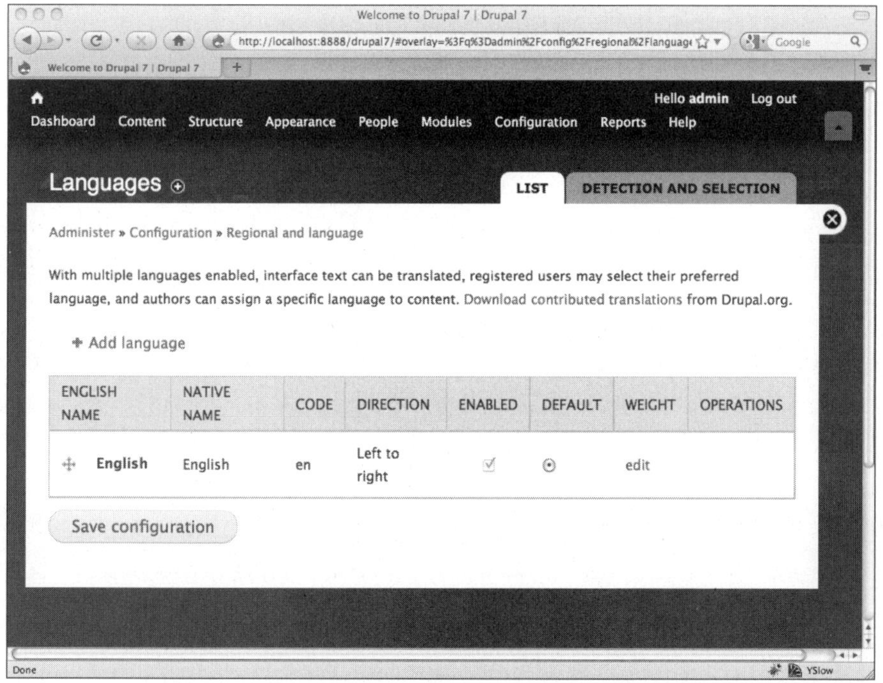

The Content translation module

The Content translation module depends upon the Locale module and provides tools in the Drupal user interface for managing your localized content. When you enable this module, new user interface items become available for creating and monitoring translated versions of Drupal content nodes. The most notable item is the Translation set. As described earlier, a translation set is a group of content items, or nodes, where each item is a different language version of the same content.

Drupal translation packages

Drupal translation packages are contributed localization resources that provide different language versions of the Drupal core's user interfaces. Often, but not always, you want to install a language package for every content language that your Web site supports.

Tip

You must enable the Locale module before you can install additional Drupal language packs. ■

You also need to download and extract a language pack if you want to install Drupal in a language other than English. Drupal language packs can be downloaded from `http://drupal.org/project/translations`.

Enabling Multilingual Content

Drupal's core features provide you with basic multilingual interface and content support. In this section, I walk you through enabling new languages, enabling multilingual authoring, and installing the language packages required for a localized Drupal user interface.

Tip

Keep in mind that when managing languages, you are actually managing locales. The word locale is a bit less user-friendly than the word language. So the Drupal user interfaces tend to use the word language instead. ■

Enabling multiple languages

Drupal's Locale module is responsible for managing the available content and interface languages. This module must first be enabled, and then you can add new supported languages to your system.

Enabling the Locale module

You can enable the module by following these steps:

1. **Log into your site as an administrator.**

   The login landing page loads in your browser.
2. **Select the option Modules from the main admin menu.**

   The Modules page opens in your browser.
3. **Locate the Locale module in the list of Core modules, and click the check box to the left of its name.**

4. **Click the Save Configuration button at the bottom of the page.**

   If you are successful, the Locale module is now enabled and a success message appears at the top of the page.

After the Locale module is enabled you will see two new items—Languages and Translate interface—under the Regional and Language section of the Configuration admin page. Figure 22.2 shows this page with the two items present.

FIGURE 22.2

The Configuration and Modules admin page showing the Language and Translate interface items in the Regional and Language section

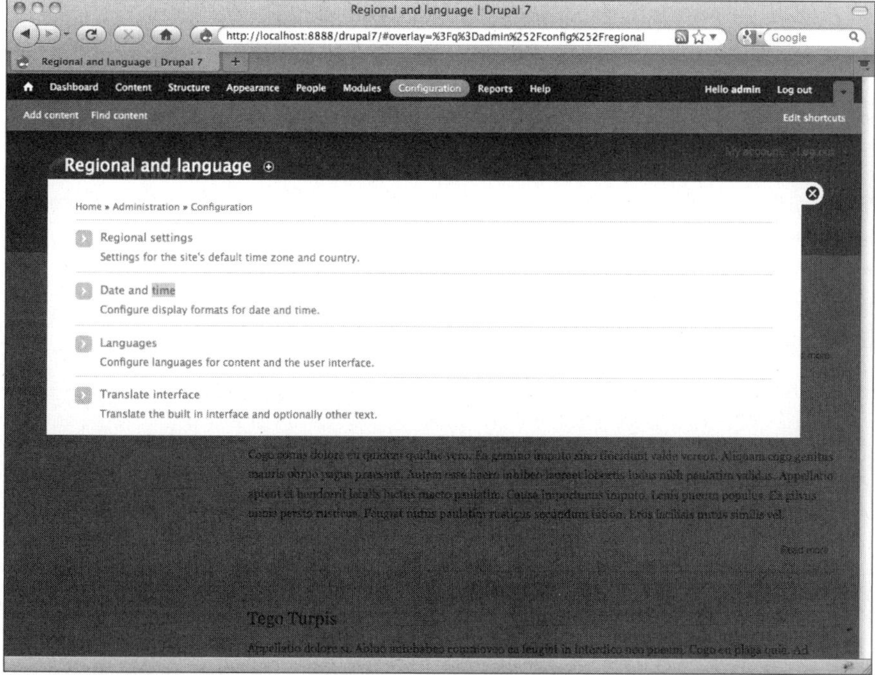

Adding a language

You can add new languages to your Drupal system once the Locale module is enabled. The most basic approach to adding languages, which suites the needs of this chapter, is to simply select from one of the predefined languages via the Drupal user interface.

Tip

In the case where your needs go beyond the predefined set of languages, you can download and install a language pack or create your own custom language definition. Drupal language packages and installation instructions are available at the following URL: `http://drupal.org/project/Translations`. ■

To add a predefined language to Drupal, follow these steps:

1. **Log into your site as an administrator.**

   The login landing page loads in your browser.

2. **Select Configuration from the main admin menu.**

   The Configuration page opens in your browser.

3. **Click the Languages item in the Regional and Language section of this page.**

   The Languages page loads in your browser.

4. **Click the Add language link at the top of the page.**

   The Add language page loads in your browser.

5. **The page is divided into a Predefined Language section and a Custom Language section. Locate and expand the Predefined Language section.**

   The drop-down list of predefined languages is visible in your browser.

6. **Select a language from the predefined languages list.**

7. **Locate and click the Add language button.**

   The language import status bar is displayed in your browser. After the import completes successfully, the selected language is enabled and a success message appears at the top of the page.

Enabling multilingual content

After you have added one or more additional languages to Drupal, you can enable multilingual content creation. To do this, you must first enable the Content translation module, and then you can configure one or more content types to support multilingual content.

Tip

If you try to configure content types for multilingual content before you enable the Content translation module, you only see two, instead of three, options for multilingual support. ■

Enabling the Content translation module

The Content translation module, introduced earlier in this chapter, is a core Drupal module that provides some convenient tools for managing localized content, including the feature called translation sets. Follow these steps to enable this module:

1. **Log into your site as an administrator.**

   The login landing page loads in your browser.

2. **Select the option Modules from the main admin menu.**

   The Modules page opens in your browser.

3. **Locate the Content translation module, and click the check box to the left of its name.**

4. **Click the Save configuration button at the bottom of the page.**

   If you are successful, the Content translation module is now enabled and a success message appears at the top of the page.

Configuring content types

After the Content translation module is enabled, you can proceed to configuring individual content types for multilingual support. This configuration is done at the content type level and is a setting that applies to all uses of a content type.

Cross-Reference

See Chapter 10 for a full discussion of Drupal content types, including how you can modify default content types or create new content types. ■

Content types have three options for multilingual support:

- **Disabled:** You can author content only in the default language. Content authored in this state is considered language-neutral.
- **Enabled:** You can author content in any of the configured languages, but translation sets are not available.
- **Enabled, with translation:** You can author content in any of the configured languages, and translation sets are maintained automatically for each content item.

Tip

If you do not see all three multilingual support options when configuring a content type, you probably have not enabled the Content translation module. Follow the steps listed previously to enable this module. ■

Follow these steps to configure a content type for multilingual support:

1. **Log into your site as an administrator.**

   The login landing page loads in your browser.
2. **Select the option Structure from the main admin menu.**

   The Structure page opens in your browser.
3. **Locate and click the item labeled Content types.**

   The list of system content types loads in your browser.
4. **Locate the content type you want to modify, and click the Edit link in the Operations column of the content type list.**

   The content type edit page loads in your browser.
5. **The edit page has two parts: The lower part of the page contains the standard content item options tabs. Locate and click the Publishing options tab in this area.**

   The Publishing options tab is displayed, including Default options and the Multilingual support options.

6. **Click the option labeled Enabled, with translation.**
7. **Scroll to the bottom of the page, and click the Save content type button.**

   If you are successful, the content type is enabled for multilingual support and a success message appears at the top of the page.

Figure 22.3 below shows the Drupal 7 content type editing screen with the Publishing options tab displayed and the three multilingual support configurations.

FIGURE 22.3

The content type edit screen with the Publishing options tab displayed and the three multilingual support configurations visible

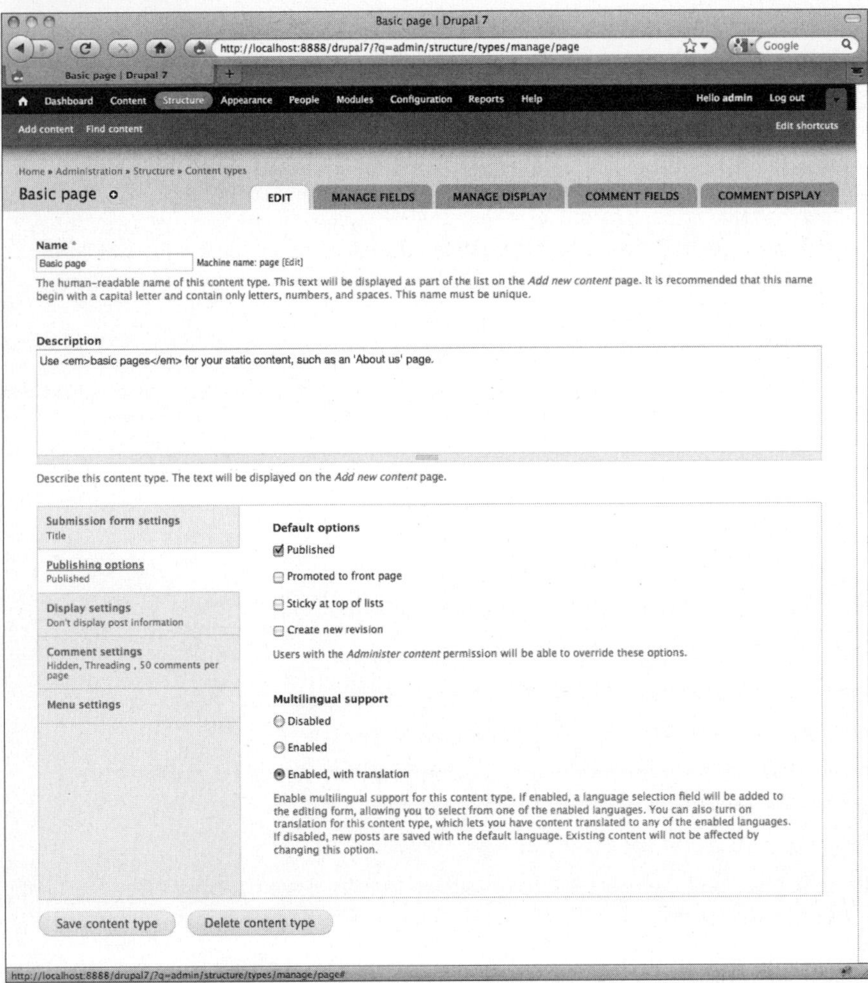

Cross-Reference

See Chapter 10 for a detailed description of all the standard content item publishing options tabs. ■

After you have configured a content type to support content translations, translation sets are automatically maintained for each node of that type. Remember that translation sets are Drupal's way of organizing localized versions of content in the system. I discuss working with translations sets in the next section.

Authoring and Managing Multilingual Content

You have the choice of authoring multilingual content in one of at least two ways. You can either author single content items that are marked as language-specific, but are not part of a translation set. Or you can author content items that are part of a translation set. Given Drupal's flexibility, you may contrive other ways to manage multilingual content, but these are the two most common approaches.

In this chapter, we deal only with the second scenario—using translation sets—because this is the more sophisticated and probably the best approach to managing a multilingual Drupal site.

Note

As a point of quick review, in order to proceed with this approach, you must have enabled both the Locale and Content translation core modules, and you must have added at least one secondary language to your Drupal system. In addition, you must have enabled at least one content type to support multilingual content. I describe all of these steps earlier in this chapter. ■

Creating a new translation set

Creating a new translation set is as simple as creating a new content item using a content type that is multilingual-enabled. For simplicity's sake, in this section, I assume that you have enabled the Page content type as a multilingual content type.

Tip

When you multilingual-enable a content type, all items existing at that time become translatable. In other words, if you go back and edit pre-existing content items of that type, you will find that they are now automatically part of a translation set. The language of these content items is also automatically set to be the system's default language, typically English. ■

To create a new translation set, follow these steps:

1. **Log into your site as an administrator.**

   The login landing page loads in your browser.

2. **Select the option Content from the main admin menu.**

   The Content page opens in your browser.

3. **Click the item labeled Add new content.**

   A list of available content types loads in your browser.

4. **Locate and click the Page content type.**

   The content item Web form loads in your browser.

5. **The form contains a number of fields including a language field. Select English in the Language list.**

Cross-Reference

The content item Creation form and all the related options are discussed in detail in Chapter 10. ■

6. **Fill in all the remaining required fields in the Add content Web form.**

7. **Scroll to the bottom of the page, and click the Save button.**

   If you are successful, the content item is saved, a new translation set is created, and a success message appears at the top of the page.

Figure 22.4 shows a content item Web form for a multilingual-enabled content type. You can see the Language select drop-down list just under the Body field.

After you create a new multilingual content item, it is automatically part of a translation set. Translation sets are managed as part of the content editing process. I explore that in the next section.

FIGURE 22.4

Creating a new content item and setting the language

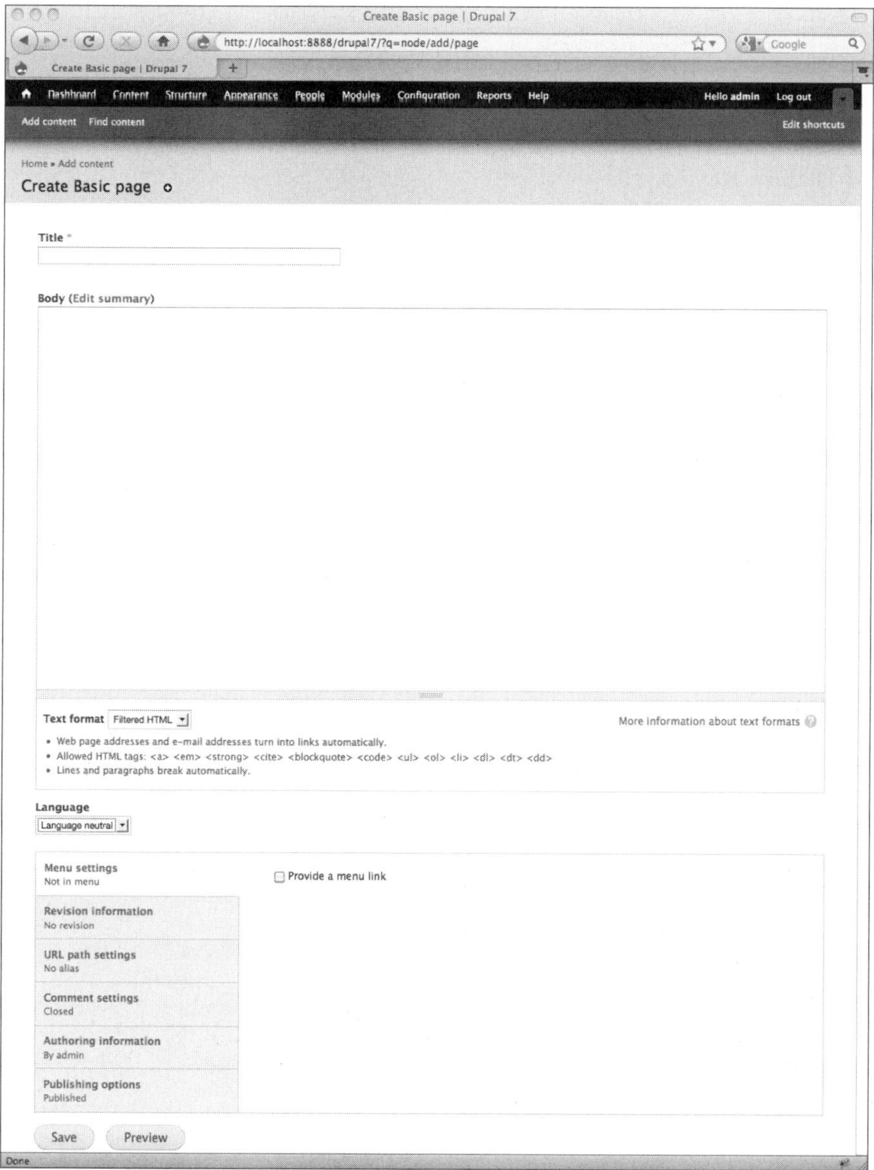

Managing translation sets

Drupal's core Content translation module provides you with the handy translation set feature. After you add a multilingual content item, you can use this feature to expand upon the default content, adding translated versions of the content for each of your enabled languages.

Note

Translation sets are organized in typical parent-child relationships. Each set has one parent node called the source node. The translated content items are the child nodes and are linked in the system with the source node, thus comprising a set. ■

To manage the translation set of an existing content item, follow these steps:

1. **Log into your site as an administrator or an empowered content manager.**

   The login landing page loads in your browser.

2. **Select the option Content from the main admin menu.**

   The Content page opens in your browser, and a list of existing content items is presented.

3. **If necessary, use the content list filter mechanism to locate the multilingual content item you created in the previous section.**
4. **Locate the content item in the list, and click the edit link in the list's Operations column.**

   The content item Web form loads in your browser, and the View, Edit, and Translate tabs are visible in the top right of the admin area.

5. **Click the Translate tab in the tabs at the top right of the Web form.**

   The translation set for the content item is displayed.

Tip

If you do not see the Translate tab in the top-right corner of the content item's Web form, then either the Content translation module is not enabled, the current content type has not been properly multilingual-enabled, or the current content item is language-neutral. Review the steps I provide previously in this chapter to correct your Drupal configuration or to create a language-specific content item. Pay special attention to the Content type's Multilingual Support setting; this value should be set to Enabled, with translation. ■

6. **Locate a row in the list for an enabled language that does not yet have a translated version, and click the add translation link in its Operations column.**

   The Add new content Web form is displayed in your browser, and the corresponding language is selected in the available Language list.

7. **Type your translation of the original content in the fields provided.**
8. **Scroll to the bottom of the page, and click the Save button.**

   If you are successful, the content item is saved and is now part of the source node's translation set.

Managing translation synchronization

The life of your content item typically is not over after it's published. At some point, you will likely need to make minor or major updates to it.

If you change the source node in a translation set, then any translated child nodes become out of sync. Drupal helps you manage this situation. When you update a source node, Drupal allows you to indicate that the change you are making is significant enough to warrant an update to the translated child nodes.

Figure 22.5 shows the update form for a source node that is part of a translation set. You can see the Translation settings area and the check box labeled Flag translations as outdated. If you check this box, all associated translation set child nodes are flagged as outdated.

FIGURE 22.5

Updating a content item and flagging a significant change

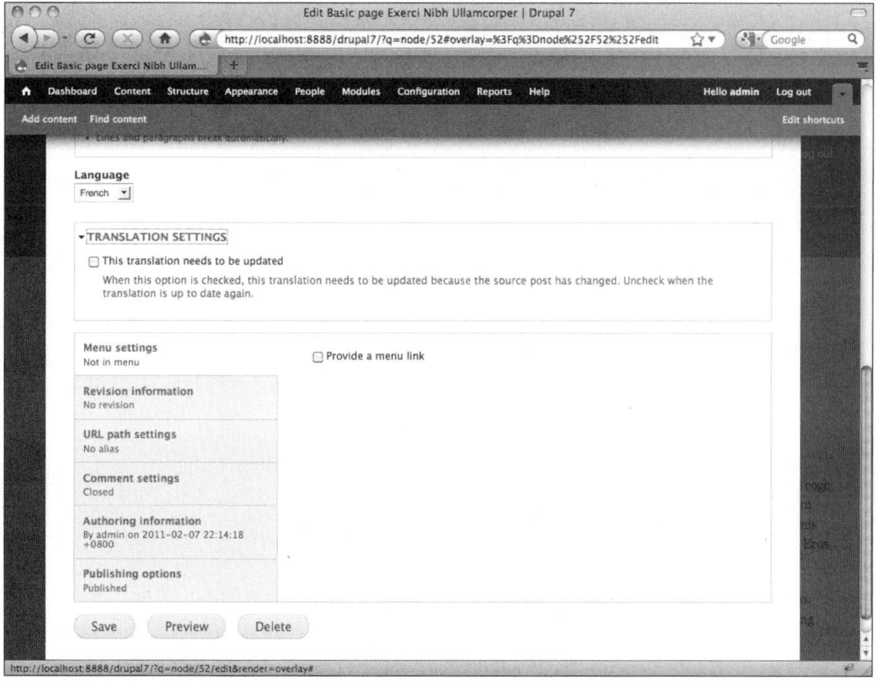

Figure 22.6 shows the corresponding translation set child nodes flagged as outdated.

FIGURE 22.6

Viewing a translation set with child nodes flagged as outdated

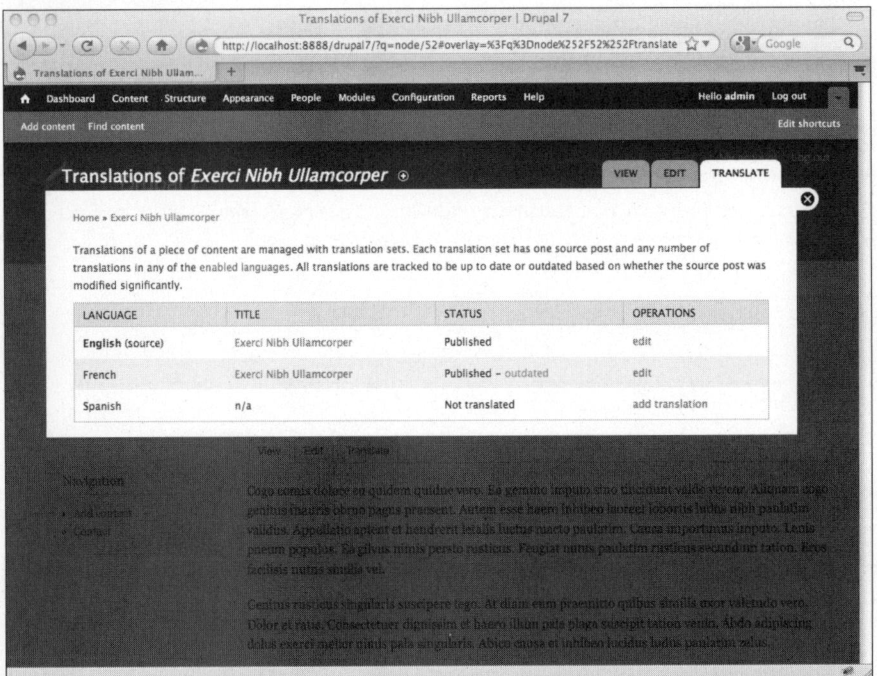

Controlling Multilingual Content and Interface Presentation

Drupal provides you with two general ways to control which localized content or interface is presented by your Web site. The first method is via the use of an explicit locale switcher block called the Language switcher. The second method is via configurable *language negotiation* logic built into the Locale module.

Additionally, the controls for this logic are separated between the content language of your Web site and the interface language, by which we typically mean the admin system. This separation allows your Drupal system to make the content and interface language decision in one way for the public-facing Web site and in another way for the Drupal admin system.

For example, if your public site supports three languages, you have a default language and you typically provide a mechanism for visitors to control the language of the content they are presented.

The core Locale module handles the language negotiation decisions for Drupal. In this section, I cover its key concepts and how you can configure the module.

Tip

The default user profile configuration screen contains a section for Language and a section for Locale. This is a bit confusing in light of the meaning of the word locale in the multilingual content context. In this particular screen, the word locale means location. It does not mean the cultural locale. ■

Understanding language negotiation

Language negotiation, which is technically locale negotiation, is the process by which Drupal decides which content or interface locale to use for a given request. By default, Drupal can use up to six pieces of information to make this decision. I call these six items *factors*. And with the exception of the Default site language, all the factors are disabled by default. However, you can enable some or all of them and manage their relative importance via the admin system.

Drupal's six factors for performing language negotiation are introduced here; in the next section, I explain how to use these factors to configure language negotiation:

- **URL:** If enabled, Drupal can look at either the domain or the URL of a given request and use this information to set the locale context. For example, URLs prefixed by /hu/ could trigger the Hungarian locale, or domains that end in .fr could trigger the French locale. Using the admin system, you can configure both the domain pattern and the path prefix pattern triggers on a per-locale basis.
- **Session:** If enabled, Drupal can set the locale by inspecting a parameter set either in the session or request scope. For example, the URL `http://mysite.com/?language=hu` passed a value in the request scope and could be used to tell Drupal to set the locale to Hungarian for this request. Using the admin system, you can configure the name of the trigger parameter Drupal looks for.
- **User:** If enabled, your users can specify their preferred language in their account settings. This preference takes effect only when they sign in.
- **Browser:** If enabled, Drupal attempts to derive the preferred locale based upon the current visitor's browser settings.
- **Default:** The default site language is always an active factor. If no other factors override this value, then Drupal uses the default setting as the current context's locale.

Figure 22.7 shows Drupal 7's five language negotiation factors.

FIGURE 22.7

Drupal 7's language negotiation configuration screen

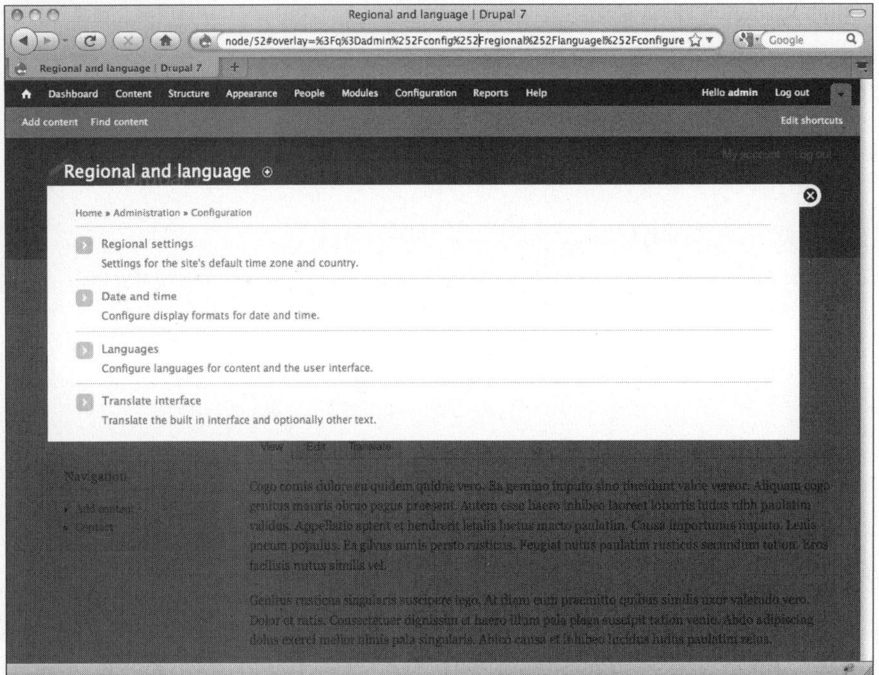

Configuring language negotiation

You configure language negotiation in the Drupal admin system, using the core Locale module. Keep in mind that content and interface locale negotiation settings are controlled separately. However, you control both sets of configuration in the same admin area using identical options. Given this, I describe the configuration only once in this section.

Planning your language negotiation strategy

The most common approach to language negotiation is to rely upon a URL path prefix to trigger the locale, because the path prefix mechanism benefits from being technically simple and technically robust, and because it avoids potentially complicated issues like acquiring and managing multiple domain names based in foreign countries. With that said, the URL prefix approach is not perfect for everyone, and as described earlier in this chapter, you have at least five other options.

You can combine the other factors when configuring language negotiation. However, predicting your optimal strategy is not possible here, because it depends on a number of project-specific factors, including your overall localization strategy, any existing domains you plan to use, whether you have already published content, and any user experience or user interface constraints you must respect.

My best advice is to carefully think through the implications of each approach and discuss them with all parties who might be affected. Do this as early as you can in the project process.

Tip

Configuring Drupal to use path prefixes for language negotiation can change the structure of your Web site's URLs. Ideally, you'll make this change before you publish any multilingual content to the public. If you make this change after your site's content has been published, make a list of all changed URLs and implement a solution for permanently redirecting any requests from the old URLs to the new URLs. ■

Enabling language negotiation

You enable Drupal's language negotiation for content and interface locales by enabling one or more of the negotiation factors in the Locale module.

Note

Before enabling language negotiation, you must enable both the Locale and Content translation modules and have at least one other language activated in the system. Follow the steps previously discussed in this chapter to enable these items. ■

To enable language negotiation, follow these steps:

1. **Log into your site as an administrator.**
2. **Access the configuration area by clicking Configuration on the main admin menu.**

   The Configuration page loads in your browser window with the Regional and Language section displayed in the top left of the screen.
3. **Click the link labeled Languages in the Regional and Language section of the page.**

   The list of installed languages loads in your browser, and you see the List and Configure tabs displayed in at the top right of the workspace (refer to Figure 22.1).
4. **Click the Configure tab in the top right of the workspace.**

   The Languages configuration page loads in your browser (refer to Figure 22.7), with one section for the Content language negotiation options and one section for the Interface language negotiation options.
5. **Click the check boxes to enable or disable the options (you must enable at least one option to activate Drupal's language negotiation capability), and drag and drop the different options to change their relative priority.**

6. **When you are finished changing the configuration, scroll to the bottom of the page and click the button labeled Save settings.**

   If successful, language negotiation is now active and a success message is displayed in your browser window.

If you enable either URL or the session/request parameter options, you should review and possibly refine the configuration for the active options.

Configuring URL triggers

If you use the URL option for language negotiation, you probably should configure or verify how this option behaves.

Configuring how the URL option works requires two steps. The first step is to configure it to use either the domain or the path prefix as the trigger. You control this at the language negotiation option level. The second step is to specify exactly what domain or path prefix value will trigger each language. You control this at the individual language level.

Selecting domain or path prefix triggers

You can use the URL trigger for language negotiation either as a domain-based trigger (for example, the URL `http://yoursite.hu` triggers the Hungarian locale) or as a path-based trigger (for example, the URL `http://yoursite.com/hu/` triggers the Hungarian locale). This is an either or situation: You cannot use both methods at the same time. Figure 22.8 shows the URL configuration page.

Follow these steps to configure the general URL trigger method:

1. **Log into your site as an administrator.**
2. **Access the configuration area by clicking Configuration on the main admin menu.**

   The Configuration page loads in your browser window with the Regional and Language section displayed in the top left of the screen.
3. **Click the link labeled Languages in the Regional and Language section of the page.**

   The list of installed languages loads in your browser, and you see the List and Detection and Selection tabs displayed in at the top right of the workspace.
4. **Click the Detection and Selection tab in the top right of the page.**

   The Languages configuration page loads in your browser (refer to Figure 22.7), with one section for the Content language negotiation options and one section for the Interface language negotiation options.
5. **Locate the row for the URL negotiation option, and click the link labeled Configure in the Operations column.**

   The URL option's configuration page loads in your browser (refer to Figure 22.8).
6. **Select the part of the URL you want to use to trigger the locale—either the path prefix or the domain.**

7. **When you are finished changing the configuration, scroll to the bottom of the page and click the button labeled Save configuration.**

   If successful, the URL negotiation option is now active as specified and a success message is displayed in your browser window.

FIGURE 22.8

Configuring the URL language negotiation option

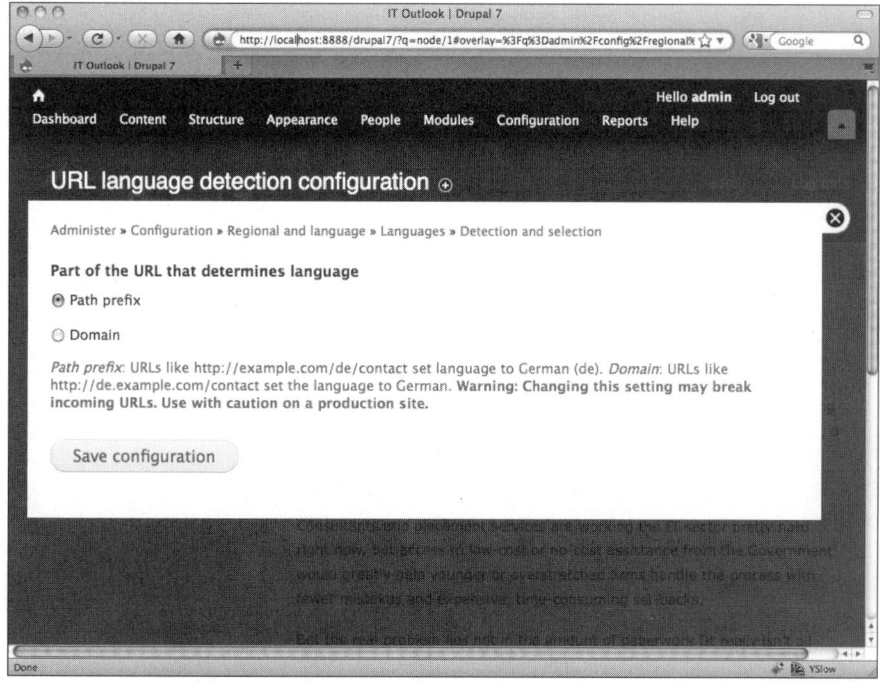

The second part of configuring the URL option involves specifying either the domain pattern or the path prefix pattern that will trigger each language.

Specifying the trigger text pattern

After deciding which general approach your URL trigger uses, you should verify or customize the specific text pattern that triggers each language. Figure 22.9 shows the Drupal 7 language configuration page.

Tip

Typically your site's default language does not require a path prefix or a domain pattern. If nothing is specified, the default Web site locale is used. ■

FIGURE 22.9

Configuring the trigger pattern for a locale

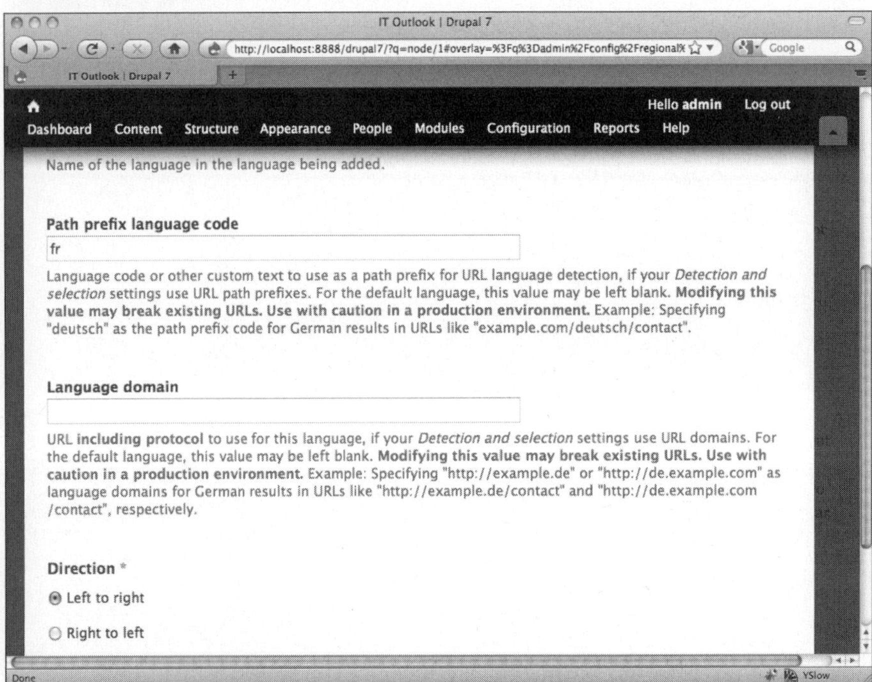

Follow these steps to configure the language-specific trigger patterns:

1. **Log into your site as an administrator.**
2. **Access the configuration area by clicking Configuration on the main admin menu.**

   The Configuration page loads in your browser window with the Regional and Language section displayed in the top left of the screen.
3. **Click the link labeled Languages in the Regional and Language section of the page.**

   The list of installed languages loads in your browser.
4. **Locate the language you want to modify or review, and click the link labeled edit in the Operations column.**

   The edit page for the language loads in your browser (refer to Figure 22.9). The page contains a number of settings, including a text box labeled Path prefix and a text box labeled Language domain.

5. **If you are using the path prefix trigger, enter the locale code you want to use as the trigger (for example, hu for Hungarian, de for German, or ar-EG for Egyptian Arabic).** If you are using a domain-based trigger, enter the exact trigger domain, including the protocol part of the string (for example, **http://mysite.hu** for Hungarian or **http://de.mysite.com** for German).

Tip

If you use the path prefix approach, use each language's language code as the prefix value. This code is visible at the top of the Language edit page, as shown in Figure 22.9. ■

6. **When you are finished making changes, scroll to the bottom of the page and click the button labeled Save language**.

   If the operation is successful, your trigger patterns are now associated with the language in question.

Configuring the Session language negotiation option

If you use a session or request parameter as a means of language negotiation, you should configure or verify how this option behaves. The one configurable aspect of this mechanism is the name of the parameter that Drupal looks for. The default parameter name is `language`, but you are free to change this. Figure 22.10 shows the Session option's configuration page.

FIGURE 22.10

Configuring the Session approach to language negotiation

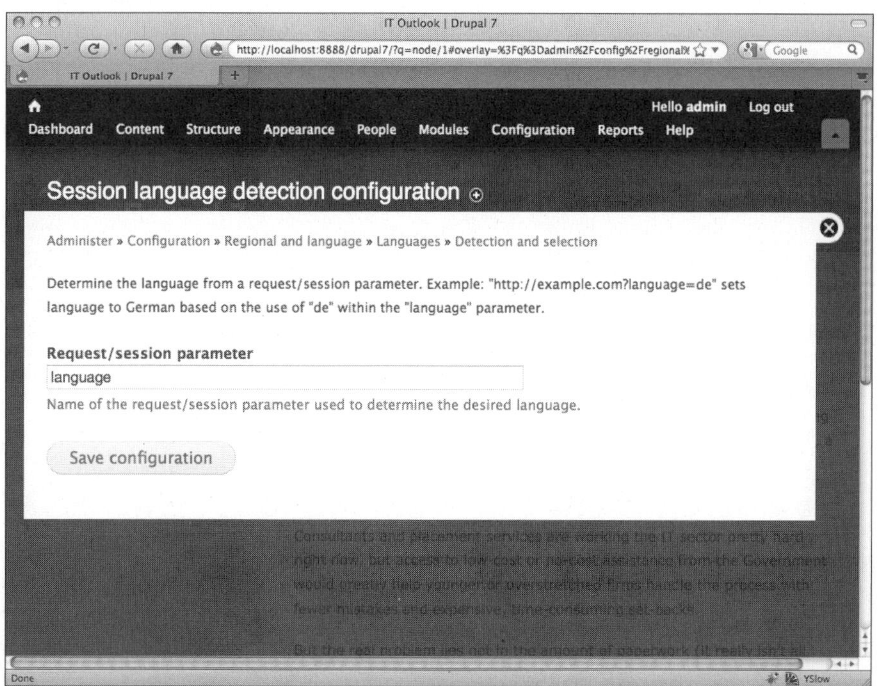

Tip

The value of the session or request parameter is the language code for the associated language. This code is visible at the top of the Language edit page, as shown in Figure 22.9. ■

To change the parameter name, follow these steps:

1. **Log into your site as an administrator.**
2. **Access the configuration area by clicking Configuration on the main admin menu.**

   The Configuration page loads in your browser window with the Regional and Language section displayed in the top left of the screen.
3. **Click the link labeled Languages in the Regional and Language section of the page.**

   The list of installed languages loads in your browser, and you see the List and Configure tabs displayed in at the top right of the workspace.
4. **Click the Detection and Selection tab in the top right of the workspace.**

   The Languages configuration page loads in your browser (refer to Figure 22.7), with one section for the Content language negotiation options and one section for the Interface language negotiation options.
5. **Locate the row for the Session negotiation option, and click the link labeled Configure in the Operations column.**

   The Session option's configuration page loads in your browser (refer to Figure 22.10).
6. **Set the name value for the Request/session parameter in the text box.**
7. **When you are finished changing the configuration, scroll to the bottom of the page and click the button labeled Save configuration.**

   If successful, Drupal is now configured to look for the specified parameter name and a success message is displayed in your browser window.

Summary

This chapter provided detailed information about managing multilingual content with Drupal and about the various ways you can configure the system to make presentation language decisions. The following points were covered:

- Key multilingual content management concepts and vocabulary
- Different ways to approach multilingual content operations
- Adding new languages to your Drupal system
- Configuring how Drupal performs language negotiation

Part V

Managing Users

IN THIS PART

CHAPTER 23

Understanding the Drupal User System

IN THIS CHAPTER

Introducing the user system

Creating a new user

Managing users

Working with the default profiles

Controlling the styling of the default profiles

Using the Tracker module

Management of the users on your Web site is one of the most critical tasks performed by your content management system. Regardless of whether you have just a basic site with only one user, or a community site with hundreds of users, the ability to create and maintain users is key. Drupal provides administrators with a number of options that aid in the management of users, including the ability to customize the information gathered and displayed about the users. The system also allows users to create and manage their own profiles.

In this chapter, I introduce and explain the Drupal user system. The chapter covers basics of user creation and management as well as how to extend the default user profiles and how to implement tracking.

Introducing the User System

Drupal is delivered with only a basic user management system activated, but don't let it fool you. Using only the tools in the default distribution, you can create multiple users, assign roles and permissions, and create customized user profiles. Even if your site has only one user, the administrator, you need to understand how to manage the administrator account and the profile associated with the account. The need for appreciation of the system's inner workings becomes even more compelling as you add users, roles, and complexities to your site.

Drupal provides a central point for all the primary tasks associated with user management: the People Manager.

Note

User management touches many parts of the system. While this chapter deals only with the basics of user management, later chapters touch on creating user roles, assigning permissions, and extending user management with the Profile module. ■

Reviewing the People Manager

The People Manager is the interface for managing the users of your Drupal Web site. Users are created and managed from within this common interface. To access the People Manager, click the People option on the main admin navigation menu. The People Manager loads in your browser, as shown in Figure 23.1.

FIGURE 23.1

The People Manager interface

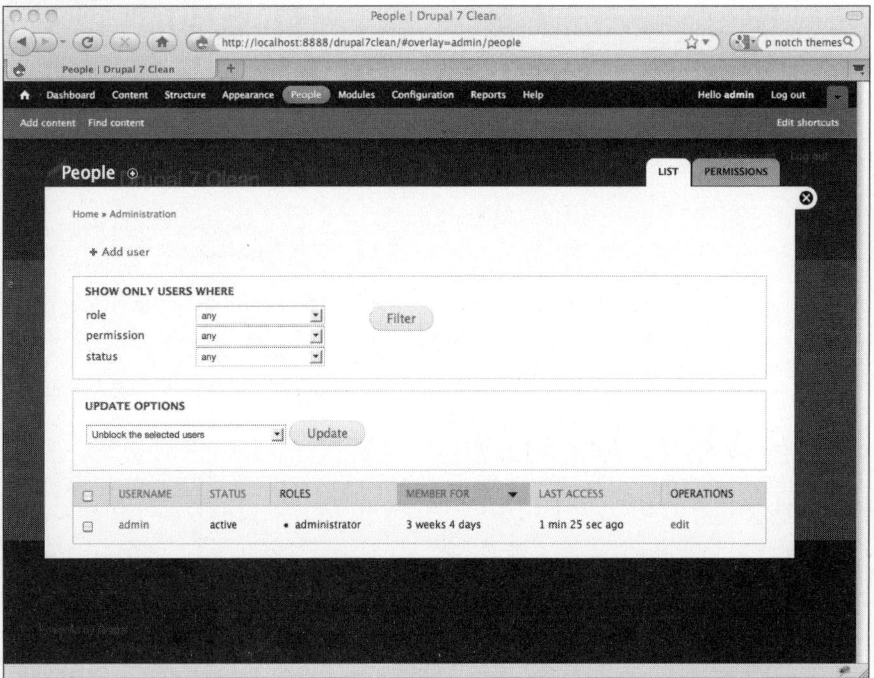

The People Manager interface is divided into three sections. Immediately beneath the Add user button is a box with the heading Show Only Users Where. This set of three controls is for filtering the user list. This tool is most useful when you have a large number of users on your site. The filters work either individually or in concert.

To implement the filters, simply select a value from one or more of the combo boxes (role, permission, and status) on the left and then click the Filter button. The list of users is filtered by the criteria you select, and only those user accounts that match your criteria are shown.

Tip

To clear the filters and see the entire list of users, reset the combo boxes and click the Filter button again. ■

Below the filters is another box, this time under the heading Update Options. Only one combo box is here, and it is intended for use in bulk operations. To use this control, select one or more users from the table of users and then choose a command from the update options combo box. To apply the command, click the Update button. Whatever operation you select is performed on all the selected user accounts. Examples of uses of this tool are shown later in this chapter.

Finally, at the bottom of the People Manager page is the table of users. The table lists all the users in the system. These columns are shown:

- **Username:** The login name of the user
- **Status:** Indicates whether the user is Active or Blocked
- **Roles:** Roles assigned to the user
- **Member for:** How long the user has been a member of the site
- **Last Access:** When the user last logged in
- **Operations:** Links to operations that can be performed on the user account

Tip

You can sort the user list by clicking the column headings. ■

Configuring Account Settings

Global user account settings are configured via the Account Settings Manager. To access the Account Settings Manager, click Configuration option on the Management menu. On the page that loads, select Account Settings under the People section of the page. The Account Settings Manager loads in your browser, as shown in Figure 23.2.

Across the top of the page are three tabs:

- Settings
- Manage Fields
- Manage Display

I discuss these in the sections that follow.

FIGURE 23.2

The Account Settings Manager

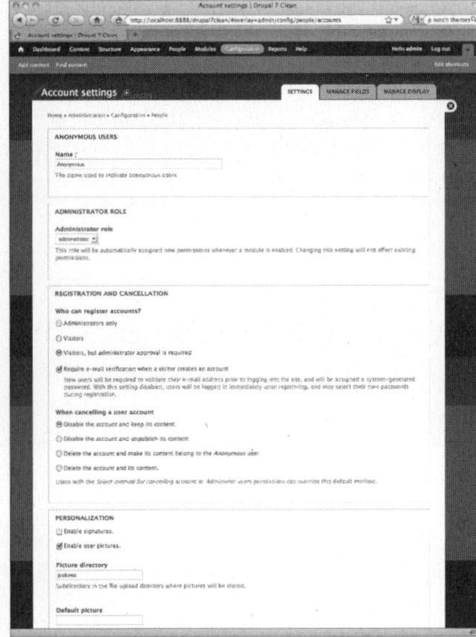

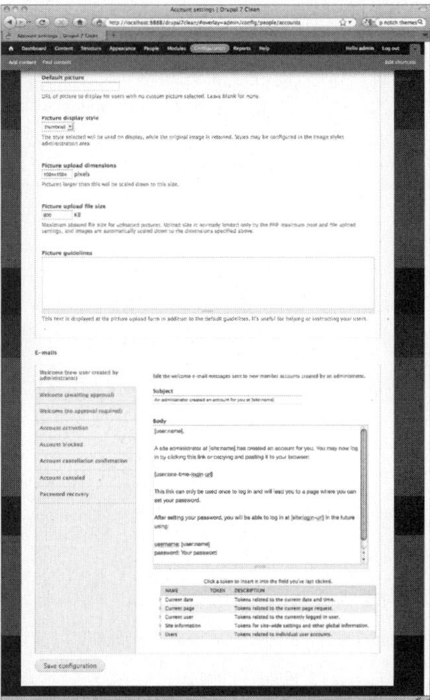

Reviewing the Settings tab

The Settings tab (refer to Figure 23.2) is the default landing page when you access the Account Settings Manager. If you are viewing one of the other tabs, you can always bring this tab to the front by clicking it.

The fields on the page are divided into five areas:

- Anonymous Users
- Administrator Role
- Registration and Cancellation
- Personalization
- E-mails

The configuration options in each of these sections are discussed in the following sections.

Anonymous Users

Only one field appears in this section of the page; it is intended to allow you to change the default label used to designate anonymous users in the system. If you want to change the default label, simply type into the blank the label you want to use and click the Save configuration button.

Administrator Role

This configuration option is provided to allow you to specify which role, if any, is automatically granted permissions when a new module is installed. The combo box contains a list of the eligible roles and includes the option to disable this feature completely, thereby forcing you to manually set permissions before any role can use a newly installed module.

Registration and Cancellation

Three configuration controls are available here. The first allows you to specify who has permission to create new user accounts. The second controls whether an e-mail notification process is required during registration. The final option controls what happens when you cancel an account.

Cross-Reference

Controlling user registration is dealt with in detail in Chapter 25. ■

Personalization

The options under this heading relate to the user's profile and personalization. These controls are available:

- **Enable signatures:** Check this option to allow users to add their own signatures to posts. This is most frequently used on sites where the comments or forum modules are active because this information show ups on the users' posts. This option is disabled by default.
- **Enable user pictures:** Check this option to allow users to upload an image to include on their profiles and on their posts. The user can control the image through the My Account page. This option is enabled by default.
- **Picture directory:** This field allows you to specify an alternative directory for the storage of user pictures. The default value is "pictures." You have no reason to change this absent special circumstances.
- **Default picture:** If you want to display a default image for users, type the path to the image in this field. The image is replaced by the user's own image if she chooses to upload one. Leave this field blank to display no default image.
- **Picture display style:** Select from the combo box the image style you want to apply to the user pictures. The options available here are dictated by the options specified in the image styles controls.

Cross-Reference

Working with images and image styles is discussed in Chapter 12. ■

- **Picture upload dimensions:** Enter a dimensions value in this field to place a limit on the maximum image dimensions that can be uploaded for the user picture. The default setting is 1024x1024. Files that exceed this value are rejected.
- **Picture upload file size:** Set the maximum permissible file size for user pictures. Files that exceed this value are rejected.
- **Picture guidelines:** In this field, enter instructions to help users with the user picture functionality. This field is relevant only if you have enabled the user picture option.

E-mails

This section of the Account Setting Manager includes the default notification e-mails sent out to users whenever various events occur. The e-mails can be viewed and edited here.

Cross-Reference

Working with notification e-mails is dealt with in more detail in Chapter 25. ■

Reviewing the Manage Fields tab

The controls on the Manage Fields page allow you to add, edit, and arrange additional fields for holding user data. The Manage Fields page content is shown in Figure 23.3.

FIGURE 23.3

The Manage Fields page

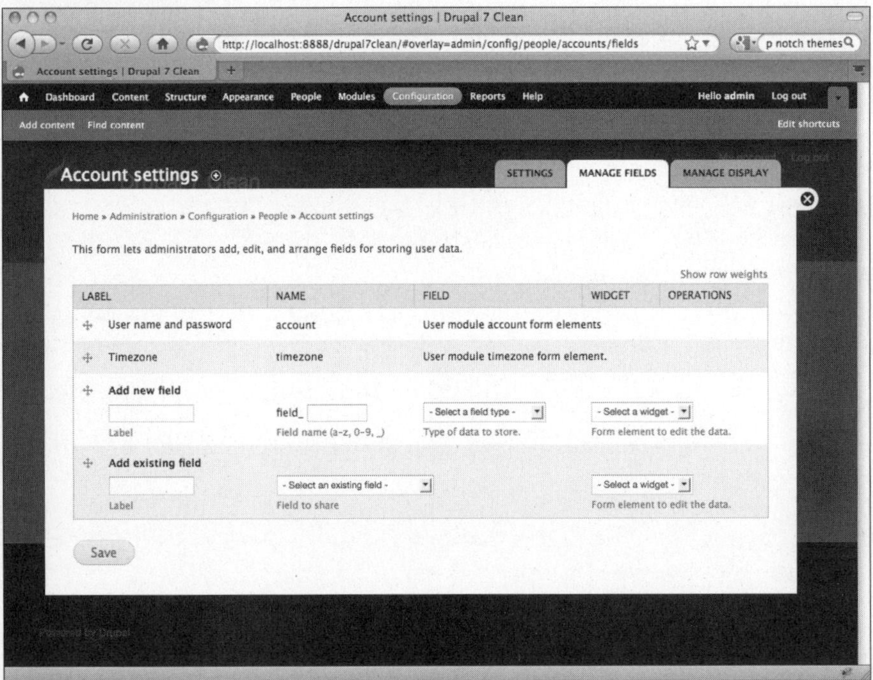

The table at the top of the page shows all the fields that are currently in the system. The table includes these columns:

- **Label:** This column contains the label that is associated with the field and displayed on the page to help users understand what to type into the field.
- **Name:** This column is the suffix of the machine readable name for the field. The prefix for all is the same: field_.
- **Field:** This column describes the type of value the field accepts.
- **Widget:** This column displays the widget, if any, associated with the field.
- **Operations:** Here you'll find links to shortcuts to perform operations on the field, if any.

Note

Widgets are interface controls used to handle the input for fields. Examples are combo boxes, text fields, text boxes, and so on. ■

Immediately beneath the listing of existing fields are controls that allow for the creation of additional fields. You can use an existing field, or you can create a completely new field to match your needs. These are your choices:

- **Add new field:** Use the controls here to create a completely new field and add it to the user profile.
  - **Label:** This label appears beside the field on the form.
  - **Field name (a-z, 0-9, _):** This is a machine-readable name for the field. Note that the field accepts only the letters a–z, the numbers 0–9 and the underscore character.
  - **Type of data to store:** Select from the combo box one of the field types.
  - **Form element to edit the data**: The selection made in the previous control dictates the options in the form element combo box. In cases where you have more than one option, you can select the widget you want to appear with the field.
- **Add existing field:** Use the controls here to add one of the existing fields in the system to the user profile.
  - **Label:** This label appears beside the field on the form.
  - **Field to share:** Select from the combo box one of the existing field types.
  - **Form element to edit the data:** The selection made in the previous control dictates the options in the form element combo box. In cases where you have more than one option, you can select the widget you want to appear with the field.

Note

To change the order in which the fields are displayed, use the crossed double arrows that precede each field. Click and drag these to rearrange the order of the fields on the page. ■

Later in this chapter, I discuss adding fields to the default profile.

Reviewing the Manage Display tab

The Manage Display page allows you to modify the position and formatting of fields on the user profiles. Click the Manage Display tab to access the page, as shown in Figure 23.4.

FIGURE 23.4

The Manage Display page showing the Custom Display Settings pane open

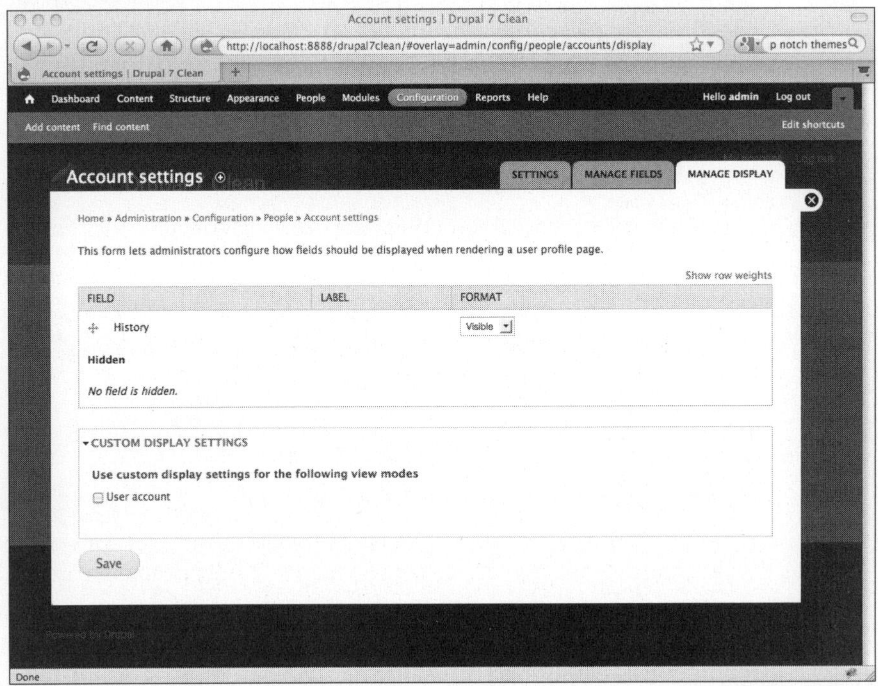

Note that the table contains only fields created using the Manage Fields functionality. Two controls are available here:

- **Label:** Select an option from the combo box to control the placement of the field relative to the default fields. The options here allow you to position the new field either above or below (inline) the other fields. There is also the option to make this a hidden field. Hidden fields are not visible to unauthorized users.
- **Format:** Select an option from the combo box to control the display of the field data. The *default* option shows it exactly the size and format specified when the field was created. *Plain text* shows you only the output in plain text format. *Trimmed* removes all extra space from the field, leaving only the field value.

The Custom Display Settings pane can be opened by clicking the name. Inside, there is only one option, which allows you to enable custom display setting for particular view modes. If you do not select this option, all modes will have the same display.

Reviewing the My Account page

All users have a My Account page. The page provides a view of the user profile, a tab for editing the user's details, and depending on the options enabled, additional tabs, as shown in Figure 23.5. The default configuration shows only the view tab and the tab that displays the user's name. If the Tracker module is enabled, you also see the Track tab, which is discussed later in this chapter.

FIGURE 23.5

This is a typical default My Account page, showing the landing page. Note the Track tab, indicating that the Tracker module is enabled.

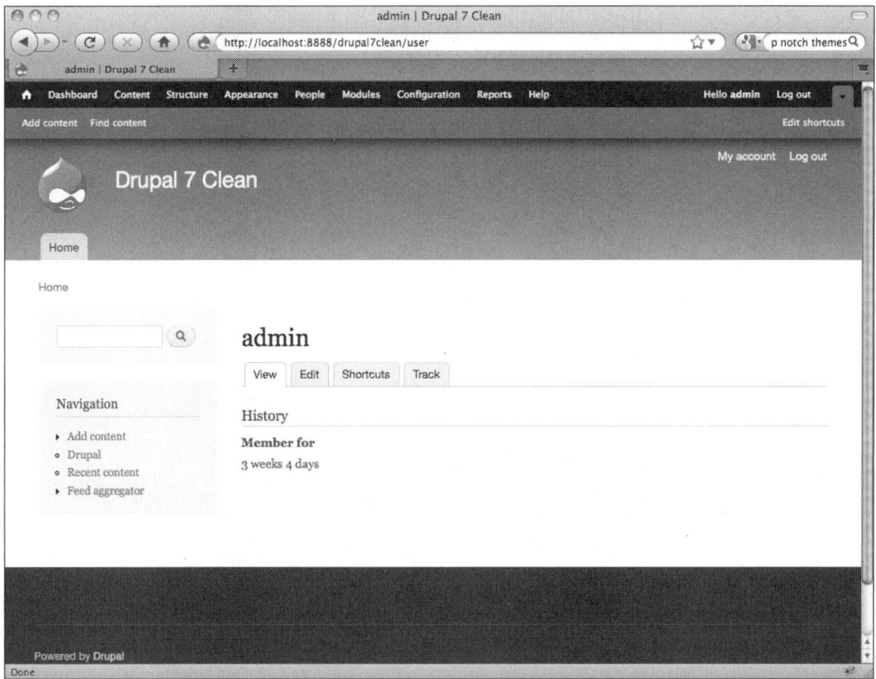

Not all tabs are visible to all users. If the viewer is not the user, or assigned to a role that grants user editing permissions, the viewer sees only the contents of the view tab. If the viewer is the user or has permission to edit the user, he also sees a link that allows for modification of the user profile information. The tab for editing is named for the user, as shown in Figure 23.6.

The options on this page enable the user to update or modify their profile. These sections are provided:

- The Account information section at the top of the page allows the users to change their e-mail address or password.

- The Picture section lets the user upload a new profile picture.
- The Locale settings enable the user to tailor the site to display dates and times in a manner consistent with the selection made from the combo box.

The user can edit the information on this page and then click the Save button to update her accounts.

FIGURE 23.6

The editing screen of a My Account page shows a user named Joe the Cat, hence the tab of the same name.

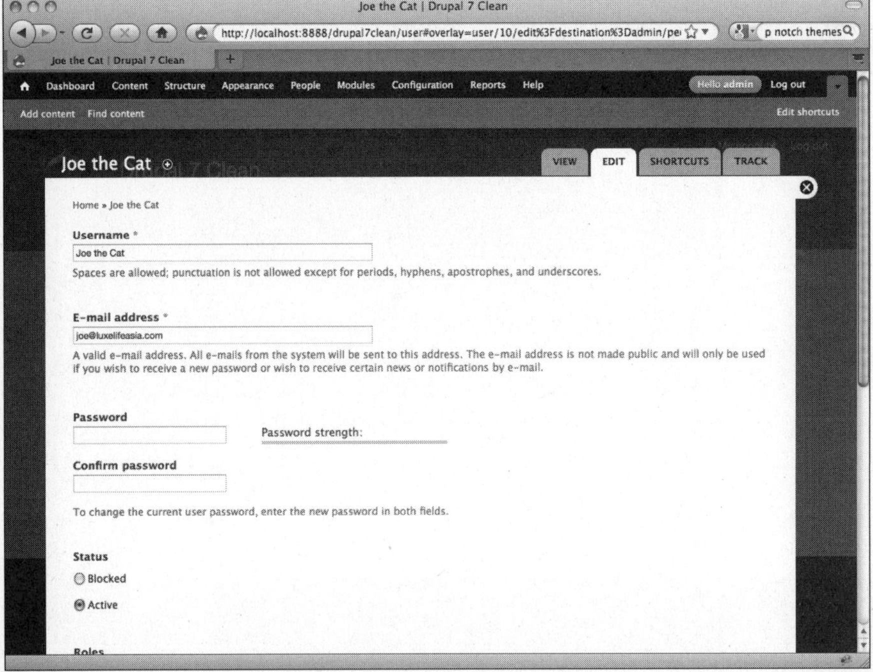

Creating a New User

User creation is subject to several different configuration settings. The settings dictate which roles can create users as well as the process that must be followed to activate the accounts. In the default configuration, users can be created from either the front end of the site or from the admin system.

Cross-Reference

Creation of users on the front end of the site is controlled by the user registration settings. User registration is discussed at length in Chapter 25. ■

You can create a new user from the admin system by following these steps:

1. **Log into your site as an administrator.**

   The admin interface loads in your browser.

2. **Select People from the Management menu.**

   The People Manager opens in your browser (refer to Figure 23.1).

3. **Click the Add user link.**

   The New User page opens, as shown in Figure 23.7.

FIGURE 23.7

The New User page

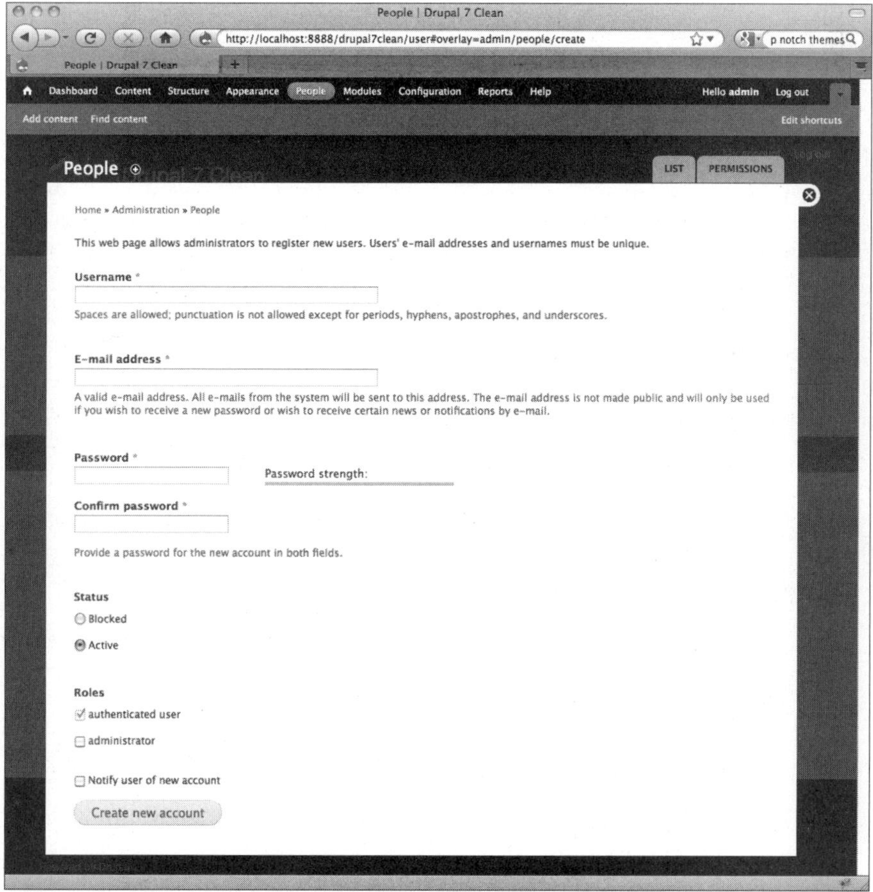

4. **Type a name for the user in the field labeled Username.**

   This is a required field.

5. **Type a valid e-mail address for the user in the field labeled E-mail address.**

   This is a required field.

6. **Type the password two times, once in the Password field and again in the Confirm password field.**

   This is a required field.

7. **Select Active or Blocked from the Status field.**
8. **Select one or more Roles for the new user.**
9. **If you want an e-mail notification sent to the user with access details, click the check box next to Notify user of new account.**
10. **Click the Create new account button at the bottom of the page.**

    If you are successful, a new user is created and a confirmation message appears at the top of the page.

There is no limit to the number of users you can create for your Web site.

Managing Users

The management of your site's users is performed most easily from the People Manager, but you also have options for performing certain tasks from the front end of the site. The latter approach is consistent with allowing users to manage their own accounts and the details displayed on the My Account page. In the sections that follow, I discuss the various options for editing, blocking, and canceling user accounts.

Editing user accounts

User accounts can be edited from either the front end of the site or from the People Manager in the admin system. In either event, you are editing the user account from the editing tab of the My Account page (refer to Figure 23.6).

To edit a user account from the admin system, follow these steps:

1. **Access the People Manager by clicking People on the Management menu.**

   The People Manager loads in your browser.

2. **Click the name of the user you want to edit.**

   The user's My Account page loads in your browser (refer to Figure 23.5).

3. **Click the user's name tab at the top of the My Account page.**

   The editing page opens (refer to Figure 23.6).

4. **Make any changes you require.**

5. **Click the Save button.**

   The system saves your changes and displays a confirmation message.

To edit a user account from the front end, follow these steps:

1. **Click the user's name.**

   The user's My Account page loads in your browser (refer to Figure 23.5).
2. **Click the user's name tab at the top of the My Account page.**

   The editing page opens (refer to Figure 23.6).
3. **Make any changes you require.**
4. **Click the Save button.**

   The system saves your changes and displays a confirmation message.

Blocking users

If you want to prohibit a user from logging into your site, you can do so by blocking the user. Blocking can only be done from the People Manager. Blocking is a temporary solution, and users who have been blocked can be unblocked by an administrator. If you want to ban the user permanently, you must cancel the account, as discussed in the next section.

To edit a user account from the admin system, follow these steps:

1. **Access the People Manager by clicking People on the Management menu.**

   The People Manager loads in your browser.
2. **Click the check box next to the name of the user you want to edit.**
3. **Select the option Block the selected users from the Update Options combo box.**
4. **Click the Update button.**

   The system blocks the user, displays a confirmation message, and changes the user's status to blocked.

To unblock a user account, follow these steps:

1. **Access the People Manager by clicking People on the Management menu.**

   The People Manager loads in your browser.
2. **Click the check box next to the name of the user you want to edit.**
3. **Select the option Unblock the selected users from the Update Options combo box.**
4. **Click the Update button.**

   The system unblocks the user, displays a confirmation message, and changes the user's status to active.

Note

Unblocking a user account results in the system sending the user a notification e-mail. ■

Canceling user accounts

To remove a user from the system, you can cancel his account. Canceling an account can be done from the front end or the admin system. This is a two-step process. After you select the option to cancel, you also must instruct the system how to handle any existing data associated with the user.

To cancel a user account from the admin system, follow these steps:

1. **Access the People Manager by clicking People on the Management menu.**

   The People Manager loads in your browser.

2. **Click the check box next to the name of the user you want to edit.**
3. **Select the option Cancel the selected user accounts from the Update Options combo box.**

   The confirmation page loads in your browser.

4. **Select the desired option for handling the user's data.**
5. **Select whether you want the cancellation to be dependent upon an e-mail confirmation.**
6. **Click the Cancel account button.**

   The system cancels the account, displays a confirmation message, and handles the user's data in accordance with the selection you made on the cancellation confirmation page.

To cancel a user account from the admin system, follow these steps:

1. **Click the user's name.**

   The user's My Account page loads in your browser (refer to Figure 23.5).

2. **Click the user's name tab at the top of the My Account page.**

   The editing page opens (refer to Figure 23.6).

3. **Scroll down to the bottom of the page, and click the Cancel account button.**

   A cancellation confirmation page loads in your browser, as shown in Figure 23.8.

4. **Select the option for handling the user's data.**
5. **Select whether you want the cancellation to be dependent upon an e-mail confirmation.**

6. **Click the Cancel account button.**

   The system cancels the account, displays a confirmation message, and handles the user's data in accordance with the selection you made on the cancellation confirmation page.

FIGURE 23.8

The cancellation confirmation page

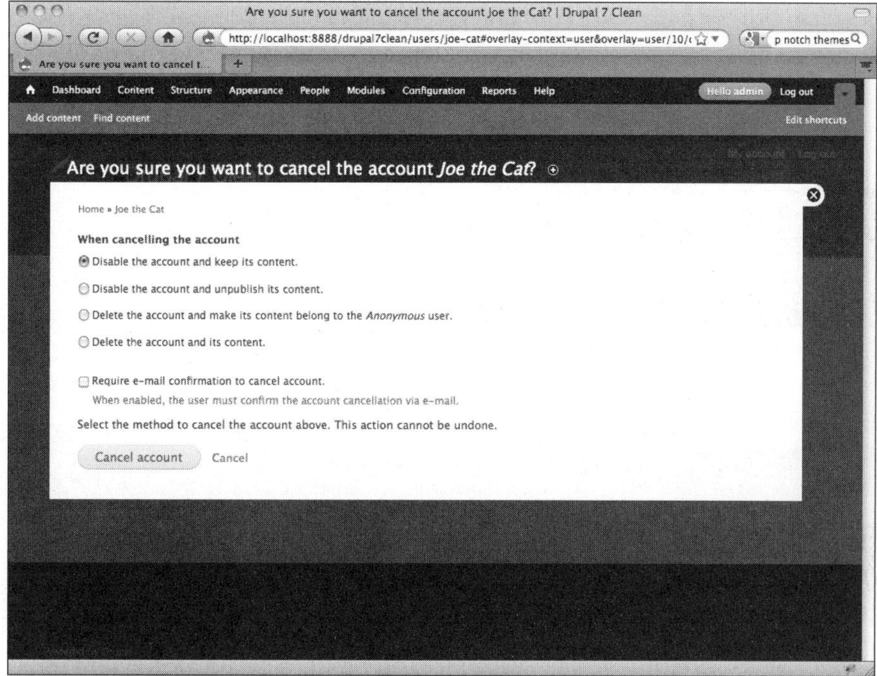

Note

If you select the option Require e-mail confirmation to cancel account, the system sends a notification e-mail to the user's registered e-mail address. The user must confirm the cancellation for it to take effect. ■

Tip

If your site permits public registration, canceling and deleting an account is not an effective way to block a user. The user can simply register again. The better course is to disable the account and block the user. ■

Working with the Default Profiles

The default user profile can be seen by accessing a user's My Account page (refer to Figure 23.5). To add fields to this page, you use the Manage Fields page in the Account Settings. To control the ordering and the display of the fields, use the Account Settings Manager and the Display Fields page. The Account Settings Manager is described earlier in this chapter. In the following, I demonstrate how to add new fields using the Manage Fields functionality.

By way of example, I am going to add a new field to the default user page. I want the users to use this new field to enter their Web site URL. To add a new field to the default user page, follow these steps:

1. **Log into your site as an administrator.**

   The admin interface loads in your browser.
2. **Click Configuration on the Management menu.**

   The Configuration page loads in your browser.
3. **Click Account Settings under the People heading.**

   The Account Setting Manager loads (refer to Figure 23.2).
4. **Click the Manage Fields tab.**

   The Manage Fields page comes to the front (refer to Figure 23.3).
5. **Scroll to the section labeled Add new field, and in the field marked Label, type "website" as the data label for the new field.**
6. **Type a machine-readable name in the field marked Field name.**

   In this case, I use the name "website."
7. **Select a field type.**

   In this example, I choose Text. The Form element automatically resets to Text field.
8. **Click the Save button.**

   The Field Settings page loads, as shown in Figure 23.9.
9. **Type a value for the maximum length of the field.**

   The default value is 255.

Caution

The Field Setting options you select cannot be changed later! ■

FIGURE 23.9

The Field Settings page

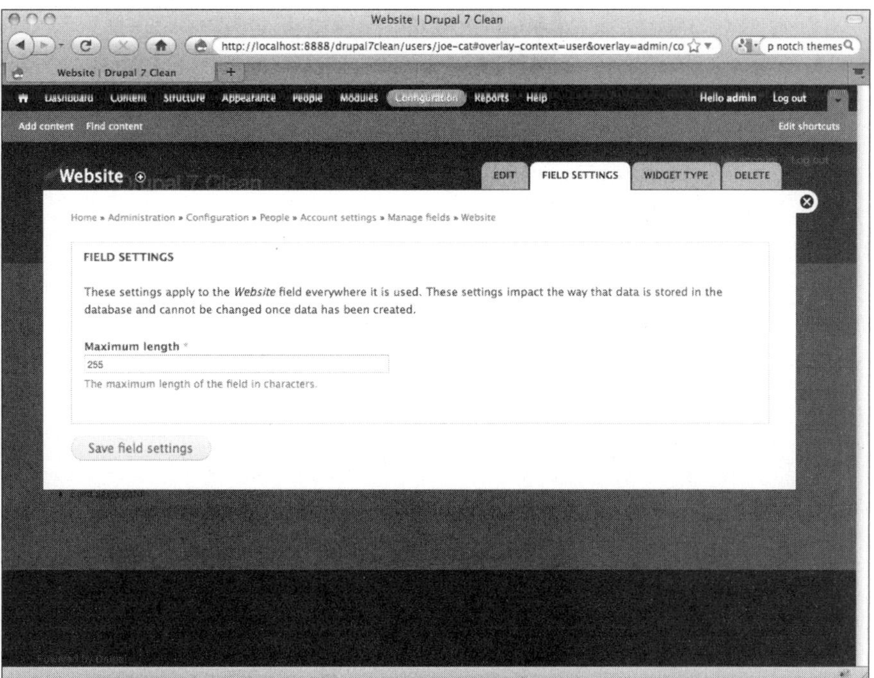

10. **Click the Save field settings.**

    The User Settings page loads in your browser, as shown in Figure 23.10.

11. **The Label is a required field, but you can use the default value "website."**
12. **I don't want this to be required, but I want to display the field on the registration form, so I check only the option Display on user registration form.**
13. **For Text processing, I leave the default value, Plain text.**
14. **Shorten this field by changing the Size of textfield value from 60 to 40.**
15. **In the Help text, add directions that will appear with the field.**

    In this case, I type: "Enter the full URL of your Web site here, beginning with http://."

16. **Use the default values for all other fields on this page.**
17. **Click the Save settings button.**

    The system creates the field and returns you to the Manage Fields page where you should see a confirmation message at the top of the page.

FIGURE 23.10

The User Settings page

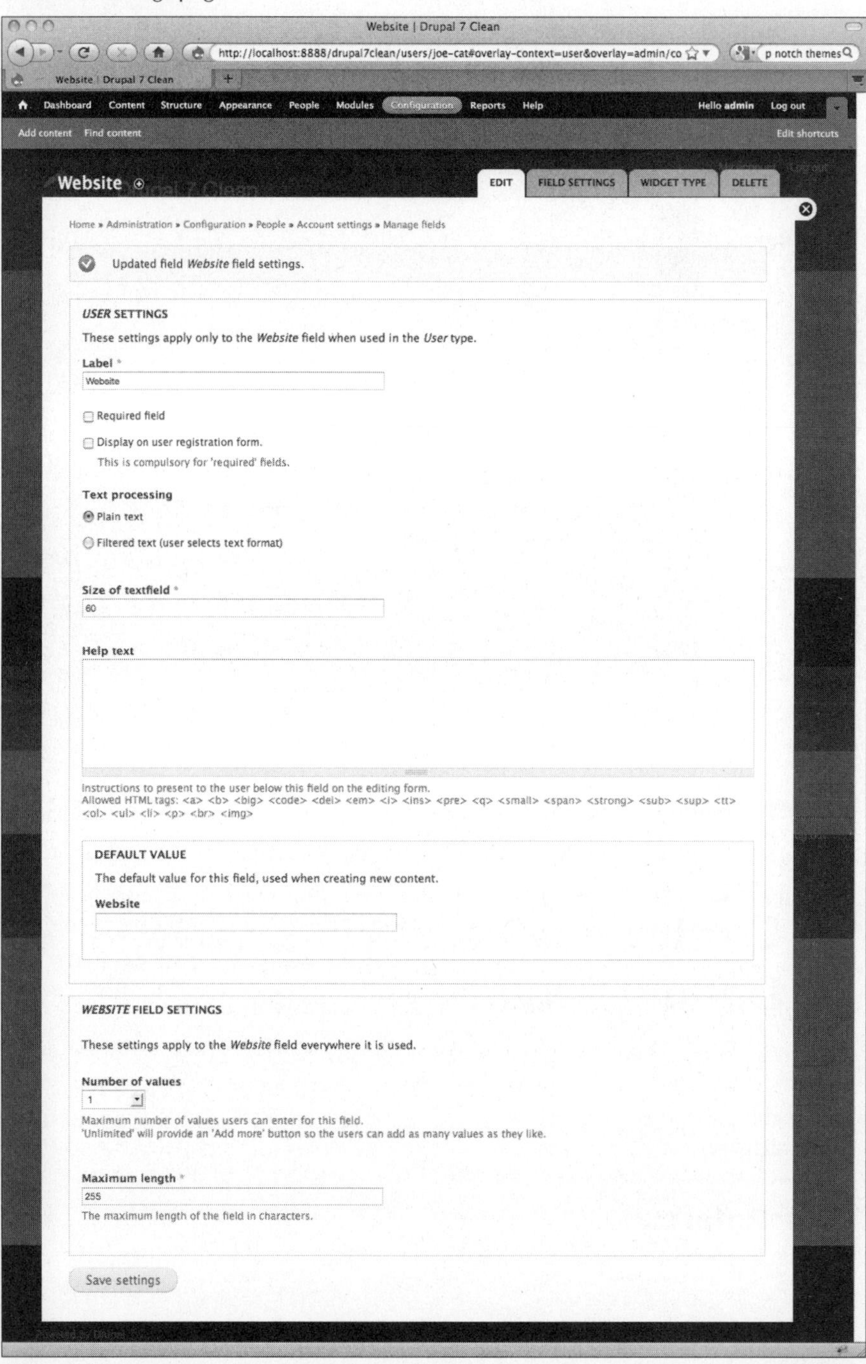

You can attach as many items as you like by repeating the process just described.

Figure 23.11 shows the user page modified with the new Web site field.

FIGURE 23.11

The user's My Account page after the addition of the new Web site field

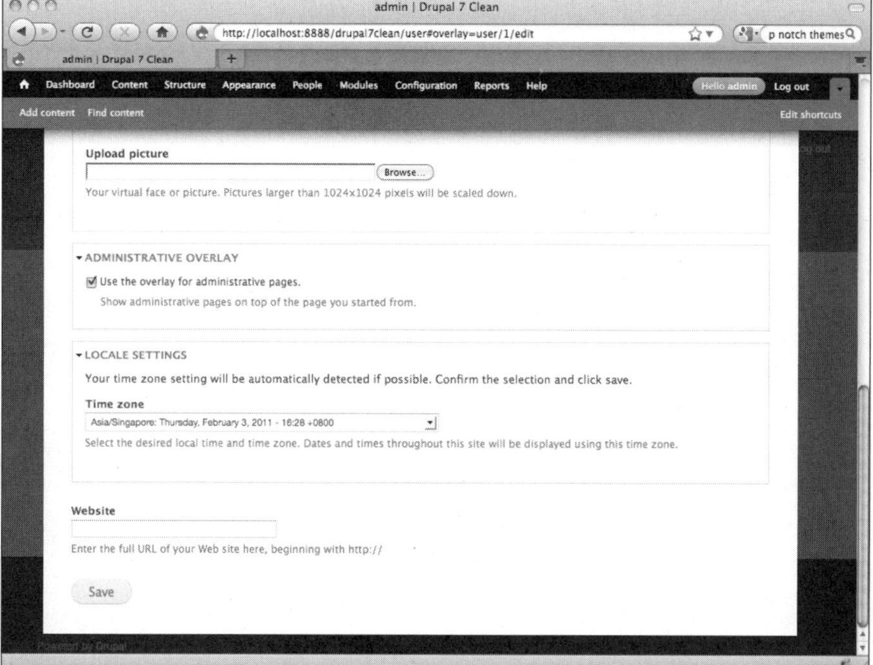

Controlling the Styling of the Default Profiles

The output associated with the user management system is primarily produced by the User module. The module provides four dedicated template files, two style sheets, and five themable functions. In the sections below, I introduce these resources, indicate their role in the display, and explain the functions and variables that are available for you to work with.

Cross-Reference

Overriding templates and working with themable functions are discussed in depth in Chapter 26. ■

Reviewing the default templates

Four dedicated templates are available for the User module. They are located at /modules/user:

- user-picture.tpl.php
- user-profile.tpl.php
- user-profile-category.tpl.php
- user-profile-item.tpl.php

Each of the templates is discussed in the sections that follow.

Reviewing user-picture.tpl.php

This is the template for controlling the display of the user profile picture. The available variables are shown in Table 23.1.

TABLE 23.1

Variables in user-picture.tpl.php

Variable	Description
$account	An array of the account information
$user_picture	The image associated with the account

Reviewing user-profile.tpl.php

The user-profile template is the key template for the presentation of all the user profile data. This template is what is seen when viewing a registered member's profile page. The variables are shown in Table 23.2.

TABLE 23.2

Variables in user-profile.tpl.php

Variable	Description
$user_profile	Prints all profile items

Note

You can use $user_profile to print all the profile items, or you can print just a subset of items. Printing a subset requires rendering one or more of the items using `render($content['field name here'])`. You need to call `render($content['field name here'])` at the conclusion to print the remaining fields. ■

Reviewing user-profile-category.tpl.php

This template controls the presentation of groups of profiles in categories. The available variables are shown in Table 23.3.

TABLE 23.3

Variables in user-profile-category.tpl.php

Variable	Description
$attributes	HTML attributes
$profile_items	All the items for the group
$title	The category title

Reviewing user-profile-item.tpl.php

This is the template for rendering profile items. This template is used to loop through and render each field that is configured for display. The available variables are shown in Table 23.4.

TABLE 23.4

Variables in user-profile-item.tpl.php

Variable	Description
$attributes	HTML attributes
$title	The field title for the profile item
$value	The value for the profile item

Reviewing the default style sheets

Two style sheets are dedicated to the formatting of the User module. Both are located at /modules/user:

- **user.css:** The primary CSS files
- **user-rtl.css:** The CSS that is applied when the site is set to display text in right-to-left orientation

Reviewing the themable functions

Five themable functions are available for user functionality; all are related to the administration of users. The functions can be found at modules/user/user.admin.inc.

- **theme_user_admin_permissions:** The theme function for the administration permissions page
- **theme_user_admin_ roles**: Controls the new role form
- **theme_user_list:** Produces the list of users
- **theme_user_permissions_description:** Produces the individual permission descriptions
- **theme_user_signature:** Produces the output of the user's signature

Using the Tracker Module

The Tracker module extends the functionality of the user profile by keeping track of the posts the user has made on the site. Tracker not only keeps a record of the posts, but it also adds a link to the My Profile page that lets the user jump to a page listing all her posts, as shown in Figure 23.12. This is particularly useful when the user is an active content contributor or when your site has a forum installed. In either case, the user can review previously submitted items and check to see whether they require changes or whether comments have been posted to the items.

FIGURE 23.12

The Tracker module in action, shown here displaying my recent posts

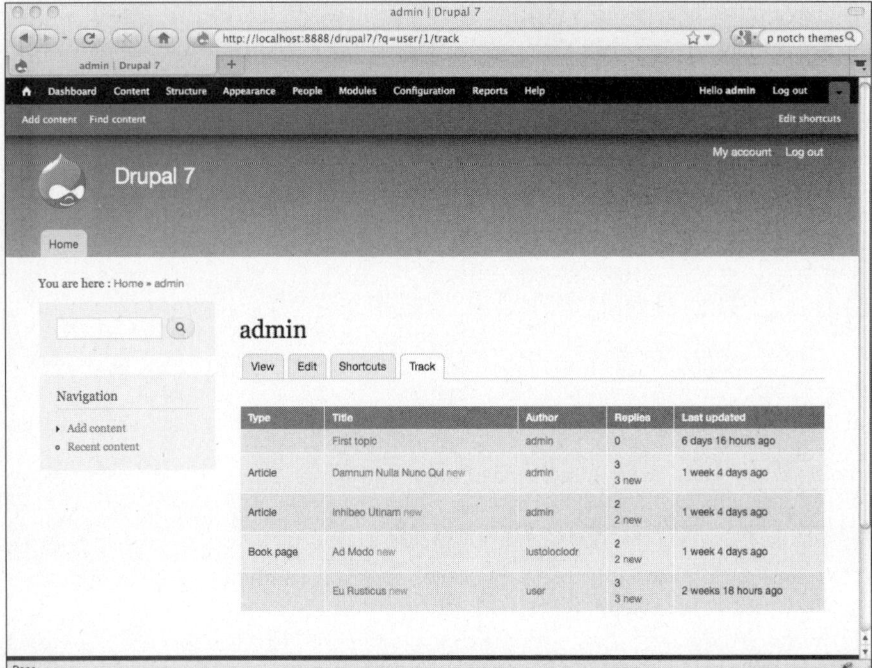

Enabling the module

The Tracker module is disabled in both the default full installation and in the simple installation profile. If you want to enable this module, you must first make sure the Comments, Text, Field, and Field SQL Storage modules are enabled, as they are required by the Tracker module.

Cross-Reference

The Comment module is discussed in detail in Chapter 15. ■

After you have enabled the required modules, you can enable the Tracker module by following these steps:

1. **Log into your site as an administrator.**

   The admin interface loads in your browser.
2. **Select Modules from the Management menu.**

   The Modules Manager opens in your browser.
3. **Click the check box next to the Tracker module.**
4. **Click the Save Configuration button at the bottom of the page.**

   If you are successful, the Tracker module is enabled and a confirmation message appears at the top of the page.

When you enable the module, a new navigation option becomes available. The option is named Recent Posts and links to a list of the most recent content items on the site. The option is published by default and appears in the default Navigation menu (refer to Figure 23.12).

Summary

This chapter addressed the use of the Upload functionality in Drupal 7. I covered these topics:

- The fundamentals of user management in Drupal
- How to create a new user
- How to edit, block, and cancel user accounts
- How to configure and customize the default user profiles
- How to affect the styling of the default user profiles
- How to enable and use the Tracker module

CHAPTER 24

Controlling User Access

Drupal gives the administrator the ability to grant or restrict access to content and functionality. User privileges are controlled through the creation of roles and the assignment of permissions. The default system includes three access roles, but you can create as many as you like and customize them to suit your needs. Proper use of roles and permissions is one of the keys to site security and the creation of work flow.

In this chapter, I review the default roles and permissions and explain how to create new roles, assign users to roles, and tailor permissions to the various roles. I also cover alternatives for achieving more granular access control at the blocks level.

IN THIS CHAPTER

Introducing Drupal's access controls

Adding a new role

Assigning users to roles

Setting permissions

Introducing Drupal's Access Controls

In the default configuration, access to the contents and functionality in your Drupal site is controlled through a combination of the roles functionality and the permissions functionality. Roles and permissions are key concepts in Drupal:

- **Roles:** Roles allow you to define a group of permissions. Users can then be assigned privileges by assigning them to roles via the Permissions Manager. The default system comes with three roles defined:
  - **Anonymous User:** This group contains users who don't have an account. For most public Web sites, this group consists of general public visitors. This is typically the largest user group.

Note

If a user is already assigned to a role, but they are viewing the site without being authenticated, they are also treated as an Anonymous User. ■

  - **Authenticated User:** This group contains users who both have an account and are logged in (authenticated). Typically, this role is used to create a class of users who can see more, or different, content and functionality than the anonymous users.
  - **Administrator:** This group contains users who have access to the back end of the site and the system's administration functionality. Typically, this is the smallest user group, with membership restricted to only the most trusted users.

Note

By default the Administrator role is the role given all the permissions in the system. This can be modified at any time from within the Permissions Manager. ■

- **Permissions**: Permissions enable you to define what each role can do and see on your site.

There are dedicated admin interfaces for both the roles and the permissions functionality. You can access both admin interfaces by clicking the People option on the Management menu and then clicking the Permissions tab. The Permissions Manager loads in your browser, as shown in Figure 24.1.

FIGURE 24.1

The Permissions Manager

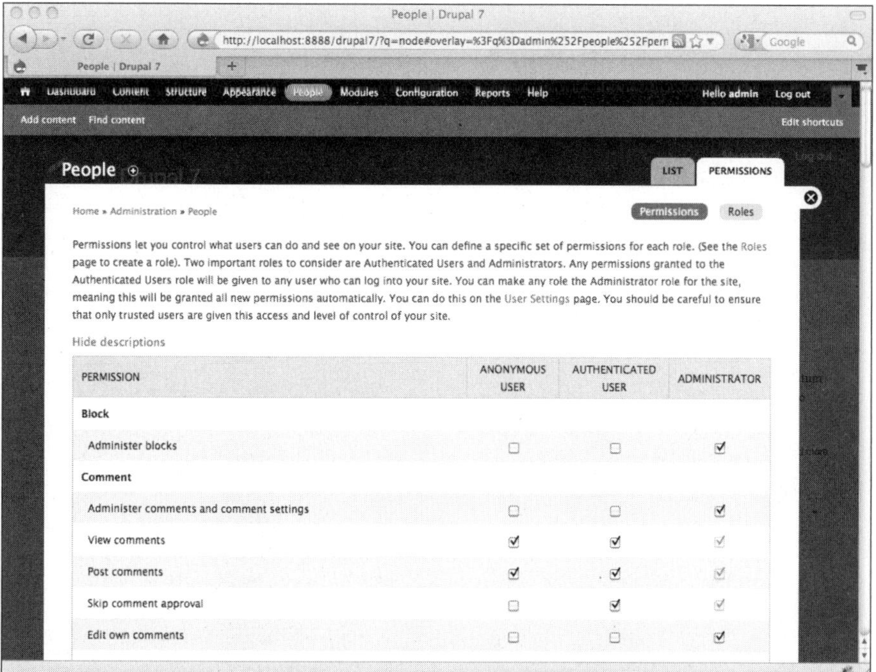

Adding a New Role

The Roles Manager is used to create, manage, and delete the roles in your Drupal site. To access the Roles Manager, click the People option on the Management menu. On the page that loads (refer to Figure 24.1), click the tab Permissions. When the Permissions Manager loads, select the button marked Roles at the top right and the Roles Manager loads in your browser, as shown in Figure 24.2.

The table shows two columns, listing the name of the roles in one and the operations available in the other. Note that two of the roles are locked; this simply means that the names cannot be modified, nor the roles deleted. The administrator role is not locked; however, the only change you can make to it is the name. The anonymous and authenticated user roles cannot be deleted. The permissions associated with all three roles can be modified by clicking the edit permissions link. Working with the permissions is discussed in the next section of this chapter.

FIGURE 24.2

The Roles Manager shows the default roles.

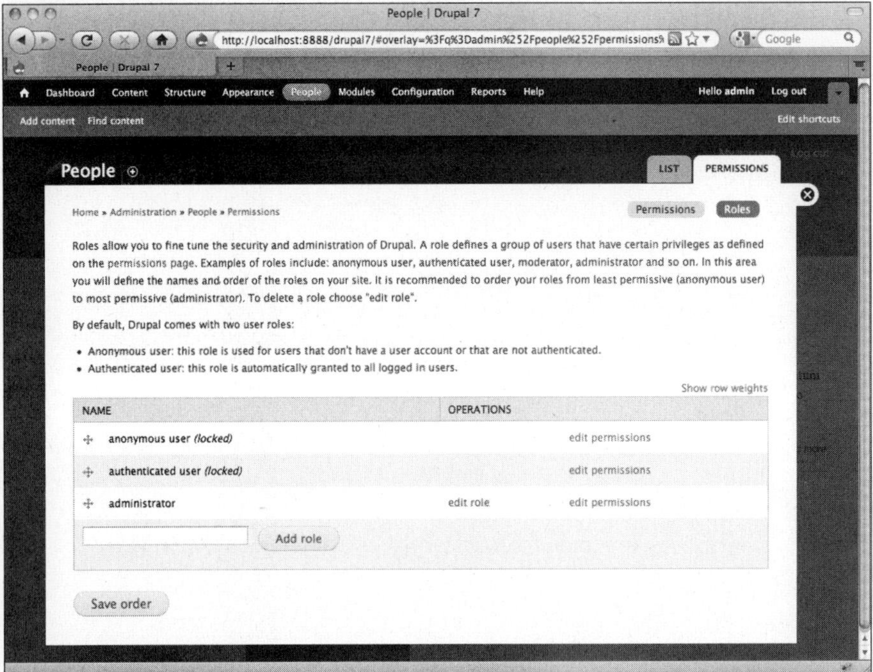

The empty field you see at the bottom of the Name column (refer to Figure 24.2) is used to create a new role.

To create a new role, follow these steps:

1. **Access the Roles Manager.**
2. **Type a name for the role in the empty field at the bottom of the Name column.**
3. **Click the Add role button.**

   If you are successful, a confirmation message appears at the top of the page and the new role is added to the table.

If you want to rename the role at any time, simply click the edit role button in the Operations column. On the page that loads in your browser, you can change the name.

The number of roles you can create for your site is not limited, nor is the number of users that can be assigned to any particular role limited. This means that you can tailor roles as closely as you like for your site. If, for example, you want to create a specific role for one specific user, you can do so with no problems.

When a new role is created, the system automatically adds it to the Permissions Manager. After you have created the role, the next logical step is to set the permissions that define the access privileges of the users assigned to that role. Clicking the edit permissions option next to the name of a role in the Roles Manager opens a permissions page specific to that particular role. Alternatively, you can view the global site permissions by accessing the Permissions Manager, as discussed in the next section.

Tip

Working with the Permissions Manager is typically more useful than using the dedicated permissions page associated with specific roles, because you can see the relationship between the roles and the connections the system forces between them. ■

To delete a role you have created, follow these steps:

1. **Access the Roles Manager.**
2. **Click the edit role link next to the name of the role you want to delete.**

   A verification page loads.
3. **Click the Delete button.**

   If you are successful, a confirmation message appears at the top of the page.

Note

You cannot delete the anonymous user and authenticated user roles. ■

Assigning Users to Roles

A user can be assigned to a role either at the time of the creation of the user account or later, by editing the user. The user pages that are visible to the administrator include a list of the roles available in the system, as shown in Figure 24.3.

To assign a user to a role, simply click in the check box next to the name of the role. Users can be assigned to more than one role. If the user is assigned to more than one role, the permissions are cumulative; that is, the user enjoys the permissions available to any of the roles to which he is assigned.

Cross-Reference

Working with users and the People Manager is discussed in detail in Chapter 23. ■

FIGURE 24.3

The user page, as seen by the administrator, shows the Roles section where users can be assigned to one or more roles.

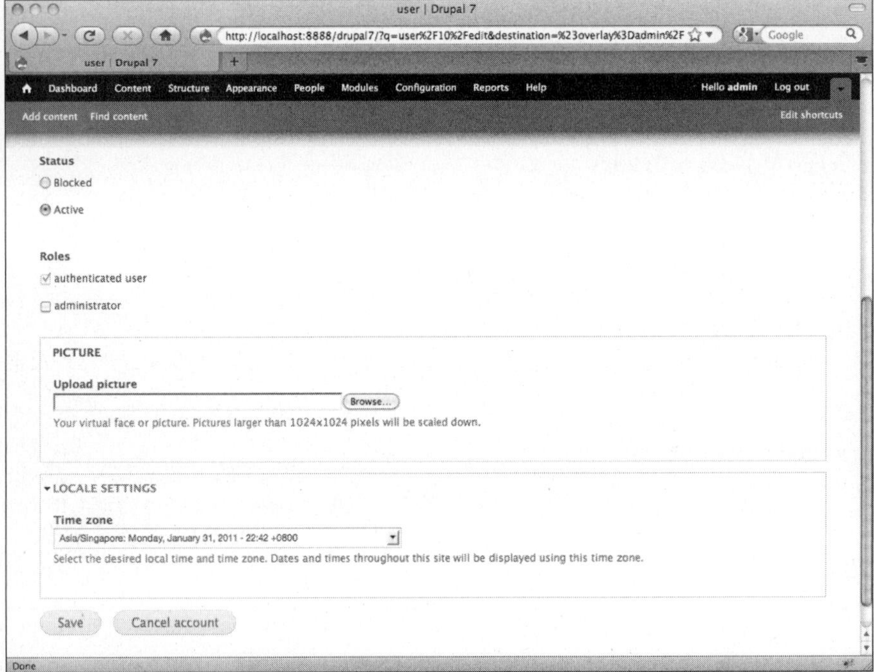

Setting Permissions

What each role can see and do on your site is controlled by the settings you specify in the Permissions Manager. To access the Permissions Manager, click the People option on the Management menu. On the page that loads click Permissions. The Permissions Manager loads in your browser, as shown in Figure 24.1, above.

Controlling global access

The interface of the Permissions Manager is dominated by a lengthy table. The table shows a column labeled Permission, which lists all the privileges available on the site. The columns to the right are for each role in the system. To grant a permission to a particular role, simply check the box in the appropriate column. To deny permission, leave the box unchecked.

Note

Permissions granted to one role are not inherited by other roles. The sole exception to this is the Authenticated User role. Any privileges you grant to the Authenticated User role are inherited by all other roles except for the Anonymous User role. ■

Cross-Reference

Roles and permissions play a key part in setting up workflow on your site. The topic of creating content management workflow is dealt with in more detail in Chapter 14. ■

Blocking IP addresses

Drupal provides site administrators with a method for completely blocking access to the site. The block is premised on the IP address of the user. The ability to block access by IP address adds a layer of security to the site and makes it possible to exclude problematic users from access to the site.

A separate interface allows for adding and managing blocked IP addresses. To access the IP Address Blocking page, click Configuration on the Management menu. On the page that loads, click the option IP address blocking. The IP Address Blocking page loads in your browser, as shown in Figure 24.4.

To add an IP address, simply type it into the IP address box and click the Add button. If you are successful, you see a confirmation message and the address appears in the table at the bottom of the page.

To delete an IP address from the list, simply click the delete link to the right of the address. When the confirmation page loads, click the Delete button and the system removes the address.

FIGURE 24.4

The IP Address Blocking page shows one IP address already added.

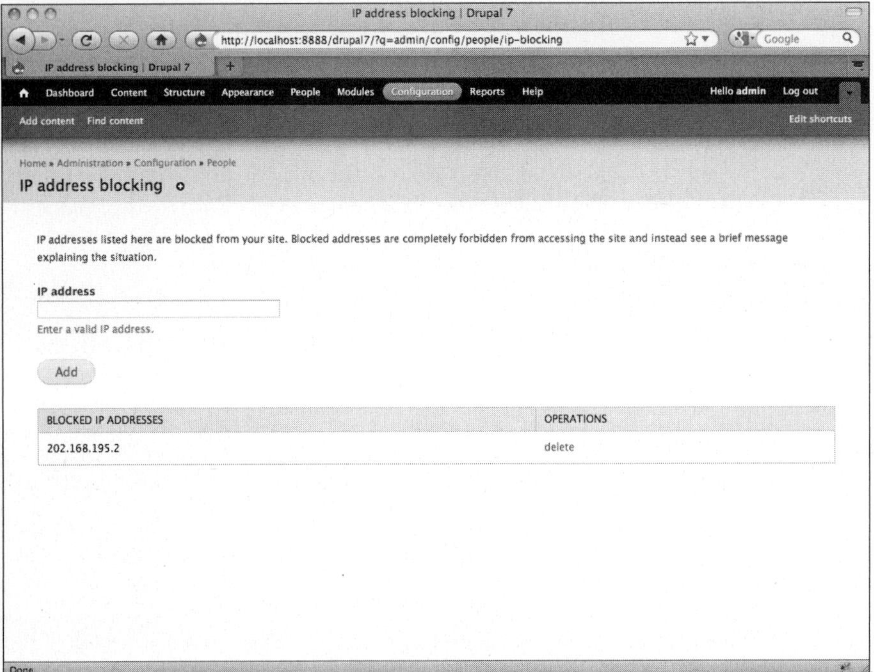

Controlling block level access

The Permissions Manager is concerned with global site permissions. Permissions can be varied at a more granular level via the Blocks Manager. Individual block visibility can be tied to the role of the user, a setting that overrides any conflicting assignments made in the Permissions Manager.

To set the visibility of a block, follow these steps:

1. **Access the Blocks Manager.**
2. **Click the configure link next to the block you want to control.**

   The block configuration manager loads in your browser.

3. **Click the Roles in the Visibility settings section of the page.**

   The control appears, as shown in Figure 24.5.

4. **Click the boxes next to the names of the roles for which you want to grant access.**

   Note that leaving all unchecked grants access to all.

5. **Click the Save block button at the bottom of the page.**

   If you are successful, the system saves the changes and displays a confirmation message.

FIGURE 24.5

The block configuration page shows the controls for restricting visibility by role.

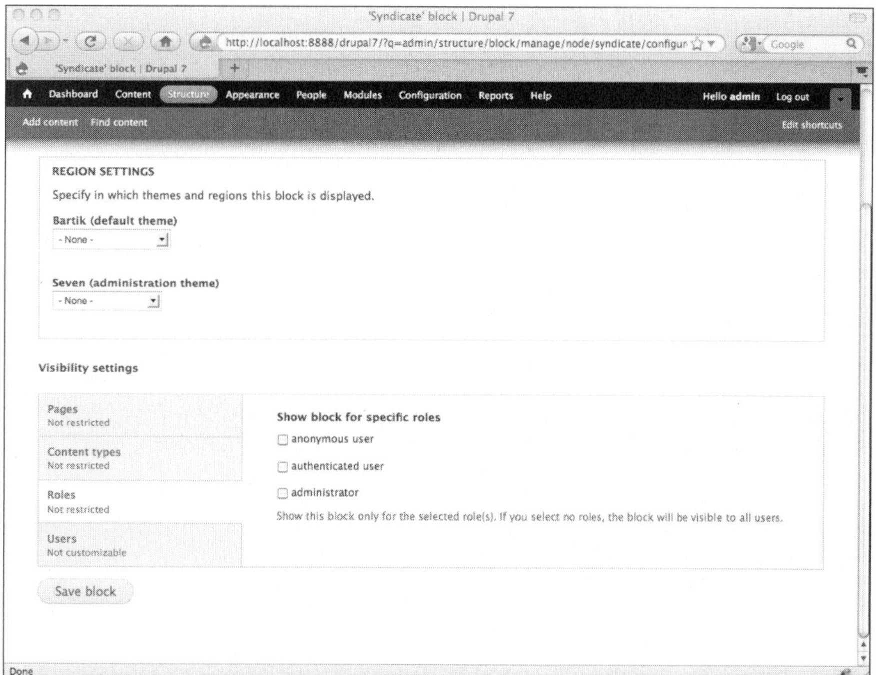

Summary

This chapter addressed user access controls in Drupal 7. I covered these topics:

- How access is controlled
- How to create new roles
- How to assign users to roles
- How to set the permissions associated with those roles
- How to block access by IP address
- How to control access at block level

CHAPTER

25

Configuring User Registration

IN THIS CHAPTER

Enabling user registration

Managing notifications

Working with the user login function

Styling the display

Adding users to your Web site can be done by either the administrator or by the users themselves. In the default system, both methods are enabled. This means that visitors to the site can create their own accounts and thereafter become members of your Web site, with all the privileges assigned to the Authenticated user role. Administrators can also create users and indeed have much greater power to assign users to roles and to give users permissions to access contents and functionality.

In this chapter, I focus on how you can use the mechanisms that allow users to register and create their own accounts on your Web site. I also cover related functions like the Login block and the Request Password functionalities.

Enabling User Registration

Drupal's default configuration allows visitors to a Web site to create their own accounts without intervention of the administrator. Obtaining a new user account is simple; a user simply clicks the Create new account link on the Login block, as shown in Figure 25.1, and then completes the form on the page that loads in the browser.

FIGURE 25.1

On the Login block, the links to both the Create new account and the Request Password functionalities are below the login form.

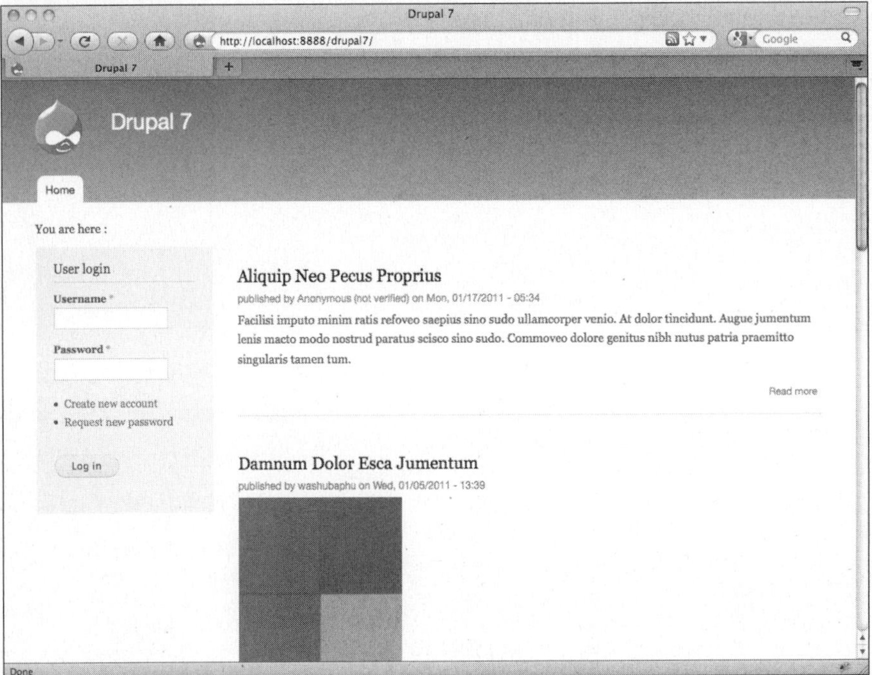

The page that loads in the visitor's browser is the User Registration page, as shown in Figure 25.2. The user must type into the form a username and a valid e-mail address, and then click the Create new account button. In response to the submission of a registration form, Drupal automatically sends to the user an e-mail containing a system-generated password. After the user receives the e-mail, he must use the password to access the site. After users have logged into the site, they can change their password if they so desire. By default, new user accounts created in this fashion are assigned to the Authenticated role.

While the default approach is certainly easy and convenient for users, it may not be optimal for your site. Options are available that allow you to create more or less secure registration processes; you can even block front-end registration completely.

FIGURE 25.2

The User Registration form

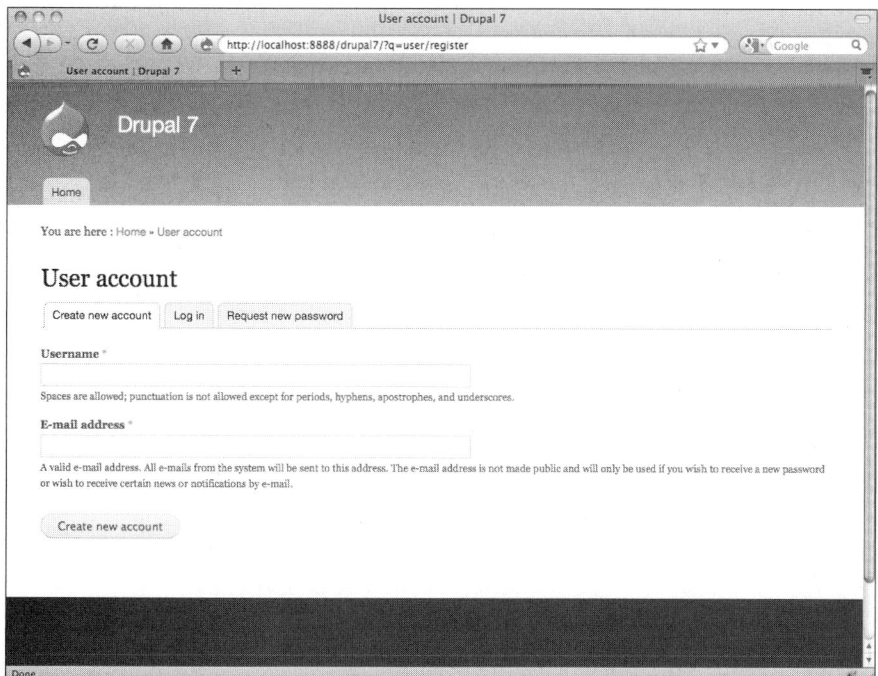

The configuration options controlling user registration are located on the Account Settings Manager. To access the manager, click the Configuration option on the Management menu. On the page that loads, select Account settings, located inside the People section of the page. The Account Settings Manager loads, as shown in Figure 25.3.

About halfway down the Account Settings page is the Registration and Cancellation section. To configure the user registration functionality, use the radio buttons displayed under the question Who can register accounts? The *Visitors* setting is the most open, allowing site visitors to create their own accounts without any oversight by the site administrators. The other two choices restrict registration. Select from either of the additional choices:

- **Visitors, but administrator approval is required:** Select this option to allow visitors to register, but unlike the default setting, administrator action is required to enable the account. Put another way, this option has the effect of turning the automatic user registration process into a user registration request, which is then subject to approval, or rejection, by the site administrator.

- **Administrators only:** This option is the most restrictive because it completely removes the option for user registration from the front end of the Web site. If you select this option, the Create a new account link is hidden on the front end and new user accounts can be created only by the site administrator.

FIGURE 25.3

The Registration and Cancellation section of the Account Settings page provides access to the controls that define who can create new user accounts.

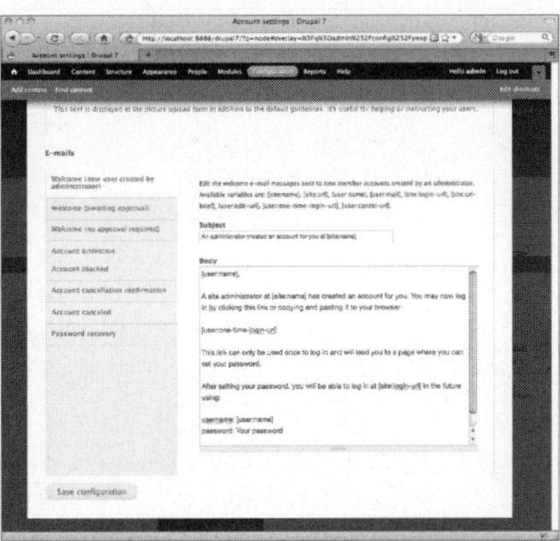

Cross-Reference

The remainder of the options on the Account Settings page are discussed in Chapter 23. ■

Drupal Authentication

Drupal's default user authentication is PHP-session-based. User credentials are stored in the site database. This basic form of authentication is sufficient for most sites, but if you need something more robust, you may want to consider implementing alternative authentication schemes.

OpenID is one of the most commonly used alternatives to the default authentication protocol. OpenID, however, is rarely used as a replacement for the default system; rather it is enabled and used to supplement the Drupal authentication system. Drupal's OpenID module is discussed in the next section of this chapter.

Tip

Another popular option is to use the Facebook Connect API for authentication. Visit Drupal.org to find modules that allow you to integrate this authentication protocol into your site. ■

If you require a more robust authentication system, you can add some third-party modules to your site, including support for LDAP.

Cross-Reference

Extending your site by adding new modules is discussed in Chapter 29. ■

Tip

If your site is expected to support a large number of authenticated users, you may want to look at external authentication protocols. If you decide to use the system default, you need to consider seriously your caching settings, or you may see some degradation in performance during periods of peak usage. ■

Using OpenID

Drupal 7 is distributed with support for the OpenID authentication protocol. If you enable this module, users who have an OpenID account can use their existing OpenID credentials to log into your Web site.

OpenID is useful in that it increases convenience for users who already have an OpenID account. Though the user still must register to get an account on your site (or be registered by the administrator), thereafter the user can use his OpenID credentials to log in, instead of having to remember a unique username and password for your site.

Note

OpenID relies on remote authentication, which means that your site must be able to communicate with an OpenID server. If your Drupal Web site is running in an intranet or other firewalled environment, it may not be able to employ OpenID without special configuration. ■

The functionality is powered by the OpenID module. The OpenID module is disabled in the default installation profiles. You can enable it easily, because there are no dependencies.

To enable the OpenID module, follow these steps:

1. **Log into your site as an administrator.**

   The admin interface loads in your browser.

2. **Select the Modules option from the Management menu.**

   The Modules Manager opens in your browser.

3. **Click the check box next to the OpenID module.**
4. **Click the Save Configuration button at the bottom of the page.**

   If you are successful, the OpenID module is enabled and a confirmation message appears at the top of the page.

Once enabled, OpenID becomes automatically available via a link below the login form. When the user clicks the Log in using OpenID link, the standard login form is replaced with an OpenID login field, as shown in Figure 25.4.

Users can click the Cancel OpenID login link to return to the default login form.

FIGURE 25.4

The OpenID login interface

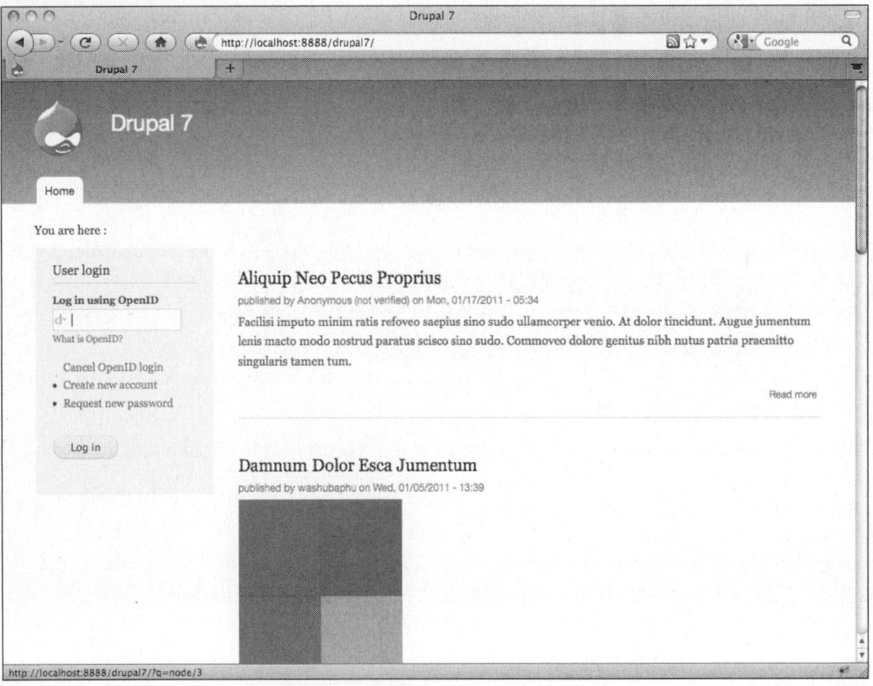

Note that before a user can use his OpenID credentials on your site, he must first associate his user account on your site with his OpenID server. This is done on the user's My Account page.

When OpenID is enabled, it adds another option tab to the My Account page. The tab displays basic information about OpenID and provides a form that can be used to associate one or more OpenID servers with the user account, as shown in Figure 25.5. A user who wants to use OpenID as a replacement to the standard Drupal username and password needs to first enter his OpenID server address on this page.

FIGURE 25.5

The OpenID tab on the My Account page

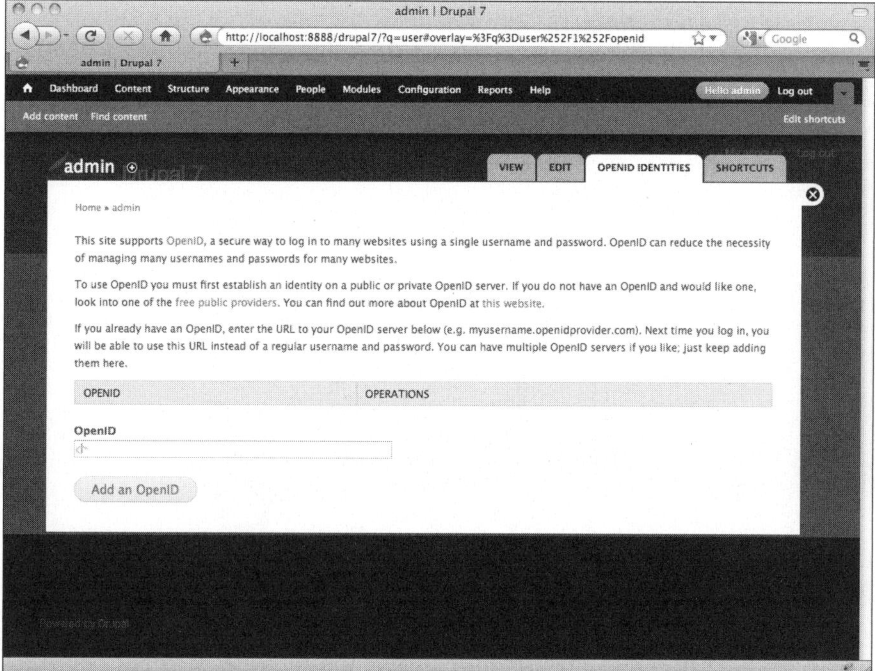

After the user has successfully paired his account on your site with his OpenID server, he can thereafter log in to your site without having to use the Drupal username and password combination.

Note

To learn more about OpenID, visit `http://openid.net/`. ■

Managing Notifications

Your Drupal system automatically generates notification e-mails in response to several circumstances. These are form e-mails, and they are sent only in response to the occurrence of specific events. In the default system, e-mails are provided for the following circumstances:

- Welcome (new user created by administrator)
- Welcome (awaiting approval)
- Welcome (no approval required)
- Account activation
- Account blocked
- Account cancellation notification
- Account canceled
- Password recovery

The system-generated e-mails are managed on the Account Settings page, as shown in Figure 25.6.

FIGURE 25.6

The E-mails section of the Account Settings page enables you to customize the system's notification e-mails.

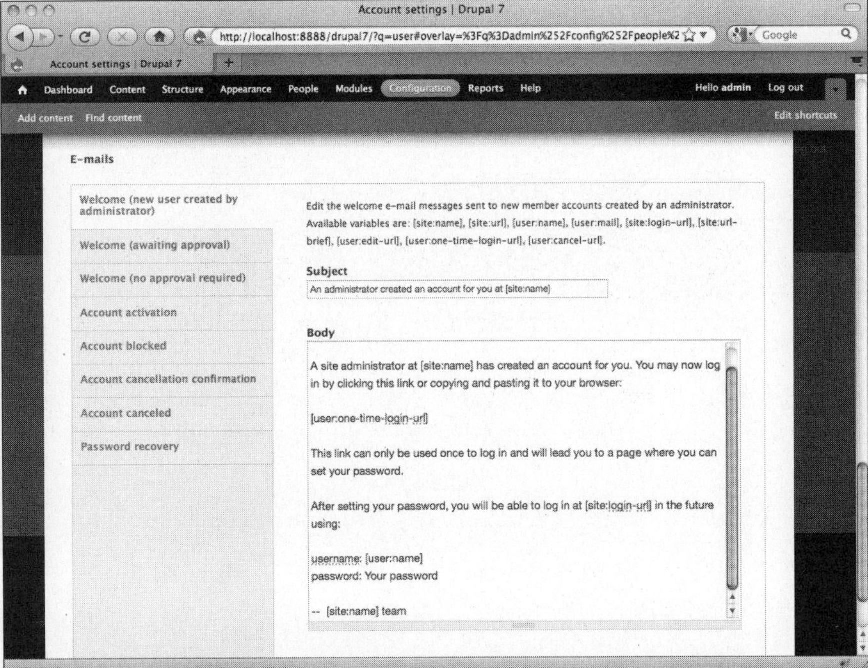

The contents of the default notification e-mails can be modified. In addition to text, they include a number of variables that allow you to control the contents of the message sent to the users.

Tip

The instructions at the top of each of the e-mail tabs include a list of the variables you can use in the e-mails. The options are: [site:name], [site:url], [user:name], [user:mail], [site:login-url], [site:url-brief], [user:edit-url], [user:one-time-login-url], and [user:cancel-url]. These variables allow you to insert dynamic text into your e-mail. The names are generally representative of the contents. If you choose to edit any of the e-mails, be careful that you don't delete variables that might be needed. ■

To modify any of the e-mails, simply make your changes in the E-mails section of the Account Settings page (refer to Figure 25.5) and click the Save configuration button.

As noted earlier in this chapter, Drupal sends verification e-mail to new users who register using the Create a new account function. If you want to disable this feature, you may do so by accessing the Account Settings page and unchecking the option Require e-mail verification when a visitor creates an account.

Note

While disabling the verification e-mail does lower a barrier to site membership, because it allows users to gain immediate access to the site, it also removes a layer of security. Though the security gained by this sort of verification process is not sufficient to stop someone intent on gaining fraudulent access, it can prevent automated bots and scripts from gaining access to your site. ■

Working with the User Login Function

The user login functionality is closely integrated with the user registration and the password request functionalities. These three functionalities typically appear together in either a block position or in the content area of the page.

Using the Login block

In the default configuration, Drupal's user login form is presented in a block. Like all other blocks in the system, the Login block can be displayed or hidden in response to the settings you specify in the Blocks Manager. The block also can be renamed and repositioned, again from within the Blocks Manager.

Cross-Reference

Working with blocks and the Blocks Manager is covered in detail in Chapter 7. ■

Using the Login page

In addition to the Login block, a login form also appears in the content area of Drupal pages. The Login page form appears as a tab at the top of the pages that display the User Registration form and the Request Password form, as shown in Figure 25.7.

If you do not want to use the Login block, you can send users directly to the Login page by adding a new Menu Item linking to the page.

Tip

Using a link to the Login page results in the user being redirected to their account page after completing the login process. In contrast, when you use the Login block, the user remains on the same page they started on when they logged in. ■

Cross-Reference

Working with menus and menu items is discussed in detail in Chapter 8. ■

FIGURE 25.7

The Login form shown here is displayed in the content area of the page.

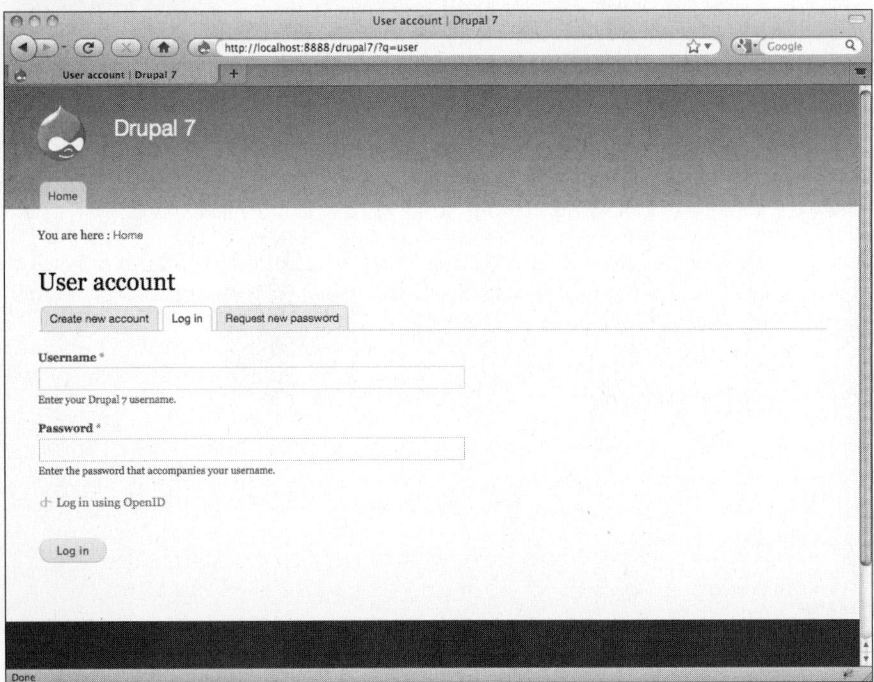

The Request Password function

Drupal provides an automated mechanism for assisting users who have forgotten their passwords. A user who needs access but cannot remember his password can click the Request new password link that appears under the Login form on the Login block (refer to Figure 25.7). Alternatively, the user can access the same function by clicking the Request new password tab on the Login page or the Create new account page, as you can see in Figure 25.8. In either event, the user is taken to the page shown in Figure 25.9.

FIGURE 25.8

The Request Password form

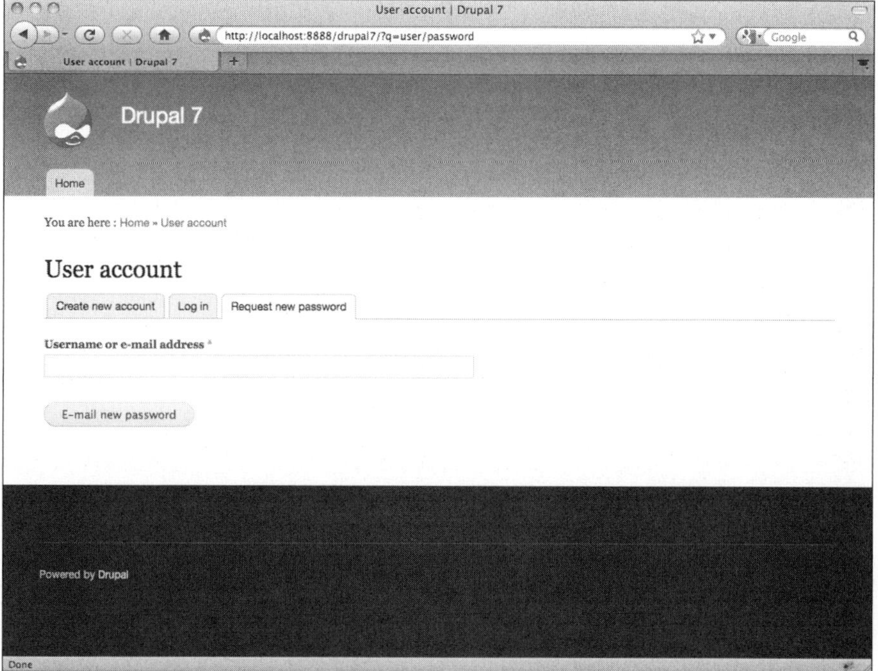

To use the function, the user simply enters either his username or registered e-mail address in the field on the form and clicks the button labeled E-mail new password. The system creates a single-use login for the user and e-mails the link to his registered e-mail address. After the user retrieves the e-mail, he can access the system by clicking the link in the e-mail. When the user clicks the link, he is taken to a page with instructions for creating a new password, as shown in Figure 25.9.

FIGURE 25.9

This page greets users when they click the link in the Password Request e-mail.

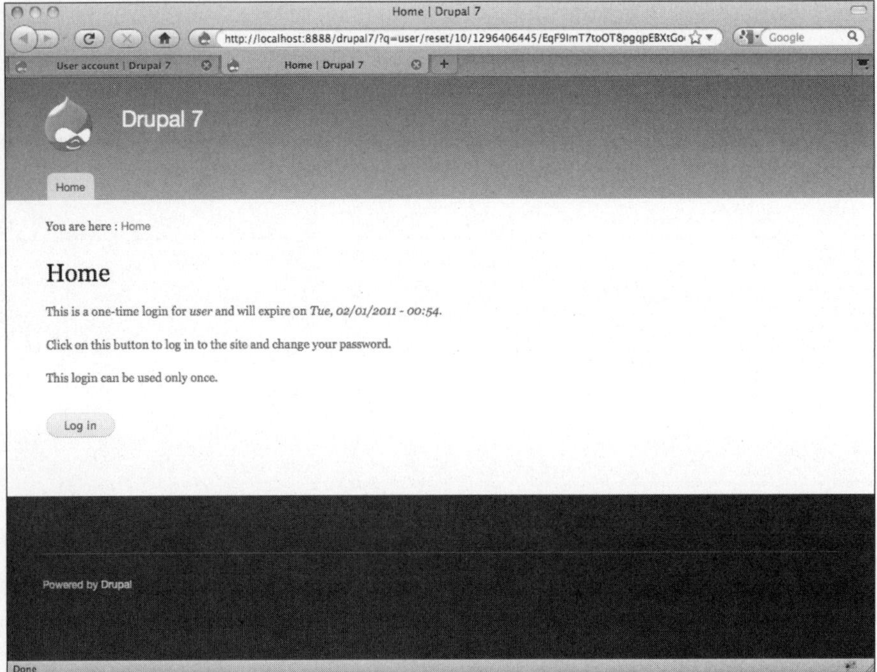

Styling the Display

There are no dedicated theming resources focused on the login, registration, and password reminder functionalities. If you want to modify the basic styling of these elements of your site, you are limited to what can be done by altering configuration settings and CSS selectors. If you want to make extensive modifications, you are forced to intercept and override the relevant functions that produce the output you see on the screen.

Note that the Login form presents two theming considerations: controlling the form display in the Login block and controlling the form display in the Login page. The User Registration form and the Password Reminder form are simpler to deal with because they appear only inside the content area of the page.

Table 25.1 lists the key functions for the login, registration, and request password forms.

TABLE 25.1

Key Functions and Their Locations and Descriptions

Function	Location	Description
user_login_block	modules/user/user.module	Produces the User Login block form
user_login	modules/user/user.module	Produces the login form seen in page view
user_register	modules/user/user.module	Produces the user registration form
user_pass	modules/user/user.pages.inc	Produces the password reminder form

Cross-Reference

Intercepting and overriding functions is covered in Chapter 30. ■

Summary

This chapter addressed user registration and related functionalities. I covered these topics:

- How to configure user registration
- How to work with the user registration form
- How to use the system-created notification e-mails
- How to work with the Login block and the Login page
- How to work with the request password form

Part VI

Customizing and Extending the System

IN THIS PART

CHAPTER 26

Customizing Drupal's Appearance

IN THIS CHAPTER

- Understanding how themes work
- Knowing the parts of a theme
- Adding new themes
- Customizing themes
- Creating a new theme
- Working with the admin theme

The Drupal CMS includes one of the most flexible and customizable systems for controlling the appearance of Web sites. The system is, however, somewhat complex and often viewed as non-intuitive. This chapter looks at the system, explains how it works, and shows how you can gain control of Drupal's theming system to create exactly what you want on the screen.

Some of the techniques discussed in this chapter require skills in HTML, CSS, and PHP. You also need an editing program that allows you to make changes to your Drupal site's theme files.

Understanding How Themes Work

A theme is a collection of files that are responsible for the look and feel of a Drupal site. Themes create the interface you see on both the front end and the back end of a Drupal site. Although a theme does not itself create the output you see on the page, it does provide the positioning and the styling for that output. The theme also can be used to select which output should be displayed and on which pages.

The layout and styling in a theme are handled by HTML and CSS. The selection of the output and the conditions placed on that output are handled by PHP. To make all this work together smoothly, Drupal relies on a theme engine known as PHPTemplate. The theme engine works behind the scenes. As a site administrator or developer, you never need to be concerned about modifying any of the files related to the PHPTemplate theme engine; the engine is part of the core and should not be modified. You do, however, need to work with HTML, CSS, and basic PHP to customize a Drupal theme.

Themes typically involve an assortment of files, some with odd file extensions. The various file types and the directory structure are discussed in the next section.

Knowing the Parts of a Theme

Drupal's theming system is quite flexible and allows the theme developer a great deal of latitude in how to approach creating and customizing themes. The PHPTemplate theming engine does much of the hard work involved in displaying the pages. As a result, only a few items are required to create a new theme. However, many options can be employed to customize the theme to your needs. All in all, the theming system can be as simple, or as complex, as you wish. The key is learning how it works and what options are available to you.

The default themes demonstrate the variety of approaches that are possible. In this section, I look at the basic parts of themes and how they are implemented in the default system.

Tip

Despite a lack of strict rules governing theme creation, certain best practices have emerged and should be respected, particularly where you expect others to use or maintain your themes. Accordingly, best practices are highlighted in the text, and you are encouraged to adopt these practices. ■

Directory structure

The default themes are kept in the `/themes` directory at the root of the Drupal installation, as shown in Figure 26.1. The `/themes` directory includes separate folders for each of the default themes: `/bartik`, `/garland`, `/seven`, and `/stark`. The directory also contains a subdirectory named `/engines` that contains the files for the PHPtemplate theme engine.

Note

In the `/themes` directory is a directory named `/tests`. The `/tests` directory contains theme files that are part of the Drupal core testing framework—that is, theme files used by the Drupal team. The themes in this file are not intended for use on the site and are not included in the administration interface. Though you aren't likely to ever use these, leave them in place. ■

If you add new themes to your Drupal installation, you can place them in either the /themes directory or inside the `/sites/all/themes` directory. A better practice is to use the `/sites/all/themes` directory, because this not only segregates your new themes from the default core themes, but it also makes those themes available to all sites. The latter is essential in cases where you are running multiple sites off one Drupal installation.

FIGURE 26.1

The directory structure relevant to themes

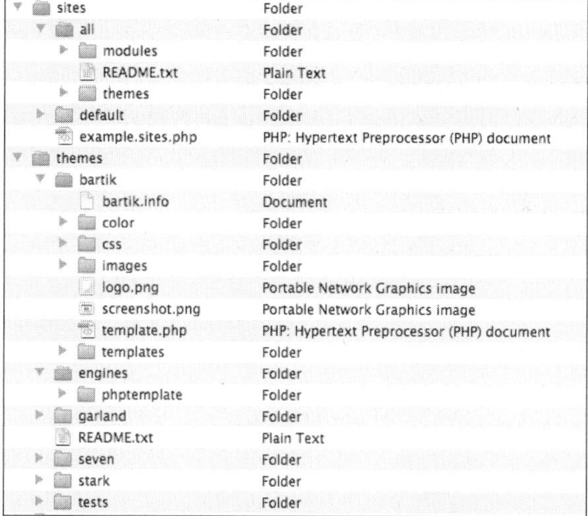

Note

With each new release, the theming system in Drupal continues to evolve. A number of refinements have been introduced in Drupal 7. Among the most noteworthy changes are the elimination of the `box.tpl.php` **file, the renaming of the primary and secondary links, and the removal of the mission statement and the footer message. There are numerous other changes. You can review a complete list at** `http://drupal.org/node/254940`. ■

Each theme always has its own distinct directory in which the files for that theme are stored. Inside that directory, you also may find additional directories. How you handle the organizational structure inside the individual theme's directory is up to you; there is no set rule concerning the creation of subdirectories inside your primary theme directory. That said, the Bartik theme directory provides an instructive best-practices example. The bartik directory contains four additional subdirectories (refer to Figure 26.1):

- **color:** Contains the files needed to implement the Color module functionality seen in the Theme Configuration Manager
- **css:** Contains all the theme-specific CSS files
- **images:** Contains all the images used by the Bartik theme
- **templates:** Contains all the Bartik theme's template files

Although none of the subdirectories are necessary to create a theme, the `/color` directory is needed to implement the optional Color module. Bartik's use of multiple directories is a convenient organizational schema. If you are creating a theme that others may have to maintain, the structure used by Bartik is useful and worth emulating.

Note

To learn how to implement the Color module functionality in your theme, check out the official documentation at `http://drupal.org/node/108459`. ■

The theme files

As noted above, a theme is a collection of files. Within that collection of files, you are likely to see a variety of file extensions. In addition to the many image formats that may appear—.gif, .jpg, .png—you also see some file types that may not be familiar. Table 26.1 lists the most common file types associated with themes and explains briefly their function.

TABLE 26.1

Extensions Used in Themes

File Extension	Purpose
.info	The theme's info file holds information describing the theme. The file is necessary for the system to identify the theme and assess its compatibility and required elements. This file type is discussed further later in this chapter.
.tpl.php	This file extension denotes a template file. These files are discussed in depth in the section that follows immediately. Although .tpl.php files are not officially required to create a theme, as a practical matter they are always present.
.js	This indicates a JavaScript file. It's not required, but is frequently seen.
.ico	This is a specialty file type used for shortcut icons; it is not required.
.php	This indicates PHP files. It's seen in themes almost exclusively in the form of the template.php file.
.css	These are cascading style sheets for the theme. Although not officially required, they are necessary if you want to have any control over your theme's styles.

In the sections that follow, I look more closely at the key files that affect the layout and styling of your themes.

The template files

Virtually all PHPTemplate-based themes include one or more template files. The template files are recognized by their unique file extension: `.tpl.php`.

Template files supply the layout frameworks for pages, groups of page, or simply parts of pages. The default Drupal system comes with a number of templates. The default templates are located in a variety of places, primarily in the various modules' directories. If the theme developer provides no template files inside the theme, the default files are used by the Drupal system.

Template files placed inside the theme directory take precedence over the default template files and are used by the system when that theme is active. This is a basic premise of Drupal theming and the key to creating custom output for individual themes. By creating custom templates to override the default templates, your output can be as simple, or as complex, as you wish.

Tip

Template files and CSS files placed in the active theme's directory take precedence over the default template and CSS files located in the core or in contributed modules. ■

The number and nature of the template files associated with a theme are the result of decisions made by the theme developer. As you look at the default theme directories, you can see a number of common templates. One of the most frequently used templates is `page.tpl.php`. The file provides a template for displaying a single Drupal page. If this file is present in a theme, it functions as the default page template. Other templates may be controlling the display of specific pages or portions of pages, but the `page.tpl.php` file is one of the key files in the theme.

Note

Another of the system's key `tpl.php` files is `html.tpl.php`. The file is a resource used by all themes in the system; it provides the `doctype`, `html`, `head`, and `body` tags for all themes. The file is located in the `/modules/system` folder. While it can be done, overriding this file is generally not recommended because it may cause unexpected results in your system. ■

Staying with the Bartik theme as an example, open the templates subdirectory inside the `/bartik` directory. Inside that subdirectory, you see a list of the templates used by Bartik:

- **comment-wrapper.tpl.php:** This template provides a container for comment-type content, including the posts in the forum.
- **comment.tpl.php:** This template provides formatting for comments.
- **maintenance-page.tpl.php:** This template provides a page that displays when the site is taken offline by the administrator.
- **node.tpl.php:** This template handles the display of nodes.
- **page.tpl.php:** This is the primary template for handling page display.

If you look inside the other theme directories, you see that each has a different approach to templates. In any case, whenever you see a template file inside the theme, you know the theme developer has included it because he wants to provide his own styling and layout, rather than relying on the system's default templates.

Note

There are other ways to override the default Drupal styling; you don't always need, or want, to create custom templates. Other approaches, and their pros and cons, are discussed later in this chapter. ■

A typical page in Drupal is composed of multiple templates working in harmony. The `page.tpl.php` template, for example, includes as part of its output multiple templates: templates for the regions, for the nodes, for the blocks, for the comments, and for the various module output seen on the screen. In the sections that follow, I discuss how you can customize any of these templates, giving you the power to control the page in whole or in part, as suits your needs.

The theme CSS

The default Drupal system includes a large number of style sheets. Most themes will include one or more style sheets that contain the style definitions that are unique to that theme. The system treats style sheets in the same way it treats templates: where no CSS is provided in the theme, the default style sheets are applied.

If you look at the Bartik theme files, you can see inside the `/css` subdirectory the following:

- **colors.css:** Styles needed for the Color module functionality
- **ie-rtl.css:** Styles needed to help ensure a consistent display for the site when viewed from the Internet Explorer browser with text orientation set for right-to-left
- **ie.css:** Styles needed to help ensure a consistent display for the site when viewed from the Internet Explorer browser in normal left-to-right orientation
- **ie6.css:** Styles needed for consistent display in the Internet Explorer 6 browser
- **layout-rtl.css:** Styles used when the test orientation of the site is set to right-to-left
- **layout.css:** Styles concerned with the layout of the page
- **maintenance-page.css:** Styles used by the maintenance page
- **print.css:** Styles that are used by the print-friendly versions of the pages
- **style-rtl.css:** Additional styles used when the text orientation is set to right-to-left
- **style.css:** A collection of the additional styles needed for the theme

The selection of CSS files varies from theme to theme, but most themes include at least a `style.css` file.

The role of the template.php file

Many themes also include a file named `template.php`. Despite the name, this file does not provide a page template for your site. Rather, the `template.php` file is used to hold a variety of more advanced snippets of code. The purpose and scope of the snippets vary from theme to theme, and there is no set requirement. Indeed, this file is not even required for a theme to function properly.

The snippets of code you see inside the `template.php` file are generally an assortment of overrides to themable functions, as well as a collection of process and preprocess functions. Put simply, the file provides a vehicle for the themer to override certain core styles and functions. Later in this chapter, I look at overriding themable functions and at dealing with process variables.

Adding New Themes

Your Drupal site comes with only a few themes, but you can add more to the installation at any time, directly from within the admin interface. New themes can be found either on the official Drupal site or an assortment of third-party sites.

Tip

Not all themes are created equal. Some themes are better at certain types of layout, others at certain types of content. For example, if you are running a directory or portal site, select a theme with sufficient regions so you can position the various blocks you need. In contrast, your requirements might be very different if you want a simple marketing site or a blog. ■

Before beginning the installation process, described below, you need to either obtain the URL of the installation file or you must download the installation file to your local machine. If you have downloaded the theme package, do not extract (unzip) it if you want to use the automatic installer in the Theme Manager.

Caution

Before you install a new theme, make sure to check for version compatibility. Themes created for Drupal 5 or Drupal 6 do not work properly with Drupal 7! Moreover, it is always a good idea to review the information on the theme project page and check to see if the theme includes a README file. Sometimes you discover prerequisites that must be met before the theme functions fully. ■

To add a new theme to the system, follow these steps:

1. **Log into your Web site as an administrator.**

   The admin interface loads in your browser.
2. **Select the Appearance option from the Management menu.**

   The Theme Manager opens in your browser.
3. **Click the Install new theme link at the top left of the overlay.**

   The theme installation page opens, as shown in Figure 26.2.
4. **If you have downloaded the theme installation package to your local machine, click the Browse button.**

   The file upload page pops up.
5. **Use the upload page box to find the installation file you want to upload; select it, and click the Open button.**

   The upload page closes, and you see the path to the installation file in the field next to the Browse button.
6. **If you have not downloaded the installation file, but you know the URL for the installation package, type it into the field marked Install from a URL.**
7. **Click the Install button.**

   The system uploads the theme and displays a confirmation message on the screen.

FIGURE 26.2

The theme installation page inside the Theme Manager

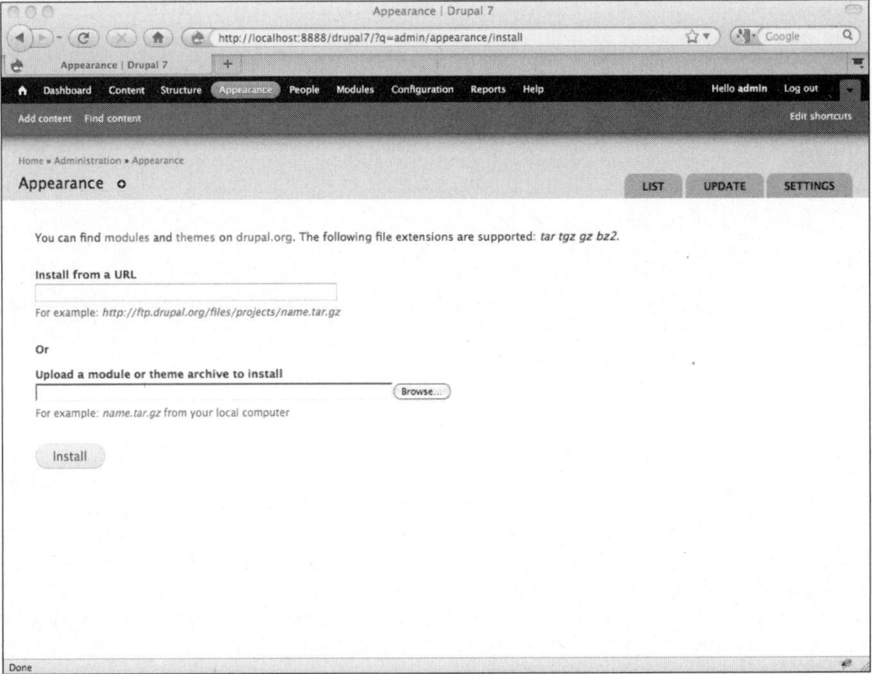

Note

You also can install themes manually by unzipping the theme package and copying the resulting directory to the `/sites/all/themes` directory on your server. ■

Note

Don't forget that the theme is not available for use until you enable it in the Theme Manager. ■

Finding New Themes

With the growing popularity of Drupal, it is not surprising that there has been an increase in the number of themes available. Some theme projects are open source and are maintained on the official Drupal site. Other themes are commercial and must be purchased from the vendor. Here are some ideas of where you can begin your search.

Drupal.org

The official Drupal site includes a repository of free themes that can be downloaded and installed on your site. For most people, this is the primary source of new theme files. The themes are searchable and can be filtered by version compatibility. Moreover, themes hosted on Drupal.org often have supplemental resources, comments, and some degree of community support. This is a great source of themes and a very good place to start your search. To learn more, visit `http://drupal.org/project/themes`.

Acquia.com

The Acquia Drupal bundle includes several unique themes. At the time of this writing, the Acquia themes could not be downloaded separately from the Acquia site; they could, however, be obtained from the themes section of Drupal.org.

Dream Template

Dream Template has more than 4,000 Web designs. The site provides designs only, not ready-to-use Drupal themes, so if you want to use a design you see here, you first need to convert it into a Drupal theme and install it on your site. Prices for their designs vary widely, depending largely on whether you want exclusive rights to the design. To learn more, visit `www.dreamtemplate.com`.

FusionDrupalThemes.com

Fusion Themes is the packaged theme business run by Top Notch Themes. Their theme packages exhibit some of the best quality code in the commercial Drupal theme space as well as some of the most versatile feature sets. Though the selection of themes is somewhat limited compared to others in this list, the themes provide a great starting point for your Drupal design. The parent company also supplies customization and custom theme development.

TemplateMonster.com

Template Monster is one of largest providers of ready-to-use commercial templates on the Web. They also provide Drupal themes. At the time of this writing, more than 500 themes are in their system, but none for Drupal 7; that is certain to change. Template Monster themes vary widely in pricing and cover an equally wide range of styles. The package you purchase should contain all the necessary elements to simply install it and go, but any customization must be done on your own. Pricing depends on whether you simply want to use the theme or if you want exclusive ownership of the theme. Note that quality varies widely in their themes and there has been some criticism of both the quality of their code and their support.

continued

continued

Theme Garden

The Drupal Theme Garden is not an official site, but it is closely aligned with the official Drupal theme releases. The themes listed on the site are drawn from the themes on the official Drupal site. The purpose of the Theme Garden is to provide you with a way to preview a Drupal theme on a live Drupal installation, without having to first download it and install it. Note that the Theme Garden site does not host the themes for download; if you find a theme you like, you need to download the theme package from Drupal.org. At the time this was written the site had yet to be updated for Drupal 7. To learn more, visit `www.themegarden.org`.

All the rest...

A search of the Web turns up a large number of theme providers. Sadly, many of them are simply reproducing the themes listed on Drupal.org. Look carefully before grabbing themes from third-party sites. If the theme exists on Drupal.org, you are better off getting the files from the official site.

Customizing Themes

Drupal themes typically include a variety of configuration options that can be controlled from within the admin system's Theme Manager. While making changes to a theme through the configuration options requires no programming skills, the options are limited and the configurable features vary from theme to theme, depending on the choices made by the theme developer when the theme was created.

If you require more in-depth customization than what is offered by the Theme Manager, you can accomplish much by simply modifying the theme's style sheets or template files. Although making changes to the code in the theme's files does require more skill, you can, with a little effort, do much.

In the sections that follow, I cover both the basic configuration options and how to make changes to the common theme files. In later sections, we look at more advanced options.

Modifying themes through configuration

The Drupal system provides the Theme Manager as a tool for site administrators to enable, disable, and configure themes. The theme customization options contained in the Theme Manager are somewhat limited, and their reach is determined by the decisions made by the theme developer; some theme developers create themes with more configuration features than others.

Default Drupal theme configuration essentially allows you to control the visibility of certain site features, like the automatic display of elements on the page or the choice of logo and shortcut icon. These are relatively minor points and the configuration options apply to all pages that use the theme. The changes are not, in other words, very granular. More complex customization requires that you work with the site's code, as discussed later in this chapter.

Note

Some contributed themes offer a richer choice of configuration options than the default themes. Some allow you to set font styling, page layout, and much more. If you want to customize your site but do not want to work with the code, seek out themes that offer the widest range of configuration flexibility. ■

In addition to the options present in the Theme Manager, you also can achieve control over the look and feel of your site and inject some variety through creative use of the Blocks Manager. Using the Blocks Manager you can show, hide, and position blocks in the regions on the page, and you can vary that presentation from page to page or from user to user.

Cross-Reference

Working with the Blocks Manager is covered in Chapter 7. ■

In Chapter 4, I covered basic site configuration, including the global and theme-specific configuration options. The upcoming discussion amplifies some points from that general chapter.

Changing page element options

To view the theme configuration options, simply access the Theme Manager and click the Settings tab. As discussed in Chapter 4, there are both global and theme-specific configuration settings. Among the options are a collection of controls related to page elements. In Figure 26.3, you can see the Toggle Display section of the theme configuration options.

Cross-Reference

The controls contained in the Toggle Display section of the theme configuration page are discussed in detail in Chapter 4. ■

Using the controls in the Toggle Display section, you can remove elements from display by your theme. By default, all the options are enabled. If you do not need or want them, uncheck the options that are unnecessary.

Changing the logo

The default Drupal themes come bundled with simple Drupal logos that are displayed by the themes. You can hide this logo by using the Toggle Display options noted above or you can upload your own logo to display by using the options in the Logo Image Settings section of the theme configuration page.

FIGURE 26.3

The Toggle Display options are used to show or hide certain page elements.

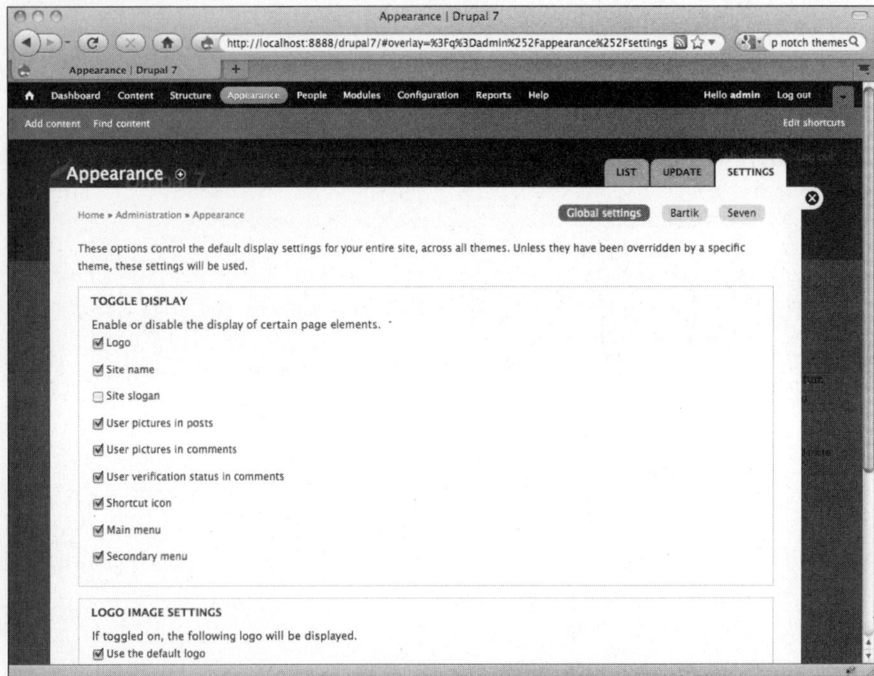

To replace the Drupal logo of the Bartik theme with the logo of your choice, follow these steps:

1. **Log into your site as an administrator.**

   The admin interface loads in your browser.

2. **Select the Appearance option from the Management menu.**

   The Theme Manager opens in your browser.

3. **Click the Settings tab on the top right of the overlay.**

   The global theme configuration page opens.

4. **Click the Bartik button at the top right of the Settings tabs.**

   The theme specific configuration page loads.

5. **Scroll down to the Logo Image Settings, and uncheck the option.**

   The logo upload fields display on the page, as shown in Figure 26.4.

6. **Click the Browse button.**

   The file upload page pops up.

7. **Use the upload page to find the image you want to upload for the logo; select it, and click the Open button.**

   The upload page closes, and you see the path to the logo image in the Upload logo image field.

8. **Click the Save configuration button.**

   The system uploads the image and displays a confirmation message on the screen.

FIGURE 26.4

The Logo Image Settings page as it appears when you elect to upload your own logo to replace the default logo

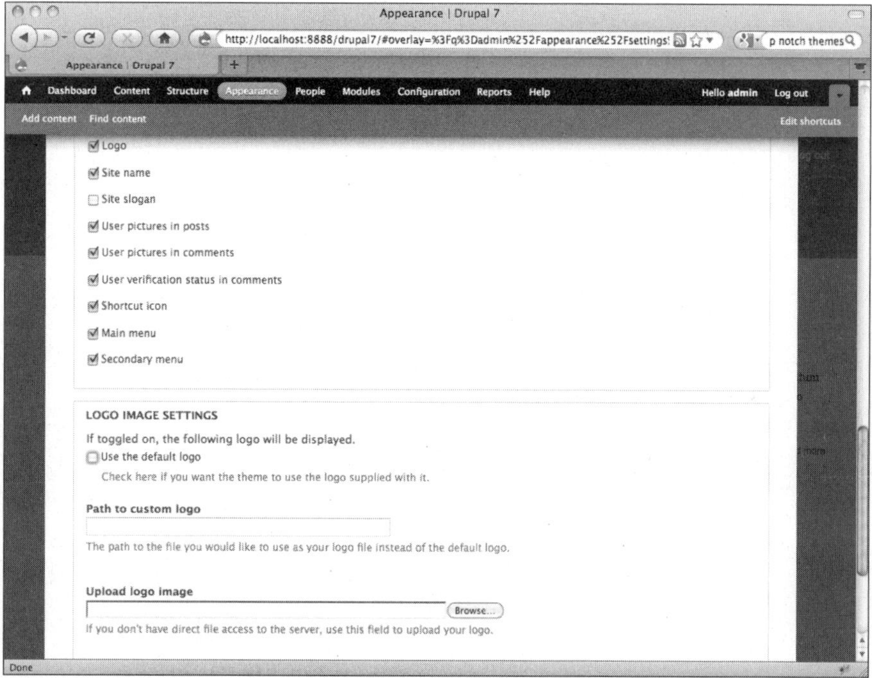

Tip

When uploading your own logo, you must pay some attention to the size and dimensions of the artwork you are uploading. The best course is to look at the dimensions of the original logo and try to upload something close, to avoid breaking the layout. The file size is also an issue because it can impact your site performance and page-loading speed; the smaller the file size, the better. ■

Using the Color module

Several of Drupal's default themes use the Color module option. The Color module allows the site administrator to adjust the colors used by the theme without having to resort to modifying the CSS; the changes can be made directly from inside the Theme Manager.

Not all themes offer the Color module. The decision of whether to include this feature is up to the theme developer. Moreover, because the functionality relies on a module, if that module has been disabled, the functionality is not available to any themes on the site.

To access the Color module controls, visit the theme-specific configuration manager. The controls are labeled Color Scheme, as shown in Figure 26.5.

Using the Color module, you can adjust the color of any of the following items in your theme:

- Main background
- Link color
- Header top
- Header bottom
- Text color
- Sidebar backgrounds
- Sidebar borders
- Footer background
- Title and slogan

Making changes to the site's color scheme is a simple matter. You simply select the name of the portion of the theme you want to modify, and then click and drag the small circles inside the color wheel.

A combo box control at the top of the list of controls (refer to Figure 26.5) contains a selection of preset color schemes. You can use one of the preset schemes as it is, or you can modify an existing scheme, or you can select the Custom option from the combo box and control all the settings yourself.

Tip

The lock icons you see next to each of the items allows you to lock the color ratio between two or more items in the color scheme; that way, as you change one color, it also affects the other colors that are locked to that control. This option simplifies creating harmonious color schemes. ■

FIGURE 26.5

The Color module controls, shown here in the theme-specific configuration page in the Bartik theme

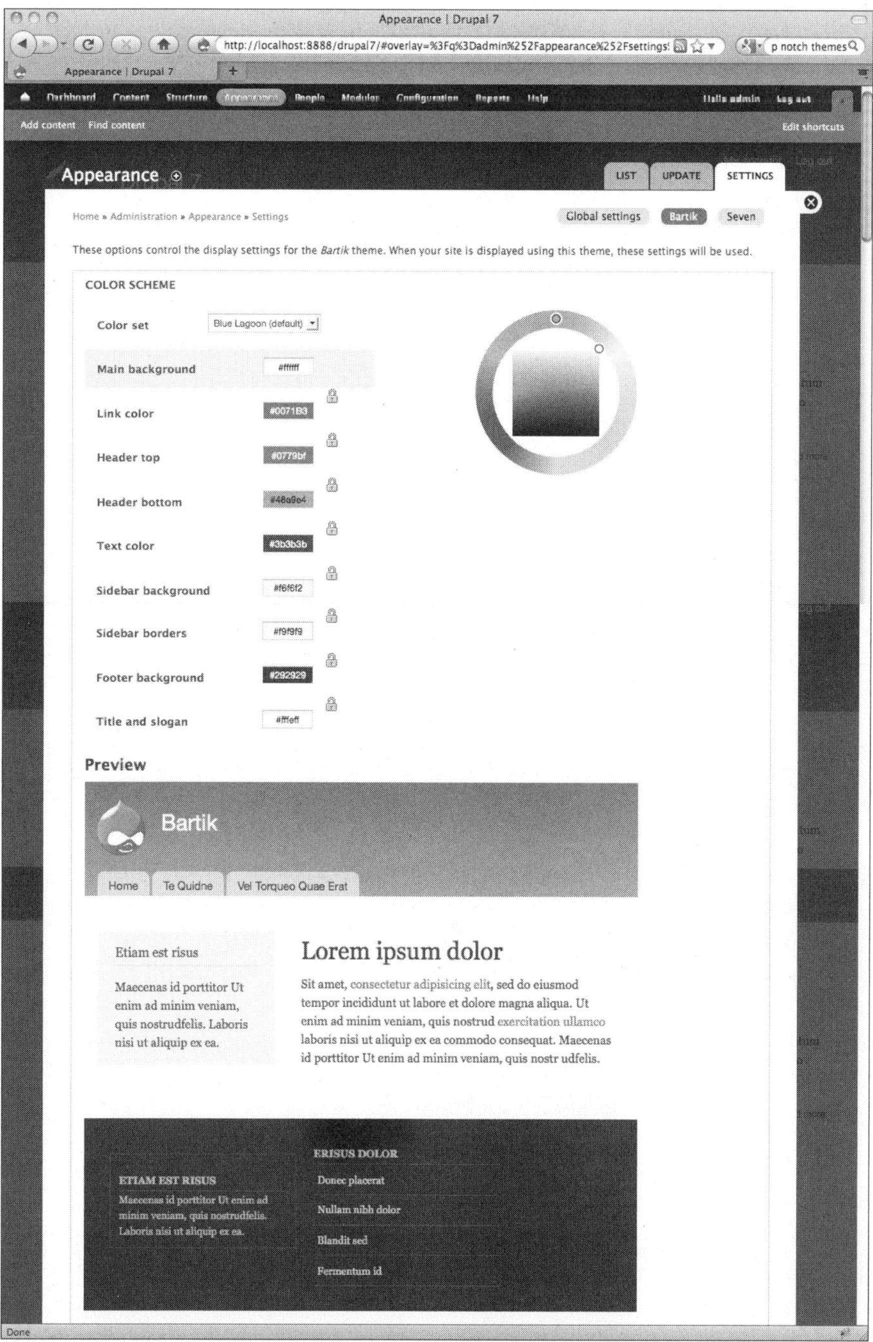

Modifying themes by changing the code

As stated in the previous section, if you want to really gain control over your themes, you need to dig into the code of the theme files. The process is not as daunting as it may sound. You can do a tremendous amount with just a little CSS knowledge. Moreover, if you are willing to invest a bit more time to learn how to work with the templates and functions, you can gain complete control over the presentation layer of your site.

Before I get into making changes to the code in the core themes, you need to learn the process involved in creating sub-themes. Even if you only plan to modify a small part of a single file contained within the default themes, you do not want to change the original theme's files. The best practice is to create a sub-theme and make your changes to it, leaving the original theme files intact.

Simply put, a sub-theme is a theme that is based upon another theme. The sub-theme inherits the resources included with the other theme, allowing you to quickly create a new theme and customize it easily. Sub-theme creation is the preferred method of customizing the default Drupal themes and is the fast and easy way to modify virtually any theme. The principal advantage of this approach is that the files of the original theme are kept intact and can be upgraded safely and without complication.

Note

The original theme upon which a sub-theme is premised is often referred to as the base theme. Certain themes have been created specifically for use as base themes. These are often called starter themes because they have a number of features that fast-track sub-theme creation and make it easy for theme developers to create advanced themes without having to do the work from scratch. ■

Let's assume you want to use the Bartik theme and that the changes you want to make are great enough that they cannot be met by simply modifying the theme configuration. Begin by creating a sub-theme to hold your changes:

1. **Access the server, and navigate to the directory where you placed the Drupal core files.**
2. **Access the /themes directory, and make a copy of the /bartik directory.**
3. **Paste the /bartik directory inside of /sites/all/themes, and rename the directory to /bartik2.**
4. **Create a new blank file and name it bartik2.css. Place it inside the /bartik2/css directory.**
5. **Rename the file from bartik.info to bartik2.info.**
6. **Open the file bartik2.info for editing.**
7. **Change the name entry from** Bartik **to** Bartik2.
8. **Change the description entry as you wish (this data appears in the Theme Manager as the theme's description text).**

9. **Delete the lines for package and version.**
10. **Add a new line:** base theme = bartik.
11. **Declare the new stylesheet by adding the line:** `stylesheets[all][] = css/bartik2.css`.
12. **Delete all other stylesheet declarations in the .info file.**
13. **Save and close bartik2.info.**
14. **Delete from the /bartik2 directory any files you do not intend to modify.**
15. **Run a search and replace on the files within the /bartik2 directory to change all occurrences of** bartik **to** bartik2.
16. **Save and close the file.**
17. **Log in to the admin system of your site.**

    The Management menu appears at the top of the page.
18. **Select the Appearance option from the Management menu.**

    The Theme Manager opens in your browser; you should see the new Bartik2 theme listed under the heading Disabled Themes.
19. **Find the Bartik2 theme, and click the Enable and set default link.**

    Bartik2 becomes the default theme.

Note

The key point you should take away is this: Do not make your changes to the core files. Preserve the integrity of the core, and segregate your changes in one place! If you want to change a file in the original Bartik theme, all you need to do now is copy that file into the new Bartik2 directory and edit it there—don't change the name. The new version of the file is used by the system in place of the original. ■

With your new version of Bartik in place (Bartik2), you can now work with impunity; the changes you make do not affect the core files, and if you should need to roll back your changes at any point, you have a backup copy of the original files. By setting Bartik2 as the active theme, you can see your changes as you work.

In the sections that follow, I use the new Bartik2 theme as our example. I go through changing the CSS and customizing the templates in that theme.

Customizing the CSS

Most aspects of your Drupal site are impacted by the styles defined in the system's CSS files. One of the easiest and most powerful ways of customizing your site is by making changes to the style sheets. Layout, text styles and sizes, colors, backgrounds, and borders are all controlled by the CSS. Indeed, you may find that many of your customization needs can be met by a combination of creative theme configuration management and CSS customization.

CSS Glossary

Before I go any further, it's worth a quick note to refresh your CSS vocabulary.

Style sheet

Style sheets are discreet files holding one or more selectors. The style sheets are found throughout the Drupal system, including in the theme directories. Style sheet files are easily recognizable because they all end with the file extension .css.

Selector

These are the style definitions inside the style sheets. For example, if you want to style the HTML tag `H1`, you add to your style sheet a selector named `H1`.

Property

These are specific attributes of the selectors. For example, if the selector is `H1`, then a typical property is `font-family`.

Value

The value is the definition given for a specific property. For example, you might define the value for the property `font-family`, as `font-family:arial;`.

Tip

Although you don't have to be a CSS ninja to work with Drupal themes, it certainly helps! The system's style sheets are numerous and complicated. Still, if you stick to the fundamental principles outlined in this chapter, you should be able to manage without much trouble. The Firebug extension for the Firefox browser also can be a big help when working with the styles. ■

CSS changes typically take one of two paths: editing the existing theme's styles or creating new styles to override some of the many default styles found in the core or in contributed modules.

Modifying the CSS inside a theme

The default themes include a number of CSS files. The files contain styles unique to the template. The Bartik theme, for example, contains a total of 10 style sheets, all located inside the /css directory. The Bartik styles are grouped by general function, with each style sheet holding only those styles related to a specific function. Most of the generic HTML and text styles are found in the `style.css` file; the selectors related to the structure of the content on the page are kept in `layout.css`.

Tip

When working with the CSS, make sure you have disabled CSS Optimization. When the feature is enabled, you may not be able to see the changes that you make, because the CSS has been aggregated and cached. You can enable the feature again after you finish your work. To learn how to handle CSS Optimization and other Performance settings, see Chapter 32. ■

You can edit the selectors contained in the theme's style sheets to suit your needs. For example, let's assume you want to change the main font style used in Bartik2; instead of using the basic serif family of fonts, you want to use something else. To make this change, do the following:

1. **Locate your Drupal installation on the server, and access the /css directory in the original Bartik theme.**
2. **Open the file style.css.**
3. **Find and copy this selector:**

   ```
   body, #site-slogan, .ui-widget {
      font-family: Georgia, "Times New Roman", Times, serif;
   }
   ```
4. **Access the /bartik2/css directory and open the file bartik2.css for editing.**
5. **Paste the selector into the bartik2.css file.**
6. **Make the changes to the font-family line of the selector to substitute the fonts you prefer.**
7. **Save your changes.**

   Your changes should now be visible on the site.

When you create a selector with the same name as one located in the base theme's style sheets or in the core, the new selector located in the active theme is given precedence over the original.

Note

In Drupal parlance, this is commonly called creating an override. ■

Similarly, if you want to override an entire style sheet in the base theme, you can do so by placing a new style sheet of the same name as the original inside the active theme's directory.

Adding new selectors is even simpler. To add a new selector to your theme, just place it inside the new sub-theme's style sheet.

Overriding styles in the core or contributed modules

The Drupal core contains a large number of style sheets. If you have added third-party modules to your site, you may also find additional style sheets contained in those modules. Don't forget that the CSS within the theme supplies only the theme-specific styling. When no style is defined in the theme's CSS, Drupal uses the styles defined in the system's many CSS files. If you cannot find the selector you want to modify in the theme's CSS, odds are good that it exists in one of the default core CSS files or in the CSS that accompanies a contributed module.

If you want to make changes to the selectors contained in style sheets outside the theme, you can do so by overriding those selectors or style sheets from within the theme. As we saw in the section immediately above, you can override a selector simply by placing your own version of the selectors inside the theme's CSS files. When more than one definition for a style exists and there is a conflict between them, Drupal gives preference to the selector that is placed in the active theme directory.

Note

It makes no difference which of the theme's style sheets you use for your CSS overrides. Although the grouped and organized style sheet structure used in Bartik is useful, it is not obligatory. If you want to override the entire style sheet from the core or a contributed module, you may do so by copying the style sheet to the theme directory and then adding the style sheet to the .info file, as discussed in the next section. The only downside to overriding the entire style sheet is that the style sheet is always loaded. If you need to make loading the style sheet conditional, you need to investigate adding it to the `template.php` file using `hook_css_alter`, as discussed at `http://api.drupal.org/api/drupal/modules--system--system.api.php/function/hook_css_alter/7`. ■

Tip

Although the system prefers that the selectors be placed in the theme's style sheets—that is, the selectors in the theme CSS take precedence over selectors of the same name located in the core or the contributed modules—don't forget that style sheets cascade. When the style is applied, the system adds together all the style sheets and applies the sum of the selector's properties. Hence, if the core provides a property for a selector that is not contradicted by the theme's definition of the selector, the system defines the style as including the uncontradicted properties even though other properties have been overridden. Overlooking the impact of style cascades is one of the most common sources of frustration when styling in Drupal. ■

Adding new style sheets

The style sheets for your theme are defined in the .info file. Look at the `bartik.info` file, located in the /bartik theme directory. In that file, notice the following lines, which include the CSS used by the Bartik theme:

```
style sheets[all][] = css/layout.css
style sheets[all][] = css/style.css
style sheets[all][] = css/colors.css
style sheets[print][] = css/print.css
```

Note the syntax used: First comes the *key* that declares that we are dealing with `style sheets`. This is followed by the *media property*, which is set off with brackets `[]`. Finally, the statements give the relative path for the style sheet.

Note

The various media types you can use are defined by the W3C standards. You can view a list of all the options by visiting `http://www.w3.org/TR/CSS21/media.html`. ■

For example, let's assume you want to create a new style sheet with styles tailored for use with mobile devices. To accomplish the task, follow these steps:

1. **Access your Drupal installation on the server and open the file bartik2.info for editing.**
2. **Create a new blank file, name it *mobile.css*, and place it inside the /css directory.**
3. **Add the following line of code, immediately below the list of style sheets.**

   ```
   style sheets[handheld][] = css/mobile.css
   ```

4. **Save bartik2.info, and close the file.**
5. **You must next clear the cache on the site for changes to the .info file to be recognized by the system. To do this, log into your site as an administrator.**

   The Management menu appears at the top of the page.

6. **Select the Configuration option from the Management menu.**

   The Configuration Manager opens in your browser.

7. **Click the Performance option under the Development group.**

   The Performance Manager opens in your browser.

8. **Click the button labeled Clear all caches at the top of the page.**

   The system clears all cached data and displays a confirmation message.

At the end of these steps, your new style sheet is ready for you to add selectors.

Note

Drupal now recommends adding new style sheets through the preprocess function `drupal_add_css`. **But this method is more complex to execute. Using the function is not a requirement; you can still add style sheets via the** `.info` **file, but in the event you are using a large number of style sheets and fear you may run up against Internet Explorer's limitation of no more than 31 style sheets, you should use this more complicated technique for including your new style sheets. Learn more by visiting** `http://api.drupal.org/api/drupal/includes--common.inc/function/drupal_add_css/7`. ■

Customizing templates

The template files in your Drupal installation can be edited using any standard Web authoring or HTML editing program. Remember, however, that it is never appropriate to edit files that are part of the core. Changing files in the core creates the risk that those files may be overwritten during patch and upgrade of the site. The better practice is to make copies of any files you need to edit and segregate those files from the core. After the files have been separated from the core, they can be modified with impunity. During the upgrade process, you need only protect that one directory from being overwritten.

Two examples are useful at this stage: In the first example, I look at modifying a template file from a theme; in the second, I look at modifying a template from within the core.

Modifying templates inside a theme

Let's assume you want to use the Bartik theme, but you want to modify extensively the logo area of the page. And let's assume the changes are great enough that they cannot be met by simply uploading your own logo through the Theme Manager or by modifying the theme's CSS.

To accomplish the task, do the following:

1. **Access the Drupal installation on the server.**
2. **Access the /templates directory inside /bartik, and copy the file page.tpl.php.**
3. **Next, open the /templates directory inside /bartik2, and paste the file you just copied. Do not change the name!**
4. **Find the section of code shown here, which is the section of the page.tpl.php file that places the logo on the page.**

   ```
   <?php if ($logo): ?>
     <a href="<?php print $front_page; ?>" title="<?php print
     t('Home'); ?>" rel="home" id="logo">
       <img src="<?php print $logo; ?>" alt="<?php print t('Home');
     ?>" />
     </a>
   <?php endif; ?>
   ```

5. **Make the changes you desire to the code.**
6. **Save your changes.**
7. **Clear your theme registry.**

   Your changes should now be visible on the site.

Tip

Clearing the theme registry is a necessary step for viewing your changes to templates. You can do this manually, or by installing the Devel module you can automate the task. After you install Devel, the module configuration includes an option to Rebuild the theme registry on every page load. ■

Overriding core templates

The default Drupal system provides templates that control the output of every area of the site. The template files are located throughout the system, most frequently inside the directories of the modules whose output they affect. As discussed, these default templates can be overridden by placing a template with the same name inside the active theme's directory.

If you want to override a default template that does not already exist inside your theme, you may do so by simply copying the template file to your chosen theme. For example, let's assume you want to provide your own styling for the blocks in your new Bartik2 theme.

Because Bartik2 does not already provide a template file for the blocks, you need to override the default template.

Follow these steps:

1. **Access the Drupal installation on the server, and locate the /modules/blocks directory.**
2. **Copy the file blocks.tpl.php to /sites/all/themes/bartik2/templates. Do not change the name!**
3. **Make the changes you desire to the code inside your new blocks.tpl.php file.**
4. **Save your changes.**
5. **Refresh the theme cache.**

   Your changes should now be visible on the site.

Tip

A useful compilation of the default core templates, together with a list of template suggestions, can be found at `http://drupal.org/node/190815`. ■

Controlling template display through template suggestions

Drupal theming employs a naming convention that allows you to gain a large amount of control over when templates are displayed. In Drupal terms, these are called *template suggestions*. The name "suggestions" is a bit deceptive, however, because these are not optional, but rather mandatory, display conditions.

The suggestions methodology is based on a naming convention that creates a hierarchy of display. The system is relatively simple to use and, when applied properly, gives you complete control of template display. Suggestions are based on a fixed formula that is explained in the Drupal documentation. A complete list of suggestions is available at `http://drupal.org/node/190815`.

For example, let's assume you want to theme the comments for your blog pages differently than comments in other areas of the site. To do so you need a template that affects only the blog comments. This is the default comments template:

```
comment.tpl.php
```

To create a template that affects only the comments to your blog content, you need to create a new template:

```
comment--blog.tpl.php
```

Note

Note the use of the double hyphen in the example above. Prior to Drupal 7, a single hyphen was used. In Drupal 7, the single hyphen is used to separate words in names, and the double hyphen is used to indicate a targeted override. ■

This new template affects only those comments attached to blog type content entries. The default `comment.tpl.php` is used in all other instances.

As mentioned earlier, the suggestions methodology is based on a hierarchy and is expressed in the naming convention. Consider the following example of the hierarchy in regard to the display of a series of page templates. The example shows the most general template suggestion first, followed in turn by more specific suggestions:

- **page.tpl.php:** The default page template that affects all pages on the site
- **page--node.tpl.php:** The template that affects only pages containing nodes
- **page--node-1.tpl.php:** The template that affects only the page containing node 1
- **page--node-edit.tpl.php:** The template that affects the page only when editing a node

You can have all the templates described above on a single site without problems. Drupal automatically prefers the more specific templates to the more general and displays the appropriate template. The key is the naming convention; get that right, and you have control over the site.

For example, let's assume you want to theme the page containing node 1. To make this work with your new Bartik2 theme, follow these steps:

1. **Access the Drupal installation on the server, and locate the Bartik2 theme directory.**
2. **Make a copy of the file page.tpl.php, and rename the copy page-node-1.tpl.php.**
3. **Make the changes you desire to the code inside your new page-node-1.tpl.php file.**
4. **Save your changes.**
5. **Refresh the theme cache.**

   Your changes should now be visible on the site, but only on the page `http://your-site.com/node/1`.

Caution

For your template suggestion to work, it must be placed in the same directory as the base template. Therefore, if you need to create a suggestion premised on a template that does not exist in your theme, you need to copy the base template to the theme directory, along with the new template suggestion. ■

Using theme functions

Not all output is themed through the use of templates. Much of the themable output is actually generated by PHP functions known as *theme functions.* Theme functions exist in multiple places in the system and can be identified by their naming convention; they are PHP functions that begin with `theme_`—for example, `theme_breadcrumb`.

Where Does the Output Come From?

Before you can override the output, you need to know what is producing it. Unfortunately, identifying the source of the output you see on the screen can sometimes be a bit of a trick.

If you know the output on the screen comes from a module, you can always look in the module directory for files ending with the proper extension: `.tpl.php`. You also can view the source of the page in hopes of finding unique CSS selectors that might help you narrow things down. These approaches, however, are both time-consuming and a source of common frustration. Moreover, simply searching for templates ignores the possibility that the output is generated by either a theme function or a preprocess function.

A much better solution is to use the Devel and Theme Developer modules. Theme Developer, once installed and enabled, can be used to locate the active theme elements and, as a bonus, list a set of possible suggestions you could use to theme the output selected. The module is a huge time-saver and well worth the effort to track it down and install it. Note that the module depends on the presence of the Devel module to work properly, so you must install both.

It is worth remembering, however, that Devel and Theme Developer are suitable for use in a development environment. The modules should never be installed and enabled on a live Web site because the information they provide can be misused.

With Theme Developer installed, you can click an item and see a list of theming elements, together with possible suggestions.

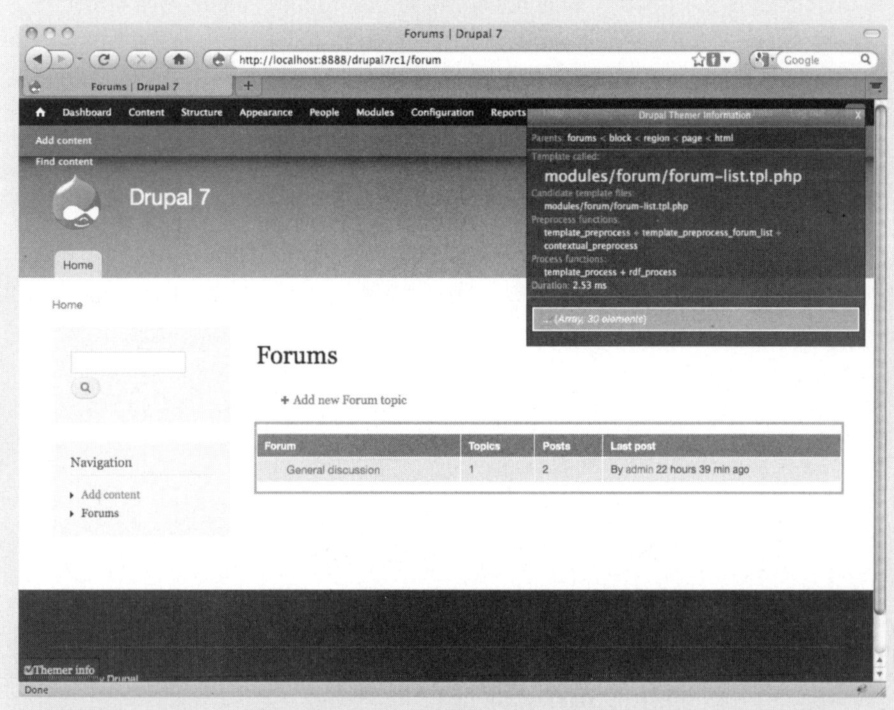

Overriding themable functions

If you discover that a bit of output you'd like to theme is produced by a theme function and you want to override that function, you can do so. Overrides for theme functions are placed in the theme's `template.php` file. Like template suggestions, themable function overrides must be named appropriately for them to work properly.

An example is the easiest way to learn this concept. Let's assume you have discovered that a bit of output you want to customize is produced by a theme function. Call the hypothetical theme function `theme_abc`. To override and customize this theme function, follow these steps:

1. **Access the Drupal installation on the server, and locate the source of theme_abc.**
2. **Copy the code for theme_abc.**
3. **Find the file template.php file, located inside /sites/all/themes/bartik2.**
4. **Paste the code for theme_abc into Bartik2's template.php file.**
5. **Rename the function from theme_abc to bartik2_abc.**
6. **Make whatever changes you need to make to customize the function.**
7. **Save your work.**
8. **Refresh the theme cache.**

   Your changes should now be visible on the site.

The key to this example is the necessity of not only copying the function into your theme's `template.php` file, but also renaming it from the generic prefix `theme` to the specific prefix `bartik2`. In other words, the override for a theme function must be named for the theme to which the override applies.

Using variable process functions

Variable process functions are primarily used to create variables that can then be used from within templates. With the arrival of Drupal 7, there are now two chances to employ this powerful function: *preprocess functions* and *process functions*. As the names imply, preprocess functions run first, followed by process functions.

Working with variable process functions requires a bit of skill with PHP and is something the vast majority of site owners will never use—even programmers resort to this only rarely; still, it is good to know the option exists. This option is most useful where you want to customize the contents of the variables that are included inside a template, or where you need to add new variables of your own for use in that template.

There are 10 expected preprocessors, and they are run in a specific order. Please visit the official Drupal documentation for details on the naming and ordering: `http://drupal.org/node/223430`.

In terms of execution, process functions are added to the `template.php` file. As indicated in the preceding section on overriding functions, process functions must be named correctly, with a prefix that matches the name of your theme.

Creating a New Theme

Although a fairly wide selection of ready-made themes exists, there may be times when the better course of action is to create your own theme, tailored closely to your needs. Typically, this is done in either of two fashions: Code the theme from scratch, or create a sub-theme. With the arrival of Drupal 7, the latter method has clear advantages in terms of both time-savings and efficiency and is the right option for most people. In this section, I touch on both methods, but I focus on how to create a new theme using the sub-themes technique.

Requirements for a theme

If you want to create your own theme from scratch, you need to know the basics. Drupal is very forgiving in terms of requirements for theme creation. There is only one required file in a PHPTemplate-based theme: the `.info` file. Although it is unlikely you would ever build a theme with only the `.info` file, it is possible.

Note

If your theme had no files other than a .info file, the theme output would be controlled by the PHPTemplate theme engine and the elements contained in the default template files and style sheets. ■

If you want to do it all yourself, follow these steps:

1. **Access the Drupal installation on the server.**
2. **Create a new directory to hold your theme files, place it inside /sites/all/themes, and give it the name you want to use for the theme.**

   For example, you may want to use `mytheme`.
3. **Create a new .info file inside the /sites/all/themes/mytheme directory, and name the new file mytheme.info.**
4. **Add contents to the .info, using as your guide the example that follows in this section.**
5. **Save your work.**
6. **Log in to the admin system of your site.**

   The Management menu appears at the top of the page.
7. **Select the Appearance option from the Management menu.**

   The Theme Manager opens in your browser.
8. **Find your new theme on the list of themes, and select Enable and set default.**

   Your new theme should now be visible on the site.

In this example, one of the key steps involves the creation of a new `.info` file. The `.info` file serves several important roles in the theme. At the most basic, the file sets the name for the theme, the theming engine to be used, and the version of Drupal required by the theme. It can additionally be used to create links to the resources needed by the theme—for example, the style sheets and scripts—and it can be used to specify certain characteristics of the theme—for example, the regions available and the features supported by the theme.

You can see how the `.info` file provides this information by reviewing the `bartik.info` file from the default Bartik theme:

```
; $Id: bartik.info,v 1.5 2010/11/07 00:27:20 dries Exp $
name = Bartik
description = A flexible, recolorable theme with many regions.
package = Core
version = VERSION
core = 7.x
style sheets[all][] = css/layout.css
style sheets[all][] = css/style.css
style sheets[all][] = css/colors.css
style sheets[print][] = css/print.css
regions[header] = Header
regions[help] = Help
regions[page_top] = Page top
regions[page_bottom] = Page bottom
regions[highlighted] = Highlighted
regions[featured] = Featured
regions[content] = Content
regions[sidebar_first] = Sidebar first
regions[sidebar_second] = Sidebar second
regions[triptych_first] = Triptych first
regions[triptych_middle] = Triptych middle
regions[triptych_last] = Triptych last
regions[footer_firstcolumn] = Footer first column
regions[footer_secondcolumn] = Footer second column
regions[footer_thirdcolumn] = Footer third column
regions[footer_fourthcolumn] = Footer fourth column
regions[footer] = Footer
settings[shortcut_module_link] = 0
; Information added by drupal.org packaging script on 2010-11-14
version = "7.0-beta3"
project = "drupal"
datestamp = "1289694732"
```

Note

The various options for the `.info` file, together with a discussion of the syntax required, are covered at `http://drupal.org/node/171205`. The default .info values are discussed at `http://drupal.org/node/171206`. ■

Even though you only need an `.info` file to create a PHPTemplate theme, if you create a new theme with only an `.info` file, you won't get a very exciting result. At the most basic, you want to add a `page.tpl.php` to create your layout and a `styles.css` for your styles; what you do after that is up to you!

Creating a custom sub-theme

While theme creation from scratch is always possible, frankly it makes little sense given that you have to reinvent the wheel. The better course is to begin with a starter theme and create a sub-theme. A sub-theme piggybacks on the templates and styles defined in an existing base theme. If you choose your base theme wisely, you not only get a complete set of basic files that are ready to use but also a collection of useful features that are already built into the theme.

Tip

Don't worry that using a sub-theme means you are limited in terms of layout. The starter themes, like Zen used in this book, are designed to provide a quick start to theme creation without imposing limitations on layout and styling. ■

Selecting a base theme

All sub-themes are premised on a base theme. Your first step should be to do a bit of research to find the most suitable base theme for your work.

You can create a sub-theme from any theme, although some require more work than others. It's best to select a theme that has the features that you want and, ideally, exhibits some of the layout and styling you want. Often, the best choice is selecting one of the themes specifically created as a starter theme. Among the candidates are the following:

- **Adaptive Theme:** This third-party theme is feature rich. The theme is well designed for maximum compatibility and includes an array of layout options and styles that can be implemented directly from the Theme Manager. It also fast-tracks sub-theme creation by providing a ready-to-use sub-theme. The only downside is that the theme has a few non-standard implementations that may make it a slightly less attractive choice if you are trying this for the first time. For experienced themers, though, this theme is hard to beat. Visit the Adaptive Theme project to learn more and download the theme at `http://drupal.org/project/adaptivetheme`.
- **Fusion:** This is a nice starter theme with numerous features and ready-to-use sub-themes. It relies, however, on the Skinr module, so if you are not familiar with Skinr, you may not want to go this way. Visit the Fusion project to learn more and download the theme at `http://drupal.org/project/fusion`.
- **Stark:** This starter theme is included in the core. It is very basic and includes few additional features. If you are looking for a clean slate, this is the right theme for your base theme.

- **Zen:** This theme has been around for years but continues to evolve and improve. The current version is tailored for use as a starter theme with a wide range of features and ready-to-go sub-themes. It's a solid choice that exhibits best practices and the choice I use in this chapter. Visit the Zen project to learn more and download the theme at `http://drupal.org/project/zen`.

Creating the sub-theme

Let's assume that you have decided to proceed by creating a sub-theme based on Zen. To get started, download the Zen theme and install it, using the instructions earlier in this chapter. After the theme files are on your server, follow these steps to create your sub-theme:

1. **Access the Drupal installation on the server.**
2. **Access your new Zen installation at /sites/all/themes/zen, and find the subdirectory named /STARTERKIT.**
3. **Copy /STARTERKIT, and move the copy to /sites/all/themes.**
4. **Rename /STARTERKIT to /zensub.**
5. **Open the file /zensub/STARTERKIT.info.txt.**
6. **Change all occurrences of STARTERKIT to zensub.**
7. **Save the file as zensub.info.**
8. **Open the file /zensub/template.php.**
9. **Change all occurrences of STARTERKIT to zensub.**
10. **Save the file.**
11. **Log in to the admin system of your site.**

    The Management menu appears at the top of the page.
12. **Select the Appearance option from the Management menu.**

    The Theme Manager opens in your browser. You should see your new theme ZenSub on the list of available themes.

Your new ZenSub theme is ready for you to begin customizing.

Customizing the sub-theme

If you look on the server, you will note that ZenSub provides subdirectories for both `/css` and `/templates`. The CSS directory contains a large number of style sheets. The templates directory, however, is empty.

Changes to the CSS should be managed directly within the style sheets contained in `/sites/all/themes/zensub/css`. The process is the same as that outlined earlier in this chapter in the section "Modifying the CSS inside a theme."

If you want to make changes to the templates, however, you need to override the base theme's templates. To do this, simply make a copy of the templates you want to modify and place them inside the `/zensub/templates` directory. Make all your changes to the new template file. Any changes made to this file take precedence over the Zen's default templates. If you want to create new templates to override core templates, follow the directions set out earlier in this chapter, in the section "Overriding core templates."

As noted earlier, ZenSub already includes a `template.php` file, so if you need override a themable function or provide for process variables, you can do so in that file.

Working with an Admin Theme

One of the big changes in Drupal 7 is the inclusion of a dedicated administration theme called Seven. Although you could always use different themes for the front end and back end of Drupal, in previous versions, the system used the same theme for both purposes. With Drupal 7, you now have a purpose-built admin theme that functions very nicely. Nonetheless, should you decide that you want to use a different theme for the administration system of your site, you can do so.

To change the admin theme of your site, follow these steps:

1. **Log into your site as an administrator.**

   The admin interface loads in your browser.
2. **Select the Appearance option from the Management menu.**

   The Theme Manager opens in your browser.
3. **Scroll down to the Administration Theme section of the page, as shown in Figure 26.6.**
4. **Select the theme of your choice from the combo box marked Administration theme.**
5. **Chose whether you want to use the same theme for both administration and content editing by using the check box labeled Use the administration theme when editing or creating content.**
6. **Click the Save configuration button.**

   The system applies the changes and displays the selected theme.

Tip

You may not want to use the administration theme for content creation and editing. If you uncheck the option, the system displays the front-end theme when you create and edit content, which often gives you a better idea what your content item will look like to site visitors. ■

Note

The overlay you see in the default admin system is the product of the Overlay module. If, for some reason, you do not want to use the overlay, simply disable that module; the theme functions fine without it. ■

FIGURE 26.6

The administration theme controls inside the Theme Manager

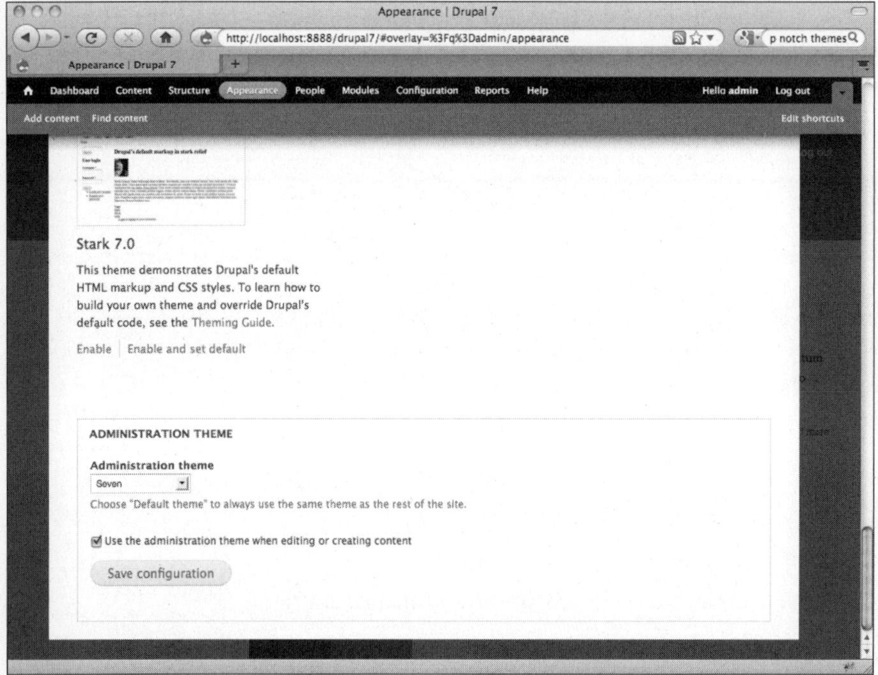

Summary

This chapter covered the basics of Drupal theming. Included in this chapter were the following topics:

- How themes work
- The anatomy of a Drupal theme
- How to use configuration to customize a Drupal theme
- How to customize a theme by making changes to the CSS and the templates
- How to override core templates and themable functions
- How to find and add new themes to your system
- How to create new themes and sub-themes
- How to change the administration theme on your site

CHAPTER 27

Customizing the Display of Content

IN THIS CHAPTER

Knowing the basic principles

Understanding Views

Understanding Panels

The content management and layout tools built into the default Drupal system provide a great deal of flexibility. Unfortunately, to enjoy the full range of the options available, you need to work with the code in the theme files. In this chapter, I look at several third-party modules that allow you to open the Drupal display options without having to be a theming ninja.

The two modules discussed, Views and Panels, combine with the custom fields functionality built into the core to allow you to extract the content items you want and then to position them dynamically on the pages of your site. The modules discussed are complex, and this chapter can only hope to touch on the many options they provide. The information presented should help you get started, but to learn more you need to explore the additional information provided on the project sites for each module.

This chapter requires you to download and install additional modules on your site.

Basic Principles

There are three ways to modify the display of content in your Drupal site. The most basic method is to use the configuration options—theme configuration and block placement—combined with creative use of the content item formatting inside the content editor. This approach is simple and requires very little advanced knowledge, but you are limited in what you can achieve.

At the other end of the spectrum is the more hardcore approach—that is, customizing the themes through CSS and the creation of overrides to the default templates. While this approach is the most flexible, you pay a price in the form of increased complexity. For many users, this is not the right answer because of the skills required.

The middle path is the use of third-party modules to do some of the hard work for you. This chapter is about two of the most common of those modules: Views and Panels.

Note

To gain more control over block formatting, you may also want to explore the Skinr module at `http://drupal.org/project/skinr`. ■

To get the most out of these modules, you must understand how the content types can be used and how you can add fields to the content types. If you understand that, then you will have three powerful tools in your hands that work together to create great content layouts:

- Use the content types to capture the information and segregate it into discrete fields that can be manipulated and styled.
- Use the Views module to group that content and prepare it for output.
- Use the Panels module to display that output on the page in the manner you choose.

Cross-Reference

Working with content types and fields is covered in Chapter 10. ■

Note

In addition to the Views and Panels modules, a number of additional modules are designed to make controlling the site output easier. Some of my favorites are listed in Chapter 29, where I discuss popular extensions. ■

Introduction to Views

In simplest terms, the Views module allows you to create, manage, and display lists of content; that may not sound like much, but it is actually quite powerful. Web sites, particularly complex Web sites, rely extensively on the creation of lists. You can see examples on many sites. When you see a block displaying the most recent articles, or a page displaying all the articles about a particular topic, or multiple pages organizing content in chronological archives, you are seeing lists at work.

The Views module is essentially an admin interface for querying your database. It provides not only the ability to create and manage lists but also the ability to control how those lists are displayed on your site. Views give you a great deal of control over how your content is organized for the users. If you have a large content site, Views can impose order on that content and make it both easier to access and more meaningful for your site visitors.

Overview of the Views framework

Understanding the conceptual framework behind Views makes it much easier to grasp what can be done and how best to do it. All views rely on a mix of the following:

- **Arguments:** Parameters that dynamically refine the view results
- **Displays:** Controls whether the view is displayed as a page or a block
- **Fields:** The individual pieces of data you choose to display in your view
- **Filters:** Used to limit the display of items in the view results
- **Relationships:** Used to create links between the fields in a view
- **Sort criteria:** Determines the order in which the view results are displayed

Note

The Views system currently in use is technically known as Views 2. Throughout this text, I refer to it simply as Views. If you have worked with Views in the past, the new system includes some changes, but it is consistent in philosophy with Views 1. Views 2 also provides the ability for you to import and convert your old Views 1 views for use in the new system. Views 3 is currently under development and will likely embody a number of changes to the way the system functions and is managed. ■

In the sections that follow, I look at how to get started with Views and how the framework is applied to create new views for your site.

Installing Views

Installing Views is no different than installing any other module, but there are related modules you need to take into account. The Views module is dependent upon the presence of an additional module, Chaos Tool Suite. Chaos Tool Suite is a set of APIs and tools to assist developers. It supplements and supports both the Views module discussed in this section and the Panels module, discussed later in this chapter.

Tip

The Chaos Tool Suite includes a number of useful utilities outside of the Views and Panels items discussed in this chapter. If you are a developer, you will appreciate the module as it speeds your work in a number of areas and improves working with AJAX and JavaScript in Drupal. You can learn more about the Chaos Tool Suite and download the module from the official project page on Drupal.org. Visit `http://drupal.org/project/ctools`. **■**

Additionally, after you install Views, it prompts you to download and install the Advanced Help module. The Advanced Help module is not necessary for you to use Views; indeed, it actually does nothing with the Views functionality itself. Rather, the Views module is bundled with additional help files and examples that can be seen only if you have the Advanced Help module installed. Therefore, if you are new to Views, I recommend you install Advanced Help. If, on the other hand, you are an experienced Views user, there is probably no reason to bother with this additional installation.

Tip

If you don't want to use the Advanced Help module, you can hide the reminder message that appears on the Views Manager by changing the configuration settings on the Tools tab. ■

To add the Views functionality to your site and have available all the options, follow the steps in these sections.

First, install the Chaos Tool Suite module:

1. **Log into your site as an administrator.**

   The Management menu appears at the top of the page.
2. **Select the Modules option from the Management menu.**

   The Modules Manager opens in your browser.
3. **Click the Install new module link at the top left of the overlay.**

   The module installation page opens.
4. **If you have downloaded the module installation package to your local machine, click the Browse button.**

   The file upload page pops up.
5. **Use the upload page to find the installation file you want to upload; select it, and click the Open button.**

   The upload page closes, and you see the path to the installation file in the field next to the Browse button.
6. **If you have not downloaded the installation file, but you know the URL for the installation package, type it into the field marked Install from a URL.**
7. **Click the Install button.**

   The system uploads the module, and you see a confirmation message on the screen.

Next, follow the same steps to install the Advanced Help module.

Finally, follow the same steps and install the Views module.

After you have all the modules installed, enable them via the Modules Manager.

Cross-Reference

Adding new modules to your Drupal system is explained in detail in Chapter 29. ■

Getting started with Views

After installing and enabling the Views and Chaos Tool Suite modules, you can access the Views Manager from the Structure link on the Management menu. Clicking the link labeled Views causes the Views Manager to load in the overlay, as shown in Figure 27.1.

FIGURE 27.1

The Views Manager displays the list of default views. I enabled the default *glossary* view; no other default views are enabled in this figure.

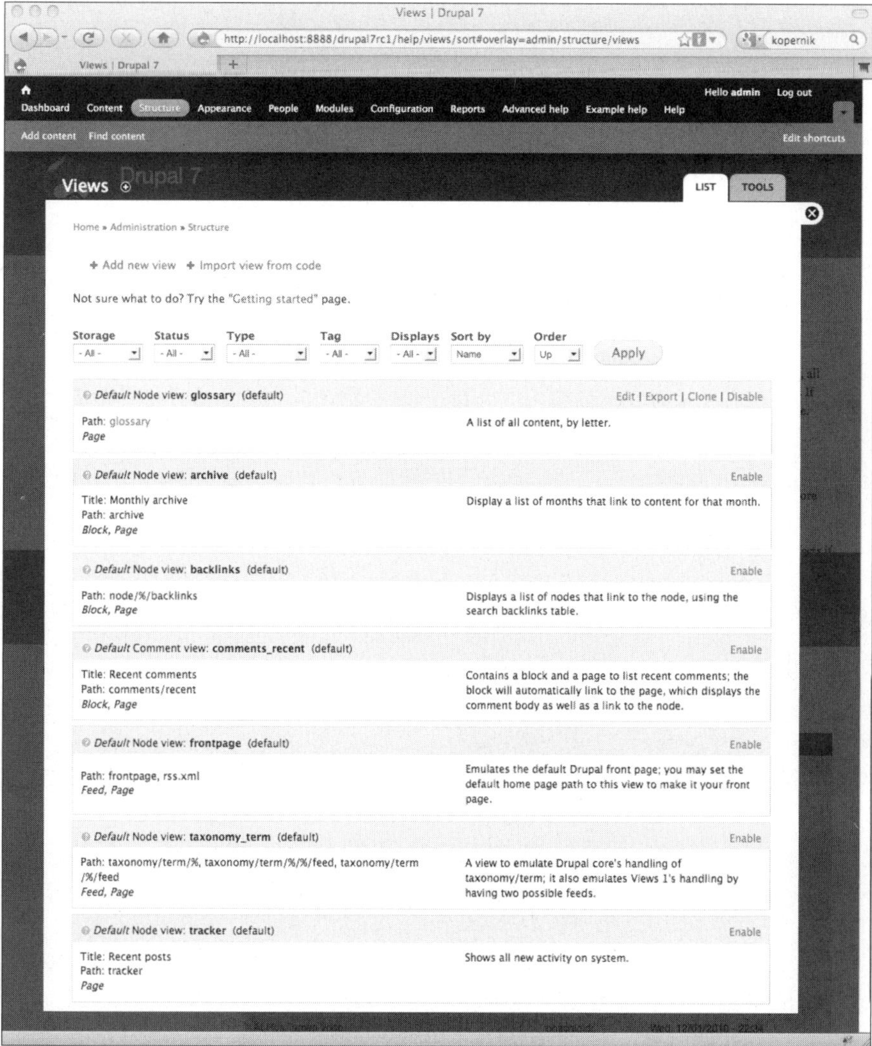

The module includes a set of default views that are ready to use. The default views address common issues and provide a starting point for your work. These are the default views:

- **Archive:** Displays a list of months that, when clicked, display a page containing a list of all the content published that month.
- **Backlinks:** Displays a list of nodes that link to individual nodes.

- **Comments_recent:** Displays a list of the most recent comments on the site. Clicking the link displays the comment and the node.
- **Frontpage:** A view that can function as the home page of your site. This view also includes an RSS feed for the page.
- **Glossary:** Creates a page listing all content, organized alphabetically. For an example, see Figure 27.2.
- **Taxonomy_term:** Creates a page or feed listing all items tagged with a particular taxonomy term.
- **Tracker:** Displays a list of the most recent activity on the site.

FIGURE 27.2

This glossary page created by the default glossary view is an example of Views output.

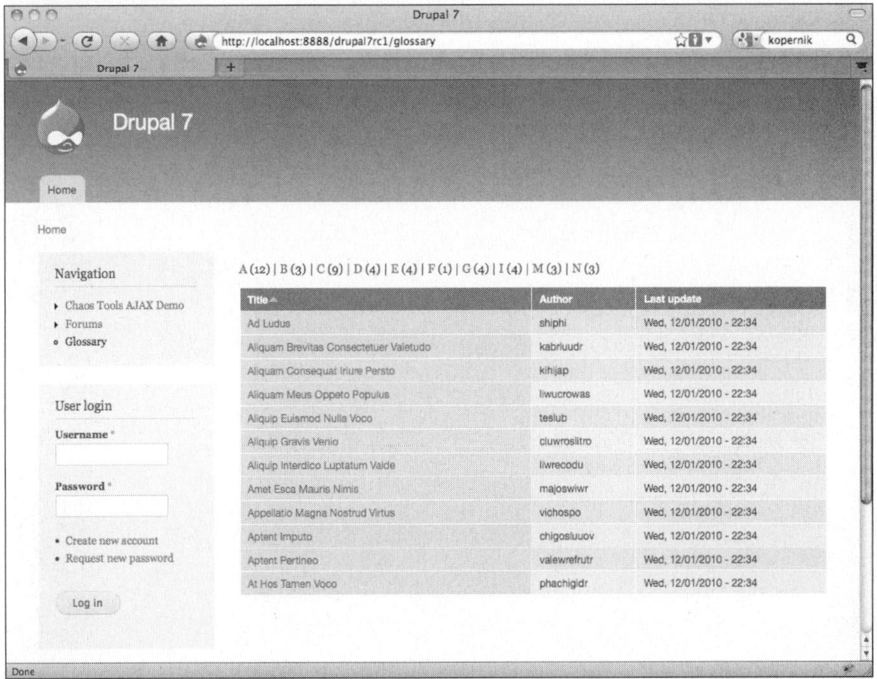

The views are disabled by default, but you need only enable them to begin using them right away. The views also can be cloned for you to customize and tailor to your needs.

Tip

If you want to modify one of the default views, I strongly recommend that you clone it first and make your changes to the cloned view. This approach preserves the default view and avoids the risk of your changes being

overwritten when you upgrade the Views module in the future. A link that allows you to clone a view is visible next to the edit link. ■

In Figure 27.1, shown earlier, you can see two tabs on the View Manager overlay. The default is List; the second tab is labeled Tools. If you click the Tools tab, you see the page shown in Figure 27.3.

FIGURE 27.3

The View Manager Tools tab

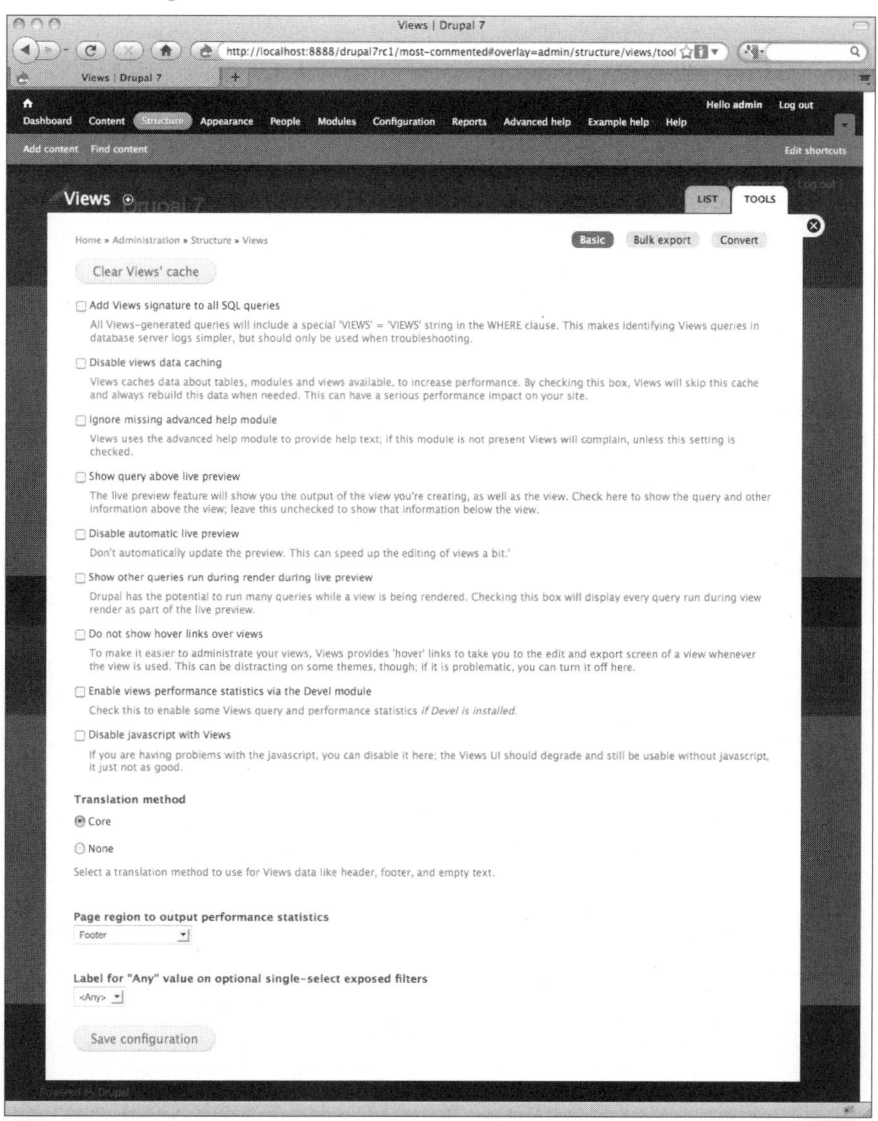

The options on this tab are explained well on the page itself, but essentially this page functions as the configuration options for the Views module. While some of the options here are relevant only during development, others are meaningful on a live site and have performance implications. At the top right, under the tabs, are three buttons:

- **Basic:** This is the default Tools page shown in Figure 27.3.
- **Bulk export:** This allows you to export your views for use on another Drupal site.
- **Convert:** This enables you to import views created with the previous version of Views, Views 1.

Tip

For most uses, the default settings in the Tools tab are sufficient. ■

Creating new views

Creating a new view is not an intuitive process. Each view has a large number of options and the combinations can seem overwhelming at first glance. The help files and the Getting started page provide some welcome assistance, but I think the best way to become comfortable with the process is through an example.

Assume you want to create a page that contains a list of the content from your site, organized according to which has the most comments. Moreover, assume that you want to show only the content of one content type: articles. The default system includes a Recent Comments block, but the configuration options are limited and won't achieve what you need. Creating a view is the answer. To accomplish this task, follow these steps:

1. **Log into your site as an administrator.**

   The Management menu appears at the top of the page.
2. **Select the Structure option from the Management menu.**

   The Structure options display in the overlay.
3. **Click the Views option.**

   The Views Manager opens (refer to Figure 27.1).
4. **Click the Add new view link.**

   The first screen of the new view wizard appears in the overlay, as seen in Figure 27.4.
5. **In the View name field, enter a machine-friendly name for the view.**
6. **The new view you want will be a node, so leave the View type control set for Node, the default.**

FIGURE 27.4

The first screen in the new view wizard

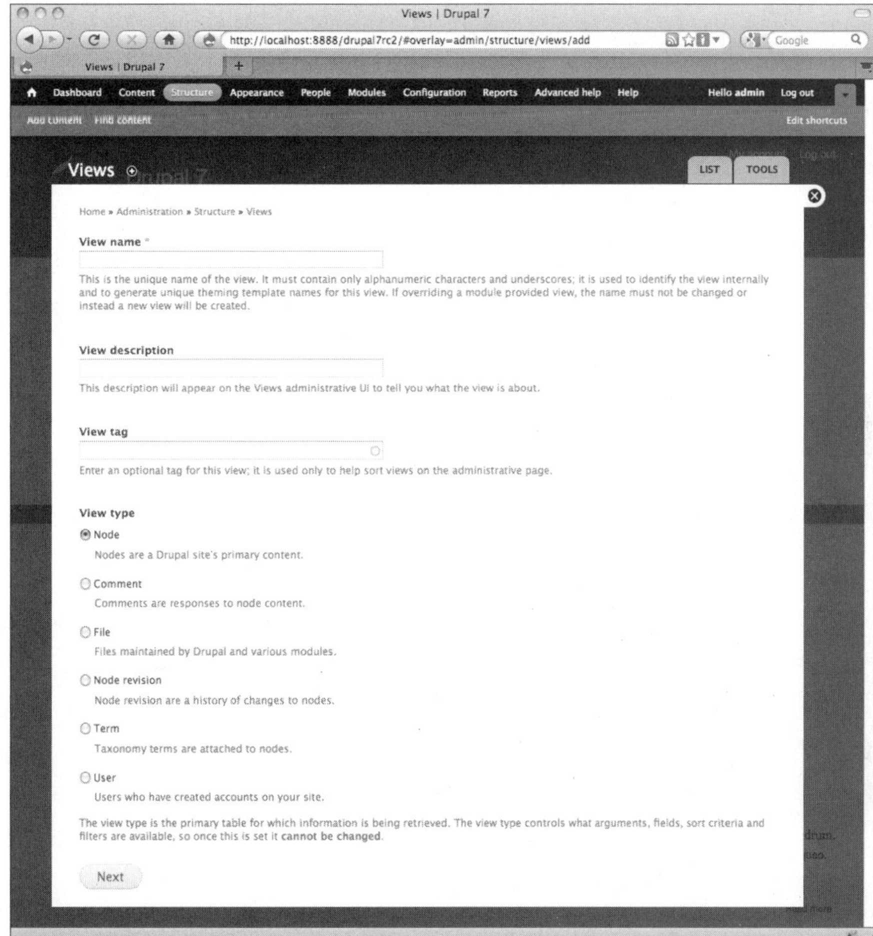

7. **Click the Next button.**

   The second screen of the new view wizard loads, as shown in Figure 27.5.

8. **Create a page display (the default option) by clicking the Add display button.**

   The Page display option is added to the view and is ready for editing.

9. **Add a path for the new view by clicking Path: None in the Page settings section of the page.**

   The Path settings show at the bottom of the page.

10. **Enter a URL for your view.**

    Use something descriptive, such as "most-comments."

11. **Click the Update button.**

    The system assigns the view page a URL.

FIGURE 27.5

The second screen in the new view wizard

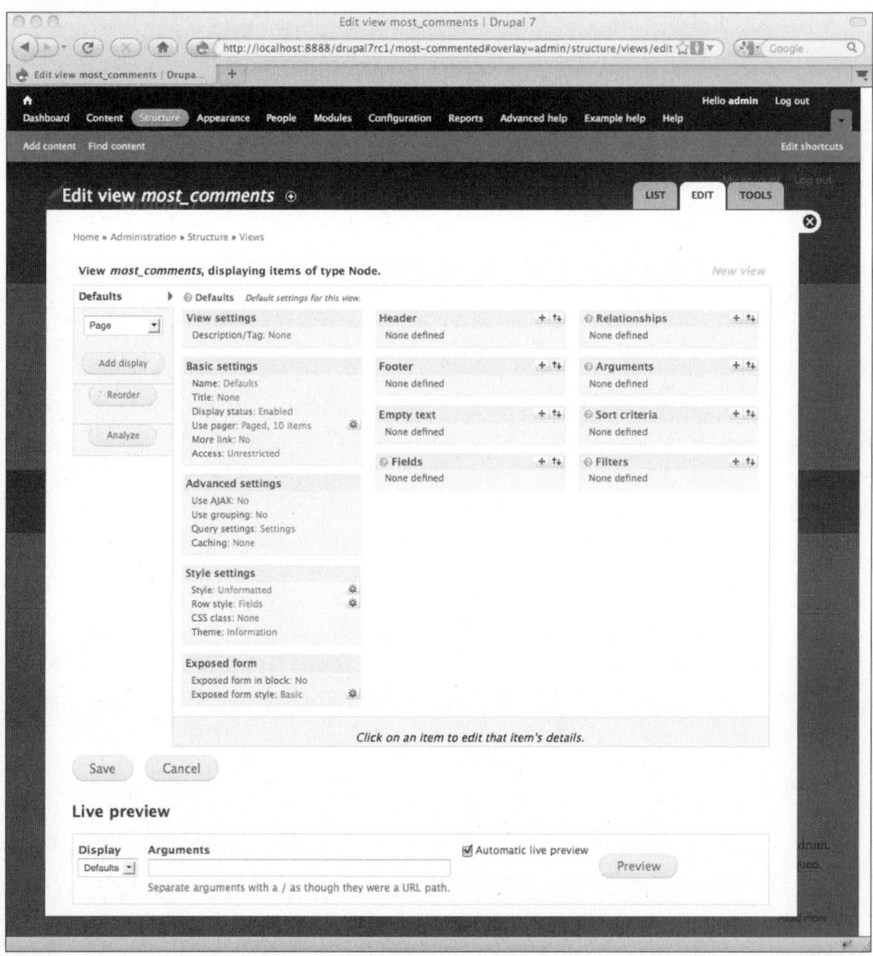

Tip

From this point forward, you can check your work by viewing the URL for the view. There is also a preview function built into the Views interface, but if you want to see the output within the context of the theme, check the URL. ■

12. **Add the view to your Navigation menu by clicking the Menu: No menu option in the Page settings section of the page.**

    The Menu item settings show at the bottom of the page.

13. **Select Normal menu entry.**

    The Menu item fields display.

14. **In the Title field, give the menu item a name—something simple like "Most Commented Articles."**

    The system assigns the title to the page.

15. **Find the Fields option on the new view page, and click the + (plus) sign.**

    The Add fields settings display at the bottom of the page.

16. **Select Node: Comment count and Node: Title.**

17. **Click the Add button.**

    The system adds the fields to the view.

18. **To add a filter to show only content of the Articles content type, find the Filters option on the new view page and click the + (plus) sign.**

    The Filters settings display at the bottom of the page.

19. **Select Node: type.**

20. **Click the Add button.**

    The system displays the Node: Type configuration options.

21. **Select Is one of and Article.**

22. **Click the Update button.**

    The system adds the filter.

23. **To add a filter to show only content that includes comments, find the Filters option on the new view page and click the + (plus) sign.**

    The Filters settings display at the bottom of the page.

24. **Select Node: Comment count.**

25. **Click the Add button.**

    The system displays the comment count configuration options.

26. **Select the option Is not equal to, and in the Value field, type the number 0.**

27. **Click Update and override.**

    The system adds the filter.

28. **Find the Sort criteria option on the new view page, and click the + (plus) sign.**

    The Sort criteria settings display at the bottom of the page.

29. **Select Node: Comment count.**

30. **Click the Add button.**

    The system displays the comment count configuration options.

31. **Select the option Sort descending.**
32. **Click Update and override.**

    The system adds the sort criteria.

33. **Click the Save button.**

    The system saves your view and displays a confirmation message.

At the end of this process, your new view editing screen should look like what you see in Figure 27.6.

FIGURE 27.6

Your new view page for the Most Comments

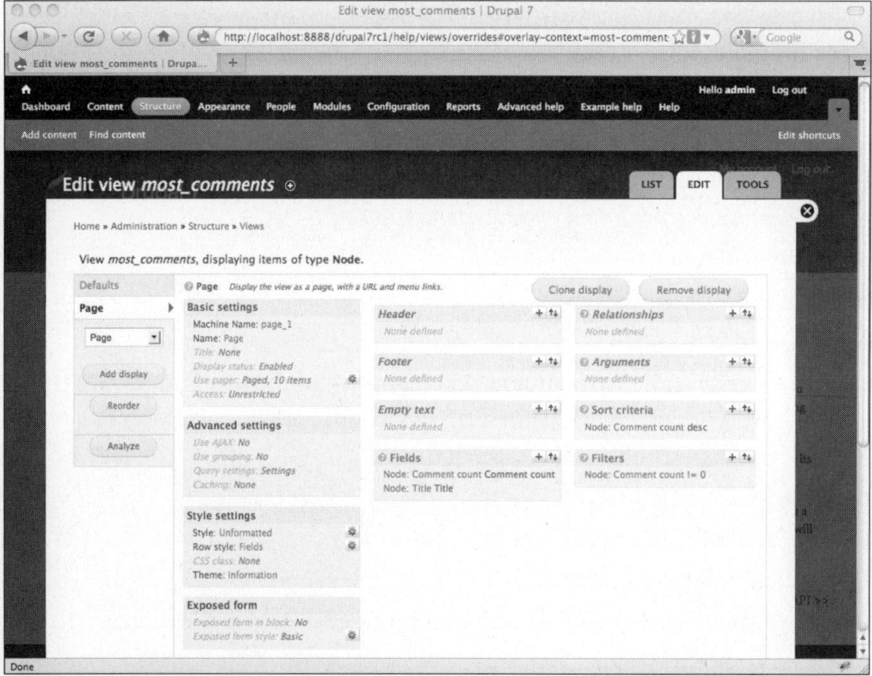

On the front end of the site, you now have a new menu link, named Most Comments, and a new page, as shown in Figure 27.7.

In the next section, I show you how to edit the view to improve the display.

FIGURE 27.7

The front end output of your new view page

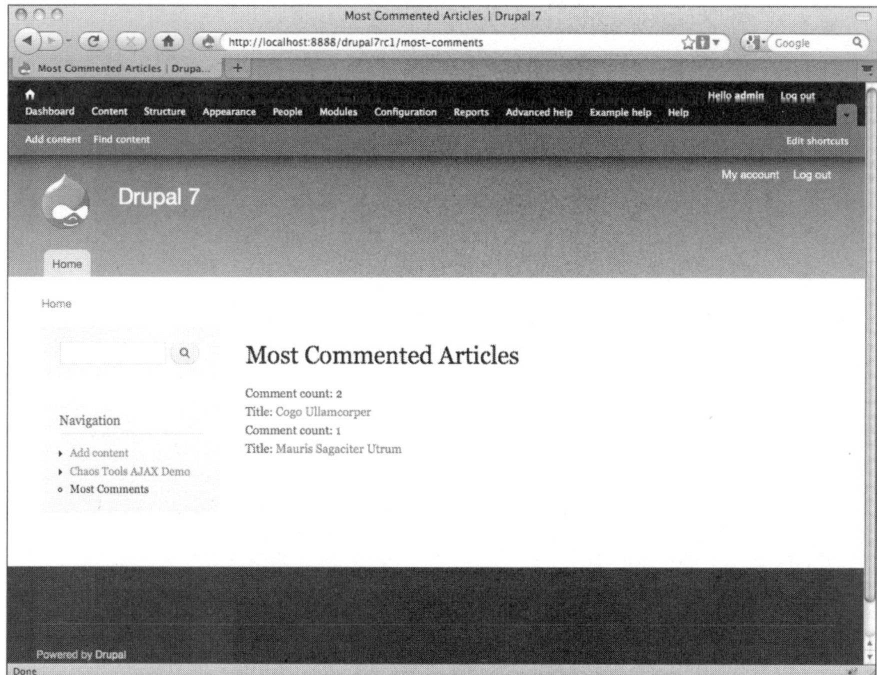

Editing and deleting views

Views can be edited and deleted from the admin system's Views Manager. In this section, I show how it can be done, using the example view created in the previous section.

The output of the view created in the preceding section has a couple of rough spots. The ordering of the items is counterintuitive (the comment count should come after the article title), and the data label for the title is unnecessary. I want to reorder the information displayed by the view and clean up the field labels.

To reorder the Comment count and Title fields, follow these steps:

1. **Log into your site as an administrator.**

   The Management menu appears at the top of the page.

2. **Select the Structure option from the Management menu.**

   The Structure options display in the overlay.

3. **Click the Views option.**

   The Views Manager opens (refer to Figure 27.1).

4. **Find the view named most_comments, and click the Edit link.**

   The view editing page opens.

5. **You want to edit the Page display, so click the Page option in the Displays column.**

   The Page display page comes to the front.

6. **Find the Fields area of the page, and click the button with the two up/down arrows.**

   The rearrange fields controls display.

7. **Click and drag the Node: Title field above the Node: Comment count field.**
8. **Click the Update button.**

   The configuration page closes.

9. **Click the Save button.**

   The system saves your changes.

Caution

Clicking the Update button does not save your changes; it merely updates the view. To save, you must click the Save button! ■

To edit the field labels, follow these steps:

1. **Log into your site as an administrator.**

   The Management menu appears at the top of the page.

2. **Select the Structure option from the Management menu.**

   The Structure options display in the overlay.

3. **Click the Views option.**

   The Views Manager opens (refer to Figure 27.1).

4. **Find the view named most_comments, and click the Edit link.**

   The view editing page opens.

5. **You want to edit the Page display, so click the Page option in the Displays column.**

   The Page display page comes to the front.

6. **Find the Fields area of the page, and click Node: title.**

   The Node: title configuration options are shown at the bottom of the page.

7. **Find the field named Label, and delete the word Title.**

8. **Click the Update button.**

   The configuration page closes.

9. **Click the Save button.**

   The system saves your changes.

The changes to the layout can be seen by visiting the page on the front end of your site. It should look similar to what is shown in Figure 27.8.

FIGURE 27.8

The newly edited Most Comments view, seen from the front end of the Web site

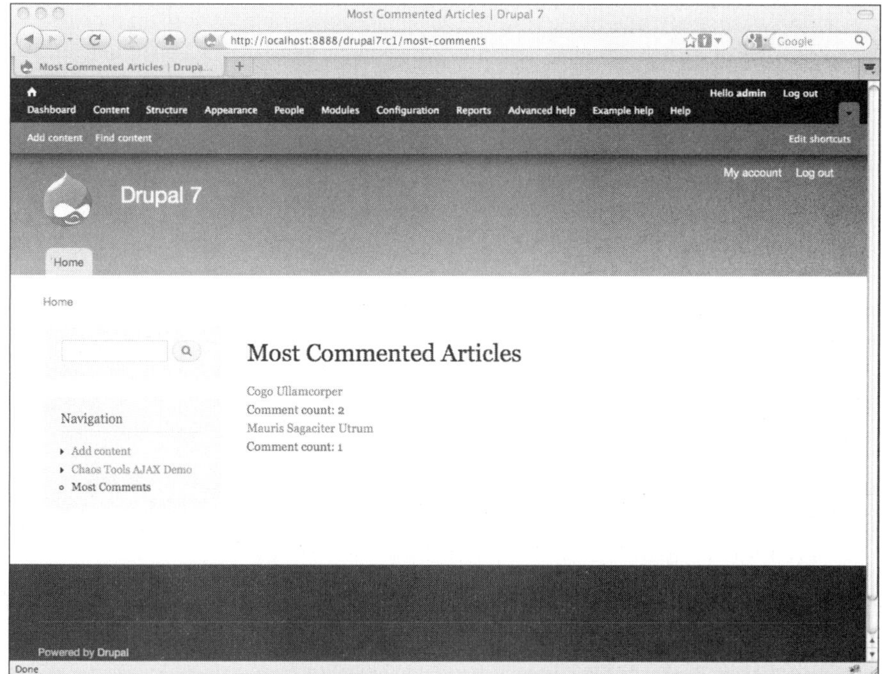

Deleting a view is even easier. Simply find the view in the list shown on the Views Manager, and click the Delete link. The system asks you to confirm the decision.

Caution

Note that after you confirm deletion, the view is gone forever; it cannot be undone! ■

Introduction to Panels

The Panels module lets you easily create reusable layouts. The beauty of it is that you don't have to work with the code and create custom themes or `tpl.php` files. The Panels admin interface is all you need; it gives you a visual way to create complex and dynamic pages.

Cross-Reference

Modifying themes by creating custom `.tpl.php` files is dealt with in Chapter 26. ■

A panel functions as a wrapper that calls content for display. Each panel is composed of panes, where you place content. The content can be a combination of blocks, views, or nodes. Moreover, the panels themselves can be created for use as blocks, nodes, or even entire pages. There is, in short, a tremendous amount of power in this module. Unfortunately, that power comes with a degree of complexity. Working with Panels can initially be rather daunting, and until you gain some experience with the system, appreciating exactly how much you can do is difficult.

In this section, I provide a brief introduction to Panels. The information helps you get started and allows you to create your first panels, but a full understanding of the system requires a much-extended treatment of the subject that is beyond the scope of this book.

Tip

The Panels module is sometimes criticized for having a negative impact on the performance of a site; however, this is rarely the case. In reality, the performance degradation is typically caused by stacking inefficient views or excessive contents inside of a panel. Regardless, Panels now provides a caching feature that allows you to cache individual panes and thereby offset any problems you might experience. To access the caching controls for a pane, click the gear icon on the pane. ■

Installing Panels

The Panels module, like Views, requires that you also install the Chaos Tool Suite module. I also recommend that you install the Advanced Help module to gain additional help files.

Note

For a discussion of the Chaos tool suite and the Advanced Help module, please see the discussion about installing Views earlier in this chapter. ■

To set up Panels on your site, and to have available all the options, follow these steps. First, install the Chaos Tool Suite module:

1. **Log into your site as an administrator.**

   The Management menu appears at the top of the page.

2. **Select the Modules option from the Management menu.**

   The Modules Manager opens in your browser.

3. **Click the Install new module link at the top left of the overlay.**

   The module installation page opens.

4. **If you have downloaded the module installation package to your local machine, click the Browse button.**

   The file upload page pops up.

5. **Use the upload page to find the installation file you want to upload; select it, and click the Open button.**

   The upload page closes, and you see the path to the installation file in the field next to the Browse button.

6. **If you have not downloaded the installation file, but you know the URL for the installation package, type it into the field marked Install from a URL.**

7. **Click the Install button.**

   The system uploads the module, and you see a confirmation message on the screen.

Next, follow the same steps to install the Advanced Help module.

Finally, follow the same steps and install the Panels module.

Note

You can download the Panels module at `http://www.drupal.org/project/panels`. ■

After you have all the modules installed, enable them via the Modules Manager.

Note

For purposes of the examples in this chapter, you do not need to enable all the options in Chaos Tools. When you are working only with basic Panels functions, you need only enable two options in the Chaos Tool Suite module: Chaos tools and Page Manager. The other options, such as Custom content panes and Custom rulesets, are really for power users who want to create reusable items for use Panels. ■

Getting started with Panels

With Panels enabled, access the Panels Manager by choosing the Panels option from the Structure option on the Management menu. The Panels Manager loads in the overlay, as shown in Figure 27.9.

Although the Panels Manager has many options, the key choices you need to get started are the top three options in the left column labeled *Create new....* The options in that column enable you to create three types of panels:

- **Panel pages:** These allow you to create complex layouts as a page, with its own URL.
- **Mini panels:** These provide a way to create content layouts that can be used as blocks.
- **Panels node:** This allows you to create a node customized and controlled by Panels.

FIGURE 27.9

The Panels Manager

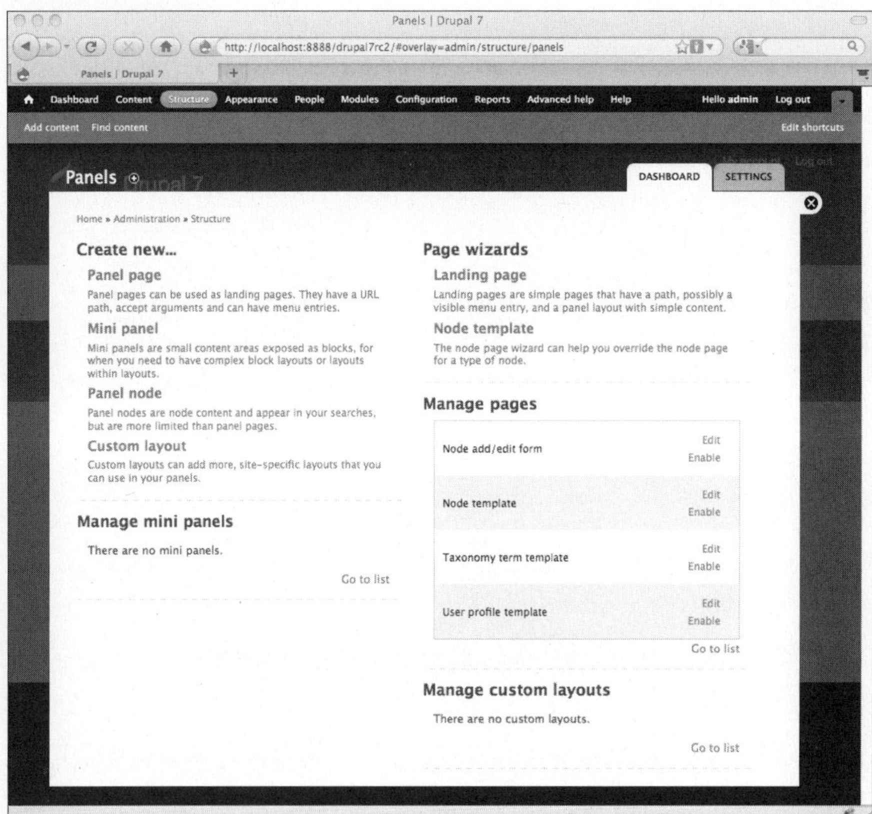

Note

After you enable Panels, the options on the Structure menu change as well. The new options match the three types of panels: Mini panels, Panel pages, and Panels node. ■

The remaining sections of the Panels Manager are largely devoted to providing a dashboard that allows you quick access to the various panels you have created. The Manage Pages section (refer to Figure 27.9) contains a list of the pages in the system, and it's a repeat of the content you can see on the Pages option on the Structure section of the Management menu.

The default Panels module (refer to Figure 27.9) comes with a set of panels that are ready to use. The existing panels are provided to override some of the key default Drupal templates. The default panels are disabled by default, but you need only enable them to begin using them right away. The panels also can be customized to your needs, giving you the ability to create overrides to the core templates, without having to create a custom `.tpl.php` file.

These are the default panels:

- **Node add/edit form:** This overrides the default Drupal interface for adding or editing nodes. It's handy for use in creating a customized content management interface for particular user or user groups.
- **Node template:** This overrides the default node template. This impacts only nodes viewed as pages. It's useful for creating custom node appearance. You can add variants to this to create nodes that are only seen when certain criteria are met.
- **Taxonomy term template:** This overrides the default template for displaying taxonomy terms. It's particularly useful for creating custom content lists based on taxonomy.
- **User profile template:** This overrides the default user profile template. It's particularly useful for creating custom user profile pages on membership sites.

The Panels Manager overlay contains two tabs (refer to Figure 27.9). The default is Dashboard; the second tab is labeled Settings. If you click the Settings tab, you see the page shown in Figure 27.10.

FIGURE 27.10

The Panels Manager Settings tab

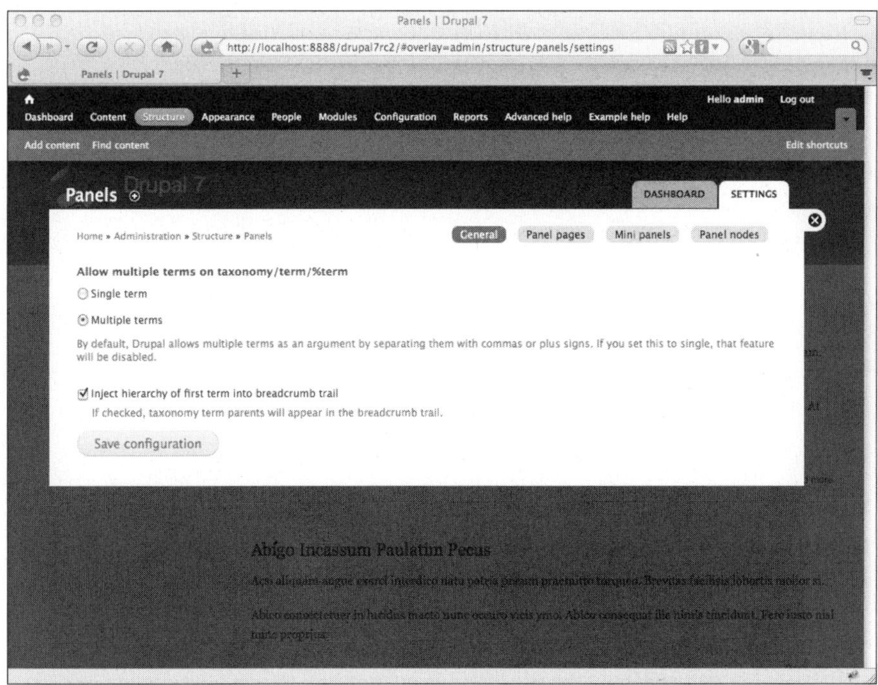

The options on this tab are explained well on the page itself, but essentially this page functions as the configuration page for the Panels module. Although some of the options here are relevant only during development, others are meaningful on a live site and have performance implications. At the top right, under the tabs, are four buttons:

- **General:** This is the default Settings page (refer to Figure 27.10).
- **Panel pages:** These allow you to configure the default behavior for new content and the available layouts for panel pages.
- **Mini panels:** These allow you to configure the default behavior for new content and the available layouts for mini panels.
- **Panel nodes:** These allow you to configure the default behavior for new content and the available layouts for panel nodes.

For most users, the default configuration in the Settings tab is sufficient and does not require adjustment.

Creating new Panels

By way of example, I take you through the steps to create a new mini panel. For my sites, I like to create a block tailored especially for my site administrators. The block contains a quick overview of critical information about changes in the site's contents and users. Although a number of individual blocks provide the information, I want to aggregate that data into one block that I can easily control and style. The solution is to use Panels to create a new mini panel that I can assign to the Dashboard of the admin interface.

To create this mini panel, follow these steps:

1. **Log into your site as an administrator.**

   The Management menu appears at the top of the page.
2. **Select the Structure option from the Management menu.**

   The Structure menu options display in the overlay.
3. **Click the Mini panels options.**

   The Mini Panels Manager opens.
4. **Click the Add button.**

   The add new mini panel page opens, as shown in Figure 27.11.
5. **In the Name field, type a machine-friendly name for the mini panel. For this example, use `admin_info`. Add a name for the administrator to see in the field Administrative title.**

FIGURE 27.11

The first step in the creation of a new mini panel

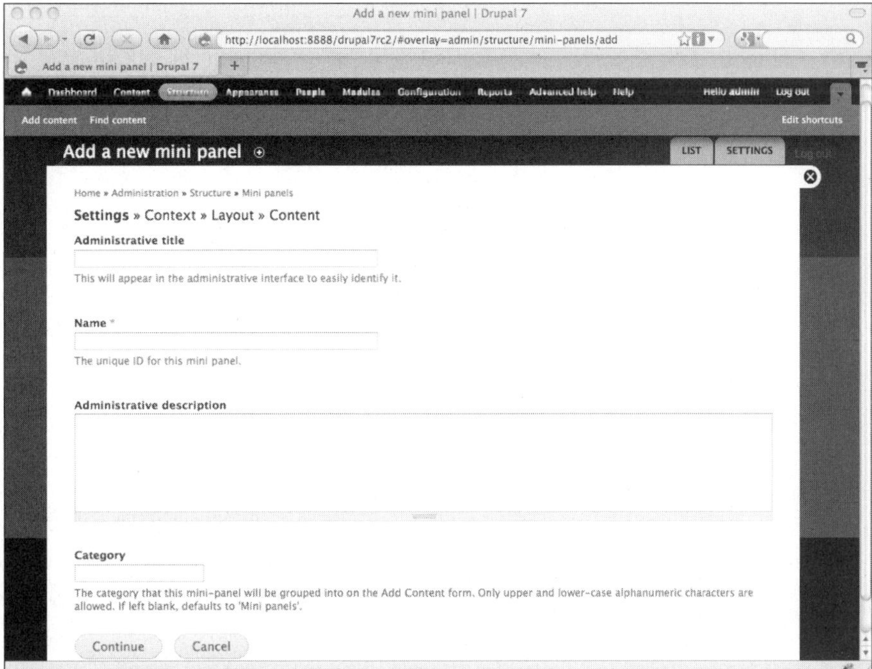

6. **Click the Continue button.**

   The second step in the add new mini panel page appears, as shown in Figure 27.12.

7. **Set the context to display the mini panel for user1 by selecting User from the Required Contexts drop-down box and clicking the Add required context button.**

   The Add required context configuration pop-up appears.

8. **On the pop-up, click the option Select a user.**

   The system displays a new field labeled Enter a user name.

9. **Enter the name used by user1 in your system.**

   User1 in my system is named Admin, so I typed Admin in the field.

Note

By selecting a specific user, I have restricted the display of this to only that particular user, not to all administrators! ■

FIGURE 27.12

The second step in the creation of a new mini panel

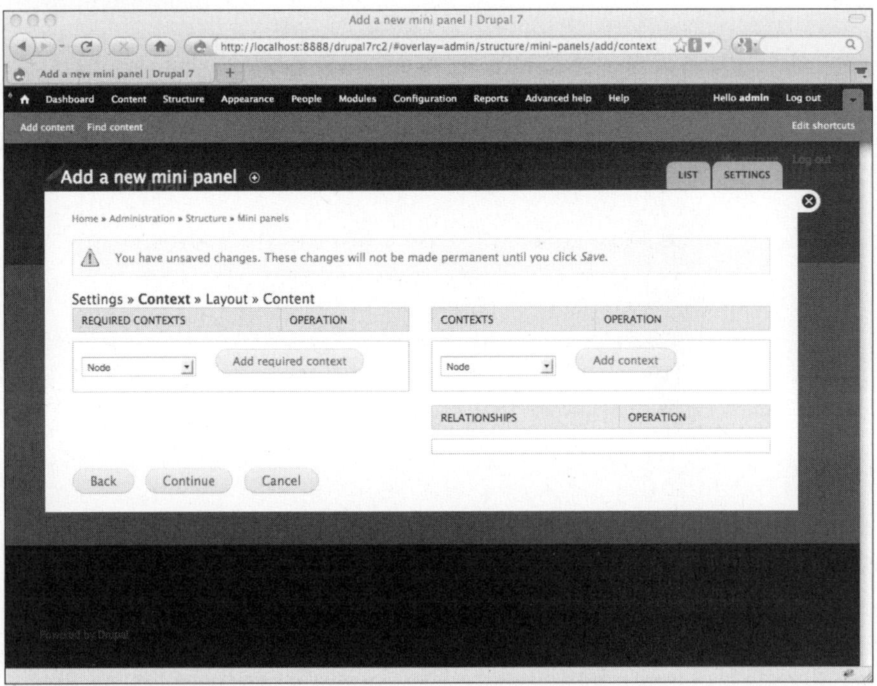

10. **Click the Finish button.**

    The pop-up closes.

11. **Click the Continue button.**

    The next step in the mini panel creation process appears, as shown in Figure 27.13.

12. **Select Columns: 1 from the Category combo box.**

    The layouts shown change.

13. **Select the Single column layout.**

Tip

Various layouts are available in single- and multiple-column formats. For the mini panel in this example, a single column is the only practical solution. The other options are very useful for pages and nodes and can be customized for your needs. ■

FIGURE 27.13

The third step in the creation of a new mini panel

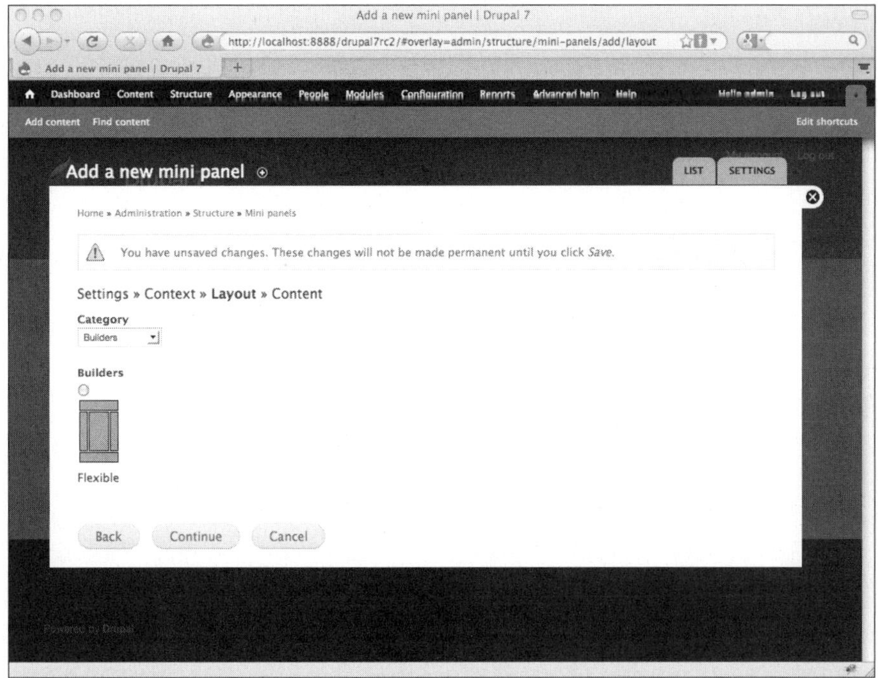

14. **Click the Continue button.**

    The final step in the mini panel creation process loads, as shown in Figure 27.14.

15. **Change the value in the Title type combo box to No title.**

    The title field disappears from view.

16. **Click the gear icon.**

    A menu appears.

17. **Click Change.**

    The panel style pop-up configuration appears.

18. **Click No style.**

Tip

The style configuration page lets you determine basic styling for the panel. If you want to use CSS to customize the display, select No style. For panel pages and nodes, you have the option to add the CSS selectors of your choice to the pane. ■

FIGURE 27.14

The final step in the creation of a new mini panel

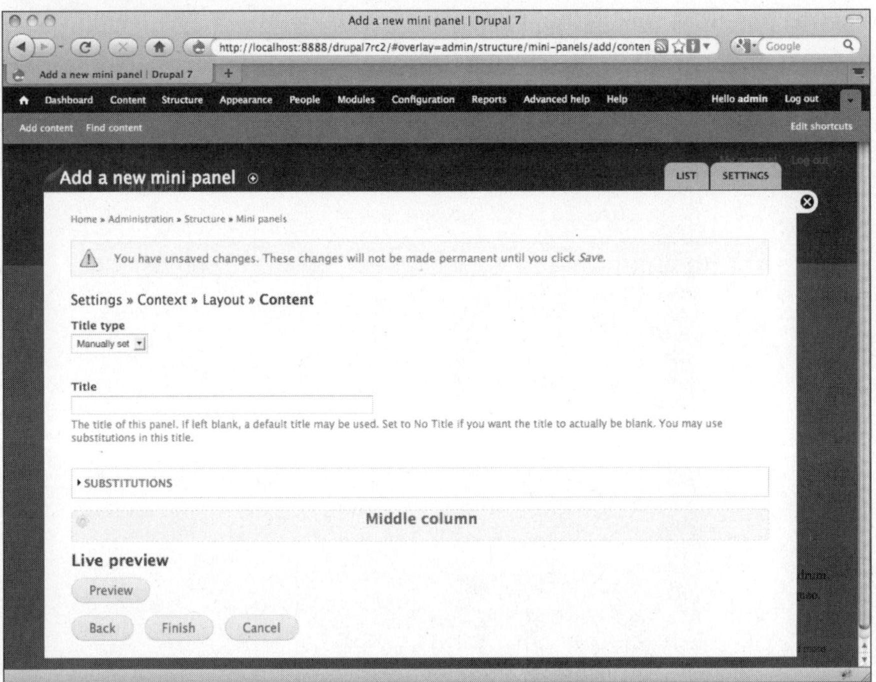

19. **Click Next.**

    The pop-up closes.

20. **Click the gear icon.**

    A menu appears.

21. **Click Add content.**

    The Add content pop-up appears.

22. **Click Widgets.**

    The Widgets options show.

23. **Click Search form.**

    The Search form configuration page opens.

24. **Click the Finish button.**

    The pop-up closes.

25. **Click the gear, and repeat the process until you have added the following contents: Who's online, Recent comments, and User menu.**

    At the end, your screen should look like what is shown in Figure 27.15.

FIGURE 27.15

The final results of adding the various content items to the mini panel

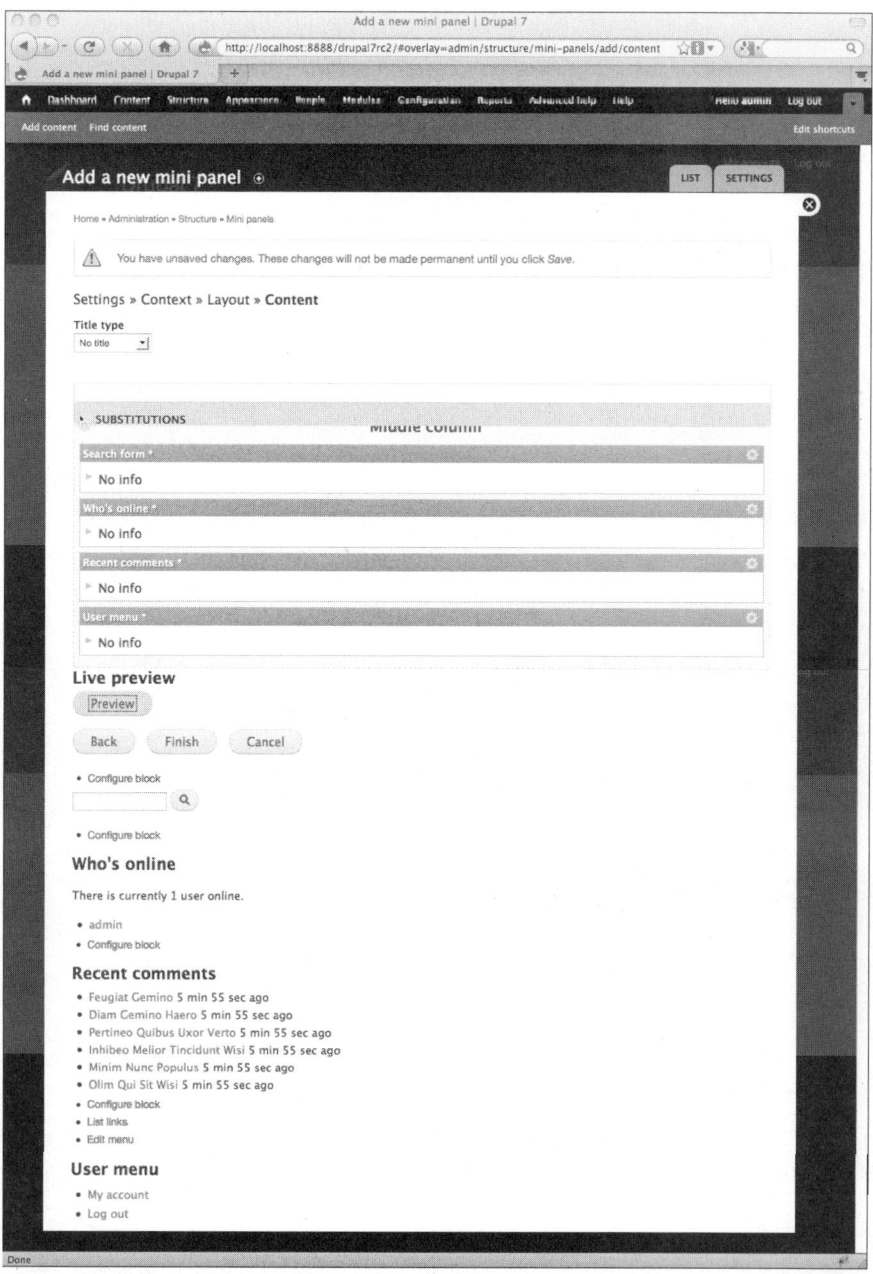

26. **Click the Finish button.**

    The system saves the mini panel and returns you to the Mini Panel Manager. If you were successful, you see a confirmation message.

Tip

Clicking the Preview button shown in Figures 27.14 and 27.15 allows you to see your work as you go. ■

The steps above take you through the creation of the mini panel. Now, to see it in action, go to the Dashboard, publish it, and remove the redundant blocks. The result should look like what you see in Figure 27.16.

FIGURE 27.16

The new Admin Info mini panel is in place on the Dashboard. I configured the block to add the title "Welcome, admin!"

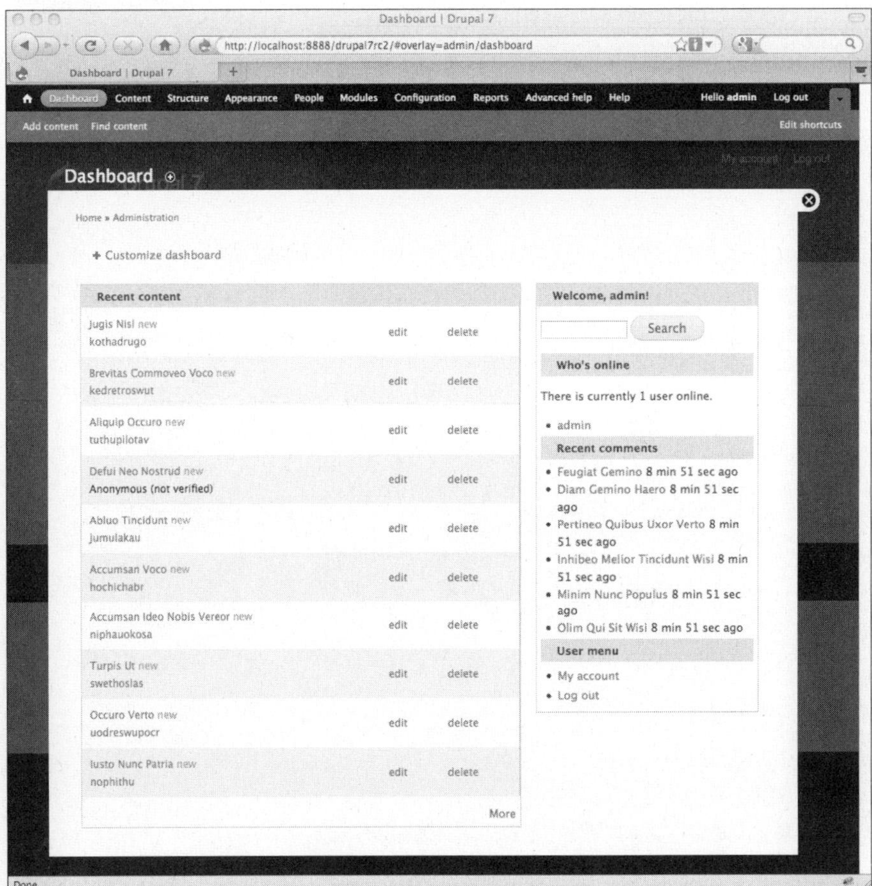

Cross-Reference

Customizing the Admin Dashboard is discussed in Chapter 3. ■

The example above shows how the Panels module can be used to create a basic block. The process for creating other types of panels is similar, though with more options for the administrator to explore.

Note

The complexity of the Panels module has inspired a number of tutorials and a fair amount of documentation. If you want to explore further, try visiting the Panels project page on the official Drupal.org site. ■

Editing and deleting panels

Editing a panel varies according to the type of panel. While a page or a node panel can be modified extensively, a mini panel is limited in its editing options. In any case, however, the process is very simple: You need only find the panel you want to modify and then click the edit button. You can make your changes on the screens that follow, and after you save them, they are done.

Deleting a panel is simple. Access the appropriate Panels Manager, find the panel you want to remove, and then click the Delete link. The system asks you to confirm the decision.

Caution

Note that after you confirm deletion, the panel is gone forever, and it cannot be undone! ■

Summary

This chapter covered how you can control and customize the output of your site using the Views and Panels modules. This chapter included these topics:

- How Views and Panels work with the core to give you control over the output
- How to install Views
- How to create your first view
- How to edit and delete views
- How to install Panels
- How to create your first panel
- How to edit and delete panel

CHAPTER

28

Customizing Drupal Functionality

IN THIS CHAPTER

Understanding basic principles

Using the right tools

Using the Drupal API

Creating a new module

Theming a module

The functionality you see and experience in Drupal is largely the province of the core and contributed modules. When you talk about customizing Drupal's functionality, you are most likely talking about customizing the modules. In this chapter, I cover the key role that modules play in Drupal and how you can customize the functionality of a Drupal site by modifying modules or by creating your own custom modules.

There are entire books devoted to the topic of creating Drupal modules and customizing Drupal's functionality. In this chapter, I cover basics and enough information to get you started.

Basic Principles

At the heart of the Drupal system are the modules. Drupal is, quite literally, modular: The modules supply the functionality on the site. Most of the modules can be enabled or disabled to allow you to tailor the site's functionality to your needs. There are, however, several core modules upon which the system relies. These core modules are key to the functioning of the system and cannot be disabled from within the admin system.

Among the key modules in the system are the following:

- **Block:** This module controls creation and management of the site's blocks. Block module documentation can be found at `http://drupal.org/handbook/modules/block`.

- **Menu:** This module powers the menu functionality and provides the interface for managing menus. Menu module documentation can be found at `http://drupal.org/handbook/modules/menu`.
- **Node:** This module manages the creation, editing, deletion, settings, and display of the main site content. Node module documentation can be found at `http://drupal.org/handbook/modules/node`.
- **System:** A number of Drupal's key functions are supplied by the System module. The module provides elements for enabling and disabling of modules and themes, the display of the administration pages, and basic site configuration. Much of what is provided by this module is relied upon by other modules. System module documentation can be found at `http://drupal.org/handbook/modules/system`.
- **User:** This module manages the user system and the login functionality. The module is also responsible for the permissions functionality. User module documentation can be found at `http://drupal.org/handbook/modules/user`.

Caution

The modules outlined above are essential to the functioning of your site. Do not attempt to modify these modules because you may crash your site! ■

The addition of new functionality to a Drupal site is accomplished through the addition of new modules. Similarly, if you want to modify the existing functionality, the odds are good that you need to modify one of the existing modules.

Cross-Reference

A complete listing of the core modules, along with descriptions, can be found in Chapter 6. ■

Modules are called by the system's framework as they are needed. Within each module, multiple events occur. You can tap into these events by using what are known in Drupal as *hooks.* The most common way to access Drupal's functionality is by accessing the hooks in the modules.

Note

Hooks are also sometimes referred to as callbacks. ■

Mastering the use of hooks is the key to customizing Drupal functionality. No matter what you want to do, odds are good that there is a hook for it. If not, you can always create your own! To implement a hook, a module simply needs to declare a function that follows the hook naming convention. For example, to implement the initialization hook, a module would declare the function `hook_init()`.

Most modules are merely collections of hooks. Hooks are provided both by the core and by the modules themselves. You also can create your own hooks and make them available for other modules to use. Once past initialization, the system steps through all the hooks in the module, calling one after the other until it reaches the end.

Note

For a variety of reasons, Drupal has not followed the course of adopting an object-oriented programming approach to PHP; rather, Drupal relies on procedural programming. Instead of relying heavily upon classes and interfaces, Drupal modules are composed largely of collections of functions. This doesn't mean you won't see objects; it simply means that OOP is not the dominant theme underlying the codeset. ■

The database in Drupal fulfills multiple purposes aside from simply storing the content. The database also holds caches, configuration information, metadata, and information on menu system structures. That said, the database does not play the central role that you might assume; it functions primarily as a place to store various bits of data. If you don't need the database for your module, you aren't forced to interact with it.

Note

Drupal 7 introduces a completely new database API. The database abstraction layer has been completely rewritten and is now based on the PHP Data Objects (PDO) library. This enables Drupal to support numerous databases, including MySQL, PostgreSQL, SQLite, MariaDB, and others. For more complete information on the role of the database in Drupal 7, visit the database API at `http://drupal.org/developing/api/database`. ■

Tip

Drupal 7 brings with it literally hundreds of changes to the system's module architecture. If you are familiar with Drupal 6 modules, then you probably want to start by reviewing the official page on converting Drupal 6 modules to Drupal 7; it provides a great summary of the impact of the changes. Visit `http://drupal.org/update/modules/6/7`. ■

The Right Tools

Having the right tools can make any job easier and faster; the same is true with Drupal. Although your preferred programming toolkit is a personal decision, the items listed in this section are of great utility value and are highly recommended to all who want to work with the Drupal codeset in any detail.

The Devel module

The Devel module is a suite of tools aimed at easing life for Drupal developers. It's hard to make a case for not using Devel (the only exception I can think is a live site). The module is a collection of helper functions, including the following:

- The ability to display a summary of all database queries for each page request (The summary also shows how many times each query ran and how long it took.)
- The ability to print arrays
- A backtrace utility

- A utility to generate sample content, users, taxonomies, and comments
- Performance logging
- The ability to view a node access summary

Devel is a powerful tool and exposes a great deal of information about your site. Although it is a great time-saver, it should not be used on a live site. Get your copy by visiting the Devel project page at `http://drupal.org/project/devel`.

Tip

You can extend the Devel module with the popular Theme Developer module. Theme Developer is a utility module that is relevant to your theming efforts and is useful both when working with theme files and during module creation. You can get Theme Developer at `http://drupal.org/project/devel_themer`. ■

The Coder module

The Coder module is a utility that performs two very useful functions:

- It reviews your source code files for compliance with Drupal coding standards and checks whether they are in line with the current Drupal API.
- It allows you to upload your module code and upgrade an old module to current standards.

Although Coder is not something you must have to work with Drupal modules, given that it makes it easy for you to create standards-compliant code, you would be foolish not to use it. Download a copy from `http://drupal.org/project/coder`.

Cross-Reference

See Chapter 29 for a discussion of how to install contributed modules to your site. ■

Drush

Drush is a command line shell and Unix scripting interface for Drupal. The Drush core enables a number of useful functions:

- The Drush Package Manager, which allows you to download, enable, uninstall, and update modules, themes, profiles, and more, from the command line
- A customized bash shell
- A utility to run cron
- A utility to dump caches
- The Drush SQL Command, which allows you to issue queries to your database

There are also additional contributed modules that integrate Drush.

If you have previously used a command line shell, you'll love Drush. If you are not experienced with a command line interface, you will find there is a bit of a learning curve to Drush, but the time savings you can gain from learning is worth the investment. You can download Drush from `http://drupal.org/project/drush`.

Note

Drush is not a module; you need to pay attention to the README for installation instructions specific to your particular OS. Don't let the project page on Drupal.org confuse you; although it looks like a module, it is not. ■

Version control

Whether you use version control is a personal choice, but if you are working with others on common code, it is hard to justify not implementing some form of version control. The Drupal project relies on the Git distributed version control system. If you are interested in becoming more involved with Drupal development, then you should make an effort to become familiar with Git. A number of Git clients are available, including an increasing number of desktop applications with usable GUIs.

Note

Setting up version control and branching under Git is beyond the scope of this book. To learn more about Git and how it is being used now by the Drupal development team, see the Git reference guide for site builders at `http://drupal.org/node/803746`**. Note that this topic is also useful for those who want to maintain a Drupal module. ■**

The Drupal API

In line with the project's focus on being developer-friendly, Drupal is one of the better documented open-source CMS systems. There is an extensive API, and the vast majority of the functions are documented using inline code documentation. Visit the full API online at `http://api.drupal.org`.

Drupal developers are expected to comply with the Drupal style manual and coding standards. As an independent developer, you may not feel compelled to follow suit, but best practices would dictate that you keep your code clean, consistent, and readable. Following the Drupal coding standards is consistent with that logic, and it has the added advantage of being a common ground with other Drupal developers. Learn more by visiting the official coding standards page at `http://drupal.org/coding-standards`.

You really have no excuse for not following Drupal standards. The Coder module, discussed earlier in this chapter, makes complying with Drupal standards painless.

Tip

A Drupal page devoted to best practices can be found at `http://drupal.org/node/360052`**. ■**

Customizing Modules

When you talk about customizing modules, you first need to decide what level of customization is required. If you only want to change the styling, it is simply a matter of overriding the themable output. You can customize the styling for any module in the system, using the techniques discussed elsewhere in this book.

Cross-Reference

To learn how to override themable output, please see Chapter 26 on customizing Drupal's appearance. ■

If, however, you need to change the way a module functions, you must make a distinction between core modules and contributed modules. You have much more latitude with contributed modules. If, for example, you want to override an entire contributed module, you can do so. In contrast, the core modules cannot be overridden in their entirety.

If you genuinely need to change the way a core module functions, you should consider two options: First, you need to decide whether Drupal is right for you. If you need to make changes to the fundamental operations of a system, you should always consider whether you have selected the right system. Second, if you are committed to modifying the core, you should set up version control and create a branch of the Drupal codeset for your use.

Note

A good place to begin research on customization of a specific module is with the Drupal community. Odds are quite good that someone, somewhere has confronted a similar issue in the past. A quick trip to the Drupal forum may provide you with a fast solution or an alternative. ■

If you want to modify the functionality of a contributed module, you should override the entire contributed module, preserving the original in case you need to roll back—and to avoid having your changes overwritten during an upgrade or patch.

To override an entire contributed module, follow these steps:

1. **Copy the module you want to override.**
2. **Change the name of the module and all references to that name inside the module's files.**
3. **Install the module.**
4. **Enable it via the Modules Manager.**

You can install the module without changing all references of the name inside the module code, but if you do not change the name throughout, you cannot install both the original module and your new customized module.

Creating a New Module

Creating a new module for Drupal is not particularly daunting. The steps are well established and relatively simple. What you put inside that module is another matter entirely. You can make your modules very complicated, introducing new hooks, multiple templates, and much more, or you can create very simple modules incorporating existing hooks and relying on default system styling; it's really up to you.

Regardless of the complexity of the functionality brought into Drupal by the module, you always follow the same basic path to module creation:

1. **Create a new module folder.**
2. **Create a .info file to provide the system with the information it needs.**
3. **Create a .module file to contain the code that provides the module's functionality.**

Although you may add other files and resources later, your module must, at a minimum, have the items listed above.

Creating a new module folder

Before you begin creating the files for a new module, you need a place to put them. In Drupal, the best place to put your custom modules is in directories inside of `/sites/all/modules`. Putting modules in this directory protects them from being overwritten during site upgrades and allows the modules to be visible to all sites, which is useful when you are running multiple sites off one Drupal installation.

Note

Some developers prefer to segregate custom modules from contributed modules by placing the custom modules either inside `/sites/default/modules` **or in a separate subdirectory at** `/sites/all/modules/custom`**. The decision is yours; there is no definitive best-practices approach on this point.** ■

Name the module directory after your module, but in machine-friendly format—that is, all lowercase, with any spaces replaced by underscores.

Next you need to create the first of two essential files for your module, the .info file.

Creating the .info file

Your new module must have a .info file. The .info file serves the following functions:

- Notifies the Drupal system of the presence of the module
- Provides information needed by Drupal to activate and deactivate the module

- Provides information about the module that is displayed in the admin interface
- Identifies the necessary files and dependencies

The `.info` file follows the `.ini` file format—that is, a collection of key pairs/values, separated by an equal sign.

Here is an example—in this case, the `comment.info` file, from Drupal's default Comment module.

```
; $Id: comment.info,v 1.14 2010/09/05 02:21:38 dries Exp $
name = Comment
description = Allows users to comment on and discuss published
   content.
package = Core
version = VERSION
core = 7.x
dependencies[] = text
files[] = comment.module
files[] = comment.admin.inc
files[] = comment.pages.inc
files[] = comment.install
files[] = comment.test
files[] = comment.tokens.inc
configure = admin/content/comment
stylesheets[all][] = comment.css

; Information added by drupal.org packaging script on 2010-12-11
version = "7.0-rc2"
project = "drupal"
datestamp = "1292101844"
```

This is what you see in this file:

- The opening line is prefixed by a semicolon. Any line that begins with a semicolon is treated as a comment and ignored by the system. The line that follows `$Id` is used to contain CVS info for the module.
- The `Name` and `Description` display in the admin system's Modules Manager. These fields are required.
- The `Package` value determines where the module is grouped inside the Modules Manager.
- The `Core` value tells us compatibility. This field is required.
- The `Dependencies` value names the other modules this module requires to function.
- The `Files` value lists the files contained within the module package.

Note

The files section of the .info file should list only those files that contain functions. Therefore, files like template files or JavaScript do not have to be listed. ■

- Configure shows the path to the module's configuration page.
- The stylesheets declaration allows you to include the CSS for the module directly from the .info file.
- The last group of information, shown after the semicolon, was automatically supplied by the packaging script.

Note

For more information on the options for the .info values and the syntax that should be used, visit http://drupal.org/node/542202. ■

Name your .info file consistently with your module directory. For example, if your module directory is named new_module, then your .info file should be named new_module.info.

After you place the .info file inside your module directory, you can see the module inside the admin system's Modules Manager. However, at this stage, the module does nothing, because it still lacks the key .module file, explained next.

Creating the .module file

The .module file does all the heavy work in your module. It contains the hook implementations that allow your module to actually do something. To understand how this works, we need an example. Here is an excerpt from the comment.module file showing the implementation of the help hook:

Note

Hooks follow a set naming convention: modulename_hookname. **In the next example, you can see the implementation of the help hook in the Comment module; the hook is named** comment_help. ■

```
/**
 * Implements hook_help().
 */
function comment_help($path, $arg) {
  switch ($path) {
    case 'admin/help#comment':
      $output = '<h3>' . t('About') . '</h3>';
      $output .= '<p>' . t('The Comment module allows users to
   comment on site content, set commenting defaults and permissions,
   and moderate comments. For more information, see the online
   handbook entry for <a href="@comment">Comment module</a>.',
   array('@comment' => 'http://drupal.org/handbook/modules/
   comment/')) . '</p>';
      $output .= '<h3>' . t('Uses') . '</h3>';
      $output .= '<dl>';
      $output .= '<dt>' . t('Default and custom settings') . '</dt>';
      $output .= '<dd>' . t("Each <a href='@content-type'>content
   type</a> can have its own default comment settings configured as:
   <em>Open</em> to allow new comments, <em>Hidden</em> to hide
```

```
existing comments and prevent new comments, or <em>Closed</em> to
view existing comments, but prevent new comments. These defaults
will apply to all new content created (changes to the settings on
existing content must be done manually). Other comment settings
can also be customized per content type, and can be overridden
for any given item of content. When a comment has no replies, it
remains editable by its author, as long as the author has a user
account and is logged in.", array('@content-type' => url('admin/
structure/types'))) . '</dd>';
   $output .= '<dt>' . t('Comment approval') . '</dt>';
   $output .= '<dd>' . t("Comments from users who have the
<em>Skip comment approval</em> permission are published
immediately. All other comments are placed in the <a href='@
comment-approval'>Unapproved comments</a> queue, until a user who
has permission to <em>Administer comments</em> publishes or
deletes them. Published comments can be bulk managed on the <a
href='@admin-comment'>Published comments</a> administration
page.", array('@comment-approval' => url('admin/content/comment/
approval'), '@admin-comment' => url('admin/content/comment'))) .
'</dd>';
   $output .= '</dl>';
   return $output;
  }
}
```

Note

The "help" example includes numerous examples of another common function, the `t()` **function. The** `t()` **function is responsible for translating strings from one language to another. You can see in the** `comment_help` **example that the** `t()` **function prefixing the literal strings of content that appear on the help page. This is the proper format for implementing this function, and it allows the system to manage the strings through the translation system.** ■

The help hook, technically `hook_help()`, is only one of many hooks implemented in the Comment module, but it's an easy-to-see example. The help hook allows the module developer to tie into the core system's help file functionality. By implementing this hook, the module developer can add help text that is automatically displayed to the site administrators when they click the help link next to the module name in the Modules Manager. Figure 28.1 shows the output generated through the use of this hook.

The help hook demonstrates how the Drupal system simplifies things for the module developer. The hook enables the developer to tap into existing system functionality, rather than having to reinvent the wheel.

Note

A complete list of the hooks available can be found in the Drupal API at `http://api.drupal.org/api/drupal/includes--module.inc/group/hooks/7.` ■

FIGURE 28.1

The help page for the Comment module shows content that was included using the help hook in the nearby sample code.

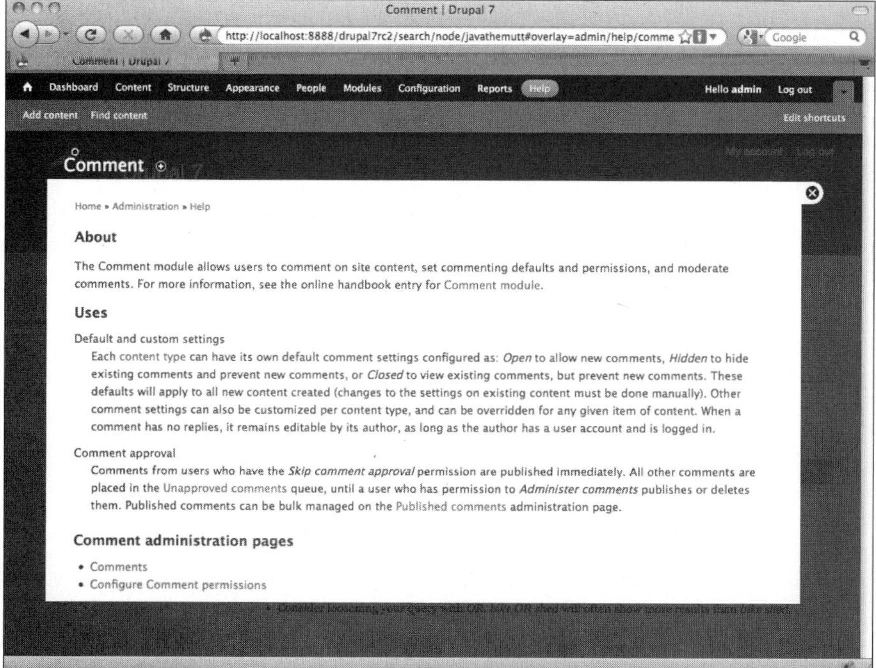

Although the help hook is a simple functionality, many other hooks offer access to more complex behaviors. Additionally, if no hook meets your needs, you can always create a new hook that your module can implement.

Interacting with the database

If you need to create a table in the database to support your module, create a `.install` file inside your module directory. The `.install` file directs the system to create the tables you need at the time the module is enabled.

The `.install` file can include multiple hooks relevant to module installation, uninstallation, or update. One of the key hooks is `hook_schema()`, which is used to manipulate the database tables. By implementing the schema and describing the database tables that your module needs, you can easily create and drop tables without having to deal with the underlying SQL statements. The `modulename_install()` function reads the schema and translates the tables and fields you describe into SQL appropriate for the database you are using.

If, on the other hand, your module needs to perform alterations to the existing database structure of another module, you need to implement a different function: `hook_schema_alter()`.

Note

The Schema API provides details on the definition structures: `http://api.drupal.org/api/drupal/includes--database--schema.inc/group/schemaapi/7.` ■

Adding blocks to a module

Drupal 7 adds a number of hooks that help you to define blocks within a module. The key hook is `hook_block_info()`, which is capable of implementing multiple blocks. The hook can also be used to specify initial block configuration settings.

Note

The hook supports a number of properties. See the Drupal API documentation to learn more: `http://api.drupal.org/api/drupal/modules--block--block.api.php/function/hook_block_info/7.` ■

In addition to `hook_block_info()`, which creates the block, you also need to implement `hook_block_view()` to build the contents of the block. The hook is called whenever Drupal needs to display the block.

Additional hooks are relevant to block creation. You may not need them all, but these are the options:

- `hook_block_configure()`: Defines the configuration form for the block
- `hook_block_info_alter()`: Changes the block definition
- `hook_block_list_alter()`: Allows you to add, remove, or modify blocks in the block list
- `hook_block_save()`: Saves block configuration changes from `hook_block_configure()`
- `hook_block_view_alter()`: Alters the content of the block
- `hook_block-view_MODULE_DELTA_alter()`: Alters content of a specific block, based on its name and delta

Theming a Module

Assuming your module has output that needs to be rendered on the screen, you need to provide either theme functions or templates to handle the display. You can use existing theme hooks, or you can create your own.

Note

If you are making theme changes to an existing module, remember that you must always clear the theme registry before you can see them! ■

Reusing existing theme hooks

When you are making decisions about how to theme your own module, you should consider reusing existing theme hooks, rather than going through the effort of creating your own. The existing Drupal system has almost 200 theme hooks, and you can reuse any of them. Many contributed modules rely on the existing core theme hooks.

Note

You can view a complete listing of the default theme implementations here: `http://api.drupal.org/api/drupal/modules--system--theme.api.php/group/themeable/7`. ■

If you have found an existing theme hook that is similar to what you need, but you want to modify it, it probably is faster to use the existing theme hook and change it using the preprocess function, discussed later in this section.

Implementing hook_theme()

If your module has output that needs to be themed, you must implement `hook_theme()` to specify the theming options for your module. `hook_theme()` is used to register the theming hooks you want to use for the module and whether those are functions or templates.

Registration is absolutely necessary for Drupal to find the theme hooks and make them available. Every module should provide a default implementation for the theme hooks it registers. If you are specifying a function, you must declare it in `hook_theme()`. If you are specifying a template, you must name the template and include the .tpl.php file in the module directory.

With the arrival of Drupal 7, you also can specify the output either by declaring variables and their values in an array or by providing a render element. For example, the `comment.module` file contains the following implementation of the `hook_theme()` function:

```
/**
 * Implements hook_theme().
 */
function comment_theme() {
  return array(
    'comment_block' => array(
      'variables' => array(),
    ),
    'comment_preview' => array(
      'variables' => array('comment' => NULL),
    ),
    'comment' => array(
```

```
        'template' => 'comment',
        'render element' => 'elements',
      ),
      'comment_post_forbidden' => array(
        'variables' => array('node' => NULL),
      ),
      'comment_wrapper' => array(
        'template' => 'comment-wrapper',
        'render element' => 'content',
      ),
    );
}
```

In the code above, a few items need to be highlighted:

- Note the naming convention: Like other hooks, there is a formula at work—in this case, `modulename_theme()`. In the code above, you can see this as `comment_theme()`.
- The code above registers multiple theming hooks for the module: `comment_block`, `comment_preview`, `comment`, `comment_post_forbidden`, and `comment_wrapper`.
- This module uses templates for only the `comment` and `comment_wrapper` hooks. In those cases where you want to use a template, you define the name of the template file, but without the .tpl.php suffix. In the example code, you see the template key followed by the base name of the template.

Note

For the declaration of the templates to work properly, you also must include proper .tpl.php files inside the module directory and the names must match those declared in the theme hook. ■

- The comment and comment_wrapper also rely upon the render element option rather than specifying variables.

Note

A list of all the parameters available to the hook can be found at `http://api.drupal.org/api/drupal/modules--system--system.api.php/function/hook_theme/7`. ■

Although the Comment module uses two templates to handle part of its output, it also uses themable functions for different output. Theme functions are named using this convention: `theme_hook`. The arguments that accompany the function are passed straight through. Themers can rely on the default styling, or they can override this function in the active theme's `template.php` file.

Looking further into the `comment.module` file, you can find an example of the implementation of a themable function to handle the output of the Comment block:

```
/**
 * Returns HTML for a list of recent comments to be displayed in the
   comment block.
 *
 * @ingroup themeable
 */
function theme_comment_block() {
  $items = array();
  $number = variable_get('comment_block_count', 10);
  foreach (comment_get_recent($number) as $comment) {
    $items[] = l($comment->subject, 'comment/' . $comment->cid,
   array('fragment' => 'comment-' . $comment->cid)) . ' <span>'
   . t('@time ago', array('@time' => format_interval(REQUEST_TIME -
   $comment->changed))) . '</span>';
  }

  if ($items) {
    return theme('item_list', array('items' => $items));
  }
  else {
    return t('No comments available.');
  }
}
```

For this code example, here are some notes:

- The function relates to the theme function named `comment_block` that was created in the example code earlier in this chapter.
- The themable functions all follow the same naming convention: `theme_theme_hook_name()`. In the code above, you can see the name `theme_comment_block`.
- The variables that follow the declaration of the function are an associative array that delineates the bits of content that you want to pass to the function.

Tip

The decision of whether to use a template or themable functions is up to you; both have advantages. Functions tend to be faster, but templates offer more flexibility and provide the option of using the preprocess function, discussed in the next section. ■

Cross-Reference

Creating templates and working with themable functions and CSS styling are topics covered by Chapter 26. ■

Using preprocess functions

Preprocess functions are used to transform raw data into variables that are usable for theming. If you want to add variables to an existing function, you also would use preprocess to make those variables available. Preprocess functions apply only to variables used as templates.

Preprocess functions require a specific naming convention: `template_preprocess_hook()`. For an example, look again to the `comment.module` file, where you can find the following, which is intended to affect the comment-wrapper template you saw created in the example code earlier in this chapter:

```
/**
 * Process variables for comment-wrapper.tpl.php.
 *
 * @see comment-wrapper.tpl.php
 * @see theme_comment_wrapper()
 */
function template_preprocess_comment_wrapper(&$variables) {
  // Provide contextual information.
  $variables['node'] = $variables['content']['#node'];
  $variables['display_mode'] = variable_get('comment_default_mode_' .
   $variables['node']->type, COMMENT_MODE_THREADED);
  // The comment form is optional and may not exist.
  $variables['content'] += array('comment_form' => array());
}
```

The preprocess function makes it easier for you to pass variables to your template and allows you to put all these statements in one place where they can be easily managed and manipulated. Relying on preprocess to supply variables for your template may initially seem more difficult, but the reality is that, across time, you will find it simpler than manipulating the theme hook all the time.

Tip

The preprocess function is also the right place to make sure that the data passed to the presentation layer is free from any potential threats to your site. Drupal makes it easy to sanitize data by providing a set of functions for that specific purpose. They should be implemented through the preprocess function. You can learn more about this process by visiting `http://drupal.org/node/933976`. ■

Summary

This chapter addressed the basics of customizing functionality in Drupal. I covered these topics:

- The key role modules play in Drupal functionality
- How to override modules
- The requirements for creating a new module
- How to set up theming for a new module
- How to use the preprocess function to add variables for theming

CHAPTER 29

Extending Your Site

IN THIS CHAPTER

How to find extensions

Working with extensions

Key extensions to address common issues

One of the defining characteristics of the Drupal CMS is its extensibility. The Drupal core includes a number of useful functions, but it's the ability to add more functionality that makes the system attractive and practical for most site owners. Third-party or "contributed" modules are a big part of the Drupal experience.

Contributed modules are available to suit a variety of functions. Some modules are very basic, others quite complicated, and still others are merely helper apps that enable other functionality. Indeed, so essential and valuable are contributed modules that few sites are deployed without at least a couple of additional extensions.

In addition to modules, contributed themes can be added to your Drupal site. Like modules, some themes are very basic, while others have many configuration options.

In the first part of this chapter, I cover how to find and install extensions for your site. The second part of the chapter includes a list of modules that are intended to address common needs.

Finding Extensions

Drupal.org includes a directory of extensions. The directory is quite lengthy and lists contributed extensions that are available for all versions of the Drupal core. The listing covers both themes and modules.

When searching for extensions, the official site should always be your starting point. An increasing number of third-party sites offer advice and information on Drupal extensions, but at the end of the day, the official project site is the best place to look for current and correct code. Figure 29.1 shows the entry page for contributed extensions listing on Drupal.org.

FIGURE 29.1

The extensions listing on the official Drupal site

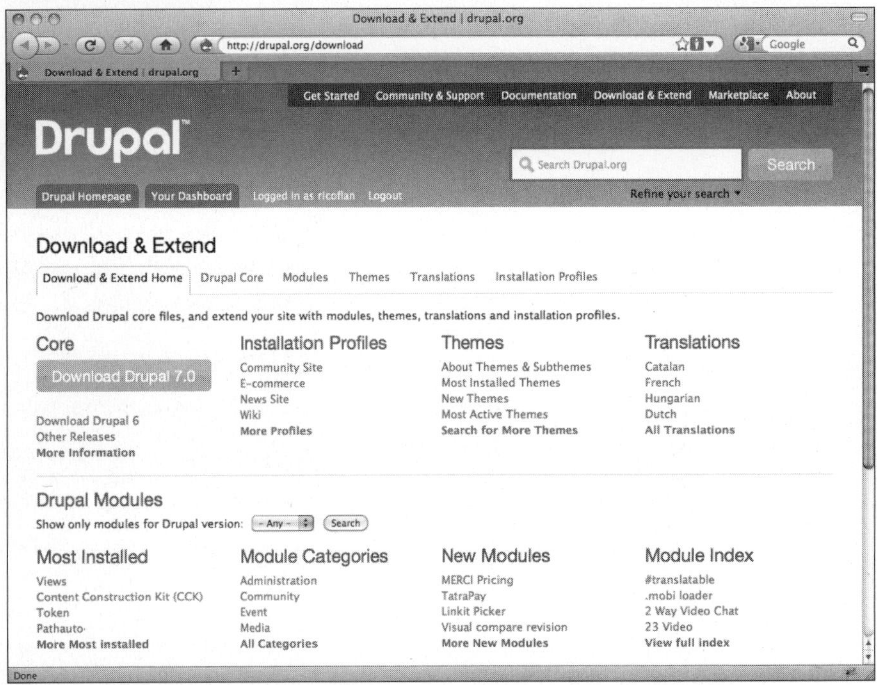

The directory breaks down the extensions by type and provides a browsable directory of the various packages for each type. The listing can be searched and filtered by version compatibility.

In addition to the short listings you see in the directory, each extension has a dedicated project page, as shown in Figure 29.2. Access the project page by clicking the name of the extension or the link labeled Find out more. The project page provides detailed information about the extension, including a description, version compatibility, documentation, and a list of issues for the extension. Additionally, any dependencies for the extension are listed on the project page. Some extensions also include a link to a live demo of the extension so you can try it out before you download it.

FIGURE 29.2

Here's a typical project page on Drupal.org. In this case, the project is the Views module.

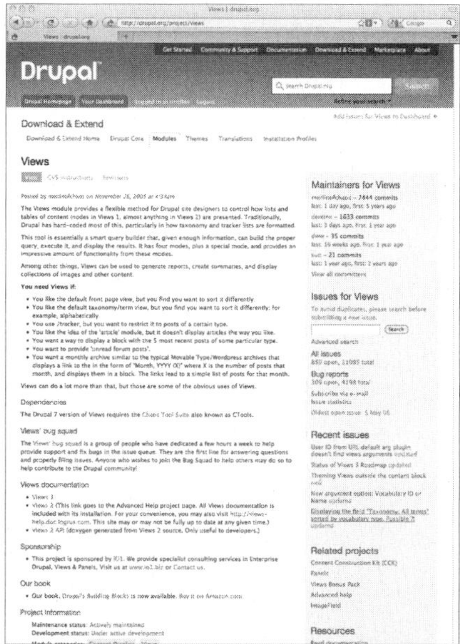

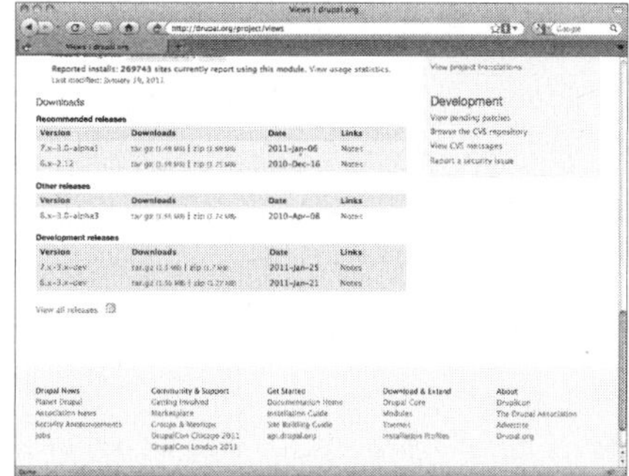

Note

Programmers who wish to contribute to the development of an extension can find CVS instructions and access on the project page. A list of the maintainers and committers for the extension is also available. If you want to become involved, start by reviewing the issues queue and then contacting the maintainers. ■

All the extensions listed on the official Drupal site are released under the open-source GPL license and are free of charge. The listings in the extensions directory identify the developer or company behind the extension and provide links to the developer's Web site and to support and documentation resources, if any.

Caution

Make sure you download only extensions that are compatible with your version of Drupal. Extensions intended for one version of Drupal are unlikely to function properly if installed on the incorrect version of the Drupal core. ■

Working with Extensions

With the arrival of Drupal 7, extension management has improved. Prior to Drupal 7, installing an extension was largely a manual process that had to be undertaken outside of the admin interface. In Drupal 7, installation can occur directly from within the admin interface, both easing and speeding the process of adding new modules and themes.

The processes for adding modules and themes are virtually identical. The steps for each, along with differences, are discussed in the following sections.

Adding new modules automatically

Additional contributed modules can be added to your site through the admin interface's Modules Manager, as shown in Figure 29.3.

Note

The automated upload functionality is provided by the Update manager module. If you do not see the link shown in Figure 29.3, make sure you have enabled the Update manager module. ■

FIGURE 29.3

The Modules Manager, showing the Install new module link

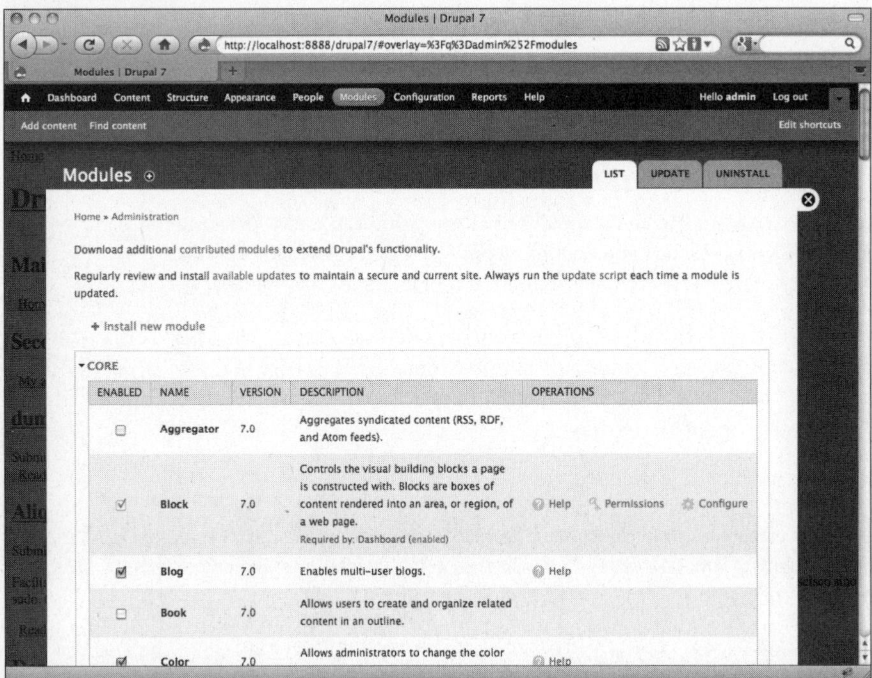

Modules can be installed either directly from a URL, that is, without first downloading the module archive, or, if you have already downloaded the module archive, you can install the module by uploading the archive from your computer.

Note

The option to install from a URL requires that your site installation have access to the Internet. You also need the URL for the package. If either of these is not available, then you must use the option that requires you to separately obtain and upload the extension's archive package. ■

To install a module using the automated installer, follow these steps:

1. **Log into your Web site as an administrator.**

   The admin interface will load in your browser.

2. **Access the Modules Manager by clicking Modules on the main admin menu.**

   The Modules Manager loads in your browser window (refer to Figure 29.3).

3. **Click the link labeled Install new module.**

   The Extension Installer loads in your browser, as shown in Figure 29.4.

FIGURE 29.4

The Extension Installer interface

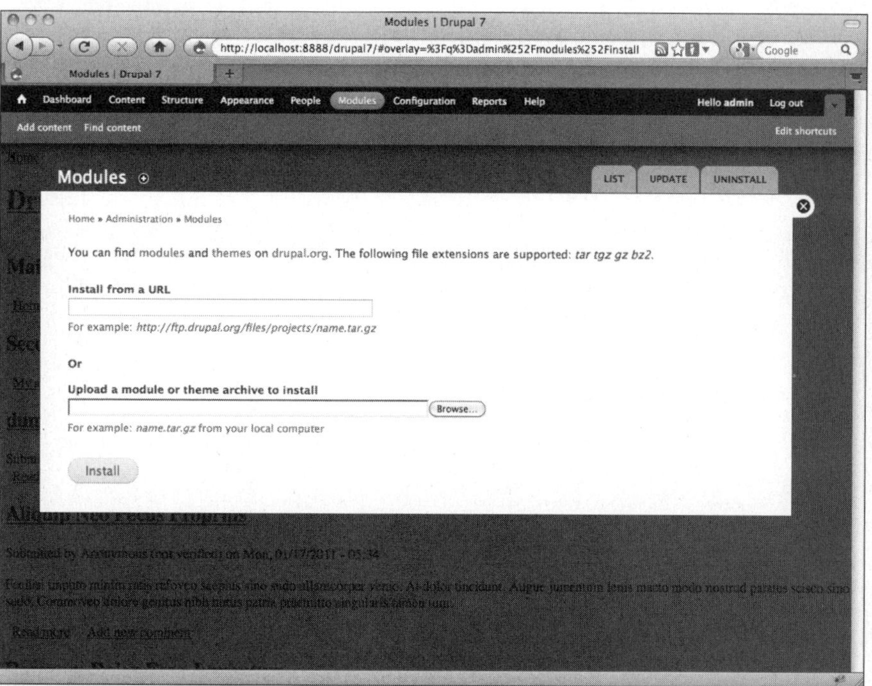

4. **If you have access to the Internet and the URL to the archive, enter the URL into the field labeled Install from a URL and move to Step 7. If you do not have access to the Internet or the URL to the archive, follow the instructions in Steps 5 and 6.**
5. **If you want to install a module from an archive you have downloaded, click the Browse button next to the file labeled Upload a module or theme archive to install.**

   The File upload page opens.
6. **Find the location of the archive, select it, and click the Open button.**

   The file upload page closes, and the name of the archive now appears in the Extension Installer.
7. **Click the button labeled Install.**

   The system now attempts to install the module. If successful, you see a confirmation message; if not, you see an error message.

After the module is installed, it appears in the listing of modules inside the Modules Manager, as shown in Figure 29.5. Before you can use the module, you need to enable it, together with any dependencies.

FIGURE 29.5

The Modules Manager, showing a newly installed module (Webform) in its default state (disabled)

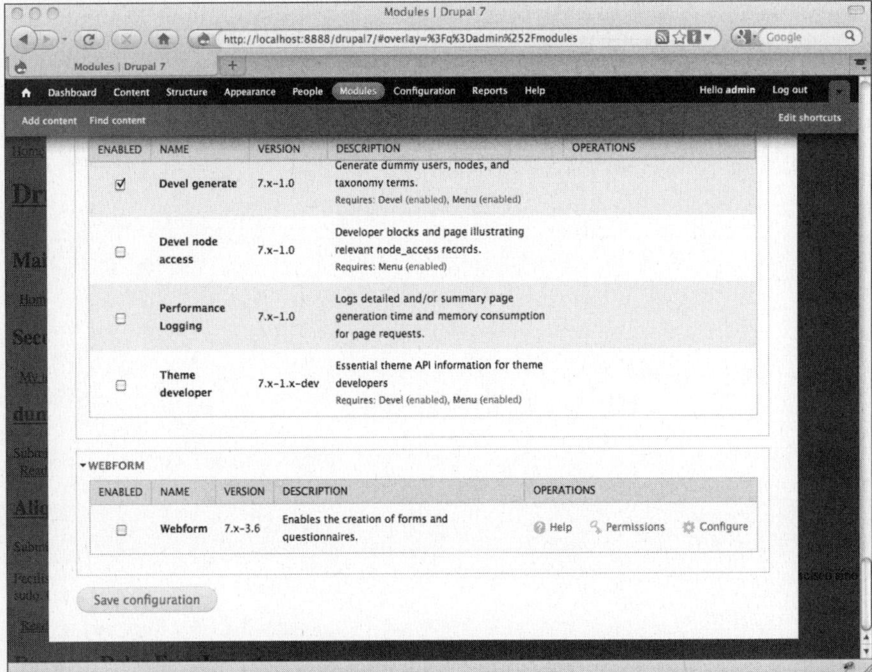

Cross-Reference

Module management is discussed in further detail in Chapter 6. ■

Adding new modules manually

If you cannot or do not want to use the automated installer discussed in the preceding section, you can install modules manually. To install a module manually, follow these steps:

1. **Download the archive file for the module.**
2. **Extract the archive locally.**

   After extraction, you should see a new directory bearing the name of the module.
3. **Connect to the server hosting your Drupal installation, either by FTP or through the use of your Web hosting control panel's file manager.**
4. **Navigate to the directory /sites/all/modules. If the /modules directory does not exist, create it.**
5. **Copy the local directory containing the module files to the /sites/all/modules directory on the server.**
6. **Log into your Web site as an administrator.**

   The admin interface loads in your browser.
7. **Access the Modules Manager by clicking Modules on the main admin menu.**

   The Modules Manager loads in your browser window.
8. **Check to see if the module you were attempting to install appears inside the Modules Manager (refer to Figure 29.5); if so, the installation has been completed successfully.**

Adding new themes automatically

Just as you can add contributed modules to your site, you also can add contributed themes. The Drupal Theme Manager provides an automated installation tool, as shown in Figure 29.6.

Note

The automated upload functionality is provided by the Update manager module. If you don't see the link shown in Figure 29.6, make sure you have enabled the Update manager module. ■

Themes can be installed either directly from a URL, that is, without first downloading the theme archive, or, if you have already downloaded the theme archive, you can install the theme by uploading the archive from your computer.

FIGURE 29.6

The Theme Manager, showing the Install new theme link

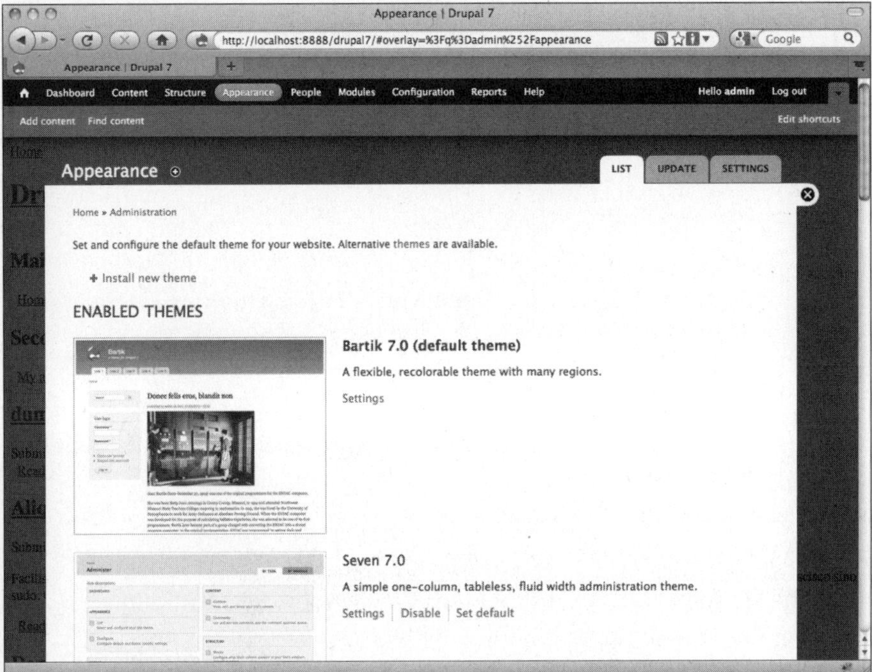

Note

The option to install from a URL requires that your site installation have access to the Internet. You also need the URL for the package. If either of these is not available, then you must use the option that requires you to obtain and upload the archive. ■

To install a theme, follow these steps:

1. **Log into your Web site as an administrator.**

   The admin interface loads in your browser.
2. **Access the Theme Manager by clicking Appearance on the main admin menu.**

   The Theme Manager loads in your browser window (refer to Figure 29.6).
3. **Click the link labeled Install new theme.**

   The Extension Installer loads in your browser (refer to Figure 29.4).
4. **If you have access to the Internet and the URL to the archive, enter the URL into the field labeled Install from a URL, and move to Step 7. If you do not have access to the Internet or the URL to the archive, follow the instructions in Steps 5 and 6.**

5. **If you have downloaded the module archive, click the Browse button next to the file labeled Upload a module or theme archive to install.**

   The file upload page opens.

6. **Find the location of the archive, select it, and click the Open button.**

   The file upload page closes, and the name of the archive now appears in the Extension Installer.

7. **Click the button labeled Install.**

   The system now attempts to install the theme. If successful, you see a confirmation message; if not, you see an error message.

After the theme is installed, it appears in the listing of themes inside the Theme Manager, as shown in Figure 29.7. Before you can use the theme, you need to enable it.

FIGURE 29.7

The Theme Manager, showing a newly installed module in its default state (disabled)

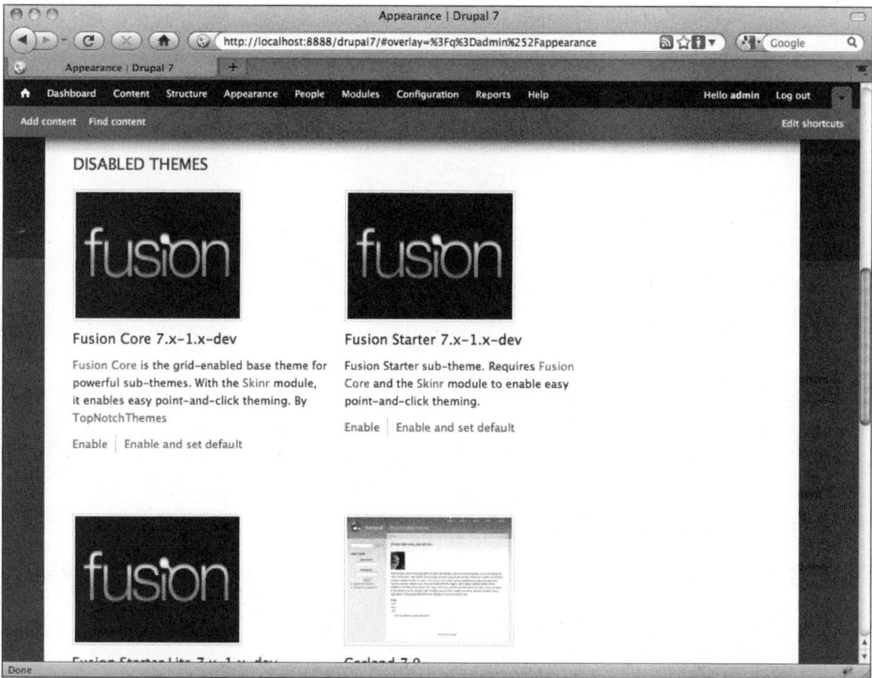

Cross-Reference

Theme management is discussed in further detail in Chapter 26. ■

Adding new themes manually

If you cannot or do not want to use the automated installer discussed in the preceding section, you can install themes manually. To install a theme manually, follow these steps:

1. **Download the archive file for the theme.**
2. **Extract the archive locally.**

   After extraction, you should see a new directory bearing the name of the theme.
3. **Connect to the server hosting your Drupal installation, either by FTP or through the use of your Web hosting control panel's file manager.**
4. **Navigate to the directory /sites/all/themes. If the /themes directory does not exist, create it.**
5. **Copy the local directory containing the theme files to the /sites/all/themes directory on the server.**
6. **Log into your Web site as an administrator.**

   The admin interface loads in your browser.
7. **Access the Theme Manager by clicking Appearance on the main admin menu.**

   The Theme Manager loads in your browser window.
8. **Check to see if the theme you were attempting to install appears inside the Theme Manager (refer to Figure 29.7); if so, the installation has been completed successfully.**

Uninstalling extensions automatically

Non-core modules can be uninstalled through the Modules Manager interface. The Modules Manager includes a tab labeled Uninstall (refer to Figure 29.3). The automatic uninstall process can be used only for contributed modules you have previously installed on the site. The modules must be disabled prior to attempting to uninstall.

To uninstall a module, follow these steps:

1. **Log into your Web site as an administrator.**

   The admin interface loads in your browser.
2. **Access the Modules Manager by clicking Modules on the main admin menu.**

   The Modules Manager loads in your browser window (refer to Figure 29.3).
3. **Click the tab labeled Uninstall at the top right.**

   The uninstall page loads in your browser, as shown in Figure 29.8.
4. **Click the check box next to the module you want to uninstall.**
5. **Click the Uninstall button.**

   The Confirm uninstall page opens.

6. **Click the Uninstall button to confirm the request.**

   The system uninstalls the module, displays a confirmation message, and returns you to the uninstall page.

FIGURE 29.8

The module uninstall page

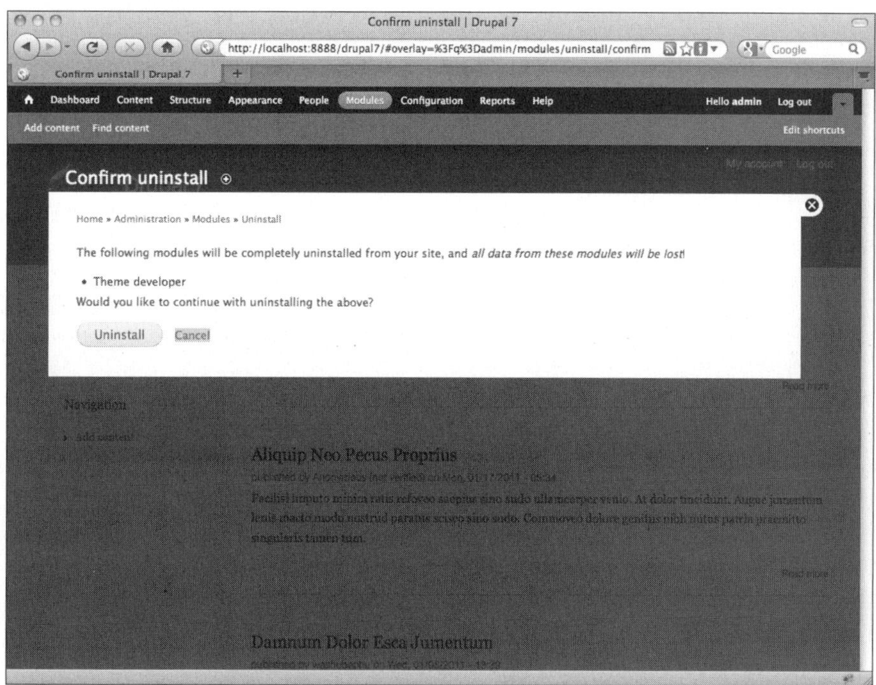

Caution

Deleting a module is permanent and cannot be undone. Uninstalling also typically wipes out any data on the module from the database. If you want to use the module again, you must reinstall it. ■

Uninstalling extensions manually

Both modules and themes can be uninstalled manually. Although manual installation is generally not problematic for themes, it can be for modules, because merely deleting the module's files from the server is not sufficient to delete any database entries associated with the module. The presence of the module's data in the database is unlikely to cause problems directly, but it isn't ideal and at the very least takes up disc space that could be used for other purposes.

To manually uninstall a module or a theme, follow these steps:

1. **Disable the module or theme from inside the admin system.**
2. **Connect to the server hosting your Drupal installation, either by FTP or through your Web hosting control panel's file manager.**
3. **Navigate to the directory /sites/all/.**
4. **To uninstall a theme, access the subdirectory /themes and delete the directory containing the theme.**
5. **To uninstall a module, access the subdirectory /modules and delete the directory containing the module.**
6. **Check to see if the module or theme you were attempting to install has been removed from the admin system; if so, the process has been completed successfully.**

Key Extensions to Address Common Issues

One of the most time-consuming aspects of module selection is finding the right tool for the job. Literally hundreds of modules are available, and sometimes you are faced with multiple options that appear to achieve your goals. Although there really is no substitute for downloading things and trying them out yourself, in this chapter I provide a list of modules that are a good starting point for addressing common needs.

Note that this is not an endorsement of one particular module over another, but rather a list of resources to help you get started.

Caution

The rate of change in the open-source world can be daunting. Developers change, projects fork, some projects get abandoned. It's impossible to say what will be here in 12 months' time. The list of modules I provide no doubt will change over time. You should always keep this in mind when you are selecting modules, and if business risk is an issue for you, do your own research and consider carefully which modules you adopt. ■

Improving content management and presentation

The modules listed in this section expand upon the Drupal system's default content management tools. The list includes both modules to enhance functionality as well as several powerful tools for controlling output. The default Drupal installation is bundled with only a text editor, so this section also lists tools to improve the system's editing functionality.

FCK Editor

`http://drupal.org/project/fckeditor`

FCK Editor is a WYSIWYG editor that replaces the plain text box used for content creation in the default Drupal installation. A number of client-side editors are available, but FCK Editor is one of the most popular due to its small size and rich feature set.

Note

At the time this was written, a module was under development to take advantage of the newest version of the editor. The new module is named CKEditor. ■

Panels

`http://drupal.org/project/panels`

The Panels module allows the site administrator to create customized layouts that can be used for predefined contexts. The creation of the layouts is simple and includes the ability to assign them to specific nodes, authors, or viewers. Panels can be used for either full pages or specific elements on the page—for example, the creation of a sidebar. The module includes its own caching mechanism and integrates well with other modules, including Organic Groups.

Printer, e-mail, and PDF versions

`http://drupal.org/project/print`

This module creates alternative versions of your nodes that allow the user to print, convert the node into a PDF, or send it by e-mail. The module includes a default style sheet that you can edit to modify the output to meet your needs. Note that the PDF functionality requires you to download and install a third-party tool.

Tagadelic

`http://drupal.org/project/tagadelic`

The Tagadelic module enables the display of a cloud of the tags used on your site. The tag cloud can be displayed as either a page or a block. The module allows you to set the font sizes to control the appearance of the cloud. The cloud entries are drawn from your taxonomy. Options include the ability to create multiple clouds based on different vocabularies.

Taxonomy Manager

`http://drupal.org/project/taxonomy_manager`

The Taxonomy Manager module provides an interface for the management of the taxonomy vocabularies in your system. The manager uses an AJAX interface to make it fast and easy to add, edit, merge, or reorder the individual terms in your vocabularies. Although you can manage your vocabularies without this module, you can work much more efficiently with this module in place! Taxonomy Manager is a time-saver and a valuable admin asset if your taxonomy is large or complex.

Views

http://drupal.org/project/views

The Views module is a smart query builder that allows you to build a query, execute it, and then display the results. The module is very powerful and makes it easy for you to add a variety of common and desirable functions to your site—for example, displaying the most recent articles or the most popular. Views gives you a great deal of flexibility, and it's one of the most effective modules for controlling display of content items on your pages.

WYSIWYG

http://drupal.org/project/wysiwyg

The WYSIWYG module is an enabling tool that allows you to easily implement your favorite client-side editor. The module supports a wide assortment of editors and plugins, including FCK Editor, jWYSIWYG, NicEdit, TinyMCE, and a number of others.

Improving administration

The modules listed in this section are intended to make managing your Drupal site easier. The list includes tools to speed administration and tools to help protect your site from SPAM and abuse.

Administration Menu

http://drupal.org/project/admin_menu

Although Drupal 7 provides a useful and usable admin theme, it may not be right for everyone. If you are looking for an alternative, the Administration Menu module may be what you are looking for. With this module installed, you can access a complete menu of administration functions from a menu bar that floats at the top of your pages. This is not an admin theme, just a device to improve accessibility to the admin menu. The menu can be configured somewhat, at least in terms of placement.

CAPTCHA

http://drupal.org/project/captcha

CAPTCHA is a challenge-response test added to forms to help cut down on invalid form submissions created by spambots or other automated scripts. The default CAPTCHA challenge is a set of letters that must be typed correctly before the system accepts the form submission. Although CAPTCHA is one of the most popular systems, you may also want to consider some of the related alternatives, such as the CAPTCHA Pack or reCAPTCHA.

CAPTCHA Pack

http://drupal.org/project/captcha_pack

The CAPTCHA Pack module is an extension of the CAPTCHA module, discussed previously. The pack adds alternatives to the letter matching format seen in the default CAPTCHA module. Alternatives includes math CAPTCHAs, where the user must perform a basic computation, text-based CAPTCHAs, where the user must supply the missing character or word, and CAPTCHAs that require the user to identify the item that does not belong.

Mollom

`http://drupal.org/project/mollom`

Mollom is an integrated solution for protecting your site against spam. The module combines CAPTCHAs with text analysis and reputation tracking. It can be configured to protect your site's contact forms, user registration forms, and forum and comment posts. The module does require registration on a third-party site. Mollom is also included as part of the Acquia Drupal installation.

reCAPTCHA

`http://drupal.org/project/recaptcha`

The reCAPTCHA system is a CAPTCHA alternative. The service is Web-based and provides a text-based challenge response test. The system includes accessibility options and also protects e-mail addresses. reCAPTCHA does require you to register your site on a third-party service, and it may not be appropriate for Drupal sites run behind a firewall.

Enhancing search

Drupal's site search can be extended and enhanced through the use of the modules listed in this section.

Apache Solr Search Integration

`http://drupal.org/project/apachesolr`

This module integrates the Apache Solr search project into your Drupal site. Solr is an open-source enterprise search platform from the Apache Lucene project. It includes powerful full-text searching, text highlighting, and faceted search. The Solr Search module provides an enhanced replacement, or supplement, to the default search functionality included in the Drupal core. To use Solr, you need to download and install additional components, and you need to make sure you meet the technical requirements for both the Solr extension and the module.

Core Searches

`http://drupal.org/project/coresearches`

The Core Searches module contains two components that allow you to remove either content search or user search from the Drupal core. The module does not provide any search functionality on its own; rather, it helps you define what can be searched on your site. If you want to use a third-party search engine, such as Solr, then installation of this module allows you to restrict the users to only the custom search.

Porter-Stemmer

`http://drupal.org/project/porterstemmer`

The Porter-Stemmer module implements the Porter stemming algorithm to improve American English language searching with Drupal's built-in search functionality. The process known as "stemming" reduces a word to its root in the search index and then returns in the search results not only the root form but also the variations on the root. The impact of this module is a search result set that is richer and typically more useful for site visitors. Note that you must re-index your site after installing and enabling this module.

Enhancing forms

The modules in this section are intended to provide additional options for form creation on your Drupal site.

Login Toboggan

`http://drupal.org/project/logintoboggan`

The Login Toboggan module enhances Drupal's user registration and login system. The module makes it easier for you to control user flow during the login process and to set landing pages and confirmation messages. You also can use the module to customize the registration form and to allow users to log in with either a username or an e-mail address.

Webform

`http://drupal.org/project/webform`

The Webform module adds a Webform nodetype to your site. The nodetype can be used to create questionnaires, contact forms, request forms, surveys, polls, and so on. Information gathered by the node can be downloaded as a .csv file. Although you can create custom forms in other ways, Webform is fast and easy and provides a good alternative for simple form creation. Note also that a related module—Webform Block—allows you to display a Webform note in a block.

Improving navigation

Site navigation tools and menus are a critical part of your Drupal site. The default menu system in Drupal contains only a limited number of display options. Through use of the modules below, you can add other options for controlling the appearance of your menus. The list also includes enhancements to the breadcrumbs function and the ability to integrate tagging and taxonomy as aids to usability.

Custom Breadcrumbs

http://drupal.org/project/custom_breadcrumbs

The Custom Breadcrumbs module is designed to help you avoid inconsistencies between the default breadcrumbs and the content shown on the page. This is most particularly an issue with output based on Views, Panels, or taxonomy terms. Through the use of this module, you can create breadcrumbs based upon parameters, thereby matching more closely the displayed content and creating more useful breadcrumbs for your site visitors.

DHTML Menu

http://drupal.org/project/dhtml_menu

The DHTML Menu module improves usability on sites that employ nested menus. The module works by using JavaScript to reduce the number of page reloads when nested menus are opened or closed. With the module enabled, nested menu items open and close without the necessity of a page reload. The module uses a cookie to keep track of menu states, so the user does not lose the menu condition when he navigates between pages.

Menu Breadcrumb

http://drupal.org/project/menu_breadcrumb

The Menu Breadcrumb module creates the breadcrumb trail based on the menu to which the page belongs. If you are relying on Drupal's menu system to impose the organizational structure on your content, this module helps keep your breadcrumbs in synch.

Nice Menus

http://drupal.org/project/nice_menus

The Nice Menus module lets you add a variety of popular menu presentation techniques to your site. The module supports three menu styles: horizontal drop-down menus, vertical menus that expand to the left, and vertical menus that expand to the right. Drop-down functionality is based on CSS. Once installed, you have the ability to place the menus in block positions and select the Drupal menus where you want the functionality to apply. You can control the appearance of the menu easily by overriding the dedicated CSS styles.

Taxonomy Breadcrumb

http://drupal.org/project/taxonomy_breadcrumb

Use this module to create breadcrumb trails based on your taxonomy vocabularies and terms. This is most useful on sites where the content is organized around the taxonomy, because it helps avoid inconsistency between the default breadcrumbs and the taxonomy-based output.

Taxonomy Menu

http://drupal.org/project/taxonomy_menu

The Taxonomy Menu module allows you to transform any of your taxonomy vocabularies into a menu. The module provides an easy way to create a hierarchical menu that is populated dynamically. Clicking the menu produces a list of articles, defined by the tags you assigned to those articles. The module integrates with the PathAuto module to create friendly URLs.

Managing media

Image galleries, slide shows, and video functionality are some of the most commonly requested functions on sites. The list in this section details a number of the options that are available for handling both still images and video files.

Album Photos

http://drupal.org/project/photos

The Album Photos module provides your site with an image album and a Flash-based slide show. The module supports a number of features, including commenting and voting on images, image uploading tools, and the ability to create multiple albums with thumbnails. Note that certain functions, including the Flash slide show, require you to install additional extensions.

Fast Gallery

http://drupal.org/project/fast_gallery

As the name implies, Fast Gallery enables quick creation of simple galleries. The module supports both still images and videos and enables you to group items together in albums. Fast Gallery generates thumbnails automatically and can work with or without the Imagecache module.

Lightbox 2

http://drupal.org/project/lightbox2

The Lightbox module adds pop-up functionality to the images on a page. When the user clicks an image, it opens the image above the page, in a lightbox. Users also can zoom in on the enlarged image. Through the configuration options, you also can use this module to create slide shows or to display HTML content.

Video

http://drupal.org/project/video

The Video module enables the uploading of video files to a Drupal site. The module supports multiple video types, including all the most popular formats. The module also supports the ability to play video in any format, including FLV, and automatically creates video thumbnails.

Video Filter

`http://drupal.org/project/video_filter`

The Video Filter module is a simple answer for embedding video in a Drupal site. With this module installed, you can embed virtually any type of video in your site by adding a tag. The module supports all the most popular services, including YouTube, Vimeo, Flickr, MySpace, Picasa, Slideshare, and Blip.tv.

Views Slideshow

`http://drupal.org/project/views_slideshow`

The Views Slideshow module allows you to turn images added to your site into a slide show. The module is highly configurable, enabling you to rotate the most recent images or the images from a selection of nodes, categories, or galleries. The module is powered by jQuery and enables you to define the filters that select the images for the shows. The Views Slideshow module requires the Views module to be installed on the site.

Enabling community

The modules in this section detail some of the most popular methods for adding community functionality and enhancing user interaction. The list includes modules that add voting, social bookmarking, and enhanced notifications for users. Also listed among the items is the Organic Groups module, which is the basis for a large number of related modules that can be installed to add further community functionality.

Comment Notify

`http://drupal.org/project/comment_notify`

The Comment Notify module enables your system to send notification e-mails to users advising them of new comments on pages where they have commented. The module supports notifications for both registered users and anonymous users.

Fivestar

`http://drupal.org/project/fivestar`

The Fivestar module was developed to provide Drupal with an easy-to-use and attractive voting widget. Fivestar enables your site visitors to vote on or rank content items. The configuration options allow you to choose the appearance of the widget and control who has access to vote. The module does require the installation of the Voting API module. The Views module is also recommended, but not required.

Organic Groups

`http://drupal.org/project/og`

The Organic Groups module adds a groups functionality to your Web site. With the module enabled, users can create and manage their own groups, allowing other members to join and to then share information across the group. Organic Groups has spawned a wide number of other extensions that build on the functionality in this module, making Organic Groups a very powerful tool in the creation of a community Web site.

Privatemsg

`http://drupal.org/project/privatemsg`

Privatemsg adds private messaging functionality to your site. Perfect for community-oriented sites, it allows users to send and receive messages to and from each other and maintains the messages in threaded conversations. Users can search and tag messages and elect to receive e-mail notifications when new messages arrive.

Service Links

`http://drupal.org/project/service_links`

The Service Links module allows you to add links to a variety of social bookmarking sites and blog search sites. The module supports the most popular services: Digg, Furl, Reddit, Facebook, Google, and so on. The options include the choice of placement of the links and the use of text or images. The links can be placed within a node or a teaser or in a block position.

Voting API

`http://drupal.org/project/votingapi`

The Voting API module provides a standardized schema for storing, retrieving, and tabulating votes. The module does not provide a voting mechanism for site users; it's an enabling module that supports other modules, like Fivestar.

Adding geolocation functionality

The Location and GMap modules can be installed to add a suite of powerful geolocation features to your Drupal site.

GMap Module

`http://drupal.org/project/gmap`

The GMap Module provides an interface to the Google Maps API. GMap can be used to create interactive maps. The package includes several related modules that allow you to integrate with Taxonomy, Views, and the Location module. A macro builder is supplied that makes it easy to create views to new maps. In order to use this module, you need a Google Maps API key.

Location

`http://drupal.org/project/location`

The Location module makes it possible to associate geolocation data with Drupal nodes or users. The module enables GeoRSS for your existing RSS feeds and integrates with the GMap Module to provide mapping that ties into data on your site. Location also integrates with Views to provide location-based filters and fields. The Location package includes a number of related modules, including the handy Location Generate, which integrates with the Devel module to enable easy testing of geolocation features on the site.

Enhancing SEO

The modules listed here provide a way to further make your site more search-engine-friendly and more user-friendly.

Global Redirect

`http://drupal.org/project/globalredirect`

The Global Redirect module provides a suite of basic functionality intended to clean up paths and aliases and to avoid potential search engine penalties for duplicate content. Global Redirect checks URLs for aliases and also checks access to the URL. The module performs a 301 redirect where the URL is not being used, directs the user to the proper page where an alias is being used, and makes sure that pages are accessed using the cleanest method.

Google Analytics

`http://drupal.org/project/google_analytics`

The Google Analytics service is one of the most widely adopted Web site traffic activity tracking systems. While you do not need a module in order to integrate Google Analytics with your site, this module does make it easy to manage your Analytics from within the administration interface of your site. The Google Analytics module provides the ability to control user segmentation and watch downloads, and it integrates smoothly with your site search. The module gives you the option to cache the Analytics code locally, thereby reducing delays in page loading.

Nodewords

`http://drupal.org/project/devel`

The Nodewords module improves the metadata options for your Drupal site. With Nodewords enabled, you have the option to set the metatags for the site as a whole and for individual pages. The module includes all the most common metadata fields, including geolocation.

Page Title

http://drupal.org/project/page_title

The Page Title module gives you control over the contents of the <title> tag for your site's pages. Using this module, you can create either patterns that automatically form the title, or you can specify the title you want to use, without being restricted to using the content's title. Given the importance of page titles in search engine rankings, this module can be a valuable addition to your site.

PathAuto

http://drupal.org/project/pathauto

The PathAuto module enables the administrator to create patterns that the system will use to automatically define path aliases for nodes, categories, and users. The ability to tailor the paths for the articles gives you the flexibility to create URLs that are optimal for your search engine marketing purposes.

Search 404

http://drupal.org/project/search404

The Search 404 module replaces your site's standard 404 "page not found" messages with a page showing search results from your site, premised on the keywords in the URL the user entered. The module improves usability by helping to mitigate errors in user input. Search 404 also supports the placement of blocks on 404 pages and can integrate both Apache Solr and Google CSE.

Site Verify

http://drupal.org/project/site_verify

The Site Verify module helps Webmasters verify site ownership for various search services. The module supports the most popular systems, including Google Webmaster, Bing Webmaster Central, and Yahoo! Site Explorer. Site Verify works with sites that require a file upload and those that require the inclusion of a specific metatag.

XML Sitemap

http://drupal.org/project/xmlsitemap

The XML Sitemap module adds to your Drupal site an XML sitemap that conforms to the sitemaps.org specification, together with tools that automate submission of the sitemaps to the various search services. Configuration options allow you to control updating, notifications, and the contents of the sitemap.

Adding ad management

If you want to run ads on your site, you need to look to a module to provide you with the functionality.

Advertisement

`http://drupal.org/project/ad`

Advertisement is a powerful tool for managing the advertising space on your Drupal site. Highly configurable, the module enables you to place ad blocks in your choice of positions, or you can automatically embed ads inside content. Numerous options are available, and Advertisement can be integrated with additional modules to provide geotargeting, caching, and support for Flash-based ads.

Google Ad Manager

`http://drupal.org/project/google_admanager`

The Google Ad Manager module is intended to simplify management of Google advertisement placements on your site. Enter your Google publisher's code, and the module enables you to place ads in blocks, which you can then assign to the position where you want them to appear.

For developers

The modules listed in this section are designed to help speed development and ease deployment of the final site. For security reasons, many of these modules should be disabled, or completely uninstalled, after the site goes live.

Backup and Migrate

`http://drupal.org/project/backup_migrate`

The Backup and Migrate module is a utility that enables you to easily back up and restore or copy your Drupal database. The module greatly simplifies migrating the site from your development installation to the live site or from one Webhost to another. Options include the ability to select what to back up, scheduled backups, and encryption. The module also integrates nicely with the Drush module.

Devel

`http://drupal.org/project/devel`

The Devel module provides a suite of useful tools for developers. Chief among its advantages is the ability to view database queries and performance data, print arrays, and assist with debugging. The module also provides a handy feature to auto-generate terms, comments, and users, thereby allowing you to quickly populate pages and features for development.

Drush

http://drupal.org/project/drush

The Drush module adds a command line shell and Unix scripting interface for Drupal. It is designed to speed the completion of common tasks, such as cron, cache clearing, and package management. You can add a Web UI by installing the Terminal module.

Theme Developer

http://drupal.org/project/devel_themer

Often referred to as "Firebug for Themers," the Theme Develop module used to be part of the Devel module suite of tools. The module injects markers into the theme code that can be viewed during development, greatly improving your ability to identify elements and the affect of your styling.

Services

http://drupal.org/project/services

The Services module allows a Drupal site to provide Web services via multiple interfaces. Service callbacks can be used with XMLRPC, JSON, JSON-RPC, REST, SOAP, AMF, and more.

Skinr

http://drupal.org/project/skinr

The Skinr module adds the ability to "skin" blocks from within the admin system, without having to work with the themes. It fast-tracks block styling and is integrated into several of the more advanced contributed themes.

Summary

This chapter addressed the process for extending your Drupal site by adding contributed modules and themes. I covered the following topics:

- Automatically and manually installing of contributed modules
- Automatically and manually installing of contributed themes
- Uninstalling extensions
- Finding extensions
- Adding extensions to address common issues

CHAPTER

30

Implementing eCommerce with Ubercart

Drupal's core system provides powerful content management functionality, but no eCommerce options. Site owners looking to add products and online sales to their Drupal Web sites must add contributed modules to achieve that functionality; most turn to the Ubercart module.

Ubercart is a powerful eCommerce plugin tailored to run on Drupal. The system is rich in features and includes everything you need to get an online storefront up and running in a single package.

In this chapter, I look at Ubercart and what you can do with it; then I take you through the basics of installing and configuring the module. I close the chapter with a look at some of the useful extensions you can use to further enhance the Ubercart system.

IN THIS CHAPTER

Knowing what Ubercart is

Obtaining and installing Ubercart

Configuring Ubercart

Store administration

Enhancing Ubercart

Note

Another interesting option is Drupal Commerce. At that time this was written the system was still in alpha but promises to be an attractive option for Drupal 7. You can learn more by visiting `http://drupal.org/project/commerce`. ■

Understanding Ubercart

Ubercart is a full-featured eCommerce system built on top of the Drupal platform. Ubercart is built entirely of Drupal modules, so it first requires a functioning Drupal Web site upon which you can install the core Ubercart package.

After you have installed Ubercart, you can enable and configure the wide variety of functionality that supports products and sales. The end result is a Web site that includes the rich content and user management features of Drupal, coupled with the ability to create and maintain a complete online shop. The entire range of features can be managed from within the standard Drupal interface, leveraging all the features and advantages of Drupal discussed in previous chapters.

Ubercart has been around for years, and there is a large and substantial community around the project. In addition to the Drupal project page, you can find a dedicated Ubercart Web site with its own support forums, system documentation, developer API, and extensive catalog of contributed modules and themes at `http://www.ubercart.org`.

Note

At the time this was written, Ubercart was not yet fully compatible with the Drupal 7 core; accordingly, the screenshots and some of the interfaces in this chapter reflect the Ubercart 2 system, as deployed on Drupal 6. ■

Features

The core Ubercart package provides a complete eCommerce solution. Although a number of contributed modules allow you to further extend the system, many shops run only the basic Ubercart core. As you will see later in this chapter, the number of options and configuration choices contained within the core is impressive. If anything, the system can be faulted for being more complex than most people need. The complexity can, however, be offset by proper theme selection and configuration of the site to implement only those features needed.

As a quick overview of what you can expect from the system, here's a listing of the primary features you find in the Ubercart core.

For customers

The core Ubercart system contains everything a visitor expects from an eCommerce Web site, including the following:

- Product categories and descriptions
- Shopping cart
- Checkout process, including single-page checkout
- Multiple payment methods
- Multiple shipping methods
- Anonymous checkout
- Automatic account creation

For site administrators

Ubercart, though a complex system, includes a number of administrator tools to help manage the complexity of running an online store. These are included in the core package:

- Order tracking
- Ability to edit orders
- Workflow process for orders (integrating shipping)
- Inventory controls
- Integration of most common payment gateways
- Integration of most common shipping platforms
- Multi-currency management
- Support for virtual products
- Configurable product attributes
- Batch import/export of products
- Integration of enhanced Google Analytics and store activity reporting

Using Ubercart

Ubercart is suitable for use either as an eCommerce solution or simply as a catalog management system. In the former usage, you implement the complete capabilities of the system, including the shopping cart and shipping and payment functionalities; in the latter usage, you simply use the system to manage and display information about products, typically in a browsable hierarchical ordering.

How you use the system depends largely on how you configure the system. You can toggle on or off most of the critical system features. The large number of discrete modules supplied with the Ubercart package means you enable only the features you want, thereby avoiding needless load on the server, while also reducing the complexity of store administration.

Note

Later in this chapter, I look at some of the common extensions you can employ with Ubercart to enhance and tailor the functionality even further. ■

Obtaining and Installing Ubercart

Ubercart, for all its complex abilities and options, is still just a module for Drupal; accordingly, you must first have a working installation of Drupal. After you have Drupal installed and configured, you can set about integrating Ubercart.

Installation requirements

Like many other advanced modules, Ubercart is dependent upon supporting modules for some of its functionality. Before you try to set up Ubercart, you must install and enable all required modules, or your Ubercart installation will fail.

Note

The Ubercart requirements can change as new and improved versions of the module are released. You should always check current requirements by visiting the project page at `http://drupal.org/project/Ubercart`. ■

The module dependencies for Ubercart in Drupal 7 have changed since Drupal 6. An Ubercart installation in Drupal 7 requires the following modules to be installed first:

- Rules
- Views

To complicate things a bit, the Rules and Views modules both have their own module dependencies, which means that before you install Rules and Views, you need to first install the following:

- Chaos tools suite (used by Views)
- Entity API (used by Rules)

So, putting it all together, you need to follow these steps to use Ubercart:

1. **Install Chaos tools suite.**
2. **Install Entity API.**
3. **Enable both modules.**
4. **Install Views.**
5. **Install Rules.**
6. **Enable both modules.**

Now, at last you are ready to install Ubercart, as discussed in the next section.

Tip

The Ubercart project also recommends that you install the Google Analytics module. Though it is not necessary for the core module functionality, it does provide site owners with enhanced reporting on site traffic and activity. Included with the Ubercart package is an optional module that enhances Google's Analytics tracking of activity within the store; it is discussed later in this chapter. ■

Integrating with an existing site

After the required dependencies have been satisfied, installing Ubercart is no different than installing any other module. Follow these steps to install Ubercart in Drupal 7:

1. **Log into your site as an administrator.**
2. **Access the Modules Manager by clicking the Modules option on the Management menu.**

   The Modules Manager loads in the overlay.

3. **Click the Install new module link.**

   The installation page loads.

4. **Either enter the URL of the installation package in the first field or click the browser button to upload the archive file from your local machine.**

5. **Click the Install button.**

   The system installs the module, and if you are successful, a confirmation message displays.

The Ubercart module is now installed on your Drupal site. The next step is to enable and configure the module.

Tip

Due to the complexity of the Ubercart module, I strongly recommend that you set up and configure your basic Drupal site first. Get everything in order on your basic site before you begin with Ubercart; otherwise, you add needless complexity to your Ubercart setup. Another option is to explore the UberDrupal installation profile. UberDrupal provides a packaged installer that incorporates the Drupal core, Ubercart, and several related modules and themes into a single installation profile. To learn more, visit the project page at `http://drupal.org/project/uberdrupal`. ■

Configuring Ubercart

Configuring any powerful eCommerce system is a significant task. Unfortunately, it is also a task many people underestimate. As you will see in the pages that follow, a number of decisions must be made. Many of the decisions have nothing to do with technology; they are business decisions relating to the product and the store operation. Before you begin configuration, make sure you have put thought into the business model and the requirements of commerce necessary for your site to be a success. If you have not thought through all these matters, you will waste time and find yourself mired in the numerous options contained in Ubercart.

To get some idea of the complexity of the system, all you need to do is visit the Modules Manager after you have completed the Ubercart package installation. Scroll down the page to the Ubercart section. Note that Ubercart presents a huge number of modules; some are required, most are optional.

Tip

If you are setting up Ubercart for a client, your best bet may be to create a questionnaire for the client to complete before you set out on configuration. The questionnaire should cover all the possible Ubercart options (and should probably also consider common extensions to Ubercart). You don't want to be making guesses on the client's behalf, and you don't want to be making phone call after phone call to pick up all the necessary bits of information you need to do your job. ■

The following core modules of the Ubercart package are required and must be enabled:

- **Cart:** Provides the shopping cart
- **Conditional Actions:** Required to help you configure conditions like shipping and tax rates
- **Order:** Needed for order management
- **Product:** Provides the product content type
- **Store:** Enables the store setup and management

To start with, enable only these modules. After you have completed the base configuration of these elements, you can begin to add optional modules and tailor the functionality to your needs.

The optional modules are grouped into four categories:

- Core (optional)
- Extra
- Fulfillment
- Payment

In the next section, I go through configuring the required core elements. In the sections that follow, I deal with each of the optional element groups in turn.

Configuring the required core

Begin by visiting the Modules Manager and enabling the five required modules in the Ubercart core. Once enabled, you should see on your Configuration Manager a link to Store Administration. If you click the link, the Store Configuration Manager loads in your browser, as shown in Figure 30.1.

Click the Configuration link to bring up the Configuration menu, as shown in Figure 30.2.

These options are on this screen:

- Cart settings
- Checkout settings
- Country settings
- Order settings
- Price handler settings
- Product settings
- Store settings

I deal with each of the configuration pages in the sections that follow.

Note

As you enable additional Ubercart options, new choices appear on this page. For example, enabling the Ubercart Catalog module results in a new configuration choice: Catalog. ■

FIGURE 30.1

Ubercart's Store Administration Manager is your starting point for many tasks, including configuration.

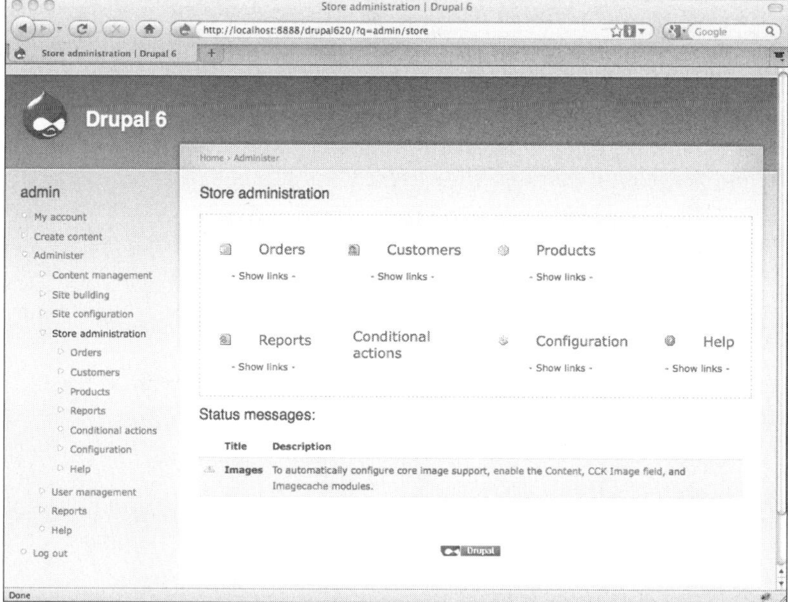

Managing Cart settings

The Cart settings control basic characteristics of your shopping cart.

To configure the cart, click the Cart settings link on the Configuration menu to open the Cart settings page. This page includes two tabs: one labeled Overview and the other labeled Edit. The default view is Overview. To make changes to the cart, click the Edit tab to bring the Cart settings editing page to the front, as shown in Figure 30.3.

The Cart settings are divided into three categories:

- General cart settings
- Cart panes
- Cart block

The controls on each page are explained in the sections that follow.

General cart settings

The options contained on this page (refer to Figure 30.3) control some of the most fundamental characteristics of your shop:

- **Add to cart redirect:** This allows you to specify the page that will be shown after the user selects to add a product to the cart. The default value shown takes the customer to the shopping cart. Leave the field blank for no redirect.

- **Minimum order subtotal:** If you want to force a minimum order value as a prerequisite to proceeding to checkout, enter that amount here. Note that this is a subtotal, before shipping, taxes, or other charges.
- **Anonymous cart duration:** Set a value for expiring the contents of the shopping cart for a non-authenticated visitor. The value can be hours, days, weeks, or even years.
- **Authenticated cart duration:** Set a value for expiring the contents of the shopping cart for a logged in (authenticated) visitor. The value can be hours, days, weeks, or even years.
- **Continue shopping element display:** The system displays a link that allows users to continue shopping from within the shopping cart. This control lets you specify the appearance of that link. Note the field at the bottom of the section that allows you to specify your own text for the link.
- **Default continue shopping link URL:** If you want to control where the user is sent if he clicks the Continue shopping link, you can enter that URL here.
- **Custom cart breadcrumb text:** Enter the label you want to appear on the breadcrumbs when the user is inside the cart.
- **Custom cart breadcrumb URL:** Specify the URL you want to link to the breadcrumb label.

FIGURE 30.2

Click the links in the Configuration menu to configure each of the individual areas.

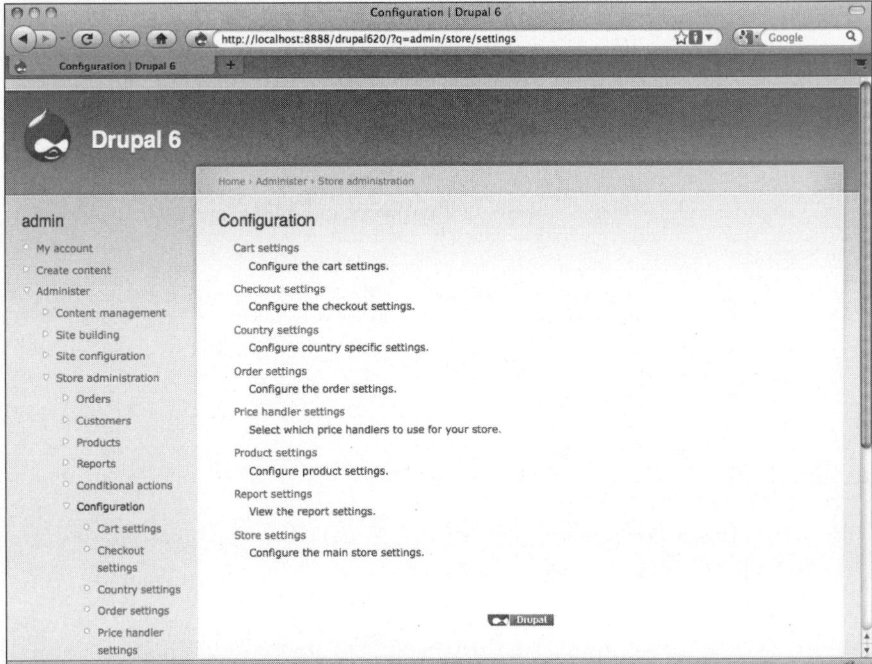

FIGURE 30.3

The changes you make in the Cart settings editing page are reflected on the overview page. Note also the links to jump between the settings, panes, and block pages.

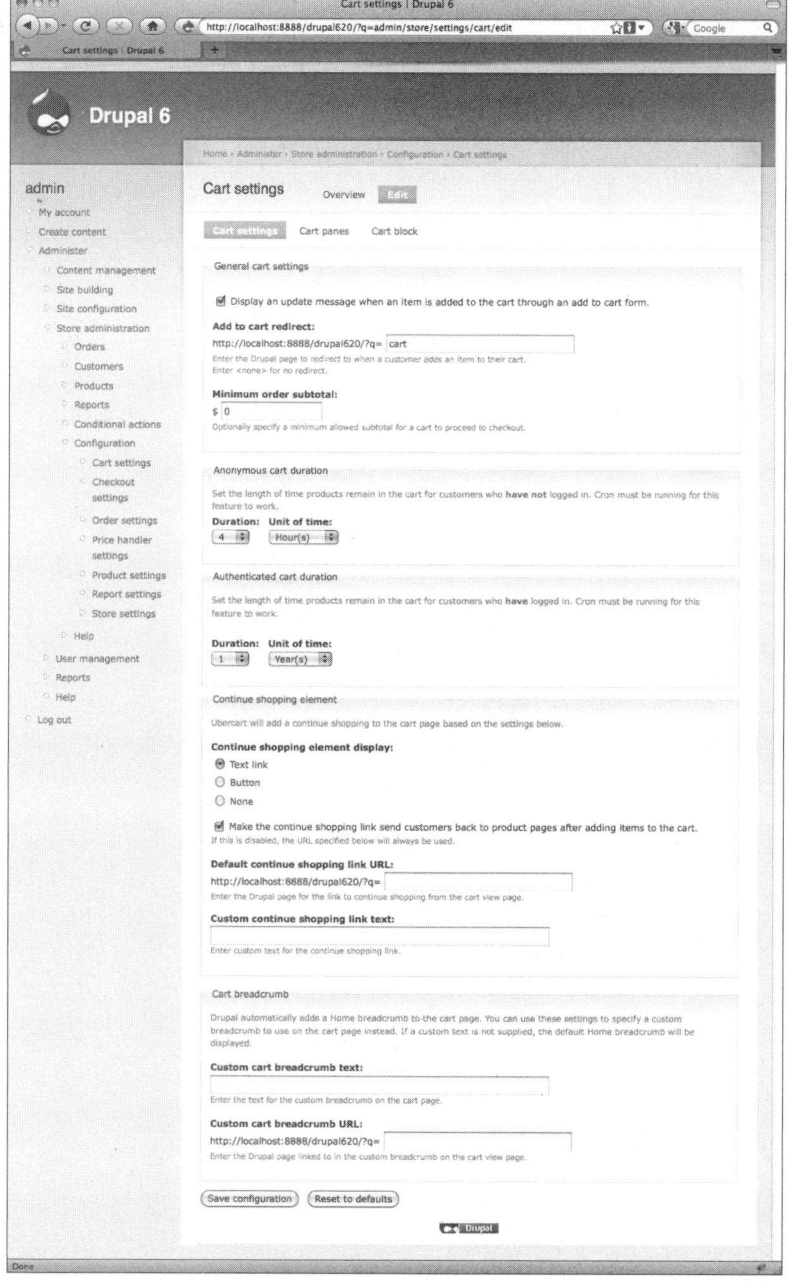

After you have made your choices, click the Save configuration button. If you want to restore the default values, click the Reset to defaults button.

Cart panes

Cart panes are the individual units of content or functionality that make up the shopping cart page. The Cart panes page lists all the available panes. At this point, before you have enabled any shipping or payment options, the only pane listed on this page is the Default cart form pane.

As you enable additional payment gateways and shipping methods, additional panes appear on this page.

Note

Do not disable the Default cart form pane; you need this for the cart to function normally. ■

Cart block

The Cart block page simply links to the Shopping cart block configuration page. Click the link given to jump to the Shopping cart block configuration page, part of the Blocks Manager. The Shopping cart block configuration page is shown in Figure 30.4.

FIGURE 30.4

The Shopping cart block configuration page is actually inside the Blocks Manager and can be accessed either from the Ubercart configuration page or directly from the Blocks Manager.

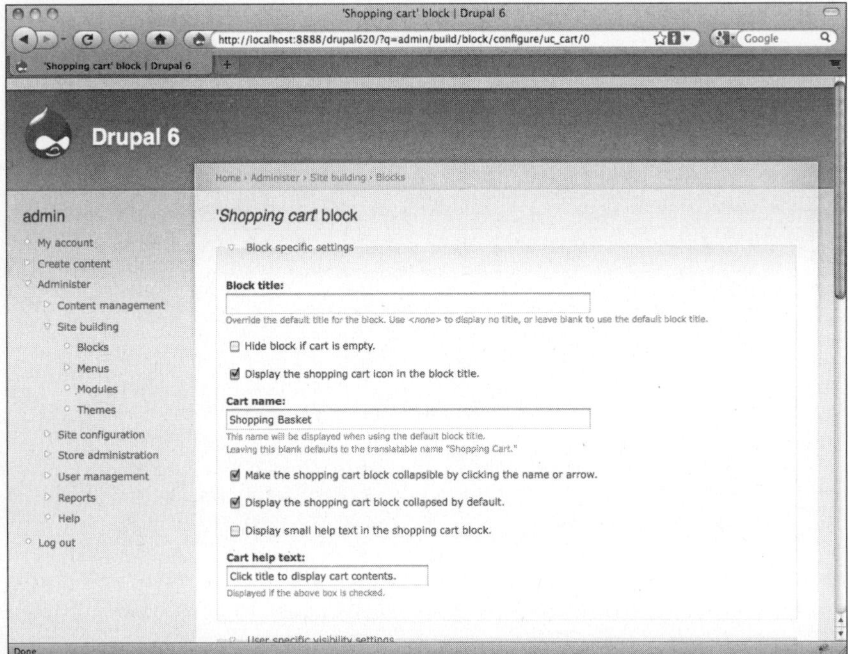

The options on this page are largely the standard choices you see in any block configuration page. The exception is the additional visibility choices relating to whether to display an empty cart and whether to allow a collapsible cart.

After you have selected your preferences here, click the Save button. The system lands you on the Blocks Manager page, so you need to go back to the Ubercart configuration menu to continue with setting up your shop.

Cross-Reference

The Blocks Manager is discussed in detail in Chapter 7. ■

Managing Checkout settings

The Checkout settings affect the checkout process customers will experience after they click the Checkout link in the shopping cart.

To configure your store's checkout process, click the Checkout settings link on the Configuration menu to open the Checkout settings page. This page includes two tabs: one labeled Overview and the other labeled Edit. The default view is Overview. To make changes to the checkout process, click the Edit tab to bring the Checkout settings edit page to the front, as shown in Figure 30.5.

The Checkout settings are divided into four categories:

- General checkout settings
- Checkout panes
- Checkout messages
- Address fields

The controls on each page are explained in the sections that follow.

General checkout settings

The controls in the top portion of the page control whether the system's checkout process is used, whether you allow anonymous checkout, and whether shipping information should be visible when the cart contains only items that are not shippable.

Tip

If you are using Ubercart only as a catalog management system, deselect the option Enable checkout. ■

The second portion of the page controls the display options for the checkout panes. Configuration of the panes content occurs on the next page of the configuration page, Checkout panes, discussed in the next section.

The final set of controls affects what happens after the customer completes the checkout process. The last option lets you specify the URL users are taken to upon completion of checkout.

FIGURE 30.5

The Checkout settings editing interface has multiple tabs at the top that allow you to jump between the different pages of the interface.

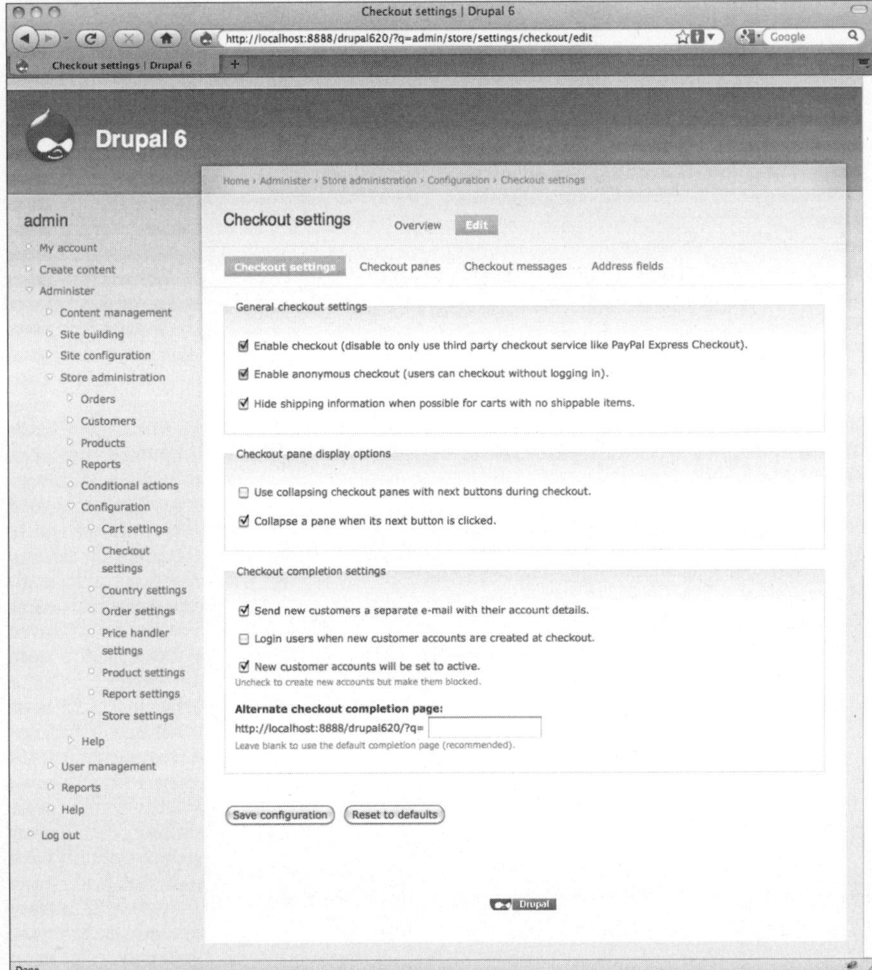

Checkout panes

Checkout panes are the individual units of content and functionality that are displayed on the checkout page. The Checkout panes page lets you control visibility of the panes. Figure 30.6 shows this page with the Customer information settings fields expanded for display.

If you do not want all the default panes to appear, unselect them by clicking the check boxes. You can also control the order of display by using the List position control in the right column, shown above.

FIGURE 30.6

To show you the Checkout panes page, I have clicked to expand the Customer information settings.

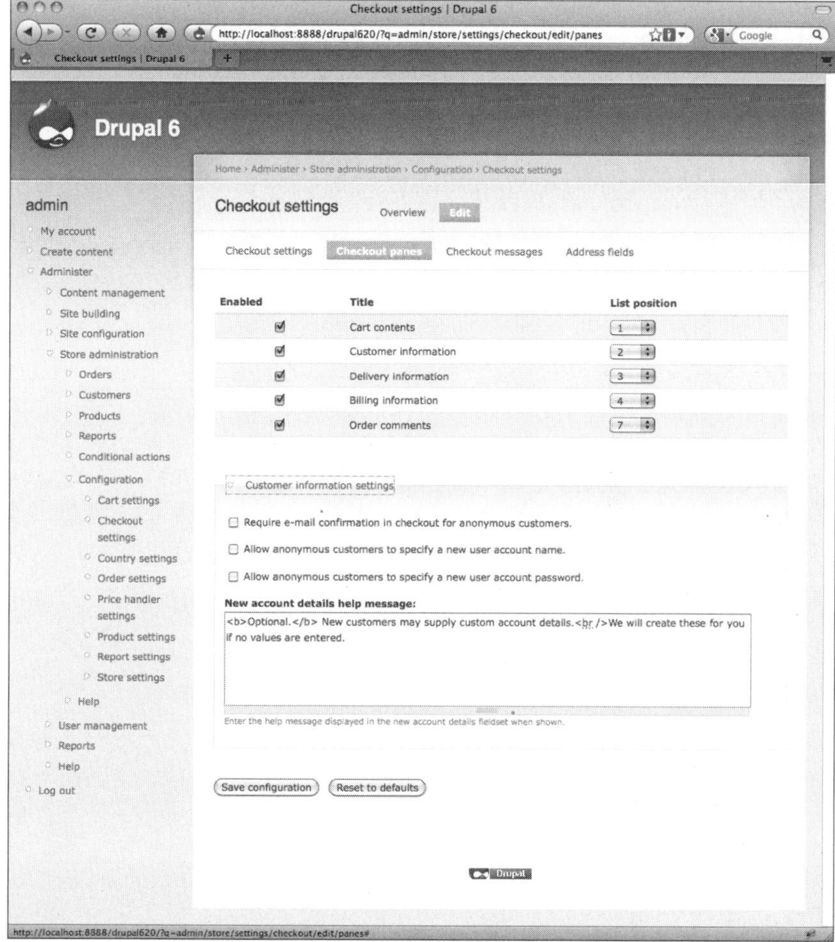

The Customer information settings area contains controls and fields that impact customer account creation. The final field lets you specify the message that will be sent to new users upon account creation.

Checkout messages

The Checkout messages page contains a list of fields that let you specify messages and instructions that will be displayed during checkout process.

Address fields

The Address fields page is, essentially, a form builder for the checkout page. Use this page to specify the information you want to gather from customers during checkout. You can disable the options you do not want to use, modify the labels shown to the customers, and determine whether specific fields are required.

Managing Country settings

The Country settings let you specify the address formats your system will support. For example, if you support shoppers in the United States, the address options for the United States will be shown to users during checkout.

Click the Country settings link on the Configuration menu to open the Country settings page. You will note that the page includes tabs—one labeled Overview and the other labeled Edit. The default view is Overview. To make changes to the cart, click the Edit tab to bring the Country settings edit page to the front, as shown in Figure 30.7.

FIGURE 30.7

The Country settings editing page

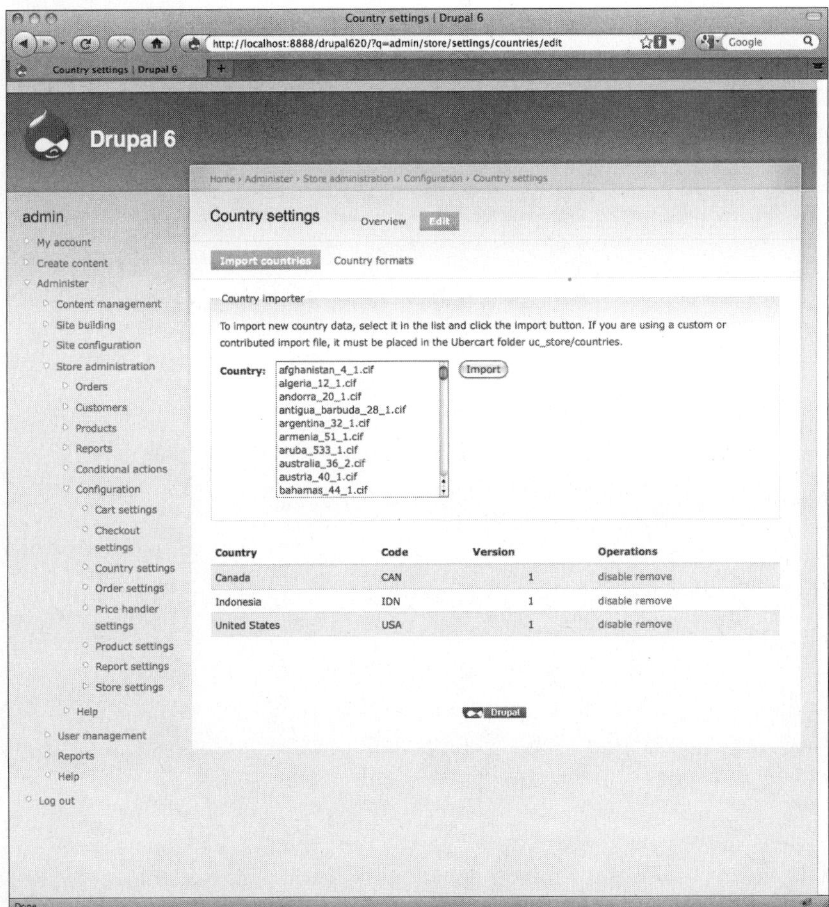

The default system has already enabled Canada and United States. To add support for another country, select the country from the box at the top of the page, then click the Import button.

The Country formats tab lets you modify the default values the system provides for each country installed.

Note

To modify country specific variables like weights and measures, visit the Store settings configuration page and click on the Format settings tab. This is discussed below. ■

Managing Order settings

Click the Order settings link on the Configuration menu to open the Order settings page. The page includes two tabs: one labeled Overview and the other labeled Edit. The default view is Overview. To make changes to the cart, click the Edit tab to bring the Order settings edit page to the front, as shown in Figure 30.8.

The Order settings are divided into three categories:

- General order settings
- Order workflow
- Order panes

The controls on each category's page are explained in the sections that follow.

General order settings

This page includes two areas. The first area simply sets the admin view preferences for your orders. The second area impacts whether the customers can see their order history and the invoice template used when invoices are viewed on the site.

Order workflow

The Order workflow page lets you create an order processing workflow on your site that matches your offline workflow. As the order moves through processing, you can update the order status through the admin system, using the states set on this page.

There are four defaults states for orders: Canceled, In checkout, Post checkout, and Completed. You can modify the labels used for these states by updating the Title field. You can change the ordering by modifying the List position. The states are then accessible to the administrator on the edit invoice page, discussed later in this chapter.

If you want to add more states to the workflow, you can do so by clicking the Create new status button.

Order panes

The Order panes page allows you to control what is displayed on the view order, edit order, invoice, and customer pages. All options are selected by default. To remove panes from view, simply deselect them. You can reorder the panes using the List position controls.

FIGURE 30.8

The Order settings editing interface includes three links that let you move between the pages of the interface.

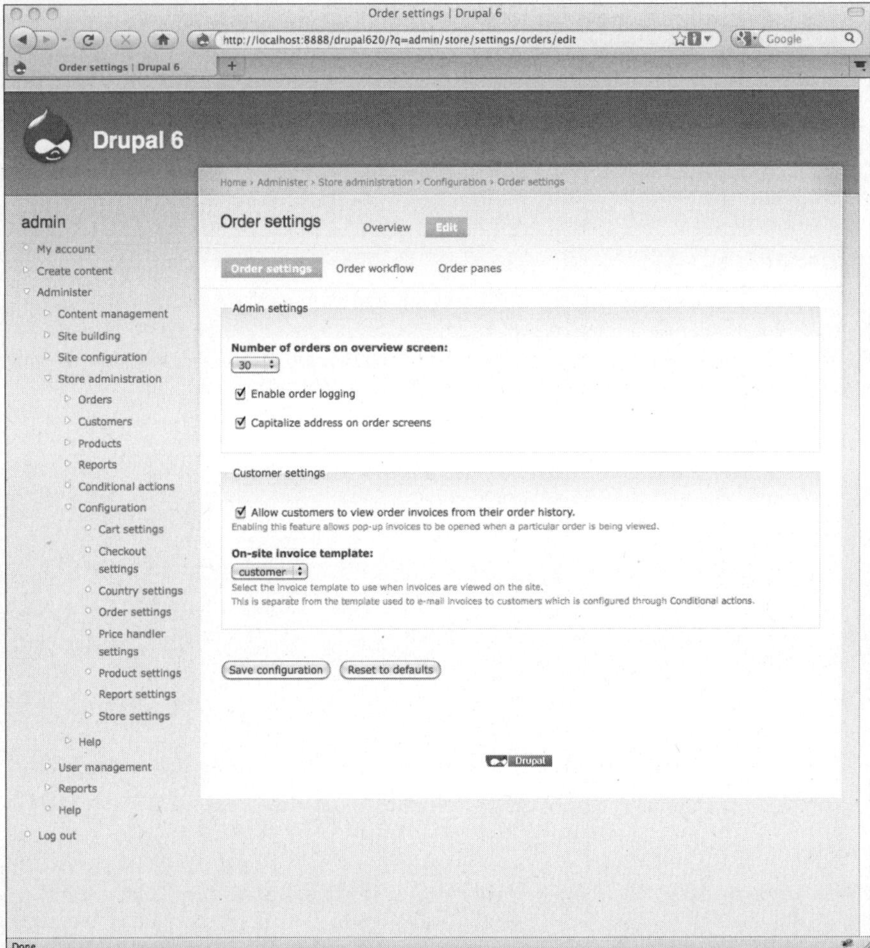

Managing Price handler settings

Click the Price handler settings link on the Configuration menu to open the Price handler settings page, as shown in Figure 30.9.

The controls on this page are limited. The Price alterers list at the top of the page includes additional price handlers, if activated.

FIGURE 30.9

The Price Handler settings page, shown here with only the default price handler activated

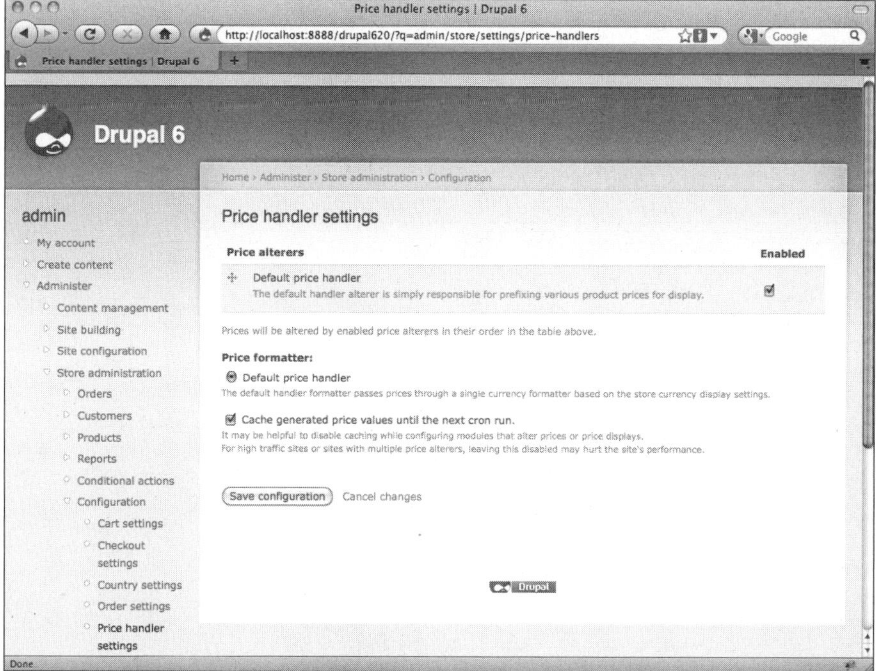

Managing Product settings

Click the Product settings link on the Configuration menu to open the Product settings page. The page includes two tabs: one labeled Overview and the other labeled Edit. The default view is Overview. To make changes to the cart, click the Edit tab to bring the Product settings edit page to the front, as shown in Figure 30.10.

The Product settings are divided into three categories:

- General product settings
- Product fields
- Product features

The controls on each category's page are explained in the sections that follow.

FIGURE 30.10

The Product settings editing page includes links at the top that allow you to jump between the three pages in this page.

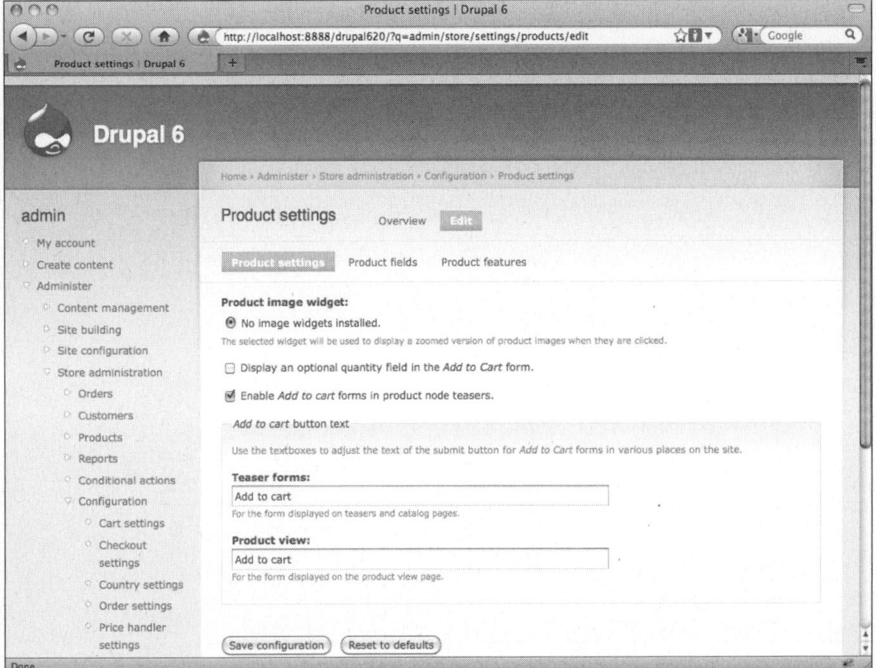

General product settings

The General product settings page affects four different areas related to products and the shopping cart.

The first field, Product image widget, shows any additional widgets added to the system that provide options for the display of products; the most common usage is widgets that enlarge or rotate product image.

Next is a check box labeled Display an optional quantity field in the Add to Cart form, which allows you to enable a field that lets customers specify the quantity of items they want to order.

The second check box, called Enable Add to cart forms in product node teasers, is enabled by default and simply provides the Add to cart link for both the teaser and the full view of the products.

The final area on this page is labeled Add to cart button text and provides two fields that let you alter the text displayed on the Add to cart buttons.

Product fields

The Product field page presents a list of the default fields available to all products and allows you to select which fields to use and control the order in which they are presented.

Product features

The Product features page enables you to control the configuration options related to the optional products features enabled on your site. In the default view, there are no additional product features enabled.

Managing Store settings

Click the Store settings link on the Configuration menu to open the Store settings page. The page includes two tabs: one labeled Overview and the other labeled Edit. The default view is Overview. To make changes to the cart, click the Edit tab to bring the Store settings edit page to the front, as shown in Figure 30.11.

The Product settings are divided into three categories:

- Contact settings
- Display settings
- Format settings

The controls on each category's page are explained in the sections that follow.

Contact settings

Use this page to provide the name and contact details for the store. The information input here is shown in multiple places on the site and in the e-mails from the store.

Note

The final field on this page lets you specify a dedicated custom help page for the store. ■

Display settings

The Display settings page includes three controls:

- **Display type for the main store administration page:** Choose your preferred option for the display of the store's administration page.
- **Primary customer address:** You can set either the customer's shipping address or the billing address.
- **Footer message for store pages:** Select one of the options for the footer. The last option provides no footer message at all.

Tip

You also can customize your footer with your own message by working with the blocks or editing the theme files. ■

FIGURE 30.11

The Store settings edit page includes links at the top right that enable you to jump between the three pages in this interface.

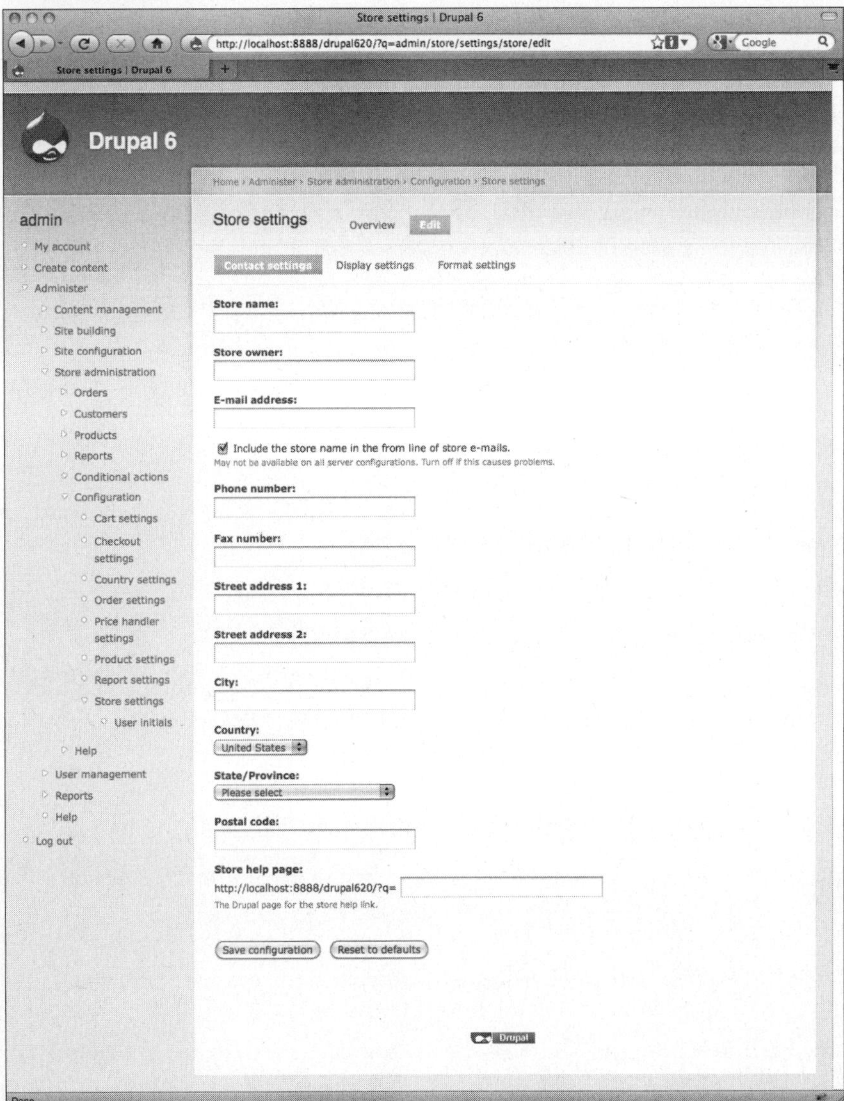

Format settings

Use the controls on the Format settings page to customize the weights, measures, and currency formats used in your store. Each of the format options is grouped into one of the following: Currency format, Weight format, Length format, or Date format. Expand the relevant section to see the options and edit them.

Core options

You can see in the Modules Manager several sets of add-ons for the Ubercart core. The section labeled Ubercart - core (optional) includes some of the most commonly used features. Many of these options relate to the type of products you provide—for example, downloadable products versus products that must be shipped. Each module is described briefly:

- **Attribute:** Enable this option to provide attributes for your products. This is useful if you have products in varying sizes, colors, or configurations that are selectable by the customers of your store.
- **Catalog:** Enable this to provide a hierarchical product catalog page and block. This option is essentially an organizational and display tool. If you have a large number of products grouped into different categories, you want to use this option. Note that you also must enable the Path module if you want to use the Catalog function.
- **File Downloads:** Enable this to provide downloadable products.
- **Payment:** This module is needed if you want to accept payment online in your shop. Enabling the module allows you to link in various payment options.

Note

The various payment gateways and options are the subject of another section of the Modules Manager, labeled Ubercart – payment, which is discussed later in this chapter. ■

- **Reports:** Enable this option, and the system gathers statistics relating to the store, users, and purchase history. This is an option most people want to use.
- **Roles:** The Roles module allows you to assign roles based on purchase histories. It's useful if you want to group your customers according to purchase behavior.

Tip

If you want to tie your pricing to the various user roles, then you want to look at installing the contributed module known as Ubercart Price Per Role, discussed later in this chapter. ■

- **Shipping:** If you need to ship products to customers, enable this module. The module is required if you want to use the Shipping Quotes module.
- **Shipping Quotes:** Enable this module if you need to provide customers with quotations for shipping fees.

Note

The various shipping options are the subject of another section of the Modules Manager, labeled Ubercart – fulfillment, which is discussed later in this chapter. ■

- **Tax Report:** Enable this module if you need to gather data on sales tax paid by customers. This module requires the Taxes module to work properly.
- **Taxes:** Enable this module if you need to charge tax to your customers.

Ubercart extras

The Ubercart – extras section in the Modules Manager lists a set of optional modules you can enable for your Ubercart store. The modules listed in the section enable enhanced functionality; none are necessary for your store, though several are quite useful. These are the options:

- **Cart Links:** Enable this module to provide links to your shopping cart from non-Ubercart nodes on your site.
- **Google Analytics for Ubercart:** Enabling this module gives you enhanced tracking of visitor activity inside your site. This is applicable only if you are using Google Analytics on your site.
- **Product Kit:** This useful module lets you package together two or more of your products into a single sales unit.
- **Stock:** If you want to monitor stock levels relative to your online sales, enable this module.

Fulfillment options

The Ubercart - fulfillment section of the Modules Manager includes modules that provide enhanced shipping options for your Ubercart store. All require you to first enable the Shipping Quotes module to function properly:

- **Flatrate:** Enable this module to provide simple flat-rate shipping fees for your store.
- **U.S. Postal Service:** Enable this to integrate the U.S. Postal Service's Rate Calculator for your store.
- **UPS:** Enable this to integrate UPS rates and services.
- **Weight quote:** Enable this to provide shipping calculations based on the weight of the order.

Tip

Enable only the fulfillment modules that are relevant to your store. If you need additional shipping modules, check the contributions section of the Ubercart site at `http://www.Ubercart.org/contrib`**.** ■

Payment options

The Ubercart - payment section of the Modules Manager includes modules that provide support for various payment gateways for your Ubercart store. All require you to first enable the Payment module to function properly; some also have additional module dependencies.

These payment modules are available in the default installation:

- **2Checkout:** Enable this to integrate the 2Checkout.com payment system.
- **Authorize.net:** Enable this to integrate the Authorize.net payment system.
- **Credit Card:** Enable this to receive payments via credit card. This does not process the credit cards for your store; it simply enables you to gather the appropriate data.

- **CyberSource:** Enable this to integrate the CyberSource payment system.
- **Google Checkout:** Enable this to integrate the Google Checkout payment system.
- **Payment Method Pack:** Enable this to provide options for payment by a variety of "traditional" payment methods, including checks, money orders, and C.O.D.
- **PayPal:** Enable this to integrate the PayPal payment system.
- **Test Gateway:** Enable this to provide a dummy payment gateway that is useful for testing your store and your shopping cart.

Tip

Enable only the payment modules that are relevant to your store. If you need additional payment modules, check the contributions section of the Ubercart site at `http://www.Ubercart.org/contrib`. ■

Store Administration

After your store is configured, you use the Store Administration Manager to deal with your products, customers, and orders. Refer to Figure 30.1 to see the links to all the store management functions. They are discussed in the following sections.

Managing products

Product management is divided between the Store Administration Manager and Drupal's content management functionality.

Creating new products

Products are created via a Drupal content type named, logically, Product. To add a new product to your store, follow these steps:

1. **Login to the admin system.**

   The admin interface loads in your browser.
2. **Select the Create Content option.**

   The Content Creation menu shows in your browser.
3. **Click the Product option.**

   The new product page appears, as shown in Figure 30.12.
4. **In the Name field, type the name you want to show to customers.**

   This is a required field.
5. **Enter a description if you want to show one to customers.**
6. **In the SKU field, enter your product's SKU (its product code).**

   This is a required field.
7. **Three pricing fields are shown on the form; the only required field is Sell price. You must give your product at least a selling price.**

FIGURE 30.12

The new product page

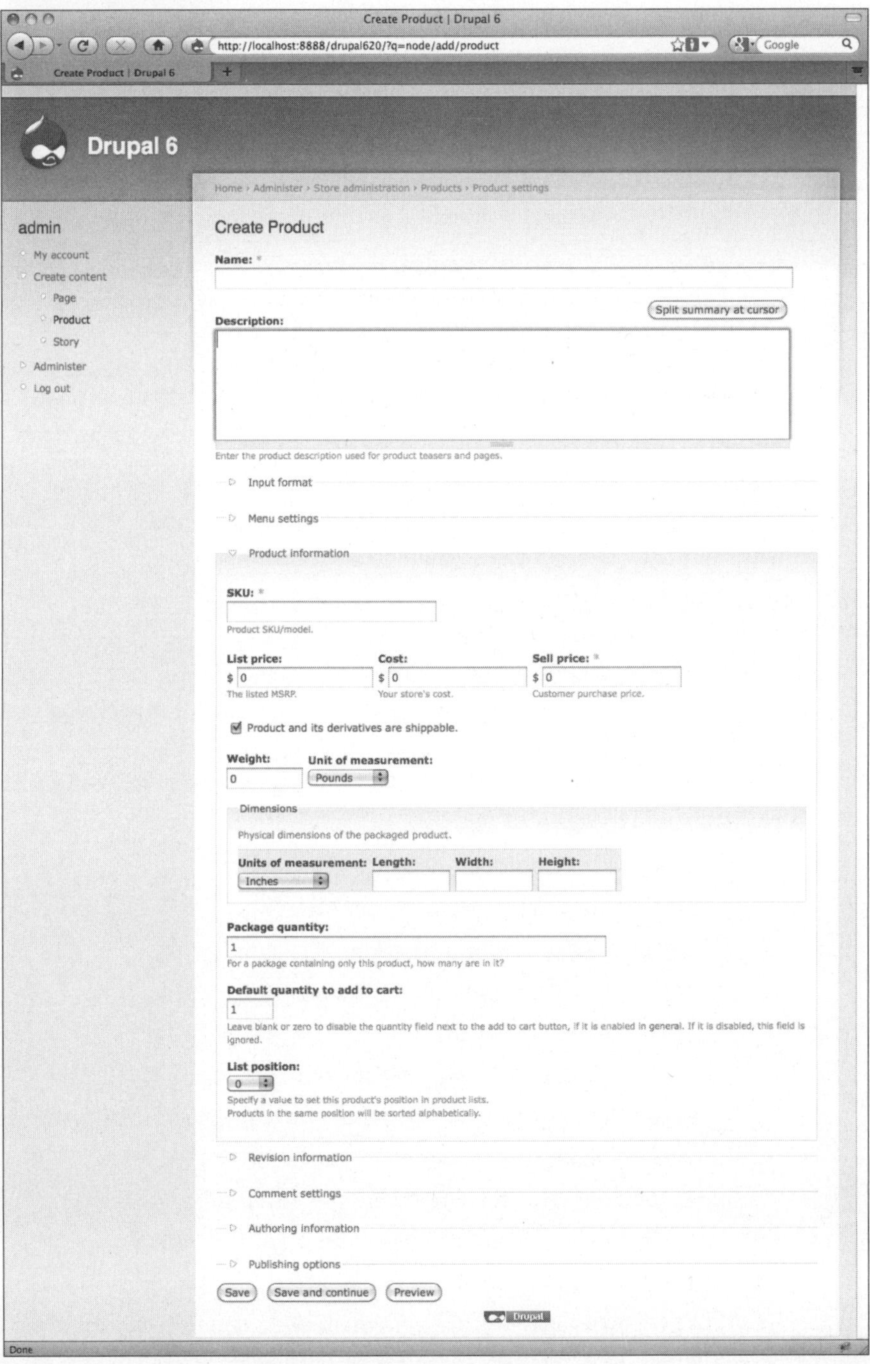

8. **If your product is shippable (not virtual), select the Product and its derivatives are shippable option.**
9. **If shipping is being charged by weight or size, complete the appropriate fields.**
10. **Complete any other desired fields.**

    All are optional.
11. **Click Save.**

    The system saves your product information and shows you a preview with a confirmation message.

After you have products in the system, you can view them easily from within the Store Administration Manager, as discussed in the next section.

Working with existing products

You can view all the existing products in your store either from the content management interface or from the Store Administration Manager. Using Ubercart's Store Administration Manager is simpler and faster, because it shows you all the products at a glance. The table in Figure 30.13 provides both a quick view of all the products and easy access to editing. Click the product name to see the product details and access a link to edit the product.

FIGURE 30.13

The Products Manager inside the Ubercart Store Administration Manager

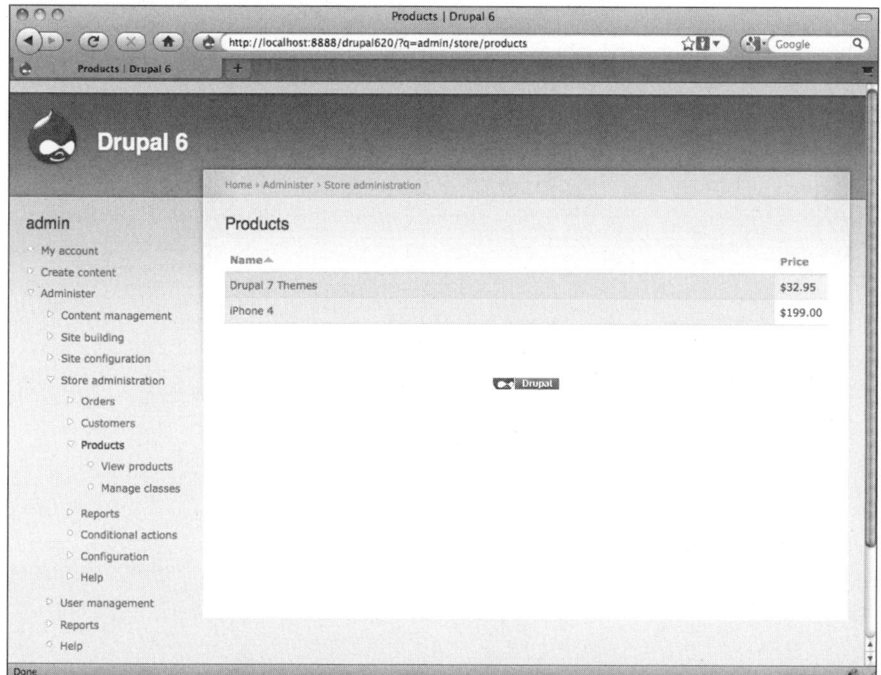

Note

If you have enabled the Catalog module, there is extended functionality associated with your products, allowing you to group them together into a hierarchy for display to customers. ■

Managing orders

Click the Orders link on the Store Administration Manager to view a listing of all the orders in the system, as shown in Figure 30.14.

The Orders Manager provides a summary view of all the orders. The filter box at the top of the page allows you to sort orders by status. Click the view icon to the left of an order to view the order details, edit the order, or view the invoice.

Figure 30.15 shows the Order view. The links at the top of the page allow you to edit the order, view the invoice for the order, or view a historical log of actions associated with this order.

At the bottom of the page (refer to Figure 30.15) are options for the administrator to add private notes to the order, to e-mail the customer, and to update the order status.

FIGURE 30.14

The Orders Manager inside the Ubercart Store Administration Manager includes links to Create order and Search orders.

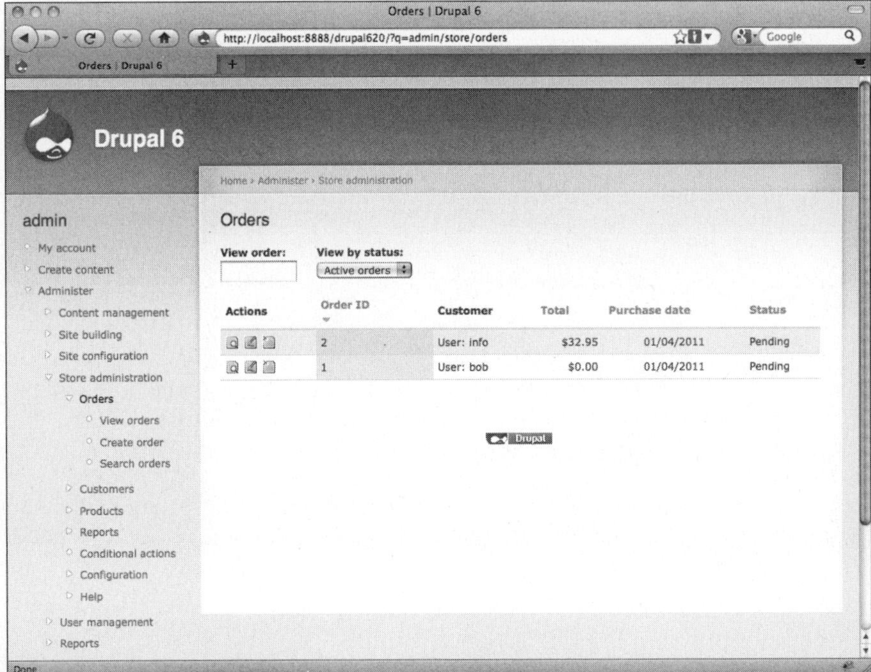

FIGURE 30.15

Viewing an order details

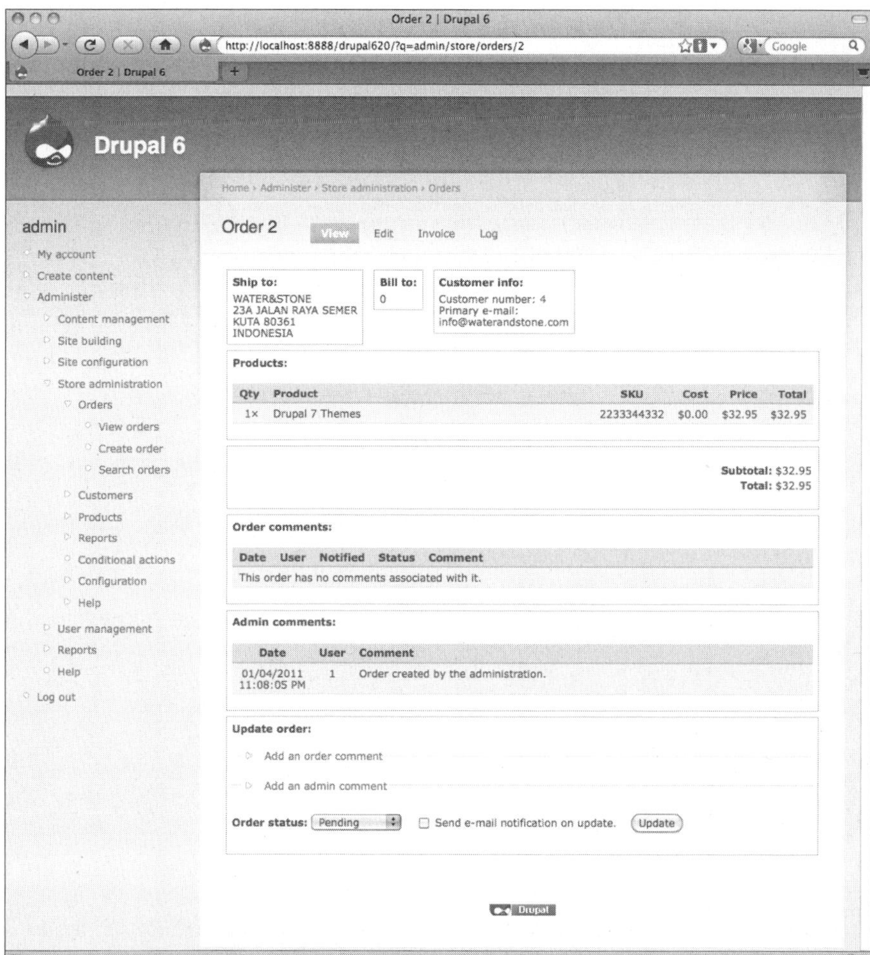

Managing customers

Click the Customers link on the Store Administration Manager to view a listing of all the customers in the system, as shown in Figure 30.16.

The Customer Manager provides a summary view of all the orders. Click the view icon to the left of an order to view customer details, edit the customer, or view the customer's order history.

FIGURE 30.16

The Customer Manager inside the Ubercart Store Administration Manager

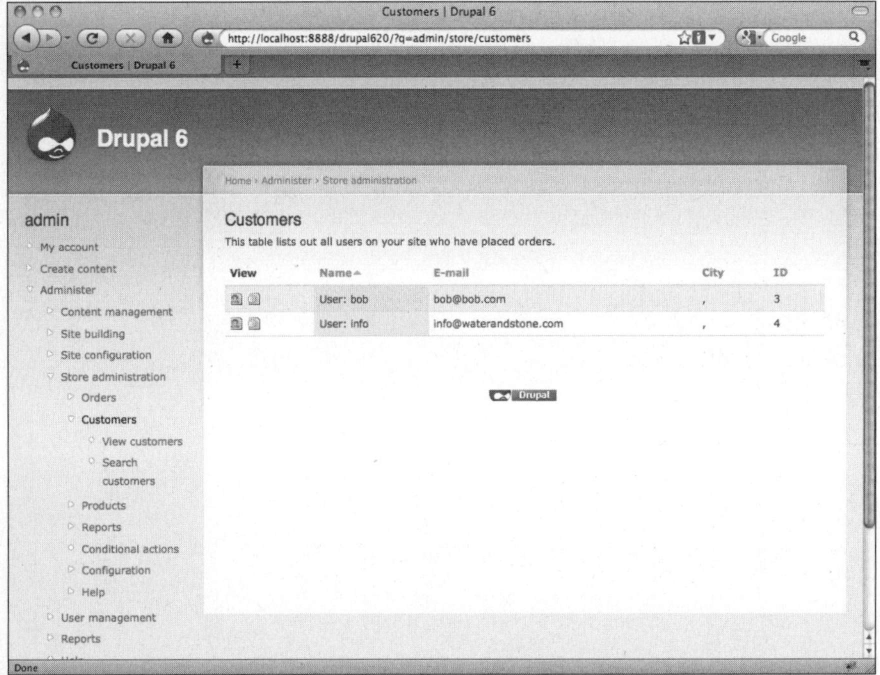

Viewing reports

The Ubercart reporting function requires that you activate the Reports module in the Modules Manager. After the Reports module is activated, the system gathers data on customer activity inside your store.

Click the Reports link on the Store Administration Manager to view your reports. The menu of reports is shown in Figure 30.17.

There are multiple reports under these headings, and you can create custom reports by using the links you find inside the Product reports and Sales reports interfaces.

FIGURE 30.17

The Reports menu inside the Ubercart Store Administration Manager

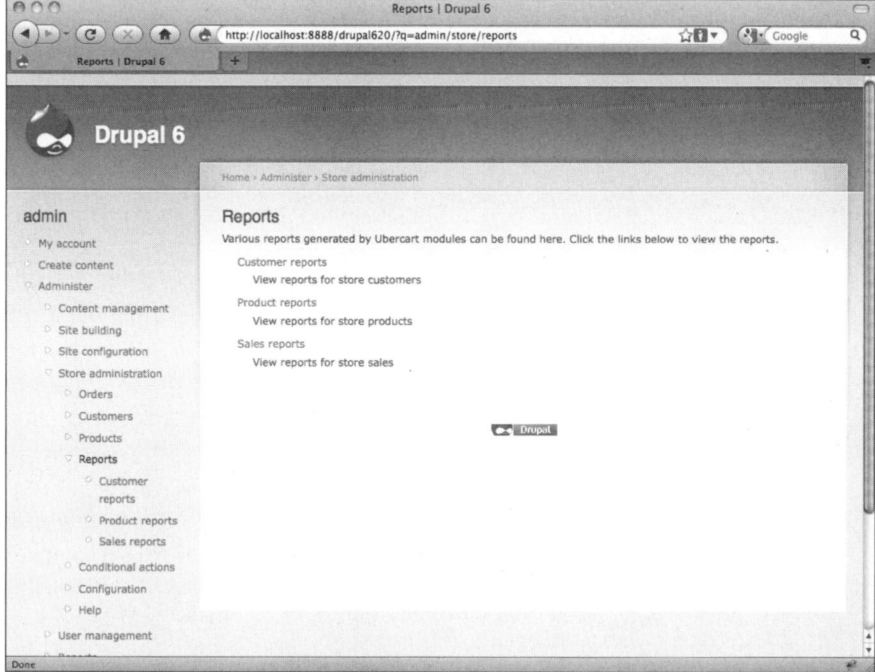

Creating conditional actions

Conditional actions are used to create custom behaviors in response to things that occur on the site. A simple example is notification e-mails to customers: When a customer completes checkout, the system sends him an e-mail.

You can use the conditional actions interface to add your own custom actions to your site. This is a fairly large topic and beyond the scope of this chapter. You can get in and experiment with this functionality with little risk, or if you prefer more guidance, go to the Ubercart site to learn more about how people use this powerful feature. Visit `http://www.ubercart.org/docs/user/7657/configuring_conditional_actions`.

Enhancing Ubercart

Quite a few community contributions are available to extend and enhance your Ubercart store. In this section, I look at a few modules that are particularly useful, with a focus on improving user experience and ease of administration.

Note

At the time of this writing, many of these modules had yet to be ported to Drupal 7. Check all for version compatibility before attempting to install them on your Drupal 7 site! ■

- **Ubercart Addresses module:** The default Ubercart system allows only one address per user. With this module, you can add support for multiple customer addresses. To learn more, visit the project page at `http://drupal.org/project/uc_addresses`.
- **Ubercart Terms of Service module:** This module makes it easy to include a terms and conditions requirement as part of the checkout process. A number of options are available, including the ability to display the terms in a pop-up. The project site is located at `http://drupal.org/project/uc_termsofservice`.
- **Ubercart Discounts (Alternative) module:** This module supports multiple discount calculations, including discounts based on the number of products purchased, percentage discounts, and fixed amount discounts. Qualification for the discount can be based on quantity, value, and role. Discounts can also be combined to create complex structures. Visit the project site at `http://drupal.org/project/uc_discounts_alt`.
- **Ubercart Discount Coupons module:** This module adds coupon-based discounts to your site. The module supports a variety of discount calculation methods as well as restrictions on use of the discounts. The system also includes a sub-module that enables the sale of coupons or the inclusion of a coupon as part of a product. View the project site at `http://drupal.org/project/uc_coupon`.
- **Ubercart Out of Stock Notification module:** If you are using the Stock module option for Ubercart, implementation of this additional module is a must. The module checks the stock levels, and if you are out of stock, it responds as you have instructed: It displays to the customer an out of stock message, hides the product, or provides a backorder option. View the project site at `http://drupal.org/project/uc_out_of_stock`.
- **Ubercart Price Per Role module:** This module enables you to tie prices to user roles; it's very useful if you want to show different prices to different users—for example, on a mixed wholesale and retail site. Visit the project site at `http://drupal.org/project/uc_price_per_role`.

- **Ubercart Product Power Tools module:** This module is concerned with simplifying the product admin section of the Ubercart store. With this module installed, you can hide unneeded fields, making product entry simpler and faster. View the project site at `http://drupal.org/project/uc_product_power_tools`.
- **Ubercart Views module:** The Ubercart Views module provides a collection of ready-to-use views tailored to the Ubercart store. The module is a time-saver that includes prebuilt views for new products, popular products, most purchased, and more. Visit the project site at `http://drupal.org/project/uc_views`.
- **UC Multiprice module:** If you are providing different pricing for different countries, the UC Multiprice module makes your life much easier. Pricing can be fixed or calculated dynamically, and it supports pricing per role. The project site is located at `http://drupal.org/project/uc_multiprice`.

Summary

This chapter addressed the basics of setting up eCommerce and product management with Drupal's Ubercart module. I covered these topics:

- The capabilities and uses of Ubercart
- How to install Ubercart
- How to configure a basic Ubercart store
- Optional core and contributed modules

Part VII

Drupal in the Enterprise

IN THIS PART

CHAPTER 31

Securing Your Site

IN THIS CHAPTER

Security best practices

Keeping up with security notices

Site security is one of the most critical issues faced by Web site owners and administrators. Open-source software like Drupal is neither more nor less secure than any other type of software. The issues that face open-source systems are essentially the same issues that face all software users. Similarly, the steps you need to take to secure your site are common to most server-based software installations.

Site owners who rely on technology alone for their security are doomed to failure. Though I emphasize it throughout the chapter, it is worth mentioning again: People are your biggest risk. To keep your site secure, you must educate users and administrators, and you need to consistently implement common-sense practices and policies.

This chapter looks at security best practices for Drupal and provides advice and tips on how to make your Drupal site secure and how to keep it secure.

Security Best Practices

Creating and maintaining a secure Web site requires attention to a variety of issues. The process starts at server setup and continues throughout the life of the site. There is no such thing as a site you can create and forget and no such thing as a site that takes care of itself. To keep your site safe, you must take affirmative steps and develop an awareness of the issues. While you cannot protect yourself from every conceivable threat, you can reduce the vulnerability of your site to a manageable level with a reasonable amount of effort.

Securing the Drupal core

Security is not one single thing; it is a process, a set of steps that need to be taken in order to achieve a result. The process begins with your server settings and the Drupal core files. If you fail to make this base level of the system secure, then additional steps are at the very least of limited effectiveness, and at the very worst, they are pointless.

Tip

The first step toward ensuring your site's integrity is also one of the easiest: Install only the most recent version of the Drupal core file packages found at the official download site, drupal.org. Do not download and install core file archives from other sites without first verifying their origins, completeness, or integrity. ■

Protect directories and files

You can take several steps to enhance the security of the directories and files on your server. The first step is adjusting the permissions to be as strict as possible without impairing use of the site. You must write-protect your critical directories. As a general rule, if you are running Drupal on the Apache Web server, then set the directory permissions to 755 and the file permissions to 644. Note that this is best done after you have fully completed your installation of the core and all extensions. You may need to make these settings more permissive if you need to install extensions in the future or if you are allowing users to upload files to your site.

Tip

Note that the ownership of files is also an important consideration. The Drupal.org site includes a good discussion of ownership and permissions issues at `http://drupal.org/node/244924`. **■**

Protect access details

Humans are your most common point of security policy failure. Admin passwords should be changed often. During the installation process, select a non-obvious name for the administrator account. Passwords also should be as secure as practicable.

In addition to controlling the access to your admin system, you need to be sensitive to the access issues that relate to your database. If you have control over the access privileges to the user accounts on your MySQL database, make sure all accounts are set with limited access.

Tip

A good administrator password should be at least seven characters in length and employ a combination of uppercase and lowercase letters, numbers, and non-alphanumeric characters. Never, under any circumstances, use words that can be found in the dictionary! This is common sense: "4tG~9fU#ss3" is much harder to crack than "tinytoons." ■

Remove unnecessary files

If you don't need a file now and you don't intend to use it, get rid of it. Logical targets for deletion include unused themes and modules you have installed and then decided not to use. If you have copied archive files (zip files or tarballs) to your server during the course of installation, make sure you get rid of those.

Protect version details

Every installation of Drupal comes with a file that details the version number being used. The file is named CHANGELOG.txt and is located at the root of your Drupal installation. Change the name of this file to keep prying eyes from discovering the version of Drupal deployed on your site; that information can be used to help them identify potential areas for attack. Don't delete the file; it contains information you may need (though this is rare!). README.txt files present a similar risk.

Maintain a sensible server setup

In an ideal world, we would all have our own dedicated servers where we could control every aspect of the system. In the real world, shared hosting is the reality for many users. Shared hosting, though certainly more cost-effective than a dedicated host, involves tradeoffs in terms of security and access privileges. Your goal should be to make the host setup as secure as possible, regardless of whether it is dedicated or shared. Exactly what you are able to do with your server varies, but you should consider the following:

- **Use Secure methods of logging in to your server, if available.** Use Secure (SFTP) or SVN for your file transfers, if available. For user authentication, use https instead of http. This helps avoid the possibility that someone can determine your username and password while you are in the process of a file transfer.
- **Turn off Register Globals.** Drupal does not need it, and it is a security risk.
- **If the mod_security module is installed on your Apache Web server, use it.** It acts as an embedded Web application firewall and provides significant protection against many common attacks. Learn more about how to use it at `http://www.modsecurity.org/`.
- **Turn safe mode off.** Safe mode is not necessary for Drupal and may cause problems with some extensions.
- **Set Magic Quotes GPC to On.**
- **Don't use PHP allow_url_fopen.** Set this option to Off.
- **Use PHP open_basedir.** Set this option to On.

Tip

Contracting with a Web host solely on the basis of price is a bad idea. Moreover, as competition has increased in the hosting space, it is becoming more of a commodity business and price points have narrowed. Instead of simply taking the cheapest host, select your host based on service levels, quality of hardware, access privileges, software installed, and backup policies. ■

Securing third-party extensions

From a security perspective, every module or theme you install on your Drupal site increases the risk you face. Each extension comes with its own set of files and potential vulnerabilities. The fact that extension quality varies wildly is a serious issue for site owners, and each extension you install brings with it a need for due diligence and ongoing maintenance. Given these issues, the first point of concern for site owners should be the issue of trust: Do you trust that the developer is capable of producing solid, secure code, and do you trust this developer to keep it patched and keep users abreast of risks as they arise? Never forget that, just like the core files, extensions have to be maintained, patched, and upgraded.

The wide variety of Drupal extensions available means that you have choices. Accordingly, before you decide to adopt a particular extension, you need to do your research. Not only should you be concerned with whether it works and looks like you want, but also whether the extension is of good quality and comes from a reputable source. There are no guarantees here, so you must do your homework and make a judgment call. Visit the developer's site. Is it professional? Is it up to date? If this is a project-based extension, check for levels of project activity and issues that have been reported but remain unfixed.

Next, before you install a new extension on a live site, test it locally. Check to make sure it installs cleanly, without error messages. Test all the various functionalities, regardless of whether you intend to use them all. Also check to see if there is documentation referenced on the extension's project page on Drupal.org, and if the extension is bundled with a README file—read it!

Finally, before installing the new extension on your live site, back up the live site. That way, if there is a problem, you can roll back and restore from the backup.

If you decide that the extension is no longer necessary and you uninstall it, check the server to make sure that the extension has uninstalled cleanly and has not left any files on your server. Many times extensions leave directories and files behind on your server, despite being uninstalled.

Cross-Reference

Uninstalling extensions is covered in Chapter 29. ■

Securing your content

While this chapter focuses on securing your Drupal installation, some site administrators also have concerns about securing the content on their sites. Security, in the context of content, is a broad topic, but typically concerns one of the following two areas:

- If your concern is about securing the transfer of data between your site and the site visitors, your best bet is to employ HTTP Secure (HTTPS). HTTPS is a protocol that encrypts requests and responses between the browser and the server. The protocol is widely used to handle the transfer of confidential or sensitive data—for example, credit card information. Implementing HTTPS is dependent upon your hosting package and your server setup. For more information, see the discussion on HTTPS on the Drupal.org site at `http://drupal.org/https-information`.

Tip

HTTPS also can be used to add another layer of protection for your admin login details. To implement this, you need to implement HTTPS for your user login. For more information about setting up HTTPS on your site, please visit `http://drupal.org/https-information`. ■

- If your concern is preventing users from inserting unsafe code into content items, then you need to implement Drupal's filters. As a general rule, you should never give untrusted users the ability to enter PHP code on your site. Indeed, to be most secure, you can block the use of HTML as well, though this is an extreme approach.

Cross-Reference

The Filter module is discussed in more detail in Chapter 4. Working with user permissions is covered in Chapter 23. ■

Note

A number of third-party modules can assist with improving security—for example, by providing enhanced session management, stricter access controls, and improvements in authentication. A list of contributed modules, organized by security topics, can be found at `http://drupal.org/node/382752`. ■

Keeping Up with Security Notices

Things change. New vulnerabilities are discovered, and new exploits are created to take advantage of them. Sometimes the rate of change is quite impressive, and it becomes a challenge to keep up with things and ensure that all aspects of your site are up to date.

Keeping up with the official announcements from Drupal.org is one of the ways you can stay informed of important news about your Drupal site. Important notices also are published on the home page of Drupal.org. Of course, if you rely on these default notifications, you will discover new alerts only when you visit Drupal.org. If you want more immediate notices, you should consider subscribing to the RSS feed or join the security mailing list. The URLs for the various official resources are included in Table 31.1.

The channel you prefer to use for alerts is entirely up to you, but the simple fact is that the only way to keep your site secure is to keep it—and its extensions—up to date. When new versions are released, do not delay in upgrading. New releases require immediate action. If you fail to upgrade your site after a security release is announced and your site is subsequently hacked, you really have no one to blame but yourself.

Tip

The Update module contained in your Drupal core is one of your best sources for notifications of new releases; make sure it is enabled and that you heed the warnings. Using the Update module is discussed in Chapter 35. ■

TABLE 31.1

Official Drupal Security Resources

Name of resource	URL
Core Security Posts	`http://drupal.org/security`
Contributed Modules Security Posts	`http://drupal.org/security/contrib`
Public Service Announcements	`http://drupal.org/security/psa`
Drupal Core RSS	`http://drupal.org/security/rss.xml`
Contributed Modules RSS	`http://drupal.org/security/contrib/rss.xml`
Security Public Service Announcements RSS	`http://drupal.org/security/psa/rss.xml`

The Drupal Security newsletter is a valuable resource. To subscribe, you must first set up an account on the Drupal.org site. After you have registered, the newsletter subscriptions can be found on the My newsletters tab of your user profile.

Tip

The Drupal Security Team typically releases security notifications on Wednesdays. ■

Note

What should you do if you find a bug in the Drupal code or a contributed module? If you discover a potential error or weakness, e-mail your concerns to the Drupal security team at `security@drupal.org`. Provide as much information as you can about the environment, the Drupal version, and the conditions that led to the appearance of the error. Do not report the error by posting it in the forum or on the module's page. ■

Summary

This chapter addressed security issues in Drupal. I covered these topics:

- Best practices for securing your site
- Securing the Drupal core
- Securing extensions
- Keeping track of security updates and information

CHAPTER 32

Managing Site Performance

IN THIS CHAPTER

Addressing typical performance concerns

Testing performance

Drupal performance management can mean different things to you depending on what scale of Web operations you are responsible for. In this chapter I provide you with an understanding of the core system's performance tuning functionality and related configuration guidance. I then take a look at a range of additional ways to improve your site's performance and review some common methods of tracking down the more subtle problems.

Addressing Typical Performance Concerns

You encounter several different types of performance issues with any dynamically generated Web site. Drupal site managers need to be concerned with these and with a number of Drupal-specific issues.

Reducing server load via caching and resource aggregation

Every time a page of your site is requested, a certain amount of computer processing and data transfer work is required to respond to the request. The more you reduce this work, the faster your site's response time is and the more visitors your site can serve at the same time. In times of high load, this can mean the difference between your site being available or being unavailable to visitors.

You control a number of important settings in the Performance section of the Drupal admin's Configure area. This section is displayed in Figure 32.1.

FIGURE 32.1

The Configure admin area showing the Development section and the Performance sub-item

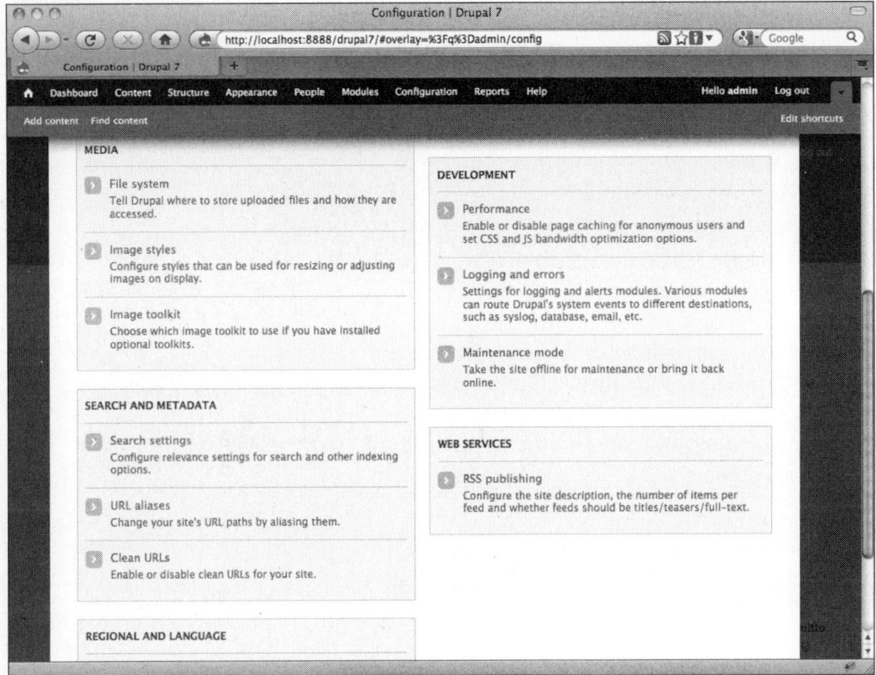

Introducing the site cache

You site's content is stored in a series of structures inside the database. These structures are quite dissimilar from the structure of a Web page. Consequently, your content must be assembled into chunks of content more similar to a Web page before it can be delivered to the site visitor. Drupal's site cache stores assembled content chunks in a format ready to deliver to the site visitors. It works at the block level, the page level, or both.

Tip

You typically leave Drupal caching turned off during development of your site. However, many people forget to re-enable caching after they launch the site. Make a review of caching settings part of your regular checklist when deploying a new project or as part of your change management processes. In addition, be sure to test your site with caching enabled before you deploy or go live. This helps you avoid unpleasant surprises during the go-live process. Enabling caching does change how your site behaves. ■

Configuring the site cache

You configure the performance and caching settings of your system in the Configure admin area. In this section, you find a Development section, and in that, a Performance sub-item (refer to Figure 32.1). The Performance sub-item is where you find all the standard site cache configuration settings, as displayed in Figure 32.2.

FIGURE 32.2

Drupal's performance configuration page, including the site cache settings

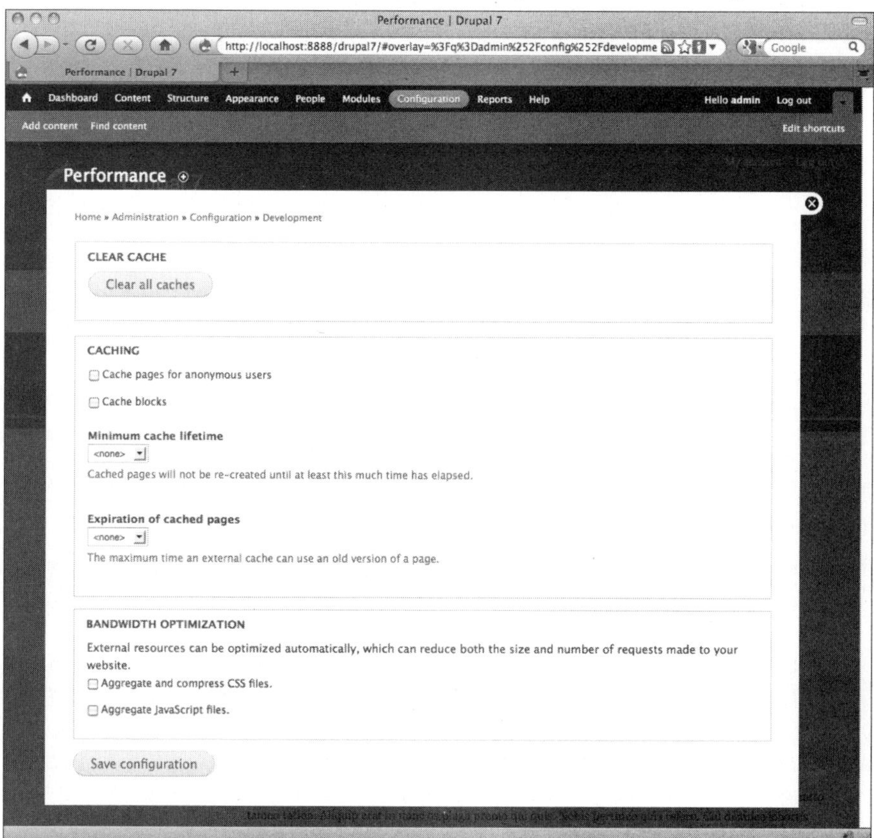

You find these items in the admin's Performance settings page:

- **Clear all caches button:** This item does exactly what it says: It removes or expires all data stored in the system's caches. You may want to use this operation to make sure you are viewing or testing the very latest changes you've made to your site.

- **Caching settings:** This section contains settings that control the behavior of the internal site cache and one setting that tries to influence external cache behavior.
  - **Cache pages for anonymous users:** If this is checked, assembled pages are cached for all anonymous (not logged in) users. This can dramatically speed up your Web site because it reduces the amount of work the server must do when serving up a page request.

Note

Caching content is much easier for anonymous users because they all share the same content access rights and can therefore typically view the same content. Caching content for authenticated users is trickier, but some contributed modules help you with this. Block caching works for both anonymous and authenticated users. ■

  - **Cache blocks:** If this is checked, Drupal caches blocks in the site cache. Blocks and pages are assembled separately, and cached blocks can be utilized for authenticated visitors.

Tip

You can use the contributed Block Cache Alter module to set granular block caching preferences. For example, you can use this module to specify the cache expire time for each block. You also can clear the block cache manually. You can download the Block Cache Alter module at `http://drupal.org/project/blockcache_alter`. **■**

  - **Minimum cache lifetime:** This setting allows you to specify a minimum amount of time that data is kept in the site cache. The longer you keep data in the cache, the more you reduce the load on your servers. Do keep in mind that the performance you gain comes at the cost of content freshness; you don't want to have a minimum cache lifetime of 12 hours for a breaking news Web site.
  - **Expiration of cached pages:** This value is used by external caches; it attempts to control how long external caching mechanisms—either yours or other peoples'—store your site's content before coming back to get a fresh copy. For example, many organizations perform some level of local Web content caching to reduce the amount of traffic passing through their firewalls. This setting tries to influence the behavior of these kinds of caches.
- **Bandwidth optimization settings:** This area influences how Drupal outputs both CSS and JavaScript resource links in each page. Without these optimizations enabled, Drupal tends to produce a large number of CSS and JavaScript resource links in the HTML document head. It's not unusual to see more than 20 such links. Each inclusion of a remote CSS or JavaScript resource implicates a request to the Web server. And most Web browsers limit the number of simultaneous requests they make to the same server, typically to between three and five simultaneous requests. If you stop to think about this, you quickly understand the importance of optimizing this behavior; the browser waits for the first set of requests to finish before making more requests. This means the requests happen in a serial, rather than parallel, manner, and that your site's pages may load quite slowly.

Tip

You should disable the bandwidth optimization settings when developing your site. Otherwise, you may not know whether you are viewing your latest changes when attempting to test them. ■

- **Aggregate and compress CSS files:** If this box is checked, Drupal does its best to aggregate all CSS files into as few resources as possible. It also compresses these files to minimize the amount of data it actually transmits over the wire for each resource request. Both of these actions can significantly improve the perceived responsiveness of your Drupal-based sites.
- **Aggregate JavaScript files:** JavaScript files are subject to the same limitations as CSS files, in terms of serial versus parallel requests from the browser. After the limit of parallel requests is reached, the browser makes requests in a serial fashion. Therefore, from a performance perspective, you probably want to limit the number of total requests whenever possible.

Reducing server load by controlling block visibility

Drupal pages typically contain a number of different blocks that together comprise a significant portion of the page's content. Blocks are a formal Drupal concept; they represent discreet chunks of content or functionality. A list of recent forum posts is an example of a block, as is a list of currently logged-in users.

Each theme has a number of page regions defined; to activate a given block, you assign it to a specific region. You can further configure blocks such that they are visible only in certain content or user contexts. For example, you can specify that a given block is visible only on the home page and only for logged-in users of a certain role.

Cross-Reference

In Chapter 7, we discuss blocks in detail, including how to manage their visibility and how to assign them to regions in each theme. ■

To enhance Drupal's performance, you should verify that each block's visibility settings correspond correctly with its actual use. This may sound like I'm stating the obvious, or even the impossible, but if you consider that theme modifications sometimes remove regions from a given template—for example, an article detail page may not have all the same regions as your home page—then this makes more sense.

The devil is in the details here. You must keep in mind that even if a given page template does not have a region defined, but the theme does have it defined and that region is in use elsewhere, Drupal still generates (or pulls from cache) the blocks for that region upon every page request. This means that the load of constructing these blocks is a complete waste of time for your server, and you may not even know it's happening, because they are never rendered in the browser.

The way to avoid this unnecessary load is to precisely define where each block should be visible. This is done in the Blocks Manager tool when editing each block's configuration, as shown in Figure 32.3. We describe this process in detail in Chapter 10.

FIGURE 32.3

Drupal's Blocks Manager tool showing the Visibility settings tab set

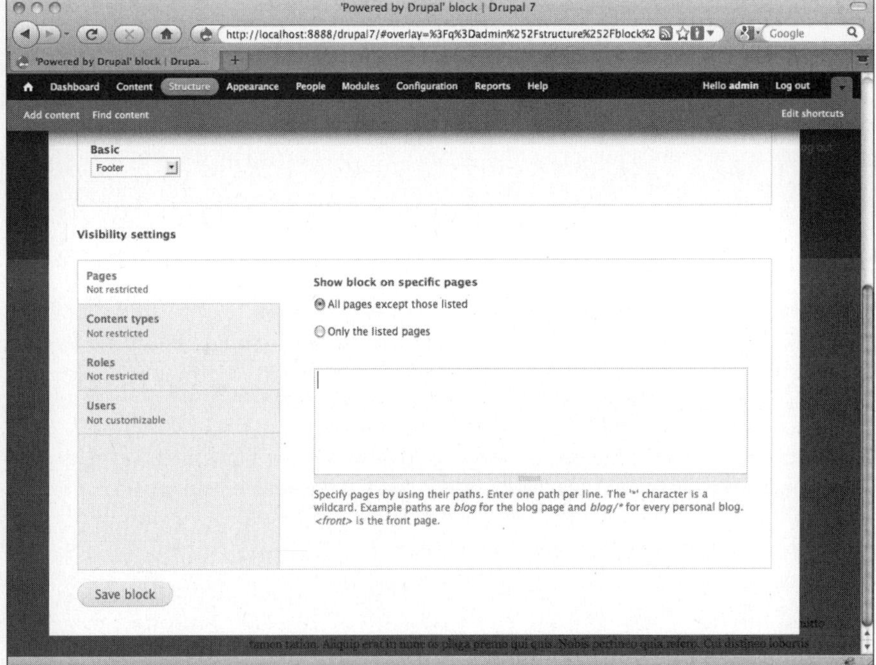

Configuring additional performance settings

Your Drupal install is likely a combination of the core system and any number of contributed modules. The core system itself is typically a mixture of enabled and disabled modules. Review these additional items when tuning your system for scalability:

- **Turn on caching or performance features in all modules:** If you are using contributed modules like Views, make sure you've enabled their native caching features. Each module differs in this regard, so run through them one at a time and make sure you are familiar with any performance features they may have. Sometimes you even find additional modules to accelerate performance.
- **Disable the Statistics module:** Unless absolutely necessary, do not run this module on your high-traffic Drupal sites. Depending on how this module is configured, it can add some significant load to your system for every page request. Most people rely upon third-party Web analytics for their higher-volume Web sites.

- **Disable the database logging module:** This core module logs a number of types of messages from your system to the database. These messages can prove quite useful. You need to evaluate whether this is a good idea in your environment. Keep in mind that writing these messages to the database adds load to your system and that you may be able to use more optimized tools to monitor your servers.

  The Drupal community documentation discusses a number of ways to monitor your system. You can learn more at this URL: `http://drupal.org/node/627162`.

- **Serve public files from public directories:** Double-check that all media files and downloads you are serving to the public are being served from public directories. If you are serving public files from private directories, you are putting unnecessary load on the system, because Drupal gets involved in the security aspects of serving private files.

- **Use Apache Lucene and Solr for search:** The Apache Foundation's Lucene search engine combined with the Apache Solr sub-project provide a powerful, effective, fully featured search tool. If your site is search oriented or if you just want to add more search features, the contributed Apache Solr Search Integration module is worth investigating. You can learn more about it at `http://drupal.org/project/apachesolr`.

- **Use memcached for cache storage:** The open-source memcached server provides a high-performance, reliable, and distributed in-memory cache infrastructure. The contributed memcache module (found at `http://drupal.org/project/memcache`) gives you the means to leverage memcached with Drupal. Using memcache speeds up Drupal because it allows you to store Drupal's cached content in fast-access RAM versus relatively slower database tables.

- **Use the Alternate PHP Cache (APC):** APC provides both low-level caching of your compiled PHP scripts—called *opcode*—and in-memory object caching, like memcached. It its role as an opcode cache APC is considered a *PHP Accelerator*. In a study published by Zend and Acquia in 2010, analysts found more than a 300 percent Drupal performance improvement just by configuring APC's PHP acceleration functionality in the Drupal environment. You can learn more about APC at `http://www.php.net/apc`. In addition, you should note that APC alternatives exist. Wikipedia has a list of known PHP accelerators at `http://en.wikipedia.org/wiki/List_of_PHP_accelerators`.

  A contributed module for Drupal 7 facilitates additional performance gains for Drupal when APC is present. This module leverages APC's ability to cache PHP application objects in shared memory, versus the default of storing them in the database. You can learn about this project at `http://drupal.org/project/apc`.

- **Use the Boost module:** This contributed module is popular for sites that deliver to mainly anonymous users. It creates a static file cache of pages that allows Drupal to significantly minimize the amount of work related to each page request. It has the advantage of working in relatively restricted environments, but like APC and memcached, configuring this module requires some advanced systems administration skills. At the time of this writing, no Boost build was available for Drupal 7, but work is in progress. The module's project page is located at `http://drupal.org/project/boost`.

- **Use the AuthCache module:** This contributed module enables caching of pages for both anonymous and authenticated visitors. Remember that standard Drupal can do some block caching for authenticated users, but it cannot do page caching for these users. AuthCache improves this situation, and it improves the performance of anonymous user page caching too. As of press time, this module was not yet released for Drupal 7, but work is in progress. You can follow the progress at `http://drupal.org/project/authcache`. Full implementation of this module is for advance Drupal administrators only because it requires special template code modifications.
- **Take control of your cron jobs:** The Drupal cron task operation is a monolithic black box. You have little control over what sub-tasks are run and when they run. You may find this undesirable. For example, you may want certain tasks to run only during quiet periods of the day. Contributed projects like Elysia Cron are working to give you more control over the situation. This can become important to tuning your server. Note that at the time of this writing, Elysia Cron was not yet available for Drupal 7, but work is in progress. You can keep tabs on the effort at `http://drupal.org/project/elysia_cron`.
- **Remove unused contributed modules:** If you are not using modules, remove them from your build. Additional modules add a bit more overhead to Drupal's operations, even if they are not active. Keep you production environment as clean as possible to reduce the clutter and the chance of confusion.
- **Use the DB Maintenance module:** This contributed module has been updated for Drupal 7. You use it to perform regular, Drupal-specific optimizations to the underlying database. Be sure to confirm that the Drupal 7 version is updated for your specific database, because Drupal can now run on a number of database types. You can download this module at `http://drupal.org/project/db_maintenance`.
- **Consider reverse proxy caching and CDNs:** If you're are running very high traffic Web sites or just want to distribute your delivery tier across a number of network nodes, you should investigate the use of reverse proxy caches like Varnish or Squid. These tools can be fine-tuned to cache significant amounts of your content on a first tier of high-performance servers, which can in turn be load-balanced and geographically distributed. Content Delivery Networks (CDNs) offer some of the same performance and reliability benefits, but they are probably more appropriate for serving larger media assets, such as videos or media files.
- **Tune your Web server, database, and file system:** This is a catchall, but my point is that one shouldn't forget to optimize Drupal's working environment. If your disks are slow or over-burdened, database reads and writes suffer. If you don't have enough memory, MySQL slows down and memcached cache requests miss. Performance optimization is the practice of a holistic perspective followed by the ability to prioritize key lever points. Don't get too hung up on modules and forsake your Web server. A recent study by Zend and Acquia demonstrated enormous Drupal performance differences with different PHP and application server environments, running on the same hardware.

Note

Technically speaking, Drupal 7 is significantly different from Drupal 6, as are many of the most used modules. Performance tuning advice for Drupal 7 and the latest generation of modules is likely to evolve considerably over the course of the next few years. If you are administering high-traffic Drupal Web sites, you should continue to keep your knowledge of the subject up to date. The best way to do this is to play an active role in the Drupal community. You can tune into the performance topics via the Drupal High Performance group's page at `http://groups.drupal.org/high-performance`. ■

Testing Performance

It's always best to be the first person to know that you have a performance or capacity problem; if you're the second person, it often means that you are entering crisis mode. With that in mind, in this section I describe how you can analyze your system's performance before it is out in the wild.

Simulating system load

Page load time is one metric worthy of your consideration, but when talking about site performance, what is most important is measuring how many people can visit your Web site at the same time. This is commonly referred to as load or capacity testing.

You probably want to answer this question of capacity for a few reasons. Most important, you want to be able to meet the needs of your audience. So, before going live with your new site, test it to make sure it can support at least the expected number of concurrent visitors. Secondly, site managers generally want to have a baseline for site performance. As your site evolves and increases in complexity, you can use this baseline to understand how a given change is affecting site performance.

Tip

Each Web site has different visitor patterns. Global sites may have several spikes of visits per day, whereas locally focused Web sites may have just one busy period per day. Take the time to understand the peaks and averages for your Web site and use this data to make your load testing realistic. ■

You find many different load testing tools in the market. A few of these include the following:

- **Apache JMeter:** An open-source, multi-threaded desktop tool that can be used to simulate user visits to your Web site. JMeter can be used to perform distributed load testing by configuring JMeter master and slave machines. Learn more about this project at `http://jakarta.apache.org/jmeter/`.
- **HP Loadrunner:** A commercial software product sold by Hewlett Packard. This tool supports a feature called Virtual User Generator (VuGen) that aims to replicate the behavior of real human visitors. The Loadrunner history and features are described at `http://en.wikipedia.org/wiki/HP_LoadRunner`.

- **The Grinder:** This open-source tool is an enterprise Java load testing framework that can be used to perform distributed Web site and application load testing. The Grinder can record actions performed by real users and use these as the basis for load testing operations. Find out more about The Grinder project at `http://grinder.sourceforge.net/`.

After you have selected and become comfortable with a load testing tool, it's time to move on. Identify the parts of your site that perform the worst and then drill down to understand the root causes.

Using the Devel module to analyze performance

The contributed Devel module, found at `http://drupal.org/project/devel`, is a Swiss army knife for Drupal developers and administrators. One of its key functions is performance analysis. You can use it to identify slow database queries, slow PHP functions, and pages that are consuming large amounts of RAM.

Note

You should not use the Devel module for performance analysis and diagnostics in your production environment. This module imposes a significant load on your system and has the potential to expose sensitive information to site visitors. Be careful about how and where you use this module. ■

After you have installed and enabled the Devel module, follow these steps to enable Devel performance diagnostics:

1. **Log into your site as an administrator.**

   The login landing page loads in your browser.
2. **Select the Configuration option from the main admin menu.**

   The Configuration's section page loads in your browser.
3. **Locate the Development sub-item in the page, and click the Devel settings link in that area.**

   The Devel module's settings page loads in your browser, as shown in Figure 32.4.
4. **Locate the Query Log section of the page, and click the box labeled Display query log.**
5. **Click the radio button to sort the query log by source.**
6. **Scroll down the page, and click the box labeled Display page timer.**
7. **Check the next box labeled Display memory usage.**
8. **Now scroll to the bottom of the page, and click the Save configuration button.**

   If the operation is successful, a success message is visible at the top of the page and your changes are now active.

FIGURE 32.4

The Devel module's configuration settings page showing the Query Log section

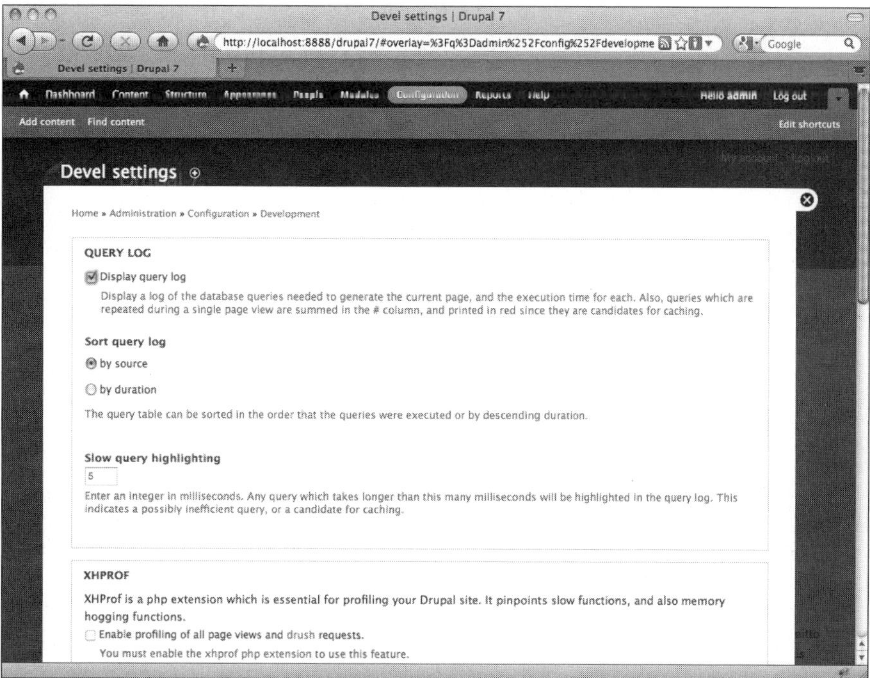

After you have enabled Devel's performance diagnostics, you see a number of outputs at the bottom of every Drupal page. These outputs can be used to identify pages that are consuming large amounts of resources or running especially intensive database queries.

If you do not see Devel's performance diagnostic outputs at the bottom of your pages, navigate to the Drupal Blocks Manager in the Structure area of the admin and ensure that the Development block is assigned to the footer or another appropriate region of the current theme.

Cross-Reference

See Chapter 7 for an introduction to the Drupal Blocks Manager tool and how you can control where blocks are rendered in the page. ■

Analyzing the performance of Views

The contributed Views module is the most used of all the contributed modules. It also has a great potential to add significant load to your server infrastructure. You have two fundamental options for tuning Views. I mentioned the first earlier in this chapter: enabling the Views cache. Just like the site cache, you can tune the amount of time that Drupal caches assembled views. If your pages with views are running slowly, be sure to verify that Views caching is enabled and consider extending the amount of time views are cached for.

When building views, you can preview the view output. This output includes the amount of time the related database queries are taking to execute. If queries are taking a long time to execute, you should first attempt to improve their performance by adjusting how the view is constructed. For example, some combinations of filters may perform much more slowly than others. Experiment with different approaches and compare the corresponding query times. Going beyond view configuration tuning, you or an experienced database administrator can analyze the slow queries and attempt to improve performance by adding new indices at the database level.

This level of tuning requires specific database skills, but the timer outputs from Views make it extremely clear whether you are making progress.

Summary

This chapter covered some more advanced topics related to Drupal performance tuning. I noted that Drupal 7 performance is an evolving story, especially because this release is very recent and significant architectural changes were made.

I discussed the following areas:

- How to enable Drupal's core performance-enhancing features, including the site cache and the ability to aggregate CSS and JavaScript resource files
- Some of the more advanced performance configurations and enhancements, especially those offered by a broad set of contributed modules
- How performance tuning is an exercise in holistic thinking and the ability to identify and prioritize key points of leverage
- How to catch performance issues before they happen using tools like the Devel contributed module

CHAPTER

33

Creating a Search Engine-Friendly Site

IN THIS CHAPTER

- Creating search engine-friendly URLs
- Managing canonicalization issues
- Adding content metadata
- Optimizing page templates
- Creating custom error pages

Search engines such as Google, Yahoo!, Bing, and others have become the doorways to the Web. The ability of these engines to accurately and meaningfully index the content of your Web site is, fortunately, something you have some control over.

The practice of search engine optimization—commonly known as SEO—is the means you have for exercising this control.

Certain SEO practices are considered by major search engine companies to be underhanded and against their rules. However, you have at your disposal a number of practices that are simple, broadly useful, and even encouraged by organizations in the search industry. I focus on these aspects of SEO in this chapter.

Tip

The folks at Google have published a SEO starter guide that you may find useful. You can access the PDF version of the guide at `http://www.google.com/webmasters/docs/search-engine-optimization-starter-guide.pdf`. ■

Drupal, like most content management systems, comes with a mixture of good and not-so-good SEO configurations. What's important to understand is that the system is configurable enough to achieve a high level of SEO. And further, with the semantic Web features that have made their way into the Drupal 7 core, the system is moving from a respectable position toward a leadership position in terms of SEO.

This chapter reviews typical SEO concerns, how you can configure Drupal to address them, and how Drupal 7 is moving in a strategic direction with regard to the next generation of SEO.

Creating Search Engine-Friendly URLs

Each piece of content in your Drupal system has an address, called a URL. Ideally, content management systems produce URLs that are easy for search engines to understand and follow, and simple for humans to read, remember, and share. Drupal's default URLs are not ideal. They are not search engine-friendly (SEF), nor are they particularly human-friendly.

Search engine-optimized URLs and human-optimized URLs are not always the same thing, but they do share some common traits. Two of these traits are:

- The URL is easy to read.
- The URL contains meaningful words.

Using a combination of core modules, contributed modules, and Web server configurations, this section walks you through a series of steps to incrementally improve the way Drupal URLs are created and managed.

Note

In the Drupal community and in the Drupal user interfaces, you may often run across the phrase "clean URLs." You can often take this expression to mean "search engine-friendly URLs," but you should note that the fundamental idea of clean URLs is simply to remove the parameters from Drupal's URLs. I clarify this in the following sections. One additional point is that the phrase "clean URLs" also refers to a specific piece of core Drupal functionality—called Clean URLs—that you access via the Drupal admin system. I discuss this in detail in the following sections as well. ■

In the worst-case scenario, Drupal's default content item URLs look something like this:

```
http://www.example.com/index.php?q=node/1
```

This isn't a terribly unfriendly URL, but it's also not considered optimal or *clean*, primarily because of the inclusion of the `?` delimiter and the following name-value parameter set (`q=node/1`).

Most modern search engines do not have a problem parsing and following such URLs, but some may still have problems parsing beyond the question mark character. This is the first point where things can be optimized, and it's precisely what Drupal's Clean URLs functionality accomplishes.

After the Clean URLs feature has been successfully configured, the previous URL looks like this:

```
http://www.example.com/node/1
```

This new "clean" URL is more search engine-friendly, and because it is both shorter and without any funny characters, it is also more human-friendly.

Enabling the Clean URLs feature

As with most content management systems, Drupal relies on what is called *URL rewriting* to translate clean URLs into the messier URLs that the system understands. Drupal relies on the Web server to do this translation work, and as such, the implementation steps for clean URLs are Web server-specific.

Tip

If you ever get stuck while trying to enable Drupal's Clean URLs, keep in mind that you can always access the dedicated documentation for this functionality at `http://drupal.org/node/15365`. ■

In this section, we cover how to implement clean URLs for two of the most common Web servers: Apache 2.2 and IIS 7. The official Drupal documentation Web site contains additional configuration guidance for other Web servers as well as useful debugging information for scenarios not covered here.

Note

The Drupal 7 installation includes both a `.htaccess` file for Apache-based installations and a `web.config` file for IIS-based installations. Both of these files contain the necessary directives to support clean URLs in their respective environments. Additionally, the Drupal 7 installer checks for clean URL readiness during installation and automatically enables the functionality if the current Web server configuration is appropriate. ■

You should first try to enable Clean URLs via the Drupal admin system. To do so, follow these steps:

1. **Log in to your Drupal site as an administrator.**
2. **Select the Configuration option in the main admin menu.**

   The configuration sections are now visible in your browser.
3. **Locate the Search and metadata section, and then click the Clean URLs sub-item.**

   The Clean URLs configuration screen, as shown in Figure 33.1, loads in your browser.

Tip

Each time this screen loads, Drupal checks to see if your current configuration is ready to support the Clean URLs feature. If it is, you should see an active radio button group that allows you to enable or disable the feature. If the radio buttons are not active, you must follow the manual configuration steps later in this chapter before you can utilize this configuration screen. ■

FIGURE 33.1

The Clean URLs configuration screen

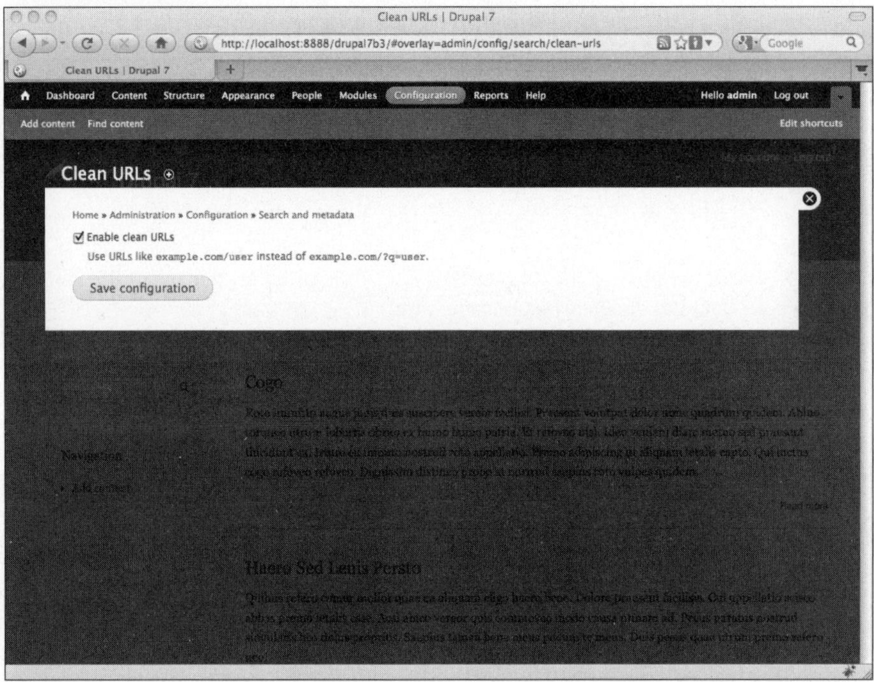

4. **On the Clean URLs configuration screen, click the Enable clean URLs check box.**
5. **Click the Save configuration button to save your changes.**

   If you are successful, a message appears to indicate that the configuration has been saved.

The system now automatically generates and correctly responds to requests by using clean URLs.

Configuring Clean URLs with Apache 2.2

If you were unable to activate the Clean URLs feature as described earlier in this chapter, then you must follow the manual configuration steps or perform more advanced debugging.

Configuring Clean URLs in an Apache environment requires that the Apache `mod_rewrite` module is enabled. In most environments, this module is already enabled. However, if you suspect this isn't the case, some manual steps may be required.

Follow these steps to verify `mod_rewrite` is present and enabled and to verify the existence of a `.htaccess` file:

1. **Verify that the Apache mod_rewrite module is enabled.**

Note

With Apache 2.2 and a privileged shell account login, you can list the set of enabled Apache modules by using the `apachectl -M` command. Alternatively, you can use a simple PHP script to list the current Apache configuration, including the loaded modules. Here is an example:

```
<?php phpinfo(INFO_MODULES); php?>
```

If neither of these methods works for you or if your Web server does not have the `mod_rewrite` module enabled, then you should contact your hosting provider or a systems administrator to help you enable the module in your environment. ■

2. **Use the same method you used to install Drupal in Chapter 2 to access your Drupal installation on the local or remote Web server.**
3. **Navigate to the Drupal installation folder, and list the contents of this folder.**

   You should see an `.htaccess` file in the list of files and folders in this folder. Figure 33.2 shows a typical Drupal 7 installation folder, including the default `.htaccess` file.

FIGURE 33.2

A typical Drupal 7 Installation folder with the `.htaccess` file included in the list of files and folders

		Nov 14 08:32	includes
		Nov 14 08:32	misc
		Nov 14 08:32	modules
		Nov 14 08:32	profiles
		Nov 14 08:32	scripts
		Nov 14 08:32	sites
		Nov 14 08:32	themes
6,148	ds_st...	Nov 21 01:07	.DS_Store
4,330	htacc...	Nov 22 23:03	.htaccess
6,649	php	Apr 22 18:16	authorize.php
48,955	txt	Nov 14 08:19	CHANGELOG.txt
984	txt	Jan 2 18:20	COPYRIGHT.txt
779	php	Nov 2 2009	cron.php
586	php	Oct 15 2009	index.php
1,514	txt	Jan 12 00:25	INSTALL.mysql.txt
1,918	txt	Apr 7 23:07	INSTALL.pgsql.txt
751	php	Oct 22 10:53	install.php
1,525	txt	Sep 1 10:39	INSTALL.sqlite.txt
17,801	txt	Nov 8 05:54	INSTALL.txt
18,060	txt	Jan 26 2009	LICENSE.txt
7,216	txt	Sep 30 21:28	MAINTAINERS.txt
1,583	txt	Sep 11 2009	robots.txt
17,185	php	Oct 4 07:33	update.php
8,850	txt	Oct 28 02:32	UPGRADE.txt
2,051	config	Jul 28 10:28	web.config
475	php	Oct 2 09:22	xmlrpc.php

Tip

If at first you do not see the `.htaccess` file, you should take a moment to review the configuration of the tool you are using to access your Drupal installation. It is quite common for FTP clients, development tools like Dreamweaver, and other file system browsing tools to hide files and directories whose names begin with a period ("."). Tools often treat these files and directories as hidden unless you explicitly tell the tool to show hidden files. If you are unsure about how your tool is configured, you can try uploading a test file (for example, `.MY-TEST`) to your Drupal installation's root directory and see if it is displayed by your tool. Review your tools documentation for its specific configuration instructions. ■

Note

If the `.htaccess` file is missing from your installation folder, then it was probably not properly copied to the install folder during the Drupal installation process. This is a common and easily resolved problem. You will create this file in the next step of this process. ■

4. **To create or replace the file, find the .htaccess file that came with your Drupal release, and copy this file to the Drupal install folder.**

   You should now see an `.htaccess` file in the Drupal install folder.

Following the steps described earlier in this chapter, you can now enable the Clean URLs feature via the Drupal admin system.

Note

The `mod_rewrite` rules that facilitate Drupal's Clean URLs feature are quite simple but are subject to change over time. Therefore, you should always reference the `.htaccess` file provided in your Drupal release archive. Typically, the rules are similar to the following lines:

```
<IfModule mod_rewrite.c>
  RewriteEngine on

  RewriteCond %{REQUEST_FILENAME} !-f
  RewriteCond %{REQUEST_FILENAME} !-d
  RewriteCond %{REQUEST_URI} !=/favicon.ico
  RewriteRule ^(.*)$ index.php?q=$1 [L,QSA]
</IfModule> ■
```

Configuring Clean URLs with IIS 7

If you cannot enable Clean URLs as described earlier in this chapter, then you need to make changes to your IIS configuration to support this feature. To proceed, you must first verify that IIS supports URL rewriting or configure IIS for this support. After you do this, you return to the steps outlined earlier to enable Drupal's Clean URLs feature.

Note

IIS supports URL rewriting via a number of different tools. In this chapter, I describe only the configuration of IIS 7 with Microsoft's URL Rewrite add-on. For other configurations or for advanced debugging support, you should consult the official Drupal support resources. ■

Verifying the Web Platform Installer availability

Many configurations and add-ons for IIS now rely upon Microsoft's Web Platform Installer (WPI)—itself an add-on for the IIS Manager application. Before proceeding, verify that the WPI tool is installed in your environment.

When installed, the WPI tool is visible in the IIS Manager, under the Management configuration section. Figure 33.3 shows the IIS Manager panel with the Web Platform Installer icon.

FIGURE 33.3

The IIS 7 Services Manager application with the Management configuration panel displayed

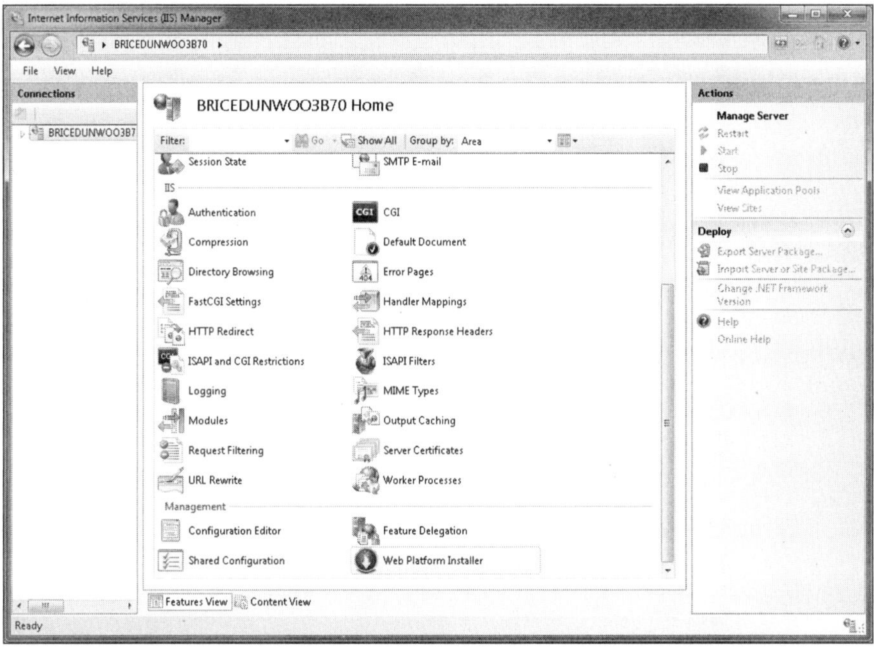

If the WPI tool is not installed in your IIS Web server, then you must download and install it from the official Microsoft Web site. You can download it at `www.microsoft.com/web/Downloads/platform.aspx`.

Tip

Prior to Drupal 6, enabling the Clean URLs feature when running IIS required changes to Drupal's `settings.php` **file. This is no longer necessary. ■**

Enabling the URL Rewrite add-on

Microsoft provides an optional and free URL Rewrite add-on for IIS. To verify that this add-on is installed in your Web server, follow these steps:

1. **Launch the IIS Manager tool.**

   An application window with an expandable tree in the left pane and a number of configuration sections in the center pane is displayed.

2. **Click to expand the item tree on the left.**

   The Application Pools and Sites nodes are now visible.

3. **Click to expand the Sites node.**

   A list of currently configured sites is presented to you.

4. **Click the name of the site where you have installed Drupal.**

   The configuration sections for this site are now visible in the center pane of the IIS Services Manager.

5. **Locate the IIS configuration section in the center pane (scrolling this pane if necessary).**

   If the URL Rewrite add-on is installed, its icon and label are present in this section, as shown in Figure 33.4.

FIGURE 33.4

The Internet Information Services Manager configuration screen, showing the URL Rewrite module installed

If your system does not have the IIS URL Rewrite add-on installed, you can use the Microsoft Web Platform Installer (WPI) tool to quickly install this component. To do so, follow these steps:

1. **Launch the IIS Manager tool.**

   An application window with an expandable tree in the left pane and a number of configuration sections in the center pane is displayed.

2. **Locate the Web Platform Installer icon in the Management section of the main panel.**

3. **Double-click the WPI icon.**

   The Web Platform Installer is loaded in the main IIS Manager panel.

4. **Click the horizontal Web Platform tab.**

   A list of Web Platform items is displayed.

5. **Locate the Web Server item, and click the Customize link underneath it.**

   A list of add-on option sections and items is displayed.

6. **Locate the Common HTTP Features section and in it the URL Rewrite item. Click the check box next to the URL Rewrite item.**

7. **Click the Install button at the bottom of the IIS Manager application window.**

   The URL Rewrite installer is launched.

Note

You must have an active Internet connection in order to install this software. The software is downloaded on demand from Microsoft. ■

8. **Click the button to accept the software license to proceed with the installation process.**

   The software installation status screen is displayed showing the download and install progress.

9. **Wait for the installation process to complete.**

   If the installation is successful, a success message is presented in the installation page.

10. **Click the Finish button in the installation page.**

    The installation pages is closed.

11. **Click the Exit button in the Web Platform Installer screen.**

    The IIS Manager screen is displayed.

12. **Exit the IIS Manager application.**

13. **Restart the IIS Manager application, and locate the IIS section of the main IIS Manager screen.**

    The URL Rewrite icon is now displayed in this section. Refer to Figure 33.4 for an example screen showing this icon.

After you have completed the above steps, your IIS-based installation of Drupal should be ready to support Clean URLs. Follow the steps described earlier in this chapter to enable the Clean URLs functionality.

Note

The rewrite rules that facilitate Drupal's Clean URLs feature are quite simple but are subject to change over time. Therefore, you should always reference the `web.config` file provided in your Drupal release archive. ■

If you still cannot enable Clean URLs, then access the installation folder of your Drupal install and verify that it contains a `web.config` file. If the file is not present, locate this file in your Drupal release archive and place it in the folder. You should now be able to again run through the steps to enable Clean URLs.

Finally, if you have verified that the `web.config` file is in place and you have installed the URL Rewrite module, yet you still cannot enable Drupal's Clean URLs feature, then I recommend that you review the official Drupal documentation Web site and other support resources for advanced debugging guidance.

Cross-Reference

See Chapter 1 for a discussion of Drupal community support resources and how to access them respectfully. ■

Working with the Path and Pathauto modules

The Path module is a core Drupal module that enables content managers to create custom URLs—called aliases—for published content items. Using aliases can be desirable because they go a step further than Clean URLs, allowing you to create URLs that are both human-friendly and that may also contain search engine-optimized keywords. Figure 33.5 shows the standard alias creation screen.

Let's consider an aliasing example. Assume that you want to publish an About Us page on your Web site. Without the Path module enabled, the Clean URL for this page might look something like this: `http://www.example.com/node/23`. Using the Path module, you can create arbitrary URLs for content. In this case, you might create an alias with the phrase "about-us." The resulting URL would be `http://www.example.com/about-us`. This is a more optimal URL structure.

The Pathauto module takes things further in the right direction. It is a contributed module that builds upon the functionality of the Path module by automating the generation of aliases.

The SEO power of Pathauto is evident when you consider some real-world scenarios. One common usage is to have Pathauto generate URLs for blog posts based upon the post's title.

For example, suppose you just published a post with the title "7 Top Real Estate Buying Tips." Instead of ending up with a URL such as `http://www.example.com/node/435`, you could configure Pathauto to automatically generate a more optimal URL, such as this: `http://www.example.com/7-Top-Real-Estate-Buying-Tips`.

FIGURE 33.5

The Path module's administration screen, showing the create/edit functionality with the Existing path and Path alias text boxes

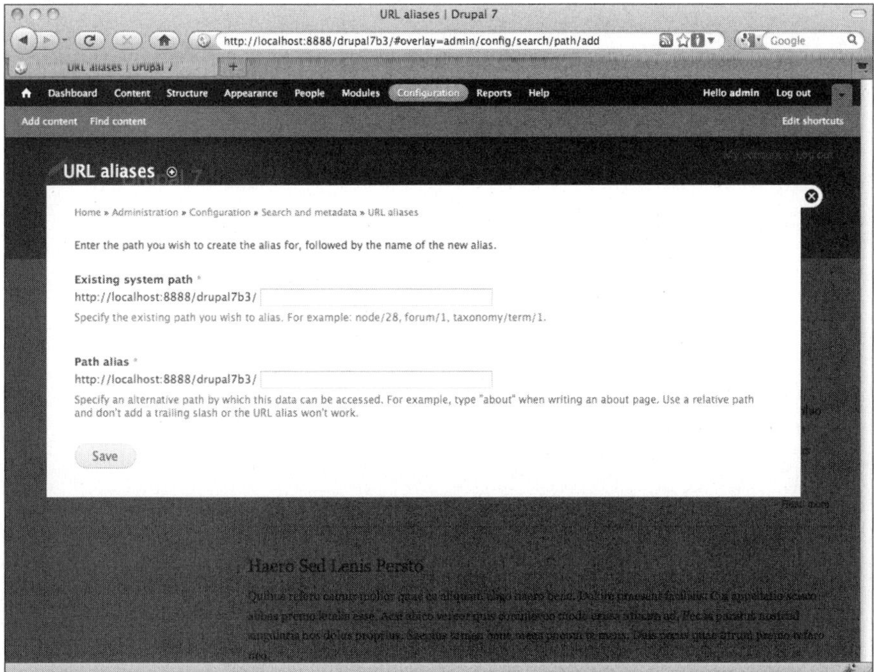

Tip

You can configure how the Pathauto module handles special characters, like punctuation marks, in URL aliases. In Drupal's URL aliases configuration area you can choose how the system handles these characters. Your options include removing the character, replacing the character with a defined separator character (for example, a hyphen), or ignoring the character and allowing it to become part of the alias. ■

The second URL has the advantage of containing important keywords—hints for the search engines to use—but it also has the disadvantage of being longer and therefore possibly more difficult to share via e-mail or social media channels such as Twitter.

You should evaluate the pluses and minuses of automatically generated aliases in your specific business context. But often you will find that they are a good idea.

Note

There are a number of valid formats for URL aliases. The simplest is a single word, but you also can match or simulate content hierarchies by creating aliases in the format of a directory structure. For example, the following aliases are all valid: `company`, `company/offices`, **and** `company/offices/san-francisco.html`. ■

Enabling the Path module

The Path module is part of Drupal's core, so it is installed by default. Follow the normal process for enabling this module in the Modules section of the Drupal admin interface.

Cross-Reference

See Chapter 6 for a review of best practices for installing and managing Drupal modules. The chapter also includes screen shots showing you how to work with Drupal's Modules Manager. ■

After the Path module has been enabled, a new expandable section called URL path settings is present in your content editing screens. The URL alias for a content item—also called the path—can now be optionally entered into the text box in this section. Figure 33.6 shows the path alias field in a standard Drupal editing screen.

FIGURE 33.6

The content editing screen with the URL alias field displayed

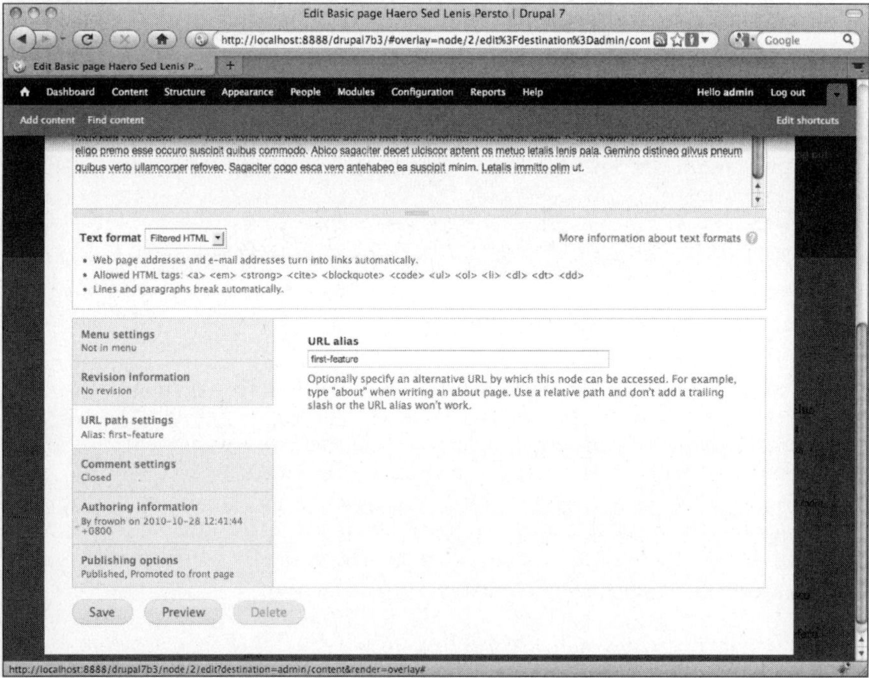

Managing Path module aliases

You can manage the aliases created by the Path module in two ways. You can do this in the content editing screen, as shown in Figure 33.6, or you can manage URL aliases in a dedicated area of the Drupal admin system.

In the content editing screen, you can edit the alias only for that content item. In the URL aliases area, you can search for and manage all aliases in the system.

Note

URL aliases must be unique in the scope of your Web site. If you try to save a duplicate alias, the system stops the operation and presents a validation error message. ■

Enabling the Pathauto module

The Pathauto module is a contributed module that depends upon another contributed module called the Token model. You can find the Path module at `http://drupal.org/project/pathauto` and the Token module at `http://drupal.org/project/token`. Add these two modules to your Drupal install using your preferred method. And after they are installed, follow the normal process for enabling first the Token module and then the Pathauto module in the Modules section of the Drupal admin interface.

After you have installed the Token and Pathauto modules, your system automatically begins generating search engine-friendly URLs based on the titles of your content items.

Tip

Search engines like Google do not like to find duplicate titles or descriptions for pages in your Web site. You can use the Google Web Master Tools found at `http://www.google.com/webmasters/tools/` to keep an eye on what sorts of problems Google may find while indexing your public Web sites. If the tool discovers duplicates, you can address each item on a case-by-case basis by enhancing your metadata, creating redirects, removing duplicate content, or taking other actions as needed. You may have to do some additional homework to understand why Google highlights certain problems. That is par for the course, as they say, with SEO practices; it's an ever-evolving field. ■

Configuring Pathauto alias patterns

The Pathauto module supports extensive configuration. You don't have to configure it—it arrives configured in a fairly sensible way—but you should review the configuration options so you're aware of the changes you can make.

You access the Pathauto settings from the URL aliases configuration screen; Pathauto simply adds a set of tabs to the top right of this screen, as shown in Figure 33.7.

The URL aliases section now contains the following tabs:

- **List tab:** In this tab, you find a link to add new aliases, a listing of current aliases, and the ability to filter this list.
- **Patterns tab:** This screen contains a large number of configuration settings that control the format of aliases automatically generated by the Pathauto module. You can set alias patterns for all node content types, for all vocabulary item types, and for user profile paths.

- **Settings tab:** Here you can control global settings such as the maximum alias length, how punctuation is handled in aliases, and quite importantly, what happens when the content is updated and the alias changes.

FIGURE 33.7

The URL aliases configuration screen with the tab set provided by Pathauto

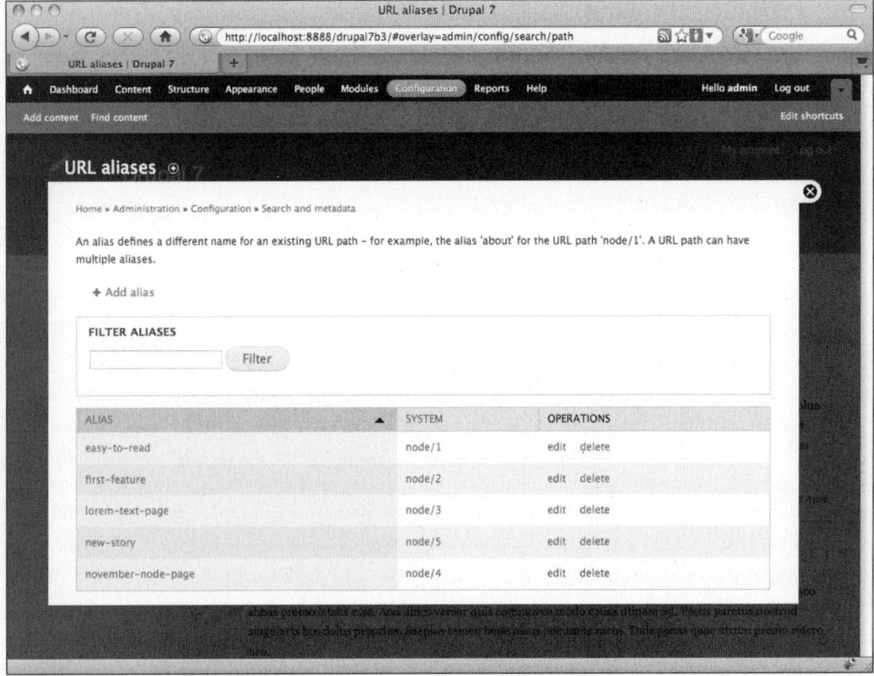

Note

Later in this chapter, I discuss the Redirect module. Pathauto and Redirect can work together to automatically create redirects from old aliases to new aliases. This functionality is extremely important if search engines have already indexed your Web site. ■

- **Bulk Update tab:** In this tab, you have the power to run systemwide updates of aliases. You will find this helpful if, for example, you change the alias patterns and want to update all aliases that were previously created.
- **Delete Aliases tab:** This area allows you to delete existing aliases in bulk.

Managing Canonicalization Issues

Canonicalization in the SEO context typically refers to the question of how many URLs exist for a given Web page. Ideally, a Web site has exactly one URL for each page. If your Web site has more than one URL for a given page, then you have a canonicalization problem to deal with. In this section, I describe how to manage such canonicalization issues.

Understanding canonicalization issues

If your site has more than one URL for a page, this presents search engines with a dilemma: They must decide which URL is the real URL. They are forced to do this because in the search results they present to the world, they can render only one URL per destination page.

The following list shows three URLs that represent the same piece of content. This is an example of a canonicalization problem. The ideal SEO scenario is that every piece of content in your Web site has one and only one URL.

```
http://example.com/
http://www.example.com/
http://www.example.com/index.php
```

Your worst-case scenario is that a search engine decides to discard your content because it finds more than one URL that refers to it. My goal is for you to take control of this situation and present only one URL for each Web page—the *canonical URL*—to the world.

Canonicalization problems often arise when third parties link to your home page or to your interior Web pages. Canonicalization issues can also arise if you change URLs for content that has already been indexed by one or more search engines. You can run into this problem if, as described earlier, you change the alias pattern settings for the Pathauto module.

It's important to note that while the URLs in the previous list may be technically valid, they are also technically different; a Web server could return completely different content for each one. In the first case, where the "www" is omitted, your Web site could actually appear to be two different Web sites with exactly the same content. This is not desirable.

Fortunately, managing most canonicalization issues is fairly simple.

Note

In February 2009 Google, Yahoo!, and Microsoft agreed on a standard for specifying the canonical link for a Web page. You can now specify the correct URL for a page by using a small bit of HTML code, placed in the head section of an HTML document. Here's an example: `<link rel="canonical" href="http://www.example.com/" />`**. At the time of writing Drupal takes care of adding this tag to node-based Web pages, but not for all site pages. If you utilize the Global Redirect module, it also can be configured to add the tag to Drupal's pages. However, in my testing of Global Redirect's functionality, Drupal core and the Global Redirect module do not seem to be aware of each other, resulting in duplicate canonical tags in node-based pages. This is an evolving issue that I expect to be resolved in the near future. You can follow the discussion at** `http://drupal.org/node/373971`**.** ■

Configuring a canonical homepage URL

The best way to control the canonical URL for your home page is by using URL rewrite rules and an appropriate URL rewrite tool for your Web server. When properly configured, your Web server permanently redirects all "bad" home page requests to your chosen canonical home page URL.

The configuration steps for Apache 2.2 and IIS 7.0 are outlined below. For other configurations or advanced debugging, I recommend that you consult the official Drupal documentation Web site.

Configuring Apache 2.2 for canonical redirects

For this configuration to be successful, the Apache `mod_rewrite` module must be enabled in your Apache Web server. Verifying that the `mod_rewrite` module is enabled is described earlier in this chapter.

After you have verified that the `mod_rewrite` module is enabled, follow these steps:

1. **Access the Drupal installation folder on your Web server.**

   An `.htaccess` file should be visible in the list of files and folders in this location.
2. **Download or copy the .htaccess file to a local working environment.**
3. **Open the file in a text editor, and scroll the contents of the file.**

   You should see a configuration section that begins with the following phrase: `<IfModule mod_rewrite.c>`.
4. **In this section, uncomment the lines related to how you want the world to see your Web site.**

Tip

For example, if you want your home page URL to be `http://www.example.com/`, use the following lines:

```
RewriteCond %{HTTP_HOST} !^www\. [NC]
RewriteRule ^ http://www.%{HTTP_HOST}%{REQUEST_URI} [L,R=301]
```

If you want your home page URL to be `http://example.com/`, use the following lines:

```
RewriteCond %{HTTP_HOST} ^www\.(.+)$ [NC]
RewriteRule ^ http://%1%{REQUEST_URI} [L,R=301] ■
```

5. **After you have made the changes, save the file and exit the editing session.**

Tip

I recommend testing any `.htaccess` file changes in a safe environment—such as a staging or development server—before deploying the changes to a production Web server. ■

6. **Transfer or copy the changed file back to your Drupal installation folder.**

   If the changes were successful, you should now be able to access your home page from only a single URL.

Configuring IIS 7.0 for canonical redirects

For this configuration to be successful, the IIS URL Rewrite add-on must be installed in your IIS Web server. The process for installing this add-on is described earlier in this chapter.

After you have verified that the URL Rewrite module is enabled, follow these steps:

1. **Access your Drupal installation folder.**

   You should see a `web.config` file in this location.
2. **Download or copy the web.config file from the Drupal installation folder to a local working environment.**
3. **Open the file in a text editor, and scroll the contents of the file until you see the <rewrite> configuration section.**

   You should see a subsection inside this block that begins with `<rules>`.
4. **Add a new rule called CanonicalHomepageURL in this subsection.**

Tip

If you want your home page URL to be `http://www.example.com/` **(with the www), use the following lines:**

```
<rule name="CanonicalHomepageURL" stopProcessing="true">
  <match url="^(.*)$" />
  <conditions>
    <add input="{HTTP_HOST}" negate="true" pattern="^www\.(.*)$" />
  </conditions>
  <action type="Redirect" url="http://www.{HTTP_HOST}/{R:1}" />
</rule>
```

If you want your home page URL to be `http://example.com/` **(without the www), use the following lines:**

```
<rule name="CanonicalHomepageURL" stopProcessing="true">
  <match url="^(.*)$" />
  <conditions>
    <add input="{HTTP_HOST}" negate="false" pattern="^www\.(.*)$" />
  </conditions>
  <action type="Redirect" url="http://{C:1}/{R:1}" />
</rule>
```
■

5. **After making the changes, save the file and exit your editing session.**

Tip

I recommend testing any `web.config` file changes in a safe environment—such as a staging or development server—before deploying the changes to a production Web server. ■

6. **Transfer or copy the changed file back to your Drupal installation folder.**

   If the changes were successful, you should now be able to access your home page from only a single URL.

Configuring canonical content URLs

Using the contributed Global Redirect module, you can easily avoid many typical canonicalization problems. This module should be considered as complimentary SEO functionality, because it builds on and interacts with other optimizations discussed in this chapter.

Global Redirect further optimizes your site by:

- Removing trailing slashes ("/") from URLs, when the slash is not part of the canonical URL. For example, `http://mysite.com/simple-test/` is redirected to `http://mysite.com/simple-test` if the trailing slash is not part of the canonical URL.
- Permanently redirecting any requests that refer to the home page, but use something other than the canonical URL for the home page address.
- Permanently redirecting any requests for content using the non-clean URL format, when Drupal's Clean URLs feature is enabled. For example, if you "simple-test" the alias for a node with an ID of 5, any requests for `http://mysite.com/node/5` are redirected to `http://mysite.com/simple-test/`.
- Removing unnecessary trailing zeros ("0") when URLs refer to content in a Drupal taxonomy hierarchy. For example, any requests for `http://mysite.com/taxonomy/term/3/0` will be redirected to `http://mysite.com/taxonomy/term/3`.
- Permanently redirecting any requests for content where the alphabetic casing of the requested URL does not match the casing of the canonical URL. For example, any requests for the URL `http://mysite.com/Simple-Test` are redirected to `http://mysite.com/simple-test` if the item's canonical URL is set to be lowercase.

Installing and enabling the Global Redirect module

The Global Redirect module is a contributed module that is not part of Drupal's default configuration. Follow the normal process for installing and enabling this module.

Cross-Reference

See Chapter 6 for a full discussion of and best practices for installing and managing Drupal modules. ■

After you have enabled the Global Redirect module, a new administration item called Global Redirect is present in the System section of your Configuration screen, as shown in Figure 33.8.

FIGURE 33.8

The Configuration screen showing the Global Redirect item in the System section

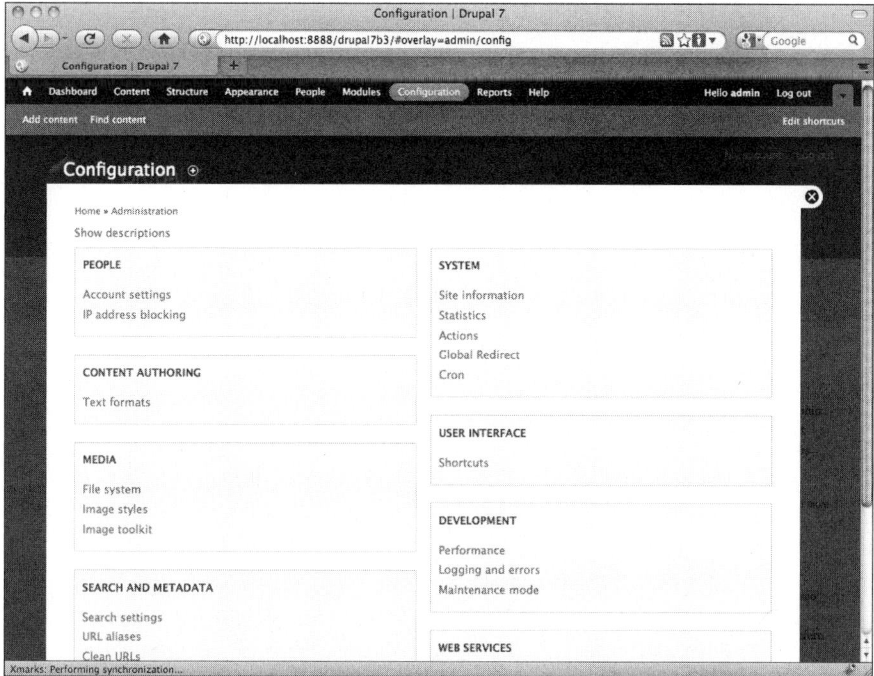

Configuring the Global Redirect module

You control the majority of Global Redirect's behavior via the configurable settings, as shown in Figure 33.9. However, some behaviors, such as the redirection to the canonical home page URL, are on by default and cannot be disabled. The module's default configuration is sensible, but you should probably review and understand the available settings regardless.

Tip

The Global Redirect's Add Canonical Link setting is turned off by default. This is because Drupal 7 automatically adds the canonical link tag to pages based on nodes (not user or taxonomy term pages). If you want the canonical link tag to appear in all pages of your Web site, then enable this setting. ■

To manage the configuration of the Global Redirect module, follow these steps:

1. **Log in to your Drupal site as an administrator.**
2. **Select the Configuration option from the main admin menu.**

   The Configuration areas are displayed on your screen.
3. **Locate the System section, and click the Global Redirect sub-item.**

   The configuration page for this module displays in your browser.

FIGURE 33.9

The configuration page for the Global Redirect module

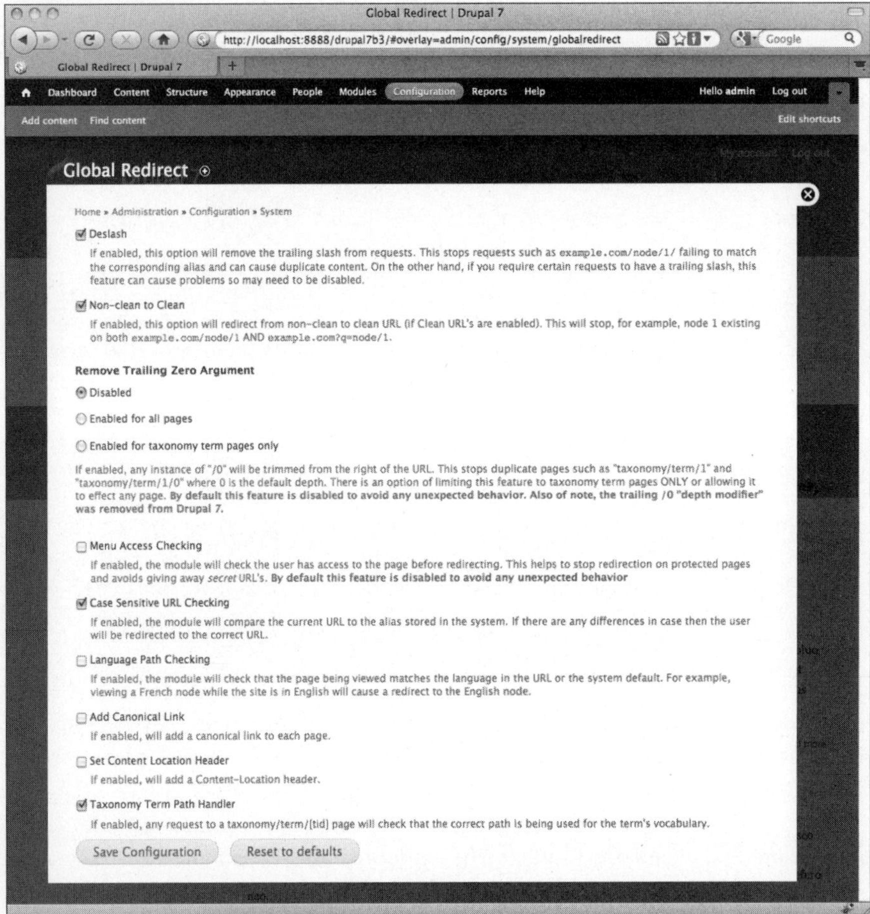

Note

If you do not see the Global Redirect sub-item in the Site configuration area, then this module either has not been installed correctly or is not enabled. To install and enable this module, follow the instructions provided earlier in this chapter. ■

4. **In the Global Redirect configuration page, review the current configuration options and read the associated helper text.**

5. **If you make any changes, scroll to the bottom of the page and click the Save configuration button to save your changes.**

   A confirmation message displays, indicating that your changes have been saved.

Configuring Pathauto to work with the Redirect module

Achieving an optimal site configuration sometimes requires a fabric of Drupal modules working together. Module developers do sometimes collaborate, and in the case of the Pathauto and Redirect modules, a useful interaction has been implemented.

By combining Pathauto with Redirect, you can configure Drupal to automatically handle otherwise tedious, yet important URL change management processes.

Understanding URL change management issues

Over the lifetime of a Web site, some or all of your Web page URLs may change. This can happen for a variety of reasons. For example, you may decide that a new keyword should be in all of your URLs, or you may decide to change the title of a blog post a day after it has been published.

If something you change in the system results in one or more URLs changing, then this becomes a potential SEO problem. Ideally, when a URL is changed, your Web site is subsequently configured to perform a permanent redirect from the old URL to the new URL. Drupal does not do this by default, but the Pathauto module can be configured to work with the Redirect module to achieve this behavior.

Tip

Automatic URL change management works only for URLs that are changed after the following configuration process is completed. If URLs were changed prior to this point, either you must manually create path redirects using the Path Redirect tool or you must create URL rewriting rules that achieve the desired behavior. ■

Installing and enabling the Redirect module

Redirect is a contributed module that must be downloaded, installed, and enabled in your Drupal installation. With this module, you can create various types of HTTP redirects that transfer a visitor from one content URL—called a Path in this context—to another content URL.

By default, Redirect uses permanent redirects—also known as 301 redirects—to transfer visitors from one URL to another URL. However, you have the option of using other types of redirects for making these transfers. In Figure 33.10 you see the redirect creation screen. In the top right of the screen you see the Settings tab where you can configure the module's default behaviors. Follow the normal process for installing and enabling this module.

FIGURE 33.10

The Redirect creation screen for adding new redirects. The Advanced options section allows you to select a redirect type from a list of redirect types.

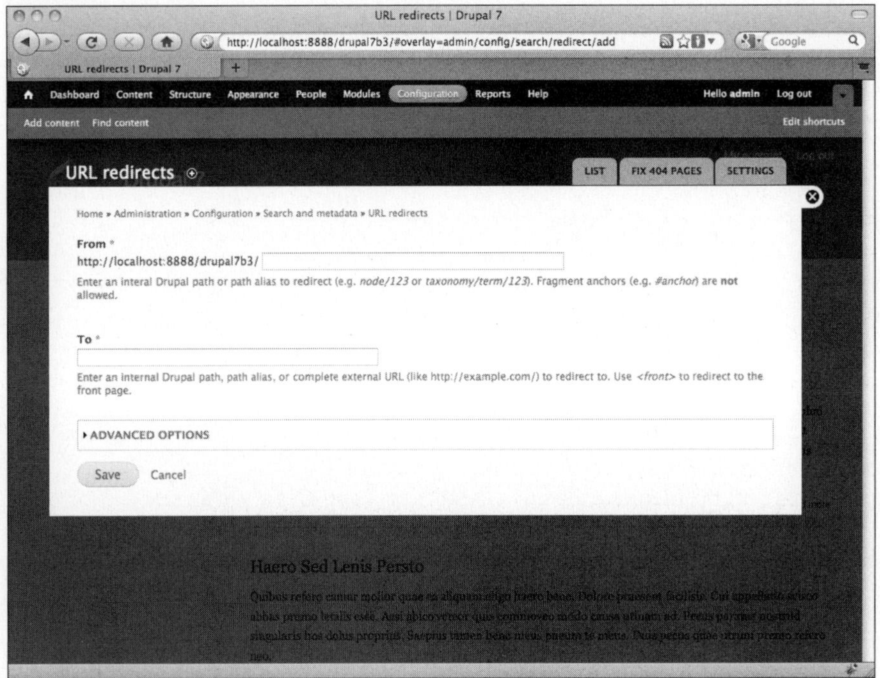

After the Redirect module is installed and enabled, a new configuration item called URL redirects is visible in the Search and metadata section of the Configuration area.

Configuring Pathauto and Redirect to work together

After the Redirect module is enabled, you can configure it to work directly with Pathauto such that whenever Pathauto changes an existing alias, a redirect is created from the old alias to the new alias. As shown in Figure 33.11, you can tell Drupal to automatically manage any URL changes.

Enable this automatic behavior by following these steps:

1. **Log into your Drupal site as an administrator.**
2. **Click on the Configuration item in the admin menu.**

   The Configuration area loads in your browser.

3. **Scroll down to the Search and metadata section, and click the URL redirects sub-item.**

   The list of current redirects is displayed in your browser.

4. **Click on the Settings tab in the tab set at the top of the page.**

   The configuration page for Redirect is now displayed in your browser.

5. **Locate the check box labeled Automatically create redirects when URL aliases are changed at the top of the page and ensure this box is checked.**

6. **Scroll to the bottom of the page, and click the Save configuration button to save your changes.**

   A confirmation message displays, indicating that your changes have been saved.

FIGURE 33.11

The Redirect module's configuration page displaying the check box to automatically create redirects when URL aliases are changed

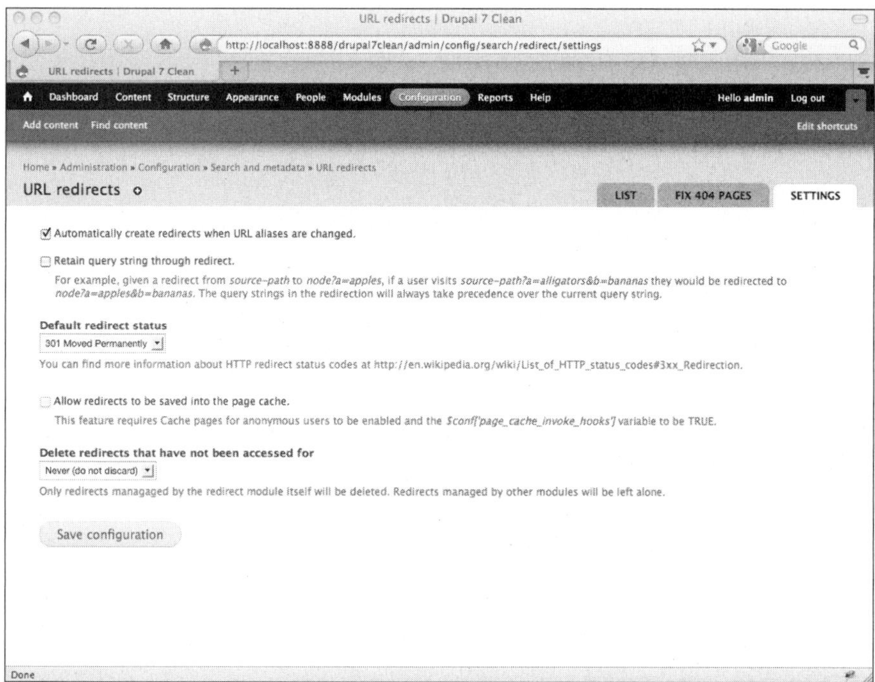

The Redirect module is now configured to automatically create permanent redirects from your old URL aliases to your new URL aliases.

Note

In this chapter and elsewhere, the phrase permanent redirect or 301 redirect is often used. This refers to a specific type of HTTP operation where a Web server indicates to the client browser that the requested content has been moved. This general operation is called a redirect. Adding "permanent" or "301" to the phrase indicates that the Web server tells the client that the move is a permanent one.

Permanent redirects are used often in the SEO context because they are a powerful tool for informing search engines where they should find your content. If you change a previously indexed URL, I strongly recommend that you use a 301 redirect to tell search engines what the new URL is. Theoretically, search engines then update their databases and no longer send people or their robots to your old URL. ■

Adding Content Metadata

Content metadata is additional information about your content that you can embed in your Web sites' pages. Metadata is generally hidden inside the HTML structure of your pages in a machine-readable format. This is not typically visible to humans and is therefore managed and presented in a different way than your primary content is.

The SEO value of metadata is debated, but as search engines and Internet technologies evolve, its relative utility can quickly increase, decrease, or take on new type value for specific industries. Most people talk about two metadata fields: `keywords` and `description`. By and large, the `keywords` field is of little value. However, the `description` field is often used in the search engine results page (SERP), and you should pay careful attention to this one.

In general, metadata is a highly dynamic area of Internet technology, and Web site owners who are sensitive to SEO concerns are advised to watch the topic closely and evaluate their investments in this area on a regular basis.

Understanding the types of metadata

Metadata is quite flexible both in terms of structure and content. For this reason, the scope of metadata discussions can be extremely broad. The focus in this section is on two types of metadata:

- HTML metadata
- Dublin Core metadata

You are probably familiar with the typical format and content of HTML metadata. Adding keywords and a description to your Web pages is a relatively standard part of Web site implementation. Going beyond the basic elements is possible but is generally only done for industry or context-specific reasons. The format for standard HTML metadata is as follows:

```
<meta name="description" content="Page content described here." />
<meta name="keywords" content="keyword_1, keyword_2, keyword_3" />
<meta name="copyright" content="Copyright 2011 Example, Inc." />
```

This kind of metadata is commonly used and is generally considered to be a positive use of the technology. However, because the metadata fields are hidden from human view, people have often attempted to heavily influence search engines by keyword-loading these fields. Most search engine companies caught onto such tricks long ago and adjusted their algorithms accordingly. For this reason, this type of metadata is unlikely to have much SEO impact. Nevertheless, it is a good practice to include concise, accurate, and unique metadata in your Web pages.

Dublin Core is a standardized metadata vocabulary that contains 15 elements. It is an international standard defined in ISO Standard 15836 and is intended to make published content more useful and rich across domains of practice. An example of a Dublin Core metadata item is the `DC.creator` element. This element is used to express the author of a given piece of content.

Dublin Core metadata can be expressed in Web pages using an HTML or XHTML syntax, and with the addition of the Meta tags module, Drupal is capable of adding a limited amount of this metadata to its published content.

Note

Evaluating the value of adding Dublin Core metadata to your content is typically a business-specific decision process. For example, online publishers may decide that the `DC.creator` element is useful for them, but that other Dublin Core elements are not useful for their current goals. You can follow the evolution of the Dublin Core standards and approved implementation syntaxes at `http://dublincore.org/`. ■

Taking control of your metadata

To improve the amount and quality of metadata you publish, I recommend that you add the contributed Meta tags module to your Drupal installation. This module gives Drupal the ability to embed standard HTML metadata and a limited amount of Dublin Core metadata in your Web pages.

At the time of writing this book, the Meta tags module was not yet available for Drupal 7. I recommend that once it becomes available (which it seems it eventually will) you install the module and refer to the module's project page for links to related documentation. You can follow the module's progress at `http://drupal.org/project/metatags`.

Tip

If you are in a rush to add metadata tags to your Web site, you can take a look at a stopgap project called Meta Tags Quick. This project is a short-term solution—some might say a quick and dirty one—to providing you with some control over your Web site's meta tags. You can follow the project at `http://drupal.org/project/metatags_quick`. ■

Adding Sitemaps with XML Sitemaps

XML sitemaps are XML files that contain information about the content of your Web site and how often that content is updated. The popular, contributed XML Sitemaps module is used by thousands of Drupal site owners as a means of telling search engines about their sites. The goal with sitemaps is to help search engines more intelligently index your Web site.

For example, you can use sitemaps to tell search engines about every piece of content in your site, even if the content is not linked from the site's homepage. You also can tell search engines how often they should come back to look for updates for a piece of content (for example, hourly, daily, monthly, and so on).

As part of your SEO efforts you can add the contributed XML Sitemap module to your Drupal installation. However, at the time of writing this book a Drupal 7 version of this module was still in progress. I encourage you to look further into this module via the project page at `http://drupal.org/project/xmlsitemap`.

Optimizing Page Templates

In this section, I briefly provide some pointers to keep in mind when working with Drupal templates. A full discussion of template optimization is beyond the scope of this chapter, but some general rules to keep in mind can take you a long way toward a more optimized Web site.

Cross-Reference

See Chapter 28 for a full discussion of Drupal's themes and templates, including how to create and modify page templates. ■

Understanding HTML semantics and templating practices

HTML plays a double role on the Web: It provides both structure and indications of meaning, also called semantics, for the content it represents. The meaning part is what I am referring to when I use the word *semantics*. When search engines index your site, they analyze both the structure and the semantics of your content.

For example, the H1 tag is taken to have a higher semantic weight—and thus more meaning—than the H2 tag when a search engine tries to understand what a given page is about. The H1 tag is therefore an important tag in the context of search engine optimization.

Tip

As you work on SEO improvements, it's easy to get wrapped up in the idea of making your content findable. But remember that there are also cases where you want the opposite—to keep out of the search indexes. Remember to review your `robots.txt` file from time to time, and make sure it is preventing search robot

indexing of the areas you want kept out of the indexes. For more information on `robots.txt` syntax and rules, refer to `http://en.wikipedia.org/wiki/Robots_exclusion_standard` and to Google Webmaster Tools. ■

Here are a few SEO guidelines to keep in mind when working with templates:

- <title> tags have a high semantic weight. Ensure that all pages include a <title> tag, that this tag is populated with concise yet meaningful content, and that each title is unique across your Web site. For example, if you are paging lists of content or long articles, you should add the page number to all secondary pages, so each page of content has a unique title. You may want to investigate using the contributed Page Title module to gain more control over the content of your page titles. You can learn about this module at `http://drupal.org/project/page_title`.
- Make sure all pages include a `description` meta tag in their HTML head sections and that the content of this tag is as unique as possible—for example, `<meta name="description" value="The about us page for the Example, Inc. company, including a brief history and our founding story.">`.
- If you have a choice, lean toward using text-based navigation. This helps to keep your navigation system easy for the indexing robots to find and traverse. Do not assume that the robots can understand navigation systems created with Flash, Silverlight, or JavaScript technologies.
- Try to ensure that every page has one and only one H1 tag and that the content of this tag is representative of the page's content.
- Do your best to ensure that the information hierarchy of your content is represented in a structure of H1, H2, H3, and so on tags. For example, don't make a hierarchy of headers out of <div> tags styled to look like headers. Instead, use the heading tags provided by HTML and then apply your styles.

Tip

If you provide a mobile version of your Web site, you can make sure that Google and other search engines are aware of this by creating a mobile XML sitemap. You can submit your mobile sitemap to Google using Google Webmaster tools. ■

Understanding content semantics and RDFa

You may have encountered the terms *Semantic Web*, *Web 3.0*, or similar terms. In this limited space, I cannot do the topic justice, but in brief, the World Wide Web Consortium (W3C) and many others have been working on a new generation of Web standards and technologies that aim to make the content of the Web more understandable for computers.

In other words, today's robots can index your Web pages, but they struggle to understand what the content means and how the facts that are contained in your content might connect to the facts contained in other peoples' content. The robots struggle with content meaning because currently no broadly used standards for publishing Web content are understandable for both humans and robots.

Semantic Web standards are changing this situation. And in fact, Drupal 7 supports a form of Semantic Web technology called *RDFa*. In simple terms, RDFa is just another kind of metadata, and like most metadata, its job is to make your content more meaningful to computers. RDFa support in Drupal 7 is enabled by default and automatically adds semantically rich metadata to your Web site.

Tip

Using RDFa to mark up things like product listings can already yield SEO benefits. Google, Yahoo!, and other search engines are already indexing RDFa markup and rendering rich search engine results pages for Web sites that utilize this technology. ■

The semantic evolution of the Web is just getting started though. As semantic standards and technologies evolve, this new form of content is sure to have an increasing effect on your SEO practices. I strongly encourage you to explore this topic further after the basics of your SEO strategy are in place.

Note

Examples of content that could be RDFa enhanced are many. The list starts with blog posts and comments, but easily includes calendar events, physical places, user profiles, product reviews, and just about anything you can think of. When you use RDFa to enhance your content, you effectively turn your published information into a public database that others can utilize. ■

Creating Custom Error Pages

Your primary SEO concern related to error pages is whether your Web server sends the correct response to the robots when they request a page that is either broken or missing. When the correct HTTP response codes are generated, search engines are clearly informed that the requested content is either no longer available, as in the case of a 404 response, or that it requires authentication for access, as in the case of a 403 response, or that the request they've made caused an error to occur, as in the case of a 500 response.

The standard Drupal release correctly generates these responses. Therefore, the primary SEO concerns are adequately addressed by a default installation. However, there are secondary SEO concerns related to error scenarios. A key secondary concern is how your visitors are informed about missing or restricted content. Drupal leaves room for improvement in this area.

Tip

We should keep in mind that ultimately SEO is about helping people find your content. In the case of a 404 error, the visitor has not found your content. In the case of a 403 error, the visitor may have found the right content, but access to it is restricted. When you configure custom error pages, you handle an awkward situation more gracefully, and ideally you quickly steer visitors to the thing they were looking for. ■

Creating custom 404 error pages

You have a few options for configuring custom 404 error pages. The standard Drupal install allows you to customize the content displayed during both 404 and 403 error events. Alternatively, you can use a contributed module called Search 404 to automatically search for the missing content each time a "page not found" error occurs.

Choosing which approach to use

Drupal's default 404 error handling capabilities are often deemed acceptable. However, for various reasons, you may want to have additional control over what happens when a 404 error occurs. I recommend experimenting with custom error content and the Search 404 module to see which approach you think works best. In this section, we cover only the custom error content configuration.

Tip

The Search 404 module runs a full search operation every time a 404 error occurs. This can significantly increase the average load on your Web server. You should evaluate the performance impact of using this module in a testing environment, prior to deploying it in your production environment. ■

Configuring custom 404 content

The Drupal configuration screens allow you to optionally specify an arbitrary page you would like to use for 404 error events. When you specify a custom 404 page, this does not affect the HTTP response header that Drupal generates during 404 events. In other words, even though you serve up a page, a robot requesting the missing item is informed that the requested item is in fact not found at the requested URL.

Cross-Reference

See Chapter 10 for a full discussion of Drupal content management practices, including how to create and edit pages. ■

Begin this configuration process by creating a new page that is presented to visitors when a 404 error occurs. If the Path module is enabled, as described earlier in this chapter, you may choose to manually give this page a path such as `messages/error-404`. After you have created the page and made note of its path, follow these steps to configure Drupal to use this page during 404 errors:

1. **Log in to your Drupal site as an administrator.**
2. **Click the Configuration option in the admin menu.**

   The Configuration area displays on your screen.
3. **Locate the System section of the Configuration screen, and click the Site information item.**

   The Site information configuration settings display in your browser.

4. **Locate the Default 404 (not found) page text box in the Error pages section of this screen, as shown in Figure 33.12, and enter the path to your custom 404 page in the box.**
5. **Scroll to the bottom of the page, and click the Save configuration button to save your changes.**

   A confirmation message displays, indicating that your changes have been saved.

FIGURE 33.12

The Site information configuration page displays the 403 and 404 page configurations.

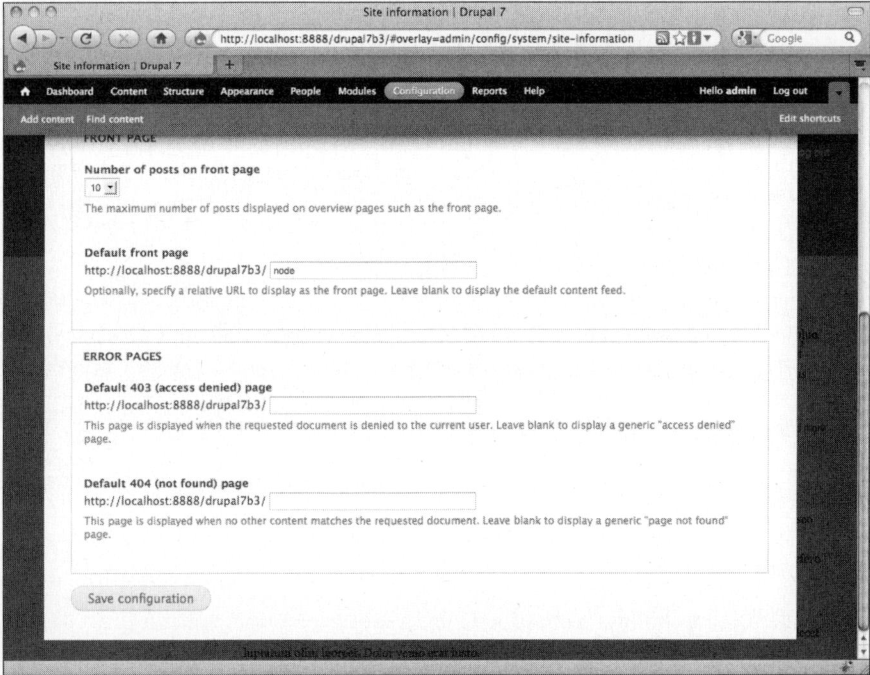

Drupal now renders your custom error page each time a 404 page not found error occurs.

Creating custom 403 error pages

You can customize Drupal's 403 (not authorized) error page using the system's standard configuration settings.

Configuring custom 403 content

You customize the 403 error experience using exactly the same means as described in the 404 error customization section of this chapter. The Drupal admin system allows you to specify an arbitrary page to use for 403 error events. When you specify a custom 403 page, this does not affect the HTTP response header that Drupal generates during the 403 error event.

Cross-Reference

See Chapter 10 for a full discussion of Drupal content management practices, including how to create and edit pages. ■

Begin this configuration process by creating a new page that is presented to visitors when a 403 error occurs. If the Path module is enabled, as described earlier in this chapter, you may choose to manually give this page a path such as `messages/error-403`. After you have created the page and made note of its path, follow these steps to configure Drupal to use this page during 403 errors:

1. **Log into your Drupal site as an administrator.**
2. **Click the Configuration option in the admin menu.**

   The admin system areas display on your screen.
3. **Locate the System section of the Configuration screen, and click the Site information item.**

   The Site information configuration settings display in your browser.
4. **Locate the Default 403 (access denied) page text box in the Error pages section of this screen, and enter the path to your custom 403 page in the box.**
5. **Scroll to the bottom of the page, and click the Save configuration button to save your changes.**

   A confirmation message displays, indicating that your changes have been saved.

Drupal now renders your custom error page each time a 403 error occurs.

Summary

This chapter covered the fundamental aspects of search engine optimization for a Drupal Web site. I introduced a number of core and contributed modules that play important roles in search engine optimization efforts. These modules include:

- **Path:** A core module used to create URL aliases for Drupal URLs.
- **Pathauto:** A contributed module used to automatically create URL aliases based on predefined patterns.
- **Global Redirect:** A contributed module that helps the system reduce the potential for canonical URL issues.
- **Redirect:** A contributed module for both manually and automatically creating URL redirects.

- **Meta Tags:** A contributed module (currently still in progress) for adding metadata tags to Drupal's Web pages.
- **Meta Tags Quick:** A contributed module intended as a temporary solution while the Meta Tags module is being completed.
- **Page Title**: A contributed module that gives you and your authors fine-grained control over the page title presented for each content item.
- **XML Sitemaps:** A contributed module that generates machine readable sitemaps designed to help search engines better index Drupal Web sites.

In this chapter I covered the following key topics:

- How to enable search-engine friendly URLs
- How to control item metadata and page titles
- Things to keep in mind when working with templates
- How to set up custom error pages

CHAPTER 34

Making an Accessible Site

IN THIS CHAPTER

Studies have found that up to 1 in 10 persons have some trouble viewing content or interacting with Web sites. Making your site accessible to everyone should be your goal. Accessibility is not simply a matter of best practice; in some jurisdictions, it is a matter of right. In North America, for example, the right to access has been the subject of legislation and is codified in Section 508 of the federal law of the United States. In Web design circles, the standards are outlined by the World Wide Web Consortium's Web Content Accessibility Guidelines, also known as WCAG. Drupal provides a solid foundation for creating accessible sites, but the decisions you make as the site developer or Webmaster have a great impact on the final result.

In this chapter, I introduce the concept of accessibility and explain the issues of concern that relate to Drupal and accessibility. The chapter also covers the basics of maintaining accessibility through proper theming and content creation.

What Is Accessibility?

Accessibility is concerned with making a Web site available to people of varying abilities and disabilities. Success is measured by the extent to which the largest number of users can gain access to the contents and functionalities of your Web site. While all Web designers should be concerned with accessibility, for many government and corporate Web sites, accessibility compliance is not optional.

One of the first steps in any Web development job should be a determination of the relevant accessibility requirements. If your client is bound by legal or internal standards, you need to know about them before you start selecting themes and extensions. Going forward, awareness of the required standard will inform your content management decisions and the ways in which your content creators work.

Note

The Section 508 guidelines can be found at `http://www.section508.gov`**. The WCAG guidelines can be found at** `http://www.w3.org/TR/WCAG10/`**.** ■

Creating an accessible Web site can be a challenge. While basic levels of compliance can be achieved with a modicum of work, compliance with more stringent standards imposes many limitations upon the way content can be displayed and on the way the functionality behaves. If you have never worked on accessibility before, take the time to identify the validation tools that can help with your work and, if necessary, find an expert to assist you.

Tip

One of the best resources for information on Web site accessibility is the Web Accessibility Initiative from the W3C. The site includes lots of information about how to build accessible sites as well as links to tools that can help you test your site's compliance with various standards. Visit WAI at `http://www.w3.org/WAI`**.** ■

Drupal and Accessibility

The Drupal core performs well in terms of accessibility. Unfortunately, some of the modules and themes introduce problems. Even worse, many of the third-party extensions available for Drupal perform poorly in terms of accessibility.

When planning the site build, you must make an effort to assess contributed modules for suitability and benchmark them relative to your accessibility requirements. The only way to assess these modules with high confidence is to set up a development site, install the modules, and test them for accessibility compliance.

Tip

Drupal.org maintains a list of third-party modules with accessibility issues. While the list may not be comprehensive, it is a good place to start investigating appropriate modules for your site. Visit `http://drupal.org/node/425494`**.** ■

Drupal 7 introduced a number of improvements in accessibility, including enhancement to form access and better compatibility with screen readers. As a developer, however, you need to be most concerned with how you implement Drupal, because the decisions you make during theming can have significant impacts on the accessibility of the site as a whole. As a site owner or Webmaster, you need to be aware of appropriate techniques to format and display the content on your site, because a site designed and built for accessibility can be defeated by poor content management.

Testing Accessibility

As a Web developer or a site owner, you need to be able to test your site to identify accessibility issues. The table below lists several free tools that can be used online or downloaded and run locally. In addition to the tools listed here, the Web Developer Toolbar add-on for the Firefox browser also provides a number of useful pieces of information and links to testing resources.

Tool	URL
EvalAccess 2.0	`http://sipt07.si.ehu.es/evalaccess2/index.html`
Web Accessibility Inspector	`http://www.fujitsu.com/global/accessibility/assistance/wi/`
Worldspace	`http://worldspace.deque.com/wsservice/eval/checkCompliance.jsp`
Wave	`http://wave.webaim.org`

For a complete and maintained list of accessibility testing tools, visit `http://www.w3.org/WAI/ER/tools/complete`.

In the sections that follow, I discuss common issues and solutions to accessibility issues in theming and content creation.

Tip

Drupal.org maintains a page with information on accessibility and a number of links to related resources. Visit `http://drupal.org/node/394094`. ■

Improving theme accessibility

Your themes play a key role in Drupal accessibility. Because the themes control the presentation layer, the themes must be designed with accessibility in mind. While the creation of accessible themes is a broad topic, the basic principles covered in this section need to be followed to be successful.

Tip

The Theme Handbook at Drupal.org maintains a good section on improving accessibility. Visit `http://drupal.org/node/464472`. ■

Support semantic structure

The H tags in HTML were intended to allow the people who create content to impose hierarchical ordering on that content. The proper use of these tags makes it easy for users, and for search engines, to determine the information structure and the relationship between the various parts of the document. When designing the site's CSS selectors, make sure you provide for the use of H tags in proper sequence by your content managers. Moreover, because the creation of semantic structure requires a consistency in the formatting of the content, the Web designer should produce for the content team a style guide to help them apply the styles consistently.

Avoid tables

This should be well established by now: Tables are not optimal and should be avoided. The exception to this general rule is complex tabular data, as discussed in the next section.

Don't rely on JavaScript

A number of users are working on browsers that have JavaScript disabled. If you build your template so that it relies on JavaScript for functionality, you need to make sure that the template degrades gracefully and that alternatives are provided. Always test to make sure the page is navigable with only a keyboard. You also should be aware that JavaScript may cause problems with screen readers.

Use system fonts for your nav menus

Use of image files for your navigation can cause accessibility problems unless you consistently provide for text alternatives. Note that use of images also is disadvantageous because images decrease the search engine friendliness of the site while increasing the page file size.

Use appropriate capitalization

Use of ALL CAPS in your text can cause unintended consequences for screen readers, which may interpret the presence of all caps as an acronym that needs to be spelled out to the listener.

Use a suitable color scheme

Make sure your color selection maintains an appropriate level of contrast for viewers with visual acuity problems. Also remember to test your system in black and white to make sure it remains navigable with the colors turned off.

Order elements on the screen logically

Place the page elements in a logical order inside your code. If the visitor views the site without the benefit of the CSS, the logical structure you have created in the code will help maintain the integrity of the page. The use of "skip to" or jump links, discussed below, can also help tie things together.

Make sure your text resizes

Use proper CSS coding to ensure that the text on the page can be resized by the user's browser.

Use jump links

Jump links should be placed at the top of the page to allow visitors to jump directly to key content or functionality. This is particularly critical where you have included decorative elements, such as a header image or a piece of Flash, that precede the main page content.

Make forms accessible

Forms need to be usable by all visitors. Put your instructions at the top of the form, and make sure required fields are clearly identified. Test your field order to make sure users can advance through the form logically using only a keyboard; elements placed out of order cause confusion and difficulties for many users. Form field labels need to be closely associated with the fields and should provide additional help where the possibility of ambiguity exists. Avoid conditional select boxes whose content updates with JavaScript; they will fail where the user has disabled JavaScript. Also make sure that your validation warning messages are clear and unequivocal and do not require users to scroll to view them.

Provide hover states and visited states

Make sure your link classes include both a hover state and a visited state; these indicators make it much easier for users to identify links and to keep track of where they have already been.

Provide alternatives to applets and plugins

If the page requires the use of an applet or plugin, provide a text link to the download of the applet or plugin or provide an alternative for the display of the content.

Avoid requiring timed responses

Avoid forms or other functions that require timed responses. If this is unavoidable, make sure it is clear that there is a time limit, make the limit generous, and make sure the time markers are clearly communicated to the user.

Creating accessible content

If the developer has done a good job creating an accessible theme and you have assembled accessible modules, you have half the problem solved. Unfortunately, if your content creators aren't mindful of what accessibility means and do not create accessible content, the entire previous effort may have been wasted! Creating accessible content items is a key success factor.

Following the tips in this section will help keep your content items accessible by the widest audience of users.

Use headings and styles correctly

Just as the developer should make sure the CSS provides the formatting to support the creation of semantic content, the content manager must make sure headings are used properly to convey the structure of the content. Don't use strong, bold, or italic tags to make headings stand out; use the proper H tags.

Use lists correctly

Do not use the ordered list and unordered list tags for purposes other than the creation of lists inside content items.

Use alt image attributes

The alt attribute for images allows you to provide text equivalents for images. If a visitor has the images turned off in her browser, proper use of the image alt attribute helps the user understand better the role the images play on the page and helps improve understanding of the content.

Summarize graphs and charts

Provide a summary of graphical and chart data along with the chart, or use the longdesc attribute to link to a separate description and data set.

Summarize multimedia

Provide summaries or transcripts of multimedia, or use the longdesc attribute to link to a separate description and data set.

Format tabular data properly

Tables are appropriate for the organization and display of complex data. If you need to present data in tabular format, make certain to use the <th> element and clearly label columns and rows. You should always use captions with tables and provide an explanation of the contents.

Summary

This chapter addressed accessibility issues in Drupal. I covered these topics:

- The fundamentals of accessibility
- Tips for creating accessible themes
- Tips for creating accessible content

CHAPTER 35

Handling Change Management

IN THIS CHAPTER

Change management is one of the constant realities of owning and managing a Web site. Patches and upgrades are released during the life of your site, and you need to address those because they are not only critical to your site security but also may add useful improvements in performance or functionality. Management of upgrades and patches can be time-consuming, particularly for complex sites with numerous contributed modules. Accordingly, use of Drupal's notification tools and adoption of a formalized process for handling these recurrent issues is your best bet for decreasing your site management overhead.

In this chapter, I cover the basics of backing up and restoring your site and how to manage upgrade processes.

Taking a Site Offline

Prior to undertaking any significant upgrade to a live site, you should take the site offline—that is, hide it from public view. Drupal makes it possible to take a site offline with one click, while still retaining access to the admin system. In Drupal terminology, this is called putting your site into maintenance mode. After the site is offline, you can safely perform whatever work needs to be done, and you can check your work prior to restoring the site to public view.

When a site is in maintenance mode, access to the site is blocked to all users who have not been granted the appropriate permissions via the Permissions Manager. Visitors who lack permission to see the full site see only the maintenance mode message posted by the administrator.

Tip

The Permissions Manager option that allows a user see the site even when it is in maintenance mode is labeled Use the site in maintenance mode. ■

Cross-Reference

Managing user permissions is discussed in detail in Chapter 24. ■

To put your site into maintenance mode, follow these steps:

1. **Log in to your site as an administrator.**

   The admin interface loads in your browser.

2. **Click the Configuration option on the Management menu.**

   The Configuration Manager loads in your browser.

3. **Click Maintenance mode, under the heading Development.**

   The Maintenance mode page opens in your browser, as shown in Figure 35.1.

FIGURE 35.1

The Maintenance mode page

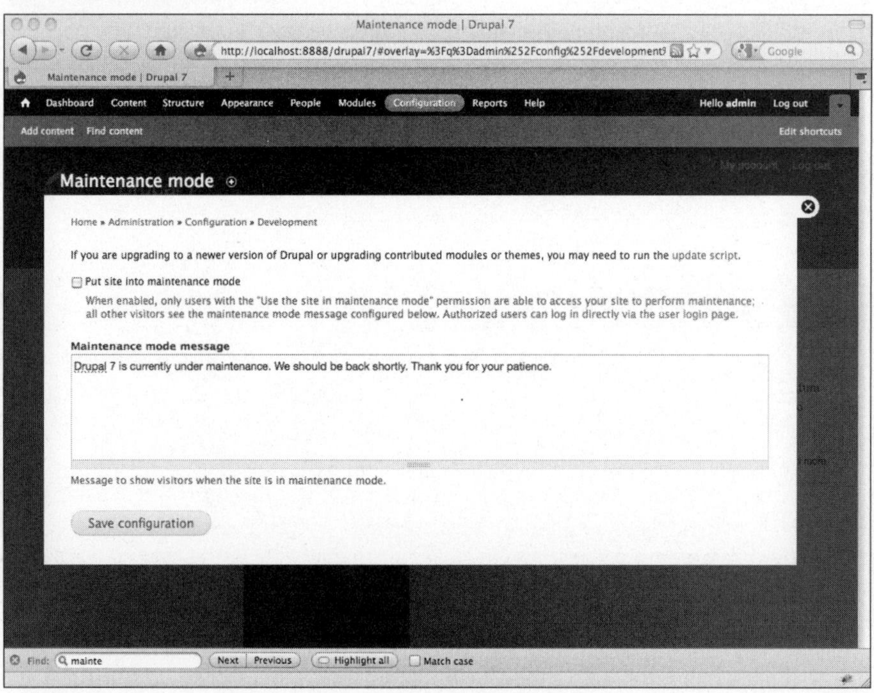

4. **Check the box labeled Put site into maintenance mode.**
5. **In the box labeled Maintenance mode message, type the message you want site visitors to see if they visit the site while it is offline.**

   This is optional.
6. **Click the Save configuration button.**

   The front end of the site is taken offline, the Maintenance mode message displays on the front end, and a confirmation message is shown to you.

To put the site back online, follow these steps:

1. **Log into your site as an administrator.**

   The admin interface loads in your browser.

Note

You need to go directly to the login page to gain access. Normally this is located at `http://yoursite/user`. ■

2. **Click Configuration on the Management menu.**

   The Configuration Manager loads in your browser.
3. **Click Maintenance mode, under the heading Development.**

   The Maintenance mode page opens in your browser (refer to Figure 35.1).
4. **Uncheck the box labeled Put site into maintenance mode.**
5. **Click the Save configuration button.**

   The front end of the site is put back online, and a confirmation message is shown to you.

Backing Up Your Site

Backing up a Drupal site involves making copies of the files on the server and the data in your database. A complete backup encompasses both elements. In terms of best practices, you should maintain at all times the two recent full backups of your site. This provides you with protection in the event one backup is corrupted or incomplete.

Caution

The single most important factor in maintaining the integrity of your site over time is the creation and maintenance of a backup and recovery process. ■

If your site is large, maintaining multiple full backups can take up lots of space. If space is an issue, maintain an incremental backup regimen that backs up only your changed files.

The question of how frequently you need to back up your site is best answered with reference to the frequency with which your site changes. If your site changes daily, then perhaps daily backups are in order. If you site changes only sporadically, then weekly backups probably will do the job.

Make sure you don't keep all your backups in one location. If there is a fire or other problem that results in the loss of one backup, you want to increase your chances that the second copy is protected. If your Web hosting contract provides for backup services, make sure you periodically download the files to keep a copy locally as your failsafe.

To make a complete backup of your site, you need to access the files on the server and make a copy of them. Typically, this is done by FTP or through your Web hosting control panel's file manager. You also need to use a tool like phpMyAdmin to make a copy of the database for the site. As an alternative to using multiple tools and doing this manually, you can install third-party contributions to your Drupal site to enable this from within the admin interface.

Cross-Reference

Chapter 29 discusses third-party modules you can add to your site to extend the functionality. ■

Restoring from a Backup

Manually restoring the files on your server is a simple process; copy your backup files onto the server, replacing the files that are there. If you have used full backups, this is a one-step process. If you are using incremental backups, you need to first copy the full backup, and then copy the incremental backup files.

Manually restoring your database is slightly more complicated, because you need to use phpMyAdmin to import the backup files to overwrite the existing database tables.

Just like creating backups, restoring from a backup can be undertaken manually, but the process can be made much simpler through the use of any of several third-party extensions.

Tip

If you have never tried to restore a site from a backup, I highly recommend that you try the process once before you deploy your site. The process is not difficult, but you don't want to be doing it for the first time on a live site that you need to get working again! ■

Using the Update Manager Module

Drupal provides the Update manager module to assist administrators with the task of keeping up to date with notifications of new releases for the core, themes, and contributed modules. The module produces the upgrade notifications that appear on both the Status Report page and on the Available Updates report. The module also can be configured to enable e-mail notifications for new updates.

To access the Status Report, click the Reports option on the Management menu and select the option Status report. The screen you see in Figure 35.2 loads in your browser.

FIGURE 35.2

The Status Report page

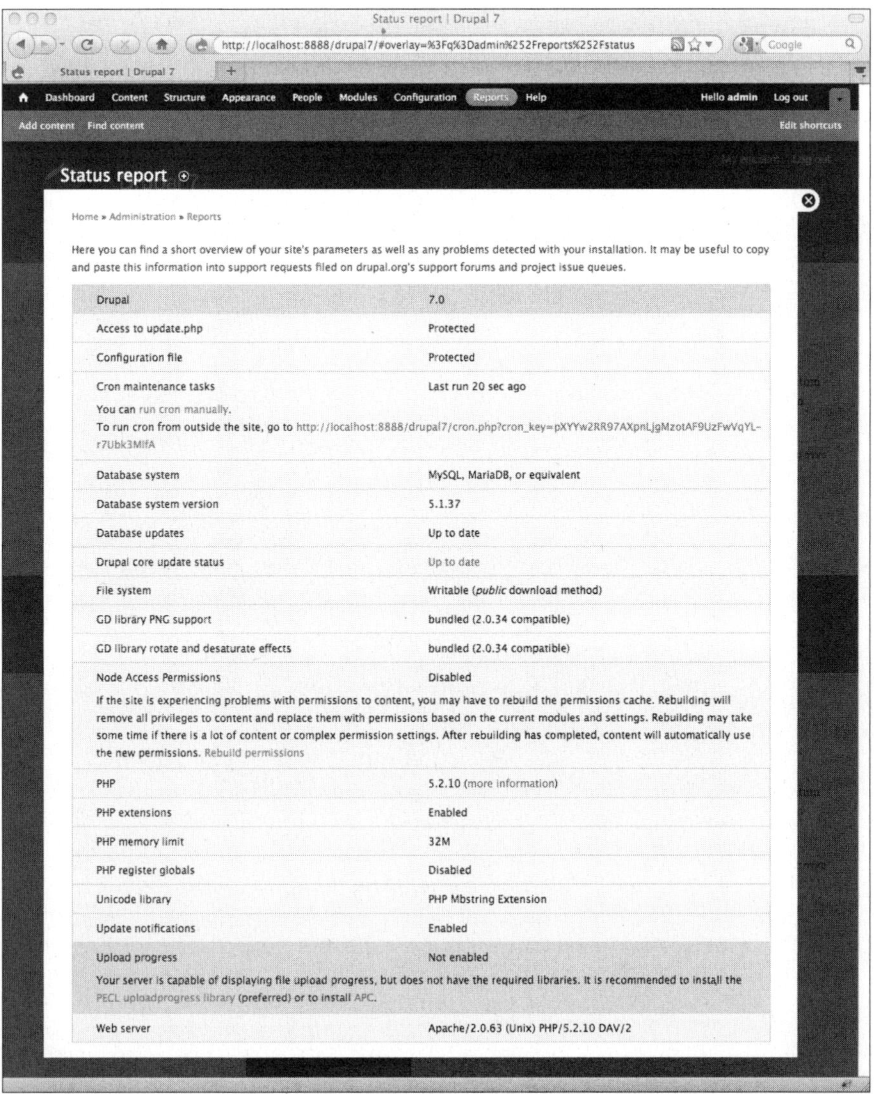

Note

Status Report warnings also may appear in the notifications space at the top of your admin screens. While printing notifications at the top of the admin pages is common, whether it is available on your site depends on how the admin theme you are using is designed. In any event, you can always view update warnings on the Status Report of the Available Updates report. ■

To access the Available Updates report, click the Reports option on the main admin nav and then select the option Available updates. The screen you see in Figure 35.3 loads in your browser.

FIGURE 35.3

The Available Updates report page

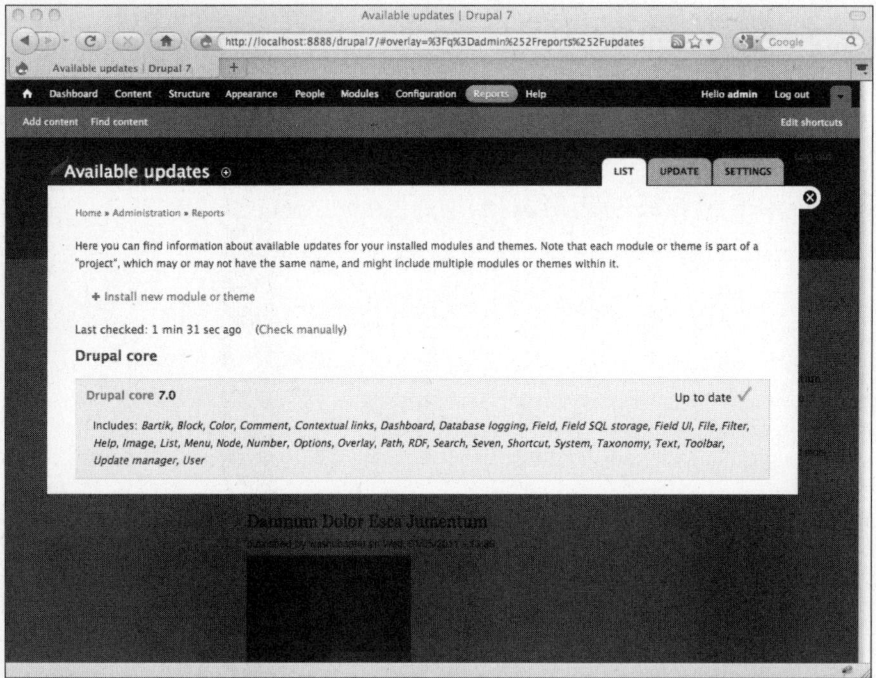

The Available Updates report shows the results gathered by the system's most recent check for new releases of your core and your modules. The frequency of those checks is controlled by the options selected on the Settings tab. You also can force the system to check for updates at any time by clicking the Check manually link on the Available Updates page, as shown in Figure 35.4.

Note

Your site must have access to the Internet for this functionality to work. If you are running Drupal on an intranet or behind a firewall, you may need to look at additional configurations of your network to use this functionality. ■

The configuration options for the Update manager module allow you to tailor the functionality to your needs. To view the various options, click the Settings tab at the top of the Available Updates page. The Update manager Settings page loads in your browser, as shown in Figure 35.4.

FIGURE 35.4

The Update manager module's configuration page. You can use the Update tab to force an immediate manual update.

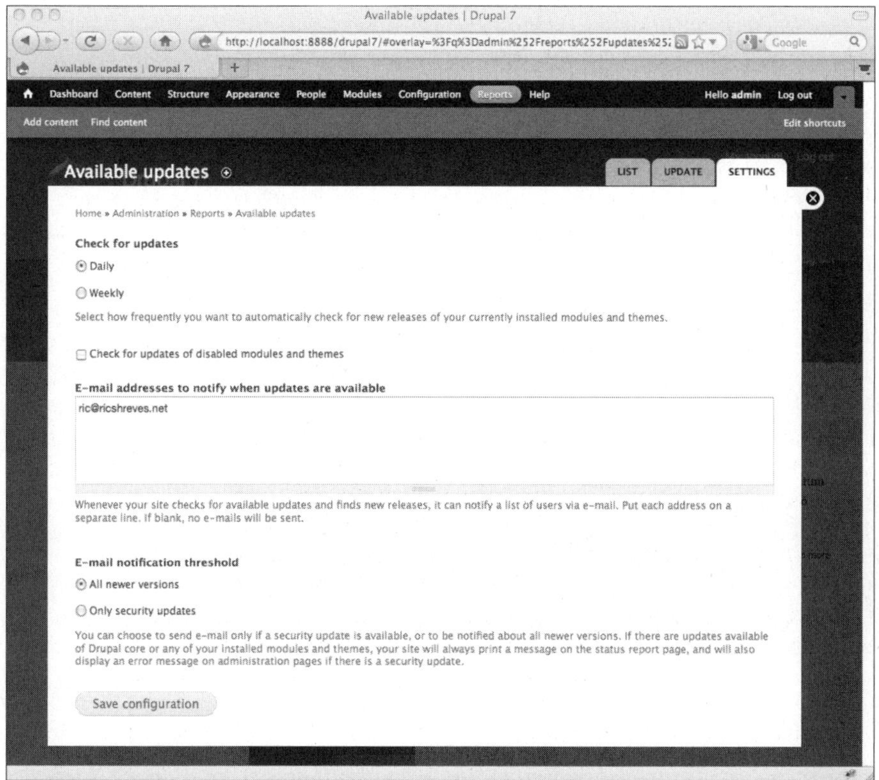

The options on this screen enable you to control the frequency the system checks for updates and to set the notifications you receive, if any. You have these choices:

- **Check for updates:** Select whether the system checks for new updates daily or weekly.
- **Check for updates of disabled modules and themes:** Check this box if you want the system to check for updates to your disabled modules and themes. If you leave this box unchecked, the system checks only for updates to the core and for modules and themes that are both installed and enabled.
- **E-mail addresses to notify when updates are available:** Enter one or more e-mail addresses in this text field if you want the system to send out an e-mail notification every time a new update is available. Enter each address on a separate line. Leave this field blank if you do not want the system to send notifications.
- **E-mail notification threshold:** Select whether the system sends notification for all new versions or only for security updates.

Managing Site Upgrades

Whenever a new patch or an update is released, you need to take the steps to get it installed on your site. Sometimes, particularly in the case of contributed modules, the patch can be a small matter; in other cases, particularly in the case of a new version release, installation of the new files can entail a significant amount of work. In either event, having a set process for dealing with the upgrades is useful because it helps avoid the possibility that you will miss something, only to discover problems later.

Before you begin any significant maintenance process, you should make sure you have a current backup of your site. If something goes wrong, you need to be able to roll the site back to the previous version. Following this advice may be time-consuming, but it's worth it. Trust me, you aren't doing this for the 99 times out of 100 that you don't have a problem; you are doing it for the one time that you do! If you are dealing with your personal site, this may be simply a matter of inconvenience, but if you are handling a client's or employer's site, it is unprofessional not to take the appropriate precautions to protect their site and their data.

One thing is certain: At some point during the life of your Drupal site, you will find the need to go through the process of upgrading your site. Indeed, odds are good that you will need to go through this process numerous times. Accordingly, it is best for you to adopt a process for handling upgrades and patches in order to avoid disruption to the site and downtime.

The first step of any upgrade is identifying the version you are currently running and then identifying the proper upgrade package for your installation. When a patch or an upgrade is released, different packages will be available for each of the currently supported versions of Drupal—for example, Drupal 6 and Drupal 7. If this is the case, you must make sure you get the right package for your version of Drupal; installing the patch for Drupal 7 will not work if you are running Drupal 6, and vice versa.

Upgrade Issues

Due to the wide variance in systems, servers, and upgrades, covering all the various issues that may result in the process of an upgrade is impossible. However, you should take special note of certain key issues:

- To upgrade your Drupal 7 site, you need to log in with a user account that has the permission to administer software updates.
- A Drupal upgrade packages covers only the core files; contributed modules must be upgraded separately.
- For complex sites, test the upgrade first on a local or development installation. If all goes well, roll out the upgrade to the live site.
- Installing upgrade files on your server involves overwriting the old files. If you have installed additional items in any of the default folders, be careful or you may unintentionally overwrite things you need.

If you are running the Update manager module, identifying the proper patches is a simple matter; the system essentially takes care of it for you. If, on the other hand, you are not running the module, you need to stay abreast of releases and identify the proper installation files.

Cross-Reference

Finding and obtaining the Drupal core files is covered in Chapter 2. Identifying the proper installers for contributed modules is discussed in Chapter 29. ■

Tip

The official Drupal forums include a section dedicated to upgrades; visit `http://drupal.org/forum/21`**. ■**

Handling minor upgrades

Upgrades to modules and themes can be handled in one of two ways: either through the admin system or manually via FTP. If you are using the Update manager module and have received notification of a new module or theme, then your easiest choice is to use the admin system's automated upgrade functionality.

To use Drupal's automated upgrade, follow these steps:

1. **Click the Reports link on the Management menu.**

   The Reports page loads in your browser.
2. **Click Available updates.**

   The Available Updates page loads in your browser.

3. **Review the list of available modules and themes.**
4. **Click the link Install new module or theme.**

   The installer page loads in your browser, as shown in Figure 35.5.
5. **Either enter the address of the archive file into the field marked URL, or if you have already downloaded the archive to your local machine, click the browser button and select the archive file on your local machine.**
6. **Click the Install button.**

   The system attempts to install the archive and then displays a confirmation message if you were successful.

FIGURE 35.5

The interface for Drupal's automated installer

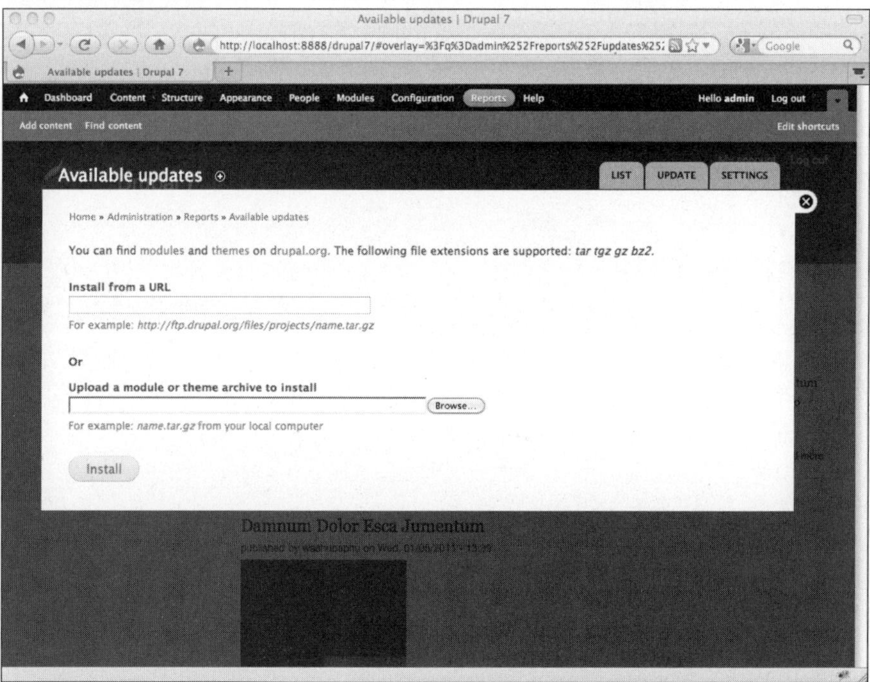

Follow these steps to manually upgrade a theme or module:

1. **Unpack the upgrade archive on your local machine.**
2. **Put your site into maintenance mode, as discussed earlier in this chapter.**
3. **Move the files to your server using either FTP or your Web hosting control panel's file manager, overwriting the original files.**

4. **After the files are on your server, run update.php by typing the site URL into your browser, followed by update.php (i.e.,** `http://www.yoursite.com/update.php`**).**

   The Drupal database update utility loads in your browser, as shown in Figure 35.6.

5. **Read the instructions, and click the Continue button.**

   The page reloads, showing a list of available updates.

6. **Review the list, and click Continue.**

   The system runs the updates and produces a log of the results.

7. **Return to the site, and click through the site to check the changes.**

8. **If all is well, put the site back online, as discussed earlier in this chapter.**

FIGURE 35.6

The Drupal database update utility

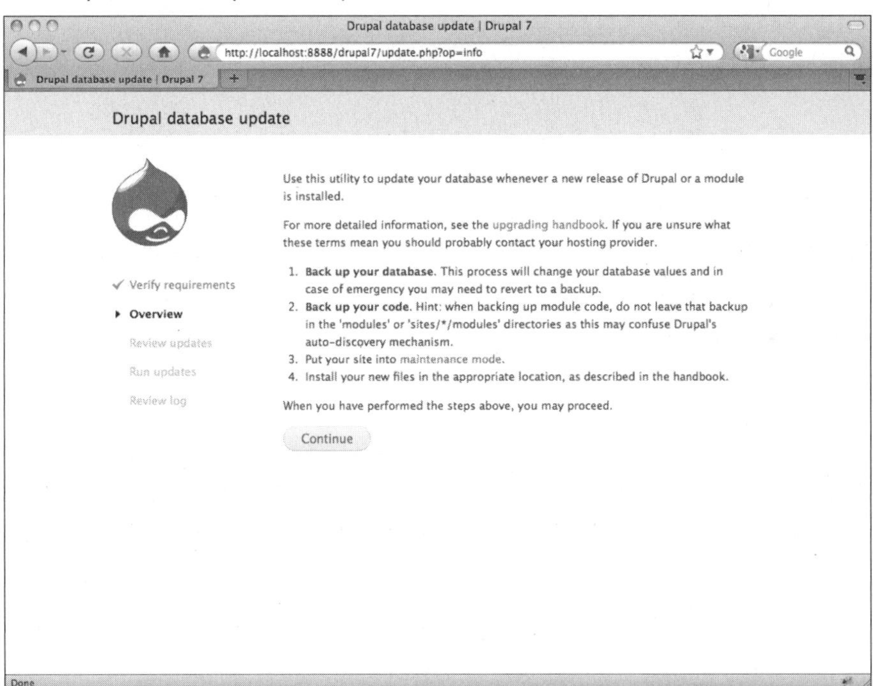

Handling major version upgrades

Before you begin a major upgrade of the Drupal core, it is essential that you make a full backup of your existing site, including your database. Set the backup to one side in the event something goes wrong and you need to restore your site. After the backup is done, it is safe to proceed with the actual upgrade process.

Major upgrades to the core have to be done manually. Follow these steps to run a major upgrade of the Drupal core:

1. **Unpack the upgrade archive on your local machine.**
2. **Put your site into maintenance mode, as discussed earlier in this chapter.**
3. **Move the files to your server using either FTP or your Web hosting control panel's file manager, overwriting the original files.**
4. **After the files are on your server, run update.php by typing the site URL into your browser, followed by update.php (i.e.,** `http://www.yoursite.com/update.php`**).**

   The Drupal database update utility loads in your browser, as shown in Figure 35.6.
5. **Read the instructions, and click the Continue button.**

   The page reloads, showing a list of available updates.
6. **Review the list, and click Continue.**

   The system runs the updates and produces a log of the results.
7. **Return to the site, and click through the site to check the changes.**
8. **If all is well, put the site back online, as discussed earlier in this chapter.**

Tip

Official Drupal upgrade instructions can always be found at `http://drupal.org/upgrade`**.** ■

Summary

This chapter addressed change management issues in Drupal. I covered these topics:

- How to take your site offline and put it into maintenance mode
- How to back up your site
- How to restore your site from a backup
- How to use the Update manager module
- How to handle minor upgrades to modules and themes
- How to handle major upgrades to the core

Part VIII

Appendixes

IN THIS PART

APPENDIX

The Directory Structure of a Drupal Installation

A complete Drupal installation includes a large number of directories and files. The directories and files reside on your server, typically, though not necessarily, in the public directory of your hosting account.

Figure A.1 is a view of the default installation of Drupal 7, with all the key directories expanded to give you the big picture of what is installed on your server.

IN THIS APPENDIX

Getting a big picture of the Drupal directories

Note

Testing directories are not expanded in the figure. ■

Cross-Reference

Appendix B provides a map of the locations of the key files and directories that you may need to locate during the customization of your site. ■

FIGURE A.1

The Drupal 7 default installation

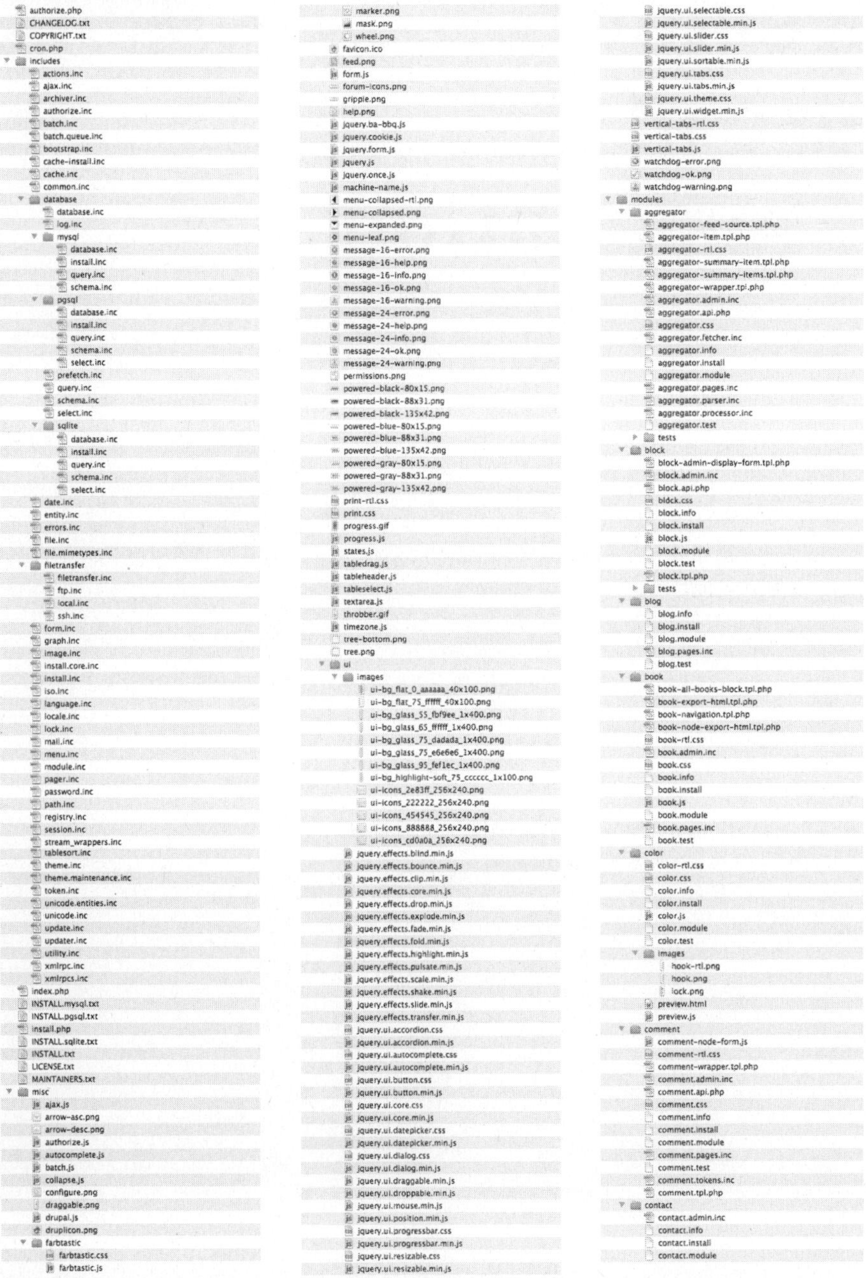

```
authorize.php
CHANGELOG.txt
COPYRIGHT.txt
cron.php
▼ includes
    actions.inc
    ajax.inc
    archiver.inc
    authorize.inc
    batch.inc
    batch.queue.inc
    bootstrap.inc
    cache-install.inc
    cache.inc
    common.inc
  ▼ database
      database.inc
      log.inc
    ▼ mysql
        database.inc
        install.inc
        query.inc
        schema.inc
    ▼ pgsql
        database.inc
        install.inc
        query.inc
        schema.inc
        select.inc
      prefetch.inc
      query.inc
      schema.inc
      select.inc
    ▼ sqlite
        database.inc
        install.inc
        query.inc
        schema.inc
        select.inc
    date.inc
    entity.inc
    errors.inc
    file.inc
    file.mimetypes.inc
  ▼ filetransfer
      filetransfer.inc
      ftp.inc
      local.inc
      ssh.inc
    form.inc
    graph.inc
    image.inc
    install.core.inc
    install.inc
    iso.inc
    language.inc
    locale.inc
    lock.inc
    mail.inc
    menu.inc
    module.inc
    pager.inc
    password.inc
    path.inc
    registry.inc
    session.inc
    stream_wrappers.inc
    tablesort.inc
    theme.inc
    theme.maintenance.inc
    token.inc
    unicode.entities.inc
    unicode.inc
    update.inc
    updater.inc
    utility.inc
    xmlrpc.inc
    xmlrpcs.inc
index.php
INSTALL.mysql.txt
INSTALL.pgsql.txt
install.php
INSTALL.sqlite.txt
INSTALL.txt
LICENSE.txt
MAINTAINERS.txt
▼ misc
    ajax.js
    arrow-asc.png
    arrow-desc.png
    authorize.js
    autocomplete.js
    batch.js
    collapse.js
    configure.png
    draggable.png
    drupal.js
    druplicon.png
  ▼ farbtastic
      farbtastic.css
      farbtastic.js
      marker.png
      mask.png
      wheel.png
    favicon.ico
    feed.png
    form.js
    forum-icons.png
    grippie.png
    help.png
    jquery.ba-bbq.js
    jquery.cookie.js
    jquery.form.js
    jquery.js
    jquery.once.js
    machine-name.js
    menu-collapsed-rtl.png
    menu-collapsed.png
    menu-expanded.png
    menu-leaf.png
    message-16-error.png
    message-16-help.png
    message-16-info.png
    message-16-ok.png
    message-16-warning.png
    message-24-error.png
    message-24-help.png
    message-24-info.png
    message-24-ok.png
    message-24-warning.png
    permissions.png
    powered-black-80x15.png
    powered-black-88x31.png
    powered-black-135x42.png
    powered-blue-80x15.png
    powered-blue-88x31.png
    powered-blue-135x42.png
    powered-gray-80x15.png
    powered-gray-88x31.png
    powered-gray-135x42.png
    print-rtl.css
    print.css
    progress.gif
    progress.js
    states.js
    tabledrag.js
    tableheader.js
    tableselect.js
    textarea.js
    throbber.gif
    timezone.js
    tree-bottom.png
    tree.png
  ▼ ui
    ▼ images
        ui-bg_flat_0_aaaaaa_40x100.png
        ui-bg_flat_75_ffffff_40x100.png
        ui-bg_glass_55_fbf9ee_1x400.png
        ui-bg_glass_65_ffffff_1x400.png
        ui-bg_glass_75_dadada_1x400.png
        ui-bg_glass_75_e6e6e6_1x400.png
        ui-bg_glass_95_fef1ec_1x400.png
        ui-bg_highlight-soft_75_cccccc_1x100.png
        ui-icons_2e83ff_256x240.png
        ui-icons_222222_256x240.png
        ui-icons_454545_256x240.png
        ui-icons_888888_256x240.png
        ui-icons_cd0a0a_256x240.png
      jquery.effects.blind.min.js
      jquery.effects.bounce.min.js
      jquery.effects.clip.min.js
      jquery.effects.core.min.js
      jquery.effects.drop.min.js
      jquery.effects.explode.min.js
      jquery.effects.fade.min.js
      jquery.effects.fold.min.js
      jquery.effects.highlight.min.js
      jquery.effects.pulsate.min.js
      jquery.effects.scale.min.js
      jquery.effects.shake.min.js
      jquery.effects.slide.min.js
      jquery.effects.transfer.min.js
      jquery.ui.accordion.css
      jquery.ui.accordion.min.js
      jquery.ui.autocomplete.css
      jquery.ui.autocomplete.min.js
      jquery.ui.button.css
      jquery.ui.button.min.js
      jquery.ui.core.css
      jquery.ui.core.min.js
      jquery.ui.datepicker.css
      jquery.ui.datepicker.min.js
      jquery.ui.dialog.css
      jquery.ui.dialog.min.js
      jquery.ui.draggable.min.js
      jquery.ui.droppable.min.js
      jquery.ui.mouse.min.js
      jquery.ui.position.min.js
      jquery.ui.progressbar.css
      jquery.ui.progressbar.min.js
      jquery.ui.resizable.css
      jquery.ui.resizable.min.js
      jquery.ui.selectable.css
      jquery.ui.selectable.min.js
      jquery.ui.slider.css
      jquery.ui.slider.min.js
      jquery.ui.sortable.min.js
      jquery.ui.tabs.css
      jquery.ui.tabs.min.js
      jquery.ui.theme.css
      jquery.ui.widget.min.js
    vertical-tabs-rtl.css
    vertical-tabs.css
    vertical-tabs.js
    watchdog-error.png
    watchdog-ok.png
    watchdog-warning.png
▼ modules
  ▼ aggregator
      aggregator-feed-source.tpl.php
      aggregator-item.tpl.php
      aggregator-rtl.css
      aggregator-summary-item.tpl.php
      aggregator-summary-items.tpl.php
      aggregator-wrapper.tpl.php
      aggregator.admin.inc
      aggregator.api.php
      aggregator.css
      aggregator.fetcher.inc
      aggregator.info
      aggregator.install
      aggregator.module
      aggregator.pages.inc
      aggregator.parser.inc
      aggregator.processor.inc
      aggregator.test
    ► tests
  ▼ block
      block-admin-display-form.tpl.php
      block.admin.inc
      block.api.php
      block.css
      block.info
      block.install
      block.js
      block.module
      block.test
      block.tpl.php
    ► tests
  ▼ blog
      blog.info
      blog.install
      blog.module
      blog.pages.inc
      blog.test
  ▼ book
      book-all-books-block.tpl.php
      book-export-html.tpl.php
      book-navigation.tpl.php
      book-node-export-html.tpl.php
      book-rtl.css
      book.admin.inc
      book.css
      book.info
      book.install
      book.js
      book.module
      book.pages.inc
      book.test
  ▼ color
      color-rtl.css
      color.css
      color.info
      color.install
      color.js
      color.module
      color.test
    ▼ images
        hook-rtl.png
        hook.png
        lock.png
      preview.html
      preview.js
  ▼ comment
      comment-node-form.js
      comment-rtl.css
      comment-wrapper.tpl.php
      comment.admin.inc
      comment.api.php
      comment.css
      comment.info
      comment.install
      comment.module
      comment.pages.inc
      comment.test
      comment.tokens.inc
      comment.tpl.php
  ▼ contact
      contact.admin.inc
      contact.info
      contact.install
      contact.module
```

```
        contact.test
  contextual
      contextual-rtl.css
      contextual.api.php
      contextual.css
      contextual.info
      contextual.js
      contextual.module
    images
        gear-select.png
  dashboard
      dashboard.api.php
      dashboard.css
      dashboard.info
      dashboard.install
      dashboard.js
      dashboard.module
      dashboard.test
  dblog
      dblog-rtl.css
      dblog.admin.inc
      dblog.css
      dblog.info
      dblog.install
      dblog.module
      dblog.test
  field
      field.api.php
      field.attach.inc
      field.crud.inc
      field.default.inc
      field.form.inc
      field.info
      field.info.inc
      field.install
      field.module
      field.multilingual.inc
    modules
      field_sql_storage
          field_sql_storage.info
          field_sql_storage.install
          field_sql_storage.module
          field_sql_storage.test
      list
          list.info
          list.install
          list.module
        tests
      number
          number.info
          number.install
          number.module
          number.test
      options
          options.api.php
          options.info
          options.module
          options.test
      text
          text.info
          text.install
          text.js
          text.module
          text.test
    tests
    theme
        field-rtl.css
        field.css
        field.tpl.php
  field_ui
      field_ui-rtl.css
      field_ui.admin.inc
      field_ui.api.php
      field_ui.css
      field_ui.info
      field_ui.js
      field_ui.module
      field_ui.test
  file
      file.api.php
      file.css
      file.field.inc
      file.info
      file.install
      file.js
      file.module
    icons
        application-octet-stream.png
        application-pdf.png
        application-x-executable.png
        audio-x-generic.png
        image-x-generic.png
        package-x-generic.png
        text-html.png
        text-plain.png
        text-x-generic.png
        text-x-script.png
        video-x-generic.png
        x-office-document.png
        x-office-presentation.png
        x-office-spreadsheet.png
    tests
  filter
      filter.admin.inc
      filter.admin.js
      filter.api.php
      filter.css
      filter.info
      filter.install
      filter.js
      filter.module
      filter.pages.inc
      filter.test
    tests
  forum
      forum-icon.tpl.php
      forum-list.tpl.php
      forum-rtl.css
      forum-submitted.tpl.php
      forum-topic-list.tpl.php
      forum.admin.inc
      forum.css
      forum.info
      forum.install
      forum.module
      forum.pages.inc
      forum.test
      forums.tpl.php
  help
      help-rtl.css
      help.admin.inc
      help.api.php
      help.css
      help.info
      help.module
      help.test
  image
      image-rtl.css
      image.admin.css
      image.admin.inc
      image.api.php
      image.css
      image.effects.inc
      image.field.inc
      image.info
      image.install
      image.module
      image.test
      sample.png
    tests
  locale
      locale.admin.inc
      locale.api.php
      locale.css
      locale.datepicker.js
      locale.info
      locale.install
      locale.module
      locale.test
    tests
  menu
      menu.admin.inc
      menu.admin.js
      menu.api.php
      menu.css
      menu.info
      menu.install
      menu.js
      menu.module
      menu.test
  node
      content_types.inc
      content_types.js
      node-rtl.css
      node.admin.inc
      node.api.php
      node.css
      node.info
      node.install
      node.js
      node.module
      node.pages.inc
      node.test
      node.tokens.inc
      node.tpl.php
    tests
  openid
      login-bg.png
      openid-rtl.css
      openid.api.php
      openid.css
      openid.inc
      openid.info
      openid.install
      openid.js
      openid.module
      openid.pages.inc
      openid.test
    tests
  overlay
    images
        background.png
        close.png
      overlay-child.css
      overlay-child.js
      overlay-parent.css
      overlay-parent.js
      overlay.api.php
      overlay.info
      overlay.install
      overlay.module
      overlay.tpl.php
  path
      path.admin.inc
      path.api.php
      path.info
      path.js
      path.module
      path.test
  php
      php.info
      php.install
      php.module
      php.test
  poll
      poll-bar--block.tpl.php
      poll-bar.tpl.php
      poll-results--block.tpl.php
      poll-results.tpl.php
      poll-rtl.css
      poll-vote.tpl.php
      poll.css
      poll.info
      poll.install
      poll.pages.inc
      poll.test
      poll.tokens.inc
  profile
      profile-block.tpl.php
      profile-listing.tpl.php
      profile-wrapper.tpl.php
      profile.admin.inc
      profile.css
      profile.info
      profile.install
      profile.js
      profile.module
      profile.pages.inc
      profile.test
  rdf
      rdf.api.php
      rdf.info
      rdf.install
      rdf.module
      rdf.test
    tests
    README.txt
  search
      search-block-form.tpl.php
      search-result.tpl.php
      search-results.tpl.php
      search-rtl.css
      search.admin.inc
      search.api.php
      search.css
      search.extender.inc
      search.info
      search.install
      search.module
      search.pages.inc
      search.test
    tests
  shortcut
      shortcut.admin.css
      shortcut.admin.inc
      shortcut.admin.js
      shortcut.api.php
      shortcut.css
      shortcut.info
      shortcut.install
      shortcut.module
      shortcut.png
      shortcut.test
  simpletest
      drupal_web_test_case.php
    files
      css_test_files
          comment_hacks.css
          comment_hacks.css.optimized.css
          comment_hacks.css.unoptimized.css
          css_input_with_import.css
          css_input_with_import.css.optimized.css
          css_input_with_import.css.unoptimized.css
          css_input_without_import.css
          css_input_without_import.css.optimized.css
          css_input_without_import.css.unoptimized.css
          import1.css
          import2.css
        html-1.txt
        html-2.html
        image-1.png
```

```
            image-2.jpg
            image-test.gif
            image-test.jpg
            image-test.png
            javascript-1.txt
            javascript-2.script
            php-1.txt
            php-2.php
            README.txt
            sql-1.txt
            sql-2.sql
          simpletest.api.php
          simpletest.css
          simpletest.info
          simpletest.install
          simpletest.js
          simpletest.module
          simpletest.pages.inc
          simpletest.test
        ▶ tests
      ▼ statistics
          statistics.admin.inc
          statistics.info
          statistics.install
          statistics.module
          statistics.pages.inc
          statistics.test
          statistics.tokens.inc
      ▼ syslog
          syslog.info
          syslog.install
          syslog.module
          syslog.test
      ▼ system
          html.tpl.php
          image.gd.inc
          maintenance-page.tpl.php
          page.tpl.php
          region.tpl.php
          system.admin-rtl.css
          system.admin.css
          system.admin.inc
          system.api.php
          system.archiver.inc
          system.base-rtl.css
          system.base.css
          system.cron.js
          system.info
          system.install
          system.js
          system.mail.inc
          system.maintenance.css
          system.menus-rtl.css
          system.menus.css
          system.messages.css
          system.module
          system.queue.inc
          system.tar.inc
          system.test
          system.theme-rtl.css
          system.theme.css
          system.tokens.inc
          system.updater.inc
          theme.api.php
      ▼ taxonomy
          taxonomy-term.tpl.php
          taxonomy.admin.inc
          taxonomy.api.php
          taxonomy.css
          taxonomy.info
          taxonomy.install
          taxonomy.js
          taxonomy.module
          taxonomy.pages.inc
          taxonomy.test
          taxonomy.tokens.inc
      ▼ toolbar
          toolbar.css
          toolbar.info
          toolbar.js
          toolbar.module
          toolbar.png
          toolbar.tpl.php
      ▼ tracker
          tracker.css
          tracker.info
          tracker.install
          tracker.module
          tracker.pages.inc
          tracker.test
      ▼ translation
        ▶ tests
          translation.info
          translation.module
          translation.pages.inc
          translation.test
      ▼ trigger
        ▶ tests
          trigger.admin.inc
          trigger.api.php
          trigger.info
          trigger.info
          trigger.install
          trigger.module
          trigger.test
      ▼ update
        ▶ tests
          update-rtl.css
          update.api.php
          update.authorize.inc
          update.compare.inc
          update.css
          update.fetch.inc
          update.info
          update.install
          update.manager.inc
          update.module
          update.report.inc
          update.settings.inc
          update.test
      ▼ user
        ▶ tests
          user-picture.tpl.php
          user-profile-category.tpl.php
          user-profile-item.tpl.php
          user-profile.tpl.php
          user-rtl.css
          user.admin.inc
          user.api.php
          user.css
          user.info
          user.install
          user.js
          user.module
          user.pages.inc
          user.permissions.js
          user.test
          user.tokens.inc
  ▼ profiles
    ▼ minimal
        minimal.info
        minimal.install
        minimal.profile
      ▼ translations
          README.txt
    ▼ standard
        standard.info
        standard.install
        standard.profile
      ▼ translations
          README.txt
    ▶ testing
    README.txt
    robots.txt
  ▼ scripts
      code-clean.sh
      cron-curl.sh
      cron-lynx.sh
      drupal.sh
      dump-database-d6.sh
      generate-d6-content.sh
      password-hash.sh
      run-tests.sh
  ▼ sites
    ▼ all
      ▼ modules
          README.txt
        README.txt
      ▼ themes
          README.txt
    ▼ default
        default.settings.php
      ▶ files
        settings.php
      example.sites.php
  ▼ themes
    ▼ bartik
        bartik.info
      ▼ color
          base.png
          color.inc
          preview.css
          preview.html
          preview.js
          preview.png
      ▼ css
          colors.css
          ie-rtl.css
          ie.css
          ie6.css
          layout-rtl.css
          layout.css
          maintenance-page.css
          print.css
          style-rtl.css
          style.css
      ▼ images
          add.png
          buttons.png
          comment-arrow-rtl.gif
          comment-arrow.gif
          search-button.png
          tabs-border.png
          menu-leaf.gif
          task-list.png
        logo.png
        maintenance-page.tpl.php
        node.tpl.php
        page.tpl.php
        print.css
        screenshot.png
        style-rtl.css
        style.css
        template.php
        theme-settings.php
      README.txt
    ▼ seven
        ie.css
        ie6.css
      ▼ images
          add.png
          arrow-asc.png
          arrow-desc.png
          arrow-next.png
          arrow-prev.png
          buttons.png
          fc.png
          list-item.png
          task-check.png
          task-item.png
          ui-icons-222222-256x240.png
          ui-icons-454545-256x240.png
          ui-icons-800000-256x240.png
          ui-icons-888888-256x240.png
          ui-icons-ffffff-256x240.png
        jquery.ui.theme.css
        logo.png
        maintenance-page.tpl.php
        page.tpl.php
        reset.css
        screenshot.png
        seven.info
        style-rtl.css
        style.css
        template.php
        vertical-tabs.css
    ▼ stark
        layout.css
        logo.png
        README.txt
        screenshot.png
        stark.info
    ▶ tests
  update.php
  UPGRADE.txt
  web.config
  xmlrpc.php
```

APPENDIX

B

Location of Key Files

IN THIS APPENDIX

Finding key files

This appendix is intended to highlight the locations of key files in the system. These files are of primary importance to developers and themers looking to identify the source of functionality or output for the purpose of intercepting and overriding them.

This is not intended to be a complete listing of all files on the site; for that, you can see Appendix A. Also note that I have not included here the files inside the themes directories.

Aggregator

The Aggregator module adds the ability to bring multiple RSS feeds into your site and group and display the output.

Module

- /modules/aggregator/aggregator.module

Style Sheets

- /modules/aggregator/aggregator-rtl.css
- /modules/aggregator/aggregator.css

Templates

- /modules/aggregator/aggregator-feed-source.tpl.php
- /modules/aggregator/aggregator-item.tpl.php
- /modules/aggregator/aggregator-summary-item.tpl.php
- /modules/aggregator/aggregator-summary-items.tpl.php
- /modules/aggregator/aggregator-wrapper.tpl.php

Blocks

The Block module powers the blocks you see on the page.

Module

- /modules/block/block.module

Style Sheets

- /modules/block/block.css

Templates

- /modules/block/block-admin-display-form.tpl.php
- /modules/block/block.tpl.php

Blog Content Type

The Blog module powers the blog content type, providing both single and multi-user blog functionality.

Module

- /modules/blog/blog.module

Book Content Type

The Book module creates the ability to transform content items into a hierarchical grouping that can be organized into "books" and navigated in sequence.

Module

- /modules/book/book.module

Style Sheets

- /modules/book/book-rtl.css
- /modules/book/book.css

Templates

- /modules/book/book-all-books-block.tpl.php
- /modules/book/book-export-html.tpl.php
- /modules/book/book-navigation.tpl.php
- /modules/book/book-node-export-html.tpl.php

Comments

The Comment module allows your users to add threaded comments to content items and in the forum.

Module

- /modules/comment/comment.module

Style Sheets

- /modules/comment/comment-rtl.css
- /modules/comment/comment.css

Templates

- /modules/comment/comment.tpl.php
- /modules/comment/comment-wrapper.tpl.php

Contact Module

The sitewide and user contact forms are created by the Contact module.

Module

- /modules/contact/contact.module

Forum

The Forum module provides the threaded discussion forum functionality.

Module

- /modules/forum/forum.module

Style Sheets

- /modules/forum/forum-rtl.css
- /modules/forum/forum.css

Templates

- /modules/forum/forum-icon.tpl.php
- /modules/forum/forum-list.tpl.php
- /modules/forum/forum-submitted.tpl.php
- /modules/forum/forum-topic-list.tpl.php
- /modules/forum/forums.tpl.php

Menus

The menus in your Drupal site are generated by the Menu module.

Module

- /modules/menu/menu.module

Style Sheets

- /modules/menu/menu.css

Nodes

The Node module is one of the key modules in the system, providing the ability to add content to the site.

Module

- /modules/node/node.module

Style Sheets

- /modules/node/node-rtl.css
- /modules/node/node.css

Templates

- /modules/node/node.tpl.php

Polls

The Polls module provides the poll voting forms and the summary output pages and block.

Module

- /modules/poll/poll.module

Style Sheets

- /modules/poll/poll-rtl.css
- /modules/poll/poll.css

Templates

- /modules/poll/poll-bar--block.tpl.php
- /modules/poll/poll-bar.tpl.php
- /modules/poll/poll-results--block.tpl.php
- /modules/poll/poll-results.tpl.php
- /modules/poll/poll-vote.tpl.php

Profile

The user profile pages are controlled by the Profile module.

Module

- `/modules/profile/profile.module`

Style Sheets

- `/modules/profile/profile.css`

Templates

- `/modules/profile/profile-block.tpl.php`
- `/modules/profile/profile-listing.tpl.php`
- `/modules/profile/profile-wrapper.tpl.php`

Search

The ability to search the contents of your Drupal site comes from the Search module. The module also controls the search results page.

Module

- `/modules/search/search.module`

Style Sheets

- `/modules/search/search-rtl.css`
- `/modules/search/search.css`

Templates

- `/modules/search/search-block-form.tpl.php`
- `/modules/search/search-result.tpl.php`
- `/modules/search/search-results.tpl.php`

System

The System module is one of the key modules in Drupal, providing a variety of functionality, styling, and configuration controls.

Module

- `/modules/system/system.module`

Style Sheets

- `/modules/system/system.admin-rtl.css`
- `/modules/system/system.admin.css`
- `/modules/system/system.base-rtl.css`
- `/modules/system/system.base.css`
- `/modules/system/system.maintenance.css`
- `/modules/system/system.menus-rtl.css`
- `/modules/system/system.menus.css`
- `/modules/system/system.messages.css`
- `/modules/system/system.theme-rtl.css`
- `/modules/system/system.theme.css`

Templates

- `/modules/system/html.tpl.php`
- `/modules/system/maintenance-page.tpl.php`
- `/modules/system/page.tpl.php`
- `/modules/system/region.tpl.php`

Taxonomy

The Taxonomy module powers the creation and management of vocabularies and the tags within them.

Module

- `/modules/taxonomy/taxonomy.module`

Style Sheets

- /modules/taxonomy/taxonomy.css

Templates

- /modules/taxonomy/taxonomy-term.tpl.php

Users

The User module provides the user registration and login system.

Module

- /modules/user/user.module

Style Sheets

- /modules/user/user-rtl.css
- /modules/user/user.css

Templates

- /modules/user/user-picture.tpl.php
- /modules/user/user-profile-category.tpl.php
- /modules/user/user-profile-item.tpl.php
- /modules/user/user-profile.tpl.php

APPENDIX

C

Installing XAMPP

IN THIS APPENDIX

Setting up a local server installation for Drupal

XAMPP is a unified software package that bundles into one installer all the necessary elements for creating a fully functional server environment. The system includes not only the basics, like the Apache Web server, the MySQL database, and the PHP language support, but also useful tools like phpMyAdmin.

XAMPP is cross-platform compatible and can be installed on Windows, Linux, or Mac. This appendix provides a step-by-step guide to installing XAMPP on a Windows machine.

At the conclusion of this process, you will have a functional server on your Windows machine that allows you to run Drupal locally.

Follow these steps to acquire the XAMPP installation package and get it set up on your local machine:

1. **Connect to the Internet, and open your browser.**
2. **Direct your browser to http://www.apachefriends.org.**

   The Web page loads in your browser.
3. **Click the main menu choice XAMPP.**

   The XAMPP page loads.
4. **Click the links XAMPP for Windows.**

   The XAMPP for Windows page loads.
5. **Click the Download link.**

   The page jumps to the Download packages list.

6. **Click either the .exe or .zip option under the heading XAMPP for Windows, Basic Package.**

   A new window opens and goes to Sourceforge.net's downloads page. The download should begin automatically.

7. **When the pop-up prompts you to save the file, click OK.**

   The software installer downloads to your computer. After it is complete, you can move to the next step.

8. **Locate the downloaded archive (.zip) package on your local machine, and double-click it.**

   The software unpacks and leaves a new file on your desktop.

9. **Double-click the new file, select the language you prefer, and click OK.**

   The installer takes you to the next screen.

10. **Select the installation location, and click the Next button.**

    The installer takes you to the next screen.

Tip

The best choice is to install this application outside your programs directory. ■

11. **Change any settings you require on the Options page or leave the default settings, and click Install.**

    All choices are optional. The installer takes you to the final screen and completes the installation.

12. **Click Finish to close the Installer.**

The installation is complete, and the software is ready to run.

To begin, simply start XAMPP from under Start ➪ Programs ➪ XAMPP. Use the Start/Stop buttons to control the servers.

To create a new Web site, simply copy the files into a directory placed inside the /htdocs directory. You can then access your new site by opening the URL in your browser, as follows: `http://localhost/sitedirectoryname`.

APPENDIX

D

Installing MAMP

MAMP is a unified software package that bundles into one installer all the necessary elements for creating a fully functional server environment. The system includes not only the basics, like the Apache Web server, the MySQL database, and the PHP language support, but also useful tools like phpMyAdmin.

MAMP is intended to run on a Mac with OSX installed. This appendix provides a step-by-step guide to installing MAMP on a Mac.

At the conclusion of this process, you will have a functional server on your Mac that allows you to run Drupal locally.

Follow these steps to acquire the MAMP installation package and get it set up on your local machine:

1. **Connect to the Internet, and open your browser.**
2. **Direct your browser to http://www.mamp.info.**

   The Web page loads in your browser.
3. **Click the main menu choice Downloads.**

   The Downloads page loads.
4. **Click the link displayed to download the software package named MAMP.**

Note

MAMP is bundled with the MAMP Pro software. While MAMP is free of charge, MAMP Pro is commercial software. Because they are bundled together, you install both, but you do not need to enable MAMP Pro if you do not want to do so. You can simply use the free version of MAMP. ■

APPENDIX D

Setting up a local development server on a Mac

5. **When the pop-up prompts you to save the installer, which is provided as a .zip file, click OK.**

   The software installer downloads to your computer. After it is complete, you can move to the next step.

6. **Locate the downloaded archive (.zip) package on your local machine, and double-click it.**

   The software unpacks and leaves a new .dmg file on your desktop.

7. **Double-click the .dmg file.**

   The file opens a new window showing the installer icon.

8. **Drag the MAMP icon into Applications directory shown in the installer window.**

   The system immediately begins to copy all the necessary files to your computer's applications directory. No confirmation appears when it is completed.

9. **Close the installer window.**

10. **Eject the installation disk.**

The installation is complete, and the software is ready to run.

To run the servers, simply double-click the MAMP icon inside the new MAMP directory. The MAMP controller opens. If the servers fail to start when you open the application, click the button Start Servers.

If the startup is successful, you see two green lights—one for the Apache Server, another for the MySQL Server. You need two green lights to use the application! When both green lights are lit, the system automatically opens the MAMP welcome page in a browser window. Note that this page contains links to all the information and utilities you need, including the phpMyAdmin tool. Typically, this page URL is `http://localhost:8888/MAMP/?language=English`.

To shut down the servers, click the Stop Servers button.

To create a new Web site, simply copy the files into a directory placed inside the `/applications/MAMP/htdocs` directory. You can then access your new site by opening the URL in your browser, as follows: `http://localhost:8888/sitedirectoryname`.

APPENDIX

E

Beyond the Book— Additional Help Resources Online

IN THIS APPENDIX

Using the help files

Finding resources online

Learning from the Drupal community

Support options for Drupal follow the pattern typical to community-driven open-source projects. Your first line of support is community help resources, that is, self-help. Those who need more assistance typically turn to vendors, either the people who built their Drupal site or other third parties who provide commercial support services.

This appendix outlines the default help options, includes a list of the official Drupal resources, and provides a brief note about options for commercial support.

The Help Files Inside Drupal

Drupal comes bundled with basic help files. Help is located in two places: the Help link on the Management menu and the context-sensitive Help links. Clicking the Help option on the Management menu takes you to a page containing a list of all the available topics, as well as links to online help resources. For site administrators, however, the context-sensitive Help links are probably the most useful help resource.

The context-sensitive links appear next to items on the various admin pages. Clicking one of the Help links displays a screen containing the help information relevant to that specific page.

Note

The default help screens are pretty basic and likely to be of the most assistance to users who are new to the system or those who use the system infrequently. ■

The Drupal help files are maintained along with the core system files. When you update your Drupal installation, your help files also may be updated, depending on the contents of the particular upgrade.

Online Help and Support Resources

Drupal is a well-documented system. In addition to a complete set of documents for site administrators, you can find tutorials, examples, and documents for theme designers and developers. Table E.1 covers some of the highlights of the official online resources.

TABLE E.1

Official Drupal Online Resources

Name	Location
The Drupal Handbooks	`http://drupal.org/handbooks`
The Official Drupal Forum	`http://drupal.org/forum`
Developing for Drupal	`http://drupal.org/contributors-guide`
The Drupal Theming Guide	`http://drupal.org/theme-guide`
The Drupal API	`http://api.drupal.org/`
Understanding Drupal—A Guide to Getting Started	`http://drupal.org/getting-started/before`
Drupal Installation Guide	`http://drupal.org/getting-started/install`
Drupal Administration Guide	`http://drupal.org/node/627152`
Drupal Tutorials	`http://drupal.org/handbook/customization/tutorials`
The Drupal IRC Channel	`http://drupal.org/irc`
Drupal Mailing Lists	`http://drupal.org/mailing-lists`
Drupal Groups	`http://groups.drupal.org/`

You also can find a variety of unofficial help resources, some more authoritative than others. One good source of information is the Scribd.com site. Scribd is a document-sharing site that includes a collection of Drupal-related documents and presentations.

Using Community Support Options

Drupal is a community-driven open-source project, meaning that all the project administrators, designers, developers, and other team members are unpaid volunteers. Unlike some other open-source projects, the Drupal project does not sell support services, training, or documentation. Getting help with a problem means turning to the community for help. The forums are the primary resource for community support.

You can access the official Drupal Community Forums at `http://drupal.org/forum`. Anyone is free to browse the forums and read the information and conversations posted there. If you want to post on the forums, however, you need to register. Registration is free and requires you to disclose only very basic information.

The first time you visit the forum, you should take a few moments to read the Forum Tips page. You can find a link to the Tips page on the front page of the forum. If you want to post a question on the forum, first run a search to determine whether the question has been asked previously. Odds are good that if you are having a problem, someone else has experienced it before and the issue has been discussed on the forums. As a matter of courtesy, check to see if it has been asked and answered before you raise the issue yet again.

Discussions on the forums are organized topically. Make sure you take a look around and get a feel for what goes where prior to posting; you can greatly increase your chance of getting a responsive answer if you post your question in the right area!

Two other community support resources exist: IRC and Drupal Groups. Internet Relay Chat, or IRC as it is commonly called, is a live chat system that allows you to log in and chat with other users in real time. Use of IRC does require an IRC client on your machine, and if you are not familiar with IRC, it can take a bit to get used to the format. Most of the IRC users are more of the "hardcore" Drupal crowd, and the discussions tend to be rather more technical that what you might find on a typical forum. That said, don't be daunted, because the IRC crowd is a valuable and knowledgeable resource.

Tip

Popular IRC clients include MIRC for Windows (`http://www.mirc.com`) and Colloquy for Mac (`http://colloquy.info/`). If you prefer, you can use a browser-based IRC client. Chatzilla is a plugin that works in the Firefox browser (`https://addons.mozilla.org/en-US/firefox/addon/16`). Opera also comes with a built-in client. ■

Drupal Groups is one of the official Drupal sites. It provides a way for people with common interests to exchange information. There are groups dedicated to technical topics, geographic regions, events, and more. If you are looking to become involved with the community, or you simply want to network and exchange information with other Drupal fans, Groups is a good option for you. To use Groups, you must first have an account at the main Drupal.org site. After you log in to the Groups site, you can join many of the groups without further delay, although some do require approval. Visit the site and explore at `http://groups.drupal.org`.

Finding Commercial Support

In the past year, the number of options for professional-level commercial support for Drupal has increased dramatically. The arrival of Acquia Drupal is one of the most interesting developments. Acquia offers support subscriptions at four different levels, from a very basic plan to a custom arrangement. The firm provides multiple channels for reaching professional assistance, including forums, tickets, and a 24x7 emergency-assistance option. If Drupal is mission critical to your firm, you can help ensure business continuity with a service like this; Acquia provides a service-level agreement and guaranteed response times. As a painless way to get started, they provide a 30-day free trial. You can learn more at `http://acquia.com/drupal-support`.

While Acquia is certainly the most visible option, if you used a vendor to build your Drupal site, you should also inquire whether they offer support services. Moreover, if you need help with a narrow issue only, or you are otherwise unwilling to enter into an ongoing support agreement, try posting a request for support on the Drupal forums, indicating that you are willing to pay for professional assistance. Such a course frequently turns up someone who is willing to provide assistance in exchange for a fee.

Index

A

Index

B

C

Index

D

E

F

G

H

I

J

L

M

Index

N

O

P

R

U

V